Cedrics

Kent, Kris, and Kim Kirchner now join their parents, Cedric and Norma, in welcoming you to Cedrics—the Twin Cities' premier international shopping experience featuring the best in world-renowned labels of men's and women's fashions. ❦ Let Kim show you gorgeous furs plus the Escada and Louis Féraud Boutiques. ❦ See sister Kris in the Gottex Resort Shop, and for clothes by Max Mara, Krizia, Rena Lange and more. ❦ Kent will introduce men to Brioni, Canali, Countess Mara, Versace and V2 by Versace.

At Cedrics, you're part of the Minnesota family!

GALLERIA ❦ 925-3424

Hurray!

TABLE OF CONTENTS

VOLUME 1 ♦ **1993** ♦ NUMBER 1

6 FROM THE EDITOR

8 PECULIARLY MINNESOTA
   Weather Statistics • **12**
   Answers to Myths About Minnesota's History • **16**
   Notable Dates in Minnesota's History • **18**
   Minnesota's Symbols • **23**
   Government • **24**
   Business • **26**
   Secondary Education • **28**
   Transportation • **29**
   Who's Who • **31**
   Special Events • **46**
   Minnesota State Parks • **58**
   Sports in Minnesota • **62**
   Casinos • **74**

Hurray! Minnesota 2

Minnesota

78 THE TWIN CITIES
   Attractions • **81**
   Lakes and Parks • **85**
   Literary Scene • **87**
   Museums • **90**
   Twin Cities Art Galleries • **99**
   Music Institutions • **101**
   Theaters • **110**
   Dance/Theater • **120**
   Venues • **123**
   Media • **136**
   Shopping • **140**
   Eater's Digest • **150**
     By Category • **183**
     By Geographic Location • **188**
   Nightlife • **194**
   Hotels/Motels • **203**
Minneapolis • 204
   History • **209**
   Neighborhoods • **211**
   Parks and Lakes • **212**

Downtown • **215**
Architecture • **223**
University of Minnesota • **228**
Warehouse District • **228**
Mississippi Mile • **232**
Main Street • **232**
St. Anthony Main • **233**
Nicollet Island • **235**

St. Paul • 236
History • **239**
Neighborhoods • **240**
Downtown • **243**
Attractions • **246**
Parks • **251**
Special Celebrations • **252**

254 THE ARROWHEAD

Duluth • **259**
North Shore • **276**
The Gunflint Trail
and BWCAW • **290**
Northern Arrowhead • **298**
Iron Range • **306**

Hurray! Minnesota

318 LAKE COUNTRY

St. Cloud Area • **321**

Lake Mille Lacs • **329**

Brainerd Lakes Area • **333**

Itasca Headwaters • **344**

West Central Minnesota • **352**

370 BLUFF COUNTRY

River Towns • **373**

Rochester • **397**

Prairie Towns • **406**

422 PIONEER COUNTRY

Mankato • **430**

New Ulm • **434**

Walnut Grove • **443**

Pipestone • **452**

Spicer/New London • **467, 468**

470 THE RED RIVER VALLEY

Fargo/Moorhead • **474**

Crookston • **480**

Thief River Falls • **482**

East Grand Forks • **484**

488 INDEX

FROM THE EDITOR

THIS BOOK IS, FIRST AND FOREmost, a labor of love. Hopefully it also will be a successful commercial enterprise. That, of course, depends on whether you find "Hurray! Minnesota" useful and recommend its purchase to others.

Its genesis goes back a few years to when my company, Dorn Communications, published two annual guidebooks — the "Minnesota Guide" and the "Twin Cities Guide." Each was fairly popular, but we quit publishing them in the early 1980s when we stopped publishing books.

"Hurray! Minnesota" is, to some extent, a combination of these two books. But it's a whole lot more. The content is more in-depth, making its utility greater. Work on this first edition — research, writing and collection of photos — has taken place over the past four years. It's been done by a dozen researchers and journalists with contributions of suggestions, information, photos and artwork from scores of people around the state.

When we first started collecting information early in 1989, we talked in terms of a 300-page book. Well, things sort of got away from us. You're holding a 500-page book. From day one, we agreed that the cover price would be as low as we could make it to give each buyer a bargain. As the book got bigger, the cover price increased. It's still as low as we can make it, given the size of the book, the fine paper on which it's printed and the use of four-color photos throughout.

All of which doesn't explain why "Hurray! Minnesota" was published. It's published simply because there's a need for a comprehensive, all-inclusive guidebook to Minnesota. The need is on the part of visitors who come for short stays or longer vacations. The need is on the part of people considering whether to make Minnesota their home . . . or who have made that decision and need a one-stop indoctrination.

The biggest need, though, is among all of us full-time Minnesotans. It's among those who have lived here a

short time and those, like me, who have lived here for more than half a century.

I have been a Minnesotan for 56 years, all of my life. Why? Because I was born and reared here and chose to stay when opportunities to go elsewhere presented themselves. Why? Because I love this place. And I know that most of my 4-million-plus fellow Minnesotans agree.

Even though I've experienced much of Minnesota, I know there is so much yet to discover, to see and do. I grew up in Mankato, becoming familiar with much of southern Minnesota through competing in sports and through working as a daily newspaper reporter for the Mankato Free Press.

I have lived in the Twin Cities for more than 30 years, enjoying much of what the metro area has to offer in quality of life. At the same time, I enjoy life at the lake near Alexandria plus

ILLUSTRATION BY ERIC HANSON

Hurray! Minnesota

business and vacation forays to points throughout the state — Duluth, the Boundary Waters, the Brainerd area, Lake Mille Lacs, Lake Vermilion and many other places.

I've fished, golfed, hunted pheasants, cross-country skied. I've followed the professional sports teams and the University of Minnesota Gophers, enjoyed the Guthrie, the Minnesota Orchestra, Saint Paul Chamber Orchestra and numerous arts offerings. I dine at some of the finest restaurants anywhere. And when I'm in Alexandria or other smaller towns, I dine at some of the finest small-town eateries anywhere, where you get the closest thing to home cooking for an incredibly low price. And I enjoy the companionship of the friendly and honest people who are the backbone of this great state. I belong to many fine organizations, including the Minnesota Historical Society, which illuminates for all of us our rich history.

Through the years I have traveled to almost every state in the country. I've had the opportunity to compare Minnesota with other states, including a lot of really fine places. But I'll stick with Minnesota.

Finally, let's consider for a minute the name of this book — "Hurray! (with the exclamation point) Minnesota." I have friends who say it's too boosterish, too corny. Yes, it is boosterish, maybe even corny. But those of us who worked on this project mean it. We're saying an unabashed "Hurray!" for a great place.

Let's celebrate this great state — its cities, villages, farms, lakes, forests, everything that it has to offer for each of us. Let's celebrate the first annual issue of this guidebook. All together now:

Hurray! Minnesota.

William J. Dorn
Editor and Publisher

Hurray! Minnesota

PUBLISHER & EDITOR
William J. Dorn

MANAGING EDITOR
Kathleen McLean

STAFF WRITER
Ginger Anderson

CONTRIBUTING WRITERS
Stephen Hererra, Laurel Lindahl,
Jack El-Hai, Deborah Johnson

RESEARCHERS
Susan Nicome, Katie Sullivan Fritz,
Julie Carlson, Jutta Streed

ART DIRECTOR
Kathleen Timmerman

ELECTRONIC PUBLISHING
White Space Design Inferno

CARTOGRAHPY
James Dahlseid

ADVERTISING SALES DIRECTOR
Marilyn P. Hanson

ADVERTISING SALES
Ginger Anderson

COVER ILLUSTRATION BY ERIC HANSON

•

"Hurray! Minnesota," the Annual Guide to Discovering & Rediscovering Minnesota, is published by Minnmedia Inc., 15 S. Fifth St., Suite 900, Minneapolis, MN 55402. Copyright © 1993 Minnmedia Inc. All rights reserved. No part of this book may be reproduced in any form or by any means without written permission of the publisher. Reviewers may quote passages in a review. All production and printing done in Minnesota.

The contents of "Hurray! Minnesota" have been researched thoroughly and every precaution has been taken to ensure accuracy. We assume no responsibility for omissions or inaccuracies. Readers are advised that businesses and institutions written about in "Hurray! Minnesota" change from time to time. Telephone ahead to verify information and for further facts about the attractions and businesses covered.

Copies of "Hurray! Minnesota" are available at book and magazine stores, gift shops, resorts and other retail locations throughout Minnesota. Or you can order from Minnmedia Inc. Mail your check to Minnmedia Inc., 15 S. Fifth St., Suite 900, Minneapolis, MN 55402. Or telephone (612) 338-1578. FAX: (612) 338-4784. Single copy price is $13.95. To the price of each copy add 91¢ for Minnesota sales tax and $1.80 for postage and handling. Total cost per book is $16.66. Inquire for quantity discount when ordering five or more copies.

• PELICAN • GULL • MILLE LACS • LONG • WHITEFISH • PEPIN •

• LEECH • OTTER TAIL • NORWAY • THIEF • DIAMOND • ALEXANDER • OSCAR • ARTICHOKE • FREEBORN • LURA •

LANTERN SKIING ON THE TRACKED AND GROOMED CROSS-COUNTRY SKI TRAIL ON THE GUNFLINT TRAIL.

PHOTO COURTESY OF MINNESOTA OFFICE OF TOURISM

• MAPLE • WINNIBIGOSHISH • UNION • THIEF • SANDWICH • TWIN •

Peculiarly Minnesota

EVERY PLACE, IT SEEMS, has something about it that you can sense, that you feel. Sometimes you like what you feel. Sometimes not. For the most part, people like what they feel about Minnesota. After being a Minnesotan for a time, you begin to understand the place and its people. "Hurray! Minnesota" is about helping newcomers and oldcomers understand and appreciate this place. It is about discovering and rediscovering Minnesota.

It is a bit of a chapbook — a book of popular tales. It is a bit of a traditional guidebook. It's meant to entertain and, at the same time, to be utilitarian. If you read through it — even give it a heavy skim — you'll understand better about Minnesota and Minnesotans. "Hurray! Minnesota" will help you "crack the code" of what makes the state and its people tick.

Minnesota is unique in that its people are almost congenitally nice. There is less meanness and mistrust than in many other places. They're friendly. But not too friendly. At least, they're not openly demonstrative in their friendliness. Some say that's because of the heavy northern European influence. German and Scandinavian are the predominant ethnic backgrounds. You have to listen carefully for a compliment. "That's not too bad" is high praise in some circles. "How's it going?" is a common greeting. "Yah, you betcha" substitutes for "yes."

Minnesotans believe strongly in education, and they have

The State of Minnesota

taxed themselves mightily over the years to have a quality educational system with opportunities for all who seek them. Native son Garrison Keillor tells of his aunt, who used to encourage diligence in learning with the admonition, "You don't want to be a $20 haircut on a 98-cent head."

Yah, you betcha, Minnesotans tell Scandinavian jokes, mostly about Ole and Lena, some even with an attempted Scandinavian accent. And when Minnesotans go to a potluck dinner they bring a "hot dish," not a casserole. When you want a soft drink in this state, it's "pop," not soda.

Minnesota is the state that gave the world waterskiing, snowmobiling, in-line roller skating, two U.S. vice presidents, more than one Miss America, Paul Bunyan and Babe the Blue Ox, the Jolly Green Giant, the Pillsbury Doughboy, Prince, Bob Dylan, Charles Lindbergh, Sinclair Lewis and Judy Garland. A Minneapolis waterfall inspired Henry Wadsworth Longfellow's "The Song of Hiawatha," iron ore from Minnesota's Iron Range provided the steel that built much of this country, and the first enclosed shopping center in the United States, Southdale, was built right here.

The name Minnesota derives from the Dakota Indian word "Minisota," meaning sky-tinted water. "Sky blue wa-

Hurray! Minnesota

Lake of the Isles, Lake Calhoun and Lake Harriet.

ter" is the more common definition. It wasn't many years ago that a local brand of beer, Hamm's, built a successful marketing campaign around the "from the land of sky blue waters" theme, featuring a friendly cartoon bear. Minnesotans who have been around for a few years can still sing the Hamm's sky-blue-waters jingle.

Minnesota's major university has a lowly rodent, the gopher, as its mascot. Its professional baseball team has won the World Series twice in recent history, while its professional football team is one of two teams to go to the Super Bowl four times and never win. The relatively new professional basketball franchise, the Minnesota Timberwolves, is appropriately named. Minnesota's wolf population of 1,600 animals is the largest in the lower 48 states. In fact, Minnesota is home to the only sizeable populations of timber wolves and bald eagles left in the United States, outside of Alaska.

Minnesota has many other natural gifts — lakes, prairies, forests, rivers, wildlife and wildflowers, grasslands, meadows, river banks and beaches.

Minnesota has prairies and grassland plains in the southwestern part of the state, coniferous and hardwood forests in the north and east, respectively, and cropland and pastures in the south and central portions. More than half of the state's land is in crops and pasture and about a third is in forests.

Water flows out of Minnesota in three directions: south to the Gulf of Mexico, north to Hudson Bay in Canada, and east to the Atlantic Ocean. The Mississippi River has its source in Itasca State Park in north-central Minnesota. At the source you can literally step from stone to stone to cross the world's third-largest river as it begins its 2,552-mile journey to the Gulf.

THE 1990 CENSUS puts Minnesota's population at 4,358,000, which ranks it 21st in population among the 50 states. The number of people in Minnesota grew 6.8 percent during the 1980s, faster than the 2.2 percent growth rate of the entire Midwest, a trend projected to continue.

About 54 percent of Minnesotans live in the Minneapolis/St. Paul metro area. There are 854 incorporated cities in the state, and about three-quarters of the population lives in cities.

When you look at a map of Minnesota, the state looks fairly tall. It's 406 miles long and 348 miles wide. Making it look

WEATHER STATISTICS

	Temperatures (Degrees F)		Total Precipitation (inches)	Snowfall (inches)	Days of Sunshine
	High	Low			
January	21.2°	3.2°	0.73"	9.0"	50%
February	25.9°	7.1°	0.84"	7.7"	56%
March	36.9°	19.6°	1.68"	9.6"	57%
April	55.5°	34.7°	2.04"	3.1"	58%
May	67.9°	46.3°	3.37"	.02"	59%
June	77.1°	56.7°	3.94"	0.0"	63%
July	82.4°	61.4°	3.69"	0.0"	72%
August	80.8°	59.6°	3.05"	0.0"	68%
September	70.7°	49.3°	2.73"	trace	60%
October	60.7°	39.2°	1.78"	.05"	55%
November	40.6°	24.2°	1.20"	5.1"	41%
December	26.6°	10.6°	0.89"	7.3"	40%

SOURCE: National Weather Service, Minneapolis/St. Paul International Airport

YES, IT DOES GET A TAD CHILLY IN THE WINTER. The mean temperature in the northern part of the state in the winter is 4 degrees F and in the southern part is 15 degrees F. The summer mean temperature is 64 degrees F in the north and 70 degrees F in the south.

But mean temperatures really don't tell the weather story in this "theater of seasons," as Minnesotans call it. In fact, "mean" is a good description of the weather extremes, both frigid and hot.

January and February are the coldest months. The warmest are July and August. The all-time low temperature was 59 degrees below zero F on February 16, 1899, in Moorhead. The record high was 114.5 degrees above zero F on July 29, 1917, in Beardsley. Temperatures alone do not depict the Minnesota weather, however. During a winter cold snap Minnesotans will be heard to exclaim, "It's not just the temperature, it's the wind chill." In a summer heat wave they'll say, "It's not just the heat, it's the humidity." Of course, they're correct in both cases. The wind chill factor can intensify winter's punishing cold. And the humidity of July and August can make a torrid summer day less bearable.

taller is the little "chimney" poking into Canada from the top of the state. It's called the Northwest Angle and is the most northerly point in the contiguous 48 states. Minnesota owns the Northwest Angle because of a mapmaker's error back in 1775. In all, the state has a land area of more than 80,000 square miles, ranking it 12th in size among all states.

The highest point in Minnesota is Eagle Mountain in Cook County in the northeastern corner of the state at 2,301 feet above sea level. The lowest point is not far away: the shore of Lake Superior at 602 feet above sea level.

Most people who know almost nothing else about Minnesota know that the state has lots of lakes and that it gets real

Hurray! Minnesota

cold in the winter. Minnesota license plates boast "10,000 lakes." Officially, Minnesota has 15,291 lakes — more lakes than any other state. A more spectacular statistic is that Minnesota has more miles of shoreline than California, Florida and Hawaii combined, more than 90,000 miles. There are 7,762 square miles of lake, which is about 9 percent of the entire area of the state.

MINNESOTA HAS FOUR distinctly different seasons, and each holds special delights to those who live here.

Spring is that time of year when Minnesotans throw open the windows and return to the great outdoors — to gardening, yard work, golf, fishing, biking and hiking. It's when lilacs exude their summery sweetness. It's when farmers get back into the fields to seed and fertilize the crops. It's time to shape up the sailboat for another season and to be able to walk out of the house without wearing a jacket.

Summer is for outdoor activities. Perhaps it's from being cooped up inside all winter, but Minnesotans hit the outdoor activities with gusto through the summer months. Not just outdoor sporting activities, but picnics, cookouts and reunions, family celebrations and community festivals. It's not surprising that Minnesota has more golfers per capita than any other state. Golfers have been chomping at the bit all winter while watching tournaments on TV.

Summer days are long, the weather warm, and the flowers, vegetables and field crops are growing. But summer is mostly the time of year when Minnesotans take to the water — either in it, on it or around it. It's "up to the lake" or "up to the cabin" for Twin Citians. It's "out to the lake" for Minnesotans elsewhere. There are lakes in every one of the 87 counties of Minnesota except one — Rock, in the southwestern corner of the state.

> A LAKE is an area of open, relatively deep water sufficiently large to produce somewhere on its periphery a barren, wave-swept shore.
>
> A POND/WETLAND is shallow and sedentary water in which vegetation can grow.
>
> DNR Division of Waters

Lake Country, in the center of the state and continuing northward into the Arrowhead region, has the heaviest concentration of lakes. The Brainerd and Alexandria areas are prime summer-cabin and second-home territory. They're also prime resort areas, catering mostly to families and groups spending one, two or more weeks at the lake.

In the summer, Minnesota lakes are for swimming, waterskiing, power boating, sailing, windsurfing and fishing. They're for walking around, biking around, in-line skating around, driving around and for sitting by.

You can feel and see fall's arrival in Minnesota. The days grow shorter and the air begins to turn nippy. The leaves stage a spectacular show of color, and the media keeps you abreast of the peak "leaf peeping" dates throughout the state, starting in the north and moving to the south.

It used to be that a sure sign of fall was the smell of burning leaves. In these more environmentally conscious times, however, leaf burning is banned, at least in the larger cities.

Fall is back-to-school time. High schools around the state launch their football seasons, playing some games on warm Indian Summer afternoons, others on crisp bundle-up evenings under the lights.

Fall is when farmers sometimes work around the clock to complete the corn harvest and when hunters take to the fields, woods and sloughs to attempt to bag their limit of pheasants, partridge, ducks, geese and other game birds. Others don bright orange outer garments and head to the woods to test their bow and arrow or gun skills to claim a deer.

Winter's cold, snow and ice can make life difficult. Minnesotans cope by staying indoors, by layering on clothes, by packing a shovel and a winter storm-survival kit in the trunk. They also survive by enjoying the weather — skating, downhill and cross-country skiing, snowmobiling, sledding and tobogganing, playing ice hockey and staging and attending a myriad of festivals and events, such as the famous St. Paul Winter Carnival and the John Beargrease Sled Dog Marathon.

Some Minnesotans take to the lakes in the winter, too. They tow little huts out onto the lake, drill holes through the ice and fish for the big ones. Some lakes turn into small villages of fish houses. Word is that a card game and an occasional nip of schnapps might be more important than the day's catch, but we wouldn't know that for sure.

Winter is credited, rightly or wrongly, with certain Minnesota achievements. The difficult winters, it's said, make Minnesotans heartier than other Americans. Perhaps this is why Minnesotans have a longer life expectancy (76.2 years) than any state other than Hawaii. The cold winter weather gets credit for causing Minnesotans to work harder and study harder, since there are fewer distractions, at least outdoors, thereby creating a very productive and well-educated work force. More than 91 percent of Minnesota youth complete high school, 20 points higher than the national average. And two-thirds of recent high school grads went on to continue their education. College entrance scores by Minnesotans consistently rank in the top three nationally. And Minnesotans support the arts to a high degree — music, theater, dance, museums — with a healthy level of attendance. The Twin Cities metro area is second only to New York in number of theaters per capita.

We shouldn't fail to mention one other thing Minnesotans do in winter. They vacation in warm-weather places, saving their time at home to enjoy the springs, summers and autumns.

The Twin Cities metro area has snow emergencies in the winter and the Metropolitan Mosquito Control District to try to rid itself of the pesky mosquito in the summer. While providing some of the best fishing in North America, Minnesota's lakes also harbor the world's ugliest fish, the eelpout, which is the subject of a festival in the community of Walker. Minnesotans tell Iowa jokes about their neighbors to the south and call their Wisconsin neighbors to the east "cheeseheads." They don't dare say anything about Dakotans (either North or South) because so many Minnesotans are former Dakotans.

Yes, Minnesotans use and enjoy the great outdoors year-round. Minnesota is top ranked in the number of recreational watercraft per capita — one boat for every six residents. It is first nationally in the sales of fishing licenses per capita. And in the winter? It's the first-ranked state for the number of snowmobiles per capita — one for every 20 residents.

FROM LATE OCTOBER 1991 to early April 1992, the Hubert H. Humphrey Metrodome in Minneapolis alone hosted three of the biggest sporting events in the world. In a little more than five months, the Twins became world champions for the second time in five years in what those who follow these things called the best, or one of the best, World Series in the long history of the national pastime. The Washington Redskins beat the Buffalo Bills 37 to 24 in Super Bowl XXVI in what people who follow these things called an incredibly boring Super Bowl. And the Blue Devils of Duke took their second straight Final Four NCAA championship in a typically exciting end to another season of college basketball.

This was all part of an incredible roll of national athletic competition hosted in Minnesota, some of it won in bidding competition, some of it won by Minnesota teams on the field of battle. In May 1991, professional hockey's Stanley Cup went to the Pittsburgh Penguins over the Minnesota North Stars in the seventh and final game at Met Center in Bloomington. Then in June 1991, Hazeltine National Golf Course in the western suburb of Chaska hosted professional golf's U.S. Open, won in a Monday playoff by Payne Stewart.

Minnesota is a cultural oasis between the coasts. It is home to the Minnesota Orchestra, the Saint Paul Chamber Orchestra, the Minneapolis Institute of Arts, the Walker Art Center, the Guthrie Theater and the Children's Theatre Company. Minnesota is home to Garrison Keillor and his "hometown," Lake Wobegon, which has turned Minnesota's small-town culture into a national phenomenon.

Minnesota has a rich community of writers, artists, composers, musicians and comedians. It is home to several of the nation's most prestigious small publishers. One estimate is that there are 40,000 professional artists living in Minnesota.

Nationally, only 5 percent of the public attends the arts frequently, which is several times a month. In the Twin Cities, it's double that figure and throughout Minnesota it's above the national average.

By law, 1 percent of the cost of state-funded buildings in Minnesota is required to be used for the purchase of art to go into the new buildings. One-third of the state's appropriation for the support of the arts is allocated to 11 multi-county arts councils.

Corporate support also has been a major factor in the growth of the arts in Minnesota. The nation's first Five Percent Club was founded in 1976 by the Greater Minneapolis Chamber of Commerce to recognize 23 companies that gave 5 percent of their pre-tax domestic profits to charity, including the arts. The program is now statewide and recognizes contributions at the 2 percent to 5 percent level and above 5 percent. Now called the Keystone Program, the program has many times more participants than when it started and has become a model for other states.

A love of the great outdoors and all of its recreational opportunities are important elements in the lives of many Minnesotans and in the state's image. Other lifestyle issues, such as low crime rates, quality education and living costs below major cities on either coast, have resulted in several organizations ranking Minnesota as one of the most desirable places to live. Cultural and recreational opportunities also help businesses to recruit talent to Minnesota.

A recent ranking by Morgan Quitno Co. of Kansas, publisher of "State Rankings and State Perspectives," placed Minnesota as the second most

The Minnesota State Snow Sculpting Competition is held each year during the St. Paul Winter Carnival.

livable state, ranking only behind New Hampshire. The rankings are based on 28 categories, among them income, crime rate, graduation rate, suicide rate, taxes, life span and unemployment rate.

In 1991 Minnesota was ranked fifth in the "green index," an environmental scorecard of the 50 states done by the Institute for Southern Studies, Durham, North Carolina. Minnesota ranked behind Oregon, Maine, Vermont and California. Minnesota was specifically praised for community health programs, groundwater protection efforts, and the "superfund" program to clean up toxic-waste dump sites and waste recycling.

Gallup Organization interviewers recently asked people in the regions of the country to single out cities in their region offering the best quality of life. Minneapolis, often cited in various quality-of-life surveys, was the Midwest winner. Interview subjects praised Minneapolis for good cultural opportunities, museums, zoos, plays, lots of sports, clean air, and lakes and parks everywhere.

PHOTO BY TIM STEINBERG/ST. PAUL WINTER CARNIVAL

Answers to Myths about Minnesota's History

MYTH: The region now known as Minnesota was an empty wilderness when the first European explorers arrived in the area during the 17th century.
Far from uninhabited, the Minnesota of the 17th century and earlier supported several groups of people, including the Dakota and Ojibwa Indians.

The Dakota had long lived at the southern end of Lake Mille Lacs and at Leech Lake. They are related to other Sioux tribes that covered the Midwest and had such names as the Winnebago, the Omaha, the Osage and the Crow. In Minnesota, the Dakota ate fresh game, including bison and waterfowl; sugar prepared from maple syrup; fish; wild rice, berries and turnips; and cultivated corn. They called their land "Minimakoce."

The Ojibwa descended from another Indian group with roots further east — the Algonquins. Other Algonquin tribes were the Blackfeet, Ottawa, Kickapoo and Cree Indians. The Ojibwa initially occupied the land at the east end of Lake Superior but gradually pushed west until their territory overlapped that of the Dakota. They, too, hunted and gathered wild rice.

In all likelihood, the first Europeans to reach Minnesota were Pierre Radisson and Médard Chouart des Groseilliers, two French explorers who may have entered the region in the 1650s. As Radisson detailed in his journals, they encountered the Dakota, perhaps near Lake Mille Lacs. Another Frenchman, the trader Daniel du Lhut, visited the town at Mille Lacs in 1679. It is difficult to know with certainty the population of Native Americans in Minnesota during those years, but they certainly numbered in the thousands.

The Dakota and Ojibwa had been preceded by other peoples. The first, sometimes called Paleo-Indians, arrived from the south around the end of the last ice age, about 10,000 years ago. They hunted mammoth and other animals that gradually met extinction as the glaciers melted and receded. With the loss of their game, the Paleo-Indians moved or died out. They left few archaeological traces behind them.

About 7,000 years ago, other people began moving in. They ate nuts, berries and small animals as well as large game. As the centuries passed, they learned to build and use stone and metal tools, weave baskets and mats, harvest and store wild rice, and grow such crops as corn and squash. They also designed and built the nearly 10,000 burial mounds that at one time dotted the Minnesota landscape; most have been destroyed during the past 150 years. At the Jeffers Petroglyphs site in present-day Cottonwood County, these early Minnesotans left another mark on the state's landscape: 1,971 painted pictures of hunters, spears in flight, and battles involving armies of figures. Other petroglyphic carvings appeared on rock faces in such places as Dayton's Bluff in St. Paul, an island in Nett Lake in Koochiching County, Reno Cave in Houston County and a bluff site near Stillwater. These groups of people left the area around A.D. 500, after which the Dakota and Ojibwa people took their place.

MYTH: Discovering the source of the Mississippi River was an easy task, simply requiring explorers to follow the river upstream.
Locating the Mississippi headwaters long obsessed Europeans and frontier Americans. Efforts to follow the river upstream often ended with the discovery of difficult rapids (such as St. Anthony Falls in present-day Minneapolis), encounters with harsh conditions, wrong

Hurray! Minnesota

turns down tributaries, or the simple realization that the search had little to offer strategically or economically. In this way, the river's source resisted discovery for nearly 200 years of attempts.

Perhaps the earliest to seek the headwaters, in the 1620s, was Samuel de Champlain, the founder of the colony of Quebec. After hearing rumors of a huge river outside his territory, he mounted an unsuccessful expedition to find the waterway. Some 50 years later, another Frenchman named Louis Jolliet became the first European to see the Mississippi River. Still, the river's source was beyond his reach.

Others came later: Pierre Charles Le Sueur, who in 1700 traveled upstream all the way from the Gulf of Mexico to St. Anthony Falls; Jonathan Carver, a British officer whose upstream expedition in 1767 veered northeast to Lake Superior; Zebulon Montgomery Pike, a U.S. army officer who erroneously identified Leech and Cass lakes as the Mississippi's sources; and the adventurous Giacomo Constantino Beltrami, leader of an 1823 effort that incorrectly selected Lake Julia as the headwaters site.

Finally, it fell to Henry Schoolcraft, a little-known writer, to make — in partnership with an Indian guide named Yellow Head — the correct identification of the true beginning of the Mississippi's course in 1832. He merged the Latin words "veritas" and "caput" (meaning "true head") to form a new name for the lake: Itasca.

MYTH: People have always viewed Minnesota's harsh winter as a drawback to living here.

Ice-fishers, skiers, skaters, hockey players and many photographers will put up a strong argument that winter weather is nothing to avoid. But many promoters of the 1860s and 1870s advanced the notion that Minnesota's annual deep freeze could actually be good for your health.

From the earliest days of statehood, government agencies, railroad companies, business associations and anybody else with a financial stake in Minnesota's growth had to grapple with the main obstacle to immigration: the win-

ORIGINS OF MINNESOTA PLACE NAMES

Bloomington: Named after Bloomington, Illinois, by settlers who arrived in 1852.

Brainerd: Named in honor of Ann Eliza Brainerd Smith, wife of the first president of the Northern Pacific Railroad.

Burnsville: Named after the Burns family, early settlers from Canada.

Duluth: Named after Daniel Greysolon du Lhut, an explorer who journeyed to Lake Superior in 1678.

Edina: Named after the Edina flour mill located within its limits, which was named after the city of Edinburgh, Scotland.

Embarrass: Named after the Embarrass River, whose name derives from the French word "embarras" (meaning "difficult," due to the driftwood that obstructed river traffic).

Hopkins: Named after Harley Hopkins, an early town postmaster.

Minnetonka: Named by Governor Alexander Ramsey, who joined the Dakota words for "big" and "water." The Dakota, however, did not use this word as a name for the lake or region.

Mound: Named for the several Indian burial mounds in the area.

New Brighton: Named after Brighton, Massachusetts.

Osseo: Named for a character in Henry Wadsworth Longfellow's poem "The Song of Hiawatha."

St. Louis Park: Named for the Minneapolis and St. Louis Railway.

White Bear Lake: Named after an Indian belief that the spirit of a bear dwelt in the lake.

NOTABLE DATES IN MINNESOTA'S HISTORY

Circa 8,000 B.C. The Paleo-Indians, Minnesota's first residents, move into the region.
1650s Pierre Radisson and Médard Chouart des Groseilliers, French fur traders, explore the area and encounter Dakota and Ojibwa people.
1680 Louis Hennepin views the Falls of St. Anthony.
1763 England takes possession of the eastern portion of Minnesota.
1783 United States assumes sovereignty of eastern Minnesota region.
1803 Western Minnesota falls under U.S. ownership with the Louisiana Purchase.
1805 Lt. Zebulon Pike arrives at the juncture of the Mississippi and Minnesota rivers and selects it as the location of Fort Snelling, which was built in 1820.
1832 Henry Schoolcraft identifies Lake Itasca as the Mississippi's true source.
1836 With the organization of Wisconsin Territory, eastern Minnesota becomes a part of Crawford County, Wisconsin.
1840 St. Paul founded.
1847 First settlements in present-day Minneapolis.
1849 Creation of Minnesota Territory.
1850 The U.S. census records 6,077 Minnesotans.
1851 As part of the Treaty of Traverse des Sioux, the Dakota Sioux sell 24 million acres of their Minnesota lands to the federal government for about $3 million, or about 12 1/2 cents per acre.
1858 Minnesota attains statehood.
1862 U.S.-Dakota Conflict results in the death of several hundred Dakota Indians and white settlers.
1865 Iron ore discovered near Vermilion Lake.
1873 Grasshoppers begin a five-year infestation of the state.
1878 A flour mill explosion in Minneapolis kills 18 people.
1889 Mayo Clinic opens in Rochester.
1891 Creation of Itasca State Park, site of the Mississippi headwaters.
1894 Forest fires destroy Hinckley and Sandstone, killing 400 people and leaving 2,200 homeless.
1900 Wheat is the most common crop on Minnesota's farms, claiming half of the cultivated acreage.
1902 George Draper Dayton opens his first retail establishment in Minneapolis at the corner of Seventh and Nicollet.
1905 Completion of the State Capitol building.

---

ter weather. At the same time, one of the nation's great health scourges of the era was tuberculosis. Physicians commonly prescribed relocation to a dry, cool climate for consumptive patients, and Minnesotans pointed out that their state provided both qualities during the winter season. As a result, people with tuberculosis flocked to Minnesota, including such a notable as Henry David Thoreau.

So many came, in fact, that Minnesota's main image nationwide during the 1860s and '70s was as a haven for sick people. "Minnesota all the year round is one vast hospital," one visitor wrote during the 1860s. "All her cities and towns, and many of her farm houses, are crowded with those fleeing the approach of the dread destroyer." A book titled "Minnesota as a Home for Invalids" sold well, while water-cure resorts, patent-medicine quacks and convalescent hotels flourished.

One effect of this influx of invalids was to create a stubborn tuberculosis problem in Minnesota that took decades to eradicate. On the other hand, some of

1906 There are 67 miles of paved roads in the state.
1918 Forest fires in Carlton and St. Louis counties claim 432 lives.
1920 Publication of Sinclair Lewis' novel "Main Street."
1927 Charles Lindbergh and "The Spirit of St. Louis" make a solo flight across the Atlantic Ocean.
1928 912 Minnesota communities have electric power.
1929 A riot erupts at Lexington Park in St. Paul during a baseball game between the St. Paul Saints and the Minneapolis Millers.
1930 Frank Kellogg, U.S. Secretary of State and a Minnesotan, receives the Nobel Peace Prize for his work on the Kellogg-Briand Peace Pact to outlaw war.
1931 A road construction crew near Pelican Rapids discovers a fossil skeleton that is about 10,000 years old; it becomes known as "Minnesota Man" (even though the skeleton proves to be a young woman's).
1931 Sinclair Lewis, a native of Sauk Centre, wins the Nobel Prize in Literature.
1937 The federal government creates Pipestone National Monument to preserve a sacred Indian rock quarry.
1943 At the peak of World War II, Minnesota's iron ore mines produce 83 million tons, an all-time record.
1948 For the first time, the value of Minnesota's manufactured products exceeds the value of farm goods.
1959 Duluth becomes an oceanic port with the completion of the St. Lawrence Seaway.
1961 Duluth and Superior, Wisconsin, joined by mile-and-a-half-long aerial lift bridge.
1963 The Guthrie Theater opens in Minneapolis.
1964 Hubert Humphrey, elected U.S. vice president, becomes the first Minnesotan to rise to national office.
1973 Governor Wendell Anderson appears on the cover of Time under the headline "The Good Life in Minnesota."
1974 Orchestra Hall opens in Minneapolis.
1979 Despite years of protest, a 436-mile power line is put into operation between Underwood, North Dakota, and Delano, Minnesota.
1983 Prince shoots his film "Purple Rain" in Minnesota.
1987 Minnesota Twins win the World Series.
1991 The Minnesota Twins are again world champions.

---

the sick did recover, and many became highly productive citizens.

MYTH: Minnesota, because of its distance from the front lines of the Civil War, played only a minor role in that conflict.

Years before the Civil War, Minnesota figured prominently in a Supreme Court case that may have made the fighting inevitable. And during the conflict, Minnesotans figured prominently in one of the war's most important battles.

The Supreme Court case was Dred Scott vs. Sanford, and it steepened America's slide into national division on the issue of slavery. Scott, a black slave born around 1800, asserted that the years he spent with his master at Illinois' Fort Armstrong and present-day Minnesota's Fort Snelling, both places in which slavery was illegal, made him a free man. The Court disagreed.

In 1836, an army physician named John Emerson, Scott's owner, traveled to Fort Snelling. The Missouri Compromise forbade slavery in this region (then a part of Wisconsin Territory), but Scott followed his master and remained a slave.

Emerson's service at the fort lasted until 1840. He and Scott went to St. Louis, and Emerson died in 1843. In 1846, while in the service of another Missouri slave-holder, Scott sued for his freedom. Finally, after 11 years of judicial dispute over his case, his suit went to the docket of the Supreme Court, where in 1857 Chief Justice Roger B. Taney declared that despite Scott's sojourns at Forts Armstrong and Snelling, the slave could not claim the citizenship of either Illinois or Wisconsin Territory. Black people, Taney pronounced, were not eligible for citizenship and had no right to sue in federal courts. The decision heightened the tension between abolitionists and advocates of slavery. Only four years later, the first Confederate shots were fired against the federal garrison at Fort Sumter, South Carolina.

That morning, on April 14, 1861, Minnesota Governor Alexander Ramsey happened to be in Washington, D.C. Immediately after hearing news of the attack on Fort Sumter and the surrender of the Union soldiers, he offered President Abraham Lincoln 1,000 Minnesota troops to fight in the war. Minnesota became the first northern state to volunteer soldiers.

The First Minnesota Volunteers filled a vital role in perhaps the most legendary battle of the war. On July 2, 1863, during the Battle of Gettysburg, the Minnesotans attacked the advancing Southern troops. While the Confederates were stopped, 47 percent of the Minnesotans were killed or wounded. The survivors, augmented by other Union troops, turned back the Southerners in a decisive second engagement on the following day.

Charles Lindbergh

MYTH: Charles Lindbergh, the Minnesotan whose solo transatlantic flight in 1927 made history, was otherwise a pretty dull guy.

In 1927, Charles Lindbergh Jr. was the world's most famous Minnesotan. Five years later, after the kidnapping and murder of his and Anne Morrow Lindbergh's young son, he was the most pitied. Before another decade had passed, World War II had broken out and Lindbergh was the most puzzling.

More than anything else, Lindbergh was a creative adventurer—a man who developed unpopular, unusual and seemingly impossible notions and put them into motion. Sometimes his ideas proved wrong and made people angry, but more often his dreams became startling and glorious realities.

Lindbergh's father, Charles Lindbergh Sr., ranked among Minnesota's most respected—but certainly not most popular—politicians of the early 20th century. For years an attorney practicing in the town of Little Falls, Lindbergh Sr. based his political career on his conviction that a cartel of bankers exerted too much influence over America's domestic and foreign policy. He won election to the U.S. Congress, but lost in a 1918 campaign to win the governorship.

Meanwhile, his son was tinkering with autos and motorcycles. The big sky above the plains near Little Falls also interested him, and he took up airplane barnstorming. In 1927, he heard about a prize of $25,000 that a man named Raymond Orteig was offering to the first pilot to fly alone from New York to Paris. Despite his lack of expertise as a navigator, Lindbergh resolved to win the prize — and did.

After this stunning success, Lindbergh did not pursue publicity and

Hurray! Minnesota

gained a reputation as a loner. With his wife, the former Anne Morrow, Lindbergh again shunned public attention in 1932 following the kidnapping and murder of their infant son. The couple moved to Europe. In the years that followed, Lindbergh developed an interest in biomedical science.

Lindbergh described his scientific work in a 1935 issue of The Journal of Experimental Medicine. Prompted by his sister's heart disease, he had begun wondering how it might be possible to keep blood circulating in the body while physicians temporarily stopped the beating of the heart to perform corrective surgery. Over several years, he and surgeon Alexis Carrel invented a three-chambered glass pump equipped with a platinum-screen filter, which in experiments proved effective in keeping a cat alive while its heart was stopped. Lindbergh's pump became known as an early artificial heart.

Nobody had expected an aviator to become a medical engineer, and even less did people anticipate Lindbergh's plunge into politics. But in the late 1930s, after meeting Hermann Goring and viewing Nazi Germany's Luftwaffe, Lindbergh publicly expressed his opinion that the Germans were militarily invincible and that America should stay out of the European war that was coming.

After the war, when the Nazis had proved quite beatable, most people forgave Lindbergh for his adventure in politics. They accepted it as another sign that the flier sometimes flew off course — an accepted risk for adventurers.

MYTH: During the post-World War II years, the suburbs of the Twin Cities inexplicably sprouted like mushrooms.
They sprouted, yes. Inexplicably, no.

The rise of Minnesota's suburbs began after the Great Depression and the outbreak of World War II, when the state's economy exploded with pent-up energy, and the Twin Cities could not contain the growth. Places like Edina, Bloomington, Roseville and Coon Rapids might have remained quiet little towns and farming communities had they been located farther from Minneapolis and St. Paul, but instead they sat within easy driving distance of the cities — making them attractive sites for the building of homes, shopping centers and businesses for the enormous number of post-war baby boom families. From a cozy area of 150 square miles in 1900, the Twin Cities metro region swelled to 800 square miles during the next eight decades.

And suburban sprawl wasn't only a Minneapolis/St. Paul phenomenon. In Duluth/Superior, the suburban population multiplied 10 times between 1900 and 1984. Fargo/Moorhead, St. Cloud, Winona, Mankato and Rochester each eventually blossomed at the edges with suburbanites.

Wherever this sprawl occurred, the automobile made it possible. All the way into the 1930s, the geographic reach of the state's major cities had extended as far as the streetcar tracks could carry it. By 1946, however, most Minnesota families owned a car, making residence within the city no longer necessary for people who wanted to enjoy the employment and cultural life available downtown. The small communities that ringed Minneapolis and St. Paul, with their wide-open fields and undeveloped tracts of land, beckoned.

By 1960, when the Twin Cities suburban population stood at nearly a half million, the suburbs had attained a second phase of growth. With thousands of homes and schools built in the preceding years, suburban communities had to pay more attention to road improvements, extensions of the sewer and water systems, and better facilities for such institutions as churches and synagogues, city government and libraries. Already altered from small towns to suburbs, the communities grew into small cities and lured businesses and services from Minneapolis and St. Paul. By the time most of the suburban baby boomers had reached early adulthood in the '70s, the places in which they had grown up had collectively roped in more than 40 percent of the employment available in the Twin Cities and most of the construction of new office towers, hotels, malls, retail strips and warehouses.

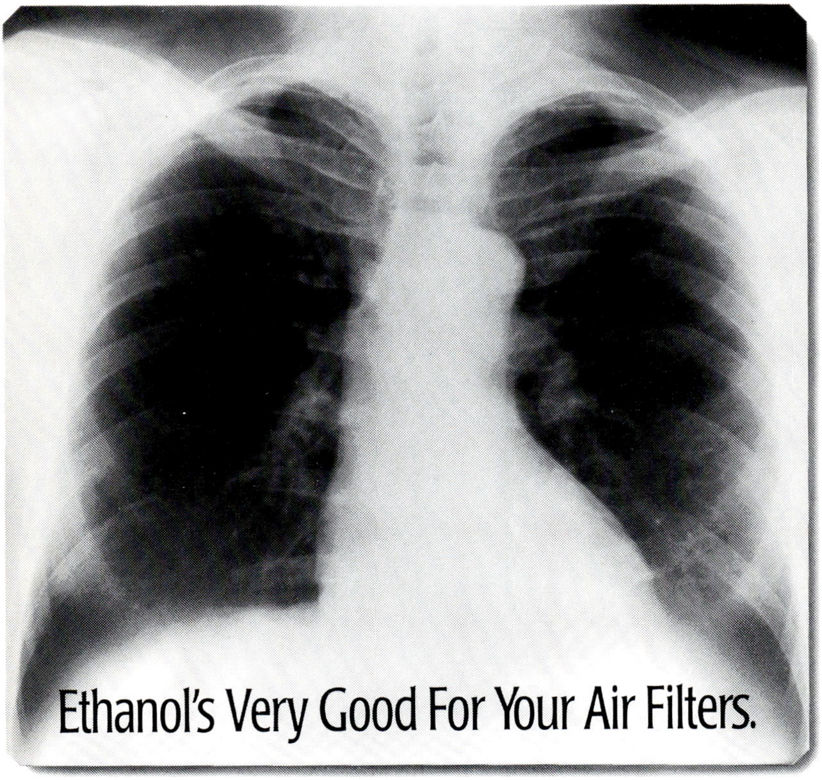

Ethanol's Very Good For Your Air Filters.

Carbon monoxide poisons your lungs. It robs them of oxygen, and causes drowsiness and nausea. The Environmental Protection Agency now says the Twin Cities and Duluth metropolitan areas have unhealthy carbon monoxide levels. Do you know where most of it comes from? Automobile exhaust. That's why you should use ethanol-blended fuel. Ethanol reduces harmful carbon monoxide emissions by up to 25 percent, and it's safe for your car. So fill up with ethanol. It'll keep your air filters running smoothly.

ethanol
Fuel For Clean Air

Sponsored by the Minnesota Corn Farmers

Minnesota's fragile state flower, the lady's slipper.

Minnesota's Symbols

THE FLAG
ROYAL BLUE IN color with a gold fringe border, Minnesota's flag has the state seal in the center with a wreath of lady's slippers around it. A ring of 19 stars surrounds the wreath, the largest star representing Minnesota, the 32nd state to join the union. Three dates are in the wreath: 1819, the date of the founding of Fort Snelling; 1858, when Minnesota became a state; and 1893, when the legislature adopted the first state flag. The current flag was adopted in 1957, replacing the earlier, more elaborate version.

THE GREAT SEAL
THE FIRST GREAT SEAL of the State of Minnesota was adopted in 1861. The seal had different variations over the years until 1983, when the legislature passed a bill that described the seal in detail. The official seal shows a barefoot farmer plowing a field near the Mississippi River, with St. Anthony Falls at the right. The farmer's ax, gun and powderhorn rest on a nearby stump, as he looks at an Indian on horseback trotting toward him. Minnesota's state motto, "L'Etoile du Nord," French for Star of the North, also appears on the seal.

BIRD — COMMON LOON
DATING BACK 60 million years, the common loon is the earth's oldest living bird species. More than 12,000 of the black and white birds live in Minnesota, giving the state a higher loon population than all other U.S. states combined, excluding Alaska. Loons can have a wing span of five feet, body length of three feet and weigh up to nine pounds. Because of their weight, loons have trouble taking off from the water. However, when flying, they can reach speeds of 60 miles per hour. Loons are excellent divers and underwater swimmers, and few fish can match their swimming ability. Their most distinctive feature is their call, which some people describe as haunting. Actually, loons make four distinct sounds: a hoot, a wail, a yodel, and a tremolo. The loon became the state bird in 1961.

TREE — NORWAY PINE
THE NORWAY PINE, also called the red pine, stands 60-100 feet tall, with a trunk 3-5 feet wide. The needles are 4-6 inches long and grow in pairs. Minnesota's largest Norway is in Itasca State Park. It's

120 feet tall and more than 300 years old. The Norway pine is a prime timber source. It was named state tree in 1953.

FISH — WALLEYE
THE WALLEYED PIKE is a favorite catch because of its fight and its good taste. Walleye are found in lakes throughout the state, but mainly the large, cool lakes of northern Minnesota. Walleyes travel in schools and usually feed at dusk and dawn. Their eyes are sensitive to light, so they go to the deep, darker waters during the day and move to shallow water at night. Minnesota's record walleye weighed 16 pounds, 11 ounces, and was about 15 years old. The walleye became the state fish in 1965.

FLOWER — LADY'S SLIPPER
THE SHOWY OR pink and white lady's slipper, a species of orchid, is one of Minnesota's rarest wildflowers. It became the state flower in 1902, and the legislature passed a law in 1922 making it illegal to pick the lady's slipper. Lady's slippers thrive in swamps, bogs and damp woods. Plants grow slowly, taking four to 16 years to produce their first flower. They bloom in late June or early July. Under the right conditions, lady's slippers have a long life span, some being more than a century old.

GRAIN — WILD RICE
A STAPLE FOOD for local Native Americans for centuries, wild rice today is a delicacy for many people. Minnesota produces 80 percent of all natural wild rice in the world. Wild rice became the state grain in 1977.

GEMSTONE — LAKE SUPERIOR AGATE
COLLECTORS FIND THE Lake Superior agate in the red glacial drift areas of central and northeastern Minnesota and along the shore of Lake Superior. This stone, a quartz mineral, became the state gemstone in 1969. Polished agates are used in jewelry making.

FUNGUS — MOREL MUSHROOM
YOU FIND MOREL mushrooms in hardwood forests throughout Minnesota in late spring. The morel is known for its delicious flavor and distinctive honeycomb pattern. It became the official state fungus in 1984.

SONG — "HAIL! MINNESOTA"
MINNESOTA'S STATE SONG is "Hail! Minnesota." In case you're at an official state function, or if you just want to impress your friends at a sing-along, here are the words:
Minnesota hail to thee!
Hail to thee our state so dear,
Thy light shall ever be
A beacon bright and clear.
Thy sons and daughters true
Will proclaim thee near and far,
They will guard thy fame and
adore thy name;
Thou shalt be their Northern Star.

GOVERNMENT

FEDERAL GOVERNMENT
MINNESOTA HAS TWO senators who serve six-year terms in the U.S. Senate. As of 1992, they were David Durenberger and Paul Wellstone. In the U.S. House of Representatives, there are eight representatives serving two-year terms.

STATE GOVERNMENT
AS WITH THE federal government, Minnesota has three branches of state government: executive, legislative and judicial.

The governor, lieutenant governor, secretary of state, attorney general, auditor and treasurer constitute the six-member executive department. They are elected independently and serve four-year terms.

The bicameral state legislature consists of the House of Representatives, whose 134 members are elected for two-year terms, and the Senate, which is comprised of 67 members serving four-year terms.

The Supreme Court, district court, probate court and municipal courts encompass the judicial arm of the state government. Judges are elected by the voters for six-year terms.

Hurray! Minnesota

The State Capitol building faces downtown St. Paul and the Mississippi.

LOCAL GOVERNMENT

MINNESOTA'S 87 COUNTIES, 855 cities and 1,802 townships provide local governmental services: fire protection, law enforcement, libraries, parks and recreation, local highway and road maintenance, water and sewer services, land-use control, economic develop-

---

STATE GOVERNMENT INFORMATION

THE "MINNESOTA LEGISLATIVE MANUAL" is updated annually and offers extensive information on the three branches of state government. Contact your state representative or the secretary of state's office at (612) 296-2805 for a copy.

- State government general information
(612) 296-6013
- State Capitol guided tours offered daily from 9 a.m. to 4 p.m.
(612) 296-2881
- State House of Representatives information
(612) 296-2146
- House of Representatives agenda and meetings hotline
(612) 296-9283
- State Senate information
(612) 296-0504
- Senate agenda and meetings hotline
(612) 296-8088

ment, airports and welfare service. Public education comes under the jurisdiction of Minnesota's 423 school districts.

The Jolly Green Giant towers above Blue Earth.

BUSINESS

MINNESOTA'S BUSINESS history is steeped in the three empires of timber, agriculture and iron. Superior transportation provided by the Great Lakes, the Mississippi River, the advent of the railroads and powerful men such as **James J. Hill** gave the state the competitive advantage to move ahead in national and international economics despite its geographic position. Timber, iron and agriculture provided the capital to build Minnesota's infrastructure.

In 1991 Minnesota was rated 16th in the nation as a manufacturing exporter and first among the states in international marketing efforts. Manufactured exports in 1990 exceeded $5.5 billion. The Twin Cities, central to this progress, have been cited as an emerging U.S. control center destined to play a key economic role nationally with other cities such as Dallas and Atlanta.

From the three basic industries, Minnesota business has expanded into manufacturing, finance, insurance and real estate, and the service industries for its major sources of income, particularly in the areas of computers and medical technology. At one time, four of the top five computer manufacturers were either headquartered in Minnesota or had major facilities located here.

In 1992 a comparative study of the public corporations in Minnesota determined the top 10 corporations as:

3M
Norwest Banks
Dayton Hudson
General Mills
Honeywell
St. Paul Companies
Super Valu
First Bank
Northern States Power
Deluxe Corporation

There were an additional 10 public companies that generated income in the billion-dollar range. Three private companies — **Northwest Airlines**, **Carlson Companies** and **Cargill** — also generated more than $5 billion in annual revenue. In fact, Cargill's reported revenue was roughly three times the top public company's revenue at $49 billion.

AGRICULTURE

FARMING WAS THE first industry in Minnesota after fur trading. In fact, farms were begun in the Red River Valley before the means to get the goods out existed. As the railroads stretched westward, the transport for produce became cost-efficient. In the late 1800s, this led to the bonanza farms of the Red River Valley that grew huge crops, first wheat and later sugar beets.

Hurray! Minnesota

By 1878 nearly 70 percent of Minnesota's tilled land was in wheat. The availability of the wheat led to the growth of food industry giants such as **General Mills** and **Pillsbury**.

The majority of farming in Minnesota is done across the southern and western portions of the state. Minnesota's first cash crops were corn, then potatoes, wheat and oats. It was in Minnesota that America's second-largest privately held corporation, the agriculture giant, Cargill, got its start in 1865.

The **Green Giant** brand name originated with the products of the Minnesota River Valley, the valley of the Jolly (ho, ho, ho) Green Giant. A 55-foot statue of the Green Giant stands in Blue Earth.

Dairy farming took precedence during the 1880s and '90s. In 1921 the dairy co-ops united to form the Minnesota Cooperative Creameries Association and the **Land O'Lakes** brand. Minnesota is still a strong dairy state. This is proven annually at the Minnesota State Fair. The all-you-can-drink milk concession of the American Dairy Association of Minnesota is the top money-making concession. (Just a tip for the true milk-drinking connoisseurs. There's a double-fudge brownie stand just across the way.) Minnesotans drink more milk per capita than people in any other state.

Agriculture, including food processing, remains the largest economic sector in Minnesota's economy. The economic value of Minnesota crops is $6 to $7 billion annually. It is estimated that the combined annual agribusiness revenue is more than $100 billion annually. The main crops farmed on Minnesota's 26.5 million acres of farmland are sugar beets, soybeans, corn and wheat with dairy as number one in the livestock area.

LUMBER

THE WHITE PINE, prize of the lumberman, was abundant in the Minnesota woods. This large tree, valued for its strong, odorless, soft, straight-grained and buoyant wood was excellent for planking, ships' masts, and paper manufacturing. The timber industry followed the virgin forests westward to Minnesota. Until 1860, lumbering was Minnesota's most lucrative business and provided the first major contribution of capital that was used to build future industries in Minnesota. People such as **Henry Sibley**, **Frederick Weyerhaeuser**, **Thomas B. Walker** and, of course, the fictional Paul Bunyan achieved fame and fortune thanks to the Minnesota woods.

Today, the lumber industry still contributes $6.2 billion annually to Minnesota's economy, employing 58,000 people. The secondary industries, particularly paper production, contribute even more. St. Cloud is the number-one lightweight-coated-paper-producing city in the nation.

MINING

DURING ITS HEYDAY, the greatest years being the 1940s and '50s, the three ranges of Vermilion, Cuyuna and Mesabi were the largest iron ore producers in the nation. The annual record for iron ore removed from the ranges was set in 1951 at more than 89 million tons.

When sources of the high-grade ore were exhausted in the 1950s, the industry reinvested to produce a lower grade of ore, taconite. Minnesota ranges are still one of the top iron ore sources in the United States.

During the last four years, production has been around 40 million tons of taconite with the industry pumping $1 billion into the state's economy and employing more than 6,000 people. For the last 10 years, more than half of the nation's annual iron ore production has come from Minnesota.

MANUFACTURING

IN 1989 THE manufacturing climate in Minnesota was ranked sixth in the nation, and Minnesota joined the ranks of states with high-intensity manufacturing. In 1987 the value added to Minnesota's economy through manufacturing was more than $22 billion.

Dominant in the sector is the manufacturing of high-technology goods such as computers, electronics and medical equipment. Minnesota is particularly strong in medical technology, thanks to its long tradition of innovative work in the medical field. The medical technology field in Minnesota owes much of its strength to such renowned institutions as the **Mayo Clinic** in Rochester and the University of Minnesota hospitals. In 1990 the top 100 high-tech manufacturers contributed $28.7 billion to Minnesota's economy.

TOURISM

MORE THAN 16 million visitors, both pleasure and business, annually explore Minnesota from the shores of Lake Superior to lake-country resorts to the wilderness of the Boundary Waters. With the opening of the Mall of America in the Twin Cities, those numbers are predicted to increase substantially, especially from the Japanese community, which already makes up 16.7 percent of the overseas travelers. Tourism has contributed as much as $6.8 billion to the economy and employs more than 98,400 people.

SERVICE COMPANIES

MINNESOTA HAS GIVEN birth to a number of America's major retailers, such as **Sears**, **Mills Fleet Farm**, **Gamble-Skogmo**, **Super Valu** and **Dayton Hudson Corporation**, one of the largest retailers in the nation.

Carlson Companies, specializing in marketing and incentive premiums, has grown into one of the largest private-service organizations under the entrepreneurial guidance of **Curt Carlson**, whose business began with his inspired marketing of **Gold Bond Stamps**. More than 50 percent of Minnesota's employment comes from the service sector.

FINANCE AND INSURANCE

MINNESOTA SERVES AS the financial center for the Midwest. The Federal Reserve Bank headquarters for the Ninth Federal Reserve District is located in Minneapolis. **Norwest Bank** and **First Bank** are the largest banks in Minnesota, each with assets totaling more than $11 billion. Minnesota has been rated among the top 10 states in venture capital funds per capita.

Incorporated in 1853, the St. Paul Companies Inc., specializing in underwriting, brokering and investment banking, is Minnesota's oldest business corporation as well as the largest medical liability insurer in the world.

FILM

THE **MINNESOTA FILM BOARD** was established in 1983 as a quasi-governmental, nonprofit commission to attract the film industry to Minnesota. Its success was demonstrated in 1990 and the first four months of 1991 when seven feature films shot here generated $14.5 million in Minnesota. Minnesota is now the fourth-largest market for film and video production in the country and creates jobs for some 5,000 people in the state. Two reasons for the Film Board's huge success in the state are the fresh locations and the more than 100 companies and 150 support services available to the industry.

SECONDARY EDUCATION

STARTING AS FAR back as 1851, with the tentative beginnings of a preparatory school that was to eventually become the University of Minnesota, Minnesota has taken pride in her students and educational system. Minnesota's colleges and universities have consistently won national recognition, with many of the colleges ranking in the top 10.

Today, along with the four campuses of the University of Minnesota, there are seven public universities and 23 private colleges and universities across the state. There are also eight private professional schools that include three seminaries and a law school; three two-year colleges; 23 community colleges; 36 technical colleges and more than 40 vocational colleges covering vocations from business and neon-sign creating to auctioneering and horseshoeing.

There are plans to merge the state college system with the community colleges and state technical colleges to form one governing body. This will create a single system with more than 62 campuses and 160,000 students.

With a high school graduation rate as high as 91 percent, which has been the highest in the nation (1987), Minnesotans have made good use of this

Hurray! Minnesota

well established secondary education system. Approximately 58 percent of Minnesota's high school graduates go on to some form of secondary education.

The University of Minnesota is one of the largest universities in the nation. Enrollment is generally around 50,000 students annually. It has consistently been ranked in the top 20 of public and private institutions in the United States. The university has more than 250 fields of study awarding more than 10,000 degrees annually, and more than 600 of those degrees are Ph.D.s. Two-thirds of the graduates from the university remain in Minnesota for their first job.

The University of Minnesota has four campuses: the Twin Cities, Duluth, Morris and Crookston. Advanced degrees are offered by the law, medical and dental schools, among others. Some of the notable institutes and research centers affiliated with the university and its programs are the Supercomputer Center, the University of Minnesota Hospital and Clinic – Variety Club Children's Hospital, and the Humphrey Institute of Public Affairs (all located in Minneapolis), the Hormel Institute in Austin, Lake Itasca Forestry and Biological Station and the university agricultural experiment stations located around the state.

The University of St. Thomas and Macalester College have been ranked as the top Midwest "up and coming" colleges in a 1991 U.S. News & World Report survey, and both Carleton and St. Olaf colleges of Northfield have been listed among the nation's top 10 small colleges. Carleton College has consistently ranked in the top 20 of national liberal arts colleges.

Many of the private colleges offer unique programs and centers for learning, such as Gustavus Adolphus College, which for the last 25 years has sponsored the Nobel Conference. This two-day, highly esteemed international conference examines different scientific disciplines every year. Another unique institution is the Hill Monastic Manuscript Library at St. John's University in Collegeville. The library is a research center dedicated to the preservation of the world's ancient manuscripts.

Most famous of the technical and vocational institutions is Dunwoody Institute in Minneapolis, a nationally acclaimed technical institute. It is reputed to be the largest of the four private industrial and technical institutions in the nation and has been providing state-of-the-art technical training for more than 75 years.

TRANSPORTATION

BY AIR

THE MOST COMMON means of long-distance travel to and from the Twin Cities is by air. The Minneapolis/St. Paul International Airport is located south of the Twin Cities on Interstate 494 and Highway 5. Allow plenty of time to reach the airport. The freeways around the airport often move slowly during peak traffic hours in the morning and afternoon.

The airport is relatively easy to navigate. It is divided into four concourses with the main terminal having an upper and a lower level. It is designed so that passengers can be dropped off at the upper level for ticketing and baggage check-in and picked up on the lower level, which houses the baggage claim areas, rental car and limousine service information.

At the lower level directly across the street from the baggage claim are the taxi and limousine stands, as well as rental car pickup. A taxi to downtown Minneapolis, which is roughly 10 miles, averages $15. To St. Paul, eight miles away, fares run around $11. There are more than 30 taxi companies serving the metro area.

Airport Express (612) 827-7777 provides a van service to Minneapolis. Round trip is $13.50; one-way is $9. To St. Paul, round trip is $10.50; one-way is $7. Rates vary, but van service also is available to many of the suburban hotels.

Metropolitan Transit Commission (MTC) buses run from the airport to downtown Minneapolis and St. Paul, but they are not express buses and can

PECULIARLY MINNESOTA

Adopt A Highway

Since May 1990 Minnesota has had an Adopt-a-Highway program, similar to programs functioning in well over half of the states. Members of some 4,000 organizations — businesses, civic groups, Scout troops, church groups, 4H clubs, even families — adopt specific lengths of highways (at least two miles long) and pledge to do at least three trash pickups each year along "their" stretch of road. Adopted highways account for some two-thirds of Minnesota's state highways. The Minnesota Department of Transportation (DOT) provides the groups with trash bags, orange safety vests and safety training. The DOT erects the signs you see along the highways crediting the organizations for their efforts. And the DOT picks up the filled trash bags.

Like most states, Minnesota has a law against littering — tossing things from your car onto the roadway or ditches or boulevards along the highways. The penalty ranges from a minimum fine of $69.20 to as high as $700. Law enforcement officers have not been known to be good-natured about littering violations.

---

take up to 45 minutes. Many of the hotels offer free transport service, so check with them when making your reservations or when you arrive at the airport.

Airline service is dominated by **Northwest Airlines**, which is headquartered in the Twin Cities. Northwest operates non-stop flights to more than 68 domestic, six international and 29 air-link destinations.

The airlines that serve the Twin Cities are:
America West (800) 247-5692
American Airlines (800) 433-7300
Continental Airlines (612) 332-1471
Delta Air Lines (612) 339-7477
KLM Royal Dutch Airlines (800) 777-5553

Northwest Airlines:
Domestic (612) 726-1234
International (612) 726-3366
TWA (612) 333-5643
United Airlines (800) 241-6522
USAir (800) 428-4322

If you're traveling by charter, many of the charter flights use the **Hubert H. Humphrey Terminal**, which is just west of the main terminal off Interstate 494.

BY TRAIN

The Twin Cities is served by **Amtrack**. St. Paul/Minneapolis Midway Station is off University Avenue at 730 Transfer Road in St. Paul. The schedule is limited. The eastbound train to Chicago leaves at 7:20 a.m. From Chicago you can transfer to trains east and south. The westbound train for Portland and Seattle leaves at midnight. Sleeper cars are available going west at very reasonable prices that include meals. (800) 872-7245.

BY BUS

Though many of the towns and cities around the state have airports, one of the most convenient means of travel within the state is by bus. There are two major bus lines serving Minnesota: **Greyhound Bus Lines** (612) 371-3311 and **Jefferson Lines** (612) 332-3224. There are terminals in St. Paul at Ninth and St. Peter streets and in Minneapolis at 29 N. Ninth St.

For travel within the metro area, the MTC provides inexpensive around-town bus service (612) 827-7733, which includes vehicles with handicapped facilities and express service to downtown, many of the malls and suburbs.

BY CAR

Some traffic rules that travelers should be aware of in Minnesota are:
■ Drivers, front-seat passengers, and all passengers ages 4-10 must wear seatbelts.
■ Infants and children under the age of 4 must be properly secured in a federally approved child carseat.
■ Headlights must be turned on any time that the windshield wipers are being used because of rain or snow.
■ Speed limits on rural interstate highways are 65 miles per hour, and on open

Hurray! Minnesota

highways, 55 miles per hour or as posted. On city streets, the limit is 30 miles per hour or as posted.

Road condition information for roads throughout the state is available from the Minnesota Department of Transportation. Taped messages with up-to-date information on road construction are available by phone 24 hours a day. From the Twin Cities area, phone 296-3076. From outside the Twin Cities area and from other states, phone (800) 542-0220. A seasonal publication, "The Get-Around Guide," has maps with a list of road construction areas and detours throughout the state. For a copy, phone (612) 296-3000.

Travel Information Centers are operated by the Office of Tourism at 11 key entry points to the state — Beaver Creek, Worthington, Albert Lea, Dresbach, St. Croix, Thompson Hill, Grand Portage, Anchor Lake, International Falls, Fisher's Landing and Moorhead. These centers are open daily from 8 a.m. to 6 p.m. from Memorial Day weekend through Labor Day. The rest of the year they are open daily from 9 a.m. to 5 p.m. (Worthington, Fisher's Landing and Grand Portage Bay centers are not open year-round; they open May 1 for the season.) Maps and brochures are available. Staff can provide directions, road and weather information, and information about attractions and vacation opportunities throughout Minnesota.

WHO'S WHO

We list here Minnesotans, past and present, still living here and living elsewhere. We list one or more of the accomplishments for which they are best known. The list is divided into general categories of media and entertainment, classical music, science/economics, film, sports, artists, writers, business, politics and miscellaneous.

MEDIA AND ENTERTAINMENT

Garrison Keillor, born and raised in Anoka, put Minnesota in the world's eye

Garrison Keillor

PHOTO BY CARMEN QUESADA

as host and storyteller on the internationally acclaimed "A Prairie Home Companion," a Minnesota Public Radio show.

Prince (Rogers Nelson), a native of Minneapolis, built himself an empire through film and music in the Twin Cities. He was director and producer of "Purple Rain," "Under the Cherry Moon" and "Graffiti Bridge."

Boone & Erickson are WCCO radio morning show personalities who are heavy on bad jokes but are the pulse of the Twin Cities for those "in the know." The morning role of Charlie Boone and Roger Erickson is carried on by **Steve Cannon** for the WCCO evening commuters.

Eric Sevareid was a member of the original CBS News broadcast team. He graduated from the University of Minnesota and was a reporter for a Minneapolis newspaper before joining CBS. He died at 79 in 1992.

Harry Reasoner, graduate of West High School in Minneapolis, had a 35-year career in network news including 13 years as co-editor of "60 Minutes." He is best remembered for anchoring election night and the major political party conventions through the '70s on ABC.

Both actress **Ann Southern** and actor **Eddie Albert** went to Central High in Minneapolis.

Actress **Loni Anderson**, runner-up for Miss Minnesota in 1961, is best known for her role in the TV sitcom "WKRP – Cincinnati."

Winona Ryder, now living in California, was originally from Winona. She played a leading part in "Beetlejuice."

Jessica Lange, from Cloquet, was nominated for an Academy Award for best actress for her role in "Frances." Another of her films, "King Kong," was filmed in Duluth.

Tippi Hedren of "The Birds" is from Minneapolis and attended West High, class of '43. Her daughter is actress **Melanie Griffith**.

The young **Charlie Korsmo** attends Breck School. He appeared as the kid in "Dick Tracy" and with Jessica Lange in "Men Don't Leave."

Richard Widmark was a native of Sunrise in Chisago County before making the big time in Hollywood.

Marlon Brando attended Shattuck Military School in Faribault.

Gig Young, an Academy-Award winner, grew up in St. Cloud. His real name was Byron Barr.

Jane Russell was born in Bemidji while her parents were visiting from North Dakota.

Arlene Dahl from Minneapolis starred in "My Wild Irish Rose," "Three Little Words," and "Inside Straight" back in the early days of film.

Patty, Maxine and LaVerne, the **Andrews Sisters**, went to North High in Minneapolis.

Pinky Lee, born in St. Paul, was a TV star of the '50s famous for his checkered coat and porkpie hat.

Actress and singer **Judy Garland** was born Frances Gumm in Grand Rapids in 1922. She was best known for her role as Dorothy in "The Wizard of Oz."

Eddie Cochran was a singer and lyricist of the late 1950s and was born in Albert Lea. Best known for "Summertime Blues" and "C'mon Everybody."

Shipstad & Johnson Ice Follies was founded in the 1920s by Eddie and Roy Shipstad and Oscar Johnson of St. Paul. A lot of practice time was spent at the St. Paul Hippodrome and on area lakes.

Guitarist and singer **Leo Kottke**

Prince

Hurray! Minnesota

recorded his first album in Minnesota in 1969.

Bob Dylan, "child of the '60s," musician and songwriter, was born Robert Allen Zimmermann in Duluth and raised in Hibbing.

Minnesota has been the home of a large number of pop music groups such as **Trip Shakespeare**, **Yanni** (New-Age music), **Husker Du**, **The Suburbs**, **Selection**, **The Wallets**, **Ipso Facto**, **The Jets**, **Bach Crow**, **Boys Club**, **The Replacements** and **The Trashmen**, who were famous for the hit "Surfin' Bird."

Singer **Karyn White** is currently in the top 40. She lives in Edina with her husband, music producer **Terry Lewis**.

Lorenzo Music is the Minnesotan who was the voice of Garfield and also did Carlton the Doorman for the "Mary Tyler Moore Show."

Julia Duffy, a native of St. Paul, is well-known for her role as Stephanie on the "Bob Newhart Show" and more recently as a cast member in "Designing Women."

A number of Minnesotans appeared in earlier TV series: **Tim Ramsey**, "Mister Roberts"; **William Demarest**, born in St. Paul, "My Three Sons"; **Linda Kelsey**, "Lou Grant"; **Robert Vaughn**, "The Man From U.N.C.L.E."; **Marion Ross**, "Happy Days"; **E.G. Marshall**, from Owatonna, "The Lawyers"; and **Karen Landry** and **Ed Flanders**, "St. Elsewhere."

Richard Dean Anderson, born in Minneapolis, played MacGyver on the show of the same name for seven seasons.

Both **Peter Graves** of "Mission Impossible" and his older brother **James Arness** of "Gunsmoke" went to Washburn High in Minneapolis.

Don Herbert from Waconia played Mr. Wizard.

Kris Kahn, a Wayzata High graduate, plays Stuart in the TV series "Coach."

TV evangelist **Dr. Billy Graham** was the former president of Bethel College in Arden Hills and founder of Youth for Christ.

CLASSICAL MUSIC

Composer **Dominick Argento** was the 1975 winner of the Pulitzer Prize for music.

Dimitri Mitropoulos was the music director of the Minnesota Orchestra from 1936 to 1949 and a champion of avant-garde composers.

Edo de Waart

Edo de Waart, born in Amsterdam, has been music director of the Minnesota Orchestra since 1986.

Stanislaw Skrowaczewski, composer, was a former music director of the Minnesota Orchestra.

Sir Neville Marriner supervised and conducted the entire soundtrack for "Amadeus." He is considered the most recorded of the Minnesota Orchestra directors. He was music director from 1979 to 1986.

James Van Demark, the classical double-bassist, is from Owatonna.

Conductor and composer **Philip Brunelle**, director of the Plymouth Music Series, was recently appointed to the board of the National Endowment for the Arts.

Eric Stokes, an iconoclastic American composer and professor at the University of Minnesota, founded the university's electronic music lab.

F. Melius Christianson composed major works of choral music and was choral conductor at St. Olaf College.

Opera singer **Judith Blegen** was originally from Minnesota.

Cornell Marneth grew up in Hopkins. One of his outstanding accomplishments was singing "Othello" at the Met.

Antal Dorati, music director of the Minnesota Orchestra for 11 years, has also conducted a large number of classical recordings.

SCIENCE/ECONOMICS

Walter Heller, onetime University of Minnesota professor, was economic advisor to presidents Kennedy and Johnson.

Norman Borlaug won the 1970 Nobel Peace Prize for his research and breeding of high-yield short-stem wheat. The University of Minnesota was his alma mater.

In 1950 **Dr. Philip Hench**, in physiology, and Edward Kendall, in medicine, both won Nobel prizes.

Walter H. Brattain and **John Bardeen** shared the 1956 Nobel prize in physics for the modern transistor.

Joseph Mazzitello, research chemist at 3M, led the development of the world's first videotape.

FILM

Sarah Pillsbury produced "Eight Men Out," "River's Edge" and "Desperately Seeking Susan."

Mark Frost moved to the Twin Cities with his family when he was 13. This playwright was co-producer of "Twin Peaks." His sister is actress **Lindsay Frost** and his father, **Warren Frost**, is an actor, author and dramatist.

James L. Brooks was the screenwriter for the "Mary Tyler Moore Show."

George Roy Hill, Minneapolis native, directed "The Sting" and "Butch Cassidy and the Sundance Kid."

The **Coen Brothers** of St. Louis Park, **Joel** and **Ethan**, co-directed "Blood Simple," "Raising Arizona" and "Miller's Crossing." They also wrote, produced and directed the Cannes Film Festival award-winning movie "Barton Fink."

Bill Pohlad produced and directed "Old Explorers" and is the son of Minneapolis business mogul Carl Pohlad.

Gordon Parks, versatile film director, author, photographer and composer, has won awards for his movie "The Learning Tree" and also for his photography. He grew up in St. Paul.

Terry Gilliam, of Medicine Lake, is the only American member of the British comedy troupe, Monty Python's Flying Circus. Most recently, he directed the much acclaimed movies "The Fisher King" and "Brazil."

Barry Morrow won an Oscar for his screenplay for "Rain Man," starring Dustin Hoffman. He grew up in Highland Park and attended St. Olaf College.

Sir Tyrone Guthrie was the director and founder of the Guthrie Theater. At the theater's opening in 1963, it was billed as the most important repertory theater outside New York.

Playwright **August Wilson**, who lived in St. Paul for several years, is a two-time winner of the Pulitzer Prize for his plays "The Piano Lesson" and "Fences."

SPORTS

Harry "Bud" Grant coached the Minnesota Vikings for 17 years.

Halsey Hall is the onetime Minnesota Twins sportscaster who could spin a tale and announce a game like no other. He originated the term "holy cow." He is a member of the Minnesota Sports Hall of Fame.

August Wilson

Hurray! Minnesota   **34**   PHOTO BY WILLIAM B. CARTER

Ray Christensen has announced more than 1,000 University of Minnesota Gopher basketball games. And **Herb Carneal** has announced more than 5,000 of the Minnesota Twins games. Both are heard on WCCO radio.

Alan Page, former Minnesota Viking and NFL Hall of Fame member, was elected to the Minnesota Supreme Court in 1992. He was a U of M regent and '91 recipient of the NEA Friend of Education award.

Jill Trenary of Minnetonka was World Figure Skating Champion in 1990 and the '88 Olympics fourth-place finisher.

Andy MacPhail is the Minnesota Twins general manager.

Rod Carew and **Harmon Killebrew**, both former Minnesota Twins, are members of the Baseball Hall of Fame. Killebrew's longest home run was hit in the old Met Stadium (now Camp Snoopy in the Mall of America) in 1967.

Kent Hrbek is a native Minnesotan and played for the Twins when they won the 1987 and 1991 World Series.

Kirby Puckett played for the Twins in the 1987 and 1991 World Series and has been one of the most popular Twins players.

Vern Gagne, champion wrestler, was the president and co-founder of the American Wrestling Association.

Minnesota's 10,000 lakes have spawned a couple of nationally famous fisherman, both from Brainerd — **Babe Winkelman** and **Al Lindner**, known for his famous Lindy Rig.

Scott and **Brennan Olson** are Minnesota brothers generally credited with the invention of in-line skates.

Dick Beardsley and **Garry Bjorklund**, champion marathon runners, both are two-time winners of Grandma's Marathon in Duluth.

Carl Eller, starting in 1964, played 16 seasons as defensive end for the Vikings.

Ralph S. Samuelson was the Lake City resident credited with introducing the sport of waterskiing in 1922. He is also credited with having made the first recorded jump on water skis in 1928.

Bronko Nagurski from International Falls is considered one of the top 101 athletes of this century. He is a member of the Pro Football Hall of Fame. In 1929 as a University of Minnesota player, he became the only player named All-American in two positions.

Bruce Smith was on the Minnesota Gophers 1940 National Championship football team and won the 1941 Heisman Trophy.

Dan Patch was the harness racer that held the record for the mile — 1:55 — for 85 years. M.W. Savage of Savage, Minnesota, purchased Dan Patch in 1903 for $60,000.

John Mariucci, the Iron Range native and hockey legend, is considered "the father of U.S. Hockey."

Kevin McHale of the Boston Celtics basketball team was a onetime Minnesota Gopher great and is a native of Hibbing.

Greg LeMond of Wayzata is a two-time winner of the Tour de France bike marathon and the second Minnesotan to be named Sportsman of the Year by Sports Illustrated.

Herb Brooks, a St. Paul native, coached the 1980 U.S. Hockey team to victory over the Soviet Union and the Olympic Gold Medal.

Terry Steinbach from New Ulm is catcher for the Oakland Athletics.

Charles "Bud" Wilkinson was a

Kirby Puckett

Minneapolis boy who coached the University of Oklahoma to 47 straight college football victories from 1955 to 1957.

Clarence "Biggie" Munn of Anoka excelled in basketball, football and track and competed in the 1932 Olympic track finals. He coached at Michigan State for seven years and is a member of the Minnesota Sports Hall of Fame.

George L. Mikan was pro-basketball's first superstar. He played for the Minnesota Lakers, winning five NBA titles in six years. He was nicknamed "Big Number 99."

Bernard "Bernie" Bierman, a graduate of Litchfield High School, coached the University of Minnesota's football team to 21 straight victories from 1932-36 and produced 15 All-American players while there.

W. "Pudge" Heffelfinger, born in Minneapolis, was a player and coach who introduced the "pulling guard" play in football where the guard left the offensive line and led interference from the ball carrier.

Patricia Jane "Patty" Berg, a Minnesotan, won her first women's Amateur Golf Championship in 1938 at 20 years old. Her first pro-championship title was in 1941.

Paul Giel was an All-American halfback for the University of Minnesota football team and member of the Minnesota Sports Hall of Fame.

Francis "Pug" Lund was an All-American back for the University of Minnesota football team under Coach Bierman.

Cindy Nelson won the bronze medal for the downhill event in Alpine skiing in the 1976 Olympics.

Tony Oliva, a Cuban, was a powerful hitter with Killebrew for the Minnesota Twins and member of the Minnesota Sports Hall of Fame.

Fran Tarkenton led the Vikings to three unsuccessful Super Bowls in 1974, 1975 and 1977. He held records for the most passes completed (3,686) and most yards gained passing (47,003) of any other pro-football quarterback.

Jim Marshall, playing for the Vikings, was tabbed a "Purple People Eater" by the media along with Carl Eller, Gary Larson and Alan Page.

Jack Morris, from St. Paul, pitched for the Minnesota Twins in the World Series in 1991 and the Toronto Blue Jays in 1992.

ARTISTS

Warren MacKenzie of Stillwater is a member of the University of Minnesota faculty and has been called one of the 12 best potters in the United States.

Paul Manship, internationally famous sculptor born in St. Paul in 1885 whose work can be seen throughout the city, created the famous Prometheus fountain, which stands in a sunken plaza at Rockefeller Center in New York City.

John Berkey of Minnetonka is the artist who painted the "old" Elvis stamp design for the April 1992 U.S. Postal Service public competition. Berkey has done many commissioned works for stamps, including one of Hubert Humphrey.

Another famous Minnesota sculptor is **Paul Granlund** of St. Peter, sculptor in residence at Gustavus Adolphus College. Granlund's work can be seen at various locations, including the World Trade Center in downtown St. Paul and Westminster Presbyterian Church in Minneapolis. "Charles Lindbergh — The Boy and the

Paul Granlund

Hurray! Minnesota   PHOTO COURTESY OF PREMIER GALLERY

Man" is located on the state capitol grounds in St. Paul.

James Earl Fraser, a Winona sculptor who died in 1953, is probably best known for designing the buffalo nickel and sculptures of the American Indian.

Painter **Seth Eastman** was stationed at Fort Snelling in 1830 and again from 1841 to 1848, during which time he did numerous oils and drawings of the Sioux and Ojibwa, creating a record of their lifestyle and activities.

Artist **Charles Biederman** of Red Wing is considered to be the founder of "structuralism," an art movement of the 1940s. He settled in Red Wing in 1942, creating and writing extensively on art theory.

St. Paul native **LeRoy Neiman** is famous for employing vivid, explosive colors, often depicting sporting events. Born in St. Paul in 1927, Neiman's works have been owned by such famous (and diverse) people as Jimmy Carter, Muhammad Ali, Orson Welles and Donald Trump.

Important in shaping the art scene in Minnesota for more than three decades were **Martin** and **Mickey Friedman**. Martin was director of the Walker Art Center in Minneapolis for 32 years and Mickey, his wife, was design curator for 21 years.

Jim Brandenburg is probably Minnesota's most famous wildlife photographer. He has been on assignments for National Geographic magazine around the world, including Africa and the Arctic.

Les Blacklock also is a famous wildlife photographer and works out of his Moose Lake home. Many Minnesota coffee tables display one of his beautiful books. His son, **Craig**, and his daughter-in-law, **Nadine**, have achieved national recognition in the same field.

Eleven Minnesotans have won the competition for design of the Federal Duck Stamp — more winners than any other state since the competition began in 1934. **Les Kouba** won in 1958 and 1967, **Ed Morris** in 1961 and 1962, and **David Maas** won in 1974 and 1982. Other Minnesotans to win are **Roger E. Preuss**, 1949; **Harvey Sandstrom**, 1954; **Arthur Cook**, 1972; **Richard Plasschaert**, 1980; **Phil Scholer**, 1983; **Dan Smith**, 1988; **Jim Hautman**, 1990; Jim's brother, **Joseph Hautman**, in 1992.

Terry Redlin of Hastings won the 1981 and 1985 Minnesota Migratory Waterfowl Stamp contests. **Jerry Raedecke** of Worthington is an ordained Lutheran minister turned artist. He has won numerous awards for his work and was named 1990 Ducks Unlimited Minnesota Artist of the Year.

Jerry Ott of Albert Lea is well known for his photorealist paintings. He gained international attention during the 1970s with his air-brushed images based on photographs.

Thomas Rose of Minneapolis, professor and director of graduate studies in studio arts at the University of Minnesota, is trained as a sculptor but works in many mediums. His artwork is in more than 50 private, corporate and museum collections and in public locations around the Twin Cities.

Fresco artists are very rare. One of them, **Mark Balma** of the Twin Cities, has been commissioned to paint frescoes in Italy's third-largest cathedral, the Basilica of Santa Maria degli Angeli of Assisi — a project expected to take 15 years. And he has been commissioned to decorate the Hall of Founders on the new downtown Minneapolis

Jim Brandenburg

campus of the University of St. Thomas at 10th Street and Harmon Place.

WRITERS

ANY DISCUSSION OF Minnesota writers must start with two international literary giants — **F. Scott Fitzgerald** and **Sinclair Lewis**. Francis Scott Key Fitzgerald, born in St. Paul in 1896, lived in a number of homes in the Summit Avenue area. The emphasis on money and social position in his youth became a recurring theme in his work, such as "The Great Gatsby." He lived in a row house at 599 Summit while revising the manuscript of "This Side of Paradise." Scott and Zelda lived at 626 Goodrich with their new baby daughter while he wrote most of "The Beautiful and Damned." Some of Fitzgerald's old haunts are still standing, including the University Club and the Commodore Hotel.

Lewis, born in 1885 in Sauk Centre in central Minnesota, was the first American to win the Nobel prize in literature, awarded in 1930. "Main Street," the literary sensation of the 1920s, enraged the people of Sauk Centre, who saw too clearly the similarities between themselves and the residents of Gopher Prairie. As his fame spread, however, the hometown residents forgave Lewis and have honored him over the years (see Lake Country section).

Maud Hart Lovelace, who died in 1980 at the age of 88, was born in Mankato and lived much of her life in Minnesota. She wrote 24 books, including the popular series of Betsy-Tacy books. The Betsy-Tacy Society's Twin Cities chapter has 92 members and there are 250 nationally.

Laura Ingalls Wilder of Walnut Grove wrote "On the Banks of Plum Creek." She is best known for the "Little House" series for children, which became the basis for the "Little House on the Prairie" television series.

Judith Guest of Edina authored "Ordinary People," which was made into a movie by Robert Redford and won an Oscar for best picture in 1980.

Susan Allen Toth of Minneapolis wrote "Blooming: A Small Town Childhood," "Ivy Days," and "How to Prepare for Your High School Reunion and Other Midlife Musings."

"A Carpet of Blue: An Ex-Cop Takes a Tough Look at America's Drug Problem," was written by former Minneapolis Chief of Police **Tony Bouza**.

"Saint Mudd," by **Steve Thayer**, is set in St. Paul during the 1930s reign of gangsters.

"A Cup of Christmas Tea," by **Tom Hegg**, illustrated by **Warren Hanson**, first became a Minnesota favorite and has since caught on nationally.

Tim O'Brien of Worthington is the author of "The Things They Carried" and the 1978 National Book Award winner for "Going After Cacciato."

John Camp of St. Paul writes under his real name — "The Empress File" and "The Fool's Run" — and under the pseudonym of **John Sandford** — "Silent Prey," "Eyes of Prey," "Shadow Prey," "Rules of Prey," a series built around Minneapolis policeman Lucas Davenport.

J. F. Powers, teacher at St. John's University in Collegeville, wrote "Morte D'Urban," the 1963 National Book Award winner. His "Wheat That Springeth Green" in 1988 was a National Book Award finalist.

Another St. John's faculty member of literary prominence is **Jon Hassler**,

Jon Hassler

Hurray! Minnesota   PHOTO BY LEE HANLEY

whose books include "Staggerford," "Simon's Night," "The Love Hunter" and "A Green Journey."

Bill Holm of Minneota authored "Coming Home Crazy: An Alphabet of China Essays."

Robert Bly, Minneapolis and Moose Lake, well-known poet, was one of People magazine's 25 most intriguing people of 1991 and is definer of the so-called men's movement with his book "Iron John."

Allen Simpson, who has written paperback mysteries under the pseudonym **M. D. Lake**, wrote "Amdens for Murder," "Cold Comfort," and "Poisoned Ivy."

Sigurd Olson of Ely, who died at the age of 83 in 1982, was a prominent figure in the environmental movement in this century. His writing captures the beauty and fragility of the wilderness. Major books include "Listening Point," "Singing Wilderness" and "The Lonely Land."

Ole E. Rolvaag, famous for his novel "Giants in the Earth," taught at St. Olaf College in Northfield. He was known for his contributions to Norwegian-American literature and his insights into the psychology of the immigrant experience in America, having immigrated to the United States in 1896 at the age of 20. His son, **Karl Rolvaag**, served a term as governor of Minnesota.

Meridel Le Sueur, now living in St. Paul, was born in 1900 and authored children's books. However, "Annunciation," the story of a young woman and the wonder of her first pregnancy, is considered to be her most accomplished work. She was prominent as a left-wing activist in the 1950s, facing criticism and blacklisting during the McCarthy era.

Novelist **LaVyrle Spencer** was born in Browerville and lives in Stillwater.

Bill Holm

She has had numerous books on the New York Times bestseller list, has four times won the Golden Medallion award for writing excellence from the Romance Writers of America, and received the Minnesota Writers Award for a favorite genre book for "Morning Glory." Author **Kathleen Woodiwiss** of Princeton, author of many books, including "Ashes in the Wind," was helpful in getting Spencer's career launched.

Kate Green of St. Paul teaches creative writing at the College of St. Catherine and at Hamline University and has authored "Shattered Moon," "Night Angel" and "Shooting Star."

Wanda Gàg of New Ulm authored and illustrated the internationally acclaimed children's book, "Millions of Cats." She died in 1946.

Carol Bly of Sturgeon Lake, born in Duluth, is a poet, essayist and author of short stories who often writes of and to women of small-town Minnesota.

Harvey Mackay, prominent Twin Cities businessman and civic leader, hit the New York Times best-seller list in 1988 with his "Swim With the Sharks Without Being Eaten Alive."

BUSINESS

DURING THE PANIC of 1873, **James J. Hill** bought the St. Paul and Pacific railroads, combined and extended them, and called the new railroad the Great Northern Railway Co.

Richard Sears began as a station agent in North Redwood for the Minneapolis & St. Louis Railroads. In 1886, at the age of 23, a sales letter he composed to sell a crate of watches marked

PHOTO BY PER BREIEHAGEN

the birth of Sears. As his business grew, he moved to Minneapolis and then to Chicago, where in 1893, after graduating from letters to ads to flyers, he joined up with Roebuck and they began to print a catalog on a regular basis offering a full line of merchandise. (See Pioneer Country section.)

In 1896, another nationally known retailer, **George Draper Dayton**, got his start. (See Minneapolis Shopping section.) **Kenneth A. Macke** has been CEO of Dayton's since 1984 and has been joined by **Stephen Watson** as president in 1990. Though Dayton's is no longer a family-run business, his descendants are still prominent in organizations and businesses in the Twin Cities, particularly in the arts, and can be considered instrumental in the overwhelming support given the arts by the business community.

John Sargent Pillsbury was an early supporter of the University of Minnesota. Another supporter of the University, **James Ford Bell**, the founder of General Mills, donated a natural history museum to the University. General Mills continues to be a profitable company under the guidance of **H. Brewster "Bruce" Atwater Jr.**, chairman and CEO, and **Mark H. Willes**, President and COO since 1988.

Sally Ordway Irvine was a benefactor to the arts and the driving force behind the creation of St. Paul's Ordway Theatre. Her grandfather, **Lucius Pond Ordway**, was a partner in Crane & Ordway Co., a plumbing and heating supply firm, and an original investor in 3M Co. Ordway supported the unprofitable 3M company for years until **William L. McKnight** and **Archibald G. Bush** joined the firm as accountants.

George Draper Dayton

William L. McKnight was chairman of the board of 3M from 1949 to 1966. The McKnight Foundation today is a major supporter of numerous nonprofit organizations.

Once head of the McKnight Foundation, **Virginia McKnight Binger** is married to **James Binger**. James, once chairman of Honeywell, manages the family real estate that includes Butler Square in downtown Minneapolis and five Broadway theaters.

Alfred A. Checchi became chairman of the board for Northwest Airlines in 1989 after organizing the buyout.

Curtis L. Carlson, the richest man in Minnesota, founded the Gold Bond Stamp Co. in 1938, the forerunner to today's Carlson Companies, now a leader in marketing incentives, hotels, travel and restaurants. **Marilyn Carlson Nelson** is now being positioned to take over the privately held company when Curt Carlson retires. She has made quite a reputation for herself already as a mover and a doer, most recently and visibly as the head of the Super Bowl Task Force.

Irwin Jacobs has been on Forbes annual list of the richest 400, thanks to business savvy and burlap bags. The Wall Street Journal coined the name "Liquidator," referring to the way he bought and resold at a profit, starting as far back as age 18 with 300 pairs of skis he bought at $13 and then sold at $39 a pair.

Jeno Paulucci is a feisty entrepreneur who sees himself as an outspoken defender of the common good. He built a financial empire in Duluth on pizzas, publishing and chow mein.

Carl Pohlad is probably best known as the owner of the world champion Minnesota Twins. Born in 1915 in Iowa, his fortune was estimated at $680 mil-

Hurray! Minnesota

lion in 1992. He has been president of Marquette Bank of Minneapolis since 1955.

Theodore Wirth was superintendent of Minneapolis parks from 1906 to 1936. He planned and supervised the development of the city parks in and around the lakes that provided for playgrounds within a quarter mile of each child and complete recreation centers within a half mile of each dwelling.

Dr. William Worrel Mayo left Europe at the age of 25 in 1845 and eventually settled in Rochester after the Civil War. He was a pioneer in surgery. He helped found St. Mary's Hospital, the first hospital in Rochester, with **Mother Alfred** of the Third Order of St. Francis. It officially opened in 1889. In 1914 the Mayo Clinic opened.

Both Mayo's sons, **Will** and **Charlie**, served as apprentices to their father from a very early age. The brothers formed a policy for the clinic of unbiased medical care, fair and equitable treatment of clinic staff and employees and a trust set up from half the annual proceeds of the clinic, which has made the clinic a leader in world medicine. Then and now, the clinic has a world-class reputation for diagnostic and state-of-the-art health care.

Charles A. Pillsbury, with the help of his uncle, **John Sargent**, and his father, **George**, founded the Pillsbury Flour Mills Co. in the early 1870s. Pillsbury was bought by a British firm in 1889, returned to American ownership in 1923 and now, once again, is owned by a British firm, Grand Met. **Ian A. Martin**, Pillsbury's current chairman and CEO, began his career with the Timex Corporation in Scotland.

James Stroud Bell was a contemporary of the Pillsburys. He managed, then

Marilyn Carlson Nelson

owned the Washburn Crosby Co., which was in flour milling. He successfully experimented with selling flour directly to the consumer through advertising. It was his son, **James Ford Bell**, who founded what is today's General Mills.

William W. Cargill and three younger brothers, **Sylvester**, **Jim** and **Sam** were the founders of what is today the largest private firm in the nation, Cargill Inc.

William R. Sweatt originally owned a wheelbarrow manufacturing plant, but he saw potential in the furnace thermostat. Years of struggle and a merger with an Indiana heating company owned by **Mark Honeywell** led to today's billion-dollar firm of Honeywell Inc. **Dr. James J. Renier** has been chairman and CEO of Honeywell since 1988.

In the second half of the 19th century, **Frederick Weyerhaeuser**, a German immigrant, established what was considered to be the world's greatest lumber empire.

Rivaling Weyerhaeuser in the same time period, **Thomas Barlow Walker** was reputed to be the largest individual owner of pine land. The Walker Art Center is part of his legacy to Minnesota.

George Hormel founded Geo.A. Hormel Co., a meat-packing firm in Austin, in 1891. Despite a major embezzlement in 1921, it has grown to be the only Fortune 500 company based in outstate Minnesota. His son, **Jordie**, a jazz musician, married actress Leslie Caron. Today's president and CEO, **Richard L. Knowlton**, worked his way through the ranks to the top job at Hormel.

Stanley Hubbard, president and CEO of Hubbard Broadcasting, sits on the Fingerhut board, three founda-

Harvey B. Ratner and Marv Wolfenson

tions, three civic organizations and one board for higher education.

J.P. Getty, once the richest man in America, was born in Minneapolis in 1892. His father, George, who was in insurance, bought an oil tract just west of Bartlesville, Oklahoma. He eventually moved his family, when J.P. was 11 years old, to Oklahoma.

C. Palmer Jaffray and **Harry C. Piper** founded the original company of Piper and Jaffray in 1913 as a commercial paper house. Both were native Minnesotans and formed their friendship, which was the basis for their future business dealings, during their period together at Yale. Today the company is run by **Addison "Tad" Piper**.

Anthony L. Andersen has been president and CEO of H.B. Fuller company since 1974.

Earl E. Bakken founded Medtronic, Inc. in 1949 and is now the director.

Winston Roger Wallin is Chairman and CEO.

The signs for **Ralph W. Burnet**'s real estate firm, Burnet Realty Inc., are seen throughout the Twin Cities.

David C. Cox is president and CEO of Cowles Media Company.

Kenneth H. Dahlberg is president of Dahlberg Inc., world-famous manufacturer of hearing aids.

Theodore Deikel, CEO of Fingerhut Companies Inc., has been commended by Jimmy Carter, Governor Quie and Mayor Hofstede.

Livio D. DeSimone was named president and CEO of 3M Company in 1991.

Lloyd Engelsma is CEO of the general contracting firm Kraus-Anderson Inc.

James D. Gabbert, founder of Games by James, is now CEO of Gabberts Furniture and Design Studio.

Pierson M. Grieve is CEO of Ecolab Inc., which provides institutional and residential services such as cleaning and lawn care worldwide.

John F. Grundhofer is chairman, president and CEO for First Bank System Inc.

Roger L. Hale is the award-winning president and CEO of Tennant Company in Golden Valley.

David A. Koch is CEO of Graco Inc., a worldwide manufacturer of pumps.

Lloyd P. Johnson is chairman and CEO of the large multibank holding company known as Norwest Corporation.

William H. Lurton is chairman and CEO and **Don C. Lein** is president of Jostens Inc., a leader in educational and recognition materials.

Anthony Luiso is CEO of International Multifoods Company.

Jim W. Lupient is CEO of the Lupient Automotive Group, which has 22 franchises in Minnesota and Wisconsin.

John E. Pearson is chairman and CEO of Northwestern National Life Companies.

Lawrence Perlman is the president and CEO of Control Data Corporation.

Harvey B. Ratner and **Marve Wolfenson** are co-owners of the Minnesota Timberwolves.

Gerald Rauenhorst is chairman and CEO of the privately held Opus Corporation, an industrial/commercial development and construction firm.

John A. Rollwagen has been chairman of Cray Research, the computer company, since 1981.

Former Minnesota State Senator **Glen Taylor** is chairman and CEO of Taylor Corporations.

Michael W. Wright is CEO of Super Valu Stores.

Hurray! Minnesota PHOTO COURTESY OF MINNESOTA TIMBERWOLVES

C. Angus Wurtele has been chairman and CEO of the Valspar Corporation since 1973.

POLITICS

Harold Stassen could well hold the record for the person who has run the most times for the office of President of the United States without winning. He has run 10 times (first in 1944 when he was in the Pacific during World War II). He was elected governor of the state when he was only 31 and served three terms from 1938-1943.

Elmer L. Andersen was governor in the 1960s. He also was a legislator, businessman, newspaper publisher, foundation president, conservationist and University of Minnesota regent. Born in 1909, he served as state senator from 1949-58. He was the last elected two-year governor of Minnesota in 1961-62.

Walter "Fritz" Mondale was vice president under Jimmy Carter. He ran and lost to Reagan in the 1984 presidential election. Now, after his loss, he has bounced back and has assumed the role, thanks in part to his WCCO interviews, as respected senior statesman.

Hubert H. Humphrey (1911-1977), Minnesota's favorite son, began his political career as mayor of Minneapolis in 1948. He later served in the U.S. Senate, was vice president under Lyndon Johnson, and waged an unsuccessful presidential campaign against Richard Nixon in 1968.

Evie Teegen, a former resident of Edina, is now the Ambassador to the Fiji Islands.

Rudy Boschwitz was U.S. Senator from Minnesota from 1978 to 1990. He founded the retail firm Plywood Minnesota in 1963.

Walter "Fritz" Mondale

Eugene Joseph McCarthy was elected U.S. Senator in 1958 and re-elected in 1964 by the largest majority ever given to a Democratic candidate in Minnesota history. Prior to that, he served in the U.S. House of Representatives from 1949 to 1957. In 1968, he challenged Johnson for the Democratic presidential nomination based on a well-supported anti-Vietnam platform.

Gus Hall was born Arvo Gus Halberg in 1910 in Virginia, Minnesota. He came from a large working-class family on the Iron Range. At 15, he was forced to quit school to help support the family. At age 17, already developing a strong sensitivity to the plight of the working class and negative feelings toward the greed and indifference represented by the large corporations, he joined the Communist Party. During the McCarthy witch-hunt, he was arrested and jailed for eight years.

After his release, he was elected general secretary of the Communist Party, an office he held until 1979. On his 70th birthday in 1981, he was awarded the Order of Lenin and the Order of Friendship Among People by the Soviet Union, the Order of Karl Marx by the German Democratic Republic, the People's Friendship Order by Czechoslovakia, and the Order of Georgi Dimitrov by Bulgaria.

The Honorable **Andrew J. Volstead** was elected to the House of Representatives in 1912. In 1919 he permitted his name to be attached to a bill that provided the means of enforcement for the Wartime Prohibition Act. The Wartime Prohibition Act prohibited the manufacture, use of materials and distribution of any alcoholic product containing .5 percent alcohol in volume.

Judge William O. Douglas, born in Maine, Minnesota, was appointed to the U. S. Supreme Court in 1939 by Franklin Roosevelt. He was the longest sitting judge. Best known for his stand in favor of civil liberty, he retired from the Supreme Court in 1975 and died at the age of 81 in 1980.

Warren E. Burger, a native of St. Paul, was appointed the 15th chief justice of the United States in 1969 by Nixon. Reagan awarded him the Medal of Freedom in 1987.

Harry A. Blackmun of Rochester was named a Supreme Court justice in 1970 on the recommendation of Chief Justice Burger. They were often referred to as the Minnesota Twins, though the name didn't really apply politically. Blackmun was the author and guardian of the Roe vs. Wade decision legalizing abortion.

Senator Dave Durenberger was elected to the Senate in 1978. He has served as a member of the Senate Finance Committee, the Environment and Public Works Committee, Special Committee on Aging, chaired the Finance Health Subcommittee and was the first Minnesotan since 1931 to chair a Senate committee: the Select Committee on Intelligence.

Frank B. Kellogg was awarded the Nobel Peace Prize in 1931 for his work on the Pact of Paris while he was secretary of state to President Roosevelt in 1925. The Pact of Paris made war illegal rather than a "legal instrument of national policy." Kellogg was raised in Olmstead County, Minnesota.

Rudy Perpich, originally a dentist from the Iron Range, held office as governor for a total of 10 years, from 1976-78 and 1982-89.

Joan Growe

Clyde H. Bellecourt, born on the White Earth Indian Reservation. is the national director for the American Indian Movement. Recently, he received the Martin Luther King Jr. Award for civil rights work in Minnesota.

Paul D. Wellstone was elected to the U.S. Senate in 1990. He is a member of the Labor and Human Resources Committee, the Energy and Natural Resources Committee, the Small Business Committee and the Select Committee on Indian Affairs.

Geri Joseph was appointed Ambassador to the Netherlands by Jimmy Carter in 1978.

Eugenia Anderson, from Red Wing, was the first woman to become a U.S. ambassador. She won her ambassadorship through hard work in the DFL ranks. Truman appointed her to serve in Denmark from 1949 to 1953. She also served as foreign minister to Bulgaria until 1964. In 1965, she was named U.S. delegate to the U.N. Trusteeship Council and special envoy for the United States.

Coya Knutsen was the country's first congresswoman. She served in the House of Representatives for two terms from 1955 to 1958.

Dr. Sidney Rand was a political appointee, under Carter in 1979, as ambassador to Norway.

Rozanne Ridgway, a St. Paul native, graduated from Hamline University to become a career diplomat. In her successful state department career, she has been an aide to Bush and ambassador to Finland.

Joan Growe was appointed secretary of state for Minnesota in 1975.

The public service career of **Karl Rolvaag** spanned more than 30 years. During that time, he served as ambas-

Hurray! Minnesota

sador to Iceland and governor of Minnesota in 1963.

Orville Freeman was secretary of agriculture under President Kennedy. He also served as DFL governor of Minnesota from 1954-60.

Ann Wynia was the former DFL majority leader in the Minnesota House of Representatives. Currently, she is commissioner of the Department of Human Services.

Sandra Hale was the commissioner of the Administration Department under Governor Rudy Perpich.

Arne Carlson was elected as IR governor of Minnesota in 1990. Previously, he was state auditor.

Floyd B. Olson had been county attorney and governor for three terms (1930-36) when he died of pancreatic cancer at the age of 45. Some say that he would have been president of the United States if he had lived longer. He was a powerful and charismatic man who could hold an audience's attention, whether in a courtroom or a saloon.

Dirilus Morrison was the first mayor of Minneapolis.

Arne Carlson

MISCELLANEOUS

MINNESOTA HAS HAD its share of beautiful women, such as former Miss Americas **Gretchen Carlson** and **B.B. Shop Waring**. **Jennifer Kline** of Minnetonka was Mrs. America and **Barbara Petersen Burwell** was Miss USA.

Minnesotans have a corner on polar expeditions. **Will Steger** and **Paul Schurke** from Ely are North and South Pole explorers. **Ann Bancroft** was the first women to the North Pole and is leading the first all-woman expedition to the South Pole.

Sister Elizabeth Kenny came from Australia as a nurse and dedicated more than 30 years of her life to the crusade against polio. Sister Kenny established the Kenny Institute, a polio treatment center in Minneapolis, in 1940.

Charles A. Lindbergh is one of America's most famous aviators. In 1929, he flew a single-engine monoplane, the "Spirit of St. Louis," on the first solo, nonstop trans-Atlantic flight from New York to Paris. Lindbergh's boyhood home outside Little Falls is maintained as a museum.

Amelia Earhart crash-landed on a remote Pacific island while attempting to circumnavigate the globe. She attended St. Paul Central High School in 1913-14.

Leonard Odell wrote the first roadside signs for Burma Shave.

Eloise Butler was a conservationist and botanist who founded the Eloise Butler Wildflower Garden in Theodore Wirth Park.

Pierre "Pig's Eye" Parrant was a whiskey merchant who staked one of the first claims in St. Paul. The first name for St. Paul was Pig's Eye; it now is the name of a locally produced beer.

Paul Bunyan is a fictional folk hero, and **Babe** is his blue ox. Folklore credits them with creating the 10,000 lakes of Minnesota during one of their rough-and-tumble games that got out of hand. William B. Laughead related and created many of the Paul Bunyan stories for the Minnesota Red River Company.

John Dillinger, notorious outlaw, spent summers in St. Paul.

Casey Jones was a Minnesota-born engineer and inspiration for the song. He was the engineer on Old Engine #201, on display in Owatonna.

45 PECULIARLY MINNESOTA

Special Events

THIS IS JUST A SAMPLING OF THE many different festivals and activities available in the state of Minnesota all year long. The Minnesota Office of Tourism publishes a complete listing each season of the festivals held in Minnesota.

In the Twin Cities call: (612) 296-5029. Outside of the Twin Cities area call: (800) 657-3700.

JANUARY
RED WING
Shiver River Days • There are lots of activities to keep you warm, such as the Uffda Triathlon — a run, ski and skate event — the moonlight ski, smoosh racing, ice/snow croquet, mutt racing spaghetti feed, chili-cooking contest and more. (612) 388-4719 or (800) 762-9516.

GRAND RAPIDS
Grand Vinterslass • The Scandinavian Celebration for the "Slaying of Winter" includes cross-country ski races, tournaments, children's activities and more. (218) 326-6619.

INTERNATIONAL FALLS
Ice Box Days • A fitting name for a festival in one of the coldest spots in the nation. Activities include smoosh race, Freeze yer Gizzard Blizzard run, Sleet Feet Obstacle Course and all kinds of games on the lake. (218) 283-9400 or (800) 325-5766.

LINDSTROM
Balloon Fest • This three-day event includes hot-air balloon events and rides, kites, sleigh rides, snowman contest and lots of good eats. (612) 257-1117.

ST. PAUL
St. Paul Winter Carnival • One of the nation's 10 leading festivals and the oldest winter celebration in the United States. It includes both public events, such as the ice castle, and neighborhood events. It is rich in heritage and tradition from the crowning of the King and Queen to the fun and mischief of the Vulcans. It was founded in 1886 as a reaction to some bad press out of New York that compared St. Paul to Siberia. Guess we showed them!! Held the second-to-last Wednesday in January through the first Sunday in February. (612) 296-6953 or (800) 488-4023. (See St. Paul section.)

FEBRUARY
PALISADE
Mid-Winter Festival • There's a parade, coronation, mukluk dance, mountain-men exhibit, games, hayrides and more. (218) 845-2604.

GRANITE FALLS
Ole & Lena Days • You won't want to miss the Ole & Lena joke contest or the lutefisk feed. There also are tournaments, a medallion hunt, flea market and old fashioned carnival. (612) 564-4081.

WALKER
International Eelpout Festival • Many different activities occur in the ice-house town that springs up on the lake for this festival, but the main event is still the eelpout fishing contest. It's lots of fun and a sight to see. (218) 547-1313 or (800) 833-1118.

ISLE
Crystal Carnival • Burly and Crystal, Isle's polar bear mascots, host the chili cook-offs, hot-air balloon races, sled hayrides, arts and crafts fair, and a $20,000 hole-in-one golf contest, all in and around Mille Lacs Lake communities. (800) 346-9375.

BEMIDJI
Mardi Gras North • Bemidji hosts a Voyageur encampment and Indian pow-wow with demonstration. There's also a costume ball, fiddle jamboree, folk festival, twilight parade and tasty goodies. (218) 751-3540 or (800) 292-2223.

NEW ULM
Fasching & Bock Beer Festival • The German heritage of this town makes for a real German celebration similar to Mardi Gras, costumes and all, held at Turner Hall. (507) 354-8850. In addition, Schell's Brewery holds the Bock Hunt, a bonfire and tour. (507) 354-5528.

Hurray! Minnesota

Introduced in 1991, the Super Ice Slide at St. Paul's Capitol Mall drew 60,000 riders over the 10 days of the St. Paul Winter Carnival.

March

Albert Lea
Annual Winter Art Show • For more than 20 years Minnesota's top artists and crafters have participated in this art show. It is held in the Skyline Mall and includes awards and entertainment. (507) 373-5665 or 373-5830.

Austin
Stories From the Heartland • Storytellers from across the country spin tails to the delight of listeners. The event

The Highland dancers at the Scottish Country Fair & Highland Games at Macalester College.

also includes a storytelling workshop. (507) 437-4563 or (800) 444-5713.

APRIL
ANNANDALE
Maple Syrup Festival • The demonstrations held in Pioneer Park include tapping, collecting, boiling and, the public's favorite, tasting the syrup with pancakes. (612) 274-8619.
MANKATO
International Festival • University and community volunteers coordinate the many national and ethnic groups that participate in a parade, dancing, talent and style shows. There are food booths and demonstrations of everything from palm reading to hair plaiting. Held in the Mankato Mall. (507) 389-1281.
COLLEGEVILLE
Swayed Pines Folk Fest • This fiddle contest has more than 60 fiddlers of all ages. There's also a craft fair, jam sessions, food and evening concert. (612) 363-2594 or 253-3620.
NEW ULM
Minnesota Festival of Music • This three-day event, sponsored by the Minnesota Music Hall of Fame, features Minnesota music makers performing a variety of music styles throughout the town, from jazz to rock, country to classical. There's even a little barbershop and bluegrass. (507) 354-7285.
ST. PAUL
Festival of Nations • Minnesota's largest ethnic celebration has more than 80 different groups represented in cafes, exhibits, demonstrations and dance. St. Paul Civic Center. (612) 647-0191.

NEW PRAGUE
Antique Show • Antiques, antiques and more antiques along with Czech-German food and costumed workers set the scene where you might make that prized discovery. (612) 758-3506.

MAY
ST. PAUL
Scottish Country Fair & Highland Games • Held the first Saturday in May, dancers, pipers and athletes compete at Macalester College along with sheepdog trials and games of brawny might. There's also arts, crafts, memorabilia and food. (612) 696-6239.
PRESTON
Trout Days • This is not just a fishing contest. In fact, among those in jogging circles, the Trout Trot (run or walk race) is the opening race for the season. There are a number of other races with something to suit everyone's ability. If running and fishing are not your line, there also is a car show, craft show, high school rodeo and a great parade. (507) 765-2156.
ST. PAUL
Cinco De Mayo • This is an outdoor fiesta in the true Latin tradition with food shows, vendors, dancing and coronation. (612) 222-6347.
HOPKINS
Mainstreet Days Fine Arts Fair • This is a fine arts and book fair that includes readings, concert and tent dance. There also is an ice cream social, food concessions and fun run. (612) 935-9365.
INTERNATIONAL FALLS
Mosquito Day • Held at Grand Mound Historical Center is a unique educational program and contest dedicated to the mosquito, Minnesota's famous pest. (218) 279-3332 or 634-2891.
SHAKOPEE
Eagle Creek Rendezvous • Held at Historic Murphy's Landing is a re-creation of the fur trade gatherings of the 1800s, including tepees, black-powder shoots and tomahawk throwing. (612) 445-6900.

At Fort Snelling, volunteers perform turn-of-the-century drills.

June
Redwood Falls
Minnesota Inventors Congress • Here's a chance to see the new inventions as they are displayed, demonstrated and judged. There's a special student inventors event and business workshops. (507) 637-2344 or (800) 468-3681.

International Falls
Prehistoric Activities Day • See demonstrations of early Indian crafts and technology such as prehistoric Indian pottery making, spearing throwing with an atlatl and more. (218) 279-3332.

St. Paul
Civil War Weekend • Experience Minnesota at the outbreak of the Civil War

in 1861 or during the war in 1864. More than 100 volunteers perform drills and skits associated with the recruiting, training and activities of the soldiers and the citizenry at the beginning of the war or during the middle years. The weekend is hosted by the Minnesota Historical Society at Fort Snelling. (612) 726-1171.

MOUNDS VIEW
Minnesota Music Festival • Held on Father's Day weekend, this is a festival of music and dancing. More than 20 bands perform at the Belrae Ballroom and in a large Bavarian tent outside. (612) 786-4630.

ROCHESTER
Minnesota Square Dance Convention • Top Minnesota and national callers announce for both square and round dancing. The hosting region changes annually. (218) 879-8766.

IRONWORLD, CHISHOLM
International Polkafest • Top polka musicians perform for continuous multi-stage polka entertainment along with the world championship polka dance contest. Oom-pah-pah to your heart's delight. (218) 254-3321 or (800) 372-6437.

EXCELSIOR
Excelsior Arts Festival • Held on the shores of Lake Minnetonka, this festival hosts more than 175 exhibitors along with food, music and entertainment. A children's tent gives the younger set a chance to try their hand at creating. (612) 474-5000.

LAKE BENTON
Saddle Horse Days • You'll have fun horsing around at this horse show, which includes competitive horse events, parade, street dance and trail rides. (507) 368-4803.

JULY

MANY CITIES THROUGHOUT Minnesota have fireworks demonstrations. Check with the Chamber of Commerce or Visitors Bureau in the area you will be visiting.

ST. PAUL
Taste of Minnesota • This festival held on the grounds of the State Capitol as part of the Fourth of July celebration is more like the ice cream social of old. There's food galore with more than 30 tents, each serving something different. There's also entertainment and, of course, Fourth of July fireworks. (612) 296-5029.

GRAND RAPIDS
Tall Timber Days • This two-day festival celebrates the influence of the past and present logging and timber industries in Grand Rapids. Included is a lumberjack show featuring world champion competitors, arts and crafts, the C-1 professional canoe race and lumber exhibitions. The U.S. National Chain Saw Championships, in which competitors are judged on their skill and creativity in carving a 6- to 8-foot log, are held during the festival. (218) 326-6619 or (800) 472-6366.

PIPESTONE
The Song of Hiawatha Pageant • This beautiful pageant takes place in an old, deep quarry that forms a three-acre natural amphitheater, and its spring-fed lake sets the stage. A cast of 200 brings to life the story of Hiawatha. The pageant is held the first two weekends of July and the first weekend of August. Performance time is at sundown, 9:15 p.m. Admission $6, 6 years and under free. (507) 825-4126 or 825-3316.

WALNUT GROVE
Pioneer Festival • This is a daytime pre-pageant activity held in conjunction with the Laura Ingalls Wilder Pageant. This festival has bluegrass, old-time and folk music. There also are demonstrations, sales, folk arts and crafts. It's a real prairie festival. (507) 274-6320.

Laura Ingalls Wilder Pageant • This is a two-and-one-half-hour live pageant performed by a cast of 50-75 area people ages 4 through 80. It is the story of the Ingalls family in 1870, based on the life of the author of the "Little House" series for children. It is held Friday, Saturday and Sunday, the first three weekends in July. (507) 859-2174 or (800) 554-1707.

IRONWORLD, CHISHOLM
Minnesota Ethnic Days • For 10 days in the month of July, Ironworld features a different ethnic group each day through its food, dance and entertainment. (218) 254-3321 or (800) 372-6437.

BRAINERD
Arts in the Park • Held in Gregory Park, this juried art show has more than 75

The milk-carton boat race is an udderly Aquatennial event.

exhibitors. Also featured are some unusual taste treats, a children's activity area and entertainment. (218) 829-2838.

Hinckley
Korn & Klover Karnival • The world champion marching bands are invited to perform. Plus, there are parades, stage entertainment, a talent show, the carnival and midway. All entertainment is free, and there is lots of it. (612) 384-7837.

Jackson
Fort Belmont Days • Over a period of a week, a variety of heritage trades and events are held in the reconstructed 1864 Norwegian civilian fort. Activities include spinning, needle crafts and blacksmithing demonstrations. (507) 847-5840.

Edgerton
Dutch Festival • Dutch dancers and floats are featured in this two-day heritage festival that includes a midway, carnival and other family entertainment. (507) 442-3080.

Pequot Lakes
Bean Hole Day • For the past 114 years on the first Wednesday after the 4th, the people of Pequot cook up 150 gallons of baked beans. The beans are served free with buns and lemonade. There is a flea market and craft show to browse through while you munch on your beans. (218) 568-8911 or (800) 950-0291.

Minneapolis
Sommerfest • This Viennese music fest is held at Peavey Plaza adjacent to Orchestra Hall. Included is a marketplace serving taste treats of Vienna and hosting dancing in the fountain area. The fest is held in conjunction with a series of concerts performed by the Minnesota Orchestra and broadcast in the plaza during the event. (612) 371-5656.

Battle Creek
Phelps Mill Summer Festival • The center of this festival is a juried arts and crafts show with more than 150 exhibitors. There are children's special events, plenty of food and the century-old flour mill is open to the public. (218) 864-5888.

Minneapolis
Aquatennial • This festival celebrating the "waters" of Minneapolis is held throughout the city highlighting city

The Minnesota State Fair, a.k.a. the Great Minnesota Get-together.

parks, lakes and rivers. Most of the 75 events that are held over a 10-day period are free and family-oriented. There are sports competitions, music, parades, food and activities for all ages. (612) 377-4621. (See Minneapolis section.)

PELICAN RAPIDS
Ugly Truck Contest • A cash prize is given for the ugliest truck. Trucks come from all over the state, lining both sides of Main Street. (218) 863-6693.

MINNEAPOLIS
Uptown Art Fair • This three-day fair held at Hennepin Avenue and Lake Street is billed as the Midwest's largest juried outdoor arts and crafts fair. More than 500 artists are expected to participate with attendance well over 300,000. Also included is a children's activity tent and evening entertainment. (612) 667-2760.

FRAZEE
Turkey Days • Turkey trot, turkey crawl, turkey barbecue and a banana split are some of the just-plain-fun things going on at this festival. Other activities include a flea market, demo derby, water fight, road rally, history pageant and lots of food. (218) 334-2661.

MONTROSE
Bavarian Sommerfest • In the Munich tradition, this three-day event is a great place to enjoy an authentic German meal, beer and music under the big tent. (612) 675-3777.

ELY
Blueberry Arts Festival • There are blueberries galore at this arts and crafts fair limited to 200 of the best national exhibitors. Ethnic food and musical presentations, family activities, canoe races and a 10-kilometer fun run make it fun for all ages. (218) 365-6123.

BLACKDUCK
Wood Carvers Festival • More than 50 wood carvers from the United States and Canada exhibit and sell their work. Music and food add to the festivities. (218) 835-4669.

AUGUST

YOUNG AMERICA
Stiftungsfest • Minnesota's oldest continuous festival was organized in 1861 by the Young America Maennerchor (men's choir). Stiftungsfest literally means "founders' day celebration" and, in the German tradition, there will be the big tent, bands, amusements and beer garden. This nationally publicized event is not to be missed. (612) 467-3676.

NISSWA
Gull Lake "Fun" Regatta • There have been more than 30 annual Fun Regattas. The two-day scow sailing event includes five races, lunches, pig roast, entertain-

ment and games for the children. Camping is available on the club grounds. (218) 963-2620.

St. Paul
Minnesota State Fair • This is everything a down-home state fair should be: 12 days of cotton candy, the midway, carameled apples, animal barns, mini-donuts, the horse show, popcorn, great-names entertainment, hot dogs, equipment displays, ice cream, rides and the all-you-can-drink milk bar (the #1 Minnesota State Fair concession stand). Lots of food and lots of fun. (612) 296-5029.

Ghent
Belgian-American Days • The Belgian sport of rolle bolle is the center of this festival, which attracts more than 2,000 spectators. Other activities include a kiddies' parade, dance and tournaments. (507) 428-3456.

Grand Marais
Fisherman's Picnic • This annual four-day festival sponsored by the Lion's Club includes a big-fish contest, loon-calling contest, fish toss, singing, street dance and an all-around good time. (218) 387-2524 or (800) 622-4014.

Red Wing
River City Days • The citizens of Red Wing host outdoor theater performances, an arts and crafts fair, live music concerts and fireworks. (612) 388-4719.

Detroit Lakes
We Fest • A three-day outdoor camping and country music festival. People from in- and out-of-state come to socialize and listen to nationally famous country singers. Attendance has topped 96,000 people listening to 35 hours of live music. This is an EVENT! (218) 847-1681.

St. Paul
Ghost Squadron Air Display • There are exhibits of original, predominantly World War II aircraft and some vehicles at the St. Paul Downtown Airport. Featured aeronautical guests and dignitaries, food and memorabilia vendors add to the festivities. (612) 455-6942.

Longville
Dog Days Celebration • This celebration has a sidewalk sale and dog show that includes awards for original categories such as the best dressed, best per-forming, and most unusual dog in town. (218) 363-2661 or (800) 756-7583.

Roosevelt
Lake of the Woods Steam & Gas Engine Show • In operation are steam threshers, antique gas tractors, and a historic Comstock Sawmill. There's also a parade of old-time steamers and tractors, antique collections and more. (218) 442-5551.

Taylors Falls
Sheepdog Trials • Competitors from throughout the United States, using only voice and whistles, guide their dogs as they herd sheep through complex courses. These amazing dogs achieve amazing things. (612) 583-2803.

Austin
Farmfest • Field demonstrations include both state-of-the-art and antique farm equipment. There's a tractor pull, including a kids' pedal pull, for prizes and points for the national event. The fest also includes farm exhibits, country music entertainment and arts and crafts sales. (507) 437-8568 or (800) 347-5863.

Statewide
Minnesota Prairie Day Celebration • Sponsored by the local communities, this is a statewide celebration, both biological and historical, of the nature of the prairie and its inhabitants. (218) 739-7576.

Ironworld, Chisholm
Iron Country Hoedown • For three days the best in country music can be heard in northern Minnesota at these concerts featuring national country music stars. (218) 254-3321 or (800) 372-6437

Scandia
Spelmansstamma • This is a true Swedish fiddling festival with master fiddlers from all over. The festival includes exhibitions, workshop, vendors and smorgasbord. (612) 645-8578 or 433-3430.

West Concord
Swissfest • Like a trip to Switzerland, this authentic festival has Alp horn blowing, international yodelers, Swiss wrestlers, Swiss flag tossing, folk dancing, many different Swiss foods and imports, and a beautiful hand-bell choir. (507) 527-2730.

Shakopee
Minnesota Renaissance Festival • Costumed players wander with you through this 16th-century village. Open week-

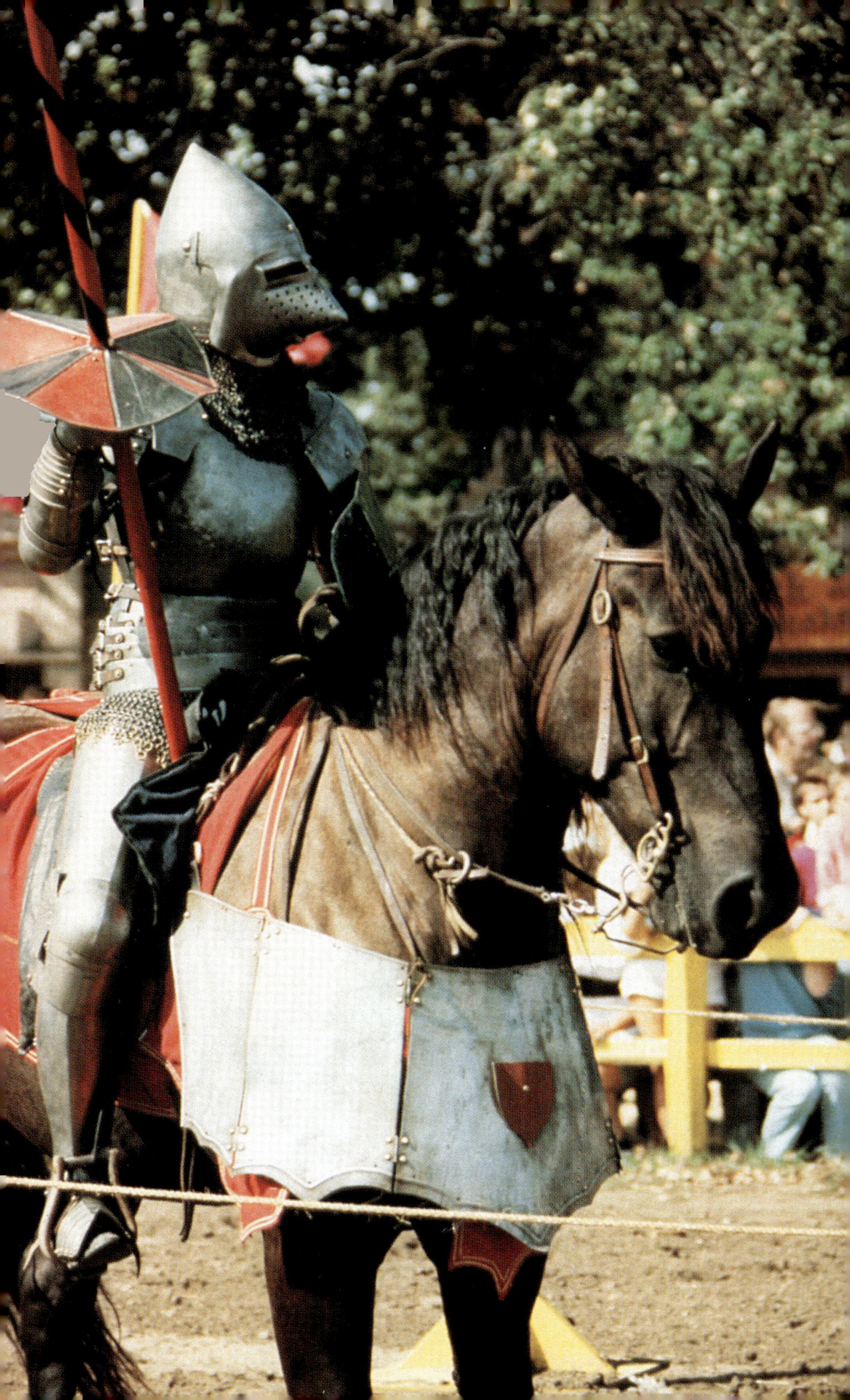

ends through August and September. Jousting, games, fine arts and crafts and unusual foods make it a real experience. (612) 445-7361.

DULUTH
Bayfront Blues Festival • Bring your blanket and lawn chairs and spend the weekend swinging to the blues. More than a dozen national and regional bands perform all day outside at Bayfront Park. Sponsored by Leinenkugel's Beer. (218) 722-4011 or (800) 438-5884.

ROCHESTER
Greek Festival • There's fun for the whole family at this traditional Greek festival of food, dancing and music held at West Silver Lake Pavilion and Park. (507) 282-1529.

ST. PAUL
AIM Powwow • A traditional American Indian Movement's gathering of nations featuring historic dancing, music, sports, art and foods. The powwow is held at Fort Snelling State Park. (612) 727-3129.

SEPTEMBER

AS THE LEAVES change across Minnesota, get your "fall colors" report from the Minnesota Office of Tourism and then head out to one of the many fall festivals across the state enjoying the colors created by the changing leaves as you go.

MINNEAPOLIS
The Jazz Party • To quote an expert, this is a "real jazz jam session performed by the best." It's fun for not only the audience, but the musicians as well, who bring along their wives and friends. There are four four-to-five-hour sessions of extemporaneous jazz performed by 25 invited musicians, who are tops in the world on their instrument. The music is mostly traditional or swing jazz of the '30s and '40s performed by unrehearsed groups of one to nine players. The party begins Friday evening and is usually held the second weekend in September. (612) 788-7194.

BLAINE
Twin Cities Collectors' Car Show • You will see more than 500 cars from the

Knight at the Minnesota Renaissance Festival.

PHOTO COURTESY OF MINNESOTA OFFICE OF TOURISM

oldest to high tech. Food concessions. (612) 434-6355.

NORTHFIELD
Defeat of Jesse James Days • A reenactment of the famous bank raid is the center of this three-day event, which includes tournaments, horse show, rodeo, storytelling, theater, arts and crafts and more. (507) 645-5604.

EXCELSIOR
Apple Days • Lots of apples, an 1800s calliope and a doll buggy/red wagon parade are some of this street festival's highlights along with food vendors, flea market and clogging demonstrations. (612) 474-6461 or 474-8116.

DULUTH
Hawk Migration Weekend • If you're lucky, you will view hundreds of thousands of hawks in migration at Hawk Ridge on the North Shore of Lake Superior. There also are enlightening evening programs and nature hikes. (218) 525-6930 or 525-5952.

LA CRESCENT
Apple Festival • Enjoy a soapbox derby, carnival, flea market and all the fun a country applefest has to offer. (507) 895-2800.

WORTHINGTON
King Turkey Days and the Great Gobbler Gallop • This celebration has been held for more than 50 years and begins with the turkeys leading the parade down Main Street. Politicians speak and turkeys race for a gobbling good time. (507) 372-2919.

WORTHINGTON
High School Rodeo • Regional student cowpunchers compete for points and a chance for the nationals. (507) 372-2919.

1992 MINNESOTA
Renaissance Festival™

Weekends & Labor Day
Aug. 14 – Sept. 26

4 miles S. of Shakopee on Hwy. 169
Open 9 am - 7 pm   **FREE PARKING**
Call 612/445-7361 for tickets & info.

PECULIARLY MINNESOTA

Octoberfest at Grandma's in Duluth.

SHERBURN
Pig Patch Days • Contests galore such as kiss-a-pig, best-looking ham hocks, and the prettiest pigs' feet. There's also mechanical pig races, a piggy/pet parade and a community pig-out. (507) 764-2607.

BROOKLYN PARK
Apple Cider Days • Apple dumplings (like no others) are best from these wood stoves. There's also cider pressing, sauerkraut making, hayrides and some good old-fashioned fun. (612) 484-9668.

FINLAND
Finn Fest • Harvest booya, bake sale and craft fair accompanied by Finnish music, dancing and horseshoe tournament. (218) 353-7700.

NEW PRAGUE
Dozinky: A Czechoslovakian Harvest Festival • This is an "old country" original festival featuring ethnic bands, costumes, dancing and singing. Also included are historical displays, demonstrations, crafts and traditional foods. (612) 758-4360.

DULUTH
Grandma's Oktoberfest • This has become a tradition as rowdy and fun as the Oktoberfest in Munich. Grandma's puts up the tent for the German beer garden with German food, beer and polka bands. (218) 727-4192.

CHANHASSEN
Fall Festival • This is a wonderful time to check out the Minnesota Landscape Arboretum via walking and tram tours. During the festival there are special classes and craft sales. (612) 443-2460.

LUVERNE
Annual Tri-State Band Festival • For more than 40 years, high school students from Minnesota, South Dakota, Iowa and Canada have competed in four classes. The event is entertaining for the entire family. (507) 283-4061 or 283-2612.

ELK RIVER
Prairie Sugar, Sorghum & Molasses • Watch while the horse-powered mill presses the sorghum and the juice is boiled down for molasses. There are also demonstrations of oxen plowing and corn shocking. (612) 441-6896.

OCTOBER
DURING OCTOBER, FOR a little oompah-pah, there are a number of Oktoberfests around the state and many local Halloween activities for young and old alike.

ALBERT LEA
A Big Island Rendezvous • Bluegrass and Native American music and dance are happening at this 250-tepee encampment. Buses will shuttle you out to Helmer Myre State Park for the food and entertainment. (507) 373-3938.

ST. PAUL
Antique Spectacular • At the fairgrounds will be hundreds of antique exhibitors from throughout the United States. (612) 771-3476.

STILLWATER
Rivertown Fall Colors Festival • On the first full weekend in October, if it's a beautiful day, this juried arts and crafts show of more than 150 exhibitors, held in Lowell Park on the banks of the St. Croix, makes a wonderful fall outing. A variety of food is available both at the show and the many excellent Stillwater restaurants. (612) 726-1171.

OWATONNA
Great Pumpkin Festival • Lots of pumpkin fun, which includes pumpkin seed and carving contests, plus square dancing, bed racing, fishing contest, arts and crafts fair and volksmarch. (507) 451-4640 or (800) 423-6466.

Hurray! Minnesota

Anoka
Halloween Festival • The "Halloween Capital of the World" has sponsored this event for more than 70 years. Included is trick or treating downtown, a grand parade, "The Big Parade of the Little People" and running/walking events to work off the sweets. (612) 421-7130.

New Ulm
Oktoberfest • Two stages hold continuous performances of both local and international singers and bands. Crafts, souvenirs, food and beverages add to the festivities. (507) 354-4217.

NOVEMBER
NOVEMBER IS THE month of arts and craft shows in preparation for Christmas giving. At the end of the month, the Christmas lights begin to shine and many cities throughout the state have events coinciding with the lighting of the lights.

Madison
Norsefest • Some won't want to miss the lutefisk supper, nor the lutefisk-eating contest (current record: 8 pounds). But there also will be a Norwegian arts and crafts show and many other activities that might be tastier to others. (612) 598-7373.

Bemidji
People's Art Festival • On display is a wide variety of unique handcrafted items for collecting or giving, produced by more than 70 artists and craftspeople from the region. (218) 751-7570.

DECEMBER
THERE ARE LIGHT displays, holiday craft fairs and local Christmas celebrations in cities around Minnesota. Call your local Chamber of Commerce for details on those in your area.

Shakopee
Folkways of Christmas • The activities at Historic Murphy's Landing include music, decorations and demonstrations of nine ethnic pioneer holidays. (612) 445-1660.

Windom
Charles Dickens' Christmas • As the audience strolls from store to store, scenes from "A Christmas Carol" are continuously played out at sites throughout Town Square with all the culinary trimmings. (507) 831-2752.

Grand Rapids
Christmas in a 1900 Logging Camp • At Forest History Center, a reconstructed logging camp is the setting for storytelling, music, wagon rides, handcrafts and demonstrations. (218) 327-4482.

Pipestone
Festival of Trees • This is a splendid holiday celebration. More than 35 trees decorated by local organizations are on display. The celebration includes carolers, Santa and Mrs. Claus, concerts, skating, sleigh rides and everything associated with winter at a country inn. (507) 825-5871 or (800) 535-7610.

Enjoy a Charles Dickens Christmas in Windom.

Minnesota State Parks

THE STATE OF MINNESOTA HAS 66 state parks and 14 state waysides. The size of the parks varies from less than 200 acres at Monson Lake Park to more than 32,000 acres at Lake Itasca. Like the state of Minnesota, the parks have a wide range of topography. Each park has its own characteristics, its own beauty and its own individual attractions. You can explore a cave, tour an iron ore mine, swim in a lake or canoe down a river. Two parks even have golf courses with club rentals.

The facilities at the parks vary. Most parks have biking, hiking, cross-country skiing or horseback-riding trails, and many have wilderness camping facilities. Other parks have swimming, boating, fishing and recreational areas. And almost half of the parks offer interpretive centers and activities to help visitors explore the beauty of nature and the many natural resources of the park. There are activities such as nature walks, movies, talks and workshops, plus Junior Park Naturalist and Explorer programs for children and young adults. Some parks even have summer entertainment programs ranging from music to storytelling.

The state parks are open 8 a.m to 10 p.m. Pets are allowed in the parks but they must be attended at all times, kept on a leash (maximum six feet) and cleaned up after. No motorized recreational vehicles are permitted in the state parks and about a third of the parks have motor and speed restrictions on their lakes.

The parks often offer some items for sale, including firewood: Gathering of firewood is prohibited in all areas of state parks. The parks system will take Visa and MasterCard or personal checks as well as cash.

To help operate and preserve the park system, minimal fees are charged for use of the facilities. All visitors need a vehicle permit, which is $4 a day or $18 for the year. The annual permit gives unlimited access year-round to all of the state parks. Nightly camping fees range in price and are determined by the degree of creature comforts offered (which in most cases means how fancy is the restroom). Walk-in rustic sites are $7, drive-in rustic sites are $8, a site with flush toilets and shower is $10, and a site with electricty is an extra $2.50, when available.

It is possible to make reservations 120 days in advance for campsites at some state parks. Otherwise, it is on a first-come first-served basis. For reservations, call (800) 765-2267.

For detailed information for all state parks:

DEPARTMENT OF NATURAL RESOURCES INFORMATION CENTER
500 Lafayette Rd.
St. Paul, MN 55155-4040
(800) 652-9747
(612) 296-6157

1 / AFTON
6959 S. Peller Ave.
Hastings, MN 55033
(612) 436-5391

2 / BANNING
Box 643
Sandstone, MN 55072
(612) 245-2668

3 / BEAR HEAD LAKE
9301 Bear Head State Park Rd.
Ely, MN 55731
(218) 365-7229

4 / BEAVER CREEK VALLEY
Route 2, Box 57
Caledonia, MN 55921
(507) 724-2107

5 / BIG STONE LAKE
Route 1, Box 153
Ortonville, MN 56278
(612) 839-3663

6 / BLUE MOUND
Route 1
Luverne, MN 56156
(507) 283-4592

Hurray! Minnesota

Map of Minnesota state parks:

- 34 Lake Bronson
- 66 Zippel Bay
- 25 Hayes Lake
- 18 Franz Jevne
- 49 Old Mill
- 3 Bear Head Lake
- 30 Judge C. R. Magney
- 24 Grand Portage
- 57 Soudan Underground Mine
- 54 Scenic
- 40 McCarthy Beach
- 10 Cascade River
- 61 Tettegouche
- 60 Temperance River
- 33 Lake Bemidji
- 20 George H. Crosby Manitou
- 28 Itasca
- 55 Schoolcraft
- 26 Hill Annex Mine
- 59 Split Rock Lighthouse
- 23 Gooseberry Falls
- 7 Buffalo River
- 53 Savanna Portage
- 39 Maplewood
- 45 Moose Lake
- 29 Jay Cooke
- 22 Glendaleough
- 12 Crow Wing
- 41 Banning
- 35 Lake Carlos
- 11 Mille Lacs Kathio
- 2 (Banning area)
- 13 Father Hennepin
- 51 St. Croix
- 5 Big Stone Lake
- 21 Glacial Lakes
- Charles A. Lindbergh
- 64 Wild River
- 56 Sibley
- 37 Lake Maria
- 27 Interstate
- 65 William O'Brien
- 44 Monson Lake
- 32 Lac qui Parle
- 1 Afton
- 62 Upper Sioux Agency
- 43 Minnesota Valley
- 17 Fort Snelling
- 19 Frontenac
- 16 Fort Ridgely
- 8 Camden
- 14 Flandrau
- 52 Sakatah Lake
- 47 Nerstrand Big Woods
- 9 Carley
- 63 / 48 O.L. Kipp
- 38 Lake Shetek
- 42 Minneopa
- 50 Rice Lake
- 58 Split Rock Creek
- 4 Beaver Creek Valley
- 6 Blue Mound
- 31 Kilen Woods
- 46 Myre-Big Island
- 36 Lake Louise
- 15 Forestville/Mystery Cave

7 / BUFFALO RIVER
Route 2, Box 256
Glyndon, MN 56547
(218) 498-2124

8 / CAMDEN
Route 1, Box 9
Lynd, MN 56157
(507) 865-4530

9 / CARLEY
Route 1, Box 256
Altura, MN 55910
(507) 932-3007

10 / CASCADE RIVER
HCR 3, Box 450
Lutsen, MN 55612
(218) 387-1543

59 PECULIARLY MINNESOTA

11 / Charles A. Lindbergh
Box 364
Little Falls, MN 56345
(612) 632-9050

12 / Crow Wing
7100 State Park Rd. S.W.
Brainerd, MN 56401
(218) 829-8022

13 / Father Hennepin
Box 397
Isle, MN 56342
(612) 676-8763

14 / Flandrau
1300 Summit Ave.
New Ulm, MN 56073
(507) 354-3519

15 / Forestville/Mystery Cave
Route 2, Box 128
Preston, MN 55965
(507) 352-5111

16 / Fort Ridgely
Route 1, Box 65
Fairfax, MN 55332
(507) 426-7840

17 / Fort Snelling
Highway 5 and Post Road
St. Paul, MN 55111
(612) 725-2390

18 / Franz Jevne
Route 3, Box 230
Birchdale, MN 56629
No phone

19 / Frontenac
Route 2, Box 134
Lake City, MN 55041
(612) 345-3401

20 / George H. Crosby Manitou
474 E. Highway 61
Silver Bay, MN 55614
Call Tettegouche: (218) 226-3539

21 / Glacial Lakes
Route 2, Box 126
Starbuck, MN 56381
(612) 239-2860

22 / Glendaleough
Highway 78
Battle Lake, MN 56551
No phone

23 / Gooseberry Falls
1300 E. Highway 61
Two Harbors, MN 55616
(218) 834-3855

24 / Grand Portage
Grand Portage, MN 55605
No phone

25 / Hayes Lake
Star Route 4, Box 84
Roseau, MN 56751
(218) 425-7504

26 / Hill Annex Mine
Box 376
Calumet, MN 55716
(218) 247-7215

27 / Interstate
Box 254
Taylors Falls, MN 55084
(612) 465-5711

28 / Itasca
Lake Itasca, MN 56460
(218) 266-3654

29 / Jay Cooke
500 E. Highway 210
Carlton, MN 55718
(218) 384-4610

30 / Judge C. R. Magney
Box 500, East Star Route
Grand Marais, MN 55604
(218) 387-2929

31 / Kilen Woods
Route 1, Box 122
Lakefield, MN 56150
(507) 662-6258

32 / Lac qui Parle
Route 5, Box 74A
Montevideo, MN 56265
(612) 752-4736

33 / Lake Bemidji
3401 N.E. State Park Rd.
Bemidji, MN 56601
(218) 755-3843

34 / Lake Bronson
Box 9
Lake Bronson, MN 56734
(218) 754-2200

35 / Lake Carlos
Route 2, Box 240
Carlos, MN 56319
(612) 852-7200

36 / Lake Louise
Route 1, Box 184
Le Roy, MN 55951
(507) 324-5249

37 / Lake Maria
Route 1, Box 128
Monticello, MN 55362
(612) 878-2325

38 / Lake Shetek
Route 1, Box 164
Currie, MN 56123
(507) 763-3256

Hurray! Minnesota

39 / Maplewood
Route 3, Box 422
Pelican Rapids, MN 56572
(218) 863-8383

40 / McCarthy Beach
7622 McCarthy Beach Rd.
Side Lake, MN 55781
(218) 254-2411

41 / Mille Lacs Kathio
HC-67, Box 85
Onamia, MN 56359
(612) 532-3523

42 / Minneopa
Route 9, Box 143
Mankato, MN 56001
(507) 625-4388

43 / Minnesota Valley
19825 Park Boulevard
Jordan, MN 55352
(612) 492-6400

44 / Monson Lake
Sunberg, MN 56289
(612) 366-3797

45 / Moose Lake
Route 2, 1000 Co. 137
Moose Lake, MN 55767
(218) 485-4059

46 / Myre-Big Island
Route 3, Box 33
Albert Lea, MN 56007
(507) 373-5084

47 / Nerstrand Big Woods
9700 E. 170th St.
Nerstrand, MN 55053
(507) 334-8848

48 / O.L. Kipp
Route 4
Winona, MN 55987
(507) 643-6849

49 / Old Mill
Route 1, Box 42
Argyle, MN 56713
(218) 437-8174

50 / Rice Lake
Route 3, Box 45
Owatonna, MN 55060
(507) 451-7406

51 / St. Croix
Route 3, Box 450
Hinckley, MN 55037
(612) 384-6591

52 / Sakatah Lake
Route 2, Box 19
Waterville, MN 56096
(507) 362-4438

53 / Savanna Portage
HCR 3, Box 591
McGregor, MN 55760
(218) 426-3271

54 / Scenic
HCR 2, Box 17
Bigfork, MN 56628
(218) 743-3362

55 / Schoolcraft
HCR 4, Box 181
Deer River, MN 56636
(218) 566-2383

56 / Sibley
800 N.E. Sibley Park Rd.
New London, MN 56273
(612) 354-2055

57 / Soudan Underground Mine
Box 335
Soudan, MN 55782
(218) 753-2245

58 / Split Rock Creek
Route 2
Jasper, MN 56144
(507) 348-7908

59 / Split Rock Lighthouse
Box 2010A, E. Highway 61
Two Harbors, MN 55616
(218) 226-3065

60 / Temperance River
Box 33
Schroeder, MN 55613
(218) 663-7476

61 / Tettegouche
474 E. Highway 61
Silver Bay, MN 55614
(218) 226-3539

62 / Upper Sioux Agency
Route 2, Box 92
Granite Falls, MN 56241
(612) 564-4777

63 / Whitewater
Route 1, Box 256
Altura, MN 55910
(507) 932-3007

64 / Wild River
39755 Park Trail
Center City, MN 55012
(612) 583-2125

65 / William O'Brien
16821 N. O'Brien Trail
Marine on St. Croix, MN 55047
(612) 433-2421

66 / Zippel Bay
Williams, MN 56686
(218) 783-6252

Sports in Minnesota

PROFESSIONAL SPORTS

THE MOST PROMINENT of the Minnesota professional sports teams is the **Minnesota Twins** baseball team, World Champions in 1987 and again in 1991. The Twins' home turf is the Hubert Humphrey Metrodome in downtown Minneapolis.

Also playing in the Metrodome is the **Minnesota Vikings** football team. Since their first season in 1961, the Vikings have had 12 Central Division Championships and won the National Football Conference Championship in 1969.

The **North Stars** hockey team plays at the Met Center in Bloomington. Since the team was founded in 1961, they have twice lost the Stanley cup in the final game — in 1981 and 1991.

The **Timberwolves** basketball team, newest of the pro teams, has its home court at the new Target Center in downtown Minneapolis. Target Center is a basketball fan's dream, designed for watching the game with a good view from every seat.

MOTOR RACING

THERE ARE NUMEROUS race tracks around the state that offer a variety of motor racing, such as stock car, motorcycle, demolition and drag racing.

Brainerd International Raceway hosts the two major events in the state — the NHRA National Drag Races and the U.S. round of the FIM World Championship Superbike motorcycle races. For more information, phone **(612) 475-1500**.

ANTIQUE CAR RUN

LAST YEAR MORE than 70 cars drove the 117 scenic miles for this annual event. It begins in New London on Friday evening with the cars parading down Main Street. The actual run begins early the next morning. There are five rest stops along the way where spectators can view the cars and talk with the drivers. The race finishes in New Brighton somewhere between 3 p.m. and 6 p.m., depending on the speed of the car and the talkativeness of the driver. A car show and the awards ceremony brunch are held on Sunday in New Brighton.

TENNIS

MINNESOTA HAS THOUSANDS of outside courts and seasonal resorts making tennis easily accessible. Recently, particularly in the Twin Cities area, the construction of indoor courts has proliferated, making this one-time seasonal sport available year-round.

Many major spectator tennis events occur in the summer months: **Pine Tree Apple Tennis Classic**, reputed to be the largest non-celebrity benefit mixed-doubles tournament in the United States; the **America's Cup**, featuring top world-ranked American players in exhibition play; and the **Minikahda Invitational**, a world-class men's tournament.

More information about tournaments and tennis in the state can be obtained from the Northwestern Tennis Association. **(612) 546-0709**.

GOLF

THOUGH GOLF IS a seasonal sport in Minnesota (from snow melt to first snow), there are numerous courses, more than 100 in the Twin Cities area and another 270 around the state, public and private, at varying degrees of challenge.

A claim to fame of many of the Minnesota courses is the water hazard. Almost all courses boast at least one never-to-be-forgotten water hazard, whether it is the "Drink" at Izatys or the 8th-hole pontoon ride to the next tee at Stonebrooke in Shakopee.

Hazeltine in Chaska was host to the U.S. Open in 1991. Other notable courses are Interlachen in Edina, Northland in Duluth, and the lake region resorts' courses, such as the challenging Grand View and Izatys courses; Madden's Resort, boasting courses of 36+ holes; the Detroit Country Club, host to the Pine to Palm Golf Classic; and the brand new

Hurray! Minnesota

18-hole championship course at Lutsen on the North Shore.

Throughout the state there are numerous Minnesota and United States Golf Association (MGA and USGA) championships and events. For a complete calendar of events, contact MGA. **(612) 927-4643** or **(800) 642-4405**.

MARATHONS

THE TOWNS AND clubs of Minnesota host many competitive walks and runs for a variety of participants. Two of the most famous are the **Twin Cities Marathon** and **Grandma's Marathon**. Both have made the top 20 marathons in the United States as determined by Runner's World magazine.

In Grandma's Marathon, more than 5,000 people run the 26.2 miles along the North Shore of Lake Superior. The race, held in June, was originally sponsored by Grandma's Saloon & Deli, located at the base of the high bridge in Duluth, and the North Shore Striders running club. Now it is a non-profit community event with more than 3,000 volunteer workers. There are a number of different races, including one for kids. There also is a spaghetti dinner open to the public in the Canal Park big tent where, after the race, musicians and entertainers perform. The entire area around Canal Park is given over to the festivities with one of the biggest post-marathon parties you'll ever see. **(218) 727-0947**.

The Twin Cities Marathon is held in October and is limited to 6,000 runners. This race, recognized as the country's most beautiful urban marathon, starts in Minneapolis and, after winding around some of the city's lakes, finishes in the shadow of the capitol in St. Paul. Like Grandma's, the Twin Cities Marathon includes in the program other races and social events for the runners, their supporters and the spectators. **(612) 673-0778**.

BIKING

BIKING IS A very popular sport in Minnesota. The entire state has trails to challenge and please most bikers, such as the 38-mile Root River Trail, which passes through Lanesboro and the scenic Southeastern Minnesota Bluff Country. There are statewide or segmented maps featuring road analysis and off-road bikeways available from the Minnesota Department of Transportation **(612) 296-2216**. The Minnesota Office of Tourism **(612) 296-5029** also has biking brochures, trail maps and guides. Information on historic corridor trails open to bikes can be obtained from the Department of Natural Resources **(612) 296-6157** or **(800) 652-9747**.

In the Twin Cities, there are numerous hiking and biking paths for both touring and exercise, such as the paths connecting parkways and lakes in Minneapolis. Information can be obtained from the Minneapolis Park and Recreation Board **(612) 348-2243**. For information on St. Paul trails, phone **(612) 292-7400**.

For those who like to ride their bike as a means of transportation, the American Youth Hostelry **(612) 659-0408** has a book outlining reasonably safe routes through the Twin Cities and the state.

THE PINES
at Grand View Lodge

Minnesota's Grandest Golf Course

Mid-week Golf Packages

Gull Lake • Brainerd, MN
1 (800) 432-3788

PECULIARLY MINNESOTA

On a clear day, you're likely to see a hot-air balloon rally anywhere in the state.

In late July, **TRAM** (The Ride Across Minnesota) takes place. Every year a different route is covered on a five-day journey across the width of the state. It is sponsored by the St. Paul Pioneer Press to raise money for the Minnesota Multiple Sclerosis Society. Average daily ride is 60 miles through some of the most beautiful and historic scenery of Minnesota. For more information, phone **(612) 870-1500** or **(800) 582-5296**.

KARE 11 Bike Classic is held late in June. This event offers five different rides from an 11-mile ride to a two-day, 300-mile marathon. Pledges go to Health One Cancer Detection and Prevention. For more information, call **(612) 336-7433**.

IN-LINE SKATING

MINNESOTA IS THE birthplace of the in-line skate. It's a natural outgrowth of the hockey player and a little of the cross-country skier who wanted to extend their workouts year-round.

The sport has progressed to the point in the state that the city ordinance now accords the responsible skater the same rights as a bicyclist on the city roadways. The in-line skater is invited to use bike paths and trails around the state and the Twin Cities. In addition, there is an in-line skating program at the Hubert Humphrey Metrodome so avid skaters can skate all winter long. **(612) 922-9000**.

There are three major races in the state: a 50 kilometer held in May at Giants Ridge, Biwabik, sponsored by National Group Outdoor Marathon Skating; the Ultra-Roll, held in conjunction with the Minneapolis Aquatennial; and the Rollerblade Summer Series in June. The latter two are held around Lake Calhoun. To date, average participation has been from 800 to 1,000 skaters.

Headquarters for the International In-line Skating Association are in the Twin Cities. For more information, call **(612) 924-2348** or **(800) FOR-IISA**.

HORSEBACK RIDING

THERE ARE MORE than 973 miles of multipurpose corridor trails available to Minnesota horseback riders. Many riders trailer their horses to these trails, but there are a number of stables around the state offering trail rides and lessons. Contact the Department of Natural Resources Trails and Waterways Unit at **(612) 296-6699** or the Minnesota Office of Tourism **(800) 657-3700** or **(612) 296-5029** in the Twin Cities.

Polo in Minnesota was organized in the early 1900s, with the first official game taking place at Fort Snelling in 1922. Today the Polo Club of Minnesota **(612) 473-3741** hosts two major tournaments at the Maple Plains Fields in the village of Independence. The first, at the beginning of August, is a benefit for the Children's Home Society. The second is the Upper Midwest Tournament, held the third week of August. Eight to 10 teams from around the nation, bringing more than 180 horses, participate over the week in elimination games. Final games are played on the weekend.

Minnesota is host to a number of rodeo events, both professional and amateur. Some of the more publicized events are the World's Toughest Rodeo held at the Met Center in February or, in June, the Buffalo Rodeo, an annual PRCA rodeo event that includes a parade and additional activities. Others such as the Northstar Stampede and the Minnesota State Championship rodeos have been held for more than 30 years running.

Around the state, there also are a number of high school rodeos for young amateurs and even a Little Britches Rodeo.

Various saddle clubs hold shows throughout the state. On any given weekend when there isn't snow on the ground, you can probably find one. For more information on most horsey events, you can call the Minnesota Horse Council at **(612) 755-4899**.

The following annual horse shows are held at the State Fairgrounds:
Horse Expo — Held at the end of April, this is a major trade show but with a lot of other activities and entertainment.
Sahara Sands — Arabian horse show.
Reigning Derby — Competition emphasizing controlling the horse, held at the end of May.
Minnesota Arabian Horse Show
Tanbark Horse Show — A major saddlebred competition.
4H Horse Show — This show is for the younger set and is held in September.
Western Saddle Club Horse Show
Minnesota Fall Arabian Festival — Held at the end of September, this is the show of shows and includes spectator events and stall decorations.
Minnesota Fall Horse Show — This hunters and jumping competition is a pre-Olympic competition.

Minnesota has quite a history in horse racing. The 1990 Kentucky Derby winner, **Unbridled**, is owned by Mrs. Frances Genter of Minneapolis. And the historically famous **Dan Patch**, the black stallion harness racer that held the record for the mile (1:55) for 85 years, was owned by Will Savage of Savage, Minnesota.

For professional spectator horse racing and pari-mutuel betting, **Canterbury Downs**, in the Twin Cities southern suburb of Shakopee, holds races from April through October. For more information, **(612) 445-RACE**.

BALLOONING

BALLOONING IS A popular sport in Minnesota all year round. There are several events, such as the Minneapolis Aquatennial, the St. Paul Winter Carnival and the Detroit Lakes Northwest Water Carnival, where balloon flight and competition can be observed.

There also are a number of outfits around the state that offer rides and lessons for a fee. Probably one of the oldest of these is the **Wiederkehr Balloon Academy** on the St. Croix River in Lakeland. Wiederkehr sells, repairs and maintains balloons along with offering training and rides. **(612) 776-5876** or **(612) 436-8172**.

Superior hiking trail at Mount Trudy Overlook near Tettegouche State Park.

SKYDIVING

FOR THOSE WHO would like a little more excitement and don't get sweaty palms when they're three steps up a ladder, there are several skydiving firms operating out of the Twin Cities. If you're brand new to the sport, you can be tandem jumping within one day. You spend a few hours learning how to land and then are strapped to a professional skydiver. You and the pro jump out of the plane together. He or she helps you control the chute, setting you gently down on terra firma once more.

ROCK CLIMBING

IN MINNESOTA, there are several places for technical rock climbing. The heights are not of real significance but the climbs vary greatly in degree of technical difficulty. Some easier climbs are found in Taylors Falls at Interstate State Park along the river. They are approximately 50 to 80 feet high. There also is the "Big Bluff" near Red Wing along the Mississippi, with its many routes up the sandstone.

In western Minnesota, Blue Mounds State Park near Luverne offers some very challenging climbs.

Along the North Shore in northeastern Minnesota are some of the highest vertical climbs with the most spectacular views, since the cliffs are right on Lake Superior. These climbs can be found at **Palisade Head** just north of Silver Bay, **Shovel Point** in Tettegouche State Park, and **Carlton Peak** near Tofte.

HIKING

THERE ARE SOME 1,840 miles of backpacking, hiking and walking trails, both wilderness and scenic, in Minnesota. Trails travel through pine forests, along sparkling lakes, through the hills and valleys of the great rivers, and across the vast plains.

Plans are under way for linkage with the **North Country National Scenic Trail**. Minnesota will be a part of this trail, which will stretch from the Missouri River in North Dakota to Lake Champlain in New York. North Country will include not only diverse and scenic landscapes but also historic sites telling the story of the settling of America and the growth of the nation. Currently, of the Minnesota portion of the trail, 68 miles running through the Chippewa National Forest are complete.

Other major trails are:
Superior National Forest — 30 trails
Minnesota Valley Trail — 36 miles
Jay Cooke State Park — 50 miles
St. Croix State Park — 127 miles
Border Route Trail — 38 miles
Isle Royale — 45 miles from end to end

Hurray! Minnesota

Whitewater rafting on the St. Louis River.

Crosby-Manitou State Park — This park has been specifically designed for backpackers.

The Minnesota Department of Natural Resources (DNR) Information Center, **(800) 652-9747** or **(612) 296-6157** has tons of information on backpacking around the state including information on the **State Parks Hiking Club**. Members of the club receive a book on the trails and can earn patches, free camping and other perks after hiking a specified number of miles. The DNR also publishes a series of brochures, Trail Explorers, which give an overview of a hiking area including geology, history and natural history.

More sources for trail information are: the Minnesota Travel Information Center **(800) 657-3700** or **(612) 296-5029**; Superior National Forest **(218) 720-5475**; Chippewa National Forest **(218) 335-2226**; or Voyageurs National Park **(218) 283-9821**.

WATER SPORTS

BEING THE LAND of 10,000 lakes, Minnesota abounds in water sports. Canoeing, kayaking, sailing, wind surfing, waterskiing, motorboat racing, whitewater rafting, swimming and, of course, fishing. There are tournaments and competitions in virtually all water sports.

CANOEING

Probably one of the most famous wilderness water playgrounds is the Voyageurs National Park and the Boundary Waters Canoe Area Wilderness (BWCAW). Most lakes are motor free, but canoes can be rented from outfitters near where you plan to begin your adventure. Overnight trippers must first obtain a permit from the park service. Reservations are advised **(218) 720-5440**. There also is a state system of 19 designated canoeing and boating rivers totaling 3,550 miles of river and lake canoe routes. The state-designated routes have access sites, campsites, portages and rest areas.

There are outfitters located around the state to help arrange your trip from supplying all services — including carrying the gear, setting up camp, and cooking the meals — to just renting you the canoe and paddles. The Minnesota Office of Tourism has a complete list of outfitters **(612) 296-5029**.

WHITEWATER RAFTING AND KAYAKING

Of the 19 designated rafting and kayaking rivers, a dozen of them have Class I or greater rapids, with as many as seven in Class II depending on the water level. Minnesota even has Class VI rapids on the Vermilion River, which flows through Superior National Forest into

Angling for muskie is a slippery business, but the big fish are a real prize.

Crane Lake. Class VI is the most difficult and dangerous, which means it is runnable only by experts in a decked boat with serious risk to life. There are portages for all rapids greater than Class III on the designated rivers.

If you would like to really get involved in the sport and aim to shoot the Class IV and V rapids, many of the outfitters have professionals, or call Superior Whitewater **(218) 384-4637**, UMD Kayak and Canoe Institute **(218) 726-7170** or Vermilion Whitewater **(612) 459-0689** and ask for Micky.

SAILING

Minnesota's 10,000 lakes are perfect for all types of sailing, from the small sunfish sailboat to deep-water yachts. More than a dozen lakes are home to as many as 20 sailing and yacht clubs. These clubs have fleets of different models of sailboats competing in regular weekly races or two-to-three-day regattas.

Most popular with the Minnesota sailors has been the scow fleet, partially because a Minnesota company, Johnson Boat Works, manufactures a complete line of recreational sailboats for sailors from 6 to 60. The racing scows are beautiful boats that have generated some of the most skilled sailors.

John Johnson created the concept of the scow or flat-bottom sailboat in 1896. Sponsored by the Grieg family of St. Paul, he built the business that is operated today by his grandson, Skip Johnson. John, quite an inventor, worked on other concepts as well. In 1903, the same year as the Wright brothers, he built a plane. He was un-

Hurray! Minnesota

able to procure financing for an engine so he flew it behind a power boat on White Bear Lake. Then in 1927, he procured the patent on the rotary snow plow, which he later sold to expand his sailboat business.

There also is a strong contingent of "keel-haulers," those who sail boats with a weighted keel or centerboard. These boats are substantially more stable in heavy winds and oftentimes have living quarters on board. Races are held around the state, but the most notable are out of Duluth and on Lake Pepin.

Other boats that are raced around the state are the Ying-Ling, J-22, or J-24 keel boats; the x-boat, primarily for the sailor under 16 years; the Flying Scott; the Hobie or catamaran, a double-hulled sailboat that really flies; and the newest member to the sailing fleet, the windsurfer. There's even a Sunfish and Laser fleet on Lake Calhoun.

WATERSKIING

Waterskiing was invented in Minnesota at Lake Pepin in 1922 by Ralph Samuelson, who imitated the action of skiing on snow by using two pine boards on the water. There are waterskiing events held throughout the state, such as the ski shows in Litchfield held during the summer. There's even a New Year's Day ski event held every year by the members of the Minnesota Water Ski Association and the Bald Eagle Water Ski club on the Mississippi River. The clubs only missed four years when the ice was too thick.

FISHING

The fishing in Minnesota is great. Minnesota is first nationally in per capita sales of fishing licenses. This is reasonable, considering there are 3,800,000 acres of fishing waters available with 144 different species to hook. The largest number of fish caught are panfish, including crappies and sunfish, which will bite at just about anything. The famous Minnesota walleye is the best eating. The northern pike is also a popular target — the largest ever caught weighed more than 45 pounds.

Minnesota has some very popular fishermen, such as Babe Winkelman, who produces a fishing program for TV, and Al and Ron Lindner, publishers of In-Fisherman, one of the largest outdoor specialty magazines, and inventors of the famous Lindy Rig.

The famous Rapala fishing lure got its start in North America with the help of Ron Weber, a businessman in Duluth. The Rapala lure was invented before World War II by Lauri Rapala, a Finnish fisherman. It was designed to imitate the swimming action of a sick or injured minnow, the first prey of a hungry fish.

Anyone 16 and older must have a fishing license to fish in Minnesota. These can be obtained from most bait stores. If you're new to the sport or just want to catch the big ones, there are guides and outfitters available around the state. The Minnesota Office of Tourism **(612) 296-5029** and the Minnesota Department of Natural Resources can provide you with detailed information **(612) 296-2959**.

One of the Minnesota rites of spring is smelting along the North Shore. Smelt are tasty or slimy, depending on who's describing. They are little fish that are caught by the thousands on "the" weekend in early April when they head up the creeks and rivers from Lake Superior to spawn. Though people gather at the streams to fish, oftentimes it's camaraderie and all-night revelry that is really the draw. Besides, who really wants to clean all those little fish, which aren't much more than a bite each. The traditional hockey tent, just north of Duluth on the Lester River, has the best beer-batter smelt you'll get anywhere. Money well spent, for a good cause.

Once simply a practical method of winter transport, cross-country skiing is now a recreation enjoyed by almost everyone.

WILDLIFE

MINNESOTA IS A great place to view and enjoy a large variety of non-game species. Thanks to the Chickadee Check-Off program, funds are set aside to maintain the habitats and educate the populace in order to insure the future of many of the varieties of mammals and birds in the state.

Minnesota DNR Nongame Wildlife supervisor Carrol Henderson **(612) 296-3344** prints a list of the prime places to view Minnesota wildlife. These locations vary from year to year, so call for the locations of the latest "in" spot.

HUNTING

MINNESOTA HAS A healthy and viable population of wild game. This includes a large variety of ducks and geese, upland game birds such as ruffed, sharp-tailed or spruce grouse, pheasants, woodcocks, Hungarian or grey partridge, white-tailed deer, fox, raccoon, rabbits, squirrel, moose and bear. The DNR maintains the licensing and sets the seasons on all hunting. For information, call **(612) 296-4506**.

WINTER SPORTS

AS FAMOUS AS Minnesota is for its summer water sports, winters supply the opportunity for almost as many sports activities. Minnesotans are avidly involved in ice fishing, skating, hockey, curling, broomball, cross-country skiing, downhill skiing, dog sledding, ice boating and snowmobiling. The Minnesota Office of Tourism has a complete list of competitive winter sports activities around the state and also a constant update on snow depths and conditions.

Dog Sledding

John Beargrease Sled Dog Marathon is a 475-mile sled-dog race from Duluth to Grand Portage and back, run along the hilly terrain of Lake Superior's North Shore through spectacular surroundings of black spruce and crystal waterfalls. The Beargrease is gaining in reputation as the largest and most famous sled-dog race outside of Alaska. The race is named after John Beargrease, who carried the mail by dog sled between Two Harbors and Grand Marais from 1887 to 1900. Racers are required to pause and pay homage at his grave in Beaver Bay as they pass by.

Cross-Country Skiing

There are more than 770 miles of state cross-country ski trails in Minnesota, with another 930 miles of Grant-in-Aid trails. The state trails are managed by the DNR, whereas Grant-in-Aid trails are managed locally with the funding coming from the Minnesota Ski Pass. To use the trails you must have a Great Minnesota Ski Pass and carry it while skiing. For pass and trail information call **(612) 296-6699**.

For a unique cross-country skiing experience, try the Minnesota Zoo in the Twin Cities suburb of Apple Valley. There are beautiful trails around the grounds past outdoor animals that love Minnesota winters. It is fun to ski past the Siberian tigers, elk, moose, or a buffalo or two. This is wilderness experience in your own back yard. For more information, call the Minnesota Zoo at **(612) 432-9200**.

Minnesota is host to a couple of cross-country ski marathons. The **Vasaloppet** is held annually in Mora, a town about an hour's drive north of the Twin Cities, and is sanctioned by the U.S. Ski Association. The race, held in February, is a challenging 58 kilometers running through the woods and meadows around Warman. For more information write or call Mora Vasaloppet, Box 22, Mora, MN 55051, **(612) 679-2629**.

The **Minnesota Finlandia** is held in March in Bemidji. It is a 100-kilometer race lasting two days. **(218) 751-0041**.

Aside from these major cross-country ski races, there are a large number of local shorter races run throughout the state. You can find one just about every weekend.

Hockey/Ice Skating

Community ice skating rinks, both indoor and out, abound around the state. On a sunny winter weekend afternoon, glide down one of the wonderful ice skating trails on a lake such as Lake of the Isles in Minneapolis or Como Lake in St. Paul.

Minnesotans are strong skaters, as demonstrated by their consistent presence in national and international skating competitions and hockey.

One of the most popular spring sporting events is the Minnesota high school hockey tournament. It is the largest high school hockey tournament in the country. Hockey starts in kindergarten with mini-mites. Kids progress to the mites, then the squirts, pee-wee, and bantam leagues on either the traveling or house teams. The ultimate is making the high school team and winning the state tournament.

Snowmobiling

There are more than 2,000 miles of state-groomed trails with another 10,200 miles of Grant-in-Aid trails. Snowmobiling started in the mid-'50s in Roseau, where the first company to manufacture snowmobiles on demand, Polaris, was founded. Arctic Cat, now Arctco, was founded next door in Thief River Falls. The trails surrounding these

> For more information on sports activities around the state, call the Minnesota Office of Tourism for a complete update. **(800) 657-3700** or **(612) 296-5029**.

two towns serve as the testing grounds for the newest machines.

The major cross-country snowmobile race in Minnesota is the three-day I-500 from White Bear Lake to Thunder Bay, Ontario. This is reputed to be the toughest of all races.

There also are a number of snowcross races throughout the state. There are two varieties of snowcross in Minnesota. One takes place on a plowed lake course. The other course is laid out on a ski hill. Each requires a little different expertise and nerve. Major snowcross events around the state are: Quadna Ski, Ely Lions Snowcross, Big Lake Winter Fest, the Chisholm Polar Bear Snowcross and the grand finale at the end of the year, the Garrison World Series Snowcross. For more information, call Motorsports Racing Plus, **(612) 786-7338**.

CURLING

Curling, of Scottish origin, is a game of skill and strategy played on ice. Stones are thrown down the ice and "swept" by one or two players of the four-man rink (team). The sweeping can adjust the speed and course of the rock in order for it to land closest to the center circle at the other end. The Duluth and Hibbing curling clubs have been host to some of the major international bonspiels, such as the Silver Broom. Besides Duluth and Hibbing, there are clubs in 16 other cities around the state. **(612) 224-7408**.

DOWNHILL SKIING

The ski areas of Minnesota offer a lot by way of amenities — food service, ski rental, snowmaking equipment, and ski schools. Some areas include live entertainment and special ski events. Among the larger of the 36 areas are:

Afton Alps, Afton. (800) 328-1328 or (612) 436-5245. 350-foot vertical drop, 18 chair lifts, one T-bar, two rope tows.

Andes Tower Hills, Alexandria. (612) 965-2455. 295-foot vertical drop, two chair lifts, two handle tows.

Buck Hill, Burnsville. (612) 435-7187. 306-foot vertical drop, four chair lifts, one T-bar, three rope tows.

Buena Vista, Bemidji. (218) 243-2231. 230-foot vertical drop, four chair lifts, one rope tow.

Detroit Mountain, Detroit Lakes. (218) 847-4708. 235-foot vertical drop, one chair lift, two T-bars, six rope tows.

Giant's Ridge, Biwabik. (800) 688-7669 or (218) 865-4143. 550-foot vertical drop, four chair lifts, one T-bar.

Hyland Hills, Bloomington. (612) 835-4604. 175-foot vertical drop, three chair lifts, three rope tows.

Lutsen, North Shore of Lake Superior. (218) 663-7281. 1,008-foot vertical drop, one gondola, four chair lifts, one T-bar, one rope tow.

Mount Frontenac, Red Wing. (612) 338-5826. 420-foot vertical drop, two chair lifts, one T-bar, two rope tows.

Mount Kato, Mankato. (507) 625-3363. 240-foot vertical drop, eight chair lifts.

Powder Ridge, Kimball. (800) 348-7734 or (612) 398-5295. 280-foot vertical drop, two chair lifts, two T-bars, three rope tows.

Quadna Mountain, Hill City on the Range. (800) 422-6649 or (218) 697-8444. 367-foot vertical drop, one chair lift, two T-bars, one rope tow.

Ski Gull, Gull Lake, (218) 963-4353. 260-foot vertical drop, one chair lift, one J-bar, three rope tows.

Spirit Mountain, Duluth. (800) 642-6377 or (218) 628-2891. 700-foot vertical drop, five chair lifts, three rope tows.

Timberlane, Red Lake Falls. (218) 253-2437. 235-foot vertical drop, four rope tows.

Wild Mountain Ski Area, Taylors Falls. (800) 447-4958 or (612) 465-7550. 300-foot vertical feet, four chair lifts, one rope tow.

Welch Village Ski Area, Welch. (612) 222-7079 or (800) 247-0769. 350-foot vertical drop, eight chair lifts, one T-bar.

Hurray! Minnesota

What does it take to be "The World's Best Aerobic Exerciser"™?

It takes a total-body exerciser.
A machine capable of exercising all the major muscle groups in your body, not simply your legs like treadmills, exercise bikes and stairclimbers.

It takes a cardiovascular exerciser.
A machine that utilizes enough muscle mass to readily exercise your heart, not simply specific muscle groups like weight machines.

It takes a weight-bearing exerciser.
A machine that utilizes the standing position to exercise the joints and long bones of the skeleton, not simply a few muscle groups like sit-down exercisers.

It takes a safe exerciser.
A machine that can't damage your knees like stairclimbers, or your back like rowers, or throw you off like treadmills.

It takes a stimulating exerciser.
A machine that's exciting and recreational to use, not monotonous and repetitive like so many other machines on the market.

It takes a NordicTrack.

Independently Adjustable Upper-Body Exerciser

Electronic Feedback

Stand-up Position

Independently Adjustable Lower-Body Exerciser

Non-Jarring Motion

Smooth, Quiet Operation

Adjustable Elevation

Patented Flywheel

Exercise machines don't get any better than this.

Call today for a
30 day in-home trial!

Models priced from $299 to $1,299.

NordicTrack
A CML Company

Call or Write for a
FREE VIDEO
& Brochure

1-800-328-5888 EXT 48AG2

Or write: NordicTrack, Dept. #48AG2,
141C Jonathan Blvd. N., Chaska, MN 55318

© 1992 NordicTrack, A CML Company • All rights reserved.

CASINOS

MINNESOTA IS FIRST IN THE NAtion in tribal gaming. At the last count in Minnesota, there were 15 casinos, 10 operated by the Chippewa tribes and five by the Sioux. There is a wide range of amenities and facilities at the casinos. Some look not unlike extensions of the neighborhood bar. Others, such as Grand Casino and Mystic Lake, have all the trappings of casinos in Atlantic City or Las Vegas.

Estimates are that in 1991 $900 million was wagered in Minnesota casinos with a gross net of $180 million to the casinos. The Minnesota casino industry is now ranked in the top 20 of Minnesota employers, employing about 8,000 people around the state. This is expected to increase to 11,000 by 1995. The average salary ranges from $5 to $8 per hour, not counting tips. About a fourth of the people the casinos employ are Native Americans.

BIG BUCKS CASINO
Cloquet
(218) 879-4691
(800) 321-0005
Big Bucks has 20 blackjack tables and more than 300 video slot machines.

MINNESOTA'S CASINOS

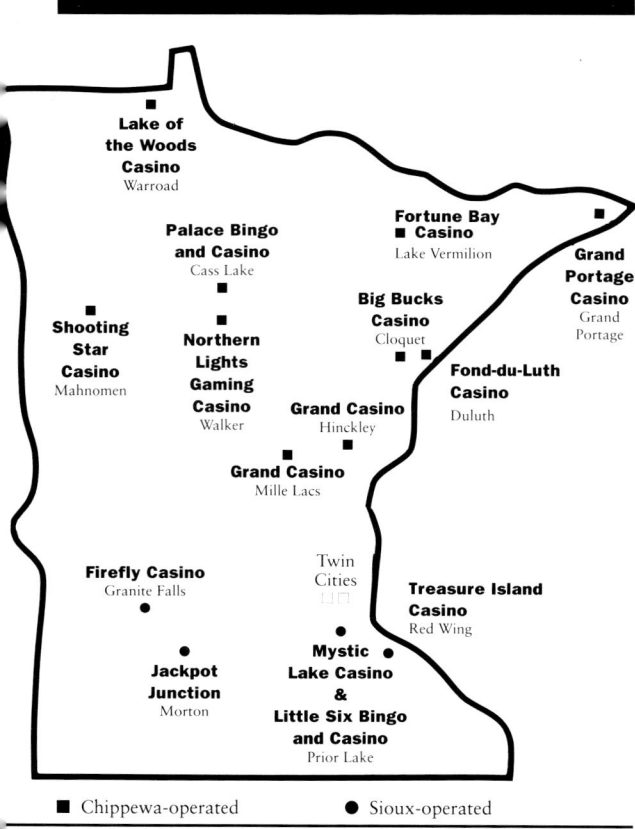

- Lake of the Woods Casino — Warroad
- Palace Bingo and Casino — Cass Lake
- Fortune Bay Casino — Lake Vermilion
- Grand Portage Casino — Grand Portage
- Shooting Star Casino — Mahnomen
- Northern Lights Gaming Casino — Walker
- Big Bucks Casino — Cloquet
- Fond-du-Luth Casino — Duluth
- Grand Casino — Hinckley
- Grand Casino — Mille Lacs
- Firefly Casino — Granite Falls
- Twin Cities
- Treasure Island Casino — Red Wing
- Jackpot Junction — Morton
- Mystic Lake Casino & Little Six Bingo and Casino — Prior Lake

■ Chippewa-operated   ● Sioux-operated

FIREFLY CASINO
Granite Falls
(612) 564-2121
(800) 232-1439
Well-lit and airy, this casino has a restaurant, 21 blackjack tables (one high-stakes) and 344 slot machines that include kino and progressive and a couple machines that could win you a car.

FORTUNE BAY CASINO
Lake Vermilion
(218) 753-6400
(800) 992-7529
Located on the beautiful shores of Lake Vermilion, this casino has 172 video slot machines with plans for more, 16 blackjack tables, a full restaurant and bar.

FOND-DU-LUTH CASINO
Duluth
(218) 722-0280
(800) 873-0280
Fond-du-Luth is located right in downtown Duluth, with plenty of shops, hotels and restaurants nearby. No blackjack tables, but

Hurray! Minnesota

Yo, Ho, Ho And A Pile Of Loot.

Treasure Island Casino is fast becoming the premiere destination for treasure seekers throughout the Midwest. And that means it's never been so easy for you to sell our Tour and Travel packages.

With numerous bus, airfare and hotel packages available, you'll find one perfect for every crew. And with the help of our tour coordinators, you'll be surprised at just how easy it is to make plans—and money.

The casino itself boasts 39 blackjack tables, high-stakes bingo and over 650 keno, poker and high-return slot machines. What's more, the Treasure Chest restaurant serves up everything from delicious entrees to savory snacks.

So set sail today. We're always open around-the-clock, every single day of the week.

Just 30 Minutes South of the Minneapolis/St. Paul Airport off Highway 61. 1-800-777-LOOT.

Must be 18 years of age to play.

Treasure Island Casino

For the pirate in all of us.

the casino does offer Minnesota Tri-Wheel, a unique bingo-type game combining roulette and craps.

GRAND CASINO
Hinckley
(612) 384-7777
(800) 472-6321
This casino is truly grand, featuring 1,450 slot machines (the most in the state), 52 blackjack tables, a buffet, a VIP lounge, fine dining, a sports bar that features country western music, a day care center and teen arcade. There also are the Royal Ascot horse-racing game and high-stakes blackjack and slots. Open 24 hours.

GRAND CASINO
Mille Lacs
(612) 532-7777
(800) 626-LUCK
Run in conjunction with the Hinckley Grand Casino, it's almost as large and has all the amenities.

GRAND PORTAGE CASINO
Grand Portage
(218) 475-2401
(800) 232-1384
The casino tends to be a little smoky, but just step out the door for the crisp cool air of the North Shore and Lake Superior. There is a lodge, marina, restaurant, hotel bar and all the amenities for a complete vacation.

JACKPOT JUNCTION
Morton
(507) 644-3000
(800) LETTER-X
Jackpot Junction has seen expansion upon expansion, but its narrow aisles also have seen a lot of excitement and a lot of wins. Prior to the opening of the Mystic Lake and Grand casinos, it was the largest and busiest of the casinos with 25,000 visitors a week. There are more than 1,100 video slot machines and live entertainment. Liquor is served.

LAKE OF THE WOODS CASINO
Warroad
(218) 386-3381
In a long, low building that used to be Morey's Fish House, this cheerful casino is peopled mostly by out-of-towners and Canadians — a Minnesota-style casino with regular and high-stakes blackjack and slot machines.

LITTLE SIX BINGO AND CASINO
Prior Lake
(612) 445-8990
(800) LITTLE-6
Little Six is the oldest bingo palace in the state, established in 1982. The new casino is to add 80 gaming tables and 1,000 video slots.

MYSTIC LAKE CASINO
Prior Lake
(612) 445-9000
(800) 262-7799
The largest casino to date in Minnesota is open 24 hours a day. Though there is no alcohol served, the food is some of the best around. For example, the executive chef monitors the quality of the food on the humongous buffet via radio communications. There are a dozen high-stakes blackjack tables among the hundreds of slots and regular blackjack tables.

NORTHERN LIGHTS GAMING CASINO
Walker
(218) 547-2744
(800) 252-PLAY
There are 12 blackjack tables with one high-stakes table, 300 video slots and a buffet-style restaurant. Liquor is served.

PALACE BINGO AND CASINO
Cass Lake
(218) 335-6787
(800) 228-6676
This bingo palace is in the process of expanding. Currently it has 12 blackjack tables, a large number of slot machines and a restaurant.

SHOOTING STAR CASINO
Mahnomen
(218) 935-2591
(800) 453-STAR
The Shooting Star has been referred to as the neon palace. It has an attached hotel, live national entertainment, a buffet, an Italian restaurant and a coffee shop. There are 24 blackjack tables, more than 850 slot machines and bingo. Liquor is served.

TREASURE ISLAND CASINO
Red Wing
(612) 388-1171
(800) 52-SLOTS
Treasure Island has 52 blackjack tables, including high-stakes tables, and more than 1,000 slot machines. There also is a large bingo hall, two buffets and a grill. No alcohol is served.

Hurray! Minnesota

B&B and Historic Inns
DIRECTORY

Jailhouse Inn Bed & Breakfast
- Victorian Decor
- 12 Rooms with Private Baths
- Whirlpools & Claw Tubs
- 7 Fireplaces
- Country Breakfasts

109 Houston 3 NW
Preston, MN 55965
507/765-2181

Lindgren's B&B Bed & Breakfast

Lindgren's Luxurious Lake Superior Log Home at Lutsen

Full BREAKFAST, Finnish SUANA, FIREPLACES, WHIRLPOOL, Charter FISHING, FALL COLORS.

Lutsen, MN 55612
(218) 663-7450

To order extra copies of
Hurray! Minnesota
Single copy $12.95 plus $2.55 for postage, shipping, handling and Minnesota sales tax = $15.40
Inquire about multicopy discount.
•
"Hurray! Minnesota"
15 South Fifth Street, Suite 900
Minneapolis, MN 55402
PHONE: (612) 338-1578

ARCHER HOUSE
Romantics: Rekindle that love affair!

Step into the warmth and comfort of a country inn. 38 rooms. 19 with whirlpools. Hiking, biking, golfing nearby. Browse in area shops.

Conference and Banquet Facilities
Gift Certificates Available

35 miles south of Twin Cities in historic Northfield, MN
(507) 645-5661   1-800-247-2235
One of Minnesota's oldest river inns.

TWIN CITIES
♦ **1900 DUPONT**
1900 Dupont Ave. S., Minneapolis, MN 55403
(612) 374-1973

METRO AREA
♦ **BLUFF CREEK INN**
1161 Bluff Creek Dr., Chaska, MN 55318
(612) 445-2735
♦ **THORWOOD AND ROSEWOOD INN**
315 Pine St. or 620 Ramsey, Hastings, MN 55033
(612) 437-3297

DULUTH AND NORTH SHORE
♦ **THE ELLERY HOUSE**
28 S. 21st Ave. E., Duluth, MN 55812
(218) 724-7639
♦ **THE MANSION**
3600 London Road., Duluth, MN 55804
(218) 724-0739
♦ **STONE HEARTH INN**
1118 Highway 61 E., Little Marais, MN 55614
(218) 226-3020
♦ **BARNUM HOUSE BED AND BREAKFAST**
2211 E. Third St., Duluth, MN 55812
(800) 879-5437

NORTHEAST
♦ **ADAM'S HOUSE**
201 E. 23rd St., Hibbing, MN 55746
(218) 263-9742

STILLWATER AREA
♦ **ASA PARKER**
17500 N. St. Croix Trail
Marine on St. Croix, MN 55047
(612) 433-5248

LAKE COUNTRY
♦ **NIMS BAKKETOPP HUS**
Route 2, Box 187A, Fergus Falls, MN 56537
(218) 739-2915

BLUFF AREA
♦ **SUNNYSIDE COTTAGE**
Route 2, Box 119, Preston, MN 55965
(507) 765-3357
♦ **QUILL AND QUILT**
615 W. Hoffman St., Cannon Falls, MN 55009
(507) 263-5507 or (800) 488-3849
♦ **CANDLE LIGHT INN**
818 W. Third St., Red Wing, MN 55066
(612) 388-6034

SOUTHWEST
♦ **LAWNDALE FARMS**
Route 2, Box 50, Herman, MN 56248
(612) 677-2687

SOUTHERN MINNESOTA
♦ **ANN BURCKHARDT'S PARK ROW BED AND BREAKFAST**
525 Park Row, St. Peter, MN 56082
(507) 931-2495

• NEW BRIGHTON • ROBBINSDALE • ARDEN HILLS • GOLDEN VALLEY •

WACONIA • FRIDLEY • FALCON HEIGHTS • MOUND • LITTLE CANADA • NEW HOPE • CRYSTAL • BLAINE

ICE SKATING ON LAKE OF THE ISLES IN MINNEAPOLIS
IS A FAVORITE WINTER PASTIME.

PHOTO COURTESY OF MINNESOTA OFFICE OF TOURISM
ILLUSTRATION BY ERIC HANSON

• LILYDALE • DEEPHAVEN • APPLE VALLEY • WHITE BEAR LAKE •

Twin Cities

THE TWIN CITIES is frequently lauded for its high caliber of education, its thriving business, sports and cultural climate, its clean air and its natural beauty. Consistently ranked one and two in quality of life and business, the Twin Cities is home to more than 30 Fortune 100 companies and is the distribution center and hub of the financial community for the Upper Midwest.

Minneapolis and St. Paul are called the Twin Cities more for their close proximity and cooperation than for any physical or demographic resemblance. St. Paul is the seat of state government and home to the flourishing "cultural corridor." Minneapolis is a shopping and entertainment hub and the site of most convention and sports activities. Both cities possess a wealth of historic buildings and a respect for the shared past that shaped them. And both cities have developed unique ways to celebrate their individuality and diversity.

St. Paul is located in Ramsey County and Minneapolis in Hennepin County. Due to recent growth and the addition of the Mall of America to the Interstate 494 corridor, the city of Bloomington, also located in Hennepin County, is playing an increasingly important role in any discussion of the Twin Cities. The seven-county metropolitan area includes 142 cities and 49

TWIN CITIES METRO AREA

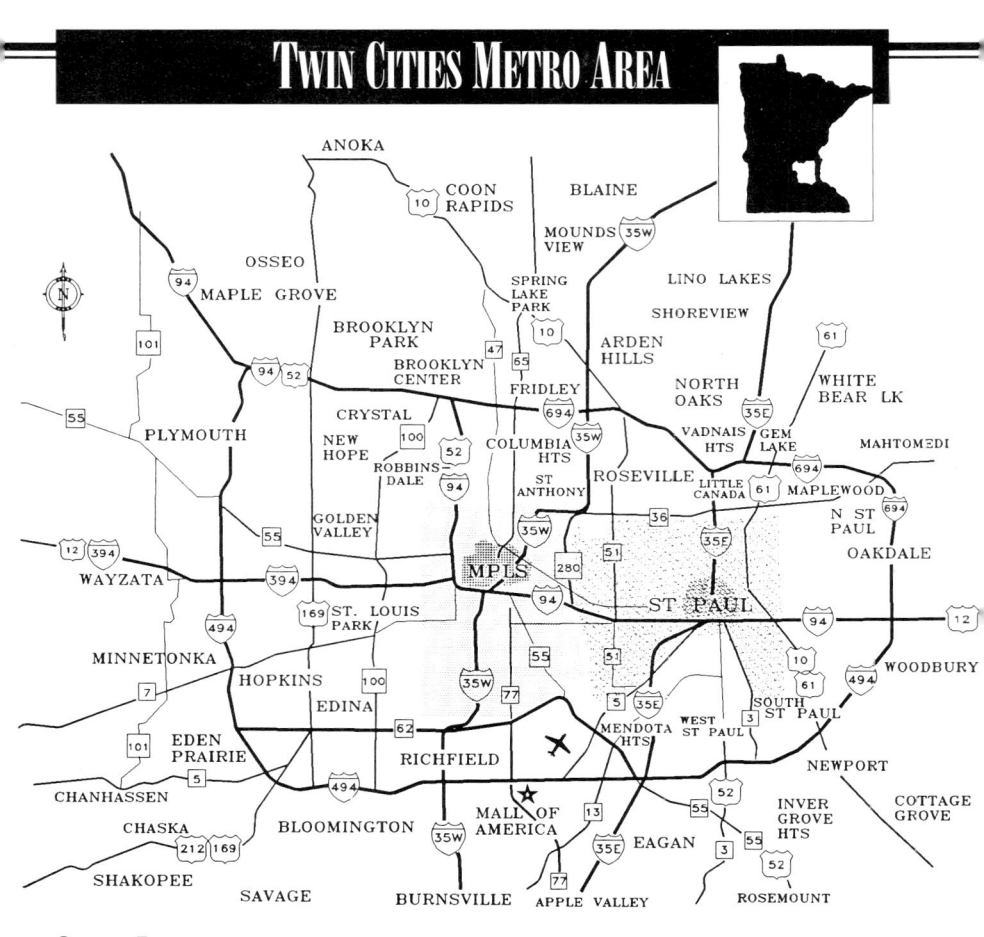

ON THE ROAD

The Twin Cities has an excellent highway system. The metro area is circled and bisected by the interconnected interstate system (this includes I-94 through the downtowns, I-494 south of the cities, I-694 north of the cities and I-394 running west from downtown Minneapolis). I-35 runs north-south between the two cities with east and west branches.

---

townships. It is among the largest metropolitan area in the United States, but ranks fourth in the nation in buying income per household. In the last census, the population of the metro area was 2,318,532, roughly half of the entire state's population. It grew by 14.7 percent in the last decade, making it the 16th-largest metropolitan area in the nation. Such growth can only be described as explosive.

The mighty Mississippi was and still is an important part of life in the Twin Cities. Once the center of economic vitality for much of the state, it is now a center for recreation as well. Both Minneapolis and St. Paul have taken steps to restore and preserve the river's beauty by establishing parks and trails along its banks, including the area surrounding Fort Snelling, the site of the confluence of the Mississippi and Minnesota rivers. The metro area also has more than its share of lakes, some connected by parks and trails, which create natural and accessible oases in the midst of the city and provide residents and visitors a chance to spend time by a lake, even if

Hurray! Minnesota

they're dyed-in-the-wool urbanites.

Both Minneapolis and St. Paul have a strong religious heritage, beginning with their early links to two explorer missionaries: Father Louis Hennepin and Father Lucien Galtier. The predominantly German, Irish and Scandinavian pioneers who first settled the Twin Cities transplanted their Lutheran and Catholic faiths to their new home. The largest Lutheran congregation in the nation is Mount Olivet Church in Minneapolis. The Cathedral of St. Paul and St. Mary's Basilica in Minneapolis are two of the most splendid examples of the Catholic faith and architecture working in tandem. Many churches throughout the metro area, apart from these, offer choral and orchestral music, Masses and performances throughout the liturgical year.

But the Twin Cities welcomes all faiths and is also made up of a number of Protestant and Jewish congregations. The Hennepin Avenue United Methodist Church, founded in 1875 and built in 1915, has a gallery filled with treasured paintings from the 16th and 17th centuries and hosts a production of "The Nativity: A Living Pageant of Christmas" each year. Temple Israel, founded in 1878, recently completed a $4 million expansion that includes a 250-seat auditorium, library and classrooms.

The following Twin Cities section contains information about history, sights, attractions and activities in Minneapolis, St. Paul and the major metropolitan area and will serve as a guide to help you enjoy your time in the Twin Cities.

ATTRACTIONS

AAMODT'S APPLE FARM
Stillwater
(612) 439-3127
Although the official data hasn't been collected yet, conservative estimates say that 6.5 out of 10 grandmas and approximately 33.3 percent of the rest of Minnesota's population take part in some sort of appling ritual during the late summer and early fall. Most of these rituals take the shape of apple pies and derive their primary substance from Aamodt's Apple Farm. Located in Stillwater, the farm grows more than a dozen varieties of apples, including Harelson. Peak season begins in mid-August and runs until the end of October. Admission is free.

HISTORIC MISSISSIPPI RIVER CRUISES
Harriet Island
St. Paul
(612) 227-1100
Every city with an attached body of water throws a huge attraction out in the middle of it and makes a ton of money taking tourists out on boats just to be near it: New York City and the Statue of Liberty. San Francisco and Alcatraz. Any

one of the Hawaiian islands and a beluga whale. (To name but three.) In the Twin Cities, we don't need any towering symbols of peace or spouting specimens of mammaldom — we've got the picturesque banks of the Mississippi River. And we've got bigger, better boats besides. The Jonathan Padelford, one of the few truly authentic sternwheelers on the Mississippi, and the Josiah Snelling will take you past the mouth of the Minnesota River and Pike Island to old Fort Snelling (excursions begin at Harriet Island Park in St. Paul.) The Anson Northrup, a four-year-old computer-built sidewheeler, and the Betsey Northrup, a party barge licensed for 462 passengers, will take you through the upper lock for a view of St. Anthony Falls and James J. Hill's Old Stone Arch Bridge (excursions begin at Boom Island Park in Minneapolis). Call for information regarding private charters, the prime rib dinner cruise, chicken and rib dinner cruise and Minneapolis Sunday brunch. Narrated excursions run daily at 10 a.m., noon and 2 p.m., Memorial Day through Labor Day. In May and

Frank Gehry's "Standing Glass Fish," 1986, in the Cowles Conservatory at the Minneapolis Sculpture Garden.

September, Saturday and Sunday at 2 p.m. Tickets: $8 (adults), $7 (seniors), $5 (children under 12).

GOVERNOR'S RESIDENCE
1006 Summit Ave.
St. Paul
(612) 297-8177
This 20-room English Tudor Revival-style home, located on St. Paul's mansion-lined Summit Avenue, was designed by architect William Channing Whitney for lumberman Horace Hills Irvine and his family in 1911. After Irvine's daughters donated the home to the state in 1965, it became Minnesota's first official governor's mansion. (Before then, Minnesota's highest elected official had to fend for himself in the housing department.) The mansion has recently undergone a $1.2 million renovation. Tours of the new and improved spaces (main and lower levels only) are free and begin every 10 minutes on Thursdays, May through October, starting at 2 p.m. and ending at 3:10 p.m.

MINNEAPOLIS SCULPTURE GARDEN
at Walker Art Center
Vineland Place
Minneapolis
Located on the fringe of downtown Minneapolis in a 7 1/2-acre verdant space adjacent to the Walker Art Center, this urban garden features sculptures of various sizes ranging from human-scale bronzes to towering steel constructions. The sculptures, which date from the early 20th century to the present, represent styles ranging from the archetypal organic abstraction of Henry Moore's "Reclining Mother and Child" (1960–1961) to the social realism of George Segal's "Walking Man" (1988). The focal point of the garden, Claes Oldenburg and Coosje van Bruggen's "Spoonbridge and Cherry" (1987–1988), is a 29-foot-high fountain that sprays over a free-form pond. Admission is free. Hours: 6 a.m. to midnight daily.

Hurray! Minnesota

PHOTO COURTESY OF WALKER ART CENTER

MINNESOTA HARVEST APPLE ORCHARD
Old Highway 169 Boulevard at Apple Lover's Lane
Jordan
(612) 492-2785
While this beautiful orchard, located on 100 acres along the Minnesota River Valley, yields dozens of varieties of "common" apples, it specializes in the obscure and experimental varieties — Mutsu, Prairie Spy, Honeygold, Jonagold, and some so experimental that they don't even have names yet. Pick your own or get them the easy way. Either way, you won't be disappointed. (Try one sliced and smothered with Minnesota Harvest's homemade caramel. You'll never eat a carameled apple on a stick again.) Besides producing apples and all of the treats that would not exist without them — apple cider, apple pie, apple strudel, apple butter (you get the picture) — the orchard offers a variety of jellies made from Minnesota Harvest's own raspberries, currents and gooseberries and honey from its own hives. The orchard also features a free petting zoo with llamas, goats, sheep, peacocks, cows, potbelly pigs and bunnies, $1 pony rides and three-minute helicopter rides for $10. The orchard is open year-round. Admission is free. Hours: 9 a.m. to 7 p.m. daily (August through October).

MINNESOTA LANDSCAPE ARBORETUM
3675 Arboretum Drive
Chanhassen
(612) 443-2460
Azaleas, lilacs, crab-apples, pines, clematis, wildflowers, roses, perennials, mums, dahlias, tropicals, orchids, crocuses, tulips, daffodils, lady's slippers. This sprawling garden that spans more than 905 acres of rolling hills, native woods and formal display gardens features 15,000 flowers and plants and 5,000 varieties of trees and shrubs. Open year-round, the Arboretum grounds are accessible by hiking trails, paved paths and a three-mile drive. Admission: $3 (adults), $1 (children under 16). The grounds are open 8 a.m. to sunset daily. Building hours: Monday through Friday, 8 a.m. to 4:30 p.m.; Saturday and Sunday, 11 a.m. to 4:30 p.m. Extended hours May through October.

MINNESOTA ZEPHYR
601 N. Main St.
Stillwater
(612) 430-3000
Dining in an elegant train car while it travels — slowly — through the beautiful countryside. Is this every romantic's dream or what? (For you non-romantics, the answer is yes.) If you are a lover of candlelight, exquisite cuisine and/or 1940s movies, one of your dreams is waiting to roll into reality at the Stillwater Depot. The Minnesota Zephyr, with three dining cars and two vista dome club cars, all restored and decorated to project an air of elegance and prestige, is your ticket to an evening or afternoon of R&R. The train departs nightly at 7:30 p.m. sharp and on Sundays at 12:30 p.m. Reservations are required. Tickets, which include an elegant four-course dinner, are $47.50. Semi-formal attire is suggested.

MINNESOTA ZOO
13000 Zoo Boulevard
Apple Valley
(612) 432-9000
According to a panel of noted wildlife experts, the Minnesota Zoo is one of the 10 best zoos in the nation. Wildlife experts, as you know, are rarely wrong — certainly, anyway, in this case. At the heart of the zoo are six trails that allow more than 1,700 mammals, birds, fish, reptiles and amphibians to live and grow in a place just like home. The Northern Trail, for instance, is home to bison, camels, moose and Siberian tigers (among others). Meet animals native to Minnesota, including beavers, owls, pumas and wolverines, or take a walk through the ZooLab, a hands-on room where you can touch select animals (i.e., the ones that won't bite you).

The newest addition to the zoo, a $2.6 million coral reef exhibit, features four shark species and more than 100 species of colorful tropical fish. The exhibit can be enjoyed from the water's surface or viewed from below through 53 feet of windows that take you into the reef. Admission: $5 (adults), $3 (senior citizens), $2 (children 3 to 12), free to children under 3. Summer hours (April through September): Monday through

The Minnesota Zoo's coral reef is a ticket to the tropics.

Saturday, 10 a.m. to 6 p.m.; Sunday, 10 a.m. to 8 p.m. Winter hours (October through March): 10 a.m. to 4 p.m. daily.

TWIN CITY MODEL RAILROAD CLUB, INC.
Bandana Square
1021 E. Bandana Blvd.
St. Paul
(612) 647-9628

Members of the Twin City Model Railroad Club — a group of model railroaders, historians, craftsmen and retired railroad personnel — have taken their passion for trains and turned it into a scale model of railroading in the United States during its heyday from the 1930s through the 1950s. This miniature railroad, along with various vignettes of Twin Cities scenes, including a reproduction of the St. Anthony Falls milling district, has been faithfully reproduced in 1/4-inch scale. Models of many famous Limiteds, including the Twin Cities Hiawatha, the North Coast Limited, the Zephyrs, the Twentieth Century Limited, the Overland Limited and the Empire Builder can be seen during the club's special shows. Admission is free. Hours: Monday through Friday, noon to 9 p.m.; Saturday, 10 a.m. to 5 p.m.; Sunday, 1 to 5 p.m.

VALLEYFAIR!
One Valleyfair Drive
Shakopee
(612) 445-7600

If your idea of fun is feeling your stomach jump up and lodge itself somewhere between your esophagus and the back of your throat, Valleyfair is the most fun you'll ever have. This 68-acre family amusement park features more than 30 rides. There's Excalibur, a roller coaster that boasts the steepest grade of any roller coaster in the world — its towering 10-story peak, 60-degree drop and maze of spaghetti curves will challenge even the strongest stomach and the bravest resolve; Thunder Canyon, a white-water river-raft ride through more than a quarter mile of rapids, waterfalls and waves; and the Corkscrew, a ride that climbs to a height of 85 feet, drops into a 360-degree vertical loop, snakes through two giant spirals and ends with a 360-degree horizontal loop (all at 50 m.p.h.) If the thought of such maniacal movement sends you reeling, don't worry: There's always Kiddie Island and Half Pint Park, designed especially to delight the younger set. If you're over 5, however, and riding Soaring Seaplanes at .05 m.p.h. isn't exactly the image you'd like to project at a densely populated theme park where you will certainly run into at least one person that you know, go see a show at the amazing Pepsi-Cola IMAX Theater or take a relaxing ride on the Minnesota River Valley Railroad, which runs through the heart of the park. There's something for everyone at Valleyfair. Admission: $16.50 (adults), $9.50 (senior citizens and children 4 years to 48 inches tall), children 3 and under are free. Open weekends in May and September and daily from June through August. Call ahead for park hours.

Hurray! Minnesota

PHOTO BY TOM CAJACOB/MINNESOTA ZOO

LAKES AND PARKS

AREA LAKES AND PARKS
HYLAND LAKE: Located in Bloomington's Hyland Lake Park Reserve, this small lake can't offer beaches, but plenty of other activities can keep you occupied. Fishing is permitted on the shoreline or off a pier. There are five miles of paved bike trails and two miles of wood-chip hiking trails near the lake. Bikes, canoes, paddleboats and rowboats are available for rent, and the **Richardson Nature Center** is located on the grounds. For more information, call (612) 941-7993.

SNELLING LAKE: This little-known lake in Fort Snelling State Park is a great place to go swimming if you don't mind the occasional 747 thundering overhead. Along with a beach, the park features 18 miles of hiking trails, five miles of paved trails, cross-country skiing, picnic areas, an interpretive center, boat and canoe landings and the historical Fort Snelling site. For more information, call (612) 725-2390.

LAKE MINNETONKA: The largest body of water in the Twin Cities area with a shoreline that runs for about 91 miles, Lake Minnetonka is actually a series of lakes and bays with names such as Priest's, Maxwell, Smithtown and North Arm. The bays, once separate little lakes, were connected by channels. In the late 1880s, the wealthy had summer homes in Minnetonka; later, they constructed year-round mansions. Today, the lake is home to people of moderate incomes as well.

Sailing, a sport introduced by wealthy New Englanders, helped make Minnetonka one of the most popular resorts in the country. For 10 cents, people could ride a trolley from the Twin Cities to the lake, then board a boat designed in the shape of a streetcar. Boating is still big business on Lake Minnetonka, as well as fishing for bass, walleye, pike and panfish.

WHITE BEAR LAKE: White Bear Lake has plenty of places for a picnic as well as playgrounds for children to frolic. The lake also features Ramsey County Beach for swimming. For bikers, hikers and in-line skaters, there is a 3.5-mile roadside trail on the west side of the lake. If you're a history buff, the Fillebrown House, an example of American picturesque architecture, is open for tours on Sundays from 1 to 4 p.m. For more information, call (612) 429-8526.

MINNESOTA VALLEY NATIONAL WILDLIFE REFUGE: The magnificent parkland of the Minnesota River Valley, which is overlooked by Fort Snelling on the bluff, is now the Minnesota Valley National Wildlife Refuge. A resource of national significance, it is a remarkable spot for wildlife in the midst of metropolitan sprawl. It stretches for 34 miles along the Minnesota River from Fort Snelling to Jordan, covering 8,000 acres.

The visitor's center, located just off Interstate 494 at the 34th Avenue exit, boasts galleries and interactive exhibits on wildlife and wildlife management as well as a 125-seat auditorium. There are several trails leading from the center: one is handicapped-accessible, and one offers a self-guided bird-watching tour that includes a fanny-pack with a bird book, binoculars and tape recorder. (612) 854-5900.

HENNEPIN PARKS
THE SUBURBAN HENNEPIN Regional Park District covers 25,000 acres of park reserves, regional parks and special-use facilities at 19 locations, all within a 30-minute drive from downtown Minneapolis. Facilities include nature centers and trails for hiking, biking and walking; fishing piers; boating and canoeing access and rentals; picnic and camping grounds; and two public golf courses. In-line skates, helmets and pads are available for rental at some parks. Daily parking permits are $4. Hennepin parks are open daily 5 a.m.

to sunset. Call (612) 559-9000.

BAKER PARK RESERVE: Located on Lake Independence in Medina, this park is just 20 minutes from the metro area. Its 2,500 acres include campgrounds, a picnic area, fishing, biking and hiking trails, horse trails, a golf course, snowmobile and cross-country ski trails. (612) 476-4666.

BRYANT LAKE REGIONAL PARK: Located in Eden Prairie, the park offers swimming, fishing, picnic areas and a non-paved boat launch with trailer parking. (612) 941-4262.

CARVER PARK RESERVE: Located at the heart of this 3,500-acre reserve in Chanhassen is the Lowry Nature Center, which offers visitors programs on the park's abundant natural resources ranging from fall bird migration and waterfowl watches to maple-syrup making and star gazing. A variety of wildlife can be seen from roads, trails, campgrounds, picnic areas and near the nature center. (612) 472-4911.

CLEARY LAKE REGIONAL PARK: Located on Highway 27 near Prior Lake, this park offers a three-season pavilion, golf, an outdoor recreation center with nature programs for the entire family, swimming, and a variety of winter activities. (612) 447-2171.

COON RAPIDS DAM REGIONAL PARK: Located on the Mississippi River in Coon Rapids, this park offers hiking, fishing, boating, picnic areas, cross-country skiing, access to the working river dam, interpretive programs, and is the site of the annual **CarpFest**. (612) 757-4700.

CROW-HASSAN PARK RESERVE: Located on the Crow River on Sylvan Lake Road (west of Rogers and County Road 116), the park is a restored prairie that replicates the early days when pioneers crossed the wilderness in their Conestoga wagons. The annual fall Prairie Fest re-creates the aura and look of those days, and the reserve offers a variety of activities year-round amid the seasonal beauties of the prairie. (612) 424-2511.

ELM CREEK PARK RESERVE: The largest park in the Hennepin Parks system, this 5,300-acre reserve near Osseo offers recreational activities year-round, including programs at the **Eastman Nature Center**. (612) 424-5511.

FISH LAKE REGIONAL PARK: This 152-acre park located in Maple Grove offers outdoor recreational facilities in a wooded lakeside setting, including challenging hills for cross-country skiers and hikers. (612) 420-3423.

FRENCH REGIONAL PARK: Located on 308 acres on Medicine Lake, this park in Plymouth features lake-based activities year-round. Hillside views of nearby downtown Minneapolis remind visitors of the park's convenient location. (612) 559-8891.

LAKE REBECCA PARK RESERVE: Located 30 miles west of Minneapolis (south of Highway 55 on County Road 50), this park offers canoeing on the Crow River and bass fishing on Lake Rebecca. Other water-based activities are set amid a rolling landscape with wetland areas that provide a haven for wildlife. This reserve is one of the prime sites for the trumpeter swan restoration program. (612) 476-4666.

MURPHY-HANREHAN PARK RESERVE: The glacial ridges and hilly terrain of this reserve make it one of the most challenging cross-country ski areas in the Twin Cities, as well as a popular spot for hiking and horseback riding. Located in Burnsville, this park is undeveloped except for the trails; interpretive programs during the spring and fall allow visitors glimpses of the park's interior and wildlife. (612) 447-2171.

NOERENBERG MEMORIAL COUNTY PARK: Formerly the estate of Frederick Noerenberg, this park is located on Lake Minnetonka and includes a formal flower garden and a boathouse of Oriental design as part of its attractions. Picnics and water-based activities are prohibited. (612) 559-9000.

NORTH HENNEPIN TRAIL CORRIDOR: A ribbon of maintained trails connects the Coon Rapids Dam Regional Park to Elm Creek Park Reserve. This 7.2-mile trail corridor provides safe and enjoyable recreation year-round, including biking, hiking, snowshoeing, cross-country skiing, ski-skating, snowmobiling and horseback riding. (612) 757-4700.

Hurray! Minnesota

LITERARY SCENE

Minnesotans love to read and write, and they willingly support and patronize the literary arts. That sort of climate has produced many writers of regional and national renown — Jon Hassler, Garrison Keillor, Howard Mohr, Bill Holm, Judith Guest, Carol Bly, Robert Bly, Patricia Hampl and J.F. Powers, to name only a few — and it has fostered a wealth of literary organizations, New Age, science fiction and antiquarian booksellers, bookstores that sponsor readings and storytelling hours, special libraries, literary collections, readings for and by writers, awards and grants programs for writers, writers' groups and independent publishers. Small presses such as Graywolf Press, Coffee House Press, Milkweed Editions, the Minnesota Historical Society Press, the University of Minnesota Press and New Rivers Press flourish in the Twin Cities. Holy Cow! Press in Duluth and Voyageur Press in Stillwater are only two small presses outside the Twin Cities that have made a name for themselves. The Hungry Mind Bookstore in St. Paul publishes the nationally recognized "Hungry Mind Review."

The literary scene in the Twin Cities? Holy Cow!

COLLECTIONS AND LITERARY CENTERS

MINNESOTA CENTER FOR BOOK ARTS
24 N. Third St.
Minneapolis
(612) 338-3634
The Minnesota Center for Book Arts (MCBA) is a space where book artists can ply their craft and exchange ideas, and where the public is invited to learn about what book artists do through classes, exhibitions and seminars on bookbinding, papermaking and printing. Both the process and the finished products are on view, as well as 19th-century printing presses, books as art objects, and current work by artists-in-residence. Faculty members include owners of small presses in the metro area and artists from a variety of media. The MCBA produces some publications, but its main purpose is to serve as a clearinghouse where newcomers to the book arts can visit and learn, and where professionals can enjoy a forum for exchanging ideas and knowledge about fine and non-traditional bookmaking.

KERLAN COLLECTION
Arthur Upson Room, Walter Library
University of Minnesota
Minneapolis
(612) 624-4576
The collection, donated to the U of M by Dr. Irvin Kerlan of St. Cloud, who died in 1963, contains galleys, artwork and manuscript pages from rare children's books, accompanied by texts illustrating how writer, artist, editor, illustrator and printer combine to make a finished book. The collection contains nearly 50,000 volumes and manuscripts in 46 different languages, and the authors represented could form a "Who's Who" of children's books. The collection, one of three in the country so extensive, is part of the Children's Literature Research Collection, which includes the Hess Collection (19th- and 20th-century dime novels), the Paul Bunyan collection (books, clippings and artifacts pertaining to Minnesota's favorite folk hero), the Beulah Counts Rudolph collection (figurines of characters from children's books), and the Rogers/Ellis collection (the works of dime novelist Edward S. Ellis). The collection is open to the public. Children are welcome but must be accompanied by an adult.

THE LOFT
Pratt Community Center
66 Malcolm Ave. S.W.
Minneapolis
(612) 379-8999
One of America's largest literary centers, the Loft is a place where Upper Midwest writers gather to discuss their craft, present their art to an audience and forge

connections to the larger literary and publishing world. It is also a place where readers come to experience, firsthand, the latest and best in contemporary writing. The Loft offers creative writing classes, writers' competitions and grants, writers' residencies, readings by nationally and locally prominent authors, children's storytelling, writers' groups and a broad variety of referral and support services for area writers. Cultural diversity in the Loft's membership and programs is encouraged and promoted.

PLAYWRIGHTS' CENTER
2301 E. Franklin Ave.
Minneapolis
(612) 332-7481
Founded in 1971 by four U of M graduate students trying to get started as professional playwrights, the Playwrights' Center is one of the Twin Cities' most stable arts groups. It has helped launch nearly 200 playwrights — among them August Wilson, Lee Blessing and Kevin Kling — and that is its continuing mission. Playwrights in all stages of development are encouraged to sharpen their work with the help of fellowships, grants and commissions awarded by the Playwrights' Center. Its annual summer workshop, Midwest PlayLabs, is one of the most important script-development programs in the country. The center's 25 core and associate members, selected by juried competitions, receive direction from workshops to staged readings. Its 270 or more playwright members are offered classes, readings and discussions with established playwrights. The general public has the opportunity to attend staged readings of unproduced and unpublished plays. Apart from the pleasure of seeing fresh work on stage, you could be watching the next August Wilson or Buffy Sedlachek get his or her start.

MINNESOTA LANDSCAPE ARBORETUM
3675 Arboretum Drive
Box 39
Chanhassen
(612) 443-2440
Named for its major benefactors, former Minnesota Gov. Elmer L. Andersen and his wife, Eleanor, the library was dedicated in 1974 and is the only horticultural-research library in the Upper Midwest. The library offers more than 1,200 current seed and nursery catalogs, plus 9,000 volumes and 350 periodicals on botany, horticulture, landscape architecture and natural history, most of which are in open stacks. Children's gardening books also are stocked.

MINNESOTA HISTORY CENTER
345 W. Kellogg Boulevard
St. Paul
(612) 296-6126
The Minnesota Historical Society's collections and libraries cover the past through the present and contain books, maps, photographs, paintings, prints, drawings, sculptures, artifacts, archeological items, manuscripts and microfilm copies of nearly every Minnesota newspaper.

LIBRARIES

THERE ARE 14 library systems in the Twin Cities with 95 branches. Area libraries offer a wide range of programming for all ages, including children's story hours, films, seminars and informational lectures. In Hennepin County, the Minneapolis Public Library and Information Center is located at 300 Nicollet Mall, (612) 372-6500. In Ramsey County, the St. Paul Public Library is located at 90 W. Fourth St., (612) 292-6311.

The University of Minnesota library system is one of the largest academic library systems in the country and has a full government documents depository library. Other academic libraries in the area have joined with the university to form College Libraries in Consortium (CLC).

COLLEGE OF ST. THOMAS CELTIC LIBRARY
2115 Summit Ave.
St. Paul
(612) 647-5723 or 647-5318
The major emphases of the library are the history, language, literature, political science, music and church history of Ireland, Scotland, Wales, the Isle of Man, Cornwall and Brittany.

JAMES J. HILL REFERENCE LIBRARY
Fourth and Market streets
St. Paul
(612) 227-9531
The library's collection of 170,000 volumes and 1,300 journal subscriptions focuses on economics and business development in the Upper Midwest.

MINNESOTA GENEALOGICAL SOCIETY LIBRARY
1101 W. Seventh St.
St. Paul
(612) 222-6929
The library revolves around tracing family histories and collects material from around the world for nearly every ethnic group and nationality, as well as current journals and newsletters from genealogy clubs. First-time visitors should call to find out what kind of information is needed to begin research into their family trees.

BOOKSELLERS

FOLLOWING IS A partial listing of metro area booksellers:

INDEPENDENTS AND SPECIALTY
ST. PAUL
Bandana Books
Bandana Square, (612) 644-0327
Hungry Mind
Grand Avenue, (612) 699-0587
Micawber's Bookstore
2238 Carter Ave., (612) 646-5506
Odegard Books St. Paul
Books for Travel
Odegard Encore Books St. Paul
Three separate stores, all in Victoria Crossing, Grand Avenue, (612) 222-2711
Red Balloon Bookshop
891 S. Grand Ave., (612) 224-8320
Shinder's
389 N. Wabasha St., (612) 227-4344
The Source Comics and Games
80 N. Snelling Ave., (612) 646-7870

SUBURBAN ST. PAUL
Little Professor Book Center
1960 Cliff Lake Road, Eagan, (612) 456-0404
Brick Alley Books
423 S. Main St., Stillwater, (612) 439-0266
Hazelden Serenity Books
Har Mar Mall, Roseville, (612) 631-8063
Lake Country Booksellers
4766 Washington Square, White Bear Lake, (612) 426-0918

MINNEAPOLIS
Amazon Bookstore
1612 Harmon Place, (612) 338-6560
Baxter's Books
608 S. Second Ave., (612) 339-4922

Brentano's Bookstore
651 Nicollet Mall, (612) 338-6808
College of Comic Book Knowledge
3151 Hennepin Ave., (612) 822-2309
Dreamhaven Books and Comics
1309 E. Fourth St., (612) 379-8924
Irish Books and Media
1433 E. Franklin Ave., (612) 871-3505
Latitudes Map and Travel Stores
Calhoun Square, 3001 Hennepin Ave. S., (612) 823-3742
Once Upon A Crime
604 W. 26th St., (612) 870-3785
The Source Comics and Games
Dinkytown, 1309 Fourth St. S.E., (612) 623-3456
Shinder's
733 Hennepin Ave., (612) 333-3628
912 Nicollet Mall, (612) 333-6942
Uncle Edgar's Mystery Bookstore, (612) 824-9984 and **Uncle Hugo's Science Fiction Bookstore**, (612) 824-6347, 2864 Chicago Ave. S.

SUBURBAN MINNEAPOLIS
The Bookcase
607 E. Lake St., Wayzata, (612) 473-8341
Frog Island Bookstore
Excelsior, (612) 474-7612

USED AND RARE BOOKS
TWIN CITIES
The Bookhouse
Dinkytown, 429 14th Ave. S.E., Minneapolis, (612) 331-1430
Dinkytown Antiquarian Bookstore
1316 Fourth St. S.E., Minneapolis, (612) 378-1286
Harold's Book Shop
186 W. Seventh St., St. Paul, (612) 222-4524
Leland N. Lien Bookseller
57 S. Ninth St., Minneapolis
(612) 332-7081
James and Mary Laurie Booksellers
251 Snelling Ave. S., St. Paul, (612) 699-1114
The Midway Bookstore
1579 University Ave., St. Paul, (612) 644-7605
Out of Print Book Shoppe
4756 Chicago Ave., Minneapolis, (612) 823-1006
Rulon-Miller Books
400 Summit Ave., St. Paul, (612) 290-0700

TWIN CITIES

MUSEUMS

ALEXANDER RAMSEY HOUSE
265 S. Exchange St.
St. Paul
(612) 296-8760
Located in the quaint pocket of the Irvine Park neighborhood near downtown St. Paul, the Alexander Ramsey House, home of the first governor of Minnesota, is a jewel among St. Paul's Victorian mansions. While it pales in size compared to the historic J. J. Hill House, located less than a mile away, the three-story mansion is fully furnished, just as it was 100 years ago. Its 15 rooms contain black walnut and hand-grained woodwork, marble fireplaces, crystal chandeliers, a dollhouse, and a rich collection of the china, silver and crystal collected by the Ramseys. Tours are led by guides dressed in period costumes and begin in the reconstructed carriage house, where you will find a wide array of Victorian items in the museum gift shop. Admission: $3 (adults), $1 (children 6 to 15), children 5 and under are free. Hours: Tuesday through Saturday, 10 a.m. to 3 p.m., with tours given on the hour. Reservations are required for large groups and Christmas holiday tours. Closed January through March.

AMERICAN SWEDISH INSTITUTE
2600 Park Ave.
Minneapolis
(612) 871-4907
You might be tempted to ask, "Where's the moat?" But don't. The former home of Swedish immigrant Swan Turnblad only looks like a medieval castle. Actually, it's a mansion built in the stately Romanesque chateau style of architecture, and it houses the largest collection of American-Swedish immigrant history in the country. Turnblad, a newspaperman who immigrated to Minnesota in 1887, once claimed that his lifelong ambition was to foster and preserve Swedish culture in America. After touring the 33-room mansion with its intricately carved oak, walnut and African mahogany panels, rare collections of copper, pewter, wood, textiles, more than 600 samples of handmade Swedish glass works, 11 Swedish stoves made of porcelainized tile, and an array of social and cultural artifacts spanning more than 150 years of the Swedish experience in America, it's obvious that this man's lifelong ambition has been realized. Admission: $3 (adults), $2 (senior citizens and students under 18). Hours: Tuesday through Saturday, noon to 4 p.m.; Wednesday, noon to 8 p.m.; Sunday, 1 to 5 p.m. Closed Mondays.

ARD GODFREY HOUSE
28 S.E. University Ave.
Minneapolis
(612) 870-8001
This 1849 home, restored by the Woman's Club of Minneapolis, is reportedly the oldest surviving frame house in the city. Located in a beautiful park overlooking the Mississippi River, the Greek Revival structure serves as a window on the past. With original fur-

---

Välkommen!

- Elaborate turn of the century mansion
- Museum Exhibits
- Cultural Center

Tue., Thur.-Sat. 12-4 p.m.
Wed. 12-8 p.m., Sun. 1-5 p.m.

THE AMERICAN·SWEDISH·INSTITUTE

(612) 871-4907

2600 Park Avenue • Minneapolis, MN 55407
Founded in 1929 by Swan J. Turnblad

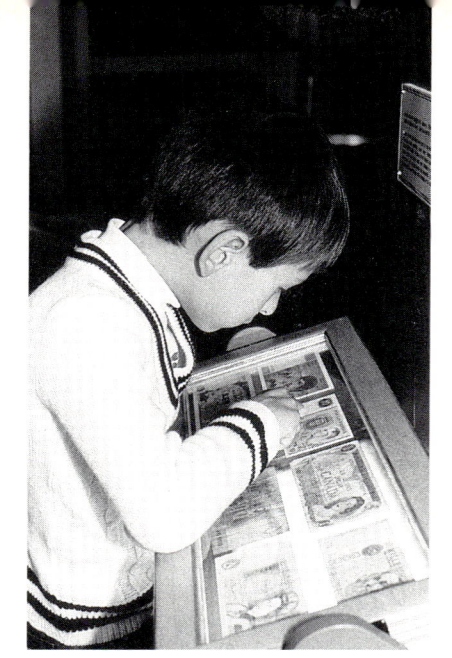

Exploring the secrets of the dollar bill in "Trading Places" at the Children's Museum.

nishings dating from 1849 and earlier and costumed guides, the only anachronism here is the air-conditioning. Admission: $1 (adults), 50 cents (senior citizens), 25 cents (students), children under 6 free. Hours: Friday through Monday, noon to 3:30 p.m., June through September. Tours are available all year round by special arrangement.

"ANTIE CLARE'S" DOLL HOSPITAL AND MUSEUM
2543 E. Seventh Ave.
North St. Paul
(612) 770-7522

Chatty Cathy lives! At "Antie Clare's" Doll Hospital and Museum. She's only one of 4,000 little dolls to grace this collection started by Clarice Erickson more than 22 years ago. Others dolls include a Creché Baby Jesus made of wax (which dates back to the late 1700s), an Alexander doll and a Shirley Temple doll — everything from antique to modern to collectibles. From the fainting couch in the parlor to the largest dollhouse in the world (a 16-by-10 1/2-foot structure built by the Minneapolis Institute of Arts and donated to the museum), "Antie Clare's" Doll Hospital and Museum is definitely charming. In addition to showcasing her collection, Erickson also has six "doctors" on staff to help fix any cosmetic ailment known to dolls, whether they be made of bisque china, vinyl, hard plastic, wax, papier maché, rubber or cloth. Admission: $4 (general); $3.50 (children 12 and under and senior citizens). Hours: Monday through Saturday, 9 a.m. to 5 p.m.

CHILDREN'S MUSEUM
1217 N. Bandana Blvd.
St. Paul
(612) 644-5305

The Children's Museum is, without question, the perfect place to free the spirited energy of those who, sometimes, seem to exist solely to try your patience. If you need a respite from the challenges of parenting, or if the sight of children — specifically *your* children — learning and having an absolutely wonderful time warms the part of your soul that frequently gets lost between cartoons in the morning and "just one more drink of water" at bedtime, bring your children to the museum and let them loose. Exhibits including "Vital Signs," an area designed to familiarize children with hospital equipment and procedures; Habitot (for children 6 months to 3 years), a crawl-through maze with bridges and tunnels; and "About the House," a cross section of a home where children can see everything that goes into making a house, are designed specifically to teach children ages 6 months to 12 years about themselves and the world around them through hands-on participation. Admission ranges from $1.50 to $3.50, depending on the season; $2.50 (senior citizens); $1.50 (1-year-olds); free for children under 1. Hours: Tuesday and Sunday, 10 a.m. to 6 p.m.; Wednesday through Saturday, 10 a.m. to 8 p.m.; Monday (June through August), 10 a.m. to 6 p.m.

GIBBS FARM MUSEUM
2097 W. Larpenteur Ave.
Falcon Heights
(612) 646-8629

This national historic site depicts life at the turn of the century as the Gibbs family — an average early-American family — lived it. The farm includes a two-story farmhouse, one-room country schoolhouse, a big red barn that houses an exhibit area, woodworking shop, veterinarian's office and a white barn with six chickens, four sheep, three ducks, two pigs and a horse named Gus. The site, which the city of St. Paul nearly turned into a parking lot in the late '40s, has never been modernized. Admission: $2.50 (adults), $2 (senior citizens), $1 (ages 2 to 18). Reservations are necessary for groups of 10 or more. Hours: Tuesday through Friday, 10 a.m. to 4 p.m.; Saturday (June through August), noon to 4 p.m.; Sunday, noon to 4 p.m. Open May through October.

GOLDSTEIN GALLERY AND COLLECTIONS
1985 Buford Ave.
St. Paul
(612) 624-7434
Located on the University of Minnesota's St. Paul campus, this design and teaching museum houses a permanent collection of more than 12,000 objects ranging from historic costumes and designer fashions to the decorative arts. The museum mounts four shows a year, including student, faculty and traveling exhibitions as well as thematic exhibits based on its collection. Admission is free. Hours: Monday through Friday, 10 a.m. to 4 p.m.; Thursday, 10 a.m. to 8 p.m.; Saturday and Sunday, 1:30 to 4:30 p.m.

HENNEPIN HISTORY MUSEUM
2303 S. Third Ave.
Minneapolis
(612) 870-1329
With four exhibition galleries, a video gallery and extensive library archives, the Hennepin History Museum's philosophy is to understand the present and anticipate the future within the context of our rich and varied pasts. "Dark Times, Bright Visions: Objects From the Hands of Dakota and Ojibwa People," for example, illustrates the survival of Dakota and Ojibwa cultures despite government assimilation policies from 1880 to 1940. "Prairie Metropolis: Life in a Northern City" orients visitors to Minneapolis and surrounding urban environments. And "Ghosts on the Freeway" is a short documentary that examines the effects of freeway construction in Twin Cities neighborhoods. These and other exhibits are available throughout the year. Call the museum for current exhibitions. Admission: $1.50 (adults), 50 cents for children 12 and under. Hours: Tuesday through Sunday, noon to 5 p.m. Closed Mondays. Group tours available by reservation.

HISTORIC MURPHY'S LANDING
2187 E. Highway 101
Shakopee
(612) 445-6900
If you need a break from the 20th century, take a step back into the daily life of the average 19th-century citizen when you visit Historic Murphy's Landing. The landing is a "living history museum," a little community of historic homes and businesses right out of the past century where costumed interpreters depict pioneer lifestyles from 1840 to 1890 through narration, demonstrations and crafts. Admission: $7 (adults), $6 (students 6 to18 years old and seniors 62 and older), children under 6 are free. Hours: Tuesday through Friday, 11 a.m. to 4 p.m.; Saturday through Sunday, noon to 5 p.m. Closed Sundays.

JAMES FORD BELL MUSEUM OF NATURAL HISTORY
10 S.E. Church St.
Minneapolis
(612) 624-1852
Let's be honest. The best part of a museum is where you can see the lifelike displays of plants, mammals and birds in their natural habitats. The James Ford Bell Museum uses these displays (a.k.a. dioramas) in that perfectly diabolical way that museums have of making something interesting and educational. While your children press their noses against the glass waiting for one of the animals to move, they'll be learning about nature, the Darwinian theory of natural selection and taxidermy. Add to it the museum's nationally acclaimed Touch and See Room — a place where you can, well, touch and see natural animal hides and furs, antlers, bones, shells, live snakes, turtles and fish (among other things) — and you've got the perfect place to spend a few educational hours. All plants and animals, by the way, are indigenous to Minnesota. Guided tours are available with a two-week advance reservation. Group reservations are nec-

Hurray! Minnesota

essary. Admission: $2 (adults), $1 (children 3 through 16 and seniors 62 and older), children under 3 are free. Hours: Tuesday through Saturday, 9 a.m. to 5 p.m.; Sunday, 1 to 5 p.m. Closed Mondays. The Touch and See room closes Tuesday through Friday at 2 p.m. Free admission on Thursdays.

JAMES J. HILL HOUSE
240 Summit Ave.
St. Paul
(612) 297-2555
The James J. Hill House is a misnomer. It really isn't a house, you see, it's a mansion. Completed in 1891 to house one of the first true moguls of Minnesota's economic development, the mansion boasts 36,000 square feet of living space including 13 bathrooms, 22 fireplaces and a 100-foot reception hall. Hill, who bought the ailing St. Paul and Pacific Railroad (later named the Great Northern) in 1878, engineered it — and the Twin Cities — to dramatic commercial success by 1893. He had this mansion built as a symbol of his massive success. Admission: $3 (adults), $1 (children 6 to 15), free for children under 6. Hours: Wednesday, Thursday and Saturday, 10 a.m. to 3:30 p.m.

HUMPHREY FORUM
University of
Minnesota
301 S. 19th Ave.
Minneapolis
(612) 624-5799
This colorful and engaging exhibit of 20th-century history, government and politics centers around one of Minnesota's most influential politicians: Hubert Horatio Humphrey. The former Minneapolis mayor, U.S. Senator and Vice President's career is documented here with lifesize photo murals, videos of his speeches and a wonderful collection of political memorabilia including two

First-century Hellenistic sculpture at the MIA.

hats he received as gifts — one from Premier Kruschev in 1958 and the other, a Stetson, from President Lyndon B. Johnson. Admission is free. Hours: Monday, 9 a.m. to 8 p.m.; Tuesday through Friday, 9 a.m. to 5 p.m.; Saturday, 10 a.m. to 3 p.m. Closed Sundays.

MCAD GALLERY
Minneapolis College of Art and Design
2501 S. Stevens Ave.
Minneapolis
(612) 874-3700
This gallery is committed to presenting and interpreting contemporary art and design through a schedule of diverse exhibitions exploring esthetic, cultural and ideological issues. Exhibitions range from student works to new and innovative pieces by local and national artists. Besides standard gallery space, there is also a catwalk off the second-floor display area where you can stand and watch students entrenched in the creative process. Admission is free. Hours: Monday through Friday, 9 a.m. to 5 p.m.; Saturday, 9 a.m. to 5 p.m.; Sunday, noon to 5 p.m.

MINNEAPOLIS INSTITUTE OF ARTS
2400 S. Third Ave.
Minneapolis
(612) 870-3200
(24-hour exhibition information)
(612) 870-3131
(program and visitor information)
With a collection encompassing more than 80,000 objects, the Minneapolis Institute of Arts (MIA) is the only comprehensive fine arts museum serving the Twin Cities and the Upper Midwest. Its encyclopedic collection of the decorative arts is at the heart of everything the museum does, with treasures including the James Ford Bell Collection of American and English Silver and nine original

The Minnesota Historical Society's new History Center houses the society's exhibits, collections, research center, educational programs and administrative offices all under one roof.

period rooms including several Colonial American rooms, a 15th-century English Tudor room and an 18th-century French salon. The museum's collectors have placed an emphasis on gathering works representative of every age and cultural tradition, spanning 4,000 years of world history. The collection contains treasures of Western art from the 14th to the 20th century, including major paintings by Rembrandt, Goya, van Gogh and Degas; sculptures ranging from prehistoric to modern times; an expansive collection of prints and drawings, including works by Toulouse-Lautrec, Roy Lichtenstein and Jasper Johns; a photography collection documenting the history of the medium from 1836 to the present, with important works by Alfred Stieglitz, Edward Steichen, Walker Evans and Ansel Adams; and an impressive textile collection including Gothic tapestries and Guatemalan weaving. Admission is free. Hours: Tuesday, Wednesday, Friday and Saturday, 10 a.m. to 5 p.m.; Thursday, 10 a.m. to 9 p.m.; Sunday, noon to 5 p.m. Closed Mondays.

MINNESOTA AIR GUARD MUSEUM
Minnesota Air Guard Base

Located at the northeast corner of the Minneapolis-St. Paul International Airport, south of Highways 55 and 62 in Minneapolis.
(612) 725-9590

This little-known museum is located about seven miles away from the Minneapolis-St. Paul Airport's main terminal. The collection of 15 planes, dating from the late 1930s to the present, includes an A-12 Blackbird (the top-secret reconnaissance plane used during the height of the Cold War in the '60s) and a P-51 Mustang fighter plane flown during World War II. All of the planes are in various stages of restoration. There is also an indoor central gallery with photos, artifacts and memorabilia chronicling the 71-year history of the Minnesota Air Guard. The adjoining gift shop sells everything from postcards and model planes to freeze-dried ice cream — the kind the astronauts eat. Admission is free. Hours: Saturday and Sunday, 11 a.m. to 4 p.m. (mid-April through mid-September) and on the second and third Saturdays of the month (October through March). Escorted tours are by appointment only, and a $1 donation is requested.

Minnesota History Center
345 W. Kellogg Boulevard
St. Paul
(612) 296-6126
The Minnesota Historical Society's vast collection of objects, artifacts and documents is breathing a lot easier these days, thanks to its new 44,000-square-foot home in the newly christened History Center. (Until recently, the society's collection was either being scrunched into one tiny exhibition space or stored at a variety of locations in and around St. Paul.) The new museum space houses a collection of more than 165,000 artifacts ranging from 10,000 B.C. to the present. Included in the collection is the snazzy purple pantsuit that Prince wore in the movie "Purple Rain" (generously donated to the museum by Prince's production staff), the 10-foot boat, "Yankee Girl," that Minnesotan Gerry Spiess sailed across the Atlantic in 1979, an oxcart from the Red River Valley and the entire back porch of Henry and Minnie Bull's 1878 Cokato home. Admission is free. Hours are Tuesday, Wednesday, Friday, Saturday, 10 a.m. to 5 p.m.; Thursday, 10 a.m. to 9 p.m.; Sunday, noon to 5 p.m. Closed Mondays.

Minnesota Museum of Art
Jemne Building, 305 St. Peter St.
Landmark Center, 75 W. Fifth St.
St. Paul
(612) 292-4355
Built in 1931, the Jemne Building, home to the Minnesota Museum of Art, is an Art Deco landmark. Thematic exhibitions from the museum's extensive collection of American and non-Western art are installed in several intimate galleries on the second and third floors. A short two-block stroll away, through the pastoral pocket of Rice Park, is the Landmark Center, which houses the museum's temporary exhibitions, often featuring new artists from the Midwest. The MMA is committed to American art that reflects the cultural diversity of this country. This commitment is apparent in the museum's extensive collection of American art and works from African, Asian and Oceanic cultures. Admission is free. Hours: Tuesday, Wednesday and Friday, 10:30 a.m. to 4:30 p.m.; Thursday, 10:30 a.m. to 7:30 p.m.; Saturday and Sunday, 1 to 4:30 p.m.

Museum of Questionable Medical Devices
219 S.E. Main St.
Minneapolis
(612) 379-4046
Most of the 250 items on display in this unusual museum have been collected by curator Bob McCoy (who has appeared with his devices on both the "Today Show" and "Late Night With David Letterman"). The rest have been provided on loan by the Food and Drug Administration, the American Medical Association's Historical Health Fraud Collection, and others. All together, the devices make up the largest collection of medical quackery in the country. Included among the charlatanry are the Nemectron, a metal-ringed device that claims to enlarge or reduce breasts (depending on your particular need), cure acne *and* rejuvenate brain cells; the Home Magneto Box, which uses electrodes and mild shocks to combat various diseases and a few minor annoyances (constipation and dandruff, among them); and McCoy's prize, the Psycograph, a metal contraption which, when worn on the head, will judge your character in less than three seconds. Admission is free; psycographic readings are $2. Hours: Monday through Thursday, 5 to 9 p.m.; Friday and Saturday, 11 a.m. to 9 p.m.; Sunday, noon to 5 p.m.

The Original Baseball Hall of Fame of Minnesota
406 S. Chicago Ave.
Minneapolis
(612) 375-9707
When the winds are favorable over the Metrodome, and the sun is swaying between the clouds, you can almost hear ethereal voices whispering: "If you build it, they will come. If you display it, they will look. If you merchandise it, they will buy." If you're a baseball fan, this place is your fantasy. Former Twins equipment manager Ray Crump has collected the most extensive assortment of baseball memorabilia this side of Cooperstown. The collection includes 10,000 autographed balls signed by baseball greats and celebrities alike (including

Babe Ruth, Frank Sinatra, and — believe it or not — the Beatles), signed World Series bats from 1955 through 1982, Rod Carew's old uniform and even the Metrodome's old artificial turf. See the bat that Mickey Mantle used to hit a home run in the 1953 All Star game. Learn about how baseballs, gloves and bats are made. Buy baseball merchandise ranging from jackets and jerseys to keychains and baseball cards. Admission is free. Hours: The museum is open during and after all Dome events as well as Monday through Friday, 9 a.m. to 5 p.m.; Saturday, 11 a.m. to 3 p.m. Closed Sundays (except when there is an event at the Dome).

Pavek Museum of Broadcasting
3515-17 Raleigh Ave.
St. Louis Park
(612) 926-8198
If you were born after, say, 1955, you ought to go to the Pavek Museum of Broadcasting for one simple reason: You can see that there was life — a very exciting, interesting and visual life — before television. Think about it: Radio, by necessity, tests the imagination. You simply can't listen to a real radio show and not visualize what's going on. The radio can't spoon-feed you like TV does. As further proof: The term "couch potato" wasn't coined until *after* 1955. Radio is an important, mind-bending medium. Joseph Pavek, an amateur radio operator who became a noted radio authority and historian, obviously knew that: His museum houses one of the nation's most extensive collections of early radio equipment and memorabilia. The collection includes thousands of radio sets, components, vacuum tubes, transmitters and receivers, broadcasting station equipment, "ham" amateur equipment, primitive crystal sets, World War I aircraft and ship-to-shore communication systems and wireless communications apparatus for the news and entertainment industries. It's all at the Pavek Museum of Broadcasting. Admission is $2 (adults), $1 (children under 13 and senior citizens). Hours: Tuesday through Friday, 10 a.m. to 6 p.m.; Saturday, 9 a.m. to 5 p.m. Closed Sundays, Mondays and holidays.

Planes of Fame Air Museum
14771 Pioneer Trail
Eden Prairie
(612) 941-2633
Absolutely the only thing more daring, more romantic and more exciting than being the pilot of an open cockpit plane is getting to ride in one. Imagine yourself in your leather helmet and goggles, your scarf blowing behind you in the wind. Maybe you're Amelia Earhart. Maybe you're the Red Baron. Whoever you are, take a trip out to the Planes of Fame Air Museum on a nice day and take a ride in a Stearman biplane. If you happen to have a fear of flying, check out the museum anyway. It houses the largest private collection of airworthy World War II planes in the world. Tours are often led by World War II veteran pilots who give firsthand accounts of famous war birds, most of which saw service in the war. The collection includes a Grumman FM-2 Wildcat, the same plane used in the battle of the Midway; the A-26 bomber that appeared in the movie "Always"; the Goodyear Corsair FGI-D that flew in the TV series "Black Sheep Squadron"; and, of course, the Stearman biplane. Admission: $5 (adults), $2 (ages 7 to17), and free for children under 7. Plane rides are $65. Hours: Friday through Saturday with tours at 11:30 a.m. and 2 p.m. Weekday tours are available by appointment. Open March through October.

Schubert Club Keyboard Instrument Museum
Landmark Center
75 W. Fifth St.
St. Paul
(612) 292-3262
If the ivories in this room could talk, you might hear stories about how Felix Mendelssohn banged too hard on the keys or about how Johannes Brahms wept when he played his famous lullaby. Not all the instruments in this collection can boast the privilege of such illustrious patronage, but they are all very special. And they are all very old. The collection of several thousand instruments includes an Italian harpsichord made in 1542, an Erard piano autographed in 1844 by Franz Liszt and the

Science Museum of Minnesota and Omnitheater.

Kisting & Son piano owned by Adolph Menzel in 1830. (Menzel was a famous French artist whose close personal friends — Felix Mendelssohn, Johannes Brahms, Clara and Robert Schumann, among them — often came over and played his piano. This piano.) The museum also includes two pianos that the public may play — a fortepiano, just like the one given to Mozart's family by a member of the German aristocracy in 1794, and a rare Art Deco piano made by Wurlitzer in 1935. There were only 12 such pianos made; this is the last one in existence. Of the collection, only 50 instruments are displayed at one time. Admission is free. Hours: Monday through Friday, 11 a.m. to 3 p.m.

SCIENCE MUSEUM OF MINNESOTA AND OMNITHEATER
30 E. 10th St.
St. Paul
(612) 221-9412

First and last, the Science Museum of Minnesota is a museum to end all museums. It is the cadillac, the caviar, the cream. It is, to borrow a quote from Judy Jetsen, "the most ut." Savvy magazine even listed it as one of the reasons why Minnesota is such a great place to raise a family. Let your kids loose in the Science Museum for a day and they might even learn something. (Don't worry, they'll be having too much fun to realize this educational component.)

How to describe this museumical icon? First of all, you know you can't go wrong when one of the first things you see is a 9-foot-7-inch dinosaur, er, Triceratops. And right across the way, down the Hall of Paleontology, there's an 82-foot-long by 18-foot-high Diplodocus, an Allosaurus and two Camptosaurs. If you wander down Anthropology Hall, you'll learn about how different cultures have met their need for food, shelter and clothing. Look for "Hmong Odyssey," an exhibit that includes a traditional Hmong dwelling, costumes, jewelry and other crafts. And, whatever you do, don't miss the Egyptian mummy. It's creepy, but it's worth it (especially if your spook stories have become dull and lifeless). Then there's "Our Minnesota," an exhibit that documents the changing environment of the state and the Experiment Gallery, a hands-on area with exhibits on waves, resonance, sound, light and air. And what museum would be complete without real live stuffed animals? This museum boasts the Bengal tiger, a family of polar bears, sloth bears, a boa constrictor and the red fox, among many others.

Finally, the Science Museum houses the Omnitheater, a 332-seat theater with a domed screen that serves to put you right in the middle of the action. Whether it's a documentary about tropical rain forests or an adventure in outer space, you'll leave feeling as though you spent the past hour in another world. (Going to the Omnitheater, it's true, is the next best thing to actually taking a vacation.) Tickets to the Omnitheater range from $5.50 (adults) to $4.50 (seniors and juniors). Admission to the museum itself is $4.50 (adults), $3.50 (seniors and juniors). Hours are Monday through Friday, 9:30 a.m. to 9 p.m.; Saturday, 9 a.m. to 9 p.m.; Sunday, 10 a.m. to 9 p.m.

The Walker Art Center with Minneapolis Sculpture Garden in the foreground.

UNIVERSITY ART MUSEUM
110 Northrup Auditorium
84 S.E. Church St.
Minneapolis
(612) 624-9876
This museum hosts a variety of thematic exhibitions throughout the year featuring works from its extensive American art collection. Contemporary and historical works dating from 1900 to 1959 include paintings by Georgia O'Keeffe, Marsden Hartley, Milton Avery, Lionel Feininger, Edward Hopper, Robert Motherwell, James Rosenquist, Roy Lichtenstein and Arthur Dove. The museum will close in April '93 and re-open in its new location at 333 East River Road, Minneapolis, in November '93. Admission is free. Hours: Monday through Friday, 11 a.m. to 5 p.m.; Sunday, 2 to 5 p.m. Closed Saturdays.

WALKER ART CENTER
725 Vineland Place
Minneapolis
(612) 375-7600
The internationally acclaimed Walker Art Center is known for its major exhibitions of 20th-century art; its presentation of vanguard music, dance, theater and film; and its innovative education programs. The Walker's permanent collection of more than 5,000 pieces features representative works from the major movements of 20th-century American and European art, with particular strengths in Abstract Expressionism, Pop Art, Minimalism, New Image painting and recent neo-Expressionism. The Walker's performing arts program, which features appearances by leading choreographers. composers and directors of experimental theater, is the largest such museum-based program in the country. Also a showcase for independent cinema, the Walker presents the most innovative and accomplished films by emerging American directors and the European avant-garde. Complementing this contemporary focus are retrospectives of the work of major filmmakers, series of rediscovered Hollywood classics and treasures from early television. Admission: $3 (adults), $2 (students 12 to 18 with ID), free to seniors, children under 12 and AFDC cardholders. Admission is free to everyone on Thursdays and the first Saturday of the month. Hours: Tuesday through Saturday, 10 a.m. to 8 p.m.; Sunday, 11 a.m. to 5 p.m. Closed Mondays.

Hurray! Minnesota

TWIN CITIES ART GALLERIES

THERE ARE MANY, MANY GALLERIES in the Twin Cities and surrounding suburbs. Listed here are just a few of the galleries that are relatively more active with special shows or in special fields. Many of these galleries are open daily, but some have individual schedules and/or are open by appointment. Call for hours.

ANDERSON AND ANDERSON
Eclectic and contemporary fine art by more than 40 regional, national and international artists. Cast metal, mixed-media, sculpture, ceramics, wall-relief, works on paper, paintings and 20th-century furnishings and interiors. 414 N. First Ave., Minneapolis, (612) 332-4889.

ART RESOURCE GALLERY
One of Minnesota's largest galleries representing professional artists in oils, acrylics, watercolor, pastels, hand-pulled prints, handmade paper textiles, photography, sculpture and fine crafts. Open six days a week. 494 Jackson St., St. Paul, (612) 222-8686.

AVERHILL HEIMDAHL GALLERY
This gallery represents the abstract expressionist paintings of former University of Minnesota and Walker Art Center teacher Ralph Brown and his students. 400 N. First Ave., Minneapolis, (612) 922-8889.

THOMAS BARRY FINE ARTS
Regional artists show contemporary sculpture, paintings, prints and photography. 400 N. First Ave., Minneapolis, (612) 338-3656.

BOCKLEY GALLERY
Contemporary art by regional and national artists. 400 N. First Ave., Minneapolis, (612) 339-3139.

CIRCA GALLERY
Contemporary artwork by regional artists in all mediums. Custom and conservation framing available. 118 N. Fourth St., Minneapolis, (612) 332-2386.

VERN CARVER GALLERY
Original landscape work by local artists in oils, pastels and watercolors. Antique prints featuring botanical, Audubon and Minnesota scenes. 1106 Nicollet Mall, Minneapolis, (612) 339-3449.

DOUGLAS-BAKER GALLERY
This gallery features paintings, drawings, sculpture and original prints, often containing elements of the visual triangle of the human figure, landscape and architecture. 400 N. First Ave., Minneapolis, (612) 332-2978.

DOLLY FITERMAN FINE ARTS
This gallery is located in a building that was once Pillsbury Library and is listed on the National Register of Historic Places. Established contemporary American and European artists are featured. 100 University Ave. S.E., Minneapolis, (612) 623-3300.

FLANDERS CONTEMPORARY ART
Paintings, sculpture and prints by contemporary regional and emerging artists as well as by artists of international recognition: Robert Motherwell, Helen Frankenthaler, Jim Dine and Andy Warhol. 400 N. First Ave., Minneapolis, (612) 344-1700.

FORUM GALLERY
Contemporary works in both sculpture and painting. Textile Building, 119 N. Fourth St., Minneapolis, (612) 333-1835.

GALLERY 416
Contemporary works of original fine art, both abstract and realism. Lazer disc monitor of limited editions and animation cells. 416 St. Peter St., St. Paul, 225-9608, or 1200 Nicollet Mall, Minneapolis, (612) 338-2913.

GEOMETRIE GALLERY
Modern furniture based on geometric forms. Full range of 20th-century classic furniture such as art deco and '50s designs. Furniture designed by international as well as regional artists. 122 N. First Ave., Minneapolis, (612) 340-1635.

GROVELAND GALLERY
Original art by regional artists presented in a Kenwood turn-of-the-century mansion. Specializing in realist paintings and drawings. 25 Groveland Terrace, Minneapolis, (612) 377-7800.

INTERMEDIA ARTS
Specializes in alternative, multimedia and performance art. 413 N. First Ave., Minneapolis, (612) 627-4449.

JAVIER PUIG DECORATIVE ARTS
Artistic furniture and other useful craft items in metal, glass and ceramics. 118 N. Fourth St., Minneapolis, (612) 332-6001.

JEAN STEPHEN GALLERIES
There are two galleries in the Conservatory: one features cartoon cells while the other is contemporary work of up-and-coming artists, both national and local. 800 Nicollet Mall, Minneapolis, (612) 338-4333

SUZANN KOHN GALLERY
Contemporary regional paintings and drawings. International Design Center, 100 N. Second Ave., Minneapolis, 341-3441, or 1690 Grand Ave., St. Paul, (612) 699-0477.

MC GALLERY
Featuring national artists working in a variety of mediums from handmade paper to ceramics and glass. Wyman Building, 400 N. First Ave., Minneapolis, (612) 339-1480.

MHIRIPIRI GALLERY
African art, sculptures and exotic wood artwork. Butler Square, 100 N. Sixth St., Minneapolis, (612) 332-7406

MINNESOTA CENTER FOR BOOK ARTS
The real art of producing a book from papermaking to printing. 24 N. Third St., Minneapolis, (612) 338-3634.

NO NAME GALLERY
Shows emerging artists and evocative, exceptional art in a wide range of mediums and forms. This is a nonprofit voluntary arts organization. 100 N. First St., Minneapolis, (612) 333-8383.

JON OULMAN GALLERY
Represents both local and national artists in photography, pastels and paintings. Wyman Building, 400 N. First St., Minneapolis, (612) 333-2386.

PREMIER GALLERY
Representing sculptor Paul Granlund as well as changing exhibits featuring Minnesota artists. 141 S. Seventh St., Minneapolis, (612) 338-4541.

RAYMOND AVENUE GALLERY
Shows both functional and sculptural crafts such as pottery, fabric, jewelry and metal work. 761 Raymond Ave., St. Paul, (612) 644-9200.

C.G. REIN GALLERIES
There are about 8,000 works in this gallery, mostly sculptures, paintings and prints of all kinds. Brandon Square, 3523 W. 70th St., Edina, (612) 927-4331.

CAROLYN RUFF GALLERY
Featuring culturally diverse works of regional and national artists. 400 N. First Ave., Minneapolis, (612) 338-8052.

SONIA'S GALLERY
Regional arts and crafts focusing on landscapes and fiber arts. Wyman Building, 400 N. First Ave., Minneapolis, (612) 338-0350.

TEXTILE ARTS INTERNATIONAL
Historic textile artworks with a network to more than 70 artists. Wyman Building, 400 N. First Ave., Minneapolis, (612) 338-6776.

THOMPSON GALLERY
Large representation of regional artists as well as national limited-edition prints. 321 N. Second Ave., Minneapolis, (612) 338-7734.

JACK WOLD FINE ARTS
Pottery, original oils and watercolors and limited-edition prints. 400 N. First Ave., Minneapolis, (612) 339-5191.

Hurray! Minnesota

Music Institutions

BACH SOCIETY CHORUS
Box 39292
Minneapolis
(612) 649-4692
The Bach Society was started in 1933 by a group of students from the University of Minnesota School of Music who wanted to sing the music of Bach. The chorus remained under the auspices of the University until 1966, whereupon it became an independent nonprofit organization. The 60- to 80-member chorus gives four or five concerts a season, including an annual holiday candlelight concert at the Landmark Center in St. Paul. (Tickets for the holiday concert range from $5 to $12.) The chorus, which performs music ranging from the 18th century to newly commissioned works, also appears with other professional groups including the Minnesota Orchestra and Lyra Concert.

BEL CANTO VOICES
1917 S. Logan Ave.
Minneapolis
(612) 377-5928
The Bel Canto Voices, established in 1976, is a diverse music program for girls grades 3 through 12 that consists of voice training as well as performance and touring experience. Nearly 150 girls and young women from around the Twin Cities metro area participate in the program that encompasses five different concert choirs. The regular performance season, which runs from September through May, includes major concerts and participation in many music and media events.

CONCENTUS MUSICUS RENAISSANCE ENSEMBLE
Box 141037
Minneapolis
(612) 379-4463
Concentus Musicus, the longest-running early-music group in the Twin Cities, specializes in the music written after Machaut and before Mozart. While the group does play some music written during the Middles Ages (A.D. 900 to 1450), most of its repertoire comes from the actual Renaissance period (A.D. 1450 to 1600). Besides maintaining a regular five-concert season, the ensemble (which also includes a smaller group called Musica Intima) also plays at the Renaissance Festival (see Festival section), private engagements and area churches. The ensemble is comprised of singers and musicians who play authentic period instruments including the lute, viola da gamba, shawm, recorder and crumhorn. Tickets are $12 (adults) and $8 (students and seniors).

DALE WARLAND SINGERS
120 N. Fourth St.
Minneapolis
(612) 339-9707
You might say that Frank Sinatra inspired Dale Warland to start what has become America's premier choral ensemble. But that wouldn't be quite right. It might be closer to the truth to say that one of Ol' Blue Eyes' famous songs expressed a sentiment that Warland, an internationally known and sought-after guest conductor and arranger, could relate to. The song in question is "My Way" and, according to Warland, that's precisely why he founded the Dale Warland Singers — to make choral music his way.

And after more than 20 successful years, an international reputation and more than 15 critically acclaimed recordings, it would seem that Warland's way has become more than just a reckless show of autonomy — it has become sweet music to choral-music lovers around the world. Warland's chorale, which consists of 40 singers, performs the

Dale Warland, founder and music director of the Dale Warland Singers.

"music of today," which includes works by composers such as Anthony Davis, Stephen Paulus, Libby Larsen and George Shearing. While the ensemble also sings the choral classics, there is a special focus on Minnesota composers and other emerging American composers. The chorale performs a five-concert subscription series annually at venues ranging from the Ordway Music Theatre and Orchestra Hall to the Colonial Church of Edina. Tickets range from $10 to $20.

ENSEMBLE CAPRICCIO
1607 Mount Curve Ave.
Minneapolis
(612) 374-3132
"Capriccio," as those of you who listened in music class will know, is the Italian word for a light, fanciful instrumental work. It is usually written in several parts, suggesting frequent changes in mood. Thus, the word "capricious" (which, as those of you who listened in English class will know, means witty and whimsical). Thus, Ensemble Capriccio. This brilliant (and, yes, capricious) string chamber trio (violin, cello, viola), made up of musicians from the Minnesota Orchestra and Saint Paul Chamber Orchestra, presents an annual three-concert series featuring guest artists of national and international acclaim. (Past guest artists include cellist Yo-Yo Ma, guitarist Sharon Isbin, pianist Lydia Artymiw and internationally acclaimed soprano Benita Valente). The ensemble plays classical and contemporary music as well as new, commissioned works by emerging and established composers. (Recent commissions include works by Paul Schoenfield and Stanislaw Skrowaczewski.) Ensemble Capriccio performs primarily at Temple Israel and the Walker Art Center. Tickets, which can be purchased at the door, are $10.

FREDERIC CHOPIN SOCIETY
Box 8131
Minneapolis
(612) 870-0604
The Frederic Chopin Society, founded in 1984, presents solo piano chamber music featuring international emerging talents as well as local artists in intimate performance settings best suited to the piano. Although the music of Chopin is presented frequently, the society's programming regularly includes the works of a variety of composers (including Mozart, Schubert, Brahms and Liszt) who are aesthetically linked to Chopin. Tickets range from $8 to $12. Season tickets, for a four-concert series, range from $32 to $40. Memberships are available starting at $15.

GREATER TWIN CITIES YOUTH SYMPHONIES
430 Oak Grove St., Suite 205
Minneapolis
(612) 870-7611
Greater Twin Cities Youth Symphonies (GTCYS) was founded in 1972 to provide young musicians (elementary age through high school) with the opportunity to become part of a symphony orchestra. Since its inception, GTCYS has become the largest youth symphony program in the world with approximately 1,000 young musicians who hail from towns within a 240-mile radius of the Twin Cities. These musicians, who participate in one of seven regular season orchestras, the summer orchestra program and the Orchestral Institute of America music camp, present formal concerts in venues including Orchestra Hall and the Ordway Music Theatre. They also perform a series of award-winning public-service concerts at Minnesota's juvenile institutions, centers for the handicapped and senior-citizen homes as well as public venues such as the Landmark Center, International Market Square and the IDS Crystal Court. Over the years, the group has taken myriad international tours to places including England, West Germany, the United Kingdom, Costa Rica, the Soviet Union, Hong Kong, Japan, China, Australia, New Zealand and Fiji.

MINNEAPOLIS CHAMBER SYMPHONY
100 N. Sixth St., Suite 935C
Minneapolis
(612) 339-0235
When you go to hear a performance by the Minneapolis Chamber Symphony, a professional orchestra of 28 musicians, you probably won't be sitting in a huge concert hall. You probably won't be outnumbered by people from a nicer suburb. And you absolutely won't be considered a ward of the state if, by

some strange freak of physiology, you have to cough during the second movement. The Minneapolis Chamber Symphony is known, you might say, for its listener-friendliness. First, it performs in accessible locations, giving those who might not otherwise attend a more formal performance the opportunity to hear classical music. Second, it is dedicated to teaching the classically untrained by featuring guest speakers who provide background information on the composers and the works to be performed.

Throughout the year, the Minneapolis Chamber Symphony produces a series of free public outdoor concerts, an affordable summer subscription concert series, a series of free holiday concerts, a winter subscription concert series and a project called the "Greater Minnesota Initiative" that seeks to provide classical music performances and music education programs to communities throughout Minnesota that are not served by professional orchestras. Tickets range from $11 to $13.50 (adults) and $5.50 to $6.75 (children, students and seniors).

Minnesota Chorale
Hennepin Center for the Arts
528 Hennepin Ave., Suite 211
Minneapolis
(612) 333-4866

The Minnesota Chorale, official chorus of the Saint Paul Chamber Orchestra, is a 150-voice symphonic chorus that was formed in 1972 to give Twin Cities musicians and singers the opportunity to perform great choral music. Besides its affiliation with the SPCO, the Minnesota Chorale also sings with the Minnesota Orchestra and gives several independent concerts a year.

Minnesota Composers Forum
26 E. Exchange St., Suite 200
St. Paul
(612) 228-1407

There's a reason why the Minnesota Composers Forum is one of the largest and most influential composer service organizations in the world. There's a reason why 600 composers from all over the world belong to the Minnesota Composers Forum. It's because everything the Minnesota Composers Forum does — from providing funds for the development of new works to producing an annual concert series — seeks to encourage and support the creation, performance and appreciation of new music. The forum, for example, is currently developing a radio program, "The Composer's Voice," which is intended to enlarge the national audience for new music and increase public recognition of living composers. This program, co-produced by Minnesota Public Radio, is due to premiere in January 1993. The forum also presents an annual five-concert series, November through June, that features works by Minnesota Composers Forum members and includes at least one ensemble of regional or national acclaim. All concerts are presented at the Minnesota History Center or Walker Art Center.

Minnesota Opera Company
620 N. First St.
Minneapolis
(612) 333-2700

When the Minnesota Opera Company (then called Center Opera) began in 1963, it quickly claimed its niche as a small, progressive, "alternative" opera company — which was fine with the St. Paul Opera Company, since its focus was fixed on producing traditional operas. The two companies coexisted peacefully for many years until they merged in 1975. The result is an opera company that is committed to producing the traditional music-theater works of Mozart, Verdi, Puccini and the like as well as newly created works that reflect the values, sensibilities and ethnic influences of contemporary culture. In other words, in any given season, you could hear an opera composed by anyone from Mozart to Dominick Argento. (Center Opera was formed to premiere Argento's commissioned work, "The Masque of Angels.") The Minnesota Opera, now the 15th-largest opera company in the nation, boasts a history that includes more world and American premieres than any other opera company in the nation. The company presents three operas a year at the Ordway Music Theatre in St. Paul with additional performances at the State Theatre in Minneapolis and the World Theater in St. Paul (see Venues section). Single tickets range from $11 (partial views) to $55. Subscriptions for a three- and four-opera series are also available.

MINNESOTA ORCHESTRA
1111 Nicollet Mall
Minneapolis
(612) 371-5600

Founded in 1903 as the Minneapolis Symphony Orchestra, the Minnesota Orchestra has maintained a distinguished national and international presence throughout its history. (As early as 1912 the orchestra was touring the United States, earning a reputation as "the orchestra on wheels.") Since its inception, the orchestra has traveled to locales around the world, including the Middle East (a 34,000 mile tour), Mexico, Australia, Hong Kong and Puerto Rico. Because of a demonstrated commitment to commissioning and performing the music of our time, the Minnesota Orchestra has received seven awards for adventuresome programming from the American Society of Composers, Authors and Publishers. Among the composers whose works have been premiered by the Minnesota Orchestra are Bela Bartok, Aaron Copland, Dominick Argento and Stanislaw Skrowaczewski. The orchestra has also presented numerous world premieres by Minnesota composers Stephen Paulus and Libby Larsen.

Maestro Edo de Waart, who has guided the orchestra since 1986, conducts subscription concerts from September through May, with performances in acoustically renowned Orchestra Hall in Minneapolis and the Ordway Music Theatre in St. Paul (see Venues section) as well as regular appearances at the Mayo Civic Center Theatre in Rochester, Minnesota, and the Benedicta Arts Center in St. Joseph, Minnesota. The orchestra's subscription concerts are broadcast nationwide on the American Public Radio network as produced by Minnesota Public Radio. Rounding out the orchestra's 52-week season are a Weekender Pops series, Young People's Concerts, an Adventures in Music series for families, Holiday Concerts, summer Cabaret Pops, an outdoor Symphony for the Cities series, and the four-week summer music festival, Viennese Sommerfest.

MINNESOTA SINFONIA
1820 S. Stevens Ave., Suite E
Minneapolis
(612) 871-1701

This 25-member chamber orchestra was formed in 1989 to help make classical music both more accessible and more affordable to the average Minnesotan. With more than 10 (mostly free) concerts a year, all at very unpretentious and easy-to-find locations, Minnesota Sinfonia seems to be doing what it set out to do. And quite nicely, too. Its performance schedule includes a winter/spring season of three or four free Sunday afternoon concerts at the Basilica of Saint Mary, a summer subscription series of four concerts ranging in price from $3 (children) to $8 (adults) and free community concerts at varying times and places throughout the spring and summer featuring everything from pops and marches to Broadway and light classics. Minnesota Sinfonia is also dedicated to educating future performers and audience members by presenting educational programs to elementary school children from local inner-city schools.

MINNESOTA'S BEST MUSIC!

One of the world's finest classical ensembles - the **Minnesota Orchestra** - presents classical and popular music in the Twin Cities' finest setting - **Orchestra Hall**. Year-round, enjoy the Orchestra and their distinquished guests. Hear popular artists like B.B. King, Johnny Mathis, and Roy Clark, and in the summer - savor two month-long musical celebrations - CABARET POPS and Viennese SOMMERFEST.

For Information, call the Orchestra Hall Ticket Office at 371-5656 or 1 (800) 292-4141

MINNESOTA ORCHESTRA
Edo de Waart, Music Director

Hurray! Minnesota

MINNESOTA YOUTH SYMPHONIES
790 S. Cleveland Ave., Suite 203
St. Paul
(612) 699-5811
Minnesota Youth Symphonies, founded in 1972, provides music programs for students first grade through college. Besides developing three full orchestras and one string orchestra, Minnesota Youth Symphonies seeks to provide its students with educational opportunities that will enhance their musical endeavors, including ear training classes (so that young musicians can learn to sight-sing music) and a master-class series led by members of the Minnesota Orchestra. Each of the ensembles performs three or more concerts a season (September through May) at various venues around the Twin Cities area. Tickets range from $7 (adults) to $5 (seniors and children).

MUSIC IN THE PARK SERIES
1333 Chelmsford St.
St. Paul
(612) 644-4234
Contrary to what its name might suggest, this acclaimed concert series does not take place in a park. Not in an outdoor park, at any rate (for which chamber music lovers should be thankful, as the series runs from October through April). The "park," in this instance, refers to St. Anthony Park United Church of Christ, the (indoor) site of Music in the Park's annual chamber music concert series. Season tickets are $45 and single tickets range from $5 to $10.

OPERA 101 THEATER COMPANY
2273 Brewster St.
St. Paul
(612) 645-2004
Opera is one of the performing arts that often gets ignored by ordinary folks because, honestly, ordinary folks tend to think that opera is only for the exceptionally elite. Opera 101 was formed in 1991 to quash this mistaken belief. The company is based on the premise that opera is as dramatically interesting as any of the performing arts. The company seeks to make opera accessible to all audiences through an approach rooted in education and dramatic development. OperaNotes, for instance, is a discussion group that assists audiences in gaining a clearer understanding of the story, theme, composer and production of each performance. And as an added bonus for those of you who avoid the opera because you are not bilingual, all of Opera 101's productions are sung in English. (Now you have no excuse.) Opera 101 produces two operas a year, one in the spring and the other in the fall. Time and place varies with each production.

PLYMOUTH MUSIC SERIES OF MINNESOTA
1900 Nicollet Ave.
Minneapolis
(612) 870-0943
Founded in 1969 by internationally renowned conductor, choral scholar and performer Philip Brunelle, the Plymouth Music Series of Minnesota has gained an international reputation for its performances and recordings of rarely heard and newly commissioned music for chorus and orchestra. As a champion of the "world of music less-traveled," Brunelle has programmed many important works that are often overlooked because the composer's name doesn't happen to be Bach or Beethoven. The 115-voice chorus and 50-member orchestra recently earned a Grammy nomination, a Gramophone Award for Best Opera Recording, and an Award for Adventuresome Programming by the American Society of Composers, Authors and Publishers. Over the years, many notable guest artists have appeared with the Plymouth Music Series, including Aaron Copland, Dave Brubeck, Sir Peter Pears and Garrison Keillor. The annual series of six concerts is produced at various venues throughout the Twin Cities including Orchestra Hall, the Historic State Theatre, Plymouth Congregational Church, Ordway Music Theatre, World Theater and the Cathedral of St. Paul. Tickets for the series are $62 and $84. Individual concert tickets are available.

SCHUBERT CLUB
Landmark Center
75 W. Fifth St.
St. Paul
(612) 292-3267
The Schubert Club began in 1882 because Governor Alexander Ramsey's daughter Marion decided that it was time for some cultural enrichment —

TWIN CITIES

The Saint Paul Chamber Orchestra during a performance, with concertmaster Romuald Tecco at lower left.

not just for herself and a few of her friends, but for the whole of St. Paul as well. So she and her friends formed "The Ladies Musicale" and set to their task. Judging from its long run, the Ladies Musicale deserves a fair amount of credit for creating the Schubert Club. Even though the name of their original group has changed, its mission of preserving recital literature remains the same. Today, the Schubert Club presents more than 50 recitals each year at the Ordway Music Theatre in St. Paul. And that's not all. The Schubert Club also sponsors an International Artist Series and free music lessons and scholarship programs for students as well as a commissioning program to ensure that recital literature will continue to grow for generations to come.

SAINT PAUL CHAMBER ORCHESTRA
Landmark Center
75 W. Fifth St.
St. Paul
(612) 224-4222

By all rights, the Saint Paul Chamber Orchestra (SPCO) is the child prodigy of the Twin Cities orchestra set. Formed in 1959 under the auspices of the Saint Paul Philharmonic, the SPCO has already found its way to the top echelon of America's major orchestras and is currently the nation's only full-time professional chamber orchestra. An ensemble of 34 virtuosic musicians with a repertoire that spans four centuries (from early Baroque to contemporary), the SPCO is internationally acclaimed for its artistry and innovative programming. As of the 1992-93 season, the SPCO has a new music director, Hugh Wolff, who has been heralded by the New York Times as "the most promising young American conductor to come along in many years."

The SPCO currently presents more than 150 concerts in a 40-week season. Concert series options include Sunday afternoon samplings of best-of-season at the Ordway Music Theatre in St. Paul and Orchestra Hall in Minneapolis; Thursday morning coffee concerts featuring primarily Baroque and classical repertoire (Ordway); Weekend Masterworks series (Ordway) and annual holiday presentations of Handel's "Messiah" in both traditional and sing-along performances.

Thursday Musical
1100 Valders Ave.
Golden Valley
(612) 333-0313

Thursday Musical (originally called "The Ladies Thursday Musicale") officially began on October 18, 1892, with a mission to create opportunities for both local musicians and audiences to perform and enjoy classical music. The organization was started by a dozen women who got together every Thursday to study and perform classical music. Today, it consists of more than 500 members including musicians, music lovers and students. Musical programs are comprised of local singers, instrumentalists and small ensembles including piano duos and string quartets. The organization keeps to a regular concert season from October through April with 12 morning and three evening concerts, all performed on Thursdays (of course) in the recital hall at Temple Israel. Concerts are also presented in members' homes as well as at venues including the Minneapolis Institute of Arts and the Swedish Institute. Season tickets, which include all morning and home concerts are $40 (adults) and $35 (seniors), evening concerts are $8 and morning concerts are $5. Thursday Musical also sponsors a Young Artist Program, which provides scholarships to students 12 to 25 years old.

Twin Cities Gay Men's Chorus
Hennepin Center for the Arts
528 Hennepin Ave., Suite 701
Minneapolis
(612) 891-9130

This 80-voice chorus, founded in 1981, produces three major concerts a year at venues ranging from Orchestra Hall to area churches. The annual season includes a spring concert of classical or contemporary composers and commissioned works, a summer concert with a lighter pops theme and a traditional holiday concert. Tickets range from $10 to $20, with discounts available to students, groups and seniors. All concerts are signed for the hearing-impaired.

Twin Cities Jazz Society
Box 4489
St. Paul
(612) 633-0329

Whenever there's a jazz-related activity going on in Minneapolis and St. Paul, the Twin Cities Jazz Society (TCJS) knows about it, most likely sponsored it and, without question, promoted it. As the only non-profit organization dedicated to "promoting and preserving America's original art form," it's their job — and since its inception in 1978, the TCJS has been doing a good one. Besides sponsoring both local and national jazz artists and producing a six-concert series each year, the society also maintains a 24-hour Jazzline that provides up-to-date information on jazz-related activities in the Twin Cities (including a weekly listing of club dates and concerts for local and incoming jazz artists). An annual membership in the Twin Cities Jazz Society is $10 (students), $15 (individual) and $20 (family). Membership includes a monthly newsletter and discounts on everything from jazz recordings to concert tickets.

University of Minnesota School of Music
Ferguson Hall
2106 S. Fourth St.
Minneapolis
(612) 626-8742

Three hundred concerts a year sounds like an insane, slightly maniacal number, but when you divide that number by several groups, including a band, chamber orchestra, a number of choirs, guitar ensembles, jazz ensembles and singers ranging in specialties from opera to jazz, it seems to work out to a manageable quota. Ensembles affiliated with the School of Music are currently performing at Northrop Auditorium and Scott Hall, but beginning in October 1993, the new 1,200-seat Ted Mann Concert Hall on campus will accommodate most performances. Most of the concerts and recitals are free and open to the public.

Wolverines
14653 Sherwood Place
Burnsville
(612) 920-3621

The Wolverines have been playing jazz, big band and swing in the Twin Cities since 1973. With five saxophones, four trumpets, three trombones, piano, bass, drums and a vocalist, the group gener-

The Minnesota State Band in 1898, with founder Christian Snelling of St. Paul (front row center). The band's first concerts in 1898 were at Como Park Lakeside Pavilion in St. Paul.

ally causes a stir wherever it plays. They generally find the most circuitous way around a melody and make you believe that they took you on the shortest trip between two points. (They're that good.) If you don't make a habit of going to great parties that make a habit of hiring great bands, you might not hear the Wolverines unless you go to the Times Bar and Cafe in downtown Minneapolis (see Nightlife section). They have a habit of playing there pretty regularly.

ZEITGEIST
275 E. Fourth St., Suite 100
St. Paul
(612) 224-7522

"Zeitgeist" is a German word that means "spirit of the times." In keeping with the spirit of its name, this four-member new-music chamber ensemble performs only the music of living composers. Leading new-music composers such as John Cage, Eric Stokes and Terry Riley have all written music for Zeitgeist, as have emerging composers including Rand Steiger, Arthur Jarvinen and Jack Vees. The unique ensemble, made up of vibes, marimba, percussion, piano, synthesizer and woodwinds, plays from a repertoire of more than 140 compositions (more than half of which were written for the group). Zeitgeist presents 12 local concerts per season at venues including the Walker Art Center, Southern Theater and Ordway Music Theatre as well as performances in venues around the world.

COMMUNITY BANDS, ORCHESTRAS AND ENSEMBLES

THERE ARE MORE than 35 bands and 25 community orchestras, dozens of classical ensembles, more than a few choral groups and a handful of once-a-year musical events in the Twin Cities. Below is a partial listing.

CIVIC ORCHESTRA OF MINNEAPOLIS
(612) 544-4930
The Civic Orchestra of Minneapolis, founded in 1952, was the first community

orchestra in the Twin Cities. Comprised of more than 60 professional and amateur musicians from around the metro area, the orchestra performs five pairs of concerts per season (September through May). Locations vary and all concerts (except for the annual benefit) are free.

MINNEAPOLIS TROMBONE CHOIR
(612) 788-3516
In one powerful performance each year (the last Sunday afternoon in February at Judson Baptist Church, Minneapolis), more than 20 professional and professional-caliber trombone players unite and play everything from Bach to jazz.

MINNESOTA FREEDOM BAND
Box 300140
Minneapolis
The Minnesota Freedom Band, comprised of gay men, lesbians, and their friends, was formed in 1982 to provide a growing community of people with the right to claim a community band. This 60-member band, a charter member of L.G.B.A. (Lesbian and Gay Bands of America), not only leads the Gay Pride Parade, it performs four concerts a year — one in winter, one in spring and two outdoor summer concerts — at various venues around the Twin Cities.

MINNESOTA STATE BAND
(612) 296-6179
As Minnesota's official community band (since 1898), the Minnesota State Band tours to national and international festivals in the summer and performs in various official capacities throughout the year.

MINNESOTA TUBACHRISTMAS
(612) 788-3516
On the first Saturday in December, in malls across America, tuba players are uniting their euphoniums, baritones, sousaphones and tubas in holiday song — thanks to a national project called "TubaChristmas." Anybody who plays a member of the tuba family — from grade school to adult, beginner to professional musician — can participate in the event by showing up for a 5 p.m. rehearsal and staying to play at the 7 p.m. performance. In the past, up to 150 musicians have participated in Minnesota's version of this holiday tuba extravaganza.

MINNETONKA ORCHESTRAL ASSOCIATION
(612) 935-4615
What began with the Minnetonka Symphony Orchestra in 1973 has grown to include a cadre of six orchestras and six choirs made up of people of all ages and abilities. The Minnetonka Orchestral Association currently lists 300 performing members, ranging in age from 6 to 90. The association is comprised of 12 ensembles: the Minnetonka Symphony Orchestra, Minnetonka Chamber Orchestra, Minnetonka Civic Orchestra, Minnetonka Youth Orchestras, Minnetonka Symphony Chorus, Minnetonka Chamber Singers, Minnetonka Children's Choirs and the Minnetonka Senior Chorale.

ONE VOICE MIXED CHORUS
(612) 344-9663
This 45-voice chorus was formed in 1988 to create an opportunity for gay men, lesbians and their friends to sing together. The chorus sings music ranging in style from classical to contemporary, with an emphasis on pieces written by gay and lesbian composers.

ROSEVILLE BIG BAND
(612) 628-0088
Founded in 1966 through Roseville Parks and Recreation, this 18-piece band plays at parks and fund-raisers, including a biannual USO-style dance held at Fleming Field in Hangar 3. (The dances, open to people of all ages and organized by the Confederate Airforce, are designed to re-create the atmosphere and music of the 1940s.)

SAINT PAUL CIVIC SYMPHONY
(612) 788-3516
Founded in 1945, the Saint Paul Civic Symphony is made up of 65 Twin Cities area musicians — both amateurs and professionals. Performances, which are mostly free, include a children's concert in December (held at the Janet Wallace Fine Arts Center at Macalester College) and a five-concert series that showcases the group's classical symphonic repertoire. The symphony's annual New Year's Eve ball, "An Evening in Old Vienna," features big band dance music, Strauss waltzes, a catered buffet and a silent auction. The gala holiday event is held at St. Paul's Landmark Center. Ticket prices start at $40.

THEATERS

BLUE WINDS THEATRE
Hennepin Center for the Arts
528 Hennepin Ave.
Minneapolis
(612) 727-3880
The Blue Winds Theatre seeks to produce plays about the American experience and how that experience affects the people who live in this country. Performances are planned for the spring, summer and fall. Box office hours are Sunday through Saturday, 9 a.m. to 6 p.m. Tickets range from $8 to $12.

C.A.S.T. THEATRE
Ford Centre
420 N. Fifth St., Suite 100
Minneapolis
(612) 338-0063
According to Charters Anderson, his C.A.S.T. Theatre (short for Charters Academy Showcase Theatre) is the only privately owned professional actors' training studio theater in the Upper Midwest. (We figure he's right, considering no one else has stepped forward to confound this belief.) Because its purpose is to train and develop actors, there is no such thing as a typical season at C.A.S.T. — from Shakespeare to Sam Shepard, this theater seeks to produce shows that will give its actors-in-training the experience they need in order to, someday, drink from that elusive fountain of success. After a three-and-a-half-year training program, Anderson's students "graduate" with a certificate and a handful of connections on both coasts. The six-show season runs year-round. Tickets range from $8 to $10.

CAMPUS LIVE THEATER
309 S.E. Oak St.
Minneapolis
(612) 378-3770
Located in the old Campus movie house on the University of Minnesota's East Bank, this relatively new theater specializes in fun, commercial shows with a focus on comedies, musicals and original shows by local playwrights. Reservations can be made through Ticketmaster at 989-5151 or by calling 378-3770 for a 24-hour recording. Tickets range from $12.50 to $15.50.

CHANHASSEN DINNER THEATRES
501 W. 78th St.
Chanhassen
(612) 934-1525
It stands to reason that "dinner theater," as a concept, was conceived only seconds after the first TV dinner made its way onto the lap of a La-Z-Boy-sitting, TV-watching American. Food and entertainment — what a perfect combination! Obviously, the people at Chanhassen Dinner Theatres know this and have been working hard (since 1968!) to perfect this concept. As an indication of their success, Theatre Crafts hails Chanhassen as "the Cadillac of Dinner Theatres," and Gourmet has called it "one of the very best" dinner theaters in the country. As the nation's largest professional dinner theater complex, Chanhassen boasts four theaters under one roof and features full-scale Broadway productions as well as smaller Midwest premieres. Box office hours: Monday through Friday, 9 a.m. to 8 p.m.; Saturday, 10 a.m. to 8 p.m.; Sunday, 10 a.m. to 6 p.m. Tickets range from $26 to $43 (dinner and show) and $14 to $25 (show only).

THE CHILDREN'S THEATRE COMPANY
2400 S. Third Ave.
Minneapolis
(612) 874-0400
Reading "The Jungle Book" over and over and over again is entertaining enough, but actually seeing Shere Kahn or Baloo or Mowgli dance in front of your eyes, well, that's cause for jubilation and wonder — no matter how old you are. The internationally recognized Children's Theatre Company has been causing jubilation and wonder in the Twin Cities, across the country and in Europe since 1964 with its spirited and imaginative adaptations of classic children's literature. As the second-largest theater for young audiences in the world (second only to the Central Children's Theater in

Hurray! Minnesota

The 1989 performance of "Alice in Wonderland" at Child's Play Theatre Company.

Moscow), nothing matches the scope of its resources and the might of its imagination. The Children's Theatre Company proves, in a wonderful, awe-inspiring way, that seeing is definitely believing. Season runs September through June. Box office hours: Monday through Saturday, 9 a.m. to 5 p.m.; Sunday, 9 a.m. to 1 p.m. and one hour before show times.

CHILD'S PLAY THEATRE COMPANY
Eisenhower Community Center
1001 Highway 7
Hopkins
(612) 925-5250

This unique theater company bills itself as "a theater by and for young people," mainly because all productions feature young actors and technicians, ages 10 to 21. The company's mainstage season features commissioned adaptations of classic children's stories. Its "Left of Center" program, aimed at adolescents over 13 years old, deals with issues relating to teenagers and growing up. Season runs September through May. Box office hours: Monday through Friday, 9 a.m. to 4 p.m. and one hour before show time. Tickets: $7 (adults), $5 (children). Group rates available.

CRICKET THEATRE
1407 S. Nicollet Ave.
Minneapolis
(612) 871-2244

The Cricket Theatre, one of a handful of its kind in the country, is (to quote a promotional brochure), "a playwright-fueled theater dedicated to the development and production of remarkable and breakthrough works by living playwrights for today's audiences." By seeking out the visionary writer and providing the support necessary to realize each writer's vision, the theater has become an exciting venue for new work — comedies, musicals, dramas — all dealing with contemporary issues. It also has become a launching pad of sorts, as many of its original productions have gone on to regional theaters throughout the country. Season runs September through June. Box office hours: Monday through Friday, 9 a.m to 5 p.m. and two hours before show time. Tickets range from $14.75 to $16.75 (adults) with $3 off for students and seniors, $9.75 (preview performances), $6 (rush).

COLLABORATIVE THEATRE
Box 1312
Minnetonka
(612) 922-4209

The Collaborative Theatre was conceived in response to a severe lack of creative opportunities for women in this otherwise thriving theater community. By supporting talented women artists in all mediums of performance — actors, directors, choreographers, dramatists, playwrights, lyricists, composers and technical experts — the Collaborative Theatre seeks to provide an intelligent forum for women's thoughts and talents that doesn't focus on their physical attributes or personal lives. The Collaborative Theatre also seeks to address serious and fundamental issues in a non-threatening, artful and entertaining way.

DUDLEY RIGGS' BRAVE NEW WORKSHOP
2605 S. Hennepin Ave.
Minneapolis
(612) 332-6620

Nothing is sacred at the Brave New Workshop, nothing. Not politics or religion or recovery or death. Not even cows. This troupe, which lampoons and lambastes everything within sight and earshot, boasts "more than thirty years of promiscuous hostility." Its trademark satirical revues and improvisational comedies — with titles including "Sex, Pies and Videogames (or the Secret of My Excess)," "Your Accountability Is Overdrawn," "Censorship of Fools (or Jesse at the Helm)" and "Touch Me Again (for the First Time)" — prove the old adage that there's always something — and someone — to make fun of. Show times: Wednesday, Thursday and Sunday at 7:30; Friday and Saturday, 8 and 10:30 p.m. Box office hours: Tuesday through Saturday, 9:30 a.m. to 9:30 p.m.; Sunday, 9:30 a.m. to 1 p.m. Tickets range from $12 to $15 (adults) and $8 to $9 (students).

EYE OF THE STORM
3929 S. Blaisdell Ave.
Minneapolis
(612) 822-7141

Jupiter is a very stormy planet. It rules education and exploration and spirituality. Summoning the planet Jupiter, they say, is like asking to be shaken up and knocked about. Eye of the Storm seeks to evoke the planet Jupiter — its thunder and its power to transform — through new theater works that focus on social and political issues that are experimental in form and/or content. Tickets range from $5 to $10.

FRANK THEATRE
2612 S. Dupont Ave.
Minneapolis
(612) 377-0501

Named after a Finnish film about 12 guys — all named Frank — this theater company is committed to producing plays that stretch the skills of the artists who create the work while challenging the everyday perceptions of the audiences who view the work. Whether it is producing a contemporary work or an older script, the theater seeks to explore social, political and cultural issues. Tickets: $12 (adults) and $8 (seniors and students).

GILBERT AND SULLIVAN VERY LIGHT OPERA COMPANY
Box 172
Minneapolis
(612) 925-9159

When Dick Fishel came to the Twin Cities in 1979, he was appalled to find that there wasn't a theater company dedicated to and crazy about Gilbert and Sullivan. So he founded one. Since then, his Very Light Opera Company has produced all of the witty and winsome duo's shows just as they would have intended them — with a large chorus, a complete orchestra and an enormously talented cast of performers who are absolutely crazy about Gilbert and Sullivan. The company sticks to a very light performance schedule as well, producing one show a year with a limited run around Easter. (Performance venue: Howard Conn Fine Arts Center, Plymouth Congregational Church on 19th and Nicollet, Minneapolis.) Tickets range from $6 to $10.

GRAND GARAGE THEATRE
324 S. Main St.
Stillwater
(612) 430-8055

This intimate (i.e., cabaret-style seating for 60) theater is eminently charming

Hurray! Minnesota

Brenda Wehle as Arkadina in the Guthrie's 1992 production of "The Sea Gull" by Anton Chekhov and directed by Guthrie Artistic Director Garland Wright.

with its wooden tables, caneback chairs and Victorian-style decor. Located in the historic Grand Garage building (which houses several interesting and eclectic shops), this theater stages smaller-scale Broadway comedies, dramas and musical revues. Box office hours: 24-hour ticket number. Tickets, which include gourmet dessert and coffee, are $15.

GREAT AMERICAN HISTORY THEATRE
30 E. Tenth St.
St. Paul
(612) 292-4323

The Great American History Theatre is a professional theater organization that exists to provide its audiences with a mirror to the lives of the people of Minnesota and a window on the lives of oth-

PHOTO BY MICHAL DANIEL   **113**   TWIN CITIES

er people in other times. It seeks to accomplish this by commissioning, producing and touring plays that dramatize the history, folklore and social issues of its own region and other locales. Whatever the subject — whether a famous St. Paul madam or a union strike on the Iron Range — the theater uses historical facts to examine contemporary issues and conditions. Box office hours: Monday through Friday, 9 a.m. to 5 p.m. Tickets: $12 to $14 (adults), $10 to $12 (seniors and students).

GUTHRIE THEATER
Vineland Place
Minneapolis
(612) 377-2224
In the spring of 1963, Sir Tyrone Guthrie directed his theater's first mainstage production. This production of "Hamlet," the story about a prince who avoided, among other things, dreams, was the realization of a dream for Guthrie. His dream was to establish a new kind of American theater where serious artists could work together, a theater that would not only provide its community with quality entertainment, but the nation with a standard of excellence for theatrical performance. His dream is still alive today as the Guthrie has become a nationally acclaimed and widely respected arena for productions ranging from classical masterpieces to contemporary American and foreign works. Box office hours: Monday through Saturday, 9 a.m. to 8 p.m.; Sundays, 11 a.m. to 8 p.m. Tickets range from $6 to $38, with discounts available to seniors, students and groups for all performances.

HEY CITY STAGE
1430 S. Washington Ave.
Minneapolis
(612) 333-1300
This recently renovated stage and adjoining restaurant have been the talk of the town ever since "Forever Plaid," a highly entertaining musical revue about four 1950s crooners, opened in the fall of 1991. After the run ends (possibly in the fall of '93), owner Sandy Hey plans to stage an equally impressive production with an equally talented cast. Go

In the Heart of the Beast Puppet and Mask Theatre holds an annual May Day Parade and Festival in Powderhorn Park.

for dinner, stay for the show. Box office hours: Tuesday through Friday and Sunday, 11 a.m. to 8 p.m.; Saturday, 2 to 10:30 p.m. Tickets are $10 (partial view) or $20 to $25.

ILLUSION THEATER
Hennepin Center for the Arts
528 Hennepin Ave.
Minneapolis
(612) 338-8371
What began in 1974 as a theater primarily concerned with mime has evolved into a theater primarily concerned with being a catalyst for social change. The Illusion Theater seeks to produce new works by new playwrights, many of which are world premieres. Whether it's a comedy or a drama, whether it's about relationships or current social issues, the only criteria for each new work is that the content serves to push the envelope a little bit closer to the edge of positive social change. Season runs from February through August. Box office: 24-hour ticket line. Tickets range from $8 to $15.

IN THE HEART OF THE BEAST PUPPET AND MASK THEATRE
1500 E. Lake St.
Minneapolis
(612) 721-2535
If In the Heart of the Beast Puppet and Mask Theatre (HOBT) has a claim to fame, it has to be those giant 20-foot rod puppets. These visually spectacular creatures march (with the help of three puppeteers) in parades and often appear at festivals around the cities. (Smaller

Hurray! Minnesota

versions of the rod puppets are used in HOBT's stage productions.) One of very few professional puppet theaters in the United States, HOBT uses the ancient tradition of puppet and mask theater to explore the events and values of contemporary society. Season runs September through May. Box office hours: Monday through Friday, 9 a.m. to 5 p.m. Tickets: $9 (adults), $5 (children).

INITIALSTAGE THEATRE COLLECTIVE
Minneapolis Theatre Garage
711 W. Franklin Ave.
Minneapolis
(612) 522-8996
Don't look for a toe-tapping, smile-inducing theater experience here. InitialStage Theatre Collective has become known for its bold treatment of controversial issues. The theater's stated mission is "to produce gritty pieces that are not only challenging to the artists involved, but to audiences as well." Judging from previous productions, this theater's unstated mission is, basically, to turn over a rock and see what's underneath it. While this method usually does not set toes to tapping, it almost always gets the brain in gear. Tickets are $6 (seniors, students and artists), $10 (adults).

JUNGLE THEATER
709 W. Lake St.
Minneapolis
(612) 822-7063
The Jungle Theater produces contemporary and classic theater works with very high production values (meaning, exactly, that staging is elaborate and complete, not sparse and experimental). The theater does do a weekly foray into the experimental realm, however, with a music/dance/theater variety show called "Balls," which runs every Saturday at midnight. (Tickets are $5.) The theater's season of six productions runs year-round. Box office hours: Monday and Tuesday, 10 a.m. to 5:30 p.m.; Wednesday through Sunday, 10 a.m. to 9 p.m. Tickets range from $10 to $16.

THE LIMELIGHT
1414 W. 28th St.
Minneapolis
(612) 871-1903
Drawing from a gaggle of 35 very funny performers, the Limelight presents ComedySportz, an improvisational comedy game show in which two teams of four comedians compete against each other for recognition and applause. While the show follows a regular format, all specific suggestions come from you and all your new friends in the audience. It's legitimate improvisational theater — no tricks, no mirrors, no wires. The show runs Thursday through Sunday at 8 p.m. Tickets: $7 (adults), $5 (students). The Limelight also features late-night productions of two-act musicals and one-act plays (usually with some sort of comedic interest). Call for information.

LORING PLAYHOUSE THEATRE COMPANY
1633 S. Hennepin Ave.
Minneapolis
(612) 332-1617
Count on the Loring Playhouse to produce theater that is intriguing, eclectic and inherently avant-garde. After all, it's not merely associated with, it's owned and operated by the same guy who runs the intriguing, eclectic and inherently avant-garde Loring Bar and Cafe. While the adjoining bar and cafe casts its bohemian shadow over the playhouse, the resident company resists categorization, stating that it "exists to provide a challenging, nurturing environment dedicated to the development of creative artists and their works through the presentation of extraordinary performing arts experiences." Tickets range from $10 to $12.50. Dinner theater packages are available.

LYRIC THEATRE
Hennepin Center for the Arts
528 Hennepin Ave.
Minneapolis
(612) 824-4935
The Lyric Theatre produces plays that have a lyrical quality. Some are plays with music, some are musicals and others possess a lyricism through language. Many of the plays produced by the Lyric Theatre are original works by local and regional playwrights and musicians. While the subject matter of these plays is broad, all themes are life-affirming and often appeal to a mature audience. For tickets or more information, call the Connection at 922-9000. Tickets range from $8 to $15.

MIXED BLOOD THEATRE
1501 S. Fourth St.
Minneapolis
(612) 338-6131
This humble theater claims to be the "greatest theater in the history of the galaxy — better than the Guthrie, closer than Chanhassen, funnier than Dudley Riggs and cheaper than McDonalds." (While we know of at least three institutions that would beg to differ with this assessment, we commend Mixed Blood for its moxie and would like to point out that all of the theaters in question are deserving of high praise.) All of Mixed Blood's productions, which range from dramas to musical revues and comedies, seek to be provocative, surprising, inexpensive and color-blind. Most of its productions are plays that are new to the area or new to the world. Box office hours: Tuesday through Sunday, noon to 8 p.m. Tickets range from $7.50 to $15.

THE MINNESOTA CENTENNIAL SHOWBOAT
on East River Road between the Washington and Franklin Avenue bridges
(612) 625-4001
In the 1800s, when riverboats were the primary means of transportation, they were also the means by which touring theater companies came to town. The University of Minnesota's Theater Department revives this tradition each summer by producing melodramas, operettas and comedies on the Centennial Showboat. While it is moored on the banks of the Mighty Mississipp', the boat never actually leaves port during a show — so put your Dramamine aside and check out a fine tradition. Box office hours: Monday through Friday, 10 a.m. to 4 p.m. Tickets range from $6 to $10.

MYSTERY CAFE
(612) 544-7404
Nicklow's
36th Ave. N. and Highway 100
Golden Valley
Bloomington Park Tavern
5221 Viking Dr.
Bloomington
Jessica Fletcher. Ben Matlock. David and Maddie. What's all in an episode's work for them will be all in a four-course meal for you at the Mystery Cafe, where you will witness a five-act comedy murder mystery in the comfortable presence of good food. Armed with a packet of clues and a pile of play money (for the purpose of bribing actors for additional clues), you will also be given an opportunity to solve the mystery. Prizes are given for the best deductions and special recognition awards for the really lame ones (meaning that even if you don't come anywhere near solving the crime correctly, you might still win something). The Mystery Cafe operates out of Nicklow's and Bloomington Park Tavern every Friday and Saturday at 7 p.m. Tickets range from $30 to $32.

NEW CLASSIC THEATRE
1822 Laurel Ave.
Minneapolis
(612) 377-4407
While the New Classic Theatre only produces one or two plays a year (usually new works and area premieres of off-Broadway hits), they're always worth waiting for, and they're always plays with good roles for actors. This is thanks entirely to the theater's artistic director, Peter Moore. Moore, a local actor, has made a career off his yuppie good looks. (One of the reasons he started the New Classic Theatre, he says, is because he wanted to play something other than a yuppie and nobody would give him the chance.) The other reason is to produce fine theater with challenging roles for local actors. Tickets are $9 (students and seniors) and $10 (adults).

NEW MUSIC-THEATER ENSEMBLE
620 N. First St.
Minneapolis
(612) 333-2700
The New Music-Theater Ensemble, a spin-off of the Minnesota Opera Company, is committed to the development, workshop and production of new operas and other forms of American music theater. Tickets range from $8 to $15.

NORTHERN SIGN THEATRE
Hennepin Center for the Arts
528 Hennepin Ave.
Minneapolis
(612) 338-7876
(612) 338-7549 (TDD)
This unique theater seeks to encourage communication between deaf and hearing people through the performing arts by

presenting all productions in American sign language and spoken English. Tickets range from $8 to $12, with discounts available for groups of 10 or more.

OLD LOG THEATRE
Box 250
Excelsior
(612) 474-5951
Nick Nolte cut his teeth at the Old Log Theatre. So did Loni Anderson and Julia Duffy (not to mention scores of other talented performers). The Old Log Theatre, which has built its reputation on presenting the best in British farce and Broadway comedy, boasts a theater that seats 655 and dining rooms that will accommodate 400 for dinner prior to each performance. It is the oldest professional theater in the Upper Midwest and the longest continuously running theater in the country. Tickets range from $12.50 to $14.50.

PARK SQUARE THEATRE COMPANY
Jemne Building
305 St. Peter St.
St. Paul
(612) 291-7005
The Park Square Theatre Company, located in the same building that houses the Minnesota Museum of Art, is in the heart of St. Paul's art district. Billed as a "classic theatre for a classic city," Park Square stages vital, accessible and entertaining productions focused on the classic repertory for diverse audiences.

PENUMBRA THEATRE
Martin Luther King Center
270 N. Kent St.
St. Paul
(612) 224-3180
Ever hear of a guy named August Wilson? (If you haven't, brush up on your Pulitzer Prize-winning playwrights.) Wilson, the author of "Fences," "Ma Rainey's Black Bottom" and "The Piano Lesson" (among others), has been closely associated with the Penumbra Theatre since it premiered his first full-length play, "Black Bart and the Sacred Hills." That was in 1982. Since then, Wilson has gone on to win two Pulitzer Prizes. And Penumbra, Minnesota's only professional black theater company, has become a theater of national stature. Its stated goal is to produce professional productions that are artistically excellent, thought-provoking, relevant, entertaining and presented from an African American perspective. Box office hours: Monday through Friday, 10 a.m. to 5 p.m. Tickets range from $8 to $16.

PLYMOUTH PLAYHOUSE
2705 Annapolis Lane
Plymouth
(612) 553-1600
The Plymouth Playhouse is a professional theater that specializes in very entertaining Broadway and off-Broadway musical comedies for people of all ages. Box office hours vary; call for recording. Tickets range from $13 to $15, with Thursday and Sunday discounts for students and seniors.

RAINBO CHILDREN'S THEATRE COMPANY
688 Selby Ave.
St. Paul
(612) 228-0854
The Rainbo Children's Theatre Company produces original, multicultural productions with a mission to combat racism and stereotypes through the performing arts. Box office hours: Monday through Friday, 1 to 5 p.m., or one hour before performances. Tickets: $7 (adults), $5 (children).

RED EYE COLLABORATION
15 W. 14th St.
Minneapolis
(612) 870-0309
If you're looking for a standard theater experience — you know, one with a plot and a pretty predictable outcome — don't go to Red Eye Collaboration. If you're interested in seeing a totally innovative approach to contemporary ideas, however, you will not be disappointed by what you find at this "experimental theater that seeks to perform original works in provocative ways." Box office hours: 24-hour ticket number. Tickets range from $6 to $12.50.

THE REFRESHMENT COMMITTEE
Seventh Place Theatre
28 W. Seventh Place
St. Paul
(612) 227-0775
A professional theater company committed to the creation and development of quality theatrical works — dramas, comedies, musical revues, children's shows —

that are based upon or reveal Biblical values and truth. Box office: Monday through Friday, 9 a.m. to 5 p.m. Ticket ranges $8 to $12. Group rates available.

SEQUOIA THEATRE
3120 S. Hennepin Ave., Suite 404
Minneapolis
(612) 823-3719
The Sequoia Theatre doesn't have a stated mission. It doesn't have a fancy theater space or a clever story about how it came to be. It does, however, have all the vowels of the alphabet in its name. And it is named after a mighty redwood tree that usually grows up to 300 feet tall — reasons enough to check out this company that concentrates on producing quality theater ranging from contemporary works to American classics. Tickets range from $8 to $15.

SOUTHERN THEATER
1420 S. Washington Ave.
Minneapolis
(612) 340-1725.
Built in 1909 to house a traditional Swedish theater (there is an identical structure still standing in Stockholm), the building at 1420 S. Washington still shows off its original proscenium arch. Since the Swedish theater closed, the space has been a trucking garage, an antique store and a restaurant, among other things. Now, of course, it is home to the Southern Theater, an exploratory theater that runs the gamut of multidisciplinary endeavors including music, theater, dance and multimedia. Being that all productions are either original or unusually executed, anything can happen at the Southern Theater — except, maybe, a classic adaptation of "Pirates of Penzance." Tickets range from $8 to $12, with special discounts for students, seniors and low-income persons.

STEPPINGSTONE THEATRE FOR YOUTH DEVELOPMENT
Landmark Center
75 W. Fifth St.
St. Paul
(612) 225-9265
The SteppingStone Theatre's mission is to use educational theater programs and stage productions to build self-esteem and confidence in children and teenagers ranging from 3 to 18 years old. All of the theater's productions are original works by local playwrights who are committed to celebrating diversity in culture and background. The four-show season runs November through July. Tickets are $5. Group discounts are available.

STEVIE RAY'S COMEDY THEATRE AND CABARET
1819 Nicollet Ave.
Minneapolis
(612) 872-0305
Stevie Ray's stage is committed to developing local talent and to stretching the boundaries of comedic performance in the Twin Cities (possibly even into Canada). It is not yet well-known, but many who have stood on Stevie Ray's stage have gone on to be quite funny in other places as well. The theater features a variety of entertainment, including performances by improvisational troupes and stand-up comedians, sketch revues, comedy variety shows and one-person productions. Open seven nights a week. Tickets range from $5 to $10.

THE THEATRE EXCHANGE
Hennepin Center for the Arts
528 S. Hennepin Ave., Suite 309
Minneapolis
(612) 333-5164
The Theatre Exchange's name refers to artistic director Julia Carey's mission to produce plays from British playwrights. Carey is originally from England and travels there frequently to look for new works to produce in the Twin Cities. Most of the plays she chooses are modern pieces that wouldn't normally have an American forum. The season typically runs from November through May.

THEATRE 65
Mail Number 4205
University of St. Thomas
2115 Summit Ave.
St. Paul
(612) 222-2329
In 1985, Margery D'Aquila, a talented and experienced actress, was 68 years old and cou!dn't get any work. All of the parts she read for — parts that called for a woman her age — were going to younger women who, through the transforming power of makeup, were made to look older. Besides that, D'Aquila realized that all the parts written for peo-

ple her age were mostly just ancillary characters created to move the story along. Most playwrights, in essence, were writing about whether the boy gets the girl — not whether the grandfather gets the grandmother. In a effort to utilize the creative talents of "chronologically advantaged" performers, D'Aquila founded Theatre 65. Since then, the company of actors (all over 50 years old) has been successfully performing musical comedies and dramas, proving by example that ageism is another harmful, separatist attitude in our society. The company performs for the general public and is also available for private bookings. Tickets range from $5 to $15.

THEATRE DE LA JEUNE LUNE
North First Avenue at North First Street
Minneapolis
(612) 333-6200
In a nutshell (and according to Mike Steele, theater critic at the Minneapolis Star Tribune): "Jeune Lune combines the classic French tradition — commedia, masks, circus, mime, Molière above all — with an American pop sensibility that takes in everything from silent films to musical comedy." However it gets there, Theatre de la Jeune Lune is definitely unique. As an example, the company's many successful productions include "Yang Zen Froggs in Moon Over a Hong Kong Sweat Shop," an original work filled with cabaret-style songs and dance about the offbeat characters who frequent a seedy bistro. Other shows, while they may sound familiar ("Romeo and Juliet," "Cyrano," "A Midsummer Night's Dream"), receive an equally unique treatment. Box office hours: Monday through Saturday, 10 a.m. to 5 p.m.; performance Sundays, noon to 5 p.m. Tickets range from $8 to $17.

THEATRE IN THE ROUND PLAYERS
245 Cedar Ave.
Minneapolis
(612) 333-3010
Founded in 1952, Theatre in the Round isn't merely the oldest community theater in the Twin Cities, it is generally considered to be one of the best community theaters in the country. Each season of 10 plays is purposely eclectic, including classics, area premieres and Broadway favorites. Box office hours: Tuesdays through Fridays, 1 to 5 p.m. At all other times, answering machine. Tickets are $5 (student rush, Sundays only) to $9.50 (adult), with discounts for students, seniors and groups.

TROUPE AMERICA
Plymouth Playhouse
2705 Anapolis Lane
Plymouth
(612) 553-1600
Venetian Playhouse
2814 Rice St.
St. Paul
(612) 484-1108
If you've ever heard of the Lovely Liebowitz Sisters, you're familiar with Troupe America. If you've never heard of the Lovely Liebowitz Sisters, you're just not familiar with big fun. Troupe America specializes in producing and promoting high-quality Broadway and off-Broadway comedies and musicals. The troupe performs regularly at the Plymouth Playhouse in Plymouth and the Venetian Playhouse in St. Paul. Tickets range from $11 to $18. Group rates are available.

UNICORN THEATRE
20 N. Fourth St.
Minneapolis
(612) 375-0854
The Unicorn Theatre's mission is to produce entertaining shows that are not only of particular interest to the gay community, but shows that aim toward a wider audience as well (translation: straight people are welcome, too). The theater runs year-round with six mainstage productions (ranging from well-known shows to the rather obscure) and five studio productions that are often new or experimental works ranging from dramas to musicals. Tickets are $10.

UNIVERSITY THEATRE
120 Rarig Center
330 S. 21st Ave.
University of Minnesota
Minneapolis
(612) 625-4001
The University Theatre presents a full slate of seven mainstage productions as well as student-produced workshops, which include actors and artists in training. Season runs late October through June. Tickets range from $7 to $9.

Dance/Theater

BALLET ARTS MINNESOTA
Hennepin Center for the Arts
528 Hennepin Ave., Suite 305
Minneapolis
(612) 340-1071
Ballet Arts Minnesota is a dance instruction studio and a performance company for both children and adults. Programs are designed for both vocational and avocational dancers with a mission "to awaken and nurture a lifelong love of the art of dance while providing excellent instruction and a broad curriculum that will thoroughly prepare those students who aspire to a career in dance." Performances, primarily in May and December, range from classical to contemporary pieces. In December each year, students from Ballet Arts along with 60 children from the Minneapolis Park and Rec program perform the "City Children's Nutcracker." Tickets range from $6 to $10.

BALLET OF THE DOLLS
1620 Harmon Place
Minneapolis
(612) 333-2792
Ballet of the Dolls is a dance theater company that performs a combination of commissioned works and adaptations of existing works ranging from the traditional to the experimental. One of two resident performing companies at the Loring Playhouse, Ballet of the Dolls is committed to contemporary ballet and to creating works that are as much about theater as they are about dance. Tickets range from $10 to $15.

ETHNIC DANCE THEATRE
1940 Hennepin Ave.
Minneapolis
(612) 872-0024
The Ethnic Dance Theatre is a performing arts company dedicated to presenting the dynamic traditions of ethnic music and dance through performance and other activities. The company of 45 artists includes singers, dancers and musicians in authentic costumes (many of which are imported) performing a full range of folk dances from Austria, Tunisia, China, Bulgaria and Hungary, among others. Tickets range from $7 to $15.

GEORGIA STEPHENS CONTEMPORARY DANCE THEATER
134 S. Prospect Ave.
Minneapolis
(612) 822-8283
Accomplished, humorous, literate, witty, cheeky, playful. These are words that seem to come up regularly in newspaper reviews of Georgia Stephens' work. Stephens, an accomplished dancer/choreographer, has become known for her use of humor, language and everyday movement in her dances. Her work is very literate. And witty. (Not to mention cheeky and playful.) Stephens' contemporary dance theater company, formed in 1989, is dedicated to creating performances that combine dance, words and music to challenge thoughts, emotions and preconceived perceptions of the world. Call for a schedule of upcoming performances.

Hurray! Minnesota

Ballet of the Dolls founder Myron Johnson (left) and company in rehearsal at their Loring Park studio.

JAWAAHIR DANCE COMPANY
1912 Norfolk Ave.
St. Paul
(612) 698-4784

The Jawaahir ("jewel" in Arabic) Dance Company performs artistic pieces based on traditional and contemporary Middle Eastern music and dance styles, including those from Arabia, Egypt, Morocco and Tunisia. The company, which was formed in 1990, is dedicated to presenting Middle Eastern dance as a living art form, bringing its rich folklore heritage to the theater stage. Tickets range from $5 to $12.

LOYCE HOULTON'S MINNESOTA DANCE THEATRE AND SCHOOL
Hennepin Center for the Arts
528 Hennepin Ave., Studio 5B
Minneapolis
(612) 338-0627

Loyce Houlton's Minnesota Dance Theatre and School has been dedicated to preparing students for professional careers in classical ballet, contemporary and modern dance since 1961. Houlton's brand of dance — sometimes referred to as "fusion ballet" — combines classically trained ballet dancers and neo-classic dance styles for an end result that is both earthy and enticing. The company produces several shows a year, including a spring show that combines the talents of student dancers and choreographers along with those of former students who are now professionals and a student show in the summer. Every December, the company teams up with the Minnesota Orchestra to perform Loyce Houlton's "Nutcracker Fantasy," the longest-running, largest-selling arts event in Minnesota.

MINNESOTA DANCE ALLIANCE
Hennepin Center for the Arts
528 Hennepin Ave., Studio 6A
Minneapolis
(612) 340-1156

The Minnesota Dance Alliance is a professional service network for dance artists in the state of Minnesota whose activities include the presentation of dance performances, financial support for members, general information distribution and referrals to dance classes and concerts. The alliance presents two concert series each year. "Short Order," which runs in the fall, is an opportunity for choreographers and other emerging artists to show new work on a shared program. "Extended Play" is a spring series that highlights new directions in the world of established and versatile dance makers by presenting the work of mature artists from the community as well as guest artists from around the country. "Bonus Track," which runs throughout the year on one Saturday a month, is a late-night showcase extravaganza including experimental and rough-cut work from a wide range of disciplines including dance, music, theater, mime, comedy, puppetry and other works emerging out of this creatively prolific community. Ticket prices are $10, with discounts for Minnesota Dance Alliance members, seniors and students.

Nancy Hauser Dance Company
1940 S. Hennepin Ave.
Minneapolis
(612) 871-9077
Founded in 1961 by the late Nancy Hauser, this company, which includes seven dancers and several apprentices, performs a repertoire of visually stunning dances as well as new works choreographed by Artistic Director Heidi Jasmin, company members and guest artists. Most works feature a modern dance style that is very accessible to people who haven't seen dance before. It's not experimental or pretentious or particularly avant-garde. But it *is* thought-provoking and thoroughly entertaining. Performances generally run in February, April, May and October. Tickets are $8.

New Dance Performance Laboratory
Hennepin Center for the Arts
528 Hennepin Ave., Suite 205
Minneapolis
(612) 341-3050
New Dance Performance Laboratory is a professional post-modern dance theater company that performs works-in-process by local and nationally prominent choreographers. This is the only dance company in the country that gives audiences an opportunity to experience exactly what goes into creating dance works by attending rehearsals (all the company's rehearsals are free and open to the public) and by actually viewing a work in process. The season runs from September through April. Work-in-process performances are $5 (adults) and $4 (students and seniors).

Pepo Alfajiri Dance and Drum Theatre
711 N. Elwood Ave.
Minneapolis
(612) 374-4244
When Senegal native Busara Whittaker moved from Atlanta to Minneapolis in the 1980s, she was disappointed to find that no one in the Twin Cities was teaching the art of African dance. Rather than mourn this cultural loss, she started Pepo Alfajiri Dance and Drum Theatre. Since 1982, the company has been performing and providing instruction in West African and Congolese dance as well as sponsoring performances and workshops from African artists including musicians, costumers, historians, dancers and drum makers.

Zenon Dance Company and School, Inc.
Hennepin Center for the Arts
528 Hennepin Ave., Suite 400
Minneapolis
(612) 338-1101
Zenon Dance is a repertory company that aims to present the commissioned works of nationally recognized modern and jazz dance choreographers. The school also offers progressive training in ballet, modern and jazz dance styles for both avocational students and professional dancers.

Zorongo Flamenco Dance Theatre
235 S.E. Bedford St.
Minneapolis
(612) 379-7361
This unique dance theater company exists to preserve the cultural heritage of Spain by promoting the art of flamenco dance, music and song.

VENUES

GUTHRIE THEATER
Vineland Place
Minneapolis
(612) 377-2224

The Guthrie is known nationally as a regional theater that produces artistically excellent work ranging from Greek tragedies and Shakespearean classics to contemporary American and foreign works. Owing largely to its rather intimate setting — 1,473 seats gathered around a thrust stage — the Guthrie is also known locally as one of the best concert venues in the Twin Cities. When it's not producing theater, the Guthrie stage is host to national acts including comedians and solo artists as well as musical groups ranging from rock-and-roll legends and R&B greats to an eclectic collection of up-and-comers.

Guthrie Theater Seating Chart

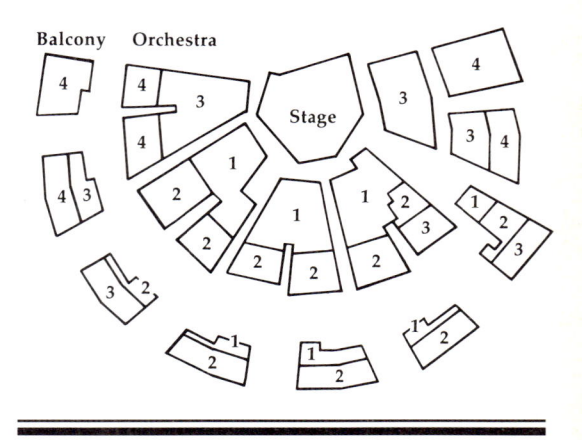

HENNEPIN CENTER FOR THE ARTS
528 Hennepin Ave.
Minneapolis
(612) 332-4478

The majestic eight-story Ohio light-sandstone building on the corner of Hennepin Avenue and Sixth Street began life more than a century ago as the Masonic Temple. At its grand opening on April 8, 1890, it was heralded as one of the finest buildings in the country, both for its architecture and its interior spaces.

The Greater Minneapolis Arts Center renovated and refurbished the building to its original splendor, and it began life anew as the Hennepin Center for the Arts in 1979. It houses restaurants, theater groups, dance companies and schools, musical groups, a publisher and various other arts organizations — some 16 in all — and rents space to other arts organizations for performances and rehearsals. The center has one of the finest dance facilities in the country and an excellent theater facility on the eighth floor, the **Bower Hawthorne Theater**. (See Theater, Music, Dance sections.)

HISTORIC ORPHEUM THEATRE
910 Hennepin Ave.
Minneapolis
(612) 339-3909

The opening program on October 16, 1921, featured all four Marx Brothers. In the 1930s, the "talkies" replaced vaudeville at the Orpheum and beginning in 1937, the primary attraction was live orchestra. The Orpheum was purchased in 1959 by Ted Mann, who brought a dozen Broadway touring productions to Minneapolis each year until 1965, when the theater was purchased by Bob Dylan (yes, *the* Bob Dylan) and his lesser-known brother. Broadway shows continued to run at the theater until 1987, although attendance and quality severely dropped.

The Orpheum was acquired from Dylan and his brother in July 1988 by the Minneapolis Community Development Agency. The theater is currently going through a major renovation — a $10.5 million project that includes building a new backstage area and a two-story addition to house dressing rooms and production offices, a new marquee, more

IN THIS HISTORIC BUILDING...

the newest, most innovative theater, music and dance performances in the Twin Cities.

For information on current performances call
332-4478

The Little Theater

illusion theater

BALLET ARTS MINNESOTA

MINNESOTA DANCE ALLIANCE

NORTHERN·SIGN·THEATRE

Loyce Houlton MINNESOTA DANCE THEATRE AND SCHOOL, INC.

NEW dance

TROUPE AMERICA INC.
Theatrical Productions, Road Shows, Convention Entertainment

The Bower Hawthorne Theater

HENNEPIN CENTER
for the arts
528 Hennepin Avenue
Minneapolis, Minnesota

Historic Orpheum Theatre Seating Chart

Main Floor

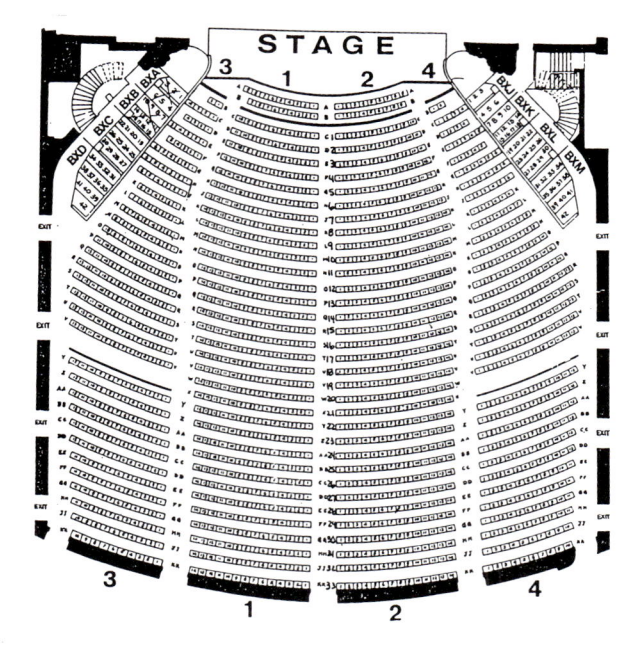

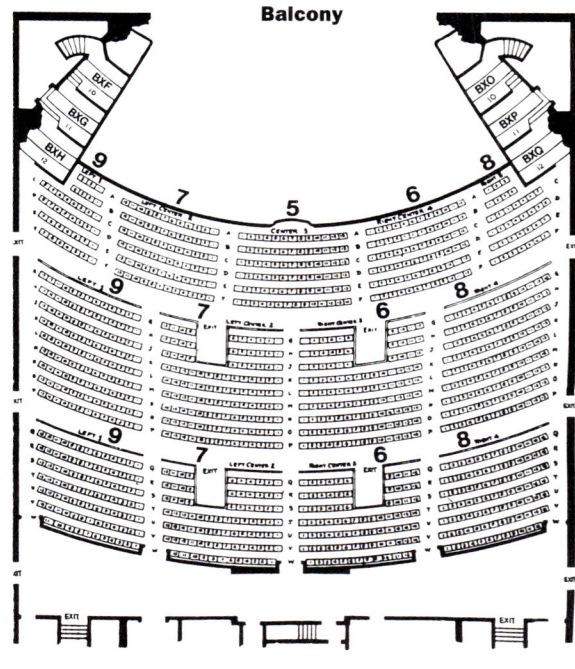

Balcony

restrooms and an overall interior facelift. Most of these changes will be made between January and November 1993 (when the theater will be closed for the renovation). When the renovation is complete, the Orpheum will be the only theater in Minneapolis with the facilities to host large touring Broadway productions. Even though the theater is somewhat worn and dilapidated now, however, there is still an appealing funkiness to the Orpheum. All in all, it's a pretty cool place to see a show.

HISTORIC STATE THEATRE
805 Hennepin Ave.
Minneapolis
(612) 339-7007

The State Theatre's ornate marquee, designed in 1991 to incorporate the style of the previous marquee (designed in 1920), is not only a jewel on Hennepin Avenue, it's physical evidence that Minneapolis' main drag is well on its way to aesthetic restoration. The Historic State Theatre first opened as a vaudeville house in 1921 and was generally considered to be one of the nation's most luxurious entertainment houses in its time. The Italian Renaissance-style theater seats about 2,200 and features painted wall murals, lots of gold leaf, crystal chandeliers, faux marble decor, molded plaster cherubs, clusters of crystal grapes, gargoyles and plaster figures representing Music, Drama and the Muse of Cinema. The theater was restored

Historic State Theatre Seating Chart

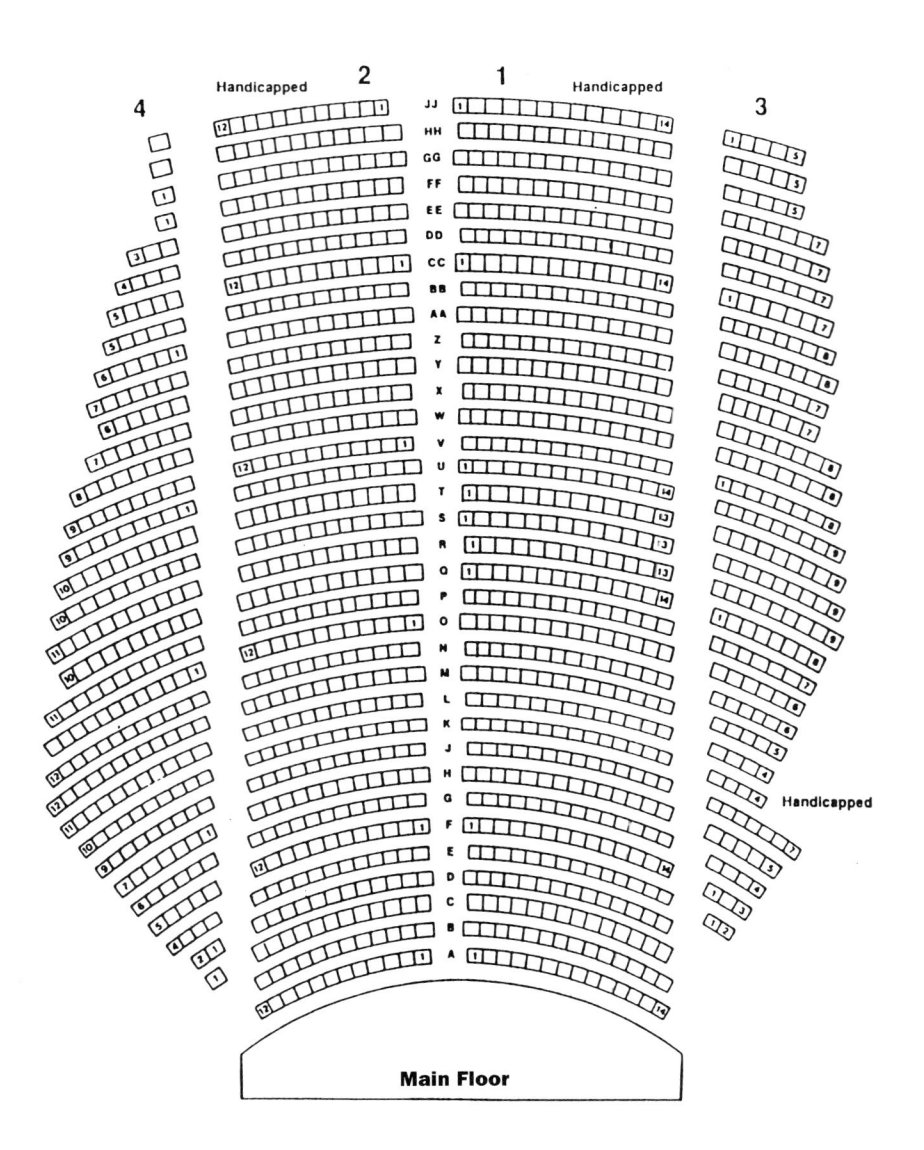

Main Floor

The flamboyant State Theatre marquee, restored to its full glory, lights up Hennepin Avenue and bids a dazzling welcome to audiences seeking a really big show.

Hurray! Minnesota

Upper and Middle Balcony

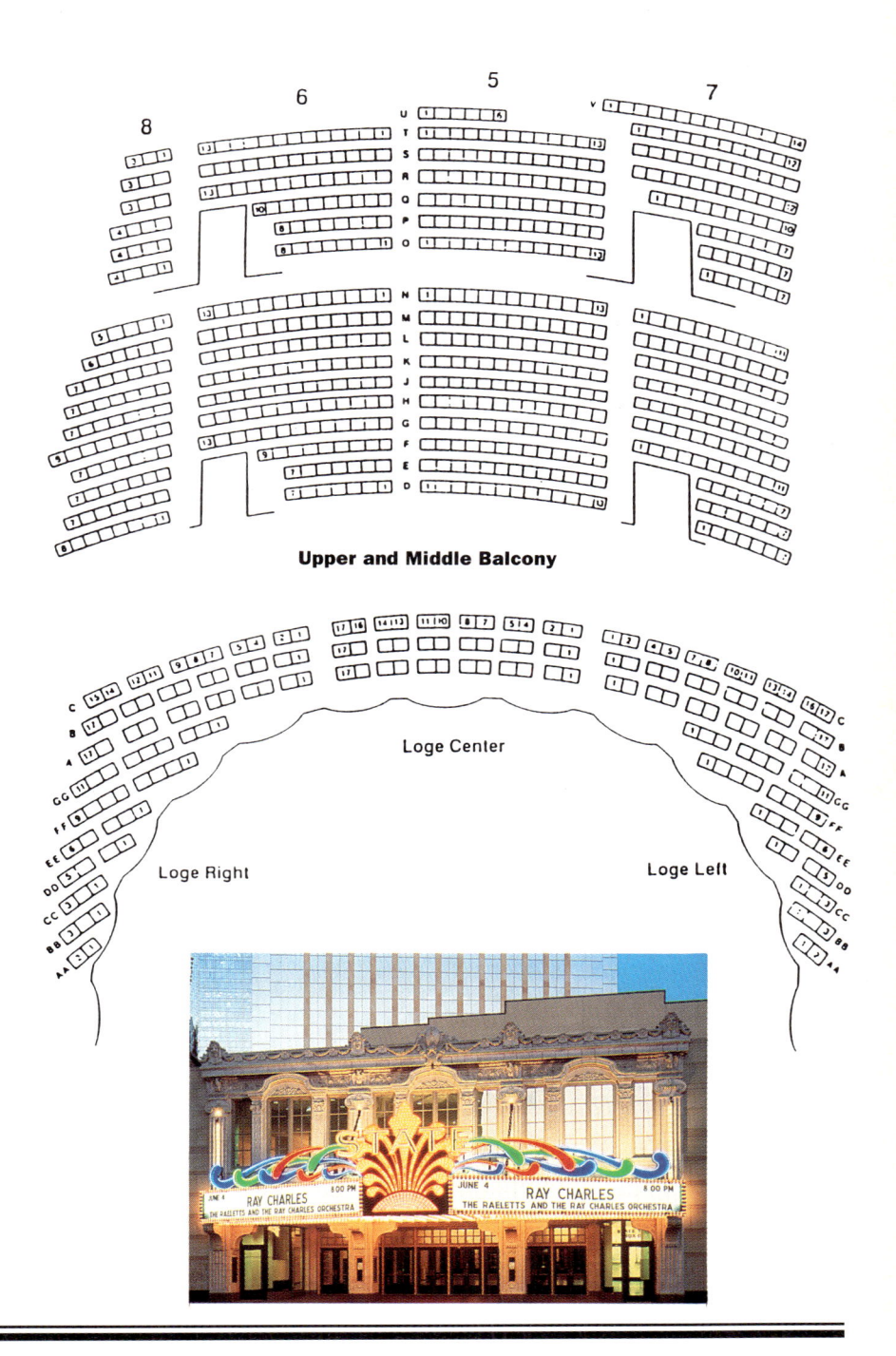

Loge Center

Loge Right   Loge Left

TWIN CITIES

Hubert H. Humphrey Metrodome

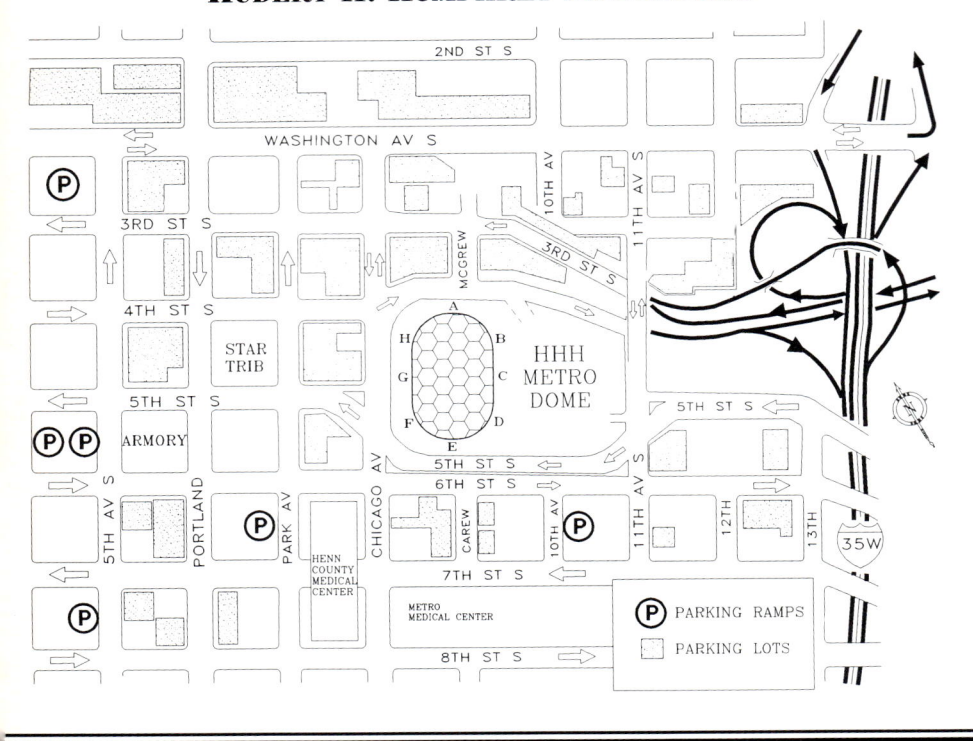

to its original opulence in 1991 and rents its stage to showcase classical music productions, Broadway plays, operas, performances from a variety of artists and, occasionally, a film classic as well.

Hubert H. Humphrey Metrodome
900 S. Fifth St.
Minneapolis
(612) 332-0386

Many Minnesotans were not pleased with the proposal to tear down the beloved Metropolitan Stadium (an outdoor arena located on the outskirts of town) and build a domed structure inside the city limits. Watching baseball and football inside a domed structure just didn't seem right to hearty sports fans who had become used to the outdoor experience. It still doesn't seem right to some — but on wintry days, you won't hear a lot of people complaining. Especially not the athletes — specifically the Minnesota Vikings — who initiated the construction of the Dome to begin with.

As the story goes, when the Vikings (football team) came to Minnesota in 1961, they signed on for 15 years. When their lease expired in 1976, they stated that they needed a covered stadium or maybe, just maybe, they'd mosey on along to greener turf. In Phoenix, perhaps. Or St. Petersburg. The next year, a commission was formed to study the feasibility of a new stadium. Ground was broken for the HHH Metrodome in 1979. The roof was inflated on October 2, 1991. And the Twins played their first game under the 290-ton woven fiberglass dome on April 6, 1982. The inside temperature was 70 degrees (which was, incidently, more than 40 degrees warmer than the temperature outside). Slowly but surely Minnesotans have come to love and accept the Metrodome — thanks, in large part, to all the attention

H.H.H. Metrodome Seating Chart

Minnesota Vikings

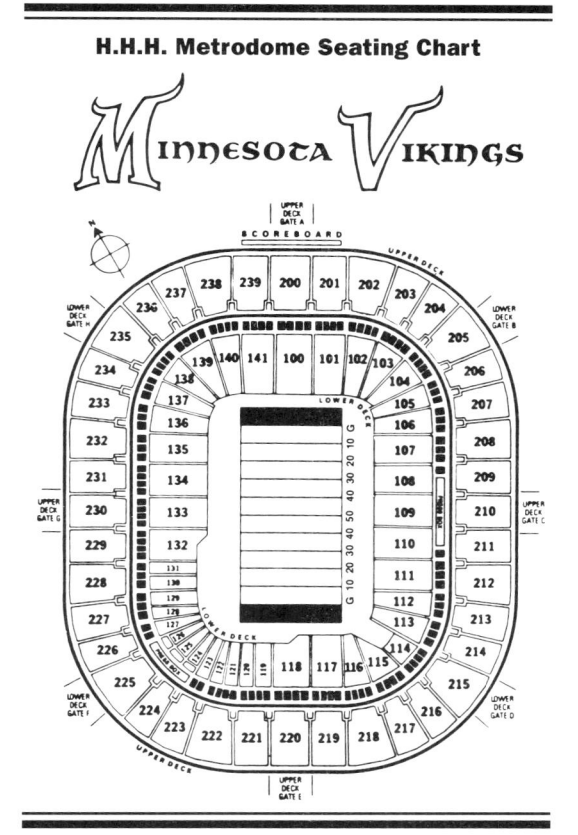

the Dome has received in recent years while playing host to the Superbowl, two World Series, the NCAA Final Four and the opening ceremonies for both the International Special Olympics and the USA Cup. Even die-hard Metropolitan Stadium fans know that it couldn't have competed with the Metrodome. Not even on a good day.

JEROME HILL THEATER
180 E. Fifth St.
St. Paul
(612) 228-9456

The building that houses the Jerome Hill Theater was built by railroad baron James J. Hill in 1916. At that time, it was called the Burlington Northern Center and had the distinction of being the largest office building in the northern United States. In the late 1960s, Burlington Northern added the Jerome Hill Theater as a conference center for the purpose of showing training and travel films. With sloped seating, cushioned chairs with plenty of personal space and wall-to-wall carpet, the 260-seat theater was not only a comfortable meeting place, but an acoustically superior viewing room as well. In 1985, the Burlington Northern Center changed its name to First Trust Center and sold the Jerome Hill Theater to Film in the Cities, an arts organization that renovated the theater and used it to show a superior assortment of foreign and art films. Film in the Cities' lease expired at the end of 1992, at which time it moved to another facility and the Jerome Hill Theater rented its space to business and community groups.

MINNEAPOLIS CONVENTION CENTER
Grant Street and Marquette Avenue
Minneapolis
(612) 335-6000

The Minneapolis City Council approved the proposal for the new Minneapolis Convention Center in 1988 so that Minneapolis would be able to respectably vie for major worldwide convention business. And why not? With respectable golf courses within driving distance, successful sports teams (not to mention a two-to-one ratio of sports fans to sports bars), four distinctive, exciting seasons and a world-class shopping mall that nearly dwarfs Atlantic City, Minnesota already had all the conventional accoutrements (OK, except year-round 70-degree temperatures) save one — a viable meeting place. Thus, the building of the Minneapolis Convention Center. The architectural minds behind this glorious building obviously knew exactly what they were doing.

From the inviting rose-brick-and-green color scheme to the exhibit halls with their 90-foot domes — everything about the building says, "Come, put on

Minneapolis Convention Center

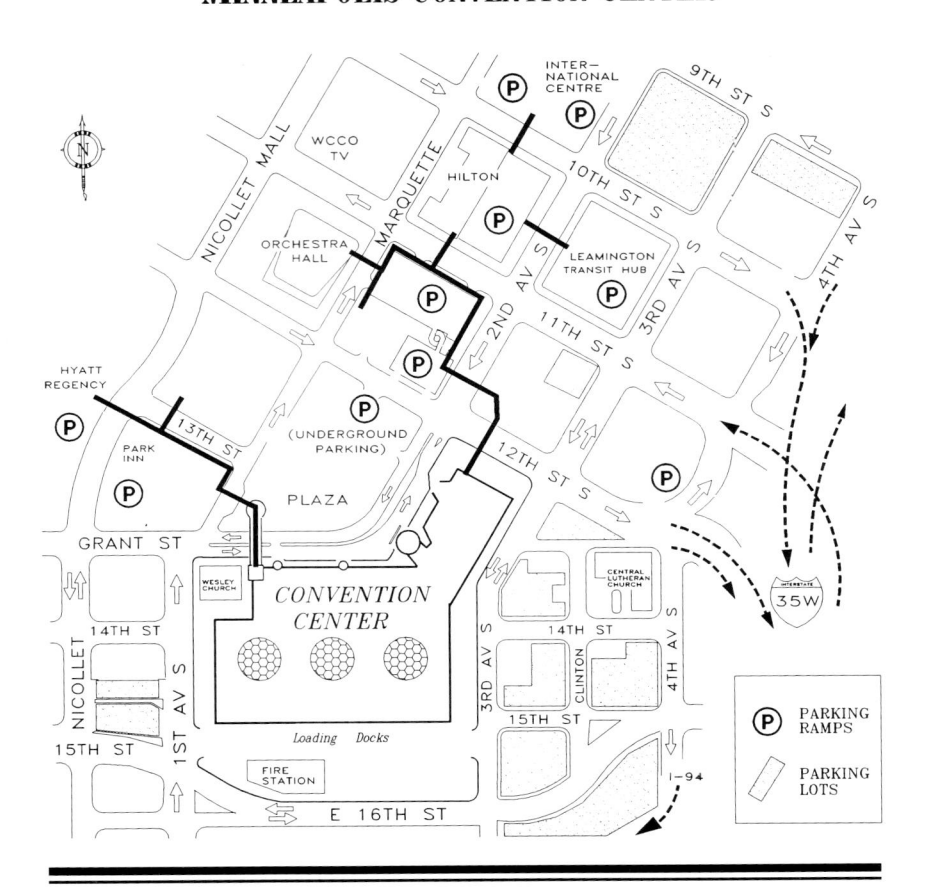

a nametag and congregate." Praised for its urban design and its user-friendliness, the convention center boasts three exhibit halls encompassing 280,000 square feet (with room for 1,500 booths measuring 10 feet by 10 feet) and two ballrooms totaling 28,000 square feet, designed to accommodate 3,600 people for meetings or 2,500 for dining. Hallways, stairwells and other miscellaneous space takes up another 367,000 square feet. It used to be that Minnesota was the last place anybody would want to book a convention. But that was before anybody knew about all of our conventional accoutrements — not to mention, of course, our new Convention Center.

MET CENTER
7901 S. Cedar Ave.
Bloomington
(612) 853-9333
Built in 1966-67 for the specific purpose of providing a hockey arena for the newly acquired North Stars, the Met Center is not a particularly beautiful space, but then, how many hockey fans are looking at the architecture? With 15,274 seats for hockey, it's big enough. With a new $3 million interior face-lift (new paint, new upholstered theater seats, new color TV monitors, new and improved lighting and more), it's state-of-the-art enough. And, doggone it, people in Minnesota love hockey. But love of one sport does not a profitable arena

Hurray! Minnesota

make. Subsequently, over the years, Met Center has opened its doors to concert-goers and events-attenders as well. In recent years, however, due to spiffier venues closer to town, Met Center has been wanting for non-hockey-related business. Until, that is, the magnificent Mall of America came to town.

Due to the commanding presence of this new neighbor, Met Center is no longer considered a long way from nowhere. Suddenly, it's a heck of a lot closer to town. In order to capitalize on this newfound geographic popularity, Met Center has hired an events management team to reestablish the facility as an entertainment center. Plans include extensive remodeling, new retail stores, restrooms, restaurants and a proposed 1,000-foot skyway link to the "Grande Mall" as well as a concentrated marketing effort to book more special events and concerts. Oh, and hockey, too.

Orchestra Hall, home of the Minnesota Orchestra and the annual Sommerfest.

NATIONAL SPORTS CENTER
1700 N.E. 105th Ave.
Blaine
(612) 785-5600

As a sports complex, this is one of the nation's finest. The likes of Carl Lewis, Jackie Joyner-Kersee, Greg LeMond and the U.S. National Men's Soccer Team have all competed here. The center also has been host to the National Weightlifting Championships, the 1990 U.S. Olympic Festival, the 1991 International Special Olympics and the 1992 U. S. Olympic Cycling Trials.

The facility includes a 170-bed dormitory, food service and full meeting facilities. The 58,000-square-foot indoor arena can house events ranging from banquets and trade shows to sport league soccer, tennis, basketball and volleyball. The indoor facilities, on 132 acres of land, include 25 regulation soccer fields, an outdoor stadium with seating for up to 25,000 and the nation's only all-wood cycling velodrome.

NORTHROP AUDITORIUM
84 S.E. Church St.
Minneapolis
(612) 624-2345

Northrop Auditorium, located on the University of Minnesota campus, is (to say the very least) a commanding structure with its massively columned facade. Built in 1929 as a convocation hall and art studio space for university students, the 5,000-seat auditorium soon became known as the Carnegie Hall of the Midwest because it was the perfect venue for showcasing the talents of classical musicians such as Sergei Rachmaninoff, Vladimir Horowitz, Igor Stravinsky and Efrem Zimbalist. Through the years, Northrop Auditorium has been home to the Minnesota Orchestra, the Metropolitan Opera's annual tour, an annual holiday presentation of "The Nutcracker" and the Summer at Northrop Festival that offers more than 20 free outdoor musical concerts every June through August. For the last two decades, it has been host to leading national and international dance companies as well as a variety of headline entertainers.

ORCHESTRA HALL
1111 Nicollet Mall
Minneapolis
(612) 371-5600

If you have vertigo or are prone to nosebleeds, it might be best to skip sitting in the third tier at Orchestra Hall. Other than that, you can't go wrong in this acoustically acclaimed concert hall. Built in 1974 to house the Minnesota Orchestra, it is the site of year-round symphony concerts, pops programs, holiday concerts, a summer festival and children's

The Ordway Music Theatre in St. Paul.

concerts — all featuring the Minnesota Orchestra and world-renowned conductors and artists. As an entertainment center, Orchestra Hall is the site of numerous Minnesota Orchestra presentations that feature the world's greatest virtuosos and ensembles, America's leading jazz musicians and popular artists, and music and dance from other countries.

The 2,463-seat auditorium was designed primarily for the symphony orchestra with its huge plaster cubes set into the ceiling and rear wall of the stage. What looks like a bad art project is really an acoustic device used to create hundreds of surfaces to disperse sound throughout the hall (so no matter where you sit — even if it's up on the third tier, you'll always be able to hear the music).

ORDWAY MUSIC THEATRE
345 Washington St.
St. Paul
(612) 224-4222

In the spring of 1981, Twin Cities arts patron Sally Ordway Irvine, nationally renowned, award-winning architect Benjamin Thompson and a delegation of four set off on a field trip to view the great performance halls of Europe. Their mission: To become visually inspired to create a similar hall in St. Paul. They visited venues in London, Venice, Milan, Vienna, Salzburg, Munich and Paris. They were visually inspired. Time magazine has described the fruit of their inspiration — the Ordway Music Theatre — as "a jewel overlooking the Mississippi" and "one of the handsomest public spaces for music in America." Anyone who has seen most of the public spaces for music in America and/or anyone who has been to the Ordway would certainly not disagree.

The Ordway presents entertainment all season long for audiences of all interests and ages: Broadway shows, drama, ballet, modern and ethnic dance, family and educational entertainment, jazz, popular and classical music and more. Besides maintaining a rigorous programming schedule of its own, the Ordway is also home to several independent organizations, including the Saint Paul Chamber Orchestra, the Minnesota Opera and the Schubert Club.

Ordway Music Theater Seating Chart

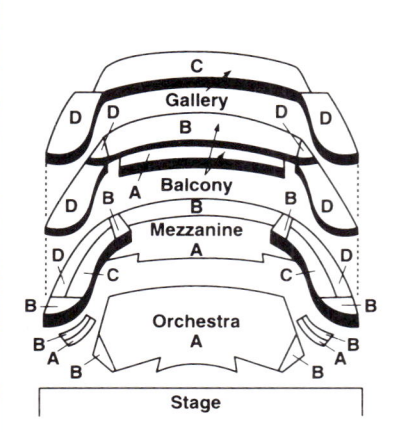

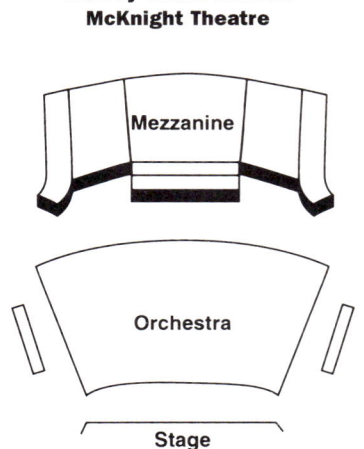

Ordway Music Theatre Main Hall

Ordway Music Theatre McKnight Theatre

Area D = partial view seating

O'SHAUGHNESSY AUDITORIUM
2004 Randolph Ave.
St. Paul
(612) 690-6700
O'Shaughnessy Auditorium, located at the College of St. Catherine, was built in 1970 as a convocation hall and a temporary home for the then-homeless Saint Paul Chamber Orchestra and Minnesota Orchestra. At the time, the SPCO was 12 years away from seeing the construction of its current home, the Ordway Music Theatre. It seems that this vested interest just might have had something to do with the fact that the ceiling on the 1,742-seat auditorium can be lowered to create a more intimate setting, perfect for chamber music. This "Eisenhower" ceiling (so named after its creator) can be raised to expose a balcony that adds 1,086 seats to the intimate chamber setting, making it the perfect venue for orchestral musings. (Hmmmm . . .)

Current programming focuses on family entertainment (the auditorium is the St. Paul home of the Children's Theatre Company) and local dance theater, as well as keeping room in its schedule for the SPCO's chamber series. (Since they've got the retractable ceiling, why not?) Tickets for O'Shaughnessy events range from $7.50 to $22, with discounts available for students and seniors.

TARGET CENTER
600 N. First Ave.
Minneapolis
(612) 673-1300
Ever since Minnesota's first professional basketball team, the Lakers, bounded off to Los Angeles in 1960, the state has been bereft of basketball. Thirty long years. No professional basketball team. In about 1984 (25 years into the 30-year bereftivation period), two local businessmen, Marvin Wolfenson and Harvey Ratner, decided that enough was enough and started to lobby for an NBA expansion team. They got one — on the condition that Minnesota build an arena specifically suited for professional basketball. So Minnesota did. The Timberwolves came. And 30 long years of professional-basketball silence came to an end.

Since 1990, the Target Center has

Target Center is a many splendored thing — in neon.

been home to the Minnesota Timberwolves, seating as many as 19,006 fans per game. When the Wolves aren't playing at home, the center hosts concerts, events and myriad family shows including the Ringling Brothers & Barnum and Bailey Circus (October), Sesame Street Live (December), Ice Capades (January) and Walt Disney's World on Ice (April).

WORLD THEATER
10 E. Exchange St.
St. Paul
(612) 290-1221

The World Theater, which seats 916, is one of the few remaining "two-balcony dramatic houses" in the country. For this alone, it is considered a treasure. Add the box seats, gilded moldings and ornaments and proscenium arch, and you have the kind of old-world charm that practically defines St. Paul. The World Theater, which opened in 1910 as the Sam S. Schubert Theater, has hosted a gamut of productions over the years — from live performances to movies. In 1986, the theater was restored to its former elegance for Garrison Keillor's live radio program called "A Prairie Home Companion." As listeners to the program grew in number, so did the World Theater's stature as a respected entertainment venue. Today, in addition to hosting Keillor's new show, "Garrison Keillor's American Radio Company," which is produced by Minnesota Public Radio and broadcast by 225 public radio stations nationwide every Saturday evening, the World Theater rents its space to groups such as the Minnesota Opera, the Minneapolis Chamber Symphony and various theater companies.

World Theater Seating Chart

Main Floor

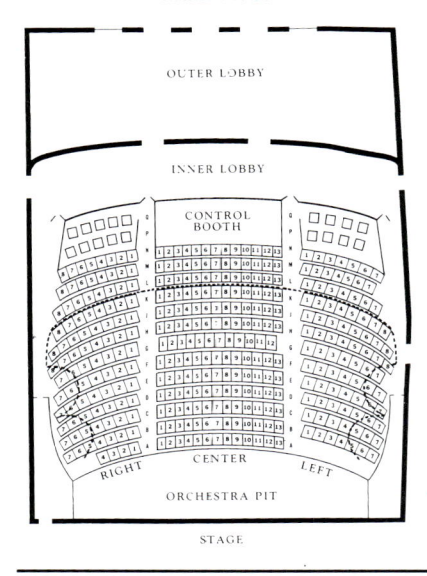

Hurray! Minnesota   PHOTO COURTESY OF TARGET CENTER

A look at the World from a box seat.

First Balcony

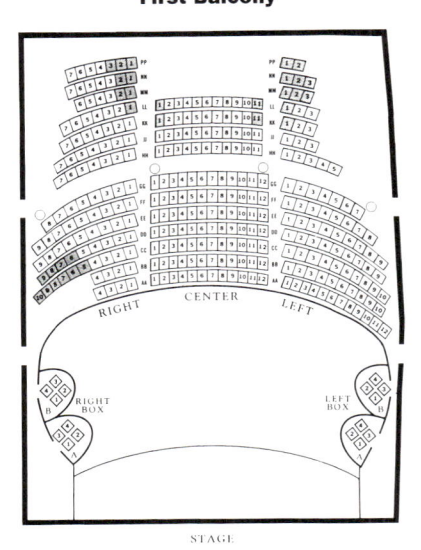

Second Balcony

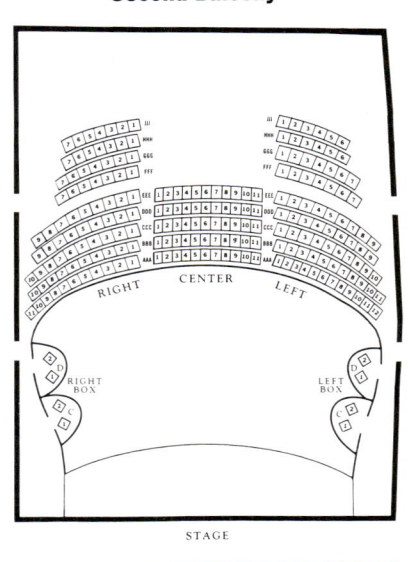

MEDIA

UNTIL RECENTLY, THE WORDS "Media circus" meant nothing to the average Minnesotan. Used to be, Minnesota was a pretty simple place. But lately, between hosting several mammoth sports events, including a couple of World Series, the Superbowl, Davis Cup, and International Special Olympics, along with visits by various political candidates, celebrities and dignitaries such as Mikhail Gorbachev and Nelson Mandela, not to mention the opening of the Mall of America and all its accompanying ballyhoo, Twin Citians have seen enough media circuses to fill the Taj Mahal — as well as a few newspaper columns, magazine articles, radio broadcasts and television newscasts. Following is a list of major media organizations that work hard to keep Twin Citians up on all the ballyhoo.

PERIODICALS

CATHOLIC DIGEST
A general-interest family magazine, the largest Catholic magazine in the world. Sold by subscription and in various Catholic churches.

CORPORATE REPORT MINNESOTA
A monthly magazine that focuses on Twin Cities businesses and the people who run them. Sold on newsstands.

MPLS./ST. PAUL
A monthly city magazine that focuses on local events, attractions, arts and events. Sold on newsstands.

MINNESOTA MONTHLY
A monthly magazine, published by Minnesota Public Radio, that focuses on life in Minnesota, public affairs, local issues, the arts, fashion and fiction. Free with an MPR membership; sold on newsstands.

UTNE READER
A nationally published bi-monthly digest of the alternative press. Sold on newsstands.

NEWSPAPERS

STAR TRIBUNE
The Star Tribune, Newspaper of the Twin Cities, has seen a lot of merges and mastheads throughout the course of its 125-year history (which, incidentally, was celebrated May 25, 1992). The Minneapolis Daily Tribune, a merger of the State Atlas and the Minneapolis Chronicle, was founded in 1867. In 1891, a group of Minneapolis investors brought a man by the name of William J. Murphy to town. As the story goes, Murphy was heading east from Grand Forks, South Dakota, where he had just spent the past several years making a success of that town's newspaper. He was on his way to seek his fortune in New York when a group of Minneapolis investors headed him off at the pass. They tracked him down in a Chicago train station, minutes before his train was leaving, and persuaded him to come to Minnesota to rescue the ailing Minneapolis Daily Tribune instead. Murphy owned and published the paper until he died in 1918. Under his leadership, the newspaper saw its first cartoon, its first half-tone engravings and even a spot of color. (Murphy left a ticy sum of money to the University of Minnesota's School of Journalism when he died. To whit, Murphy Hall.)

Another notable newspaper man, John Cowles Sr., bought the Minnesota Daily Star in 1935 and then the Minneapolis Journal in 1939. Thus, the Minneapolis Star-Journal. In 1941, the Star-Journal merged with the Tribune, becoming the Minneapolis Tribune (morning edition) and Minneapolis Times (evening edition). In 1947, the Star-Journal became the Minneapolis Star and 35 years later, all of the papers merged to become the Minneapolis Star Tribune. In 1987, the Minneapolis Star Tribune became the Star Tribune, Newspaper of the Twin Cities, making it the only major metropolitan newspaper in America without the name of a city on its masthead. The paper currently publishes three editions — a Minnesota state edition, a Minneapolis edition and a St. Paul edition. It publishes the 14th-largest Sunday

Hurray! Minnesota

newspaper in the country and the largest between Chicago and the West Coast with a circulation of 685,975. The daily newspaper is the 19th-largest metropolitan newspaper in the country with a circulation of 412,871.

Pulitzer Prize winners:

1990 – Lou Kilzer and Chris Ison for "Fire Story: Arson in St. Paul," a two-part investigative report on a local arson ring
1968 – Nick Kotz, national reporting (Washington bureau)
1959 – William Seaman, photography
1958 – Clark Mollenhoff, national affairs reporting
1954 – Richard Wilson, national reporting (Washington bureau)
1948 – Nat Finney, international affairs reporting (Minneapolis Tribune)

THE ST. PAUL PIONEER PRESS

Minnesota was a full-fledged territory for only seven weeks before James Madison Goodhue, a lawyer-turned-newspaperman from New Hampshire, dispatched its first newspaper on April 28, 1849. Goodhue's paper was called, appropriately, the Minnesota Pioneer. He had intended to call it "The Epistle of St. Paul," but changed it, saying, "We found so many little Saints in the territory, jealous of St. Paul." The Minnesota Pioneer was a four-page, six-column sheet that proclaimed the motto: "Sound Principles, Safe Men and Moderate Measure." Six months after its inception, the motto was changed to "Democratic Principles, Democratic Men and Democratic Measures," a variation that foreshadowed its merger in 1855 with the St. Paul Daily Democrat. The paper was renamed the St. Paul Pioneer and Democrat until 1863 when it changed its name to become the St. Paul Daily Pioneer. At this time, the other paper in town, the St. Paul Daily Press, was two years old.

The Pioneer, with a circulation of 1,500, and the Press, with a circulation of about 1,100, were the strongest papers in Minnesota during the Civil War years. When they consolidated for economic reasons in 1875, it was a surprise to readers of both papers. The new merger, however, proved immediately successful. In its first year, the St. Paul Pioneer Press ran the two biggest stories of the century — The Battle of Little Big Horn and the Jesse James gang's Northfield Bank robbery.

In the 100 years since Custer's Last Stand, the Pioneer Press has seen enough acquisitions, mergers and subsequent name changes to make a tired copywriter's eyes blur. To chronicle them further would be insane (sorry, George Thompson/St. Paul Dispatch, C.K. Blandin/Pioneer Press and Dispatch, Knight Newspapers and Ridder Publications/Knight-Ridder). The current rendition of St. Paul's daily paper, the St. Paul Pioneer Press, continues to build upon the values of Minnesota's early pioneers. It's a rag that would make James Madison Goodhue proud. (Oh, its daily circulation is 207,000 and the Sunday circulation is 280,000.)

Pulitzer Prize winners:

1986 – John Camp for "Life on the Land," a series of articles about a southern Minnesota farm family
1988 – Jacqui Banaszynski for "AIDS in the Heartland"

OTHER NEWSPAPERS

CITYBUSINESS
Weekly editions for Minneapolis and St. Paul provide in-depth coverage of business news and issues affecting Twin Cities businesses and businesspeople. Sold on newsstands.

CITY PAGES
Weekly arts, entertainment, news and features. Free.

DOWNTOWNER
Weekly chronicler of life and work in downtown St. Paul. Free.

MINNESOTA WOMEN'S PRESS
Bi-monthly newspaper focusing on women's issues and concerns. Free.

SKYWAY NEWS
Arts, entertainment, news, features and people profiles targeted specifically toward downtown and suburban workers. Free.

TWIN CITIES READER
Weekly arts, entertainment, news and features. Free.

RADIO STATIONS

Minnesota Public Radio (KSJN 99.5 FM / KNOW 91.1 FM) is, without question, the vanguard in public radio. Since its first broadcast on January 22, 1967, MPR has been producing broadcasts that have won more than 400 awards for news and cultural programming (including the prestigious Peabody, Grammy, Ace and Edward R. Murrow awards) and providing the visionary leadership that has created a successful model for other public radio stations in the United States.

A few of MPR's most significant accomplishments include: helping to create Radio Talking Book, the nation's first information service designed for the blind and visually handicapped, which broadcasts readings from newspapers, magazines, and newly released books; serving as incorporator and founder of National Public Radio; providing the corporate umbrella for the formation of American Public Radio; developing the nation's most successful public radio program, "A Prairie Home Companion" (host Garrison Keillor went on to appear on the cover of Time magazine); providing the leadership to ensure that the public radio satellite system in America was developed as a multi-channel system capable of both transmitting and receiving, rather than as a single one-way system broadcasting out of Washington, D.C.; and co-producing the first live marathon international remote broadcast from the United States, spotlighting Twin Cities culture, politics, business, arts and popular music scene. (The 33-hour broadcast, co-produced with the British Broadcasting Corporation's Radio 3, was heard by 120 million listeners throughout the United States, United Kingdom and other parts of the world.)

Currently, MPR's national programs include "Garrison Keillor's American Radio Company"; "Saint Paul Sunday Morning," the most popular classical music program on public radio in this country; "Sound Money," which offers advice and strategies for personal finance and investment; "Pipedreams," a program showcasing the majesty and diversity of the pipe organ; and the annual Christmas broadcast of "A Festival of Nine Lessons and Carols," aired live from King's College Chapel in Cambridge, England, to public radio listeners across the country. Each year, MPR also produces a full season of broadcasts of both the Saint Paul Chamber Orchestra and the Minnesota Orchestra.

WCCO Radio (830 AM) is a Minnesota phenomenon. With audiences that number one million weekly and ratings nearly twice as high as its closest competitor, WCCO is the darling of Minnesota radio stations, mostly because it's so "Minnesota." It's trustworthy, like your dog or your best friend. And it's comforting — much like a hot cup of cocoa on a cold winter night. When WCCO reports the news and information, it sort of comes out sounding like advice from your grandpa. The station is the local source for really significant things such as school closings (on snowy mornings, it's true, 98 percent of the school-aged children in WCCO's broadcast area are tuned in and praying to hear the name of their school announced over the air) and severe weather reports.

WCCO not only knows its audience, it treats that audience like family. And for that, it has won five Peabody awards (the highest honor in broadcasting) and has consistently ranked as the number one AM/FM station in the upper Midwest since it first went on the air. The station began broadcasting in 1922 as WLAG, "The Call of the North." Two years later, the station was sold to the Washburn Crosby Company (now known as General Mills) and took on its new owner's initials — WCCO. Washburn Crosby initially bought the station because somebody in marketing had this crazy idea that advertising Gold Medal flour over the radio just might give it an advantage over its competitor, Pillsbury flour. The marketing person with the crazy idea was right: Gold Medal flour advanced. And so did WCCO Radio. Since its humble beginnings, WCCO Radio has been known for its on-air personalities (and *their* personalities). Broadcasting greats such as Cedric Adams and Clellan Card set a precedent for excellence and humor that continues today.

Hurray! Minnesota

WCCO's "Good Morning Show" crew (left to right): Eric Eskola, Sid Hartman, Charlie Boone, Roger Strom, Karen Filloon, Dave Lee and Roger Erickson.

AM STATIONS
WDGY 630 AM, country western
WCCO 830 AM, news and information
KJJO 950 AM, country
KMZZ 980 AM, album-oriented rock
WMIN 1030 AM, original hits of the '40s, '50s and '60s
KFAN 1130 AM, all-sports station
KNOW 1330 AM, news and information
KLBB 1400 AM, the music of your life
KQRS 1440 AM, classic rock
KBCW 1470 AM, country western
KSTP 1500 AM, news/sports/talk
KKCM 1530 AM, contemporary Christian
KYCR 1570 AM, contemporary Christian

FM STATIONS
KBEM 88.5 FM, jazz
KMOJ 89.9 FM, urban contemporary
KFAI 90.3 FM, community radio
KNOW 91.1 FM, news and information
KOOL 107.9 FM, oldies
KQRS 92.5 FM, classic rock
KRXX 93.7 FM, today's new rock
KS95 94.5 FM, adult contemporary
KNOF 95.3 FM, gospel
KTCZ 97.1 FM, adult or alternative album rock
KSJN 99.5 FM, classical
WCTS 100.3 FM, Christian broadcasting
KDWB 101.3 FM, top 40
KEEY 102.1 FM, country western
WLTE 102.9 FM, soft adult contemporary
KJJO 104 FM, country

TWIN CITIES TELEVISION
TV STATIONS (NETWORK AND LOCAL)
KTCA Channel 2, public
WCCO Channel 4, network (CBS)
KSTP Channel 5, network (ABC)
KMSP Channel 9, network
KARE Channel 11, network (NBC)
KTCI Channel 17, public
KLGT Channel 23, local network
KITN Channel 29, local network (FOX)

THE TWIN CITIES offers viewers a variety of programming on its network stations, three of which — WCCO, KTCA and KSTP — have recently garnered 23 Emmy Awards. Several cable companies provide the metro area with a full range of cable programming.

WCCO TV, the television counterpart to WCCO Radio, is owned by CBS Inc. Hubbard Broadcasting owns KSTP television and radio. KTCA and KTCI are public television stations that produce local programming as well as provide national and international programs. Since the completion of its new headquarters in downtown St. Paul in 1989, the Minnesota TeleCenter, KTCA/KTCI has been able to expand its programming and production capabilities and give each station its own identity.

Of the local-access cable channels, Metro Cable Network Channel 6 is a fairly successful non-commercial network reserved for alternative, arts, education and public affairs programming, and it reaches a significant audience.

SHOPPING

THE TWIN CITIES IS A SHOPPER'S mecca. The **Mall of America**, which opened in August 1992, is the largest covered retail shopping mall in the nation. Referred to as the megamall, at 2.6 million square feet of retail space, it is of mega proportions.

Placed conveniently around the Twin Cities are four other major shopping malls whose retail space ranges from .9 to 1.6 million square feet. **Southdale**, the first covered shopping mall in the nation, was built in 1956. These malls are all anchored by **Dayton's**, which in 1992 is celebrating its 90th anniversary. Dayton's, a division of the Dayton Hudson Corporation, one of America's largest general merchandise retailers, was a part of Southdale when it first opened.

With the success of Southdale and the expansion of the suburbs, three more Dales (as they are referred to locally) — **Brookdale** (1962), **Rosedale** (1969), **Ridgedale** (1974) — were built. **Burnsville Center** was the last in 1977. Besides the large suburban malls, there are two excellent downtown shopping districts in St. Paul and Minneapolis, both with indoor centers. (See St. Paul and Minneapolis sections.)

REGIONAL CENTERS

BROOKDALE CENTER
Highway 100 and Brooklyn Boulevard
Brooklyn Center
(612) 566-6672
Brookdale features the four major department stores of Sears, J.C. Penney, Carson Pirie Scott and Dayton's, which are joined by more than 50 clothing and specialty stores.

BURNSVILLE CENTER
35W and County Road 42
Burnsville
(612) 435-8181
Burnsville, the second largest of the center malls, has a food court with more than 16 restaurants on the promenade level. The mall is anchored by Carson Pirie Scott, J.C. Penney and a newly remodeled Dayton's. There are dozens of specialty, gift and jewelry shops and more than 45 apparel stores.

RIDGEDALE SHOPPING CENTER
12401 Wayzata Boulevard
Minnetonka
(612) 541-4864
Ridgedale is anchored by Dayton's, J.C. Penney, Sears and Carson Pirie Scott and has nearly 100 other retail outlets.

ROSEDALE SHOPPING CENTER
W. Highway 36 and Fairview Ave. N.
Roseville
(612) 633-0872
Roseville is one of the Twin Cities' busiest malls and 99 percent occupied. The largest stores are Dayton's, Carson Pirie Scott, J.C. Penney and Montgomery Ward.

SOUTHDALE CENTER
66th St. and France Ave.
Edina
(612) 925-7885
When Southdale opened its doors in 1958, it had 800,000 square feet of retail space. The recent remodeling of the center, which included a new Dayton's store, brought the retail space to 1.6 million square feet. Southdale is anchored by Dayton's, Carson Pirie Scott and J.C. Penney. There are more than 150 retail establishments on the four levels of this premier mall.

NEIGHBORHOOD CENTERS

AS WELL AS the larger malls, the Twin Cities has a number of smaller but often unique shopping centers. Many are housed in historic buildings, such as St. Anthony Main and Riverplace (see Downtown Minneapolis section) and Bandana Square. There are many more centers located in suburban neighborhoods in the metro area.

INTERNATIONAL MARKET SQUARE (IMS)
100 Second Ave. N.
Minneapolis
(612) 338-6250
International Market Square (IMS), at 100 Second Avenue North in downtown

Hurray! Minnesota

Southdale Center in Edina is the world's first enclosed shopping mall.

Minneapolis, is a design center with as many as 90 showrooms of innovative products and services from wallpaper and furnishings to light and bathroom fixtures. The building has eight floors with a five-story atrium in the center. The first five floors have showrooms with displays divided between office and business, residential and architectural supplies.

Here you will find the latest in kitchen technology, imaginative solutions to building or remodeling projects or high-tech designs for environmental entertainment centers. Though not the place to shop for bargains, it is the place to find distinctive furnishings, materials and accessories as well as state-of-the-art architectural supplies.

Sales are through trade professionals only. So to purchase any of the products you must first contract with a design professional. A number of reputable design services are located in the building, such as the **American Society of Interior Designers** and the **Institute of Business Designers**.

Market Hall, in the center atrium, contains **Shel-bea's Deli and Sundries** and the **Atrium Cafe International Restaurant**. Both only serve lunch. However, the center courtyard of the building is often rented out for large parties and events with the food catered by the Atrium.

BANDANA SQUARE
1021 Bandana Boulevard E.
St. Paul
(612) 642-1509

Retail, dining and entertainment establishments are housed in the old brick buildings that were once the repair shops for the Northern Pacific Railroad and are now on the National Register of Historic Places.

EDEN PRAIRIE CENTER
8301 Flying Cloud Drive
Eden Prairie
(612) 941-7650

This mall is anchored by Sears and Carson Pirie Scott and has a skyway to Target. There's a food court and more than 75 retail and service stores.

EDINA
The **Galleria** is one of three small shopping malls just west of Southdale in Edina. Anchored by **Gabberts Furniture** (927-1500), the upscale Galleria houses many fine home furnishing and accessory shops along with more than 25 designer fashion stores. **Centennial Lakes Plaza** on 76th and France Avenue, located in a beautiful setting of pools and pagoda-like buildings, features the 25,600-square-foot **Computer City SuperCenter** (844-0080) along with other restaurants, shops and service stores.

50TH AND FRANCE
At 50th Street and France Avenue you'll find a concentration of professional services and retail stores with lots of free parking. In this village-like setting is exceptionally convenient shopping that includes access to bookstores, dry cleaners, dentists, doctors, attorneys, 20

Uptown
Calhoun Square at the corner of Hennepin Avenue and Lake Street forms the hub for the Uptown shopping district. Here you will find unique and eclectic shopping for original and unusual fashions, along with great restaurants and coffeehouses.

clothing stores, **Lund's** grocery store, a post office, galleries, gift and accessory shops and the Edina Cinema.

Grand Avenue and Victoria Crossing
St. Paul

There's an eclectic group of shops at this crossroads and up and down Grand Avenue carrying original items from children's clothing and books to kitchen accessories and antiques.

Maplewood Mall
Interstate 694 and White Bear Ave.
Maplewood
(612) 770-5010

The mall's avenues, with more than 100 retailers, join the three department stores of Sears, Kohl's and Carson Pirie Scott. On the upper level there is a food court with 13 fast-food choices.

Northtown Mall
University Ave. and Highway 10
Blaine

This mall in the northern suburbs is anchored by Carson Pirie Scott and Montgomery Ward. There also are large Kohl's and Woolworth stores along with a large and varied number of service and retail shops.

Hurray! Minnesota

PHOTO BY RICH RYAN

St. Anthony Main and Riverplace
Minneapolis
Located in historic riverside warehouses, St. Anthony Main and Riverplace feature unique specialty clothing and gift shops along with excellent restaurants and live entertainment.

Wayzata
Downtown Wayzata is located on Lake Minnetonka. The lake lends itself to the relaxed atmosphere cultivated by the merchants who have produced a vacation spirit to go with the shopping experience. Along Lake Street, facing the lake, are a number of specialty and apparel shops, including **Winona Knits** (476-1798) with its fabulous sweaters. In the Wayzata Bay Shopping Center is The **Foursome** (473-4667). This department store, founded in 1935, is one of the last family-run department stores in the state and carries clothing for the entire family.

FOOD
Byerly's and **Lund's** are Minnesota's homegrown, upscale grocery stores. Both have eight locations around the

Twin Cities. The St. Louis Park Byerly's is the most remarkable of the stores, with thousand-dollar chandeliers over the frozen-foods freezers, subdued lighting and plush-carpeted aisles. You can find just about any unique or gourmet grocery item at this Byerly's, along with a liquor store, deli, restaurant, gift shop and flower shop.

Not surprisingly, the Twin Cities has its share of ethnic food grocers, such as **Cossetta's Market and Pizzeria** (222-3476) in St. Paul, the premier of Italian pizza parlors and delicatessens, or **China Market** (331-3343) on Hennepin Avenue in Minneapolis, purveyor of the most exotic of Oriental vegetables, foods and seafood.

Ingebretsen's Scandinavian Foods and Gifts (729-9333) does a wonderful job of providing the Twin Cities Scandinavians with foods from their native lands. And since 1954, nationally known **Kramarczuk's Sausage Company, Inc.** (379-3018), on East Hennepin in the St. Anthony neighborhood, serves the best in Polish sausage, blood sausage and homemade frankfurters. Another old-timer, only this time in St. Paul, is **Gleason's Specialty Shoppe** (222-6914) on St. Peter Street. Founded in 1918 by John Gleason, a coffee roaster, Gleason's provides the Twin Cities with the finest coffee, teas and fresh roasted peanuts, as well as specialty baking items such as candies, chocolates, fresh spices, jellies, candied fruits and European cooking utensils.

Surdyk's (379-9757), on East Hennepin Avenue and University Avenue Northeast, is the grocery store of liquor stores with one of the best selections of wines at the most reasonable prices in the Twin Cities. But **Hennepin Lake Liquor Store** (825-4411) on West Lake Street is a secret worth discovering. It is here that unique and hard-to-find wines, at prices oftentimes lower than at the vineyards themselves, can be found. Ask for Phil. He'll steer you to some of the best vintages.

During the summer, there are two **Farmers' Markets** in Minneapolis and two in downtown St. Paul. On Thursday, Nicollet Mall becomes a country fair of vegetables and flowers, and farmers gather each morning at Lyndale and Glenwood avenues in Minneapolis. In St. Paul on Thursday mornings, a market is held at Seventh and Wabasha and on weekend mornings one is held at East Fifth and Wall streets.

ANTIQUES

THE TWIN CITIES is blessed with numerous antique dealers. Antique buffs should visit the 11 dealers under one roof at the **Antique Corner** on West 50th Street and Xerxes Avenue South. But Hopkins has the really big antique malls, **Treasures Antique Mall** (930-0477) at 1115 Excelsior Ave. E., with 45 dealers and 9,000 square feet of merchandise, and **Mainstreet Antique Mall** (931-9748) at 901 Main Street, where 50 dealers display their wares.

There are two multiple-floor locations — one in Minneapolis (722-6000) and one in St. Paul (646-0037) — for **Antiques Minnesota**, which bills itself as "recycling America's past" and the largest dealer in Minnesota with 16,000 square feet of furniture.

St. Paul, particularly along West Seventh Street near downtown and Payne Avenue on the East Side, is a great place to find a number of stores that carry authentic and valuable antiques.

Don't miss **Architectural Antiques** at 801 Hennepin Ave. in Minneapolis. It is loaded with items that have been saved from the wrecking ball, such as huge fireplaces, statuary, brass doorknobs, stained glass windows, sinks and loads of doors in all shapes and sizes.

BARGAINS

THE TWIN CITIES has consignment shops for everything from designer and children's clothing to toys, furniture and sporting goods. **Rodeo Drive** (920-0188) on Excelsior Boulevard carries designer labels for both men's and women's fashions and also has a second store featuring children's clothing. **Play It Again Sports**, with more than a dozen locations, will sell that piece of equipment you just never got around to using or that the family's youngest outgrew.

For brand-name bargains, there are

Hurray! Minnesota

manufacturers' outlet malls at **Medford Outlet Mall** (35W south of the Twin Cities), **Manufacturer's Marketplace** in Woodbury (Interstate 94 and Highway 19) and, recently opened in Branch just north of the Twin Cities (Interstate 35 and Minnesota 95), **Tanger Factory Outlet Center**, each with up to 30 stores. Here no middleman handles the merchandise, so savings from 20 to 75 percent can be had on the latest in clothes and merchandise from such manufacturers as Naturalizer, Liz Claiborne, Geoffrey Beene, Farberware, Fieldcrest Cannon and Oshkosh B' Gosh.

At locations throughout the state, **Target**, a division of Dayton's, carries trendy but inexpensive clothing as well as household items and accessories. Recently two **Target Greatland** stores were opened featuring more than 140,000 square feet of concentrated fashions. One store is in Apple Valley, a suburb south of the Twin Cities, and the other is in Plymouth, a suburb northwest of Minneapolis.

Brand new to the Twin Cities is **Filene's Basement**. Filene's offers upscale department store merchandise at almost violently low prices in four locations, including one in the Mall of America.

SPECIALTY STORES

INTERESTING SPECIALTY stores abound in the Twin Cities. There are stores representing almost every country or region in the world, from the continent of Africa to the little island of Bali. A few with a European flavor are: the **Dublin Walk** (338-5203) at 1200 Nicollet Mall, featuring Belleek china, crystal and Irish traditional sweaters and gift items; **American Swedish Museum Shop** (871-3004); **Scandia Imports** (339-6339); **Harriett of London** (339-4011) and **John McLean Co.** (228-9746), both carrying British clothing and teatime items; the **Wunderbar** (454-2156) for Bavarian clothing; and **Europa Riverplace** (378-9619) for Baltic and East European decorative items.

Minnesota also has a number of unusually good homegrown enterprises that have achieved national attention such as **Bachman's** (861-7600), which specializes in decorative floral products. The main floral center at 6010 Lyndale Ave. S. has an outstanding selection of plants and related products on display. **Hoigaard's** (929-1351), which opened up an awning shop almost 100 years ago, is one of the best stores in the Twin Cities to shop for leisure furnishings and sports and recreational clothing and equipment.

Another centennial store is the **Hudson Map Co.** (872-8818), founded in Minneapolis in 1892 by Horace B. Hudson. The company draws and publishes maps, while its store at 2501 Nicollet Avenue sells these, other maps and map-related items. For music-related items, there's the **Electric Fetus** (870-9300), started up in the late 1960s in the days of the flower children. It features an extensive selection of compact discs, tapes and records. And last but not least, if you're looking for an authentic Minnesota souvenir, **Hello Minnesota** (339-5996) is the store with loons and lady's slippers galore, as well as clothing and art objects reflecting your visit to the state.

Have You Been To Rodeo Drive?

Designer Consignment Boutiques
Men • Women • Maternity • Children

Anne Klein, Ralph Lauren, Donna Karan, Armani, Ungaro, Hugo Boss, Claiborne, Florence Eisman, Heartstrings, Baby Dior

Rodeo Drive

Men & Women
4110 Minnetonka Blvd, Minneapolis
Mon.-Fri. 10-8; Sat. 10-6; Sun. 12-5
920-0188

Children
3058 Excelsior Blvd, Minneapolis
Mon. & Thurs. 10-8;
Tues., Wed., Fri., & Sat. 10-6
920-6046

Snoopy overlooks his playground at the Mall of America.

MALL OF AMERICA
Interstate 494 and Highway 77
(612) 883-8800

Referred to as the "Mount Rushmore of Shopping" and the "Taj Mall," the Mall of America gives new meaning to the terms "shop till you drop" and "power shopping." In the 2,468,000 square feet of retail space, not only are there four major department stores presenting their best in merchandise and service, but there also are more than 240 stores along the connecting avenues. There are 40 women's apparel stores alone. The three miles it takes to house all these stores are highlighted by thousands of skylights, 800 trees, 3,000 plantings, 44 escalators and 17 elevators, not to mention 3.5 miles of handrailing.

At 4.2 million square feet, the mall is the largest complex of its kind in the United States. Maximum capacity is estimated at around 67,000 people. But as large as it is, it is not overwhelming. Four distinct "themes" divide the space into a manageable sequence of small spaces that make it easy to find your way and very people-friendly.

The mall is symmetrically laid out, similar to a fort. The large department stores of **Nordstrom**, **Bloomingdale's**, **Sears** and **Macy's** are located on each of the four corners. A three-level mall avenue with row upon row of unique specialty shops connects the four large corner stores. Each avenue has a different decorating theme providing diversity to the eye and visual orientation.

There are plazas in front of each of the department stores and also plazas at the midpoint of each of the four "avenues." Each plaza has its own unique shape and design, from Japanese-type fish ponds to Golf Mountain and Market Tower. The plaza in the center of the east side is referred to as the Rotunda and, like a town hall, is the location for major mall activities. The six-acre Knott's Camp Snoopy, like the hole of a donut, is located in the center.

But shopping is not all the mall has to offer. It is really a shopping, entertainment and recreational facility that incorporates the concept of entertainment shopping in a big way. For starters, there are **Knott's Camp Snoopy**; **Golf Mountain**, a two-level miniature-golf course; **Lego Imagination Center**, the most spectacular Lego model show in the world; and **enTRAINment**, a monument to Lionel trains and a spectacular treat for any train lover.

There is a fourth level only on the south and east sides, which contains the **Upper East Side** entertainment complex and **Mall of America 14** with its 14 big screens and 4,000 seats. Upper East Side has bars and nightclubs catering to a broad range of American music tastes, such as New Orleans-style **Fat Tuesday's**, country western **Gatlin Brothers Music City** and **America's Original Sports Bar**, part of America Live, a five-club music and sports complex. (See the Nightlife section.)

In addition, the mall, the major stores and Upper East Side all host events and national entertainers. And many of the stores have amusement and entertainment centers as an integral part of the store, such as MSP Airport Drive-in on the third floor of Bloomingdale's. This entertainment center for children includes 14 computers, activity tables, a puppet theater and a "drive-in" movie with stationary kiddie cars for watching the latest Disney film or the dolphins at the Minnesota Zoo.

There's **Oshman's Super Sports USA** with a silicone skating rink, a putting green and full-swing driving range, archery range, tennis/racquetball court and regulation basketball hoop for a few practice shots. Though there is no gambling in the mall, **Grand Casino** has a shop to teach people how to play blackjack and other games. And it offers free shuttle service from the mall to its two gambling facilities, which are about an hour and a half away.

There are many unique specialty shops carrying items you won't find anywhere else. There's **Alamo Flags**, **Bare Bones**, with working skeletons for the ghoul or doctor in the house, **Darts 'n' Pool**, **Everything's a $1.00**, **Painted Tipi**, **Kiwi Beach** and original apparel shops such as **Comfortwear** or **Valerie Fitzgerald's**.

The mall has more than 30 restaurants, nine of which are full service and seven of which have entertainment. There also are two food courts on the third level of the south and north sides.

The mall places heavy emphasis on customer service, providing strollers and wheelchairs at no charge and renting electronic convenience vehicles and US West pagers and cellular phones. There's the **Pepsi Pick-up**, a free tram service, operating on the third level. And at each entrance is general information that can provide language interpretation, message services and a computer system for locating lost children (or adults). There also are help phones, package pickup, lockers, family rooms, an urgent care center and emergency car service.

Parking is relatively easy and convenient at the mall with none of the 12,750 spaces more than 300 feet from one of the eight entrances. That means that no matter where you park, you won't be more than a football field away from an entrance. The two ramps are located on the east and west sides of the mall. The parking areas in the east ramp are named for the states east of the Mississippi and in the west ramp for the states west of the river. Know your geography and you won't get lost. There also are smaller surface lots in front of the four major stores and on the north and south sides. The most convenient parking for access to the Upper East Side is in the east side parking ramp.

As convenient as the parking is, the public transportation system is even more so. There is a special entrance for buses on the lower level of the east side that will put you immediately in the mall. MTC (Metropolitan Transit Com-

Paul Bunyan and Babe surprise many visitors to Camp Snoopy.

mission) has added express routes from both downtowns and a number of park-and-go lots in the suburbs.

KNOTT'S CAMP SNOOPY

At Knott's Camp Snoopy in the center of the mall, everything you see and hear adds to the illusion that it is summertime, 70 degrees and you're outside enjoying the Minnesota woods. (This will be great during the Minnesota winter.) Camp Snoopy, with its park-like natural setting of trees and winding paths, is a counterpoint to the hard linear architecture and fast pace of the mall avenues and stores. With more than 400 trees standing from 10 to 30 feet high and 30,000 blooming plants, Camp Snoopy has the largest indoor planting in the world. There are creeks and fountains throughout the park. The rock used to form the creek beds and mountains is modeled after the rocks found at Taylors Falls in the St. Croix Valley. This Minnesota summer camp, overseen by Snoopy, can accommodate 10,000 people, and it's loaded with entertainment.

It is fitting that Snoopy was chosen as mascot for the camp since **Charles Schultz**, the creator of Snoopy and the Peanuts comic strip, is a native Minnesotan. His dog, Spike, was the prototype for the first Snoopy. The Guinness Book of World Records calls Peanuts the world's most popular comic strip.

In the camp are seven merchandise outlets and 16 rides that include a state-of-the-art roller coaster; a log chute with flume-drops of 40 feet and a memorable meeting with an animated Paul Bunyan and Babe the Blue Ox; the most beautiful of merry-go-rounds, the Americana Carousel; traditional bumper cars; and lots of rides for the younger visitors.

There also are three entertainment theaters: the Ford Playhouse, the Northwood Stage and the Wilderness Theater. They present everything from classic audience-hissing melodramas and children's plays to trained animal shows, 3-D movies and musical entertainment.

Stadium Club, a sports restaurant, **Hormel Cook Out Food Court**, **Mrs. Knott's Kitchen** and the **Silver Stein-Festhaus**, a hearty German-style stube with a year-round beer garden, are highlights of the 14 dispensers of food and sociability in the camp. Don't miss Mrs. Knott's traditional homemade fried chicken with mashed potatoes and gravy that's been served at Knott's Berry Farm since 1934.

Admission to the park is free. For the rides and shows, automatic ticket sellers dispense point passes with a cash par value per point of 50 cents. Admission varies from two to five points.

Sports trivia buffs will be impressed with the fact that the seven acres of park sit on the site where the old Metropolitan (Met) Stadium, home to the Twins and Vikings, stood from 1956 to 1981. Harmon Killebrew hit his longest home run (522 feet) in 1967 at Met Stadium. There is a brass plate on the site of the old home plate, which is next to the Northwood Stage. The seat where the longest home run ball landed is to be suspended in its place at the other end of the park, so fans can judge for themselves the distance the ball flew.

REACH THE READERS OF "Hurray! Minnesota"

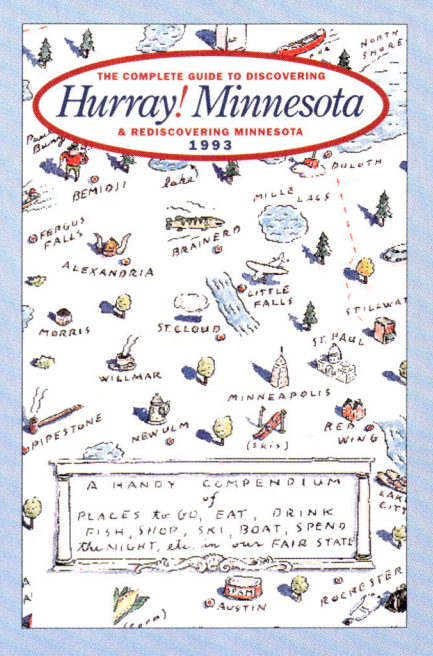

"Hurray! Minnesota" is an annual publication prepared for Minnesota's four-million plus residents, as well as the hundreds of thousands of tourists, conventioneers and business travelers. "Hurray! Minnesota" reaches readers through bookstores, magazine sellers, gift shops, relocation divisions of realtors, corporate human resources departments, Chambers of Commerce, convention and visitors bureaus, hotels and motels, major convention groups and numerous other outlets throughout the state.

•

For further information or to place an ad in the 1994 edition, contact Marilyn Hanson, director of advertising sales, at:

"Hurray! Minnesota"
15 South Fifth Street, Suite 900
Minneapolis, MN 55402
(612) 338-1578
Fax: (612) 338-4784

Eater's Digest

THE TWIN CITIES METRO AREA has a wide range of restaurants to suit just about anyone's taste. For this reason, Eater's Digest has evolved into a guide that lists more than 400 restaurants in the Twin Cities. After a glance at the Eater's Digest, you will quickly discover that in the Twin Cities you aren't limited by a lack of variety.

However, this hasn't always been the case. Over the last decade, dining in the Twin Cities has matured. Restaurants representing cuisine from around the world have opened their doors in the metro area. Paella from Spain, Tandoori chicken from Afghanistan and nouveau cuisine such as spicy-Asian-chicken pizza from California are only a few examples of the ethnic dining available.

While in Minnesota, there are plenty of opportunities to eat Minnesotan. Restaurants that serve Minnesotan/Midwestern cuisine such as the **Dakota Bar and Grill** and the **Nicollet Island Inn** are popular in the Twin Cities. At the Dakota Bar and Grill, the menu items such as thyme-marinated pork with blueberry sauce and broiled fillet of walleye with wild rice are served with only the freshest Midwestern ingredients. A country-style inn with 24 guest rooms, the Nicollet Island Inn features beef-pork meatloaf with mushroom gravy and garlic mashed potatoes, sauteed pheasant with corn sauce and other Midwestern fare.

A spectacular view of the Twin Cities skyline is possible from restaurants in either of the two downtowns. While in St. Paul, enjoy a view of the Mississippi River, State Capitol and St. Paul Cathedral at **Le Carrousel**, the cities' only revolving restaurant. Le Carrousel is known for more than its view — the service and American cuisine will not disappoint. **Windows on Minnesota**, located on the 50th floor of the IDS tower in downtown Minneapolis, is a fine-dining restaurant with an innovative approach to traditional fare. For instance, the lobster ravioli with artichoke and sun-dried tomato or sea scallops with cilantro butter sauce and red-and-black-bean salad are both flavorful choices. After enjoying one of the many tantalizing desserts, the Windows on Minnesota lounge is a great place to top off a romantic evening with dancing.

"M" is for steakhouse in the Twin Cities. Ironically, several steakhouses in the metro area begin with the letter M. There are three in downtown Minneapolis alone: **Manny's Steakhouse**, **Morton's of Chicago** and **Murray's**. Murray's has been downtown since 1946. Though it serves American cuisine other than steak, Murray's is famous for its Silver Butter Knife Steak. The newest steakhouse in Minneapolis is Morton's of Chicago, a chain restaurant with national acclaim. If you are looking for superb service and healthy portions, Morton's is the place for you. Manny's Steakhouse opened in 1988 and is a locally owned New York-style steakhouse. Again, Manny's will not disappoint with its dry-aged beef and quality service. Operating for more than 40 years in St. Paul, **Mancini's Char House** has earned local recognition. At Mancini's, you will enjoy steak or lobster and live entertainment nightly.

From steakhouses to African cuisine, the Twin Cities has it all. If you have never tried the flavors from western Africa, a trip to **Dupsy's African Cuisine** is the perfect opportunity. You will find well-known ingredients such as okra and black-eyed peas prepared with unfamiliar flavors and in unfamiliar ways. While dining at Dupsy's, try the egusi, a spicy stew with beef, melon seeds and greens or the moyinmoyin, a custard made from black-eyed peas. **Fair Oaks** is the restaurant to visit if you are curious about the cuisine from northern India. The decor at Fair Oaks is nothing out of the ordinary, but the food is. Some of the dishes to try are the Tandoori chicken, samosas, flat bread, and for dessert, the mango ice cream.

If ethnic food isn't what you're looking for and elegant dining is, try the **510 Restaurant**. This contemporary French/American restaurant is located across the street from the Guthrie Theater in the graceful 510 Groveland Building. The menu ranges from an eight-course meal to a three-course pre-theater dinner for patrons combining dinner with an evening at the Guthrie. While at the 510 Restaurant, the tenderloin of lamb with fig sauce or the stuffed breast of duck with port wine and pistachios are excellent choices.

The nightclub atmosphere of **Yvette** is another way to enjoy the evening. A jazz trio plays while you dine at this fine Continental restaurant. Yvette features such culinary delights as Chateaubriand with bearnaise sauce and grilled chicken breast in a rosemary-Chardonnay wine sauce.

If barbecued food is more your style, then the place to visit is **Market Bar-B-Que**. This restaurant is a tradition and has been open for more than 45 years. Market Bar-B-Que is one of the rib hot spots in town — the autographed photos on the wall are testimony. Bob Hope, Sugar Ray Leonard and Bob Dylan are just a few of the well-known visitors. Market Bar-B-Que specializes in St. Louis-style pork and Texas beef ribs as well as broiled items and salads.

About an hour's drive beyond the Twin Cities metro area is **Schumacher's New Prague Hotel**. This world-class restaurant and hotel features gourmet dishes from central Europe. Schumacher's was recognized as one of the 12 best inns of 1990. The specialties at Schumacher's are the traditionally rich and heavenly, such as caraway duck, roasted rabbit and stuffed goose.

This is just a sampling of the array of dining choices in the Twin Cities. Eater's Digest is a comprehensive guide designed to provide you with a thorough look at the dining experiences available in the Twin Cities metro area and beyond. For your convenience, Eater's Digest is divided into three listings: by alphabet, by category and by geography. The abbreviations and symbols used in the descriptions of restaurants are explained in a key located in several places throughout the guide. Enjoy.

ALPHABETICAL

ACROPOL INN
Greek and American eatery with 50 specialties including moussaka, arnakie exoheko, tiropeta and spanakopeta. Wine and beer served. 11am-9pm M-Th, -10pm F and Sa. *!!* No credit cards. 748 Grand Ave., St. Paul, 298-0151.

AFTON HOUSE INN
Caesar salad and homemade desserts in two different dining rooms. Entertainment – F and Sa. Lunch: 11:30am-2:30pm M-Sa. Dinner: 5-10pm M-Th, -11pm F and Sa; 4-9pm Su. Su brunch: 10am-2pm. Su brunch cruises. *!!* V/MC/DI. Afton (four miles south of Interstate 94 off Highway 95), 436-8883.

AL BAKER'S
Casual affordable dining in a nostalgic atmosphere. Entrees span all tastes with ribs, chicken, steak, seafood, burgers and Mexican dishes. 11am-11:30pm M-Th, -12:30pm F and Sa, -10:30pm Su. Su brunch: 9:30am-1pm. *!!* AE/V/MC/DC. Yankee Doodle and Pilot Knob roads off Interstate 35E, Eagan, 454-9000.

ALEXANDER'S RESTAURANT
A casual comfortable atmosphere featuring a variety of original salads, sandwiches, and soups. Breakfast: 7-10:45 am M-F. Lunch: 11am-3pm M-F. Box lunches and personalized catering also available. *!* V/MC. 714 Second Ave. S., Mpls., 339-2893.

AL'S BREAKFAST
An institution near the University of Minnesota campus since 1950. Menu items include hash browns, omelets and eggs Benedict. No liquor. 6am-1pm M-Sa; 9am-1pm Su. *!* No credit cards. 413 14th Ave. S.E., Mpls., 331-9991.

AMERICAN PIE
This restaurant features Chicago-style, deep-dish and flat pizzas, salads, sandwiches and

---

AE = American Express / V = VISA / MC = MasterCard / DI = Discover / DC = Diners Club / CB = Carte Blanche
! = less than $10 / *!!* $10-$18 / *!!!* $18-$28 / *!!!!* more than $28

151 TWIN CITIES / EATER'S DIGEST

homemade desserts. No liquor. Minnesota Law Center, Nicollet Mall – 7am-7pm M-F. Grant St. – 11am- 10pm M-Th, -11pm F and Sa; 2pm-9:30pm Su. *!* AE/V/MC/DC. 107 W. Grant St., Mpls., 871-1669. Minnesota Law Center, Nicollet Mall, 514 Nicollet Mall, Mpls., 332-6428.

America's Harvest
Dine in the atrium on fresh bakery items and from a menu that changes seasonally. Piano entertainment in the Atrium Lounge. 6:30am-10pm daily. Su brunch: 11am-2pm. *!!!* AE/V/MC/DC/CB/DI. Northland Inn, 7025 Northland Drive (Interstate 94 and Boone), Brooklyn Park, 536-8300.

Anchorage
This restaurant offers an extensive seafood menu including Anchorage broth, salmon en'croute, mahi mahi and surf 'n' turf. Dancing and entertainment. Breakfast: 6:30-11am M-F; 7:30-11am Sa and Su. Lunch: 11:30am-2:30pm M-Sa. Dinner: 5:30-10pm Su-Th, -11pm F and Sa. Su brunch: 10:30am-2:30pm. *!!!* AE/V/MC/DC/CB/DI. Metrodome Hilton, 1330 Industrial Boulevard, Mpls., 379-4444.

Annie's Parlor
Old-style ice cream parlor serving hamburgers, hand-cut fries, malts and homemade hot-fudge sundaes. Liquor served at Hennepin Ave. St. Paul – 11am-9pm Su-Th, -11pm F and Sa; noon-midnight Su. 14th Ave., Mpls. – 11am-11pm M-Th, -midnight F and Sa; noon-11pm Su. Hennepin Ave. – 11am-11pm M-Th, -1am F and Sa; 11am-10pm Su. *!* AE/V/MC/DC/CB/DI. 406 Cedar Ave., St. Paul, 339-6207. 313 14th Ave. S.E., Mpls., 379-0744. 2916 Hennepin Ave., Mpls., 825-4455.

Anthony's Wharf
Seafood restaurant with a view of the Mississippi River and the city skyline. The menu includes swordfish, shrimp, little neck clams, snow crab legs and live Maine lobster in addition to steak and chicken dishes. Call for hours. *!!* AE/V/MC/DI. St. Anthony Main, 201 Main St. S.E., Mpls., 378-7058.

Antonio's Pasta and Steak House
Italian-American restaurant featuring veal Marsala, prime rib, porterhouse and New York strip steaks. 6am-1pm M-F; 6:30am-1pm Sa, -11:30pm Su. Dinner: 5:30-10pm daily. *!!* AE/V/MC/DC/CB/DI. Hotel Seville, 8151 Bridge Road, Bloomington, 830-1300.

Applebee's
Neighborhood bar with basswood decor and menu items that include a variety of burgers, salads and sandwiches. 11am-1am M-Sa; 11am-midnight Su. Su brunch: 11am-3pm. *!* AE/V/MC. Eden Prairie, 942-7993; Northtown Center, Blaine, 784-8086; Southtown Center, Bloomington, 881-8845; Brookdale Center, Brooklyn Center, 566-1003; Brooklyn Park, 424-2730; Burnsville Center, Burnsville, 435-2545; Calhoun Village, Mpls., 925-3403; Maplewood Mall, Maplewood, 770-0604; New Hope, 533-1870; Ridgedale Center, Minnetonka, 544-5540; Spruce Tree Center, St. Paul, 642-9757.

Apples
An informal American restaurant offering homemade soups and desserts. Fresh turkey and beef roasted on premises. 11am-9pm M-Sa. *!!* V/MC. 1260 Town Centre Drive, Eagan, 683-9145.

Arabian Nights
You may eat communal- or American-style in this authentic Middle Eastern restaurant. While eating one of the traditional Middle Eastern entrees such as hummus, shawirma, curried lamb or chicken, you will be entertained by belly dancers. 11am-11pm daily. *!* AE/V/MC. 2523 Nicollet Ave., Mpls., 872-0523.

Arboretum Tea Room
With a view of the arboretum grounds, this cafeteria-style restaurant serves soups, sandwiches, desserts and teas. No liquor. Hours vary according to the seasons. *!* No credit cards. 3675 Arboretum Drive, Chanhassen, 443-2460 ext. 959.

Arnold's Hamburger Grill
With a '50s-'60s interior, this restaurant features hamburgers, sandwiches, salads and hand-dipped malts. No liquor. Mpls.—11am - 11pm M-Sa, -10pm Su. Other locations – 11am-10pm Su-Th, -11pm F and Sa. *!* V/MC. Burnsville, 894-3350; Coon Rapids, 755-4480; Crystal, 535-8777; Mpls., 338-7143; Minnetonka, 474-9042; Richfield, 869-6263; North St. Paul, 451-9012.

Atrium Cafe International
Perfect for business or pleasure luncheons under the skylights of International Market Square. Your choice of gourmet-style buffet or menu. 11:30am-2pm M-F. *!* AE/V/MC/DC/DI. International Market Square, 275 Market St., Mpls., 339-8000.

Austin's
This restaurant serves prime rib and dry-aged beef and chops. Fresh seafood daily. Lunch: 11:30am-2:30pm M-F. Dinner: 5:30-10pm M-Th, -11pm F and Sa. Reservations recom-

Hurray! Minnesota

mended. !!! AE/V/MC/DC/CB/DI. Interchange Tower, 600 S. Highway 169, St. Louis Park, 542-8822.

AWADA'S RESTAURANT AND LOUNGE
Casual dining offering American appetizers, salads, gourmet burgers and chicken breast sandwiches. Other entrees include fresh fish, steak and Lebanese-style shish kebab and tabouli. Lunch: 11am-2:30pm M-Sa. Dinner: 5-9pm M-Th, -11pm F and Sa; 3-8pm Su. ! AE/V/MC/DI. 199 E. Plato Boulevard, St. Paul, 293-9111.

AZUR
Avant-garde restaurant serving French-Mediterranean entrees from filet of beef with Provencal herb crust and shallot sauce to sauteed snapper with stewed artichokes and garlic. Boasts of having the longest bar in Mpls. Lunch: 11:30am-2:30pm M-Sa. Dinner: 5:30-10pm M-Sa. !!! AE/V/MC/DC. Fifth Floor, Gaviidae Common, 651 Nicollet Mall, Mpls., 342-2500.

BAD HABIT CAFE
This coffeehouse is filled with old books and contemporary magazines, making it a great place to sit and ponder life. In addition to the obvious (coffee), try the unusual; soups, sandwiches, salads, muffins and the delicious cheesecake. 7am-11pm M-Th; noon-3am Sa, -6pm Su. ! Hamm Building, 418 St. Peter St., St. Paul, 224-8545.

BACKSTREET GRILL
This diner is a throwback to the past. Each table hosts a jukebox and the menu features hamburgers, fries, malts and homemade pies. No liquor. 6am-8pm M-F; 8am-8pm Sa, -2pm Su. ! No credit cards. 195 S. Robert St., St. Paul, 228-1526.

BALI HAI
American, Chinese and Polynesian restaurant complete with waterfalls, canoes and Hawaiian lithographs featuring menu items from ribs, shrimp, and egg rolls to chicken wings, Hawaii Five-O and flaming ambrosia. Polynesian show T and Sa. 11am-10pm Su-Th, -1am F and Sa. ! AE/V/MC. 2305 White Bear Ave., St. Paul, 777-5500.

BARBARY FIG
Mediterranean restaurant that features meals of North Africa and southern France. Daily specials include entrees such as Moroccan bastilla, grilled vegetables with aioli, and leg of lamb with juniper berries and fresh rosemary. Wine and Beer. Lunch: 11:30am-2pm M and W-Sa. Dinner: 5-9pm Su-M and W-Th; 5:30-10pm F and Sa. !! V/MC. 720 Grand Ave., St. Paul, 290-2085.

BARNEY'S UNDERGROUND
(Formerly Acapulco Bar and Grill.) A traditional American restaurant that serves pub food – sandwiches, chicken wings and specialties such as prime rib sandwiches and French onion soup. 11:30am-1am Tu-Sa and Su-M during special arena events ! AE/V/MC. Sixth and Hennepin, lower level, Mpls., 371-0828.

BEANERY CAFE
Located on Lake Minnetonka, this cafe features fish, shrimp and pasta, in addition to burgers and malts. 5-10pm M-Th, -11pm F; 3-11pm Sa, -10pm Su. Su brunch: 11am-2pm. ! AE/V/MC/DI. 3746 Sunset Drive, Spring Park, 471-8595.

BEIJING
A Szechuan restaurant that is thought to be one of the best in town. The usual fare of Szechuan food with many wonderful specials not listed on the menu. 11am-10pm M-Th, -11pm F and Sa; noon-10pm Su. ! AE/MC/V/CB/DC. Westwind Plaza, 4773 Highway 101 at Highway 7, Minnetonka, 933-6361.

BENCHWARMER BOB'S
Sports bar with 15 TVs. Menu features burgers, chicken, steaks and chili. 11am-11pm M-Th, -midnight F and Sa, -10pm Su. ! AE/V/MC/DC/DI. 8078 Brooklyn Boulevard, Brooklyn Park, 493-2979.

BENJAMIN'S
Family-style restaurant with a casual atmosphere serving breakfast, soups, salad bar, sandwiches, dinner and Su brunch. No liquor. 7am-9pm M-Sa; 8am-8pm Su. ! V/MC. Edina, 926-7743; Minnetonka, 470-9809; Roseville, 639-0633; St. Louis Park, 544-2074; Kelly Inn, St. Paul, 222-1956; Shakopee, 445-0310; Columbia Heights, 574-2722.

BENNIGAN'S
Traditional meals in a casual setting. Includes salads, sandwiches, burgers, pasta, Cajun dishes, chicken, steak and seafood. 11am-12:30am daily. Sa and Su brunch at Bloomington, Su only at St. Louis Park. Both Bennigans' offer two-for-one cocktails seven days a week 11am-7pm and 10pm-midnight. ! AE/V/MC/DC/CB/DI. 1800 W. 80th St., Bloomington, 881-0013. 6475 Wayzata Boulevard, St. Louis Park, 593-5024.

BIFF'S SPORTS BAR AND GRILL
Informal sports bar with 27 pool tables, game room and eight electronic dart games. Full restaurant and bar with crab legs special on Sa

and Su. DJ on F and Sa. *!!* AE/V/MC. 7777 Highway 65, Spring Lake Park, 784-9397.

BIGELOW'S
Dining in a relaxed setting. Menu includes steaks, prime rib and fresh seafood. Live music and dancing on F and Sa. 6:30am-10pm M-Su. Su brunch: 10am-2pm. *!!* AE/V/MC/DC/CB/DI. Sheraton Midway, Interstate 94 and Hamline, St. Paul, 642-1284, ext. 521.

BIGSBY'S CAFE
Urban cafe featuring soups, luncheon entrees, hot and cold sandwiches, muffins, salads and desserts. 7am-8pm M-F. *!* AE/V/MC/DI. 701 Fourth Ave. S., Mpls., 338-0023.

BILLY'S BAR AND GRILL
Casual dining in a century-old historical setting. Full menu featuring steaks, pasta, Mexican, burgers and your favorite cocktails. Friday night fish fry. 11am-10pm Su-Th, -11pm F and Sa. *!* AE/V/MC. 214 Jackson St., Anoka, 421-3570.

BILLY'S LIGHTHOUSE
Overlooking Long Lake, this restaurant features fresh seafood, fettuccine a la mer, beef Burgundy, prime rib and Grand Marnier roast duckling. The saloon offers burgers and appetizers. Hours vary seasonally. Su brunch: 10am-2:30pm. *!!* AE/V/MC/DC/CB. 1310 W. Wayzata Boulevard, Long Lake, 473-2355.

BILLY'S ON GRAND/VICTORIA CAFE
Full-service bar and grill with menu items including daily and nightly specials, ribs, seafood, steaks, chicken and burgers. Four- season patio with fireplace. Kitchen open 11am-12:30am daily. *!!* AE/V/MC/DC/DI. Victoria Crossing East, 857 Grand Ave., St. Paul, 292-9140.

BISCAYNE BAY
Serving innovative fresh-fish specials created by our Mobile Four Diamond and American Culinary Federation award-winning chef. Lobster creations with an artistic flair, beef tenderloin with bourbon glaze, veal medallions with cherry-shallot sauce and fresh fish beyond compare. 6:30-10pm daily *!!!* AE/V/DC/CB/DI. Airport Hilton, Interstate 494 at 34th Ave., Bloomington, 854-2100.

BLACK FOREST INN
Informal Bohemian German restaurant offering beef goulash, Wiener schnitzel, Hungarian sauerbraten, hasenpfeffer, homemade bratwurst and desserts. 11am-midnight M-Sa; noon-11pm Su. *!* AE/V/MC/DC/DI. 26th and Nicollet, Mpls., 872-0812.

BLUE FOX INN
Serving a variety of meals including chicken Kiev and peppercorn steak. Live music F and Sa. Karaoke sing-along M-F. Lunch: 11am-2pm M-F. Dinner: 4-9:30pm M-Th, -10:30pm F and Sa. *!!* V/MC/DC/CB/DI. 3833 Lexington Ave. N., Arden Hills, 483-6000.

BLUE NILE
With a menu that represents Ethiopia and the Middle East cuisine, this restaurant serves steak tartare, lentil dishes and cubed lamb with onions and jalapeno. Beer and wine. 11am-10pm M-Th, -11pm F; 9am-11pm Sa, -10pm Su. *!* V/MC/DI. Lake and Lyndale, Mpls., 823-8029.

BLUE POINT RESTAURANT AND OYSTER BAR
Located in scenic Wayzata, specializing in fresh ocean fish, seasonal fresh crab, live large lobsters and the best selection of fresh oysters in the Twin Cities. Like stepping onto the Eastern seaboard. 4-10pm M-Th, -11pm F and Sa. *!!!* AE/V/MC/DC. 739 E. Lake St., Wayzata, 475-3636.

BOCA CHICA
A family tradition worth tasting, since 1964. Serving a variety of Mexican cuisine – tacos, tostados, enchiladas and also chile rellenos, quisados, flautas, moles, tamales and more. Full bar serving margaritas and many of your favorite Mexican beers. 11am-10pm M, -10:30pm Tu-Th, -midnight F and Sa; 10am-10pm Su. Su brunch: 10am-2pm. *!!* AE/V/MC. 11 Concord St., St. Paul, 222-8499.

BOCCE
An upscale Italian sports bar serving, with style, burger, pasta and pizza as well as dinner entrees. 11:30am-1am M-Sa; 10am-1am Su. *!!* AE/V/MC/D. Butler Square, 100 N. Sixth St., Mpls., 332-1600.

BOMBAY BICYCLE CLUB
Eclectic menu including prime rib, fettuccine shrimp, and chicken smothered with cheese, mushrooms and onions. Dancing Th-Sa. 11:30am-1am M-Sa; 11am-midnight Su. *!* AE/V/MC/DI/DC. 199 Northtown Drive, Blaine, 786-0380.

BOMBAY PALACE
Northeastern and southern Indian cuisine, specializing in Tandoor cooking. All-you-can-eat buffet features 11 items that includes three vegetable and two meat dishes, rice and bread. 11am-9pm M-Th, -10:30pm F and Sa. *!* V/MC. 1424 Nicollet Ave., Mpls., 872-7044.

BOSTON GARDEN
Informal restaurant offering spaghetti, homemade soups, lasagna, milk shakes, desserts and

breads. Wine and beer. 6am-9pm M-Sa; 8am-8pm Su; Su brunch: 10am-2pm. ❕ AE/V/MC/DI. 1019 Main St., Hopkins, 933-7827.

BOUNDARY WATERS
A variety of dishes from char-grilled chicken and beef, daily fish selections, and mandarin-chicken salad to cream-of-wild-rice soup, grilled fresh fish and pasta. Wine and beer at Southdale; full bar at Ridgedale. Southdale – 11am-8:30pm M-F, -5pm Sa; noon - 4pm Su. Ridgedale – 11am-8:45pm M-F, -4:45pm Sa; noon-4:45pm Su. ❕ AE/V/MC/DI. Dayton's Southdale, Edina, 924-6737. Dayton's Ridgedale, Minnetonka, 591-6727.

BRIAN'S SEAFOOD CASA
Internationally prepared fresh seafood and fish entrees are served. Each month the menu changes to represent the cuisine of a different international region. One month the theme will be Caribbean, and the next you may find dishes from the Mediterranean or South and Central America. Pasta dishes, steak and chops are also served. Entertainment W-Su. 4:30pm-midnight M-Sa; 10am-midnight Su. Su brunch: 10am-2pm. ❕ AE/V/MC/DI. 2901 S. Hennepin Ave., Mpls., 824-1490.

BRINE'S
Each location features hot and cold deli sandwiches, bratwurst, chili, steak and eggs, soups and hamburgers. Stillwater – 8am-9pm daily; Su brunch: 8am-noon. St. Paul – 7am-5pm M-F ❕ AE/V/MC at Stillwater, no credit cards at St. Paul. 219 S. Main St., Stillwater, 439-1862. 9 W. Fifth St., St. Paul, 227-8663.

BRIT'S PUB
Nestled in downtown Minneapolis, while offering a taste of a trip to a British pub. Menu includes homemade popovers, shepherd's pie, and a wide variety of malt scotches and ports. 8am-1am M-Sa, -midnight Su. Afternoon tea served between 2:30-4pm M-F. ❕❕ AE/V/MC/DC/CB/DI. 1110 Nicollet Mall, Mpls., 332-3908.

BROOKDALE INN
A variety of dishes from char-grilled chicken and beef, daily fish selections, and mandarin-chicken salad to cream-of-wild-rice soup, grilled fresh fish and pasta. Wine and beer. 11am-8pm M-F, -4pm Sa; noon-3pm Su. ❕ AE/V/MC/DI. Dayton's Brookdale, Highway 100 and Brooklyn Boulevard, Brooklyn Center, 569-6727.

BUFFALO CANTINA
This new restaurant brought its own grill to Minnesota — an authentic Texas pit barbecue where beef brisket is slow-cooked for 17 hours.

You can also order a barbecue rib platter, half chicken, a sausage platter, Tex-Mex items and sandwiches. Take-out on the lower level at the Buffalo Gap. 11:30am-1am daily. ❕ AE/V/MC. Mississippi Live, main floor, 1 S.E. Main St., Mpls., 331-6788.

BUGSY'S
At the site of the now-defunct Players, Bugsy's serves up oversized salads, pastas, hot and cold sandwiches, burgers and homemade soups. 11am-1am daily. ❕ AE/V/MC/D. 315 N. First Ave., Mpls., 341-3953.

BURGUNDY ROOM
Serving broiled steaks and a variety of sauteed items. Lunch: 11:30am-1:45pm M-F. Dinner: 5:30-9pm M-Th, -10pm F and Sa. ❕❕❕ AE/V/MC/DC/CB/DI. Best Western Drovers Inn, 701 S. Concord St., South St. Paul, 455-3600.

THE BUTTERY
Sandwiches, soups, salads and hot entrees such as lasagna, beef stroganoff and chicken are served. 11:30am-1am M-Sa, -midnight Su. ❕ AE/V/MC. 395 N. Robert St., St. Paul, 222-5861.

CACTUS WILLIES TEX-MEX GRILL
Pepitos-owned neighborhood restaurant offering gourmet burritos, char-grilled chicken, nachos and burgers. 10am-10pm M-Th, -11pm F-Sa; 11am-10pm Su. ❕ No credit cards. 5001 34th Ave., Mpls., 721-2936.

THE CAFE
Dine in the atrium while feasting on our barbecued walleye fillet, coo coo pie, homemade ice cream and other traditional American fare. 6:30am-11pm daily. ❕❕ AE/V/MC/DC/CB/DI. Third floor, Radisson Plaza Hotel, 35 S. Seventh St., Mpls., 339-4900.

THE CAFE
Serving Continental-American meals, this restaurant offers veal, stuffed fillet and pasta. Breakfast: 6:30am-11:30am M-F, -1pm Sa and Su. Lunch: 11:30am-2:30pm M, -4:30pm Tu-F. Dinner: 4:30-9pm Tu-Th, -10pm F and Sa. ❕❕ AE/V/MC/DC/CB. Saint Paul Hotel, 350 Market St., St. Paul, 292-9292.

CAFE BRENDA
Cafe serving gourmet natural foods from the Mediterranean, Asian and ethnic American cultures. Vegetarian and seafood specials daily. Wine and beer. Lunch: 11:30am-2pm M-F. Dinner: 5:30-10pm M-Th, -11pm F and Sa. ❕❕ AE/V/MC. 300 First Ave. N., Mpls., 342-9230.

CAFE CARABELLA
Continental restaurant serving breakfast, lunch and dinner. Sandwiches, salads and light-

healthy fare are served, as well as a full dinner menu from fresh fish to our "all you can eat prime rib special" every evening. Su brunch never to be forgotten. 6:30am-10pm daily. !! AE/V/MC/DC/CB/DI. Airport Hilton, I-494 at 34th Ave., Bloomington, 854-2100.

CAFE DI NAPOLI
Established in 1938, this cafe serves Italian and American cuisine including pizza, spaghetti, lasagna, salads and manicotti. 11am-11pm M-Th, -11:30pm F and Sa. ! AE/V/MC/DC/CB. 816 Hennepin Ave., Mpls., 333-4949 or 333-9019.

CAFE LUXEFORD
Jazz at the Luxx. Newly remodeled cafe with updated menu serving shrimp fettuccine, broiled walleye and grilled chicken. Breakfast, lunch and dinner are served. 6:30am-10pm Su-Sa. Live jazz 8:30pm-12:30am Tu-Sa. !! AE/V/MC. Hotel Luxeford, 11th at LaSalle, Mpls., 332-6800.

CAFE SFA
A bustling cafe serving homemade pastas, salads, sandwiches, soups and desserts. 11am-4pm M-Sa. ! AE/V/MC. Saks Fifth Avenue, fourth floor, Gaviidae Common, 655 Nicollet Mall, Mpls., 333-7200.

CAFE UN DEUX TROIS
Paris and New York bistros have influenced this restaurant's decor and cuisine. The upscale flavor makes it a perfect place for an elegant lunch. The menu features traditional bistro fare such as French onion soup, escargot a' la Bourguignonne, steak and French fries as well as grilled lamb with a garlic and tomato comfit. 11am-10pm M-Th; 5-10pm F and Sa. !! AE/V/MC/D. 114 S. Ninth St., Mpls., 673-0686.

CAFE LATTE
Gourmet cafeteria featuring pasta salads, stews, soups, European tortes, triple-layer turtle cakes, fruit tortes and espresso drinks. Wine and beer. 10am-11pm M-Th, -midnight F; 9am-midnight Sa, -10pm Su. Sa and Su brunch: 9am-noon. ! AE. 850 Grand Ave., St. Paul, 224-5687.

CAFFE SOLO
Featuring an Italian menu, this restaurant, coffee house and bakery specializes in pastas and breakfasts. 7am-1am M-Th, -3am F and Sa, -11pm Su. ! No credit cards. 123 N. Third St., Mpls., 332-7108.

CAIRO CAFE
In the heart of downtown Minneapolis, this cafe offers a Middle Eastern menu with items including falafel, kebabs and rabbit. 11am-9pm daily. !! No credit cards. 704 Hennepin Ave., Mpls., 338-6810.

CALHOUN'S AMERICAN GRILL
Informal restaurant with a menu including a variety of sandwiches, and half-chicken cooked with matzo balls. 11am-11pm M-Sa; 8am-9pm Su. Sa and Su brunch: 8am-2pm. ! AE/V/MC/DI/DC. Calhoun Beach Club, 2730 W. Lake St., Mpls., 926-4985.

CAPERS
Restaurant featuring pasta and pizza, fresh fish, seafood and Italian entrees. No liquor. 11am-10pm M-Th, -11pm F; 8am-11pm Sa; 10am-10pm Su. Su brunch: 10am-2pm. !! AE/V/MC. 2221 W. 50th St., Mpls., 927-4416.

CARAVAN SERAI
"The first Afghani restaurant in the United States" offers traditional dining under a tent on cushions. The menu includes lamb, beef, shrimp and vegetarian entrees. Featuring traditional Tandoori clay oven cooking over open charcoal. Beer and wine. Lunch: 11am-2:30pm M-F. Dinner: 5-10pm Su-Th, -11pm F and Sa. !! AE/V/MC/CB/DC. 2175 Ford Parkway., St. Paul, 690-1935.

CARAVELLE
Serving Chinese and Vietnamese dishes such as lobster and sugar-cane shrimp. Wine and beer. St. Paul – 11am-9pm M-Th, -10pm F and Sa. Mpls. – 11am-9pm Su-Th, -10pm F and Sa. ! V/MC/DC. 799 University Ave., St. Paul, 292-9324. 2529 Nicollet Ave., Mpls., 871-3226.

CECIL'S DELICATESSEN AND RESTAURANT
Featuring deli favorites like matzo-ball soup, potato latkes, cabbage borscht, burgers, sandwiches, freshly baked breads and homemade cream pies. St. Paul – 9am-8pm daily. Mpls. – 9:30am-6:30pm M-F; 10:30am-6pm Sa. ! V/MC. 651 Cleveland Ave. S., St. Paul, 698-0334 or 698-6276. City Center, 40 S. Seventh St., Mpls., 341-0170.

CEDAR STREET CAFE
Comfortable, warm, American restaurant featuring homemade soups, beef pot pie, sandwiches, salads, pecan pie and apple walnut cake. No liquor. 6am-3pm M-F. No credit cards. Minnesota Building, 46 E. Fourth St., St. Paul, 292-0874.

CHAMPP'S
Sports bar with hardwood floors, high ceilings, windows and nine TVs. Offering burgers, pasta, salads, chicken sandwiches, desserts, malts and shakes. Minnetonka and Larpenteur – 11am-1am M-Sa, -midnight Su. St. Paul – 11am-10pm daily. Richfield – 11am-11pm M-

Hurray! Minnesota

Sa, -10pm Su. Appetizers served at all locations until midnight M-Sa, -11pm Su. *!* V/MC. 7701 Plymouth Road, Minnetonka, 546-3333. Sibley Plaza, 2431 W. Seventh St., St. Paul, 698-5050. Market Plaza, 790 W. 66th St., Richfield, 861-3333. 1734 Adolphus St., 35E and Larpenteur, 487-5050.

CHAPMAN'S SCOREBOARD
Our all-new sports bar features 13 TVs plus the big screen. All-new menu including an immense salad bar. 11am-1am M-Sa, -midnight Su. *!* AE/V/MC/DC. Two blocks north of Crosstown on Shady Oak Road, Minnetonka, 935-6537.

CHART HOUSE
Overlooking Lake Kingsley, this restaurant serves steaks, prime rib, seafood and poultry. Lunch: 11:30am-2:30pm daily. Dinner: 5-10pm M-Sa; 3-9pm Su. Su brunch: 10am - 2pm. *!!!* AE/V/MC/DC/CB/DI. 11287 Klamath Trail, Lakeville, 435-7156.

CHEERS ON SIXTH STREET
It's not the original Cheers in Boston, but it is a pretty popular place. Homemade chips are the trademark. Other offerings include burgers, a chicken breast sandwich and a daily special which might be prime rib, seafood, a sandwich or chicken breast salad. 11am-1am daily. *!* AE/V/MC. 23 N. Sixth St., Mpls., 332-7680.

CHEROKEE SIRLOIN ROOM
This family-run restaurant dating back to the 1930s features fresh Alaskan salmon, walleyed pike, jumbo shrimp and specializes in sirloin steak. Su brunch: 10am-2pm. St. Paul – 11am-2:30pm and 5-11pm M-Sa; 3-10pm Su. Eagan – 11am-9pm M-W, -10pm Th-Sa; 10am-9pm Su. *!!* AE/V/MC/DC/CB. Cedar Ave. at Cliff Road, Eagan, 454-6744. 886 Smith Ave. S., St. Paul, 457-2729.

CHESSEN'S DELI AND BAR
This is a full-service, New York-style deli and bar. It is known for its 6 oz Reuben sandwich. Received the Power Breakfast Award in 1990. 7am-1am M-Sa. Kitchen open until 10pm. *!* AE/V/MC/DC. 310 Fourth Ave. S., Mpls., 338-2755. Chessen's Too, 330 Second Ave. S., Mpls., 341-8136.

CHEZ BANANAS
Caribbean restaurant with a flair for the eccentric. Menu items include garlic-cream scallops, jerk chicken, beef filet calypso, spicy Caribbean barbecue. Wine and beer. 11:30am-10pm Tu-Th, -midnight F; 5-11pm Sa, -9pm Su, -10pm M. *!!* V/MC. Textile Building, 129 N. Fourth St., Mpls., 340-0032.

CHEZ COLETTE
1930s brasserie features traditional entrees from the French provinces. Coq au vin from Burgundy, oysters and lobster from Brittany, quiche from Lorraine and garlic sausage from Paris. Pianist entertains nightly. Breakfast: 6:30-11am M-F; 7-11:30am Sa. Lunch: 11:30am-2pm M-F; noon-2pm Sa. Dinner: 5:30-10pm M-Th, -11pm F and Sa. Su brunch: 11am-2pm. *!!* AE/V/MC/DC/CB. Hotel Sofitel, 5601 W. 78th St., Bloomington, 835-0126.

CHEZ DANIEL
A bistro-style French restaurant offering escargot, steak au poivre and roast duckling. 11am-10pm M-Th, -11pm F and Sa; 10:30am-9pm Su. *!!* AE/MC/V/DC. Embassy Suites Hotel, 2800 W. 80th St., Bloomington, 888-4447.

CHEZ PAUL
Informal country-French dining offering chicken breast stuffed with lobster, grilled lamb chops, chilled strawberry souffle and grapefruit-Bavarian creme. Wine and beer. Lunch: 11:30am-2:30pm daily. Dinner: 5:30-10pm Su-Th, -11pm F and Sa. Lighter menu in the bistro: 7am-10pm Su-Th. Dining room *!!!* Bistro *!* V/MC/DC. 1400 Nicollet Ave., Mpls., 870-4212.

CHI-CHI'S
Mexican restaurant with a menu featuring burritos, chajitas (charbroiled strips of chicken on a sizzling blackened skillet) and chimichangas. DJ and dancing nightly at Richfield and Brooklyn Center. Brooklyn Center – 11am-10:30pm Su-Th, -midnight F and Sa. All others – 11am-11pm M-Th, -midnight F and Sa, -10pm Su. Su brunch: 11am-2pm. *!!* AE/V/MC/DC/DI. Anoka, 427-1970; Brooklyn Center, 561-0550; Burnsville, 435-7117; City Center, Mpls., 339-0766; Eden Prairie, 942-5544; Maplewood, 770-6888; Minnetonka, 473-0770; Richfield, 866-3433; St. Paul, 644-1122.

CHILI'S
Family-style restaurant serving chili, Caribbean salad and charbroiled fajitas. 11am-10pm. *!* AE/V/MC/DC/CB/DI. 1840 W. County Road B2, Roseville, 633-7718. 7801 Normandale Boulevard, Bloomington, 831-

---

AE = American Express / V = VISA / MC = MasterCard / DI = Discover / DC = Diners Club / CB = Carte Blanche
! = less than $10 / *!!* $10-$18 / *!!!* $18-$28 / *!!!!* more than $28

You Can Contribute to *Hurray! Minnesota*

We are now preparing the 1994 edition of "Hurray! Minnesota." You are invited to submit information regarding museums, entertainment, historic sites, festivals and celebrations, recreational activities and destinations, parks and lakes, sporting events, nightlife and dining spots, and hotels, resorts and B&Bs, as well as facts, trivia and/or historic notes about the state.

■

Updates, additions and/or corrections of existing entries are welcome.

■

Color slides, black-and-white photographs and original work by photographers will be considered, but the publisher will assume no responsibility for submissions unless accompanied by a self-addressed stamped envelope.

■

Address all correspondence to:

"Hurray! Minnesota"
15 South Fifth Street, Suite 900
Minneapolis, MN 55402
(612) 338-1578

1201. 8057 Brooklyn Boulevard, Brooklyn Park, 425-1550. 1800 Beam Ave., Maplewood, 773-9501. 14161 Aldridge, Burnsville, 898-3101.

CHOO CHOO BAR AND RESTAURANT
A 1909 caboose inhabits a depot-inspired dining room. Featuring chicken wings, barbecued ribs, seafood and Italian dishes. Stand-up comedy F and Sa. 11am-11pm M-Th, -1am F and Sa; noon-11pm Su. !! AE/V/MC. 160 Railway St., Loretto, 479-3565.

CHRISTOS
Greek restaurant offering traditional favorites like moussaka, spanakopita and shish kebab. Many specialties of the house hail from Cyprus. Wine and beer. 11am-10pm M-Th, -11pm F; 4-11pm Sa, -9pm Su. ! V/MC. 2632 Nicollet Ave., Mpls., 871-2111.

CIATTI'S ITALIAN RESTAURANT
Authentic Italian cuisine and a fine dining atmosphere. A large menu features delicious northern and southern Italian dishes priced reasonably. !! AE/V/MC. Mpls., 339-7747; Burnsville, 892-7555; Eden Prairie, 944-5181; Falcon Heights, 644-2808; Maplewood, 770-6691; St. Paul, 292-9942; Edina, 920-3338. Su brunch available at some locations.

COGNAC MCCARTHY'S
This bistro offers country-French breakfasts, French-Cuban rotisserie chicken, fresh mussels, reddened whitefish, steak, chops and homemade desserts. 9am-11pm M-Sa, -9pm Su. ! AE/V/MC. 162 N. Dale St., St. Paul, 224-4617.

COPPER STEIN
Informal dining offering such American cuisine as barbecued ribs, seafood and steak. 6am-9:30pm M-Th, -10:30pm F; 7am-10:30pm Sa; 8am-2pm and 5-9:30pm Su. !! AE/V/MC/DC. 5635 Manitou Road, Excelsior, 474-5805.

CORBY'S
Restaurant with a British flavor in downtown Hudson. Offering seafood, lamb and a unique cuisine with a European flair. Lunch: 11:30am-2pm, M-F English pub food. ! Dinner: 5-10pm, Tu-Su. !!! AE/V/MC/DC. 417 Second St., Hudson, WI, (715) 386-1610.

COSSETTA'S
Featuring Italian entrees, this deli market and pizzeria offers salads, pizza and sandwiches. Wine and beer. 11am-10pm M-Sa, -8pm Su. ! No credit cards. 211 W. Seventh St., St. Paul, 222-3476.

COUNTRY HOUSE
This restaurant specializes in steaks. Live music played Th-Sa. Lunch: 11am-2pm M-F. Dinner:

5-10pm daily. *!!* AE/V/MC. 10715 S. Shore Drive, Medicine Lake, 546-4655.

COYOTE CAFE
Southwestern restaurant offers such specialties as enchiladas, chili and a varied selection of omelets and frittatas. 11am-9pm M-Th, -11pm F and Sa; 9am-9pm Su. *!* AE/V/MC. Hennepin Ave. and Sixth St., Mpls., 338-1730.

DA AFGHAN
Voted the best Middle Eastern restaurant '88, '90 and '91. Serving Afghani dishes in surroundings intriguingly decorated with tapestries. Entrees include chicken, kebabs and organically raised lamb. Lunch: 11am-3pm M-F. Dinner: 5-10pm M-Th, -11pm F and Sa. *!!* AE/V/MC/DC. 929 W. 80th St., Bloomington, 888-5824.

DAKOTA BAR AND GRILL
This restaurant serves traditional Midwestern fare with Midwestern ingredients. Menu items include thyme-marinated pork loin with a maple-blueberry sauce, broiled fillet of walleye with wild rice, and excellent desserts. 5-10:30pm M-Th, -11:30pm F and Sa; 5:30-9:30pm Su. *!!* AE/MC/V/DC/DI. Bandana Square, 1021 Bandana Boulevard E., St. Paul, 642-1442.

D'AMICO CUCINA
Elegant Italian restaurant with a changing menu. Specialties include Italian peasant dishes, fish, lamb and pasta. Live entertainment: Th-Sa. Dinner: 5:30-10pm M-Th, -11pm F and Sa; 5-9pm Su. Open at 5pm on Timberwolves nights. *!!!!* AE/V/MC/DC. 160 Butler Square, Mpls., 338-2401.

DAVANNI'S
Offering New York-style hand-pounded, thin-crust, and deep-dish pizzas, as well as 15 hoagies and a salad bar. Wine at some locations. Beer at all. *!* No credit cards. Twelve metro area locations, call the Connection at 922-9000 for details.

DAY BY DAY
Home-cooked breakfasts are served all day; the green earth special with hash browns, broccoli, eggs, cheese and onion is a particular favorite. Also served are basic vegetarian fare as well as croissant sandwiches, salads and burgers. 6am-8pm M-W, -10pm Th and F, -3pm Sa; 7am-3pm Su. No credit cards. *!* 477 W. Seventh St., St. Paul, 227-0654.

THE DECO
With a view of the Mississippi River, this restaurant features a menu of Scandinavian salads, smoked salmon, hot entrees, soups, fresh cardamom and cinnamon rolls. Regular menu and buffet served 11:30am-2pm Tu-F. Su brunch: 11am-1pm. *!!* AE/V. Jemne Building, 305 St. Peter St., St. Paul, 228-0520.

DELITES OF INDIA
This restaurant features 50 dishes from the Punjab that include pranthas, Indian flat breads and curries, in addition to homemade mango, rose and almond ice cream. Wine and beer. Lunch: 11:30am-2pm Tu-Su. Dinner: 5-9pm Tu-Su, -9:30pm F and Sa, -8:30pm Su. Su brunch: 11:30am-2pm. *!!* AE/DC/CB. 1123 W. Lake St., Mpls., 823-2866.

DIAMOND THAI CAFE
This restaurant caters to people with a stomach for spicy food. Features pod prig kieng-pork, beef, chicken, shrimp or tofu stir-fried with cashews, onions, hot peppers, water chestnuts, bamboo shoots and vegetables. No liquor. 11am-9:30pm M-F; noon-9:30pm Sa; 11am-8pm Su. *!* AE/V/MC. 1423 Washington Ave. S., Mpls., 332-2920.

DIXIE'S BAR AND SMOKEHOUSE GRILL
This restaurant offers Tex-Mex, Cajun, American and southern-style cuisine with such menu items as blackened fish, coconut shrimp, hickory-smoked barbecued ribs, skin-on fries and key lime, pecan and mud pies. 11am-11pm M-Sa; 10am-midnight Su. Su brunch: 10am-2pm. *!!* AE/V/MC/DC/CB. 695 Grand Ave., St. Paul, 222-7345.

DOCK CAFE
On the shore of the scenic St. Croix River, this restaurant features fresh fish, choice beef, a variety of pasta specials, and homemade soups and desserts. Lunch: 11am-3:30pm daily. Dinner: 5-9pm Su-Th, -10pm F and Sa. *!!* AE/V/MC/DC/CB. 425 E. Nelson Ave., Stillwater, 430-3770.

DOVER
Great food and all that jazz. New American cuisine. 6am-10pm daily. All-new complimentary happy hour buffet and selected drink specials 5-7pm M-F. Live jazz 8pm-midnight Tu-Su. Su brunch: 11am-2pm. *!!* AE/V/MC/CB. Sheraton Park Place Hotel, Interstate 394 Vernon Xenia Exit, Mpls., 542-1060.

AE = American Express / V = VISA / MC = MasterCard / DI = Discover / DC = Diners Club / CB = Carte Blanche
! = less than $10 / *!!* $10-$18 / *!!!* $18-$28 / *!!!!* more than $28

Duggan's Bar and Grill
Featuring prime rib cooked slowly in rock salt, this restaurant also offers fresh pastas, stir-fried entrees, Cajun dishes and fresh fish. Lunch: 11am-2:30pm M-Sa. Dinner: 5-10pm M-Th, -11pm F and Sa, -9pm Su. Su brunch: 11am-2pm. !! AE/V/MC/DC. 5916 Excelsior Boulevard, St. Louis Park, 922-6025.

Du Jour
(Formerly Le Peep.) Specializes in such breakfast dishes as panhandled eggs served in a skillet with peasant potatoes and vegetables. No liquor. 6:30am-2:30pm M-F; 7am-2:30pm Sa and Su. ! AE/V/MC. 89 S. 10th St., Mpls., 333-1855. Colonnade, Highway 12 and Turners Crossroad, Golden Valley, 591-5033; Saint Paul Center, 444 Cedar St., St. Paul, 228-0805.

Dupsy's African Cuisine
Featuring the foods of western Africa. Serving dishes such as Jollof rice, coconut rice, curry, egusi (a spicy beef stew) and fufu. 11am-9pm M-Th, -10pm F and Sa; 1-7pm Su. ! No credit cards. 474 University Ave., St. Paul, 225-1525.

Eddie Webster's
English manor restaurant featuring seafood, poultry, sandwiches and steaks. Live music in the Cabaret. 11am-11pm M-F; 5-11pm Sa; 4-9pm Su. !! AE/V/MC/DC/DI. 1501 E. 78th St., Bloomington, 854-4056.

Eddington's
American cafeteria-style restaurant offering homemade soups, bread sticks and muffins, plus sandwiches and a salad bar. No liquor. City Center – 6:30am-8pm M-F; 10am-6pm, Sa. St. Paul – 7am-3pm M-F. Pillsbury – 6:30am-4pm M-F. Minnetonka – 8am-8pm M-Th and Sa, -10pm F. ! No credit cards. 40 S. Seventh St., Mpls., 332-4062; 385 Cedar St., St. Paul, 228-0427; Pillsbury Center, 200 S. Sixth St., Mpls., 338-5747; 12987 Ridgedale Drive, Minnetonka, 591-9586.

Ediner
Dine on hamburgers, malts, salads and homemade soups in a 1940s atmosphere complete with diner car and jukebox. Liquor at Calhoun Square. Galleria – 9am-9pm M-F; 8am-9pm Sa, -8pm Su. Calhoun Square – 9am-10pm M-Th, -11pm F; 8am-11pm Sa, -10pm Su. ! AE/V/MC/DI. Galleria, France Ave. S. at W. 69th, Edina, 925-4008; Calhoun Square, 3001 Hennepin Ave., Mpls., 822-6011.

Edwardo's
Specializing in Chicago-style stuffed pizza, this colorful restaurant features thin-crust and stuffed pizzas, in addition to salads, spaghetti and linguine. Wine and beer. 11am-11pm Su-Th, -midnight F and Sa. Su brunch: 11am-4pm. ! AE/V/MC. Symphony Place, 1125 Marquette Ave., Mpls., 339-9700. 2633 Southtown Drive, Bloomington, 884-8400.

Egg and I
Exhibiting the works of local artists each month, this restaurant features breakfast and egg dishes, such as omelets, eggs Benedict and sourdough pancakes, Belgian waffles and Mexican eggs. No liquor. 6am-3pm M-F; 8am-3pm Sa and Su. ! No credit cards at Mpls. AE/V/MC at St. Paul. 2704 Lyndale Ave. S., Mpls., 872-7282. 2550 University Ave., St. Paul, 647-1292.

Eleven East Cafe
Casual American-style cafe offering fresh seafood and salads. 6:30am-10pm daily. Su brunch: 10:30am-2pm. !! AE/V/MC/DC/CB/DI. Radisson Hotel, 11 E. Kellogg Boulevard, St. Paul, 292-1900.

Ellington's (Crown Sterling Restaurant)
Art-deco restaurant featuring an American menu with International specialties. Lunch: 11am-2:30pm M-F. Dinner: 5-10pm Su-Th, -11pm F and Sa. !! AE/V/MC/DC/CB/DI. Eighth floor, Crown Sterling Suites Hotel, 425 S. Seventh St., Mpls., 339-7995.

El Meson
First and only authentic Spanish Latin restaurant in the Twin Cities. The house specialty is the paella. A must-try are the shrimp Victoria, arvoz con pollo, garlic chicken, rice with black or red beans, fried plantains and yucca. No liquor. 11am-10pm Tu-F; noon-10pm Sa; 4-9pm Su. !! AE/V/MC. 3450 Lyndale Ave. S., Mpls., 822-8062.

Elsie's Restaurant and Lounge
Scottish restaurant offering taco salad, chicken, liver, seafood, steaks, prime rib, barbecued pork ribs, homemade soups and tapioca pudding. 11:15am-10pm M-Th, -11pm F and Sa, -8pm Su. ! 721 Marshall St. N.E., Mpls., 378-9702.

El Torito
Assortment of Mexican dishes including seafood fajitas and all-you-can-eat luncheon buffet. 11am-11pm M-Th, -midnight F and Sa. 10am-10pm Su. Su brunch: 10am-2pm. ! AE/V/MC/DC/CB/DI. 6440 Wayzata Boulevard, Golden Valley, 544-3406.

Emily's Lebanese Deli
Offering such Lebanese dishes as baked kibbi, lamb shish kebabs, tabouli salad and flat

ORDER ADDITIONAL COPIES OF "HURRAY! MINNESOTA"

I wish to order additional copies of "Hurray! Minnesota" at $13.95 each. Minnesota residents add 6.5 percent sales tax (91¢ per book). Add $1.80 per book for postage and handling.

_____	Copies at $13.95	$ _____
	6.5% MN sales tax, per copy	$ _____
	Postage & handling, per copy	$ _____
	Total	$ _____

Mail this card and your check or credit card information to: "Hurray! Minnesota"
15 S. Fifth St., Suite 900
Minneapolis, MN 55402

☐ VISA   ☐ Mastercard

CREDIT CARD NUMBER _____   EXPIRATION DATE _____

SIGNATURE _____

Ship to:
NAME _____

ADDRESS _____

CITY _____ STATE _____ ZIP _____

PHONE (___) _____

Inquire about quantity discount when ordering five or more copies of "Hurray! Minnesota" by phoning Minnmedia Inc. at (612) 338-1578.

ORDER ADDITIONAL COPIES OF "HURRAY! MINNESOTA"

I wish to order additional copies of "Hurray! Minnesota" at $13.95 each. Minnesota residents add 6.5 percent sales tax (91¢ per book). Add $1.80 per book for postage and handling.

_____	Copies at $13.95	$ _____
	6.5% MN sales tax, per copy	$ _____
	Postage & handling, per copy	$ _____
	Total	$ _____

Mail this card and your check or credit card information to: "Hurray! Minnesota"
15 S. Fifth St., Suite 900
Minneapolis, MN 55402

☐ VISA   ☐ Mastercard

CREDIT CARD NUMBER _____   EXPIRATION DATE _____

SIGNATURE _____

Ship to:
NAME _____

ADDRESS _____

CITY _____ STATE _____ ZIP _____

PHONE (___) _____

Inquire about quantity discount when ordering five or more copies of "Hurray! Minnesota" by phoning Minnmedia Inc. at (612) 338-1578.

bread. No liquor. 9am-9pm M, W, Th and Su -10pm F and Sa. *!* No credit cards. 641 University Ave. N.E., Mpls., 379-4069.

EMPORIUM OF JAZZ RESTAURANT AND LOUNGE
Featuring live jazz Th-Sa nights, this restaurant serves seafood, steaks and New Orleans meals. 11am-9pm M-W, -9:30pm Th, -10pm F and Sa; 3-9pm Su. *!!* AE/V/MC/DC. 1351 Sibley Memorial Highway, Mendota, 452-1830.

ESTEBAN'S
Mexican restaurant offering traditional to exotic fare. Fajitas, pork chops with Cajun topping, rib-eye and stuffed shrimp wrapped in bacon. Featuring an indoor patio setting. 11am-9pm Su-Th, -10pm F and Sa. *!!* AE/V/MC/DC/CB/DI. 324 S. Main St., Stillwater, 430-1543.

EXCELSIOR PARK TAVERN
Overlooking Lake Minnetonka, this restaurant serves pizza, hamburgers and sandwiches. 11am-11pm M-Th, -midnight F and Sa. Su brunch: 11am-2pm. *!* AE/V/MC/DC/CB. 685 Excelsior Boulevard, Excelsior, 474-1113.

FABULOUS FERNS'S BAR AND GRILL
An eclectic restaurant offering a gourmet meal, but not for a gourmet price. The menu features such items as chicken with leeks and mustard, salmon with sun-dried tomatoes, catfish fingers in a roasted red bell pepper sauce. 11am-10pm M-Th, -11pm F and Sa. 10am-10pm Su. Su brunch: 11am-3pm. *!* AE/V/MC/DI. 400 Selby Ave., St. Paul, 225-9414.

FAIRFIELD INN
Serving seafood, walleye, prime rib and stir-fry chicken or join us for our famous buffet. Buffet: 5-8pm daily. 6am-10:30pm M-F; 7am-11pm Sa and Su. *!!* AE/V/MC/DC/CB/DI. Marriott Hotel, 2020 E. 79th St., Bloomington, 854-7441.

FAIR OAKS
Dishes of north India such as Tandoori chicken and samosas. 7am-9:30pm Su-Th, -10:30pm F and Sa. *!* AE. Fair Oaks Hotel and Restaurant, 2335 Third Ave. S., Mpls., 871-2000.

FAR EAST
Authentic Szechuan and Hunan cuisine. Featuring such specialties as the sliced leg of lamb and Szechuan-style sauteed scallops in garlic sauce. Reputed to be "the best in the Twin Cities" by Mpls/St. Paul magazine. Wine and beer. 11am-9:30pm M-Th, -10pm F and Sa; 4-9:30pm Su. *!* No credit cards. 5033 France Ave. S., Edina, 922-0725.

FAVORÉ RISTORANTE
Serving a complete Italian menu with original antipasto and pasta. Fun bar with happy-hour specials to meet and greet after work. *!!* 11:30am-10pm M-Th, -11pm F and Sa. Closed Su. World Trade Center, St. Paul, 228-9788.

FESTIVAL
American cuisine. Pianist M-Sa nights. Lunch: 11:30am-2:30pm M-F. Dinner: 5-11pm M-Sa. *!!!!* AE/V/MC/DC/CB/DI. Radisson Plaza Hotel, 35 S. Seventh St., Mpls., 339-4900.

FIFTH AT FIFTH
This restaurant attracts the neighborhood artists with healthful meals and homemade breads. The menu change daily, but while you're there look for entrees such as pasta with artichoke hearts and fresh basil, curried mock duck and salad Nicoise. 7am-2:30pm M-F. *!* No credit cards. 420 N. Fifth St., Mpls., 333-3072.

50'S GRILL
Old-style supper consisting of homemade meat loaf, smoked pork chops, chicken, burgers and malts. Beer is served. Delicious desserts featuring fresh apple, wild-blueberry and cherry pies; chocolate fudge, turtle and German chocolate cakes. Desserts made entirely from scratch. 11am-10pm Su-Th, -11pm F and Sa. *!* V/MC. 5524 Brooklyn Boulevard, Brooklyn Center, 560-4947.

FIGLIO
Trendy restaurant serving California-Italian meals such as burgers with stracchino cheese, homemade pasta and a variety of gourmet pizzas. 11am-2am M-Sa; 11:30am-1pm Su. *!!* AE/V/MC. Calhoun Square, 3001 Hennepin Ave., Mpls., 822-1688.

FILLY'S SPORTS BAR AND GRILL
Informal sports bar with burgers, sandwiches and appetizers. 11am-11pm daily. *!* V/MC/DI. Chanhassen Bowl, 581 W. 78th St., Chanhassen, 934-6603.

FINE LINE MUSIC CAFE
Featuring a dinner menu with entrees such as pan-fried Minnesota walleye cheeks and grilled breast of chicken with tarragon mushroom sauce. Live music nightly by local and national talent. 5-10pm M-Th, -midnight F; 6pm-midnight Sa, -10pm Su. Su brunch: 12:30-2:30pm

---

AE = American Express / V = VISA / MC = MasterCard / DI = Discover / DC = Diners Club / CB = Carte Blanche
! = less than $10 / *!!* $10-$18 / *!!!* $18-$28 / *!!!!* more than $28

with live gospel music. !! AE/V/MC/DC/CB. 318 First Ave. N., Mpls., 338-8100.

FITZGERALD'S
Overlooking Mears Park, this restaurant offers stir-fry, mesquite-grilled fresh fish, steaks, salads, prime rib, seafood and freshly baked desserts. 11am-10pm M-Th, -11pm F and Sa. Light menu until 11pm M-Th, midnight F and Sa. Su brunch: 10:30am-2:30pm. !! AE/V/MC/DC/CB. Galtier Plaza, 175 E. Fifth St., St. Paul, 297-6787.

510 RESTAURANT
A time-honored tradition of elegance and grace located just across the street from the Guthrie Theater in the beautiful 510 Groveland Building. Contemporary French and American cuisine. Special menu for pre-theater dining. Formal service. Excellent wine list. Valet parking. Available for private parties. Dinner: 5:30-10pm M-Sa. !!!! AE/V/MC/DC/CB. 510 Groveland Ave., Mpls., 874-6440.

FOREPAUGH'S
Choose to dine from a selection of nine rooms in a Victorian mansion. Menu items include wild boar, walleye, veal, poultry, beef and fresh seafood. Lunch: 11:30am-2pm. M-F. Dinner: 5:30-9:30pm M-Sa; 5-8:30pm Su. Su brunch: 10:30am-1:30pm !! AE/V/MC. 276 S. Exchange St., St. Paul, 224-5606.

FRANCESCA'S BAKERY AND CAFE
Informal Italian restaurant featuring Italian breads, torta rustica and whole-grain muffins. No liquor. 7am-5:30pm M-F; 7:30am-5pm Sa and Su. ! No credit cards. 518 Selby Ave., St. Paul, 227-5775.

FREIGHT HOUSE
Listed on the National Register of Historic Places and overlooking the St. Croix River, this restaurant serves steak, burgers, fish, chicken Dijon and arcola chicken salad. Dancing nightly. 11am-8pm Su-Th, -10pm F and Sa (winter). 11am-10pm daily (summer). !! AE/V/MC/DC/CB/DI. 305 S. Water St., Stillwater, 439-5718.

FRESHMARKET
This Neiman Marcus-owned restaurant has a bit of home-store Texas flavor sprinkled throughout the menu. There are many healthful entrees such as spicy Southwestern cuisine, pasta dishes, soups, sandwiches and salads. 11am-5pm M-Sa. ! AE. Gaviidae Commons, fourth floor, 505 Nicollet Mall, Mpls., 339-2600.

FUDDRUCKER'S
Home of the "world's greatest hamburger" with more than 29 toppings from which to choose. Also serving grilled chicken sandwiches, hot dogs, fish, soups and malts. 11am-10pm Su-Th, -11pm F and Sa. ! AE/V/MC. 3801 Minnesota Drive, Bloomington, 835-3833. 2740 Snelling Ave. N., Roseville, 636-3833. 6445 Wayzata Boulevard, St. Louis Park, 593-3833.

GALLERY 8
Located in the Walker Art Center, this cafeteria serves sandwiches, sourdough-French bread, salads, soups, fresh fruit, poppy seed cheesecake, shortbread and creme brulee. Wine and beer. 11:30am-3pm Tu-Su. ! No credit cards. Walker Art Center, Vineland Place, Mpls., 374-3701.

GALLIVAN'S
Elegant dining with such entrees as prime rib, steaks and seafood. Live entertainment nightly. 11am-1am M-Sa. !! AE/V/MC/DC. 354 Wabasha St., St. Paul, 227-6688.

GARDEN CAFE
Informal Tex-Mex dining with entrees including gourmet pizzas, burgers and a breakfast buffet. 6am-2pm M-F; 7am-2pm Sa and Su. Dinner: 5-10pm daily. !! AE/V/MC/DC/CB/DI. Wyndam Garden Hotel, 4460 W. 78th St. Circle Drive, Bloomington, 831-3131.

GARDEN OF SALONCIA
This cafe with a high-ceiling store front in a 19th-century building offers wonderful Greek sandwiches, soup, salads and homemade pastries such as baklava and boughasta with lemon-cream or hazelnut filling. 11am-9pm M-Th, -10pm F and Sa. Call for Su hours. ! No credit cards. 19 Fifth St. N.E., Mpls., 378-0611.

GASTHAUS BAVARIAN HUNTER
Old-World cuisine served in a traditional Bavarian atmosphere. Wiener schnitzel, sauerbraten, pork roast, beef roast and potato and bread dumplings, and red cabbage. Polka band two evenings a month. Strolling accordion

---

The 510 Restaurant
★★ Award Winning ★★
Fine Dining
Fine Wines
Great Service
874-6440
510 Groveland, Minneapolis

Hurray! Minnesota

player leads German sing-along F nights and Su afternoons. Lunch: 11am-2pm M-F. Dinner: 5-9pm M-Th, -10pm F; noon-10pm Sa, -8pm Su. Su brunch: noon-4pm. *!!* AE/V/MC/DC. 8390 Lofton Ave., Stillwater, 439-7128.

GASTOF ZUR GEMUTLICHKEIT
Serving such German specialties as rouladen and schnitzel. Live German music seven days a week. Open 11am daily. Closing times vary. Su brunch: 10:30am-3pm. *!!* AE/V/MC/DC. 35 mile west of Mpls. on Highway 12, Montrose, 675-3777.

GIORGIO
Informal authentic Italian restaurant offering a variety of pasta as well as chicken, pork and beef entrees. There is a wide selection of appetizers. Wine and beer. Lunch: 11am-2pm Su-Th; limited menu 2-5pm. Dinner: 5-10pm Su-Th, -11pm F and Sa. Sa and Su brunch: 10am-2pm. *!!* No credit cards. 2451 Hennepin Ave., Mpls., 374-5131.

GIPPER'S ALL-AMERICAN SPORTS BAR AND GRILL
Serving Cajun-chicken sandwiches and stir-fry chicken salads. 11am-11pm M-Sa; 10am-10pm Su. *!* AE/V/MC/DC/CB/DI. 4608 Excelsior Boulevard, St. Louis Park, 927-8719.

GLADSTONE CAFE AT LANDMARK CENTER
Offering soups, salads and sandwiches. Wine and beer. 9am-2:30pm M-F. *!* No credit cards. Landmark Center, 75 W. Fifth St., St. Paul, 227-4704.

GLUEK'S
German beer hall serving everything from brats, Wiener schnitzel and barbecued ribs to chicken, walleye, sandwiches, steak and burgers. 11am-midnight M-Sa; 4:30pm-midnight Su. *!* AE/V/MC/DC/DI. 16 N. Sixth St., Mpls., 338-6621.

GOOD EARTH
Healthy meals served in a smoke-free environment. Menu includes homemade soups, pita sandwiches, cashew chicken salad, stir-fry dishes and homemade baked goods — all with natural ingredients. Wine and beer. Calhoun Square – 11:30am-9:30pm M-Th, -10pm F; 9:30am-10pm Sa, -9pm Su. Galleria – 9am-10pm M-Sa, -8:30pm Su. Roseville – 7am-10pm M-Th, -11pm F and Sa, -9pm Su. *!* AE/V/MC. Calhoun Square, 824-8533; Galleria, 925-1001; Roseville, 636-0356.

GOODFELLOW'S
Specialties from all regions of the country, including wild-rice fritters, grilled salmon with horseradish and South Dakota venison.

Lunch: 11am-2:30pm M-F. Dinner: 5:30-9pm M-Th, -10pm F and Sa. *!!!* AE/V/MC/DI. Fourth floor, Conservatory, 800 Nicollet Mall, Mpls., 332-4800.

GRANDMA'S SALOON AND DELI
Decorated with an eclectic array of antiques and other oddities, this restaurant serves sandwiches, pasta specialties, steak, onion rings, salads and homemade cheesecake. Dancing W-Sa. 11:30am-10:30pm M-Th, -11:30pm F and Sa; 4-10pm Su. *!!* AE/V/MC. 1810 Washington Ave. S., Mpls., 340-0516.

GREEN MILL
Featuring deep-dish, thin-crust and stuffed pizza. This restaurant also serves pasta dishes, calzone, sandwiches and burgers. Wine and beer. 11am-11pm Su-Th, -midnight F and Sa. Call for hours on Su. *!* AE/V/MC/DC. 8266 Commonwealth Drive, Eden Prairie, 944-3000. 52 Hamline Ave. S., St. Paul, 698-0353. 2626 Hennepin Ave., Mpls., 374-2131. 4501 France Ave. S., Mpls., 925-5400.

GULDEN'S SUPPER CLUB
All American, chicken, ribs and steaks. Seafood buffet on F. Prime rib buffet on Sa. 11am-9:30pm Su-Th, -11pm F and Sa. Su brunch. *!* AE/V/MC/DC. 2999 N. Highway 61, Maplewood, 482-0338.

GUSTINO'S
Italian restaurant with a singing wait staff. Menu features entrees from the northern region of the country, including cioppino, cassata Milanese, and meat and seafood dishes in white wine cream sauces. 6-10pm M-Th, -11pm F and Sa; 6-8pm Su. *!!!* AE/V/MC/DC/CB. Marriott City Center, 30 S. Seventh St., Mpls., 349-4000.

HAMLINE'S
"An island of humanity in a sea of glass." Opened in 1926, one of the first hole-in-the-wall restaurants in downtown Mpls. Traditional American food is served such as homemade soups and desserts, sandwiches, salads and breakfast items. The menu changes daily. 5:30am-2pm M-F; 8am-1pm Sa. Closed on weekends during baseball season. *!* No credit cards. 512 Nicollet Ave., Mpls., 333-3876.

HARBOR VIEW CAFE
Dining in a 19th-century tavern offering chicken, lamb and seafood. Schedule varies seasonally; closed Tu-W and winter months. *!!* No credit cards. First and Main St., Pepin, WI, (715) 442-3893.

HEARTTHROB CAFE
'50s and '80s memorabilia adorn this popular

163 TWIN CITIES / EATER'S DIGEST

restaurant. Entrees include I Want My Baby Back ribs, Little Anthony and the Appetizers and Steak, Rattle and Roll. 11:30am-11pm M-Th, -midnight F and Sa; noon-8pm Su. *!* AE/V/MC. Saint Paul Center, 30 E. Seventh St., St. Paul, 224-2783.

Hey City Cafe
A cafe for the '90s – grand windows and bright decor. Serving lighter dishes such as pasta, pizza and sandwiches, coffee and desserts. 11am-11pm Tu-Th, -midnight F; 5pm-midnight Sa; 11am-10pm Su. *!* AE/V/MC/DC/CB/DI. 1430 S. Washington Ave., Mpls., 333-1300.

Hoops on Hennepin
A combination sports bar and nightclub with 17 TV monitors, big screen and full satellite capabilities for all major sporting events. Menu includes specialty sandwiches and appetizers. DJ and dancing nightly. 11am-1am daily. Su brunch: 11am-2pm. *!* AE/V/MC/DC. 1110 Hennepin Ave., Mpls., 375-1900.

Hopkins House
Specializing in prime rib, this restaurant offers seafood and salad bar. Live music and dancing M-Sa. 11am-9pm M-Sa. Su brunch: 10:30am-2pm. *!!* AE/V/MC/DC. 1501 Highway 7, Hopkins, 935-7711.

Hubert's
Located across from the Metrodome, this sports-oriented restaurant serves hamburgers, soups and salads. 11am-1am daily. *!* AE/V/MC/DC/CB/DI. 601 Chicago Ave., Mpls., 332-6062.

Hunan Garden
Chinese restaurant featuring Hunan, Mandarin and Szechuan meals. Entrees include tea-smoked duck, princess chicken and Peking duck. 10:30am-9:30pm Su-Th; 11am-10:30pm F and Sa; 2:30-9:30pm Su. *!!* AE/V/MC/DC. 380 Cedar St., St. Paul, 224-7588.

Hungry Horse
This restaurant serves seafood, chicken and steaks. Lunch: 11am-2pm M-F. Dinner: 5-10pm M-Th, -11pm Sa, -9pm Su. *!!* AE/V/MC/CB/DC. 8395 Flying Cloud Drive, Eden Prairie, 943-8173.

Ichiban Japanese Steak House
Featuring teppanyaki table-side cooking in a Japanese-garden atmosphere. 4:30-10pm Su-Th, -10:30pm F and Sa. *!!!* AE/V/MC/DC/CB/DI. 1333 Nicollet Mall, Mpls., 339-0540.

Italian Pie Shoppe and Winery
Offering a variety of pizza, salad and other Italian meals. Wine and beer. Both locations 11am-10pm M-Th, -midnight F and Sa. Eagan – 1-10pm Su. St. Paul – 4-10pm Su. *!* AE/V/MC. 1438 Yankee Doodle Road, Eagan, 452-4525. 777 Grand Ave., St. Paul, 221-0093.

It's Greek To Me
Greek restaurant serving moussaka, souvlaki, dolmades, sandwiches, soups, spanakopita and lamb entrees. Wine and beer. 11am-11pm daily. *!* V/MC 626 W. Lake St., Mpls., 825-9922.

Ivories
American dishes from pizza to lobster served in a supper club atmosphere. Pianist during evenings Tu-Sa. Lunch: 11am-2pm M-F. Dinner: 5-10pm Tu-Th, -11pm F and Sa. *!!* AE/V/MC/DC. 605 Waterfront Park, Suite 150, (Highway 169 N.) Mpls., 591-6188.

Jacob's 101 Lounge and Restaurant
Northeast Mpls. neighborhood bar and grill. Lebanese and American meals including tabouli salad, kibbi nayee, shis taouk, walleyed pike, steaks, shrimp and prime rib. 7am-10:30pm M-Sa. *!!* AE/V/MC. 101 Broadway St. N.E., Mpls., 379-2508.

Jakeeno's
Italian restaurant featuring Jack Keegan's family recipe for thin crust pizza with your choice of toppings. 11:30am-11:30pm Tu-Sa; 4-11:30pm Su-M. *!* No credit cards. 3555 Chicago Ave., Mpls., 825-6827.

Java
This Egyptian and American restaurant serves fresh gyro sandwiches, rabbit, combination-meat plates and baklava. For entertainment and a cultural escape, there are belly dancers on F and Sa evenings. Egyptian music is played daily. 11am-10pm daily, -11pm F and Sa. *!* No credit cards. 2801 Nicollet Ave., Mpls., 870-7871.

Jax Cafe
An award-winning chop house favorite of Minnesota since 1933. Private parties 20-300. Pianist Th-Sa. 11am-11pm M-Sa; 3:30-9pm Su. Su brunch: 10am-3pm. *!!* AE/V/MC/DC/CB/DI. 1928 University Ave. N.E., Mpls., 789-7297.

J.D. Hoyt's
A country roadhouse in the warehouse district offering Cajun, charcoal and hickory-smoked entrees. 7am-3pm M-Sa. Dinner: 5-11pm M-F, -11:30pm Sa; 4:30-10:30pm Su. Su brunch: 11am-2pm. *!!!* AE/V/MC/DC/CB/DI. 301 Washington Ave. N., Mpls., 338-1560.

Jenning's Red Coach Inn
Serving seafood, chicken and chops. Pianist F and Sa. 11:30am-10pm M-Th, -10:30pm F and Sa. *!!* AE/V/MC/DC/CB. 4630 Excelsior Boulevard, St. Louis Park, 927-5401.

JERUSALEM'S
Middle Eastern restaurant serving shawirma, hummus, falafel, baba ganoush, baklava and krima. Wine and beer. 11am-11pm daily. *!* V/MC. 1518 Nicollet Ave., Mpls., 871-8883.

JOE SENSER'S SPORTS GRILL AND BAR
Upscale sports-oriented bar serving hot dogs and burgers as well as steak and seafood. 11am-1am M-Sa, -midnight Su. *!* AE/V/MC. 4217 W. 80th St., Bloomington, 835-1191. 2350 Cleveland Ave. N., Roseville, 631-1781.

THE JOLLIET
With a view of the IDS Crystal Court, this restaurant offers American meals. *!!* AE/V/MC/DC/CB/DI. Third floor, Marquette Hotel, 710 Marquette Ave., Mpls., 332-6374.

JOSE'S CHEEKS AND CHEERS
Informal Mexican and American restaurant with a casual dining atmosphere. Serving nachos, tacos, burritos, American skillets, sandwiches, salads, pizza and more. Mpls., Mendota Heights and Burnsville – 11am-11pm Su-Th, -midnight F and Sa; St. Paul – 11am-11pm M-Th, -midnight F and Sa; noon-11pm Su. *!* AE/V/MC/DC. Butler Square, 100 N. Sixth St., Mpls., 333-5265. 825 Jefferson Ave., St. Paul, 227-6315. 857 Sibley Memorial Highway, Mendota Heights, 451-0160. 3809 W. Highway 13, Burnsville, 894-6541.

J.P. MULLIGAN'S
Offering Mulligan stew as well as quiche, crab legs, veal, prime rib, sandwiches, steaks and burgers. Piano lounge and pub. 11am-1am Sa; 9am-10pm Su. Su brunch: 9am-1pm. *!!* AE/V/MC/DC/CB. 3005 N. Harbor Lane, Plymouth, 559-1595.

J.P.'S
Family-oriented restaurant serving traditional breakfast fare as well as malts, burgers, clam chowder, fried chicken and sandwiches. Beer. Edina – 5am-11pm daily. Eden Prairie – 6am-9pm daily. *!!* No credit cards. 5125 Vernon Ave. S., Edina, 929-2685. 9589 Anderson Lake Parkway, Eden Prairie, 941-9680.

JUANITA'S RESTAURANTE MEXICANO
Mexican cafe featuring tacos, burritos and enchiladas. No liquor. 11am-8pm Tu-Th, -10pm F; 9am-2am Sa, -5pm Su. *!* No credit cards. 201 Concord St., St. Paul, 290-2511.

KABUKI JAPANESE RESTAURANT
Serving chicken teriyaki, sashimi, sushi, steak, seafood and tempura shrimp amid traditional Japanese decor. Lunch: 11am-1:30pm M-F. Dinner: 5-9pm M-Th, -9:15pm F and Sa. *!!* AE/V/MC/DC. 6534 Flying Cloud Drive, Eden Prairie, 941-5115.

KAFFE STUGA
Scandinavian fare including smoked fish, smorgasbord buffet, sandwiches, baked goods and soups. Braille menu available. 6:30am-10:30pm M-F; 7am-10:30pm Sa, -10pm Su. *!!* AE/V/MC/DC/CB/DI. Radisson Hotel South, Interstate 494 and Highway 100, Bloomington, 893-8473.

KEEFER COURT
A true Hong Kong noodle shop and Western/Chinese bakery. 11am-6pm W-M. *!* No credit cards. 326 Cedar Ave., Mpls., 340-0937.

KEYS
Featuring breakfast all day, this restaurant also offers roast beef, chili, salads, breads, cakes and pies for lunch and dinner. Brooklyn Park – 6am-8pm M-F; 7am-12:30pm Sa and Su. Crystal – 7am-8pm M-F, -noon Sa and Su. New Brighton – 6am-3pm M-F; 7am-12:30pm Sa; 8:30am-12:30pm Su. Lexington Ave. – 6am-9pm M-F; 7am-9pm Sa and Su. Raymond Ave. – 5 am-3pm M-F; 7am-noon Sa; 8:30am-noon Su. Robert St.– 6:30am-2:30pm M-F; 8am-noon Sa and Su. White Bear Lake – 7am-10pm Tu-Sa, -2pm Su, -3pm M. *!* No credit cards. 8465 W. Broadway, Brooklyn Park, 493-2232. 6408 Bass Lake Road, Crystal, 533-3679. 1192 Fifth Ave., New Brighton, 636-0662. 1682 Lexington Ave. N., Roseville, 487-3530. 767 Raymond Ave., St. Paul, 222-4083. 2208 Fourth St., White Bear Lake, 426-2885.

KHAN'S MONGOLIAN BARBECUE
Chef will stir-fry your selection from five meats, 10 vegetables and 10 sauces while you wait. Wine and beer. 11am-9:30pm M-Th, -10pm Sa; 5-9pm Su. *!!* AE/V/MC. 418 13th Ave. S.E., Mpls., 379-3121. 2720 N. Snelling Ave., Roseville, 631-3398.

KHYBER PASS
Authentic Afghani restaurant offering flavorfully spiced lamb, chicken kebabs and vegetarian entrees. Wine and beer. Lunch: 11am-2pm Tu-Sa. Dinner: 5-9pm Tu-Sa. *!* No credit cards. 1399 St. Clair Ave., St. Paul, 698-5403.

KIKUGAWA
Traditional Japanese dining in this restaurant

AE = American Express / V = VISA / MC = MasterCard / DI = Discover / DC = Diners Club / CB = Carte Blanche
! = less than $10 / *!!* $10-$18 / *!!!* $18-$28 / *!!!!* more than $28

serving sukiyaki, tempura, sushi, seafood, beef and chicken. Lunch: 11:30am-2pm daily. Dinner: 5-10pm M-Th, -11pm F and Sa; noon-9pm Su. *!!* AE/V/MC/DC. Riverplace, 43 Main St. S.E., Mpls., 378-3006.

KINCAID'S
This restaurant specializes in steak and seafood entrees. Also featuring Nebraska corn-fed beef, prime rib, chicken, fresh oysters, salmon and fresh pasta. Lunch: 11am-2:30pm M-Sa. Dinner: 5-10pm M-Th, -11pm F and Sa, -9pm Su. Su brunch: 10am-2pm. *!!!* AE/V/MC. Normandale Lake Office Park, 8400 Normandale Lake Boulevard, Bloomington, 921-2255.

KING AND I
Thai restaurant offering lemon grass soup, shrimp, walleye and stir-fry dishes. Wine and beer. 11am-11pm M-Sa. *!* AE/V/MC. 1034 Nicollet Mall, Mpls., 332-6928.

KING'S INN
Offering fresh seafood in addition to steaks and appetizers. 11am-11pm M-Sa. Closed Su. *!!* AE/V/MC/DC/CB/DI. West of Interstate 494 on Highway 7, Minnetonka, 938-4800.

KINHDO
Vietnamese restaurant serving spicy chicken, sauteed beef with potatoes, pork, Vietnamese chow mein and soups. Beer. 11am-9pm M-Su, -10pm F and Sa. New Hope closed Su. 6345 Penn Ave. S., Richfield, 861-2491. 2755 Hennepin Ave., Mpls., 870-1295. 2709 Winnetka Ave. S., New Hope, 544-8440.

KOZLAK'S ROYAL OAK
Overlooking the Royal Oak Garden, this restaurant serves filet mignon, prime rib, walleye, pheasant and homemade gelatos and sorbets. Strolling musicians at Su brunch. Lunch: 11am-2:30pm M-Sa. Dinner: 4-9:30pm M-Th, -10:30pm F and Sa, -8:30pm Su. Su brunch: 10:30-2pm. *!!* AE/V/MC/DC/CB. 4785 Hodgson Road, Shoreview, 484-8484.

KRISTY'S
Breakfast, lunch and dinner are served at this fine restaurant. Menu items range from a buffet for breakfast to seafood for dinner. 7am-11pm daily. Su brunch: 10am-1:30pm. *!* AE/V/MC/DC/CB/DI. Radisson Hotel, 12201 Ridgedale Drive, Minnetonka, 593-0000.

KUPPERNICUS
A distinctive coffeehouse offering fresh-ground coffee, juices, pastries and deli items. A renovated warehouse with a warm airy environment that is furnished with sofas, coffee tables and armchairs. 6:30am-11pm S-Th, -2am F and Sa. *!* No credit cards. Located at the southeastern corner of the St. Paul Farmer's Market. Broadway and Prince. 308 Prince St., St. Paul, 290-2718.

LA CASITA
This Mexican restaurant features tacos, enchiladas and fajitas. 11am-10:30pm M-Th, -11pm Sa, -10:30pm Su. *!!* AE/V/MC. 5085 Central Ave. N.E., Columbia Heights, 571-7784.

LA CORVINA
Mexican and Latin restaurant specializing in dishes like sea bass, shrimp Creole and enchiladas suizo. 11am-10pm M-Sa. *!* AE/V/MC/DC/CB/DI. 1570 Selby Ave., St. Paul, 645-5288.

LA CUCARACHA
Mexican restaurant offering enchiladas suizo, chicken mole, chile relleno, guacamole and huevos rancheros. Wine and beer. 11am-11pm Su-Th, -1am F and Sa. *!* AE/V/MC/DC/CB. 36 S. Dale St., St. Paul, 221-9682.

LAN XANG
Vietnamese and Thai dishes such as flavorful broth with rice noodles and beef or fried noodles with shrimp. 11am-9pm M-Sa; 4-8pm Su. *!* No credit cards. 1844 Central Ave., Mpls., 788-1750.

LAKE ELMO INN
Continental restaurant with country decor serving roast duckling, seafood, veal and hickory-smoked ribs. Lunch: 11am-2pm M-Sa. Dinner: 5-10pm M-Sa; 4:30-8:30pm Su. Su brunch: 10am-2pm. *!!!* AE/V/MC/DC/CB/DI. 3442 Lake Elmo Ave. N., Lake Elmo, 777-8495.

LAKE STREET GARAGE
Restaurant decorated with a cab from a 1942 tow truck. Menu items include malts and pizza. Wine and beer. 11am-10pm M-Th, -11pm F; noon-11pm Sa. *!* No credit cards. 3508 E. Lake St., Mpls., 729-8820.

LA TERRASSE
Informal French dining atmosphere serving French onion soup, scallops au gratin, steak au poivre, salads, sandwiches, pastries and more. 11am-midnight M-Th, -1am F and Sa; 10:30am-midnight Su. Su brunch: 10:30-2:30pm. *!!* AE/V/MC/DC. Hotel Sofitel, 5601 W. 78th St., Bloomington, 835-1900.

LATOUR
Relaxing atmosphere with regional American and Continental cuisines. Featuring specialties such as pan-fried lobster, tournedos of veal, and roast rack of lamb Provencal. Classical pianist nightly. Dinner: 6-10pm M-Sa. Su brunch: 10:30am-2pm. *!!!* AE/V/MC/DC/

CB/DI. Registry Hotel, 7901 24th Ave. S., Bloomington, 854-2244.

LE BISTRO CAFE
Serving French and American food including crepes and quiches. 11am-9:30pm M-Th, -10pm F, -9pm Sa; 10am-5:30pm Su. Su brunch: 10am-2pm. ! AE/V/MC/DI. Rosedale Shopping Center, West Highway 36 at Fairview, Roseville, 636-0953.

LE CAFE ROYAL
This French restaurant offers fresh fish, flambes and gueridon sommelier service. Lunch: 11:30am-2pm M-F. Dinner: 6-10pm M-Sa. !!! AE/V/MC/DC/CB. Hotel Sofitel, 5601 W. 78th St., Bloomington, 835-1900.

LE CARROUSEL
With a view of the Mississippi River, this revolving restaurant atop the Radisson Hotel offers seafood, steaks, grilled chicken entrees and flaming desserts. Pianist nightly. Lunch: 11:30am-2pm M-F. Dinner: 5:30-10:30pm M-Th, -11:30pm F and Sa. !!! AE/V/MC/DC/CB/DI. 22nd floor, Radisson Hotel, 11 E. Kellogg Boulevard, St. Paul, 292-1900.

LEEANN CHIN
Cantonese and Szechuan cuisine served in buffet-style contemporary setting. Lunch: 11am-2:30pm M-Sa (M-F at International Center). Dinner: 5-9pm M-Th, -10pm F and Sa at all locations. 5-9pm Su at Bonaventure only. Sa brunch: 11am-2:30pm. Su brunch: 11:30am-2:30pm at Bonaventure and Union Depot. !! AE/V/MC. Bonaventure, Highway 12 and Plymouth Road, Minnetonka, 545-3600. Union Depot Place, 214 E. Fourth St., St. Paul, 224-8814. International Center, 900 Second Ave. S., Mpls., 338-8488.

LEE'S VILLAGE INN
Home-style cooking featuring roast turkey, hot popovers and pecan pie. Wine. Pianist Tu-Su. Lunch: 11am-4pm M-Sa. Dinner: 4-8:30pm Tu-Sa; 8:30am-7:30pm Su. Su buffet: 8:30-11:15 am. !! AE/V/MC/DI. 800 S. Cleveland Ave., St. Paul, 698-0724.

LEXINGTON
A timeless tradition in the heart of historic Grand Avenue. Choose from formal dining or pub atmosphere. A favorite meeting place that is known for its good food. 11am-11pm M-Sa; 9am-9pm Su. !! AE/V/MC/DC/CB. 1096 Grand Ave., St. Paul, 222-5878.

LIDO CAFE ITALIA
For more than 35 years, this restaurant has been specializing in homemade Italian cuisine. Call for hours. Su brunch: 10am-1:45pm. !

AE/V/MC/DC/DI. 2801 Snelling Ave. N., Roseville, 636-9721.

LINCOLN DEL
This restaurant features a wide selection of deli items including Reuben sandwiches, blintzes, knishes, gefilte fish, matzo ball soup and a variety of desserts. St. Louis Park – 7am-11pm M-Th, -1am F and Sa; 7:45am-11pm Su. Bloomington – 6:45am-1pm M-Th; -midnight F and Sa; 8am-10pm Su. !! V/MC. 4100 Lake St., St. Louis Park, 927-9738. I-494 and France Ave. S., Bloomington, 831-0780.

LINDEY'S PRIME STEAK HOUSE
This restaurant offers a wide variety of steak entrees. 5-10:30pm M-Th, -11:30pm F and Sa. !! No credit cards. 3610 Old Snelling at County Road E, Arden Hills, 633-9813.

LION'S TAP FAMILY RESTAURANT
Informal surroundings serving a variety of burgers and fries for more than 30 years. Beer. 11am-11pm M-Th, -midnight F and Sa; 11:30am-11pm Su. ! No credit cards. 16180 Flying Cloud Drive, Eden Prairie, 934-5299.

LIVING ROOM
Modern bar and restaurant with elegant decor. The gourmet menu varies weekly. One week it is French and Italian cuisine, the next it may be Venezuelan. Featuring pasta, seafood and meat entrees. Live entertainment nightly. Lunch: 11am-3pm M-F. Dinner: 5:30-11pm M-Th, -midnight F and Sa. Call for Su hours. !! AE/V/MC/DC. 256 First Ave. N., Mpls., 343-0360.

LOMBARD'S
This American restaurant features seafood, steaks and salads. DJ and dancing nightly at adjoining Northern Lights nightclub. Breakfast: 6-11am M-F; 7-11am Sa. Lunch: 11am-2pm M-Sa. Dinner: 5-10pm daily. Su brunch: 9am-2pm. !! AE/V/MC/DC/DI. Holiday Inn Minneapolis North, 2200 Freeway Boulevard, Mpls., 566-8000.

LONE STAR GRILL
Southwestern restaurant offering real Tex-Mex smoked beef brisket, beef and pork ribs and Mexican entrees. Sports bar including three large-screen TVs. Happy hour: 4-6pm daily. 11:30am-11:30pm M-Sa; 11:30am-10pm Su-Th, -11pm F and Sa. ! AE/V/MC. 11032 Cedar Lake Road, Minnetonka, 540-0181.

LOON CAFE
Restaurant and bar situated in the heart of downtown Minneapolis serving four varieties of chili in addition to burgers and spicy Mexican dishes. 11am-11pm M-Sa; 5-11pm Su. !

AE/V/MC/DC/CB. 500 First Ave. N., Mpls., 332-8342.

LORD FLETCHER'S ON LAKE MINNETONKA
Overlooking Lake Minnetonka, this restaurant features fresh seafood, walleyed pike, prime rib and pasta. Entertainment nightly. Indoor and outdoor dining. 80 boat slips. Lunch: 11am-2:30pm M-Sa. Dinner: 5:30-10pm M-Sa; 4:30-9pm Su. Su brunch: 11am-2pm. *!!* AE/V/MC/DI. 3746 Sunset Drive, Spring Park, 471-8513.

LORETTA'S TEA ROOM
Serving stroganoff, chicken pie, Swiss steak and goulash. Lunch: 11am-2pm M-F. Dinner: 5-7:30pm Tu, W, F. Su brunch: 11am-2pm. *!* No credit cards. Enter on 26th St. and Park Ave., Mpls., 871-1660.

LORING CAFE
Bohemian bar overlooking Loring Park serves shrimp with pears, green peppercorns and lemon chicken. Wine and beer served in cafe, full bar next door. Lunch: 11:30am-2:30pm M-F. Dinner: 5:30-10:30pm Su-Th, -midnight F and Sa. *!!!* V/MC. 1624 Harmon Place, Mpls., 332-1617.

LOTUS
Vietnamese restaurant offering wok-cooked dishes such as imperial chicken, barbecued mock duck, tofu dishes, egg rolls and seafood entrees. Hennepin and St. Paul – 11am-10pm Su-Th, -11pm F and Sa. Oak St. – 11am-10pm M-Sa. Edina and Burnsville – 11am-9pm M-Th, -10pm F and Sa. Grant St. – 11am-9pm M-Sa. *!* No credit cards. 3037 Hennepin Ave., Mpls., 825-2263. 313 Oak St., Mpls., 331-1781. 3907 W. 50th St., Edina, 922-4254. 1917 E. Cliff Road, Burnsville, 890-5573. 867 Grand Ave., St. Paul, 228-9156. Limited seating at 113 W. Grant St., Mpls., 870-1218.

LOWELL INN
Each dining room offers a different selection of entrees such as escargot, lobster, walleyed pike, fish, pork, lamb and chicken. Breakfast: 8-10:30am daily. Lunch: noon-2:30pm daily. Dinner: 6-9pm daily. *!!!!* V/MC. 102 N. Second St., Stillwater, 439-1100.

LOWRY'S
This intimate restaurant features seafood, beef dishes and pasta. Wine and beer. 11am-10pm M-Th, -11pm F; 4:30-11pm Sa; 10am-9pm Su. Sa brunch: 11am-2pm. Su brunch: 9am-2pm. *!!* AE/V/MC. 1934 Hennepin Ave., Mpls., 871-0806.

LUCIA'S
This restaurant offers potato watercress soup, smoked chicken terrine with honey mustard,

pasta and homemade ice creams. Menu varies weekly. Wine and beer. Lunch: 11:30am-2:30pm Tu-F. Dinner: 5:30-9:30pm Tu-Th, -10pm F and Sa, -9pm Su. Sa and Su brunch: 10am-2pm. *!!* V/MC. 1432 W. 31st St., Mpls., 825-1572.

LUFRANO'S ITALIAN RESTAURANT
Featuring northern and southern Italian dishes. Homemade bread and pastries. *!* No credit cards. 4257 Nicollet Ave., Mpls., 823-5788.

LYON'S PUB
Inspired by pubs in England, this establishment offers fish and chips, Philly cheese-steak sandwiches and burgers. Dancing nightly. Restaurant – 11am-11pm M-Sa. Bar – 11am-1am M-Sa; call for Su hours. *!* AE/V/MC/DC/CB. 16 S. Sixth St., Mpls., 333-6612.

MAD CAPPER SALOON AND EATERY
Victorian-style pub offering burgers, deli sandwiches, chili and soups. 11am-1am M-Sa; noon-midnight Su. *!* AE/V/MC/DI. 224 S. Main St., Stillwater, 430-3710.

MAI VILLAGE
Vietnamese restaurant featuring seven courses of beef dishes. Wine and beer. 11am-10pm M-F; 10am-10pm Sa and Su. *!* V/MC. 422 University Ave. W., St. Paul, 290-2585.

THE MALT SHOP
Old-fashioned malt shop serving burgers, Greek and T-bird's nest salads, homemade soups, sheepherder pita-pocket bread sandwiches and malts. No liquor. Live music frequently. 11am-10:30pm M-Th, -11pm F; 8am-11pm Sa, -10:30pm Su. *!* V/MC/DC/DI. 809 W. 50th St., Mpls., 824-1352. Interstate 94 and Snelling Ave. S., St. Paul, 645-4643.

MAMA D'S
Specializing in Italian dishes such as linguine, manicotti, veal Parmesan and fettuccine Alfredo. Wine and beer. 10:30am-8:45pm M-Th, -9:45pm F; 4-9:45pm Sa. *!!* AE/V/MC. 821 Raymond Ave., St. Paul, 646-7774.

MAMA MIA'S RISTORANTE
Italian restaurant offering porchetta, pasta, pizza, calzone, salads and desserts. Wine and beer. Open 7am daily for breakfast. *!* All credit cards. 1420 Nicollet Ave., Mpls., 872-2200.

MANCINI'S CHAR HOUSE
Providing lobster and steaks for more than 40 years. Live entertainment W-Sa. 5pm-11pm Su-Th, -midnight F and Sa. *!!* AE/V/MC. 531 W. Seventh St., St. Paul, 224-7345.

MANNING'S CAFE, MANNING'S IN THE PARK, MANNING'S STONEHOUSE
This family-operated restaurant enterprise has

been offering steaks, chicken and onion rings since 1932. Wine and beer at Mpls. – 7am-1am M-Sa; 10:30am-1am Su. St. Paul – 6:30am-8pm M-F; 7:30am-8pm Sa and Su. St. Anthony – 7am-9pm M-Th, -10pm F; 8am-10pm Sa. *!* AE/V/MC. 2200 Como Ave. S.E., Mpls., 331-1053. 2264 Como Ave., St. Paul, 641-0808. 2700 Highway 88, St. Anthony Village, 789-5863.

MANNY'S STEAKHOUSE
As its name suggests, this restaurant offers dry-aged beef in addition to chicken and seafood dishes. 5:30-10pm M-Th, -11pm F and Sa; 5:30-9pm Su. *!!!* AE/V/MC. Hyatt Regency Hotel, 1300 Nicollet Mall, Mpls., 339-9900.

THE MANOR
Serving a variety of dishes such as chicken Kiev, orange roughy and lobster tail. Live music Tu-Sa; dancing W-Sa. 11am-1am M-Sa. *!!* AE/V/MC/DC. 2550 W. Seventh St., St. Paul, 690-1771.

MARIE CALLENDER'S RESTAURANT AND BAKERY
More than 35 varieties of pie in the bakery. Restaurant serving soups, sandwiches, pasta and hamburgers. 11am-10pm M-Th, -11pm Sa and Su. Su brunch: 10am-2pm. *!!* AE/V/MC/DI. County Road 42 and Nicollet Ave., Burnsville, 435-2880.

MARIO'S RISTORANTE
Italian cuisine including lasagna, fettuccine Parmesan, chicken cacciatore, eggplant and pizza. Wine and beer. 11am-11pm M-Th, -midnight F; noon-midnight Sa, -11pm Su. *!* AE/V/MC/DC/CB/DI. 3748 23rd Ave. S., Mpls., 721-3555.

MARKET BAR-B-QUE
This restaurant specializes in St. Louis-style pork and Texas beef ribs. Also serving barbecued chicken, broiled pork chops, Cajun shrimp and a number of barbecue items. Mpls. – 11:30am-2:30am M-Sa; noon-midnight Su. Minnetonka – 11:30am-midnight M-Sa; noon-11pm Su. *!!* AE/V/MC/DC/CB. 1414 Nicollet Ave., Mpls., 872-1111. 15320 Wayzata Boulevard, Minnetonka, 475-1770.

MARTHA'S VINEYARD
Featuring fresh seafood entrees like walleye, salmon, orange roughy, shrimp, scallops and oysters on the half shell. The menu also includes steaks, prime rib and chicken. DJ nightly. Breakfast and lunch 6:30am-2pm M-F; 7am-2pm Sa and Su. Dinner: 5:30-10pm daily. *!!!* AE/V/MC/DC/DI. Holiday Inn West, 9970 Wayzata Boulevard, St. Louis Park, 593-1918.

MATIN
A Vietnamese restaurant that features imperial mock duck, spicy chicken, shrimp soup, curry dishes and egg rolls. No liquor. Lunch: 11:30am-2:30pm. Dinner: 4:30-10:30pm daily. *!* 2411 Hennepin Ave., Mpls., 377-2279.

MAXWELL'S CAFE
This New York-style cafe is well-situated for catching a meal or a drink before an event at the Dome. Gourmet burgers, Philly steak sandwich and a wide variety of salads are served. 11am-midnight M-Sa; 11am-10pm Su. *!* AE/V/MC/D/DC. 1201 S. Washington Ave., Mpls., 340-9738.

MAXWELL'S ROADHOUSE
A modern-day roadhouse atmosphere with outdoor seating in the back. Maxwell's serves sandwiches, gourmet burgers and a wide variety of salads. Noon-11pm daily. *!* AE/V/MC/D/DC. 1111 S. Washington Ave., Mpls., 340-9738.

MAYSLACK'S POLKA LOUNGE
The menu includes one-pound roast-beef sandwiches dipped in garlic sauce. Full menu served 11am-11pm daily. Live polka music 4-8pm Su. 11am-11pm daily. *!* No credit cards. 1428 Fourth St. N.E., Mpls., 789-9862.

BEST RIBS!

"Best Ribs in Town" – Newsweek 1/27/92
MPLS. STAR/TRIBUNE
MPLS./ST. PAUL MAGAZINE

SINCE 1946

MARKET BAR-B-QUE®

Real pit-smoked ribs.
872-1111   **475-1770**
1414 Nicollet Mall   Hwy. 12, 1/2 mile
Downtown Mpls.   W. of 494, Mtka.

Mama Mia's RISTORANTE

Hey, That's Italian!!!

**EAT IN OR TAKE OUT.
DELIVERY, TOO!
872-2200**
1420 NICOLLET (1 blk. from Convention Center)

McCormick's
Offers a variety of dishes including steaks, gourmet sandwiches, Minnesota trout, homemade pasta, burgers and ice cream. 6:30am-11pm M, -midnight Tu-Sa, -10pm Su. Su brunch: 10am-2pm. !! AE/V/MC/DC/CB/DI. Radisson Hotel Metrodome, 615 Washington Ave. S.E., Mpls., 379-8888.

McGuire's
Serving seafood, steaks and prime rib. Live music and dancing Tu-Sa. Breakfast: 6:30am-2pm M-F; 7am-2pm Sa and Su. Lunch: 11am-2pm daily. Dinner: 5-10pm M-Th, -10pm F and Sa. Su brunch: 11am-2pm. !!! AE/V/MC/DC/CB. 1201 West County Road E, Arden Hills, 636-4123.

Meadows
This restaurant features fresh seafood and wild game from the northern plains. Including smoked meats and a three-fowl sampler. Piano bar. Complimentary parking. 5:30-10pm M-Th, -11pm F and Sa. !!! AE/V/MC/DC/CB. Radisson Hotel Metrodome, 615 Washington Ave. S.E., Mpls., 379-8888.

Mediterranean Cruise Cafe
Serving the cuisine of the countries along the Mediterranean from Greece to Palestine. Excellent shawirma, kebabs and lamb dishes. Jamal, Hussein and Pappa David have been operating this authentic restaurant for 12 years. A trip to the Mediterranean without the plane time. Belly dancers F and Sa. If you're lucky, Xllona will be dancing. 11am-10pm M-F; noon-10pm Sa and Su. !! AE/V/MC. Highway 13 and Cedar Ave., Eagan, 452-5991.

Mick's
This restaurant features moderately priced comfort food such as burgers, grilled chicken, meatloaf, chicken pot pie, salads, pastas and soup. Desserts such as the chocolate layer cake with cream-cheese/chocolate frosting, banana cream pie or the cream pie of the month are must-try menu items. 11am-11pm M-Th, -1am F and Sa; 10am-11pm Su. ! AE/V/MC/DC. 40 S. Seventh St., Mpls., 375-0560.

Mediterranean Feast
Mediterranean restaurant featuring marinated lamb, falafel, hummus, pocketbread sandwiches, kebabs and gyros. 9am-11pm daily. Su brunch: 11am-2pm. ! AE/V/MC/DI. 701 W. Lake St., Mpls., 827-1488.

The Minneapolis Bar and Grill
Offering the most complete menu in the city! In addition to serving its famous steaks, burgers, sandwiches, barbecued ribs and seafood, the restaurant also features Mexican and Italian cuisine. Enjoy a full menu selection at breakfast along with breads and pastries prepared fresh daily. Appetizers all day with selected appetizers priced at $2.50 during happy hour. 7am-10pm M-Th, -midnight F; 11am-midnight Sa, -11pm Su. ! AE/V/MC/DC/DI. 514 Nicollet Mall, Mpls., 338-0335.

Minnesota Zephyr
Elegant dining train with five dining cars offering three hour excursions through the St. Croix River Valley. Serving a four-course white linen dinner with a choice of three entrees (game hen, flounder or prime rib). Departure at 7:30pm F and Sa, 11:30am Su. Afternoon excursions. !!!! V/MC/DI. 601 N. Main St., Box 573, Stillwater, 430-3000. Reservations only.

Mirror of Korea
This restaurant offers spicy entrees as well as stir-fried dishes. No liquor. 11am-9:30pm M-F; noon-9:30pm Sa. ! V/MC. 3117 E. Lake St., Mpls., 721-3069.

Monte Carlo Bar and Grill
Serving a variety of sandwiches, chicken salads and steaks. 11am-1am M-Sa; 10am-midnight Su. Su brunch: 10am-4pm. !! AE/V/MC/DC. 219 Third Ave. N., Mpls., 333-5900.

Morton's of Chicago - The Steakhouse
Aged prime steaks, whole Maine lobsters, fresh fish and prime rib done to perfection. Lunch: 11:30am-2:30pm M-F. Dinner: 5:30-11pm M-Sa, 5-10pm Su. !!!! AE/V/MC/CB/DI. 555 Nicollet Mall, Mpls., 673-9700.

Mr. D's Ribs
A true rib place, offering smoked juicy ribs with lots of flavor. Also offering barbecued beef, pork and hot sausages, catfish and barbecued chicken. Take out. ! No credit cards. 486 N. Robert St., St. Paul, 291-2300.

Mudpie Vegetarian Restaurant
This restaurant offers vegetarian meals including the veggie burger, salads, soups and Middle Eastern dishes. Wine and beer. 11am-10pm M-Th, -11pm F; 8am-11pm Sa, -10pm Su. ! AE/V/MC. 2549 Lyndale Ave. S., Mpls., 872-9435.

Muffin Man
Besides baked goods, this restaurant serves soup and sandwiches. No liquor. Smoke free. Mpls. – 7am-10pm daily. Town Square – (baked goods only) 7am-6pm M-Sa. ! No credit cards. 2300 Hennepin Ave., Mpls., 374-5573. Town Square, 444 Cedar St., St. Paul, 227-2717.

Muffuletta in the Park
This cafe features pasta, grilled shrimp, stuffed breast of chicken, tortellini, Roma salmon and

veal battuta. Lunch: 11:30am-2:30pm M-F, - 3:30pm Sa. Dinner: 5-9pm M-Th, -10pm F and Sa. Su brunch: 10:30am-2pm. *!!* AE/V/MC. Milton Square, 2260 Como Ave., St. Paul, 644-9116.

MURRAY'S
Since 1946, this restaurant has specialized in a variety of steak meals including the Silver Butter Knife Steak, fresh fish, seafood and chops. Violin and pianist. M-Sa evenings. 11am-10:30pm M-Th, -11pm F and Sa; 4-10pm Su. Tea: 2-4:30pm M-Sa. *!!!!* AE/V/MC/DC/CB/DI. 26 S. Sixth St., Mpls., 339-0909.

MY LE HOA
A true Chinese restaurant offering such dishes as minced seafood lettuce wrap, baked quail, bird's nest soup and hot pot dishes. 10:30am-10pm Sa and Su. *!* V/MC/DC. 2900 Rice St., Little Canada, 484-5353.

MY PIE
Specializing in deep-dish and stuffed pizzas. Wine and beer at Edina. No liquor at Golden Valley. 4-10pm Su-Th, -midnight F and Sa. *!!* AE/V/MC/DC. 3501 W. 70th St., Edina, 920-4444. Pizza delivery and takeout only at 5410 Wayzata Boulevard, Golden Valley, 544-5551.

Spend Some Time In An Institution.

If the world has left you a little crazy, come to Murray's Restaurant. For 40 years we've given people safe asylum from the dog-eat-dog world. With extraordinary food. Experienced service. And a truly inviting atmosphere. So visit Murray's soon. And get the kind of treatment you deserve.

Murray's
26 S. 6th 339-0909

© 1986 Murray's

NaiSmith's
Home away from home for the Timberwolves, this sports bar serves soup, spicy Oriental salad, tuna platter salad, grilled swordfish and a variety of full or half sandwiches, including grilled cheese, prime rib and club house. 11am-1am M-Sa; 10:30am-1am Su. Target Center, first level, 600 N. First Ave., Mpls., 673-8080.

Nam
This restaurant features such Vietnamese dishes as hot-and-spicy chicken, egg foo young, shrimp lo mein and beef curry. No liquor. 11am-8:30pm M-Sa. ! AE/V/MC. 1005 Nicollet Mall, Mpls., 332-3666.

Nankin
Offering Mandarin and Cantonese cuisine since 1919. Lunch and dinner buffet: 11am-3pm and 5-9pm daily. 11:30am-9:30pm M-Th, -11pm F and Sa; noon-8pm Su. !! AE/V/MC/DC. 2 S. Seventh St., Mpls., 333-3303.

Neon Lunch
This jazzy cafe serves delicious pasta, chef, Caesar and fruit salads, sandwiches and two hot entrees each day. 7:30am-3pm M-Th, -2:30pm F. ! No credit cards. 155 S. Fifth Ave., Mpls., 339-0370.

New French Cafe and Bar
Warehouse district restaurant offering a variety of French dishes, including French bread baked on the premises. Casual menu at the New French Bar. Breakfast: 7-11am M-F. Lunch: 11:30am-1:30pm M-F. Dinner: 5:30-9:30pm M-Sa, -9pm Su. Late-night supper: 10pm-midnight F and Sa. Sa and Su brunch: 8am-2pm. !!! AE/V/MC/DC. 128 N. Fourth St., Mpls., 338-3790.

New Horizons
A Middle Eastern and American restaurant that serves gyros, tabouli salad, stuffed grape leaves, spinach pie and saharre (chicken stuffed with ricotta cheese). 6am-10pm M-Th, open 24 hours on F and Sa. ! V/MC/D/CB. 1015 W. Lake St., Mpls., 827-6211.

New Riverside Cafe
With a wide selection of menu items, this restaurant stirs up everything from vegetarian entrees to wok dishes. No liquor. 7am-11pm M-Th, -midnight F; 8am-midnight Sa. Su brunch: 9am-1:30pm. ! No credit cards. 329 Cedar Ave., Mpls., 333-4814.

New Sexton Cafe
This cafe features numerous recipes for those who love omelets. No liquor. 6am-3pm M-F; 7am-2pm Sa and Su. ! No credit cards. 527 S. Seventh St., Mpls., 333-6617.

Nguyet
Vietnamese restaurant featuring egg rolls, sauteed shrimp and won-ton soup. Wine and beer. 11am-9pm M-Sa. ! No credit cards. 823 W. Broadway St., Mpls., 522-4156.

Nicklow's
Restaurant serving such Greek delights as saganaki or hot seafood salads. Live entertainment W-Sa. 11am-1am M-Sa. !! AE/V/MC/DI. Highway 100 and 36th Ave. N., Crystal, 529-7751.

Nicklow's Cafe and Bar
Overlooking Laddie Lake, this restaurant offers American and Greek menu items like the New York T-bone and gyros. 11am-9pm Su-Th, -10pm F and Sa. !! AE/V/MC/DI. 8466 Central Ave. N.E., Spring Lake Park, 784-8566.

Nicollet Island Inn
On an island in the Mississippi River adjacent to downtown Minneapolis, this country-style inn features contemporary American cuisine and 24 beautiful guest rooms. Breakfast: 7-10am M-Sa. Lunch: 11:30am-2pm M-F, -3pm Sa. Dinner: 5:30-10pm M-Th, -11pm F and Sa; 4:30-9pm Su. Su brunch: 9:30am-2pm. !! AE/V/MC/DC/CB/DI. 95 Merriam St., Mpls., 331-3035.

Nikki's Cafe
Cafe and bar serving gourmet pizza, pasta, salads and entrees. Featuring live music nightly. 11am-11pm M-Th, -midnight F and Sa; 11:30am-11pm Su. Su brunch: 11:30am-2:30pm. !! AE/V/MC. 107 Third Ave. N., Mpls., 340-9098.

The 90's at Noon
The new spot for a creative lunch in downtown Mpls. You get great show-us-your-chops meals and drinks plus big, big fresh-sliced sandwiches. 8am-1pm M-Sa; 10am-1pm Su. ! AE/V/MC/DI/DC. 408 Hennepin Ave., Mpls., 333-7755.

Nora's
Restaurant adorned with historic photos of local scenes serving roast turkey sandwiches, seafood, chicken, soups and fresh-prepared popovers. 11am-10pm daily. ! V/MC/DI. 2107 E. Lake St., Mpls., 729-9353. 3118 W. Lake St., Mpls., 927-5781.

Normandy Village
For more than 40 years, this restaurant with the atmosphere of a 16th-century Norman Inn has been serving seafood, steaks, ribs, Caesar salad and desserts. Breakfast: 6-11am. Lunch: 11:30am-2pm daily. Dinner: 5-10:30pm M-Sa, -10:15pm Su. !! AE/V/MC/DC/CB/DI. Hotel

Normandy, 405 S. Eighth St., Mpls., 370-1400.
No Wake Cafe
Located on the Mississippi River, this barge-style restaurant offers a menu that includes scones, muffins and burgers. Wine and beer. 7am-2pm M-F; 5-9pm W, -10pm F; 8am-10pm Sa; noon-10pm Su. *!* No credit cards. No reservations. 100 Yacht Club Road, St. Paul, 292-1411.

Nye's Polonaise Room
Polish and American restaurant featuring spare ribs, sauerkraut, potato dumplings, cabbage rolls and piroghi. Polish wine, beer and vodka. Polka band F and Sa evenings. 11am-11:30pm M-Sa. *!!* AE/V/MC/DC. 112 Hennepin Ave. E., Mpls., 379-2021.

Oak Grill
Traditional food served including burgers, steaks and poultry entrees. Fresh-baked popovers are a must. 11am-7pm M-F, -3pm Sa. *!!* AE/V/MC/DI. 12th floor, Dayton's, 700 Nicollet Mall, Mpls., 375-2938.

Odaa
Homemade East African food prepared fresh and preservative free. Specialties include steak tartare and many vegetarian dishes served authentically on communal trays and eaten with buddeena. Mango juice, spiced tea, specialty African coffees and desserts. 11am-10pm M-Th, -11pm F and Sa; 3-9pm Su. *!!* AE/V/MC. 408 Cedar Ave., Mpls., 338-4459.

O.J.'s
Watch sports on cable TV or play videos. Then sit outside on the patio or in the atrium for a hoagie, huge taco salad, burger or one of the hot lunch specials. *!* AE/V/MC/DC. 11am-1am daily. Galtier Plaza, 175 E. Fifth St., St. Paul, 225-8105.

Ol' Mexico
Mexican restaurant featuring pocket tacos and chimichangas. Karaoke sing-along W-Sa at Roseville. Live entertainment W-Sa at Woodbury. 11am-10pm M-Th, -11pm F and Sa; 11am-9pm Su. *!!* AE/V/MC/DC. Lexington Plaza Shopping Center, 1754 Lexington Ave. N., Roseville, 487-2847. 1690 Woodlane Drive, Woodbury, 738-7122.

Old City Cafe
Serving Israeli dishes such as chumus and falafel. A choice of 15 Middle Eastern salads. No liquor. 11:30am-8:30pm M-Th, -2pm F;

8pm-midnight Sa. *!* No credit cards. 1571 Grand Ave., St. Paul, 699-5347.

Olive Branch
Enjoy homemade soups and fresh daily entrees or choose from a wide selection of sandwiches and salads. 6:30am-10pm M-Sa; 8am-10pm Su. *!!* AE/V/MC/DC/CB/DI. Best Western Drover's Inn, 701 S. Concord St., South St. Paul, 455-3600.

Olive Garden
Italian restaurant with a menu featuring entrees from northern and southern Italy. Unlimited refills of Italian salad, breadsticks and nonalcoholic beverages. 11am-10pm Su-Th, -11pm F and Sa. *!!* AE/V/MC/DC/CB/DI. 4701 W. 80th St., Bloomington, 831-0404. 1749 Beam Ave., Maplewood, 773-0200.

Oliver's
This English pub offers Mexican and American entrees, including tortillas, fajitas and burritos. Eight different beers on tap. 4-11pm M-W, -midnight Th-Sa; 5-11pm Su. *!* No credit cards. 2007 Lyndale Ave. S., Mpls., 871-5591.

Olympics Cafe
Greek and American cafe featuring gyros, shish kebabs, chicken, burgers and barbecued beef sandwiches. Catering available. 11:30am-1:30am M-Th, -2am F and S; 1-11pm Su. *!* No credit cards. 527 Hennepin Ave., Mpls., 332-1375.

Origami
Situated next to a Haitian art gallery, this restaurant specializes in Japanese food and features a sushi bar. Lunch: 11:30am-2:30pm M-F. Dinner: 5-10pm M-Th, -11pm F and Sa. *!!* AE/V/MC/DI. 30 N. First St., Mpls., 333-8430.

Original Pancake House
Offers a variety of breakfast entrees including baked German pancakes, souffle omelets and apple pancakes. 7am-3pm daily. Sa and Su brunch: 7am-3pm. *!* AE/V/MC/DC. 3501 W. 70th St., Edina, 920-4444.

Pagoda
Cantonese and Szechuan restaurant serving lemon chicken and Hong Kong steak. 11am-9pm M-Th, -10pm F; 4-10pm Sa; Closed Su. *!!* AE/V/MC. Highway 120 and County Road E., White Bear Lake, 777-8333.

Palomino
Euro-Metro bistro featuring Mediterranean taste in an atmosphere of polished hardwoods.

AE = American Express / V = VISA / MC = MasterCard / DI = Discover / DC = Diners Club / CB = Carte Blanche
! = less than $10 / *!!* $10-$18 / *!!!* $18-$28 / *!!!!* more than $28

173 Twin Cities / Eater's Digest

Featuring brick-oven pizza and oak-fired rotisserie for spit-roasted chicken, prime rib and seasonal game. Free parking after 5pm. Lunch: 11:15am-2:30pm M-Th; 11:30am-2:30pm Sa and Su. Dinner: 5-10pm M-Th, -11pm F and Sa; 4-9pm Su. Bar: 11:15am-12:30am M-F; 11:30am-12:30am Sa, -10pm Su. *!* AE/V/MC. Skyway level, Ninth and Hennepin, Mpls., 339-3800.

PAM SHERMAN'S BAKERY AND CAFE
Uptown cafe serving roast chicken, vegetarian lasagna, pasta with fresh pesto. Delicious homemade desserts and bakery items such as raspberry mousse cake, triple-chocolate cake and low-fat breads. No liquor. 7am-10pm M-Th, -11:30pm F and Sa; 8am-10pm Su. *!* No credit cards. 2914 Hennepin Ave., Mpls., 823-7269. 1204 Harmon Place, Mpls., 672-9121.

PANNEKOEKEN
Specializing in pannekoekens and Belgian waffles. No liquor. 6am-11pm Su-Th, -midnight F and Sa. *!* AE/V/MC. Bloomington, 884-4007 and 881-5635; Brooklyn Park, 561-4430; Columbia Heights, 571-8661; Fridley, 571-6646; Southdale Square, Richfield, 866-7731; Roseville, 633-9621; West St. Paul, 455-1653; Ridge Square, 525-1338; Fargo, ND, (701) 237-3559; Tower Square, 943-2804; Maplewood, 779-7844; Long Lake, 476-8821; Rochester, (507) 287-0717.

PAPAYA'S
Offering a wide selection of sandwiches, salads and pizzas in a tropical setting. 6:30am-11pm daily. *!* AE/V/MC/DC/CB/DI. Fifth floor, Marriott City Center, 30 S. Seventh St., Mpls., 349-4000.

PARKER HOUSE
Restaurant featuring prime rib, steaks and seafood. 11:30am-10pm M-F; 5-10pm Sa, -9pm Su. *!!* AE/V/MC/DC/CB/DI. 1318 Highway 13, Mendota, 452-1881.

PARK TAVERN
For more than 30 years, this restaurant has offered its famous hamburgers in addition to a variety of sandwiches and pizza. 6:30am-1:30am M-F; 8am-1am Sa. Sa and Su brunch: 9am-2pm. *!* AE/V/MC. 3401 Louisiana Ave. S., St. Louis Park, 929-6810.

PATRICK MCGOVERN'S PUB AND RESTAURANT
Featuring real home-cooked turkey with real mashed potatoes and gravy. It's wonderful*!* Also chili, homemade sandwiches, soups and desserts. 11am-10pm M-Th, -11pm F; 8am-10pm Sa. *!!* AE/V/MC/DI. 225 W. Seventh St., St. Paul, 224-5821.

PEARL GARDEN
Serving Szechuan and Cantonese cuisine and seafood specialties. 11am-10pm daily. *!!* AE/V/MC/DC/CB. 905 Hampshire Ave. S., Golden Valley, 541-0610.

PEARSON'S EDINA RESTAURANT
Family-owned restaurant serving baked chicken, Swedish meatballs, fresh-broiled salmon, soups, cakes, pies and pastries for more than 50 years. 7am-9:30pm M-Sa; 9am-7pm Su. *!* AE/V/MC/DC/DI. 3808 W. 50th St., Edina, 927-4464.

PEPITOS TEX-MEX BAR AND GRILL
Family-owned and operated Mexican restaurant specializing in spicy pork, chicken mole, huevos rancheros, nachos lupitas and homemade tortillas. Open stage comedy Su 9-11:30pm. 11am-11pm Su-Th, -midnight F and Sa. Su brunch: 11am-3pm. Bar open until 1am every night. Catering available. *!!* AE/V/MC. 4820 Chicago Ave., Mpls., 822-2104.

PEPITOS MEXI-GO DELI
Unique faster food alternative offers Pepitos homemade Mexican specialties to go, such as tacos, gourmet burritos, enchiladas, nachos lupitas and burgers. 10am-10pm M-Th, -11pm F and Sa; 11am-10pm Su. *!* 4624 Nicollet Ave., Mpls., 825-6311.

PERFUME RIVER
Vietnamese restaurant with meals such as imperial chicken, chow mein, rice noodle salad and spring rolls. 11am-10pm M-Th, -11pm F; noon-11pm Sa, -10pm Su. *!* No credit cards. 324 Cedar Ave., Mpls., 332-0892.

PETER'S GRILL
A Minneapolis institution since 1914, this restaurant offers steak, seafood, homemade soups, pies, cakes and pudding. No liquor. 7am-8pm M-F; 8am-4pm Sa. *!* No credit cards. Baker Center, 114 S. Eighth St., Mpls., 333-1981.

PIAZZA'S ITALIAN RISTORANTE
Italian restaurant featuring spaghetti, manicotti, ravioli, veal Marsala, chicken parmigiano, homemade sausage and pizza. Strolling accordion player Sa. Dine in or take out. Beer and wine. 11am-9:30pm M-F; 4-9:30pm Sa and Su. *!* AE/V/MC. Highway 55 and Boone, Golden Valley, 542-8107.

PICCADILLY
With a view of White Bear Lake, this restaurant offers seafood, steak and ribs. Prime rib is the house specialty. Featuring all-you-can-eat dinners W (chicken), F (fish) and Su (turkey).

5-10pm Tu-Th, -10:30pm F and Sa; 4-8pm Su. Su brunch: 10:30am-2:30pm. *!!* AE/V/MC. 70 Mahtomedi Ave., Mahtomedi, 426-3455.

PICKLED PARROT
Unique decorations fill this restaurant offering Southern, Southwestern and Caribbean meals. Live entertainment. 11am-1am M-Sa; Su hours vary. *!!* AE/V/MC. 26 N. Fifth St., Mpls., 332-0673.

PING'S SZECHUAN BAR AND GRILL
Serving Szechuan, Mandarin, Cantonese and Peking dishes, specializing in duck. Also offering pop chicken, sesame beef and fried pot stickers. Wine and beer. Lunch buffet: 11:30am-2pm M-F. 11am-9pm M-Th, -10pm F and Sa. *!!* AE/V/MC/DC. 1401 Nicollet Ave., Mpls., 874-9404.

PIZZERIA UNO
Featuring deep-dish pizza, this restaurant also offers an American and Italian menu. 11am-midnight daily. *!* AE/V/MC. Ridgedale, Minnetonka, 544-2777; Edina, 925-5005.

PLUMS NEIGHBORHOOD GRILL AND BAR
Offering burgers, chicken sandwiches, coconut beer shrimp, homemade chicken soup and the house specialty, Cajun pork tenderloin. Dancing W-Sa. Noon-11pm M-Sa; 10am-9pm Su. *!* V/MC/DC. 480 Snelling Ave. S., St. Paul, 699-2227.

POLO
Contemporary Italian restaurant featuring fresh fish, veal, chicken and more than 20 pasta dishes. Lunch: 11:30am-4pm M-F. Dinner: 4-10pm M-Th, -11pm F; 5-11pm Sa; 3-10pm Su. Su brunch: 9am-3pm. *!!* AE. 9920 Wayzata Boulevard, St. Louis Park, 545-0041.

PORT OF BEIRUT
Lebanese restaurant featuring gyros, tabouli and grilled kebabs in addition to vegetarian entrees. Belly dancing F and Sa. Wine and beer. 11am-9:30pm M-Th, -10:30pm Sa; closed Su. *!* AE/V/MC. 1385 S. Robert St., West St. Paul, 457-4886.

POULET
Offering a wide selection of international chicken entrees. 7am-10pm M-F; 8am-10pm Sa. Su brunch: 8am-3pm. *!!* AE/V/MC/DC. 2558 Lyndale Ave. S., Mpls., 871-6431.

PRACNA ON MAIN
Next to the Mississippi River, this restaurant serves grilled chicken breast, steak sandwiches, oyster pasta, spinach salad and burgers. 11:30am-10pm daily. *!!* AE/V/MC/CB/DI. St. Anthony Main, 117 Main St. S.E., Mpls., 379-3200.

PRONTO RISTORANTE AND CAFFE PRONTO
Pronto Ristorante is a Minneapolis dining institution offering northern Italian cuisine in an elegant, sophisticated setting. Caffe Pronto is a casual restaurant featuring 30 varieties of pasta as well as pizzas. Caffe – Lunch: 11:30am-2pm M-F. Dinner: 5-10pm M-Th, -11pm F and Sa, -9pm Su. Ristorante – 5:30-10pm M-Th, -11pm F and Sa, -9pm Su. Ristorante *!!!*, Caffe *!!* AE/V/MC. Hyatt Regency Hotel, 1300 Nicollet Mall, Mpls., 333-4414.

THE PURPLE ONION
An American bistro with great homemade foods. Award-winning chef features flaming rib-eye peppercorn steak, salmon and raspberry chicken. Also serving sandwiches, pizzas and burgers. Happy hour all day M-F. Satellite sports and dancing nightly. *!* AE/V/MC/DC/DI/CB. 5001 W. 80th St. at Highways 494 and 100, Bloomington, 835-5686.

Q. CUMBERS
All-you-can-eat soup and salad bars offer muffins, fresh fruit and frozen yogurt as well as hot entrees. Wine and beer. Muffins, coffee and juice 7:30-11am daily. 11am-9pm Su-Th, -10pm F and Sa. *!* V/MC. Centennial Lakes Plaza, 7465 France Ave. S., Edina, 831-0235. Crossroads Mall, County Road B2 and Snelling, Roseville, 628-0350.

QUAIL ON THE HILL
Authentic Parisian-style French restaurant in St. Paul historic Cathedral Hill area. Five minutes from downtown. Free parking. Wine and beer. Lunch: 11:30am-2:30pm M-F. Dinner: 5:30-10:30pm M-Sa. *!!* V/MC. 371 Selby Ave., St. Paul, 291-1236.

QUEEN OF EXCELSIOR
For brunch this floating restaurant offers caramel rolls and chicken a la king on a pastry shell with scrambled eggs. Dinner menu items include breast of chicken with rice, fresh vegetables and custard flan. Moonlight cocktail cruises with live music. Dinner cruises: 6:30pm F and Sa. Cocktail cruises: 9:30pm F and Sa. Su brunch cruises: 11:30am-1:30pm. All cruises weather-permitting. *!!!* AE/V/MC. 10 Water St., Excelsior, 474-2502.

RAINBOW CHINESE
A Cantonese cafe serving sweet and sour items, soups and rice with toppings. 11:30am-10pm M-Th, -2am F and Sa, -9pm Su. *!* AE/V/MC/DC/CB. 2750 S. Nicollet, Mpls., 870-7084.

RADISSON CAFE AND CONFERENCE DINING ROOM
An eclectic Euro-style bistro and bar serving

European- and American-inspired foods and baked goods in a casual atmosphere. Grilled meats, poultry, fresh seafood and homemade pasta. 6:30am-10pm M-Th, -11pm F; 7:30am-11pm Sa; 7am-10pm Su. *!!!* AE/V/MC/DC/CB/DI. Radisson and Conference Center, Northwest Business Campus, 3131 Campus Drive, Plymouth, 559-6600.

Red Lobster
Specializing in seafood dishes, this restaurant offers more than 100 items from which to select. 11am-10pm Su-Th, -11pm F and Sa. *!!* No personal checks. AE/V/MC/DC/DI. Blaine, 786-7667; Brooklyn Center, 561-6188; Burnsville, 435-2552; Golden Valley, 546-7300; Roseville, 636-9800; Maplewood, 770-8825; Bloomington, 888-8102; West St. Paul, 552-0700.

Red Sea
Featuring hot and spicy Ethiopian and Eritrean dishes. All fresh ingredients with no preservatives or artificial flavor. No liquor. 11am-1am daily. *!* V/MC. 320 Cedar Ave. S., Mpls., 333-1644.

Ristorante Luci
Italian trattoria offering pasta, homemade mozzarella and a variety of breads and desserts. Fresh fish daily. Fixed-price four-course dinner. 5-9:30pm M-Th, -10:30pm F and Sa. *!!* No credit cards. 470 Cleveland Ave. S., St. Paul, 699-8258.

River Room
Steaks, pasta and fresh fish. Featuring wild rice soup, popovers and salads. 11am-7:30pm M-F, -3pm Sa; 11am-2:30pm Su. *!!* AE/V/MC/DI. First floor, Dayton's, Seventh and Cedar, St. Paul, 292-5174.

River's Edge
Along the Apple River, this restaurant offers Wisconsin trout, chicken Alfredo and features frog legs. Pianist entertains nightly. Seafood buffet: 5:30pm F; prime rib and crab buffet: 5:30pm Sa. Noon-9:30pm Su-F; 4-11:30pm Sa. Su brunch: 11am-2pm. *!!!* AE/V/MC/DC/DI. Highway 64, Somerset, WI, (715) 247-3305.

Riverview Supper Club
Offering chicken teriyaki, ribs and Cajun chicken. Dancing F and Sa. Dinner: 4pm-1am daily. *!!* AE/V/MC/DC/CB. 2319 West River Road, Mpls., 521-7676.

Roper's Restaurant
Country-western informal restaurant with blackened catfish, jumbo shrimp and steaks. A different special each week. Large dance floor, game room and bar. Local high-profile musical entertainment. 5-11pm Tu-Sa. *!* AE/V/MC. 3720 E. River Road, Fridley, 781-3377.

Rose's Vietnamese Cuisine
Menu entrees include chicken, beef, pork, seafood and vegetarian dishes. Wine and beer. 11am-9pm M-Sa. *!* No credit cards. Sibley Plaza, 2447 W. Seventh St., St. Paul, 690-1061.

Rosen's Bar and Grill
Downtown sports bar serving an extensive menu of soups, salads, sandwiches, burgers and pastas. 11am-11pm daily. *!* AE/V/MC/CB/DC/DI. Kickernick Building, 430 First Ave. N., Mpls., 338-1926.

Rosewood Room
Elegant dining with entrees such as cilantro shrimp, steak and sauteed breast of duck. Pianist F and Sa. Breakfast: 7-11am. Lunch: 11:30am-2pm. Dinner: 6-10pm M-Th, -10:30pm F and Sa. Closed Su. *!!!* AE/V/MC/DC/CB/DI. Omni Northstar Hotel, 618 Second Ave. S., Mpls., 338-2288.

Rossini's Trattoria
Italian restaurant and espresso bar offering pasta, soups and breads. Wine. 7am-4pm and 5-10pm M-F; 11am-10pm Sa *!* V/MC/DC. Centennial Lakes Medical Building, 7373 France Ave. S., Edina, 831-2276.

Royal Orchid Thai Restaurant
Voted number one Thai restaurant by the Twin Cities' top food critics in Mpls/St. Paul magazine, Aug. '91. Wine and beer. 11:30am-10pm Su-Th, -11pm F and Sa. *!!* V/MC. 1835 Nicollet Ave., Mpls., 872-1938.

Rudolph's Bar-B-Que
Featuring a variety of barbecued ribs served with spicy coleslaw. Lyndale Ave. – 11am-midnight M-Sa; 10am-2am Su. Hennepin Ave. – 11am-11pm M-Th, -1am F and Sa, -10pm Su. St. Paul – 11am-1am M-Sa, -10pm Su. Su brunch: 10am-2pm at Lyndale Ave; 11am-3pm in St. Paul. *!!* V/MC. 1933 Lyndale Ave. S., Mpls., 871-8969. 815 Hennepin Ave. E., Mpls. 623-3671. Galtier Plaza, Jackson St., St. Paul, 222-2226.

Rusty Scupper
Offering prime rib, steaks, seafood, fresh fish and pasta. DJ and dancing Saturday night. 5-10pm M-Th, -11pm F and Sa; 5-9pm Su. *!!* AE/V/MC/DC/CB/DI. 4301 W. 80th St., Bloomington, 831-5415.

Sahari
This restaurant serves Middle Eastern, Greek and vegetarian food. Moussaka, hummus, gyros and a wide selection of vegetarian dishes are served. Winter hours: 11am-9pm M-Th, -10pm

F and Sa; 5-9pm Su. Summer hours: 11am-10pm M-Th, -11pm F and Sa. ! AE/V/MC/DC/CB/DI. 1831 Nicollet Ave., Mpls., 870-0071.

SAIGON
Vietnamese restaurant serving vegetarian combination platters, chicken curry with lemon grass, mock duck and chicken wings. Call for hours. ! No credit cards. 317 W. 38th St., Mpls., 822-7712. 3035 Lyndale Ave. S., Mpls., 827-8918. Knollwood Mall, 8332 Highway 7, St. Louis Park, 938-7788.

SAMURAI STEAK HOUSE
A Japanese teppanyaki house. The chef cooks your meal at the table-top grill while you watch. Featuring sesame chicken, shrimp and steak. 5-10pm M-Th, -11pm F and Sa; 4:30-8:30pm Su. !! AE/V/MC/DC/D. 850 S. Louisiana, Golden Valley, 542-9922.

ST. CLAIR BROILER
Featuring fabulous burgers, sandwiches and desserts along with omelets and breakfast dishes served all day. No liquor. 6:30am-midnight M-F; 7am-midnight Sa and Su. ! No credit cards. 1580 St. Clair Ave., St. Clair and Snelling, St. Paul, 698-7055.

ST. JAMES HOTEL
With a view of the Mississippi River, this hotel offers dining options that vary with the individual dining settings. Port of Red Wing – Lunch: 11am-2pm M-Sa. Dinner: 5-9:30pm nightly. Su brunch: 11am-2pm. Call for Veranda hours. Port !! Veranda ! AE/V/MC/CB/DI. 406 Main St., Red Wing, 227-1800. Outside the Twin Cities, (800)252-1875.

ST. MARTIN'S TABLE
Serving lunch only, this vegetarian restaurant serves spinach ricotta sandwiches, breads, soups, salads and carrot cake. Volunteer wait staff contributes tips to charity. Live music Sa. No liquor. Pastries and coffee are served 9:30am-5pm M-Sa. Lunch: 11:30am-2:30pm M-Sa. ! No credit cards. 2001 Riverside Ave., Mpls., 339-3920.

ST. PAUL GRILL
With a view of Rice Park, this American restaurant and bar features fresh seafood and grilled dry-aged beef. Lunch: 11am-2pm M-Sa. Dinner: 5:30-11pm Tu-Sa, -10pm Su-M. Late night bar menu until midnight daily. Su brunch: 11am-2pm. !! AE/V/MC/DC/CB. Saint Paul Hotel, 350 Market St., St. Paul, 22-GRILL (224-7455).

SAJI-YA
This Japanese restaurant offers sushi, chicken teriyaki, teppanyaki, tempura shrimp and features knife-flashing table-side cooking. Lunch: 11am-2pm M-F. Dinner: 5-10pm M-Th, -11pm F and Sa, -9pm Su. !! AE/V/MC/DC. 695 Grand Ave., St. Paul, 292-0444.

SAKURA TRADITIONAL JAPANESE RESTAURANT
Japanese dining including tempura, teriyaki and sushi. Wine and beer. Lunch: 11:30am-2:30pm M-Sa. Dinner: 5-9:30pm M-Th; 4:30-10pm F and Sa; 4-9:30pm Su. !! AE/V/MC/DC/CB. Galtier Plaza, 175 E. Fifth St., St. Paul, 224-0185.

SAN ANTONIO GRILL
A honky-tonk of some distinction. Open-air atmosphere. Offering award-winning mesquite fajitas, Texas barbecued beef, carnitas and other traditional fare. 11am-10pm M-Th, -11pm F and Sa, -8pm Su. ! AE/V/MC/DC/DI. Third level, Saint Paul Center, 30 E. Seventh St., St. Paul, 290-9047.

SASHA'S DELI AND GRILL
Overlooking Lake Minnetonka, this fine restaurant serves delicious salads, pastas and features a fresh catch of the day. 8am-9pm M-Sa; 10am-3pm Su. !! AE/V/MC. 294 E. Grove Lane, Wayzata, 475-DELI.

SAWATDEE
This Thai restaurant serves a traditional menu including spicy curries, paradise chicken wings, fresh fish, spring rolls, seafood and Pad Thai noodles. 11am-10pm Su-Th, -11pm F and Sa. !! AE/V/MC/DC/DI. 607 Washington Ave. S., Mpls., 338-6451. 8501 Lyndale Ave. S., Bloomington, 888-7177. MarketHouse, 289 E. Fifth St., St. Paul, 222-5859.

SCHUMACHER'S NEW PRAGUE HOTEL
Our world-class restaurant and hotel features gourmet central European dishes. Recognized as one of the 12 best inns of 1990 and featured in national, regional and international publications. Schumacher's is known as Minnesotans' favorite out-of-town restaurant. 7am-9pm daily. !!! AE/V/MC/DI. 212 W. Main St., New Prague, 445-7285 (metro area) or (612) 758-2133.

SCULLY'S BROILER AND BAR
Serving fresh fish, pasta, steaks, sandwiches and salads. 6am-11pm M-Th, -midnight F and Sa; 5-9pm Su. Su brunch: 11am-1pm. !! AE/V/MC/DC. 1321 E. 78th St., Bloomington, 854-0101.

SERGEANT PRESTON'S SALOON AND EATERY
A restaurant featuring hundreds of combinations of creative sandwiches, plus homemade

soups, garden-fresh salads and award-winning appetizers. Cocktails featuring freshly squeezed oranges and grapefruits. One of the cities' largest outdoor cafes. Su all-you-can-eat brunch. Delivery available. 11am-1am daily (earlier for Vikings games). *!* AE/V/MC/DC/CB. 221 Cedar Ave., Mpls., 338-6146.

SERLIN'S CAFE
Offering a variety of menu items under $10. The price of dinner includes soup and pie. No liquor. 6am-7:30pm M-Sa. *!* No credit cards. 1124 Payne Ave., St. Paul, 776-9003.

700 EXPRESS
Lower-level eatery offering American dishes and featuring the Marketplace Sampler (cream cheese, meats and salads) and fettucine czarina. Wine and beer. 11am-8pm M-F, -5pm Sa; noon-5pm Su. *!* AE/V/MC/DI. Lower level, Dayton's, 700 Nicollet Mall, Mpls., 375-2684.

SHANNON KELLY'S
Something for everyone featuring ribs, chicken, steak and shrimp. Centrally located to Ordway, Science Museum and Civic Center. Live piano nightly. 11am-1am M-Sa. *!* AE/V/MC/DI. Sixth and Wabasha, St.Paul, 292-0905.

SHELLY'S WOODROAST
Northwoods oasis in the city, offering wood-roasted meats and fish as well as specialty appetizers, soups and salads. Fresh homemade desserts. 11am-10pm Su-Th; -midnight F and Sa. Su brunch. *!!* AE/V/MC/DC. Highway 12, west of Turner's Crossroad, St. Louis Park, 593-5050.

SHERLOCK'S HOME
English pub serving such favorites as toad-in-the-hole and ploughman's lunch with a microbrewery on premises. Lunch: 11am-2:30pm M-F. Light fare: 2:30-5:30pm M-F; 11am-5:30pm Sa; 4-10pm Su. Dinner: 5:30-10pm Su-Th, -11pm F and Sa. *!!* AE/V/MC/DC. Crosstown Highway and Shady Oak Road, Minnetonka, 931-0203.

SHILLA STONE BBQ
Featuring Korean dishes such as kim-chee chigay casserole, mandoo dumplings and bin dae kuk (mung bean pancakes). 11am-9:30pm T-Sa; noon-9:30pm Su. *!* No credit cards. 694 N. Snelling, St. Paul, 645-0006.

SHIPSIDE
Nautical-inspired restaurant offering a variety of seafood delights including king crab and shrimp. Lunch: 11:30am-2pm M-F. Dinner: 5:30-10pm M-Sa. Su brunch: 10:30am-2pm. *!!* AE/V/MC/DC/CB. Radisson South, Interstate 494 and Highway 100, Bloomington, 835-7800.

SHOREWOOD INN
Overlooking Moore Lake, this restaurant features a selection of menu items ranging from gyros and kebabs to chicken and seafood. Live music M-Sa. 11am-10pm M-Th, -11pm F and Sa. *!!* AE/V/MC/DC/CB. 6161 Highway 65, Fridley, 571-3444.

SHUANG CHENG
Offers Cantonese and Szechuan cuisine. Live lobster and fresh seafood flown in daily. 11am-10pm M-Th, -11pm F and Sa. *!* V/MC. 1320 Fifth St. S.E., Mpls., 378-0208.

SIDNEY'S PIZZA CAFE
Specializing in pizza, pasta and dessert, often of the unusual variety, such as Asian spicy chicken pizza, coconut chicken pasta, or apple pie pizza. All pasta is homemade. 11:30am-11pm Su-Th, -midnight F and Sa. *!* AE/V/MC. 2120 Hennepin Ave., Mpls., 870-7000.

SIGNATURE CAFE
Offering Mediterranean and Egyptian food such as vegetarian sandwiches and seafood dishes. No liquor. Lunch: 11am-2pm M, -3pm Tu-F; 10am-3pm Sa. Dinner: 5-9pm Tu-Sa; 10am-noon Sa. *!!* AE/V/MC. 130 Warwick St., Mpls., 378-0237.

SKYROOM
Overlooking Minneapolis, this sky-high, exciting express restaurant features a variety of dishes at five unique food concepts: the Eighth Street Deli; Pizza and Pasta; the Chickery; Grill It; and a colossal salad bar. Pianist daily. Wine and beer. 11am-3pm M-Sa. *!* AE/V/MC/DI. 12th floor of Dayton's. Nicollet and Seventh, Mpls., 375-4559.

SNUFFY'S MALT SHOP
Malt shop reminiscent of days gone past, serving burgers, fries and malts. Kids receive special treatment and have their own menu. St. Paul – 11am-9pm M, -10pm Tu-Sa. Roseville – 11am-10pm M-Th, -11pm F and Sa. Both locations noon-9pm Su. *!* No credit cards. 244 Cleveland Ave. S., St. Paul, 690-1846. 1125 Larpenteur Ave. W., Roseville, 488-0241.

SORREL'S
Italian restaurant serving scaloppine Marsala, fettuccine fruiti de mer and fresh salmon. Lunch: 11:30am-2pm M-F. Dinner: 6-10pm M-Sa. Su brunch: 9:30am-1:30pm. *!!* AE/V/MC/DC/CB/DI. Marriott Hotel, 2020 E. 79th St., Bloomington, 854-7441.

SORRENTO
Authentic lasagna, fettuccine Alfredo, chicken Parmesan, pizza and spaghetti made by owner Rossetta Virgilio, who was born just outside

Sorrento, Italy. 7am-5pm M-F. *!* No credit cards. Soo Line Building, skyway level, 105 S. Fifth St., Mpls., 376-0696.

SPIKE'S SPORTS BAR
Watch sports on TV or play pool, electric golf or basketball. Menu items include grilled chicken salad sandwich, fresh fruit with yogurt dressing, Greek tuna salad, chili, navy-bean soup, burgers and other basket food. 11:30am-11pm daily. *!* AE/V/MC/D/DC. Hyatt Regency Minneapolis, 1300 Nicollet Mall, Mpls., 370-1242.

SRI LANKA CURRY HOUSE
Offering such Sri Lankan specialties as a selection of beef, shrimp and lamb curries. Live music Sa. Wine and beer. Lunch: 11:30am-4pm Th-F; 1-4pm Sa. Dinner: 5-10pm M-Th, -11pm F and Sa, -10pm Su. *!!* V/MC/DC. 2821 Hennepin Ave., Mpls., 871-2400.

STACY'S SEA GRILL
Seafood restaurant with a menu including seafood Newburg and swordfish. Live music and dancing Th-Sa. 6:30am-10pm M-T, -11pm W-F; 7am-11pm Sa and Su. Sa and Su brunch. *!!!* AE/V/MC/DC/DI. Marriott Hotel, 5801 Opus Parkway, Minnetonka, 935-5500.

STEAK AND ALE
This restaurant with Old English decor serves steak, Creole blackened entrees, broiled shrimp, fresh fish and prime rib. Bloomington – Lunch: 11am-2pm M-Sa. Dinner: 5-10pm M-Th, -11pm F and Sa; noon-10pm Su. Roseville – Lunch: 11:30am-2pm M-F. Dinner: 5-10pm M-Th, -11pm F and Sa; noon-10pm Su. *!!* AE/V/MC/DC/CB/DI. 2801 Southtown Drive, Bloomington, 884-0124. 1893 Highway 36, Roseville, 633-9083.

STEAMBOAT INN
Overlooking the St. Croix River, this restaurant's specialty is prime rib of beef. The menu of 45 items includes blackened red snapper, bronzed halibut and duckling. Piano bar. Summer hours – Lunch: 11:30am-2pm M-F. Dinner: 4:30-9pm M-Th, -10pm F and Sa; noon-9pm Su. Su brunch: 10am-2pm. Chicken and fish fry buffet: 4:30-9pm F. *!!* AE/V/MC/DC/CB/DI. 307 N. Lake St., Prescott, WI, (800) 262-8232.

STUART ANDERSON'S CATTLE CO.
Specializing in prime rib as well as sirloin, filet mignon, chicken, steaks, ribs, Alaskan crab and lobster. Lunch: 11am-4pm M-F. Dinner: 4-10pm M-Th, -11pm F and Sa; noon-10pm Su. *!!* AE/V/MC/DC/DI. Bloomington, 835-1225; Fridley, 571-5087; Minnetonka, 541-1430; Roseville, 636-4145.

THE STUDIO
Cafeteria offering usual and unusual food carefully prepared on site. Soup, salads, spinach pie, vegetable lasagna and Chinese chicken with walnuts as well as breads and desserts. Menu changes daily. Wine and beer. 11:30am-2:30pm Tu-Su. *!* No credit cards. Minneapolis Institute of Arts, 2400 Third Ave. S., Mpls., 870-3180.

SUNSETS
With a view of Lake Minnetonka, this restaurant serves a variety of dishes including stir-fries, salads, steaks and pasta. Breakfast: 7-10:30am M-Sa. Lunch: 11am-4:45pm M-Sa. Dinner: 5pm-midnight M-Sa; 3-11pm Su. Su brunch: 9:30am-2pm. *!!* AE/V/MC. 700 E. Lake St., Wayzata, 473-LAKE.

SUNSHINE FACTORY
This restaurant offers an eclectic menu with entrees from champagne chicken breast and scallop fettuccine to barbecued ribs and seafood. Lighter fare in the bistro. Lunch: 11:15am-2:30pm M-Sa. Dinner: 5:15-11pm daily. Bistro: 2:30pm-1am M-F; 11am-1am Sa; noon-midnight Su. Su brunch: 10:30am-2pm. *!!* AE/V/MC/DC. 7600 42nd Ave. N., New Hope, 535-7000.

SUN SUN CHINESE RESTAURANT
Rated as one of the best Chinese restaurants in the Twin Cities by the Reader in 1990. Cantonese, Szechuan and Peking food are served. There are almost 100 menu items ranging from stir-fry dishes to lobster. 11am-9pm M-F; 4-9pm Sa; 12:30pm-9pm Su. *!* No credit cards. 854 W. University Ave., St. Paul, 291-0212.

SUZETTE'S CAFE EXCEPTIONALE
Featuring steaks, chicken, seafood and pasta. Live jazz Th-Sa. 11am-10pm M-Th, -1am F and Sa; 11am-8pm Su. Su brunch: 10am-2pm. *!!* AE/V/MC/DC. 498 Selby Ave., St. Paul, 224-5000.

SWEENEY'S SALOON AND CAFE
Menu ranging from burgers, prime rib and chicken to pasta, scallops and crab legs. 11am-11pm Su-W, -midnight Th-Sa. Sa and Su brunch: 10am-2pm. *!* AE/V/MC. 96 N. Dale St., St. Paul, 221-9157.

AE = American Express / V = VISA / MC = MasterCard / DI = Discover / DC = Diners Club / CB = Carte Blanche
! = less than $10 / *!!* $10-$18 / *!!!* $18-$28 / *!!!!* more than $28

SWISS ALPS
Restaurant featuring classic French and Continental entrees done to perfection. The Continental atmosphere will have you reminiscing about your last trip to Europe. Lunch: 11am-2:30pm daily. Dinner: 5:30-10pm Tu-Sa. *!!* V/MC/DC/CB. 771 Cleveland Ave., St. Paul, 690-5765.

SZECHUAN STAR
Cantonese, northern Chinese and Hong Kong-style dishes including imperial shrimp, orange chicken and Peking duck. Wine and beer. 11am-10pm M-Th, -11pm F and Sa, -9pm Su. Sa and Su brunch: 11am-3pm. *!!* AE/V/MC/DC/DI. 3655 Hazelton Road, Edina, 835-7610.

TABLE OF CONTENTS
This restaurant serves grilled ocean fish, duck breast and pork tenderloin among other fresh and eclectic offerings. Menu varies around four entrees and chicken breast. Lunch: 11:30am-2pm M-F; noon-2pm Sa. Dinner: 5:30-9:30pm M-Th, -10:30pm F and Sa. Espresso and baked goods served between lunch and dinner. *!!* No credit cards. 1648 Grand Ave., St. Paul, 699-6595.

TAM'S BAMBOO HOUSE, TAM'S EAST GARDEN, TAM'S RICE BOWL
Serving Cantonese and Szechuan meals. Bamboo House – 11:30am-10pm daily. East Garden – 11am-10pm M-F; 5-10pm Sa and Su. Rice Bowl – 11am-9:30pm Su-Th, -11:30pm F and Sa. Dim sum Su brunch: 11am-1pm at Rice Bowl. *!!* 7321 Zane Ave. N., Brooklyn Park, 560-2600. 328 S. Third St., Mpls., 338-1022. 1160 Fireside Drive, Fridley, 784-4402.

TANDOOR
Indian restaurant offering curries, kebabs, Tandoori chicken and lamb with spinach prepared in tandoor (clay) ovens. No liquor. Lunch: 11:30am-2pm M-F. Dinner: 5-9pm M-Sa. *!!* AE/V/MC. 210 Hennepin Ave. E., Mpls., 378-2055.

TANG'S GINGER CAFE
East-meets-West restaurant that serves contemporary Oriental cuisine. The menu features traditional Oriental appetizers such as spring rolls and pot stickers as well as unusual entrees such as shrimp soba salad with cashew pesto and cinnamon orange lamb mu shu. 11:30am-10pm M-Th, -11pm F and Sa; 5:30-10pm Su. *!*, some items *!!* AE/V/MC/D/DC. 1310 Hennepin Ave., Mpls., 339-2890.

TAY DO
A Vietnamese restaurant with offerings such as pho, egg rolls and bo nuong vi. 11am-9pm M-F; 9am-10pm Sa. *!* No credit cards. 1821 University Ave., St. Paul, 644-1384.

TAXXI
American bistro specializing in local and regional food. 6:30am-10:30pm seven days a week. *!!* AE/V/MC/DC/CB/DI. Hyatt Regency Hotel, 1300 Nicollet Mall, Mpls., 370-1234.

T-BIRDS
This '50s-inspired restaurant serves french-fried finger foods, T-burgers, sandwiches and T-Birds tea. DJ and dancing nightly. 2pm-1am M-F; 11am-1am Sa and Su. *!* AE/V/MC. 3035 White Bear Ave., Maplewood, 779-2266.

TEJAS
Informal Southwestern restaurant offering shrimp enchiladas, smoked-chicken nachos and freshly squeezed margaritas. 11am-10pm M-Sa; noon-5pm Su. *!!* AE/V/MC/DI. Lower level, Conservatory, 800 Nicollet Mall, Mpls., 375-0800.

TEQUILABERRY'S CALIFORNIA RESTAURANT
Sandwiches, salads, steaks and seafood. The loft features an all-you-can-eat prime rib special. Lunch: 11am-4pm M-Sa. Dinner: 4-10pm M-Th, -10:30pm F and Sa; 3-10pm Su. Su brunch: 10am-3pm. Loft – 5-10pm M-Th, -11pm F; 4-11pm Sa, -10pm Su.*!!* AE/V/MC/DI. 133 N.W. Coon Rapids Boulevard, Coon Rapids, 780-1850.

T.G.I. FRIDAY'S
Informal dining in a creatively decorated restaurant. Serving American food such as onion rings, Cajun chicken sandwiches and hot-fudge sundaes. 11am-1am M-Sa; 10am-1am Su. Su brunch: 10am-3pm. *!!* AE/V/M/DC/CB/DI. 5875 Wayzata Boulevard, St. Louis Park, 544-0675. 7730 Normandale Boulevard, Bloomington, 831-6553. 2480 Fairview Ave. N., Roseville, 631-1101.

TIMES BAR AND CAFE
American bistro featuring a seasonal menu. Innovative sandwiches soups, stews, salads and full entrees. 11am-12:30am M-Sa. Su jazz brunch: 11am-3pm. *!!* AE/V/MC/DI. 1036 Nicollet Mall, Mpls., 333-2762.

TIN CUP'S
Operating since 1923, this restaurant/bar has burgers, steaks and chicken. 11:30am-10pm M-Th, -11:00pm F and Sa; 11:30-9pm Su. *!* AE/V/MC. 1220 Rice St., St. Paul, 489-7585.

TINUCCI'S
Featuring week-night specials such as ribs and chicken on Tu, Italian cuisine W, old-style chicken and dumplings on Th, fish on F, and prime rib Sa. 11am-9:30pm Tu-Th, -10pm F;

Hurray! Minnesota   **180**

4:30-10:30pm Sa. Su brunch: 10am-3pm. *!!* AE/V/MC. 396 21st St., Newport, 459-9011.

T.K. NICK'S
Casual dining featuring American cuisine such as steaks, seafood and light pastas. Experienced bartenders serving excellent drinks. 11am-11pm M-Sa. Su brunch: 9am-2pm. *!!* AE/V/MC/DC/CB/DI. Located on the northeast corner of Highway 100 and 55, 521-8825.

TO CHAU
Featuring Vietnamese dishes both familiar and exotic with savory, spicy sauces and unusual dessert drinks. 11am-9pm Su-F, -10pm Sa. *!* No credit cards. 823 University Ave., St. Paul, 291-2661.

TONKIN
A Vietnamese restaurant serving chicken chow mein, chicken wings, fried rice and excellent egg rolls. 11am-8:30pm M-Th, -10pm F and Sa; call for hours on Su. *!* AE/V/MC. 345 N. Wabasha St., St. Paul, 227-4020.

TOP HAT LOUNGE
This bar and restaurant serves sandwiches, tacos and lunch specials, which may include roasted chicken, baked ham or lasagna. 10am-midnight M-F; 11am-midnight Sa and Su. *!* AE/V/MC. 134 E. Fifth St., St. Paul, 228-1347.

TOROS OF ASPEN
Mexican restaurant and bar serving Mexican favorites like fajitas, seafood enchiladas and enchiladas grande. Also an extensive American menu. Live music F and Sa, occasionally W. Reservations accepted. 11am-10:30pm M-Th, -11pm F; 3-11pm Sa; 5-10pm Su. *!* AE/V/MC/DC/CB. 6001 Shady Oak Road, Minnetonka, 938-9100.

TOULOUSE
French-Mediterranean cafeteria-style eatery serving salad Nicoise, pizza, grilled sourdough and sandwiches. Su brunch. Wine and beer. 11am-3pm daily. *!* AE/V/MC/DC. Fifth floor, Gaviidae Common, 651 Nicollet Mall, Mpls., 342-2700.

TOUR DE FRANCE
Three-time winner Greg LeMond is part owner of this restaurant featuring an international menu of healthy meals including Szechuan salmon and Black Angus strip steak. Smoke-free. Wine/beer. Lunch: 11:30am-2pm Tu-F. Dinner: 5:30-9:30pm Tu-Th; 5-10:30pm F and Sa. *!!!!* AE/V/MC. 4924 France Ave. S., Edina, 929-1010.

TRIESTE CAFE
A Mediterranean ethnic deli. A truly great find. Italian-style hoagies, falafel, soups, chili, baked goods and outstanding gyros that fill you␣up but not out. 6:30am-5pm M-F; 9:30am-2pm Sa. *!* Next to the Pacific Club at #9, 10 S. Fifth St., Mpls., 333-4658.

TRIGGER'S
Overlooking 750 acres of woods, this restaurant offers regional dishes made from regional sources. Serving ring-necked pheasant, duck with blueberry sauce and wild rice soup. Lunch: 11:30am-4pm W-Su. Dinner: 5:30pm-midnight Tu-Su. *!!* AE/V/MC/DC. Minnesota House and Hunt Club, 2920 E. 220th St., Prior Lake, 447-2272.

T.R. MCCOY'S
'50s-'60s-inspired restaurant serving fried chicken, barbecued ribs as well as burgers, fries and malts from the soda fountain. 11am-10pm Su-Th, -midnight F and Sa. *!!* AE/V/MC/DI. 7850 University Ave. N.E., Fridley, 571-4724. Interstate 94 and Century Ave., Woodbury, 731-0018.

TROUT HAUS
The catch of the day is yours*!* Try your luck in one of the heated arenas during the winter or in one of the 33 outdoor ponds in the summer. All fishing equipment supplied and no license is required. Also serving chicken, ribs and steak. 11:30am-9pm daily. *!!* V/MC. 14536 W. Freeway Drive, Forest Lake, 464-2964.

TULIPS
French-style bistro serving lamb chops, veal, steaks, chicken, sauteed swordfish and scallops steamed in vermouth. Lunch: 11:30am-3pm M-F. Dinner: 5-11pm daily. *!!* V/MC/DC. 452 Selby Ave., St. Paul, 221-1061.

TWO GUYS FROM ITALY
Italian restaurant featuring dishes from the northern and southern regions of the country such as veal, poultry and seafood specialties, pasta and pizza. Wine and beer. 11am-9pm Su-Th, -10pm F; noon-10pm Sa. Lunch buffet: 11am-2pm M-F. Su brunch: 11am-2pm. *!!* AE/V/MC/DC. 4660 Highway 61, White Bear Lake, 429-6787. 7495 France Ave. S., Edina, 831-3031.

TWO PESOS
This Mexican restaurant features homemade guacamole and tortillas in addition to fajitas. Beer and margaritas. 10:30am-2am M-Sa, -midnight Su. *!* V/MC. No personal checks. 1320 W. Lake St., Mpls., 825-8264.

T. WRIGHT'S
Specializing in prime rib, this restaurant also offers steaks, walleyed pike, burgers and a huge salad bar. Call for hours. *!!* AE/V/

MC/DC. Minnetonka Boulevard and Highway 101, Wayzata, 475-2215. 5800 Shingle Creek Parkway, Brooklyn Center, 560-7880.

URBAN WILDLIFE BAR AND GRILL
Saloon with open grill offering chicken, kebabs, burgers, sandwiches, fries and appetizers. 11:30am-1am daily. *!* AE/V/MC/DC. 331 Second Ave. N., Mpls., 339-4665.

VENETIAN INN
Offering the finest in Italian dining. Celebrating our 63rd "delicious" year. Noon lunches and candlelight dining. 11:30am-10pm M-Sa. *!!* AE. 2814 Rice Street, Little Canada, 484-7215.

VESCIO'S ITALIAN RESTAURANT
For more than 35 years featuring lasagna, spaghetti, ravioli, fettuccine Alfredo, pizza, chicken Romano and much more. Wine and beer at Mpls. and St. Louis Park. Cocktails at Burnsville. Burnsville – 11am-10pm M-Th, -11pm F and Sa; noon-9pm Su. Mpls. – 11am-10pm Tu-Th, -12:30am F and Sa; 3-10pm Su. St. Louis Park – 11am-10pm M-Th, -11pm F and Sa; noon-9:30pm Su. *!* AE/V/MC at Mpls., plus DC/DI Burnsville and St. Louis Park. 14300 Burnhaven Drive, Burnsville, 892-6700. 406 14th Ave. S.E., Mpls., 378-1747. 4001 Highway 7, St. Louis Park, 920-0733.

VILLAGE HOUSE/QUE VIET
This Vietnamese restaurant offers such dishes as asparagus and crab soup, egg rolls and red snapper in a sweet-sour sauce. Wine and beer at Lilydale. *!* No credit cards. 2211 Johnson St. N.E., Mpls., 781-4744. 969 Sibley Memorial Highway, Lilydale, 452-5018. 6100 Brooklyn Boulevard, Brooklyn Center, 560-0215.

VILLAGE WOK
Well known to students and faculty members of the U of M for Cantonese dishes. This restaurant features walleye, sole and fresh Chinese produce. Traditional American foods and money-saving rice plates are also available. 11am-2am daily. *!* AE/V/MC/DC. 610 Washington Ave. S.E., Mpls., 331-9041.

VINA
Vietnamese restaurant serving abalone dishes, red snapper, Vietnamese salads, egg rolls and rice pancakes. No MSG. No liquor. 11am-8pm Su-Th, -9pm F and Sa. 12pm-8pm Su at the St. Paul location only. *!* No credit cards. 756 Cleveland Ave. S., St. Paul, 698-8408. 6401 Nicollet Ave., Richfield, 866-5334.

VINEYARD
Menu items include steaks, lobster, shrimp, fresh vegetable dishes and prime rib. 11am-10pm M-Th, -11pm F; 4-11pm Sa; 11:30am-10pm Su. *!!* AE/V/MC/DI. West Highway 10 and Thurston Ave., Anoka, 427-0959.

WADSWORTH'S
This restaurant features steaks, chops and poultry cooked on a wood-burning grill. 5:30-10pm M-Sa. *!!!* AE/V/MC/DC. Northland Inn, 7025 Northland Drive, Brooklyn Park, 536-8300 ext. 6051.

W.A. FROST AND CO.
This restaurant offers fresh fish, pasta salad and lemon chicken in a Victorian building with an adjoining fireside parlor and an outdoor garden patio. 11am-midnight M-Sa; 10:30am-midnight Su. Su brunch: 10:30am-2:30pm. *!!* AE/V/MC/DI. 374 Selby Ave., St. Paul, 224-5715. Reservations recommended.

WATERS BAR AND GRILL
With an early 1900s decor, this restaurant features old-fashioned burgers, clubhouse sandwiches, Reubens, chicken wings, chef salads and desserts. 11am-10pm M-Th, -11pm F-S. *!!* AE/V/MC/DI/DC. 119 Washington Ave. N., Mpls., 333-1675.

WHITE LILY
Featuring Vietnamese dishes including hot-and-spicy chicken and seafood and beef. Wine and beer. 11am-9:30pm M-Th, -10:30pm F and Sa; 4:30-9:30pm Su. *!* No credit cards. Crocus Center Mall, 758 Grand Ave., St. Paul, 293-9124.

WHITNEY GRILLE
Classic American cuisine featuring smoked duck tart, venison, jallapeno shrimp and Washington state sturgeon. Pianist nightly. Reservations advised. Breakfast: 6:30-10:30am M-F; 7-10:30am Sa. Lunch: 11am-3pm M-Sa. Dinner: 5:30-10:30pm daily. Su brunch: 9:30am-2:30pm. *!!!* AE/V/MC/DC/CB. Whitney Hotel, 150 Portland Ave., Mpls., 339-9300.

WILLOW GATE
Specializing in Cantonese, Szechuan and Hunan cuisine, this restaurant offers smoked sesame chicken, moo goo gai pan, chow mein, steamed fish and smoked tea duck. Wine and beer. 11:30am-9pm M-Th, -10:30pm F and Sa; 4-9:30pm Su. *!* V/MC. 767 Cleveland Ave. S., St. Paul, 699-3141. 1885 W. Perimeter Drive, Roseville, 628-0990.

WINDOWS ON MINNESOTA
With a sky-high view of Minneapolis, this restaurant offers roast duck with green-peppercorn sauce and roast rack of lamb. Also available are seafood and steak combinations. 5pm-midnight, last seating 10:45pm daily. Su

brunch: 10:30am-3pm. !!! AE/V/MC/DC/CB/DI. Top of the IDS Tower, Eighth St. and Nicollet Mall, Mpls., 349-6250.

WOOLEY'S
Serving roast duck, steak, veal, smoked fish and poultry. Lunch: 11am-2pm M-Sa. Dinner: 5-10pm M-Sa, -9pm Su. Su brunch: 11am-2pm. !!! AE/V/MC/DC/CB/DI. 7901 34th Ave. S., Bloomington, 854-1010. 175 E. 10th St., St. Paul, 224-5111.

YANGTZE
Featuring Hunan, Cantonese, Szechuan and Mandarin meals such as sesame beef, Hunan triple crown, tangerine beef and seafood bird's nest. Full-service bar. 11am-10pm M-Th, -11pm F; 10am-11pm Sa, -10pm Su. Dim sum brunch: 10am-2pm Sa and Su. !! AE/V/MC. 5625 Wayzata Boulevard, St. Louis Park, 541-9469.

YVETTE
This restaurant features filet mignon, dry-aged beef, Chateaubriand with bearnaise sauce, and pheasant. Live music and dancing Tu-Sa nights. 11am-11pm M-Th, -midnight F-Su. Su brunch: 11am-4pm. !!! AE/V/MC. Riverplace, 65 Main St. S.E., Mpls., 379-1111.

CATEGORY

AFRICAN
Barbary Fig
Blue Nile
Dupsy's African Cuisine
Odaa
Red Sea

AMERICAN
Afton House Inn
Al Baker's
Alexander's Restaurant
American Harvest
Annie's Parlor
Applebee's
Apples
Arnold's Hamburger Grill
Atrium Cafe International
Awada's Restaurant and Lounge
Backstreet Grill
Barney's Underground
Beanery Cafe
Benjamin's
Bennigan's

The finest in
Dining
Music
Dancing

Featuring live music and dancing
Tuesday thru Saturday by Colette and Company

Featuring fresh seafood flown in daily from Boston plus aged steak, veal, lamb, free range chicken, pheasant, and pasta dishes. Also featuring the best outside cafe in Minneapolis.

Kitchen opens daily at 11 a.m. to 11 p.m. Monday thru Thursday; to midnight Friday and Saturday; to 10 p.m. Sunday's Bar open until 1 a.m.

At Riverplace ● 65 Main St. SE, Minneapolis ● Phone 379-1111

Bigsby's Cafe
Billy's Bar and Grill
Billy's Lighthouse
Billy's on Grand/Victoria Cafe
Blue Fox Inn
Boundary Waters
Brookdale Inn
Brine's
Buffalo Cantina
Bugsy's
Burgundy Room
The Buttery
The Cafe
Cafe SFA
Calhoun's American Grill
Cecil's Delicatessen and Restaurant
Cedar Street Cafe
Chart House
Cheers on Sixth Street
Chessen's Deli and Bar
Chili's
Choo Choo Bar and Restaurant
Cognac McCarthy's
Copper Stein
Coyote Cafe
Dakota Bar and Grill
Day by Day
Dock Cafe
Dover
Eddie Webster's
Ediner
Eleven East Cafe
Ellington's
Excelsior Park Tavern
Fairfield Inn
Festival
50's Grill
510 Restaurant
Fitzgerald's
Freight House
FreshMarket
Fuddrucker's
Gallivan's
Gladstone Cafe
Good Earth
Goodfellow's
Grandma's Saloon and Deli
Gulden's Supper Club
Hamline's
Harbor View Cafe
Heartthrob Cafe
Hey City Cafe
Hopkins House
Hungry Horse

Ivories
Jax Cafe
J.D. Hoyt's
Jenning's Red Coach Inn
The Jolliet
J.P. Mulligan's
J.P.'s
Keys
Kincaid's
Kozlak's Royal Oak
Kristy's
Kuppernicus
Lake Street Garage
Le Bistro Cafe
Le Carrousel
Lee's Village Inn
Lexington
Lion's Tap Family Restaurant
Lombard's
Loon Cafe
Lord Fletcher's on Lake Minnetonka
Loretta's Tea Room
Lowell Inn
Lyon's Pub
Mad Capper Saloon and Eatery
The Malt Shop
Manning's Cafe, Manning's in the Park, Manning's Stonehouse
The Manor
Marie Callender's Restaurant and Bakery
Market Bar-B-Que
Maxwell's Cafe
Maxwell's Roadhouse
Mayslack's Polka Lounge
McCormick's
McGuire's
Meadows
Mick's
Minneapolis Bar and Grill
Minnesota Zephyr
Monte Carlo Bar and Grill
Mr. D's Ribs
Muffin Man
Murray's
Neon Lunch
Nicollet Island Inn
The 90's at Noon
Nora's
Normandy Village
No Wake Cafe
Oak Grill
Olive Branch
Oliver's
Pam Sherman's Bakery and Cafe

Hurray! Minnesota

Pannekoeken
Papayas
Park Tavern
Patrick McGovern's Pub and Restaurant
Pearson's Edina Restaurant
Peter's Grill
Piccadilly
Plums Neighborhood Grill and Bar
Pracna on Main
The Purple Onion
Queen of Excelsior
River Room
River's Edge
Riverview Supper Club
Roper's Restaurant
Rosewood Room
Rudolph's Bar-B-Que
St. Clair Broiler
St. James Hotel
St. Paul Grill
Sasha's Deli and Grill
700 Express
Sergeant Preston's Saloon and Eatery
Serlin's Cafe
Shannon Kelly's
Shelly's Woodroast
Shorewood Inn
Skyroom
Snuffy's Malt Shop
Steamboat Inn
Sunsets
Sweeney's Saloon and Cafe
Table of Contents
Taxxi
T-Birds
Tequilaberry's California Restaurant
T.G.I. Friday's
Times Bar and Cafe
Tin Cup's
Tinucci's
T.K. Nick's
Top Hat Lounge
Trigger's
T.R. McCoy's
T. Wright's
Urban Wildlife Bar and Grill
Vineyard
Wadsworth's
W.A. Frost and Co.
Waters Bar and Grill
Whitney Grille
Windows on Minnesota
Wooley's

ASIAN
Bali Hai
Beijing
Caravelle
Diamond Thai Cafe
Far East
Hunan Garden
Ichiban Japanese Steak House
Kabuki Japanese Restaurant
Keefer Court
Khan's Mongolian Barbecue
Kikugawa
King and I
Kinhdo
Lan Xang
Leeann Chin
Lotus
Mai Village
Matin
Mirror of Korea
My Le Hoa
Nam
Nankin
Nguyet
Origami
Pagoda
Pearl Garden
Perfume River
Ping's Szechuan Bar and Grill
Rainbow Chinese
Rose's Vietnamese Cuisine
Royal Orchid Thai Restaurant
Saigon
Saji-ya
Sakura Traditional Japanese Restaurant
Samurai Steak House
Sawatdee
Shilla Stone BBQ
Shuang Cheng
Sun Sun Chinese Restaurant
Szechuan Star
Tam's Bamboo House, Tam's East Garden, Tam's Rice Bowl
Tang's Ginger Cafe
Tay Do
Tonkin
To Chau
Village House/Que Viet
Village Wok
Vina
White Lily
Willow Gate
Yangtze

BREAKFAST
Al's Breakfast
Caffe Solo
Egg and I
Du Jour (formerly Le Peep)
New Sexton Cafe
Original Pancake House
Pannekoeken

CAJUN
Dixie's Bar and Smokehouse Grill
Emporium of Jazz Restaurant and Lounge
J.D. Hoyt's

CARIBBEAN
Chez Bananas
Pickled Parrot

CONTINENTAL
The Cafe
Cafe Carabella
Forepaugh's
Lake Elmo Inn
Latour
Suzette's Cafe Exceptionale
Swiss Alps
Yvette

DELI
Cecil's Delicatessen and Restaurant
Chessen's Deli and Bar
Emily's Lebanese Deli
Grandma's Saloon and Deli
Lincoln Del
Sasha's Deli and Grill
700 Express
Trieste Cafe

ECLECTIC
Bad Habit Cafe
Bocce
Bombay Bicycle Club
Brian's Seafood Casa
Cafe Brenda
Cafe Luxeford
Cafe Un Deux Trois
Duggan's Bar and Grill
Emporium of Jazz Restaurant and Lounge
Fabulous Fern's Bar and Grill
Fifth at Fifth
Figlio
Fine Line Music Cafe
Garden Cafe
Hey City Cafe
J.D. Hoyt's

Living Room
Loring Cafe
Lowry's
Lucia's
Muffuletta in the Park
New Riverside Cafe
Nikki's Cafe
Palomino
Pickled Parrot
Poulet
Radisson Cafe and Conference Dining Room
Sidney's Pizza Cafe
The Studio
Sunshine Factory
Table of Contents
Tour de France

FISH/SEAFOOD
Anchorage
Anthony's Wharf
Biscayne Bay
Blue Point Restaurant and Oyster Bar
King's Inn
Martha's Vineyard
Red Lobster
Scully's Broiler and Bar
Shipside
Stacy's Sea Grill
Trout Haus

FRENCH
Azur
Chez Colette
Chez Daniel
Chez Paul
Cognac McCarthy's
510 Restaurant
Forepaugh's
La Terrasse
Le Bistro Cafe
Le Cafe Royal
New French Cafe and Bar
Quail on the Hill
Suzette's Cafe Exceptionale
Toulouse
Tulips
Windows on Minnesota

GERMAN
Black Forest Inn
Gasthaus Bavarian Hunter
Gastof Zur Gemutlichkeit
Gluek's
Schumacher's New Prague Hotel

Hurray! Minnesota

GREAT BRITAIN
Brit's Pub
Corby's
Elsie's Restaurant and Lounge
Sherlock's Home

GREEK
Acropol Inn
Christos
Garden of Saloncia
It's Greek to Me
Nicklow's
Nicklow's Cafe and Bar
Olympics Cafe

INDIAN
Bombay Palace
Delites of India
Fair Oaks
Tandoor

ITALIAN
Antonio's Pasta and Steak House
Boston Garden
Cafe Di Napoli
Caffe Solo
Capers
Ciatti's Italian Restaurant
CocoLezzone
Cossetta's
D'Amico Cucina
Favoré Ristorante
Figlio
Francesca's Bakery and Cafe
Giorgio
Gustino's
Italian Pie Shoppe and Winery
Jakeeno's
Lido Cafe Italia
Lufrano's Italian Restaurant
Mama D's
Mama Mia's Ristorante
Mario's Ristorante
Olive Garden
Piazza's Italian Ristorante
Polo
Pronto Ristorante and Caffe Pronto
Ristorante Luci
Rossini's Trattoria
Sorrel's
Sorrento's
Two Guys From Italy
Venetian Inn
Vescio's Italian Restaurant

MEDITERRANEAN
Azur
Mediterranean Cruise Cafe
Mediterranean Feast
Palomino
Trieste Cafe

MEXICAN
Boca Chica
Cactus Willies Tex-Mex Grill
Chi-Chi's
El Torito
Esteban's
Jose's Cheeks and Cheers
Juanita's Restaurante Mexicano
La Casita
La Corvina
La Cucaracha
Oliver's
Ol' Mexico
Pepitos Tex-Mex Bar and Grill
Pepitos Mexi-Go Deli
Toros of Aspen
Two Pesos

MIDDLE EASTERN
Arabian Nights
Blue Nile
Cairo Cafe
Caravan Serai
Da Afghan
Emily's Lebanese Deli
Jacob's 101 Lounge and Restaurant
Java
Jerusalem's
Khan's Mongolian Barbecue
Khyber Pass
Mediterranean Cruise Cafe
New Horizons
Old City Cafe
Port of Beirut
Red Sea
Sahari
Signature Cafe
Sri Lanka Curry House

PIZZA
American Pie
Davanni's
Edwardo's
Green Mill
Italian Pie Shoppe and Winery
My Pie

Nikki's Cafe
Pizzeria Uno
Sidney's Pizza Cafe

POLISH
Mayslack's Polka Lounge
Nye's Polonaise Room

SCANDINAVIAN
The Deco
Kaffe Stuga

SELF-SERVICE
Arboretum Tea Room
Cafe Latte
Cossetta's
Eddington's
Gallery 8
Q. Cumbers
Skyroom

SOUTHWESTERN
Buffalo Cantina
Cactus Willies Tex-Mex Grill
Coyote Cafe
Dixie's Bar and Smokehouse Grill
Garden Cafe
Lone Star Grill
Pickled Parrot
Roper's Restaurant
San Antonio Grill
Tejas

SPANISH
El Meson

SPORTS BAR
Benchwarmer Bob's
Biff's Sports Bar and Grill
Bocce
Champp's
Chapman's Scoreboard
Filly's Sports Bar and Grill
Gipper's All-American Sports Bar and Grill
Hoops on Hennepin
Hubert's
Joe Senser's Sports Grill and Bar
Lyon's Pub
NaiSmith's
O.J.'s
Rosen's Bar and Grill

STEAK
Austin's
Bigelow's
Cherokee Sirloin Room
Country House
Gallivan's
Kincaid's
Lindey's Prime Steak House
Mancini's Char House
Manny's Steakhouse
Morton's of Chicago - The Steakhouse
Parker House
Rusty Scupper
Steak and Ale
Stuart Anderson's Cattle Co.

VEGETARIAN
Cafe Brenda
Delites of India
Good Earth
Mudpie Vegetarian Restaurant
New Riverside Cafe
Sahari
St. Martin's Table
Signature Cafe

GEOGRAPHIC LOCATION

DOWNTOWN MINNEAPOLIS
Alexander's Restaurant
American Pie
Anchorage
Arnold's Hamburger Grill
Atrium Cafe International
Azur
Barney's Underground
Bigsby's Cafe
Bocce
Bombay Palace
Brit's Pub
Bugsy's
Cactus Willies Tex-Mex Grill
The Cafe
Cafe Brenda
Cafe Di Napoli
Cafe Luxeford
Cafe SFA
Caffe Pronto
Caffe Solo
Cafe Un Deux Trois
Cairo Cafe

Hurray! Minnesota

Cecil's Delicatessen and Restaurant
Cheers on Sixth
Chessen's Deli and Bar
Chez Bananas
Chez Paul
Chi-Chi's
Ciatti's Italian Restaurant
Coyote Cafe
D'Amico Cucina
Diamond Thai Cafe
Du Jour (formerly Le Peep)
Eddington's
Edwardo's
Ellington's Crown Sterling Restaurant
Festival
Fifth at Fifth
Fine Line Music Cafe
510 Restaurant
FreshMarket
Gallery 8
Garden of Saloncia
Gluek's
Goodfellow's
Gustino's
Hamline's
Hoops on Hennepin
Hubert's
Ichiban Japanese Steak House
J.D. Hoyt's
The Jolliet
Jose's Cheeks and Cheers
Keys
Khan's Mongolian Barbecue
King and I
Leeann Chin
Living Room
Loon Cafe
Lotus
Loring Cafe
Lyon's Pub
Mama Mia's Ristorante
Manny's Steakhouse
Market Bar-B-Que
McCormick's
Maxwell's Cafe
Maxwell's Roadhouse
Meadows
Mick's
Minneapolis Bar and Grill
Monte Carlo Bar and Grill
Morton's of Chicago - The Steakhouse
Murray's
NaiSmith's
Nam

Nankin
Neon Lunch
New French Cafe and Bar
New Sexton Cafe
Nikki's Cafe
The 90's at Noon
Normandy Village
Oak Grill
Olympics Cafe
Origami
Palomino
Pam Sherman's Bakery and Cafe
Papaya's
Peter's Grill
Pickled Parrot
Ping's Szechuan Bar and Grill
Pronto Ristorante
Rosen's Bar and Grill
Rosewood Room
Rudolph's Bar-B-Que
Sawatdee
700 Express
Skyroom
Sorrento
Spike's Sports Bar
The Studio
Tam's
Tang's Ginger Cafe
Taxxi
Tejas
Times Bar and Cafe
Toulouse
Trieste Cafe
Urban Wildlife Bar and Grill
Waters Bar and Grill
Whitney Grille
Windows on Minnesota

RIVERPLACE/ST. ANTHONY MAIN/ MISSISSIPPI LIVE
Anthony's Wharf
Buffalo Cantina
Kikugawa
Nicollet Island Inn
Nye's Polonaise Room
Pracna on Main
Tandoor
Yvette

UPTOWN
Annie's Parlor
Brian's Seafood Casa
Calhoun's American Grill

Delites of India
Ediner
Figlio
Good Earth
Kinhdo
Lotus
Lucia's
New Horizons
Pam Sherman's Bakery and Cafe
Sri Lanka Curry House
Two Pesos

SOUTH MINNEAPOLIS
Applebee's
Arabian Nights
Black Forest Inn
Blue Nile
Caravella
Christos
Egg and I
El Meson
Fair Oaks
Giorgio
Green Mill
It's Greek to Me
Java
Jerusalem's
Lake Street Garage
Loretta's Tea Room
Lowry's
Lufrano's Italian Restaurant
Mario's Ristorante
Matin
Mediterranean Feast
Mirror of Korea
Mudpie Vegetarian Restaurant
Muffin Man
Nora's
Oliver's
Pepitos Mexi-Go Deli
Perfume River
Poulet
Rainbow Chinese
Red Sea
Royal Orchard Thai Restaurant
Rudolph's Bar-B-Que
Sahari
Saigon
Sidney's

SOUTHWEST/50TH AND FRANCE
Capers
Far East

Green Mill
J.P.'s
Lotus
Pearson's Edina Restaurant
Tour de France

SOUTHDALE/CROSSTOWN
Benjamin's
Boundary Waters
Ciatti's Italian Restaurant
Ediner
Good Earth
My Pie
Original Pancake House
Pannekoeken
Pizzeria Uno
Q. Cumbers
Rossini's Trattoria
Szechuan Star
Two Guys From Italy

494/SOUTH SUBURBS
Al Baker's
Arnold's Hamburger Grill
Antonio's Pasta and Steakhouse
Applebee's
Apples
Arboretum Tea Room
Arnold's Hamburger Grill
Benjamin's
Bennigan's
Biscayne Bay
Cafe Carabella
Champp's
Chart House
Cherokee Sirloin Room
Chez Colette
Chez Daniel
Chi-Chi's
Chili's
Ciatti's Italian Restaurant
Da Afghan
Eddie Webster's
Edwardo's
Emporium of Jazz Restaurant and Lounge
Fairfield Inn
Filly's Sports Bar and Grill
Fuddrucker's
Garden Cafe
Green Mill
Hungry Horse
Joe Senser's Sports Bar and Grill
J.P's

Hurray! Minnesota

Kabuki Japanese Restaurant and Lounge
Kaffe Stuga
Khan's Mongolian Bar-B-Que
Kincaid's
La Terrasse
Latour
Le Cafe Royal
Lincoln Del
Lion's Tap Family Restaurant
Lotus
Manning's
Marie Callender's
Mediterranean Cruise Cafe
Olive Branch
Pannekoeken
Parker House
Pepitos Tex-Mex Bar and Grill
Port of Beirut
The Purple Onion
Rose's Vietnamese Cuisine
Rusty Scupper
Sawatdee
Schumacher's New Prague Hotel
Scully's Broiler and Bar
Shipside
Sorrel's
Steak and Ale
T.G.I. Friday's
Trigger's
Vescio's Italian Restaurant
Vina

West Suburbs
Applebee's
Austin's
Beanery Cafe
Beijing
Benjamin's
Bennigan's
Billy's Lighthouse
Blue Point Restaurant and Oyster Bar
Boston Gardens
Boundary Waters
Champp's
Chapman's Scoreboard
Chi-Chi's
Choo Choo Bar and Restaurant
CocoLezzone
Copper Stein
Country House
Dover
Duggan's Bar and Grill
Du Jour (formerly Le Peep)
Eddie Webster's

Eddington's
El Torito
Excelsior Park Tavern
Fuddrucker's
Gastof Zur Gemutlichkeit
Gipper's All-American Bar and Grill
Good Earth
Hopkins House
Hungry Horse
Ivories
Jenning's Red Coach Inn
J.P. Mulligan's
King's Inn
Kinhdo
Kristy's
Leeann Chin
Lincoln Del
Lone Star Grill
Lord Fletcher's
Lotus
Market Bar-B-Que
Martha's Vineyard
My Pie
Nicklow's Cafe and Bar
Olive Garden
Park Tavern
Pearl Garden
Piazza's Italiano Ristorante
Pizzeria Uno
Polo
Queen of Excelsior
Radisson Cafe and Conference Dining Room
Saigon
Samurai Steak House
Sasha's Deli and Grill
Shelly's Woodroast
Sherlock's Home
Stacy's Sea Grill
Sunsets
Sunshine Factory
Tam's
T.G.I. Friday's
T.K. Nick's
Toros of Aspen
T. Wright's
Vescio's Italian Restaurant
Village House/Que Viet
Yangtze

Northeast Minneapolis
Champp's
Emily's Lebanese Deli
Jacob's 101 Lounge and Restaurant
Jax Cafe

Jakeeno's
La Casita
Lan Xang
Lindey's Prime Steakhouse
Mayslack's Polka Lounge
Nguyet
Riverview Supper Club

Downtown St. Paul
Annie's Parlor
Bad Habit Cafe
Benjamin's
Brine's
Buttery
The Cafe
Caravelle
Cecil's Delicatessen and Restaurant
Cedar Street Cafe
Chi-Chi's
Cossetta's
Day by Day
The Deco
Du Jour (formerly Le Peep)
Eddington's
Eleven East Cafe
Favoré Ristorante
Fitzgerald's
Forepaugh's
Gallivan's
Gladstone Cafe
Heartthrob Cafe
Hunan Garden
Le Carrousel
Leeann Chin
Mancini's Char House
Mr. D's Ribs
Muffin Man
No Wake Cafe
O.J.'s
Patrick McGovern's Pub and Restaurant
River Room
Rudolph's Bar-B-Que
St. Paul Grill
Sakura Traditional Japanese Restaurant
San Antonio Grill
Sawatdee
Shannon Kelly's
Tonkin
Top Hat Lounge
Wooley's

Grand Avenue/Cathedral Hill
Acropol Inn
Barbary Fig
Billy's on Grand/Victoria Cafe
Cafe Latte
Cognac McCarthy's
Dixie's Bar and Smokehouse Grill
Fabulous Fern's
Francesca's Bakery and Cafe
Green Mill
Italian Pie Shoppe and Winery
Kuppernicus
La Corvina
La Cucaracha
Lexington
Lotus
Old City Cafe
Quail on the Hill
St. Clair Broiler
Saji-ya
Suzette's Cafe Exceptionale
Sweeney's Saloon and Cafe
Table of Contents
Tulips
W.A. Frost and Co.
White Lily

Highland Park
Caravan Serai
Khyber Pass
Lee's Village Inn
Plums Neighborhood Grill
Ristorante Luci
Shilla Stone BBQ
Snuffy's Malt Shop
Swiss Cafe
Vina
Willow Gate

University Avenue/Midway
Applebee's
Bigelow's
Chi-Chi's
Dupsey's African Cuisine
Egg and I
Keefer Court
Mai Village
Malt Shop
Mama D's
Signature Cafe
Tin Cup's

St. Anthony Park/ Bandana Square
Dakota Bar and Grill
Manning's
Muffuletta in the Park

West Side of St. Paul
Awada's Restaurant and Lounge
Backstreet Grill
Boca Chica
Cherokee Sirloin Room
Juanita's Ristorante Mexico

University of Minnesota/ Dinkytown/West Bank
Al's Breakfast
Annie's Parlor
Grandma's Saloon and Deli
Hey City Cafe
New Riverside Cafe
Odaa
St. Martin's Table
Sergeant Preston's Saloon and Eatry
Shuang Cheng
Sun Sun Chinese Restaurant
Tay Do
To Chau
Village Wok

East Suburbs
Afton House Inn
Bali Hai
Burgundy Room
Champp's
Ciatti's Italian Restautant
Gulden's Supper Club
Lake Elmo Inn
Pagoda
Piccadilly
Serlin's Cafe
Tinucci's
T.R. McCoy's

694/North Suburbs
American Harvest
Applebee's
Arnold's Hamburger Grill
Benchwarmer Bob's
Benjamin's
Biff's Sports Bar and Grill
Billy's Bar and Grill
Blue Fox Inn
Bombay Bicycle Club
Brookdale Inn
Champp's
Chi-Chi's
Chili's
Ciatti's Italian Restaurant
Elsie's Restaurant and Lounge

50's Grill
Fuddrucker's
Good Earth
Gulden's Supper Club
Jose's Cheeks and Cheers
Keys
Khan's Mongolian Barbecue
Kozlak's Royal Oak
La Corvina
Le Bistro
Lido Cafe Italia
Lindey's Prime Steak House
Lombard's
McGuire's
My Le Hoa
Nicklow's
Ol' Mexico
Pannekoeken
Q. Cumbers
Roper's Restaurant
Shorewood Inn
Snuffy's Malt Shop
Steak and Ale
Stuart Anderson's Cattle Co.
T.G.I. Friday's
T.R. McCoy's
T-Birds
Tam's
Tequilaberry's California Restaurant
Trout Haus
Two Guys From Italy
Venetian Inn
Village House/Que Viet
Vineyard
Wadsworth's
Willow Gate

Stillwater
Brine's
Dock Cafe
Esteben's
Freighthouse
Gasthaus Bavarian Hunter
Lowell Inn
Mad Capper Saloon and Eatery
Minnesota Zephyr

Wisconsin
Corby's
Harbor View
River's Edge
Steamboat Inn

NIGHTLIFE

THE TWIN CITIES IS A MECCA FOR the night owl and boasts more studios per square foot than any other city except, of course, Music City in Nashville. With so many musicians in the metro area, there is a need for music hot spots. The Twin Cities isn't shy when it comes to obliging such a demand. In this listing of nightclubs, comedy clubs, dinner theaters, cabarets and more, there are nearly 200 entertainment venues. Nightlife in the Twin Cities is not only plentiful, but diverse. From the **Loring Bohemian Bar**, where you will find anything from R&B to the world beat, to live country bands at **Roper's**, there is something for everyone in the Twin Cities.

The number of clubs has grown even larger over the last year with the opening of **Mississippi Live** and the **Mall of America**. Both are multiple-club entertainment venues that offer everything from disco to comedy. Mississippi Live has 15 nightclubs and restaurants under one roof for one cover charge. On the third level of the Mall of America, the Gatlin brothers have opened **Gatlin Brothers Music City**, and several other clubs and restaurants offer lively entertainment and inventive cuisine.

Downtown Minneapolis has its share of clubs to offer the late-night entertainment seeker. **The Fine Line Music Cafe**, **Glam Slam** and **First Avenue and 7th Street Entry** are just a few. All three offer live local and national talent. The Fine Line will keep you entertained even on Sunday morning with brunch and gospel music. At Glam Slam, you can dance to a DJ or listen to such nationally acclaimed artists as Prince or Ziggy Marley. It is difficult to keep up with the array of first-rate bookings at First Avenue and 7th Street Entry. The diversity of acts includes rock, heavy metal, reggae, funk, blues and more, all set against the backdrop of Prince's film "Purple Rain."

Nationally known comedians appear at Scott Hansen's Comedy Galleries, which are located in downtown St. Paul and at St. Anthony Main in Minneapolis: **Comedy Gallery Minneapolis**, **Comedy Gallery St. Paul**, **The Padded Cellar** and **Wild Bill's Comedy Safari**. Besides comedy acts at the galleries, the Padded Cellar offers one-person acts and musical shows, and Wild Bill's Comedy Safari is an experimental workshop full of comedy fun.

Jazz and R&B are alive and well in the Twin Cities. There are several jazz clubs around the metro area such as **Suzette's Cafe Exceptionale** in St. Paul, **Emporium of Jazz and the**

Hurray! Minnesota

Mariner Restaurant in Mendota and **Cafe Luxeford** in downtown Minneapolis. All offer exceptional jazz, with Dixieland at the Emporium of Jazz and local and touring acts at Suzette's and the Luxeford. For traditional R&B, the **Blues Saloon** is the place to be. Located in a renovated warehouse in St. Paul, the Blues Saloon has atmosphere and a large dance floor for the true R&B fan.

The Twin Cities metro area also boasts the largest professional dinner theater complex in the country, **Chanhassen Dinner Theatres**. For more than 20 years, Chanhassen Dinner Theatres has offered musicals such as "Hello Dolly" and "Me and My Girl" as well as plays such as "Shirley Valentine." There are four theaters under one roof at Chanhassen Dinner Theatres, where professionally produced musicals and plays are performed year-round.

The Twin Cities offers myriad possibilities for entertainment. This nightlife section gives you a taste of the diversity that exists in the metro area. For your convenience, the guide is divided into the following 15 categories: R&B • Jazz • DJs/Dancing • Country Western/Country Rock/Bluegrass • Folk/Ethnic • Rock/Pop • Gay/Lesbian • Nonalcoholic • Comedy • Exotic Dancing • Ballrooms • Piano Bars • Dinner/Music/Nightclubs • Dinner/Theater/Cabarets • Multiple Entertainment Venues. Have an evening filled with fun.

R&B

BLUES ALLEY
This bar features a variety of local R&B artists F-Sa nights. Every Su jam with the house band. Cover on F-Sa. 15 Glenwood Ave. N., Mpls., 333-1327.

THE BLUES SALOON
Local and touring artists perform Th-Su. Located upstairs in a renovated warehouse, this bar has a large dance floor for the true R&B fan. Jam every M night. Cover varies. 601 N. Western Ave., St. Paul, 228-9959.

BROWN DERBY
Blues jam session every Th night and Su. Live rock on F-Sa. Karaoke on W. No cover. 567 Stryker Ave., St. Paul, 291-9632.

BUNKER'S MUSIC BAR AND GRILL
A variety of R&B and funk bands play Th-Sa. Popular local artists perform regularly on Su-W. Covers varies. 761 Washington Ave. N., Mpls., 338-8188.

FIVE CORNERS
Small, Chicago-style club that features local R&B and reggae bands nightly. Cover varies. 501 Cedar Ave., Mpls., 338-6424.

RAGIN' CAJUN
R&B as well as some rock played W-Sa by local artists. Cover. 1351 Sibley Highway, Mendota, 452-1830.

ST. ANTHONY EAST
Live blues W and Sa nights. Contemporary dance tunes Th, country music on F and a variety of bands M-Tu. This bar is a melting pot for artists from all genres. No cover. 400 Hennepin Ave. E., Mpls., 623-9478.

WHISKEY JUNCTION
Live music by local artist every night of the week. "We do the blues" as well as country rock and rockabilly. Dance floor. No cover. 901 Cedar Ave., Mpls., 338-9550.

JAZZ

BILLY'S ON GRAND/VICTORIA MUSIC CAFE
This music cafe features acoustic jazz as well as blues and folk music Tu-Su. Billy's has pool tables, video games, darts and a patio on Grand Ave. Cover rarely. 857 Grand Ave., St. Paul, 292-9140.

BOCCE
This upscale sports bar features late-night jazz with local artists on F and Sa. No cover. 100 N. Sixth St., Mpls., 332-1600.

CAFE LUXEFORD
Local and touring artists perform nightly at this popular spot for jazz. The cafe has a French flavor with a dash of New Orleans spice thrown in for good measure. Jam session M. No cover. Hotel Luxeford, 1101 LaSalle Ave., Mpls., 332-6800.

D'AMICO CUCINA
Jazz is played in the lounge of this elegant Italian restaurant F and Sa nights. No cover. 100 N. Sixth St., Mpls., 338-2401.

DAKOTA BAR AND GRILL
Open nightly featuring traditional mainstream jazz by local and national artists. This nationally renowned restaurant and bar features fine dining. No cover. Bandana Square, 1021 E. Bandana Boulevard, St. Paul, 642-1442.

EMPORIUM OF JAZZ AND THE MARINER RESTAURANT
Dixieland jazz played F and Sa in this seafood restaurant and bar. Cover. No cover for dining patrons. 1351 Sibley Memorial Highway, Mendota, 452-1830.

FITZGERALD'S
In this bar that overlooks Mears Park jazz is performed F and Sa night. Minimal cover. 175 E. Fifth St., St. Paul, 297-6787.

J.P. MULLIGAN'S
Local jazz and blues singers perform F and Sa nights. No cover. 3005 Harbor Lane, Plymouth, 559-1595.

NIKKI'S CAFE
Live music played nightly by local artists. Light jazz and blues W-F. Country on Tu. No cover. 107 Third Ave. N., Mpls., 340-9098.

NOSTALGIA
In the Seven Corners area, this bar and restaurant offers jazz Th-Sa. No cover. 247 Cedar Ave., Mpls., 330-0926.

RAGTIME TAVERN
Live jazz is performed on Th nights. Look for musical/comedy cabaret on Sa night. No cover. 712 Washington Ave. S.E., Mpls., 331-3315.

SUZETTE'S CAFE EXCEPTIONALE
Local and touring groups perform jazz W-Sa nights at this French-Continental cafe. Cover varies. 498 Selby Ave., St. Paul, 224-5000.

TIMES BAR AND CAFE
This cafe offers jazz and blues by local artists nightly to an eclectic crowd of music lovers. No cover. 1036 Nicollet Mall, 333-2762.

WHITNEY HOTEL
In the elegant Whitney Grille local jazz and blues musicians play M-Sa; seasonally in the outdoor Garden Plaza F-Su. No cover. 150 Portland Ave., Mpls., 339-9300.

YVETTE
Classic jazz music while you dine in this popular bistro on Tu-Sa after 8pm. No cover. Riverplace, 65 S.E. Main St., Mpls., 379-1111.

TWIN CITIES JAZZ SOCIETY
JazzLine - 633-0329.

DJS/DANCE CLUBS

AFTER THE GOLD RUSH
DJ spins the top 40 dance music W, F and Sa. No alcohol served on teen nights, Th and Su. Cover varies. Live band occasionally on Th and Su. 7539 W. Point Douglas Road, Cottage Grove, 458-0636.

ALLEYGATORS
Different entertainment every night. Top 40 dance music F and Sa. Country W and Su. Ladies night Tu. Cover varies. Highway 494 and Bass Lake Road, Maple Grove, 553-9111.

BARNEY'S UNDERGROUND
Progressive dance music W-Sa night. Minimal cover on weekends. Sixth and Hennepin, Mpls., 371-0828.

BE-BOP CAFE
DJ spins the '50s, '60s and early '70s greatest hits nightly. Live music Tu. Cover varies. 1009 109th Ave. N.E., Blaine, 754-2424.

CHEERS ON SIXTH
Dance to the top 40 W-Su night. A popular venue after a Target Center event. No cover. 23 N. Sixth St., Mpls., 332-6780.

COCO'S
This lounge offers dance music Tu-Sa night. Karaoke on W and Sa. No cover. Holiday Inn Roseville, 2540 Cleveland Ave. N., Roseville, 636-4567

EDDIE WEBSTER'S BONKERS
DJs for local radio stations play the top 40 Tu-Sa. Country on Su. Cover varies. 1501 E. 78th St., Bloomington, 854-4056.

FILLY'S NIGHTCLUB
DJs play top 40, pop, rock and requests Th-Sa. Th ladies night. Live music occasionally on F and Sa, may have more during the fall and winter months. Minimal cover. Chanhassen Bowl, 581 W. 78th St., Chanhassen, 934-6603.

FLAMINGOS
DJ plays top 40s dance music M-Sa. Occasionally live music, call ahead. Happy hour 4-7pm daily. No cover. Airport Hilton, 3700 E. 80th St., Bloomington, 854-2100.

GABBY'S SALOON AND EATERY
This bar and restaurant is two floors: sports bar on first level, and three bars and dance floor upstairs. DJ nightly. W country rock night. Th is ladies night. Cover varies. 1900 N.E. Marshall St., Mpls., 788-8239.

GORDON'S
In Scotees Lounge disco music plays F and Sa nights. Th nights karaoke. No cover. 7725 Zane Ave., Brooklyn Park, 561-7660.

GRANDMA'S SALOON AND DELI
This popular restaurant and night spot has DJ play top 40 dance music W-Sa. There are three levels to Grandma's with dancing on the first, casual dining on the second and billiards on the third. Cover varies. 1810 Washington Ave. S., Mpls., 340-0516.

HOGGSBREATH BAR
The original cowboy bar in the Twin Cities. DJ plays top 40 seven nights a week on a large

Hurray! Minnesota

dance floor. Country M, Th and Sa. Cover varies. 2504 N. Rice St., St. Paul, 484-7067.

HOLLYWOOD HOLLYWOOD
Music nightly at this newer night spot. DJ spins the top 40 on Sa and R&B on F. Live bands occasionally on Tu and Th. Cover varies. Galtier Plaza, 175 E. Fifth St., St. Paul, 291-1480.

HOOPS ON HENNEPIN
DJ spins the progressive top 40 every night. No cover. 1110 Hennepin Ave. S., Mpls., 375-1900.

HOT ROD'S
Top 40 and dance music played nightly by DJ. Sports bar. Karaoke every Sa. No cover. University and Snelling, St. Paul, 646-3020.

LORD FLETCHER'S ON LAKE MINNETONKA
Live bands perform in Granddaddy's Lounge on weekends. DJ spins top 40 and karaoke during the week. No cover. 3746 Sunset Drive, Spring Park, 471-8513.

MAXWELL'S ROADHOUSE
Live bands occasionally on weekends. DJ plays rock, jazz and blues nightly. No cover. 1111 Washington Ave. S., Mpls., 340-9738.

MERMAID
DJ spins the current top 40 dance music seven days a week. There is also a sports bar, dining room and bowling alley. 2200 Highway D, Mounds View, 784-7350.

MINGLES
Top 40 and dance music played by DJ Th-Sa night after 9pm. 61 W. Little Canada Road, Little Canada, 484-6501.

NORTHERN LIGHTS
DJ plays top 40 seven nights a week. Karaoke Tu and Su. Cover W-Sa. Holiday Inn, 2200 Freeway Boulevard, Brooklyn Center, 566-8000.

THE PC
(The Pacific Club renamed.) DJ every night and occasionally live music. Dance to progressive rock, jazz and reggae in a casual atmosphere. Cover varies. Lumber Exchange Building, 10 S. Fifth St., Mpls., 339-6206.

PERIMETER DANCE GALLERY
On weekends dance to progressive top 40 played by a DJ Th-Sa. Cover after 10pm. 254 Second Ave. N., Mpls., 332-0918.

PLUMS NEIGHBORHOOD GRILL AND BAR
DJ plays contemporary dance music W-Sa. No cover. 480 Snelling Ave. S., St. Paul, 699-2227.

RAVELS
Dance to the top 40 or your request by DJ Tu-Sa. Karaoke on W. No cover. Registry Hotel, 7901 24th Ave. S., Bloomington, 854-2244.

R. BERRY'S
DJ spins a variety of music nightly. Male dancers once a month. Country on W. Live bands play occasionally. Cover on F and Sa. 7721 W. 147th St., Apple Valley, 431-7777.

SH-BOOM
DJ plays the hits of the '50s, '60s, '70s, '80s and '90s nightly. Occasionally live music on W. 14917 Garrett Ave., Apple Valley, 432-1515.

STONEHOUSE
Dance to the top 40 and more Tu-Sa night. No cover. Municipal Liquors, 2700 Highway 88, St. Anthony, 788-7499.

T-BIRDS
DJ plays top 40 and oldies seven nights a week. Cover Th-Sa. Maplewood Square, Maplewood, 779-2265.

UNDERGROUND BAR
DJ plays top 40 dance music on W, F and Sa nights. No cover. 412 14th Ave. S.E., Mpls., 331-7506.

WALLABY'S LANES AND NIGHTCLUB
A variety of music is played by a DJ throughout the week from county rock to top 40. Karaoke on Su. Occasionally live bands. Cover Th-Sa. Central Plaza Mall, 45th Ave. N.E. and Central Ave., Columbia Heights, 571-9005.

WEBER'S
DJ spins the '60s-'90s as well as country, rock and your request Tu and Sa. Karaoke Th and F. No cover. 2497 Seventh Ave., North St. Paul, 777-5521.

WILLIAM'S UPTOWN
William's is an entertainment complex that showcases progressive music by local and touring bands Tu and Th-Sa. There is a dance floor and restaurant as well as live blues at the Cabaret and reggae at 2911 W. Hennepin Ave., Mpls., 823-6271.

WINDOWS ON MINNESOTA LOUNGE
While dancing to contemporary music, the view of the Twin Cities from the top floor of the IDS tower is impressive. DJ plays M-Sa. No cover. 50th floor, IDS Tower, Eighth and Nicollet, Mpls., 823-6217.

WINNER'S NIGHTCLUB
Dance to the top 40 Tu-Su. No cover. Best Western Canterbury Inn, 1244 Canterbury Road, Shakopee, 445-3644.

COUNTRY WESTERN/ COUNTRY ROCK/BLUEGRASS

BUCKBOARD SALOON
Live country bands perform nightly at this spirited dance saloon. No cover. 469 N. Concord St., South St. Paul, 455-9955.

CANYON COUNTRY BAR AND NIGHTCLUB
Upscale country western and country rock by both live bands and DJ Th-Su. Karaoke on W. Su no alcohol. Cover varies. World Trade Center, 30 E. Seventh St., St. Paul, 224-2783.

CHEERS 2 YA
Music every night of the week. Live country bands perform W-Sa and DJ plays Su-Tu. Cover varies. 911 First Ave. E., Shakopee, 445-3820.

COWBOY
This bar mixes live music with progressive country disco. Country blues Su. Cover varies. 400 Third Ave. N., Mpls., 333-1006.

COUNTRY HOUSE
Live country rock Th-Sa. Dance floor. No cover. 10715 S. Shore Drive, Medicine Lake, 546-4655.

DULONO'S PIZZA
Featuring live bluegrass and folk bands on F-Sa. No cover. 607 W. Lake St., Mpls., 827-1726.

GATLIN BROTHERS MUSIC CITY GRILLE
This 22,500-square-foot Gatlin Brothers-owned restaurant and nightclub features live country music and Southern-style cooking. Mall of America, I-494 and 77, Bloomington, 858-8000.

HOMESTEAD PICKIN' PARLOR
Jam sessions Tu and W evening and Sa afternoons. No cover. 6625 Penn Ave. S., Richfield, 861-3308.

LALLY'S ON 10
Live country bands every W-Sa. Cover varies. 6937 Highway 10, Anoka, 427-8740.

MIRAGE
Live country rock bands play W-Sa. Live rock on Su-Tu. Cover varies. 2609 26th Ave., Mpls., 729-2387.

ROBERT'S
Live country music seven nights a week. Swing on F and Sa. Cover varies. Off Highway 10, 2400 County Road H2, Mounds View, 786-5654.

RON'S NORTH END DEPOT
Live country and blues bands perform Th-Sa nights. DJ plays a variety of music Su-W. Dance floor. No cover. 1638 Rice St., St. Paul, 489-8262.

ROPER'S
Live bands play country western Tu-Sa. 3720 East River Road N.E., Fridley, 781-3377.

STARK'S SALOON
Dance on one of two large dance floors to local and touring bands on W-Sa and to a DJ on Tu-Su. Learn to two-step in Western-dance classes for a fee. Cover on weekends. Highways 55 E. and 149 S., Eagan, 454-8251.

STRYKER'S AND HOPKINS BOWL
Local country bands play Th-Sa. Karaoke on Tu. Dance floor. Western-dance lessons on Su, W and Th for a fee. No cover. 107 Shady Oak Road, Hopkins, 938-4090.

STUDLEY'S
Local and regional country western bands keep the dance floor moving Th-Sa. DJ plays country music Su and W. Cover varies. 3020 W. 133rd St., Shakopee, 445-8112.

FOLK/ETHNIC

CEDAR CULTURAL CENTER
Ethnic and folk music as well as dance is performed here ranging from Cajun to African; join in on some of the dancing. Call for details and ticket prices. 416 Cedar Ave., Mpls., 338-2674.

LORING BOHEMIAN BAR
World sounds such as Russian retro, French cabaret or flamenco performed nightly. Poetry reading every first and third Tu. Often jazz and R&B are played. No cover. 1626 Harmon Place, Mpls., 332-1617.

HALF-TIME REC
Irish music and food W-Sa. Boccie ball, pool and darts. Cover varies. 1013 Front Ave., St. Paul, 488-8245.

IRISH WELL
Live Irish folk music by local and touring bands M-Sa. Enjoy Irish dining and dance as well as waltzes on Th-Sa. No cover. Twins Motor Inn, 1975 University Ave., St. Paul, 645-7162.

THE NEW RIVERSIDE CAFE
Acoustic and vocal artists from Tu-Sa. No cover. Cedar and Riverside, Mpls., 333-4814.

ST. MARTIN'S TABLE
Folk and acoustic on Sa at this cafe. St. Martin's Table is a nonprofit eatery that donates to different hunger causes. No cover. 2001 Riverside Ave., Mpls., 339-3920.

ROCK/POP

ARCHIE'S IN HOPKINS
Local bands playing the top 40 and classic rock nightly. No cover. 1022 Main St., Hopkins, 935-7718.

Hurray! Minnesota

Blainbrook Entertainment Center
Dance to live rock and country rock Th-Sa. Male dancer on Th. This is a large entertainment center with disco sound and light show, bowling lanes, sports bar and game room. 1200 Central Ave. N.E., Blaine, 755-8686.

Cabooze
Live entertainment nightly. R&B, reggae and rock as well as world beat are played with vigor and volume. Cover varies. 917 Cedar Ave., Mpls., 338-6425.

Charley Goodnight's
Dance to live music Tu-Sa. Karaoke Su-M. No cover. Best Western Northwest Inn, I-94 and Highway 81, Brooklyn Park, 566-8855.

Charly's
Classic rock and roll and top 40 Tu-Sa, played by local bands Th-Sa. Cover varies. 924 S. Robert St., West St. Paul, 457-2607.

Fernando's
Get a peek at some of the new local bands that play rock and blues nightly. Cover varies. 1501 E. Lake St., Mpls., 721-2107.

First Avenue and 7th Street Entry
Music on the cutting edge — progressive, alternative, metal and ethnic — by nationally known bands. DJ keeps everyone dancing Su. New bands Tu. There are three stages at this popular night spot. 701 N. First Ave., Mpls., 338-8838.

400 Bar
Diverse local bands perform R&B, reggae, rock and pop. Cover varies. 400 Cedar Ave., Mpls., 332-3383.

Glam Slam
DJ dance club or live concerts depending on bookings. Varied format of regionally and nationally acclaimed artists. Open Tu-Sa. Cover varies. 110 N. Fifth St., Mpls., 338-3383.

Garrity's
Good ol' rock and roll to the current hits performed by live bands F and Sa. The rest of the week a DJ keeps things hopping. No cover. 1696 White Bear Ave., Maplewood, 777-6961.

Hexagon Bar
Dance to the top 40 at this neighborhood bar. Local bands perform W-Su. No cover. 2600 27th Ave. S., Mpls., 722-3454.

Hopkins House
Rock and roll, top 40 and some oldies by local bands nightly. Cover varies. 1501 Highway 7, Hopkins, 935-7711.

Iron Horse
This is the place to be for rock and heavy metal. Live bands play nightly. Cover varies. County Road 81 and Bass Lake Road, Crystal, 533-2503.

Kicks
Upscale club playing the top 40 T-Sa. DJ plays country on Tu and top 40 on W. Local bands Th-Sa. Cover varies. Marriott Hotel, 5801 Opus Parkway, Minnetonka, 935-5500.

K.J.'s
Classic rock and roll is featured by live bands nightly except M. No cover. 9011 University Ave. N.E., Blaine, 786-1014.

Lyon's Pub on Grand
Listen to a variety of bands on Su and M ranging from acoustic to rock. Live dance music Tu, and DJ keeps the dance pace moving W-Sa. No cover. 788 Grand Ave., St. Paul, 224-1787.

Mainstreet Bar and Grill
Classic and current hits by live bands Tu-Sa. No cover. 814 Main St., Hopkins, 938-2400.

The Manor
In the main dining room, music of the '40s and ballroom W-Sa. In the back room, rock and pop Tu-Sa. No cover. 2550 W. Seventh St., St. Paul, 690-1771.

Maplewood Fun Mall
An entertainment complex with a sports bar, pizza parlor, billiards club, and Doo Wah Ditty's, where live bands are booked three nights a week. Look for rock or country on one of two stages. Cover varies. English St. and Frost Ave., Maplewood, 774-8787.

McCready's
A variety of music is featured here throughout the week. Live progressive and dance music as well as reggae, R&B and rock. Cover varies. 300 S. Third St., Mpls., 340-0173.

Mendota Saloon
Rock and roll, classic and current by live bands on F-Su. Cover on F and Sa. 1352 Highway 13, Mendota, 452-9582.

Mirage
Every night live hard rock to heavy metal. Cover varies. 2609 26th Ave. S., Mpls., 729-2387.

Nicklow's
Features live country rock and Motown Th-Sa. No cover. Highway 100 and 36th Ave., Crystal, 529-7751.

Nick's Live
Acoustic music Tu-Th. Weekend live entertainment and dancing. No cover. Days Inn, 1780 E. County Road D, Maplewood, 770-2811.

O'GARA'S
Nightly, there is music at the banjo bar in the front of the club and live rock and dancing in the back. R&B and alternative rock is featured in the Garage. Cover varies. 164 N. Snelling Ave., St. Paul, 644-3333.

PAULY'S SPORTS BAR AND RESTAURANT
Mixture of rock and roll and R&B Th-Sa. Cover. 401 W. 78th St. Chanhassen, 934-3030.

PEPPPERCORNS
Featuring live bands that play the top 40 W-Sa. No cover. 1178 Arcade, St. Paul, 776-2314.

PK'S PUB
A variety of music is played here with R&B on W, and rock on F and Sa. Su there is old-time music. No cover. 230 Front Ave., St. Paul, 488-4473.

THE POODLE CLUB
Top 40 in a neighborhood bar atmosphere. Live bands play frequently. No cover. 3001 E. Lake St., Mpls., 722-1377.

RYAN'S
Heavy metal nightly featuring local and national talent. Cover varies. Fourth and Sibley, St. Paul, 298-1917

SERUM'S GOOD TIME EMPORIUM
Classic rock by local bands Th-Su. DJ plays the same Tu and W. Cover F and Sa. 213 Jackson St., Anoka, 421-7522.

SNEAKERS
Live classic and current rock W-Sa. Karaoke on Tu. Cover on weekends. 9946 77th Ave. N., Maple Grove, 424-5731.

GAY/LESBIAN

GAY 90'S
There isn't a lack of variety here. There are eight venues in this entertainment complex: a piano lounge W-Sa; a show lounge featuring female impersonators F and Sa; two DJ bars with dancing; a strip bar; a leather bar; a drinking bar; and a lesbian bar. No cover. 408 Hennepin Ave., Mpls., 333-7755.

CLUB METRO
A variety of dance music is featured Tu-Su at this new club. Karaoke M. No cover. 733 Pierce Butler Road, St. Paul, 489-0002.

KEENAN'S
Live rock and jazz bands perform here on F and Sa nights. No cover. 620 W. Seventh St., St. Paul, 227-3840.

RUMOURS
DJ mixes top 40, oldies, country and your request and keeps the dance floor packed M-Sa. Enjoy the piano bar F and Sa. No cover. 490 N. Robert St., 224-0703.

THE SALOON
DJ plays a little bit of everything every night of the week. Progressive M and funk on W. Underwear night first Tu every month. No cover. 830 Hennepin Ave., Mpls., 332-0835.

TOWNHOUSE COUNTRY
Dance to recorded country western music nightly. Take dance lessons Tu-Su at no charge. 1415 University Ave. W., St. Paul, 646-7087.

NONALCOHOLIC

HABITAT OF MINNEAPOLIS
By day a coffeehouse, by night a dance club. DJ mixes a blend of music from the '80s with current hits to progressive and rock. Country Th. Occasionally live bands. Cover varies. 407 W. Lake St., Mpls., 827-6277.

NEW UNION
Contemporary Christian bands play throughout the week. Call for time and ticket information. 507 E. Hennepin Ave., Mpls., 379-2825.

SLICK'S ALTERNATIVE
Live music from the '50s, '60s and '70s, rock or country F and Sa. Karaoke W. Western dance classes Th. Cover on F and Sa. 2450 36th Ave. N.E., St. Anthony.

COMEDY

ACME COMEDY COMPANY
National artists perform Tu-Sa at 8pm and F and Sa at 10:30pm with open-stage night on M. Cover. 708 N. First St., Mpls., 375-1111.

BIG TEN COMEDY GALLERY
Comedy on F and Sa nights, open night 8:30pm Sa. Cover. 4703 Highway 10, Arden Hills, 633-7253.

COMEDY GALLERY MINNEAPOLIS
National comedians perform at this popular club that draws large crowds. Nightly 8pm and 10:30pm F and Sa. Cover. St. Anthony Main, 219 Main St. S.E., 331-JOKE.

COMEDY GALLERY ST. PAUL
National talent performs nightly 8pm and twice nightly on F and Sa 8pm and 10:30pm. Galtier Plaza, 175 E. Fifth St., St. Paul, 331-JOKE.

COMDEYSPORTZ
Let the games begin, improvisational competitions between teams of comedians. Th-Sa. Cover varies. 1414 W. 28th St. Mpls., 871-1903.

DUDLEY RIGGS' BRAVE NEW WORKSHOP
This comedy playhouse, a Twin Cities institution, joyfully satirizes every facet of 20th-century life. Nothing is sacred. Improvisation is at

Hurray! Minnesota

its best W-Su night. Cover varies. 2605 Hennepin Ave., Mpls., 332-6620.

THE PADDED CELLAR
A variety of comedy entertainment Tu-Su from one-person acts to musical shows. Cover varies. St. Anthony Main, 219 Main St. S.E., Mpls., 331-JOKE.

STEVIE RAY'S COMEDY THEATER AND CABARET
In this nonalcoholic comedy club, local talent plays nightly. Improv M nights. Cover varies. 1819 Nicollet Ave., Mpls., 872-0305.

TOTALLY BONKERS COMEDY CLUB
Comedians Sa nights. Cover. Holiday Inn, Highway 55 and I-94, Plymouth, 559-1222.

WILD BILL'S COMEDY SAFARI
An experimental workshop for stand-up comics. Never the same show twice. Cover. M-Sa at 9pm. St. Anthony Main, 219 S.E. Main St., Mpls., 331-JOKE.

WILLIAM'S CABARET
Comedy cabaret with national and regional comedians. Tu- Su. Cover varies. 2911 W. Hennepin Ave., Mpls., 823-6271.

EXOTIC DANCE

DEJAVU NIGHTCLUB
315 N. Washington Ave., Mpls., 333-6333.

LAMPLIGHTER LOUNGE
W. 160 Larpenter Ave., St. Paul, 489-9200.

PAYNE RELIEVER
899 Payne Ave., St. Paul, 771-4215.

SOLID GOLD
Adult entertainment with dancers on several stages and female boxing and wrestling. 115 S. Fourth St., Mpls., 341-2332.

BALLROOMS

BEL RAE BALLROOM
Ballroom or contemporary dance music. Cover. Dance lessons free with cover charge Th-Su. Highway 10 near 35W, Mounds View, 786-4630.

MEDINA ENTERTAINMENT CENTER
A variety of live dancing music from ballroom to country. Friday and Saturday in ballroom and Checkers Lounge. Cover varies. 500 Highway 55, Medina, 478-6661.

SHAKOPEE BALLROOM AND BANQUET CENTER
Country western lessons and live music most Friday nights. Special seasonal events. Cover varies. Shenandoah Road and Fourth Ave. E., Shakopee, 445-0412.

PIANO BARS

BUGSY'S
Dueling pianos Tu-Su in this American cafe and bar. 315 Hennepin Ave., Mpls., 341-3953.

CHEZ COLETTE LOUNGE
Background piano music in this intimate lounge M-Sa. Hotel Sofitel, 5601 W. 78th St., Bloomington, 835-1900.

THE MANOR
Lively piano bar with sing-along W-Sa. In the back of this restaurant and bar there is rock and pop Tu-Sa. 2550 W. Seventh St., St. Paul, 690-1771.

T.K. NICK'S
Piano bar with sing-along W, F and Sa nights. 604 N. Lilac Dr., Golden Valley, 521-8825.

NYE'S POLONAISE LOUNGE
Polka and old-time music as well as sing-along piano bar F and Sa. No cover. 112 Hennepin Ave. E., Mpls., 378-9857.

DINNER/MUSIC/NIGHTCLUBS

ANCHORAGE LOUNGE
A variety of talent performs from one-man shows to top 40. No cover. Minneapolis Metrodome Hilton, 1330 Industrial Boulevard, 331-1900.

BALI HAI
Polynesian revue featuring traditional music and dance Tu-Sa. No cover. 2305 White Bear Ave., Maplewood, 777-5500.

BUNGALOW INN
Enjoy classic tunes from the '50s through the '80s while dining. Dance floor. No cover. 1151 Rivercrest Road N., Lakeland, 436-5005.

THE CHART HOUSE
Enjoy a variety of live music from jazz to top 40 while dining F and Sa. Dance floor. Cover added to dinner. 11287 Klamath Trail, Lakeville, 435-7156.

DOVER RESTAURANT AND BAR
Dine and dance to a variety of live music Tu-Sa. No cover. Sheraton Park Place Hotel, 5555 Wayzata Boulevard, St. Louis Park, 542-8600.

FINE LINE MUSIC CAFE
Often featuring regional and nationally acclaimed artists. Music seven nights a week and gospel music at Su brunch. Cover varies. 318 N. First Ave., Mpls., 338-8100.

IVORIES
Piano/cabaret and show tunes Tu-Sa at this popular restaurant and lounge. No cover. 605 Waterfront Park (Highway 169 N.), Mpls., 591-6188.

THE MANOR
Lively piano bar with sing-along W-Sa. In the back of this restaurant and bar there is rock and pop Tu-Sa. Cover varies. 2550 W. Seventh St., St. Paul, 690-1771.

MCGUIRE'S LOUNGE
After dinner, dance to live top 40 music W-Sa. Tu recorded music. No cover. Ramada Hotel and Conference Center, 1201 W. County Road, E. Arden Hills, 636-4123.

NYE'S POLONAISE LOUNGE
Polka and old-time music as well as sing-along piano bar F and Sa. No cover. 112 Hennepin Ave. E., Mpls., 378-9857.

SHOREWOOD RESTAURANT AND LOUNGE
Dance to the top 40 in the lounge. Live music W-Sa. Recorded music M and Tu. No cover. 6161 Highway 65, Fridley, 571-3444.

TOROS OF ASPEN
A variety of entertainment throughout the week ranging from strolling mariachis to jazz or top 40. Cover W, F, and Sa in the Loft. 6001 Shady Oak Road, Minnetonka, 938-9100.

DINNER/THEATER/CABARET

CHANHASSEN DINNER THEATRES
Dine while enjoying the play or only see the show at the largest professional dinner theater in the metro area and the nation. There are four theaters under one roof where the performances range from comedies to musicals. Call for ticket prices. 501 W. 78th St., Chanhassen, 934-1525.

HEY CITY STAGE AND CAFE
In this '50s-style diner, the musical comedy Forever Plaid plays Tu-Su. Late night cabaret F and Sa. Limited dinner menu and alcohol served in the theater. Call for ticket prices. 1430 Washington Ave., Mpls., 333-9202.

LORING PLAYHOUSE
This theater is situated around the corner from the Loring Bar and Cafe on the second floor of the Gold Bond Stamp Building. The dance company Ballet of the Dolls performs here regularly. Also, there are several theatrical productions throughout the season. Call for current season events and ticket prices. 1633 S. Hennepin Ave., Mpls., 332-1617.

MYSTERY CAFE
Participate in a murder-mystery while dining at Nicklow's Cafe or aboard a cruise at Excelsior (seasonal). Call for schedule and ticket prices. Nicklow's, Highway 100 and 36th Ave., Crystal, 529-7751. Bloomington Park Tavern, 785 Excelsior Boulevard, 521-7660.

MULTIPLE ENTERTAINMENT VENUES

MALL OF AMERICA
(612) 883-8800
The largest mall in America features several entertainment venues. Besides **Gatlin Brothers Music City**, which seats 500 for live entertainment, there are eight other restaurants and clubs. The **Gatlin Brothers Music City Grille** is the place to go for home-style Southern cooking, and for traditional American fare try **Players**. There is **America's Original Sports Bar**, where you can play indoor basketball, pool or darts. You can dance at **Puzzles** while the DJ spins the top 40 and more (occasionally live bands). **Knuckleheads** is the place to see up-and-coming comedians. There are two other bars to visit: **Hooters** and **Fat Tuesday**, where Mardi Gras is celebrated all year in this New Orleans-style bar.

MISSISSIPPI LIVE
(612) 331-3589
One cover charge allows entry into 11 night-clubs and four restaurants. At **Buffalo Gap Barbecue 'n Blues** you can listen to a blues jam session and order ribs cooked on the Texas-style barbecue pit. There are three other restaurants to try: order traditional Mexican fare such as tacos and burritos at the **Cabo Taco**; try the pizza or hamburgers at the **Twin City Diner**; **Buffalo Cantina Pit & Grill** features Southwestern cuisine with a DJ that plays country and rock. The nightclub scene ranges from an upscale karaoke club at **Cats and Co.** to **Platinum**, a two-level dance club that mixes top 40 with reggae and the oldies. **Fat Cats** is a private club with a special entrance. Dance to a live country band at **Billy Bob Barnett's Country Nights**. At **River Rats** sing along to dueling pianos. Dance to the top 40 at **Global Go Go**. **Magic** features magic shows on the hour. For those who are looking for something nonalcoholic, try **Minnesota Fire and Ice**, where specialty coffees and flavored waters are served. Video monitors keep sports and rodeo fans up to date with recent events at **Billy Bob Barnett's Billiards & Sports**. At **Mississippi Live Midway**, play video games, billiards or a dancing piano like the one in the movie "Big." Buy T-shirts and gifts at **Mississippi Live Retail**.

Hurray! Minnesota

HOTELS/MOTELS

There are hundreds of hotel and motel accommodations at all price ranges throughout the metro area. Best Western, Holiday Inn, Marriott, Hilton and Radisson hotels, Motel 6, Days Inn, Super 8 Motel, Excel Inn and Red Roof Inns are all represented with one or more establishments.

Counting the large hotels alone, the Twin Cities has more than 5,000 rooms in downtown Minneapolis and another 8,700 in the metro area. The largest hotel in the area is the new **Minneapolis Hilton and Towers** (612) 376-1000, adjacent to the Minneapolis Convention Center with more than 800 rooms. The **Hyatt Regency Minneapolis**, 1300 Nicollet Mall (612) 370-1234, and the **Radisson Hotel South and Plaza Tower**, located south of the city, each boast the most meeting space at 60,000 square feet.

Other prominent hotels in downtown Minneapolis are the **Marquette** at Seventh and Marquette (612) 332-2351; the **Minneapolis Marriott City Center**, 30 S. Seventh St. (612) 349-4065; the **Radisson Plaza Hotel Minneapolis**, 35 S. Seventh St. (612) 339-4900; **Park Inn International**, 1313 Nicollet Mall (612) 332-0371; and the **Omni Northstar Hotel** at 618 S. Second Ave. (612) 338-2288. Smaller and offering a more personal atmosphere are the **Nicollet Island Inn** on Nicollet Island (612) 331-1800 and the **Whitney Hotel** at 150 Portland Ave. (612) 339-9300.

In St. Paul, there is the **Radisson Hotel St. Paul**, 11 E. Kellogg Blvd. (612) 292-1900 and, still retaining the flavor of the Fitzgerald era after recently being remodeled, the **St. Paul Hotel** at 350 Market St. (612) 292-9292.

In the metro area, there is a concentration of accommodations in Bloomington in the vicinity of the airport and Mall of America. And farther west of the airport, off Interstate 494 and Highway 100, are the **Radisson Hotel South and Plaza Tower** (612) 835-7800 and the French-influenced **Hotel Sofitel** (612) 835-1900. North of the cities along Interstate 694 is the **Northland Inn and Executive Conference Center** (612) 536-8300.

For information on accommodations in the Twin Cities and around the state, the **Minnesota Office of Tourism** has comprehensive booklets on Minnesota motels, hotels and bed and breakfasts. (612) 296-5029 or (800) 657-3700.

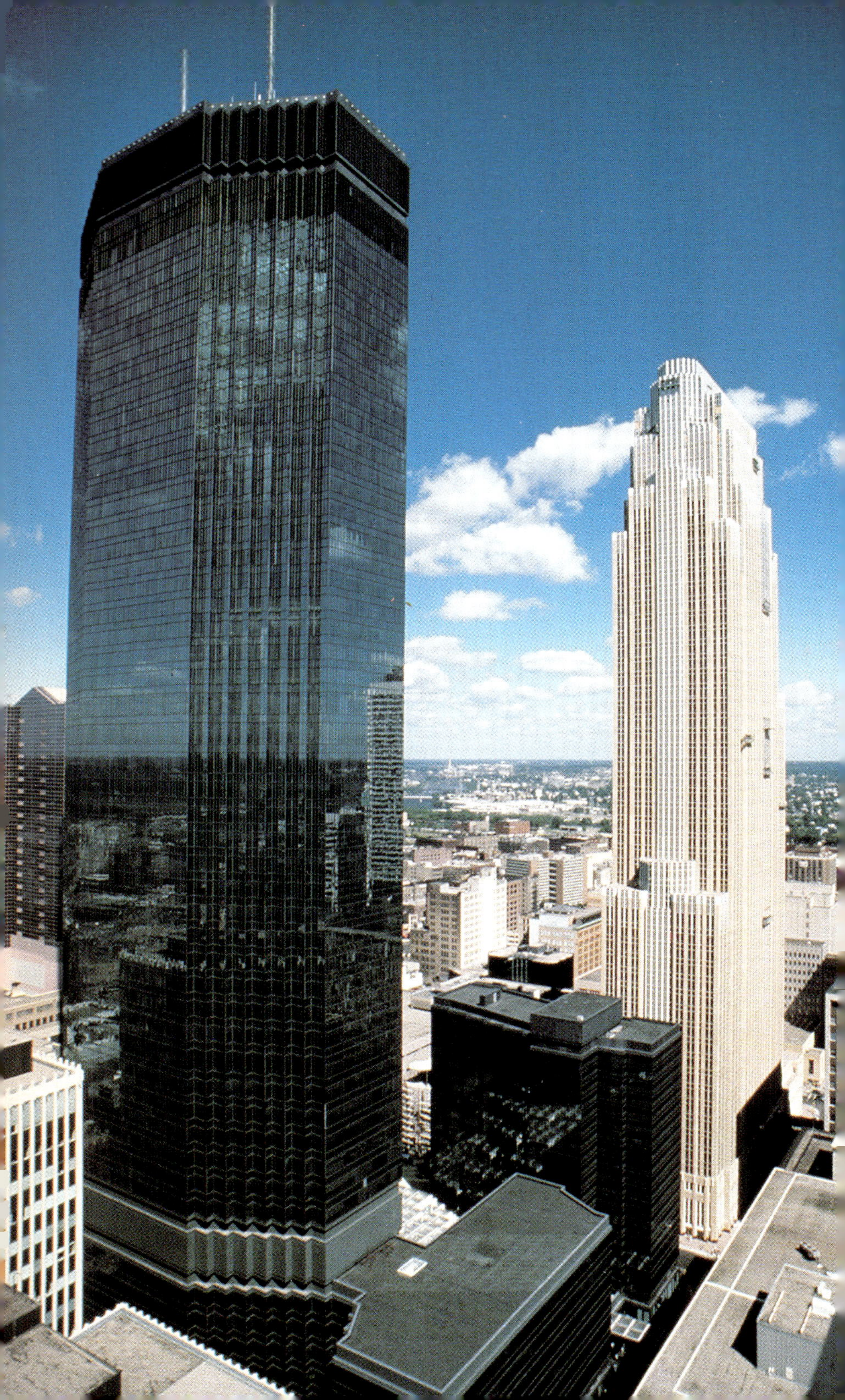

MINNEAPOLIS

SEVERAL YEARS AGO, MINNESOTA humorist/writer/radio personality **Garrison Keillor** took a crack at clarifying a century-old issue: "The difference between St. Paul and Minneapolis is the difference between pumpernickel and Wonder Bread." Keillor refers to the common, and not unfounded, perception that St. Paul is more ethnically varied and a Catholic stronghold, while Minneapolis is primarily Scandinavian and Lutheran. The differences between the "twin" cities run deep and have roots in their age, history of settlement, geography, religion and business. Yet those same variances in attitude and background also serve to tie the cities together; St. Paul and Minneapolis, as the Twin Cities, make their differences work for, rather than against, them.

Long before it was paired with St. Paul, Minneapolis began its life as the twin cities of Minneapolis and St. Anthony, located on the west and east banks of the Falls of St. Anthony, respectively. Known as "the Mill City" and "the City of Lakes," both then and after it was officially named, Minneapolis was first settled by transplanted New Englanders with an eye for the business opportunities presented by the waterpower the falls generated. The occupancy rights of the "squatters" on both banks of the falls were finally honored by Congress in 1855, but by 1852 the two settlements had merged into one: Minneapolis.

Once they were joined by a permanent bridge, built by **Franklin Steele** and his partners in 1855, the areas on both sides of the river grew with amazing rapidity. By 1860, the village of Minneapolis had a population of more than 10,000. St. Paul boosters got a shock when the 1890 census showed beyond a doubt, even after a bitterly contested recount, that the upstart town near St. Anthony Falls had a larger population — 46,000 compared with St. Paul's 42,000. St. Paul has never regained its initial superiority of numbers, and the friendly rancor between St. Paul and Minneapolis on many other issues has persisted through the decades.

Minneapolis' Yankee and Midwestern pioneers were followed by waves of immigrants from Scandinavia, Germany and the United Kingdom: farmers, businessmen and job-seekers looking for a fresh start in life. The jobs were increasingly plentiful, as the mills generated separate but interdependent business opportunities for coopers, furniture-makers, food marketers, dry-goods purveyors, bankers, doctors and undertakers. After the railroads began to serve the area, which had until then been dependent upon and restricted by the river's reach, more homesteaders, entrepreneurs and laborers from Europe and the East Coast entered the area, bringing more businesses and development in their wake.

The railroads opened up further business opportunities, enabling Minneapolis mills and storage depots to process agricultural products from the Dakotas and western Minnesota and ship them to markets farther south and east. By the close of the Civil War, a dozen or more sawmills were powered by the falls, producing 100 million board feet of lumber a year. Production continued apace until the turn of the century, when the apparently limitless forests of north-central Minnesota and western Wisconsin were near depletion. The city's dozen-odd flour mills, also powered by the falls, were producing more than 250,000 barrels of flour a day by 1870, as well as spawning a number of food- and feed-processing, machinery-manufacturing and flour-packaging enterprises. The number of industries and the proliferation of the railroads caused the city's growth to spread away from the river,

The IDS Building and the Norwest Tower dominate the skyline of downtown Minneapolis.

The C.C. Washburn flour mills in December 1893.

and as the job market increased, so did the population.

In the midst of all the flour and lumber milling and the hubbub accompanying the growing pains of a town rushing through its infancy and flinging itself headlong into adolescence, something amazing was happening in Minneapolis that set the tone for all its subsequent successes. The fortunes accrued from the mills and their attendant industries were, happily, falling into the hands of some of the city's greatest civic leaders and private benefactors. They bequeathed to Minneapolis an indelible legacy of generosity and common sense, because they understood that a community with an enlightened, responsible citizenry makes for a sound business climate.

Many of these early benefactors, well-educated Easterners with a strong sense of moral and civic responsibility, funneled vast portions of their wealth back into the adopted city that had given them so much, in the sure knowledge that they would see a sound return on their investment. The imprint of private and corporate giving to arts and civic institutions begun in those early days gave Minneapolis an enviable cultural climate and economic foundation that guided the city ably through its struggle toward adulthood.

John Sargent Pillsbury, a New England retailer, invested in the flour-milling business run by his nephew, **Charles**, in the 1850s. The **C.A. Pillsbury Co.** (now known as the Pillsbury Co.), became one of the world's great food companies, and successive generations of Pillsburys have served as community, cultural and political leaders. **John S. Pillsbury** himself was a major contributor to the fledgling University of Minnesota and served as a longtime regent. He was also elected three times as governor of Minnesota.

Cadwallader C. Washburn and **John Crosby** were partners in the **Washburn Crosby Co.**, founded by Washburn in 1866, which became known to the world as **General Mills, Inc.** During the 1880s, Washburn helped transform the city into the nation's foremost grain-milling complex. Successive generations of both early partners have played significant roles in the city's development.

Thomas B. Walker, one of the community's early lumber-milling magnates and another transplanted Yankee, turned a large portion of his milling fortune into civic and cultural improvements, in-

Hurray! Minnesota

cluding the **Minneapolis Public Library**, park systems, the local symphony orchestra and his namesake, the **Walker Art Center**, which originated with his extensive private collection begun in the 1870s. Walker's heirs donated land adjacent to the center for the renowned Guthrie Theater in the mid-1960s.

William Wallace Cargill, a 21-year-old Scotsman from Wisconsin, went to work for a grain company in Iowa, quickly became a partner and then the owner of **Cargill Elevator Co.** By the 1880s, he had moved to Minneapolis. Cargill had also taken on a partnership with the MacMillan family, and succeeding generations of the two families have continued to own and operate the giant privately held multinational conglomerate, as well as contribute to the arts and civic organizations in the Twin Cities.

3M Company was founded in Two Harbors in 1902, but didn't take off until it came up with a waterproof sandpaper and the first masking tape in the 1920s. Shortly after, it produced Scotch Brand transparent tape, and the rest is history. Two men who joined the firm — **William McKnight** in 1907 and **Archibald G. Bush** in 1909 — both lent their name and fortunes to foundations that provide millions of dollars in grant money each year to worthy projects, individuals and arts organizations.

Minneapolis and St. Paul became the cultural mecca of the Midwest, a blessed relief to Midwesterners living far from the lights and attractions of such cities as Chicago, New York or San Francisco. By the turn of the century, people and commerce were drawn to these twin river towns from the Dakotas, northern Iowa, western Wisconsin and rural Minnesota.

Minneapolis offered many delights to visitors: the Minneapolis Athenaeum, a precursor to the public library, opened its doors in 1859; the Minneapolis YMCA opened in 1866; and the Pence Opera House, billed as the "playhouse for pioneers," offered its glittering programs beginning in 1867. Minneapolis installed a Chamber of Commerce in 1881, electric lights in 1882, electric streetcars and its first "skyscraper" (the 12-story Guaranty Loan Building, which had electric lights, Turkish baths and a string orchestra that played on the roof deck) in 1889, the Grand Opera House in 1882, the Minneapolis School of Art in 1886, and the Minneapolis Symphony Orchestra in 1903. The 32-story **Foshay Tower**, dedicated in 1929, was the tallest building west of Chicago. Already flourishing in business, civic, cultural and educational areas, Minneapolis was also a solid hometown for citizens who appreciated clean air, safe streets, big-city amenities and communities with schools, churches and lovely, tree-lined streets.

The importance of preserving and maintaining the natural beauty of this city of lakes was not lost on the city's founders, either, and they demonstrated their usual prudence and vision in several ways. Both Minneapolis and St. Paul bought the land running along the river between Fort Snelling and the main Twin Cities campus of the University of Minnesota (near the St. Paul line in southeast Minneapolis) and developed it into a verdant parkway. Hennepin County, which includes the city of Minneapolis and several of its western and southern suburbs, began developing one of the largest county park systems in the nation. (The Minneapolis parks system was recently named best in the country at the National Recreation and Park Association Congress.)

Maine natives **Charles Loring**, the city's first commissioner of parks, and **Horace Cleveland**, a landscape architect, directed the city's purchase of several large parcels of land for use as public parks during the 1880s. Loring also recruited **Theodore Wirth** from Connecticut as second superintendent of Minneapolis parks in 1905. Among the acreage belonging to the public as a result of their foresight was the land surrounding Minnehaha Falls near Fort Snelling, the land flanking Minnehaha Creek, and the land around the five largest lakes inside the city limits — Calhoun, Cedar, Nokomis, Harriet and Lake of the Isles, which had been a good-sized tract of swampland southwest of downtown before it was dredged.

As the years went by, Minneapolis faced many of the problems that plague

The Aquatennial celebration in full sail.

major cities. Two world wars and the Great Depression caused predictable hardship at home; a corrupt police force during Prohibition and a corresponding rise in local yellow journalism soured the climate and led to assassinations and political embarrassment. Teamster strikes in the 1930s ended in pitched street battles and **Governor Floyd B. Olson** declared martial law. The racial and ethnic conflicts inflamed by national social upheavals took their toll on the city as Minneapolis reached maturity.

But conflicts quite often produce leaders and solutions. While Franklin D. Roosevelt was trying to pull the country out of the Depression and then World War II, a young man named **Hubert H. Humphrey** was elected mayor of Minneapolis in the mid-1940s and cleaned up the police force, as well as helping form the state's liberal Democratic Farmer Labor party. The DFL quickly became the dominant political party in what had always been a Republican stronghold.

In 1950, as Minneapolis faced its centenary, its population was 500,000 and it was on the threshold of great achievement and change. The population was fleeing to the suburbs, forcing innovative retailers such as **George Draper Dayton**, whose store had stood for years on the corner of Seventh and Nicollet, to come up with the outrageous idea of building an enclosed shopping mall, **Southdale**, in the suburb of Edina — the first of its kind anywhere. The mills were gone, but the great companies spawned by the mills remained, in addition to other healthy industries. Minneapolis was set to move forward.

Today, four major-league sports franchises call Minneapolis home: the **Minnesota North Stars**, the **Minnesota Twins**, the **Minnesota Vikings** and the **Minnesota Timberwolves**. Three stadiums, two located in downtown Minneapolis, serve as venues. Breakthroughs in medicine and health-care technology at the University of Minnesota and other local medical and scientific centers have drawn nationwide attention. The internationally acclaimed **Minnesota Orchestra**, **Walker Art Center** and **Guthrie Theater** remain at the forefront of the city's cultural life and have been joined by the **Minneapolis Institute of Arts** and a host of theater, dance and performance art companies, museums, historical societies and musical organization that flourish and find support in a city that loves the arts.

Minneapolis celebrates its lakes and its joie de vivre with an annual summer festival — **Aquatennial**. The Aquaten-

Hurray! Minnesota PHOTO BY MERLIN QUIGGLE

nial is an appropriate annual summer festival for the City of Lakes. Held each year since 1940 in July, the festival boasts more than 75 different family events from wacky milk-carton boat races and grandiose sand-sculpture competitions to golf and croquet tournaments and fireworks.

The events have varied over the years but always included the royalty competition for the Queen of the Lakes crown, the Grande Day Parade and Torchlight Parade, which have had as many as 250,000 spectators. There also are arts and crafts festivals, concerts, young and old fishing tournaments, sailing regattas, skateboard races, banquets, a not-to-be-missed downtown block party, challenge swims, a bike festival, a water-ski show, picnics and a powerboat classic.

Back in 1940, after consulting the weather almanacs, the Aquatennial committee chose the third week in July as the period most likely to be sunny. Every year since, more than one million people celebrate the Aquatennial throughout the city.

Gene Autry, cowboy movie star, was the celebrity grand marshal in the Aquatennial's first year, which included a WCCO radio live broadcast of "Melody Ranch," Autry's weekly radio program. **Vice President Richard Nixon** also served as grand marshal for the 1958 parade. Other notable visitors to the Aquatennial included actors **Jimmy Stewart** and **James Arness**, actress **Jayne Mansfield**, singer **Eddie Fisher**, and **Bob Barker** hosting a "Truth or Consequences" broadcast in Southdale in 1957.

As time marched on, so did the music presented during the Aquatennial. It began with singing cowboys in the early '40s to big bands and crooners such as **Gordon MacRae** in 1947. In 1958 there was the Aqua Hop at Loring Park and in 1967 there was Minneapolis' forerunner to Woodstock held at the Minneapolis Auditorium, a three-day event featuring **Shadows of the Knight**, the **Electric Prunes**, **Buffalo Springfield** and the **Jefferson Airplane**.

Today the Aquatennial is run by a small full-time staff. The commodore, president, general festival chairman and five vice-commodores are volunteers along with almost a thousand more.

HISTORY

THE FIRST WHITE man to see the only falls on the Mississippi River was **Father Louis Hennepin** in the late 1600s. He named them after his patron saint, Anthony of Padua. Hennepin described the falls as "terrible" and "astonishing," even after having seen Niagara Falls on an earlier North American expedition. In 1778, a Connecticut Yankee named **Jonathan Carver** described St. Anthony Falls as an "astonishing work of nature," 250 yards across, 30 feet deep from lip to cauldron and audible as far as 15 miles away (later explorers found his measurement of the falls to be slightly exaggerated). "A more pleasing and picturesque view cannot . . . be found throughout the universe," Carver wrote.

Father Hennepin

From the mid-1600s on, the upper Mississippi territory was part of the holdings of the French, Spanish and English governments and finally, as part of Thomas Jefferson's Louisiana Purchase in the early 1800s, the property of the United States. Lewis and Clark explored the territory and in 1805 the federal government dispatched **Lt. Zebulon Pike**, explorer and frontier soldier, to purchase land for a fort on the upper Mississippi River. Pike signed a treaty with Sioux **Chief Little Crow** that ceded to the U.S. government nine miles of land on both banks of the Mississippi River from the point where the river was joined by the Minnesota River to the Falls of St. Anthony. (The government promised Little Crow 1 1/4 cents per acre, though payment was delayed for a considerable time. For 60 gallons of liquor and $4,000, Pike also purchased, in 1805, all the Minneapolis lakes and adjacent land, most of St. Paul and the land where the Mississippi and Minnesota rivers come together.)

In 1819, **Lt. Col. Henry Leavenworth** was ordered to establish a fort, and the following year construction was completed under the command of **Col. Josiah Snelling**, for whom the fort is named. Snelling ordered construction of a sawmill and a grist mill at the Falls of St. Anthony in order to supply lumber and fresh flour to the fort.

Because of Snelling's perspicacity, the fort that was established to protect American fur interests in the region led the way to the diversified exploitation of St. Anthony Falls. Small groups of settlers from New England and the more eastern and southern parts of the Midwest began to congregate on both banks of the falls, though civilian settlement was prohibited until the early 1850s, when treaties with the local Indians were ratified.

Squatters and land speculators, also in violation of federal authority, had already begun a settlement east of the falls called **Pig's Eye**. (Later named St. Paul, the settlement was located about 10 miles downriver from the falls and thus provided a natural terminus for steamboat traffic on the upper Mississippi, enabling it to become a commercial center early on. St. Paul was named the territorial capital in 1849.)

Entrepreneur **Franklin Steele** built the first private commercial sawmill on the west bank of the falls in the early 1840s with the assistance of Maine millwright **Ard Godfrey**. A short time later, a man named **Roswell Russell**, using lumber from that mill, built the first frame house at the site, which became St. Anthony's first legitimate store. By 1850, the population of St. Anthony was about 300, and the community was incorporated.

On the west side of the river, in 1850, **John H. Stevens** secured the rights to build what was the first permanent home in Minneapolis. Steele helped open the west bank to settlement by establishing, in conjunction with the military, the site's first ferry service between the east and west banks and by promoting Stevens' claim. (It was in Stevens' home in 1852 that former Philadelphian **Charles Hoag** suggested the name for the community: "Minneapolis," a combination of "minne," the Indian word for water, and "polis," the Greek word for city. He suggested the "h" as an aid to pronunciation, but it was soon dropped.)

By the 1920s, the city's once-mighty lumber milling industry had all but disappeared, followed by a leveling off of the flour-milling industry. But by this time, so many industries had been generated by these two pioneer concerns that the city's economy was assured of stability. Through a process of merger and concentration, the Twin Cities' millers perpetuated themselves in a handful of large, multinational companies that remained in Minneapolis and continued to spark enough diversification to keep the local economy healthy.

Also, by 1900 Minneapolis had established itself as the retail hub of the Midwest through the creativity of people such as **George Draper Dayton**, who constructed a six-story building on the corner of Seventh and Nicollet at the turn of the century that shortly became synonymous with full-service department store shopping throughout the Upper Midwest; **Elizabeth Quinlan**, an Irish immigrant and clerk, who, with another clerk named **Fred Young**, founded the city's first ready-to-wear women's clothing store in 1894; and a Scotsman named **William Donaldson**, whose "glass block" on Nicollet Avenue was one of the most dazzling emporiums in the region. (**Donaldson's** department stores were mainstays of the city's home-based retail community until their purchase in 1988 by Chicago-based **Carson Pirie Scott**.)

Communication also blossomed during the early part of the century. The Washburn Crosby milling company bought a two-year-old radio station called WLAG in 1924. The company changed the station's call letters to **WCCO**, for Washburn Crosby Co., and its first commercial jingle was for a product called **Wheaties** breakfast cereal. During the next decades, WCCO, under independent management, became one of America's mightiest stations, beaming its signal to points all across the country. In 1948, under the direction of the **Stanley Hubbard** broadcasting company, **KSTP** provided the region's first commercial television service. Within a short time, all three major networks were represented by Twin Cities-based stations.

Six months after the end of World War II, a former navy engineer named **William Norris** and a small group of engineers and technicians formed a company called **Engineering Research Associates (ERA)** and set up shop in a former radiator plant in south Minneapolis. The company soon had a contract to develop the first general-purpose computer system for the federal government. Atlas, as the system was called, propelled ERA industry competitors into the computer age. ERA developed into the **Sperry Univac** division of the **Sperry Rand Corporation**, while Norris set off on his own in 1957 and formed **Control Data Corporation**.

Meanwhile, a man on the north end of town named **Earl Bakken** was developing the world's first wearable, battery-powered cardiac pacemaker. His company, **Medtronic Inc.**, became the world's largest manufacturer of implantable pacing devices. In the late 1930s, a man named **Curtis Carlson** combined the idea of trading stamps and the grocery business into what became the multinational **Gold Bond Stamps**.

The climate in Minneapolis has sustained many such stories of successful and innovative strides taken in business and the arts. Creativity flourishes in this city that was founded and nurtured by hardy, visionary pioneers who poured their energies into promoting the present and preparing for the future.

Neighborhoods

THE CITY'S EARLIEST residential neighborhoods were clustered among the mills and other industrial and commercial establishments along both sides of the river. As the business activity increased, so did the need for greater residential space, which was developed to the south and west of the original industrial sites. The working class congregated in the affordable housing relatively close to their jobs, as was the case in most growing cities, and the more affluent citizens began to build their homes away from the center of commerce. New arrivals lived in places such as Bohemian Flats near the mills along the west bank of the river, while their employers lived on Park Avenue, Lowry Hill, or near the lakes.

Since the first wave of settlers to Minneapolis in the 1840s, various communities have established and retained the flavor of ethnic diversity. Northeast Minneapolis is a combination of Southern and Eastern European backgrounds, with large numbers of Polish, Ukrainian, Czech and Italian surnames fronting small businesses and family-run establishments. The "regular" streets of Northeast have recently served as the background for the films "Equinox" and "Baboon Heart."

Southeast Minneapolis is the center of a large student population flanking the University of Minnesota, including **Dinkytown** and **Stadium Village**. On the border between Northeast and Southeast stands **Our Lady of Lourdes Catholic Church**, the oldest Catholic parish in the city and one of the oldest buildings in the city. Southeast includes the **Prospect Park** residential area, which is one of few areas with winding streets rather than the developer's grid that predominates in other parts of the city. The "witch's hat tower," positioned on one of the three highest elevations in the city limits, is a familiar landmark of the Prospect Park neighborhood, which presents an aspect of calm in the midst of the industrial activity that abounds in the Midway district to the north and east.

South Minneapolis is primarily marked by the Scandinavian immigrant experience, including the West Bank, or Cedar-Riverside area surrounding the university campus on the west side of the river. Though retaining a flavor of the 1960s hippie presence and housing a continuous student population, the area has for years celebrated the Swedish and Norwegian past in events such as the **Snoose Boulevard Festival**.

The **Uptown** area along East Hennepin, an upscale compilation of shops, restaurants and movie theaters showing art-house films, has become a gravitation point for black-clad youth sporting the latest styles in hair and dress, as well as anyone seeking the hip and trendy.

Around the great chain of large lakes contained within the urban setting of Minneapolis and spreading outward toward the suburbs, the city's neighborhoods take on an elegance to match the fine homes and spacious yards. Many of the city's neighborhoods are inextricably connected to the lakes and corresponding parks around which they sprang up, such as **Kenwood**, **Calhoun Beach** and **Calhoun Village**, **Bryn Mawr**, **Lowry Hill**, **East Isles**, **Linden Hills** and **Lynnhurst**.

Others have retained the flavor of the working-class or middle-class roots that shaped them, such as **Loring Park**, a neighborhood located at the edge of downtown with Loring Park and Loring Lake at its center. It includes a mixture of the city's most- and least-expensive housing, its newest and oldest. Apartments, condominiums and townhouses predominate in this small, somewhat bohemian community adjacent to the Walker Art Center, the Guthrie Theater, the Basilica, the Loring Cafe and Playhouse and a variety of small shops and businesses.

Parks and Lakes

Minneapolis boasts approximately 170 parks, with a total acreage of 6,385, and it contains 18 lakes. Throughout the summer months, the parks host concerts, theater, movies, dance, storytelling, lessons in swimming, sailing, windsurfing, boating, tennis and golf, water exercise instruction, programs for teens, children and people with disabilities, horticulture workshops and nature tours, lessons on ecology and the preservation of native wildlife resources, and a variety of other programs and activities. For a weekly update on information and activities, call the **Leisure Line** at (612) 348-PARK. For further information: **Minneapolis Park and Recreation Board**, 310 Fourth Ave. S., Minneapolis, MN 55415 (612) 348-2142. For information on the city lakes, call (612) 348-2243.

CEDAR LAKE: Originally called Lake Leavenworth after **Col. Henry Leavenworth**, the first commander of Fort Snelling, Cedar Lake was later renamed for the red cedars that originally grew on its shores. Many new cedars have since been replanted. The lake is accessible from Lake of the Isles via the canal. (Before the canal to Lake of the Isles was excavated, the level of Cedar was several feet higher and part of the current northwest shore was an island.) Cedar is the only lake in the city with private lake access. There is a canoe rack on Cedar Point, a fishing dock on the south point, guarded beaches at Southeast and Cedar Point, and an unguarded beach in the northeast area. The northeast area includes many unmarked trails and is something of a haven for unsanctioned activities such as nude bathing, hobo camps and mountain biking — all against park regulations. Cedar Lake is 170 acres with 2.9 miles of shoreline and a maximum depth of 65 feet.

LAKE OF THE ISLES: Originally a marshy lake with four islands, the area was dredged in the 1890s (most of the parkland around the lake sits on the resulting fill). The two southern islands were joined to the mainland, where they now form part of the shoreline. The two northern ones were reshaped and now form a bird and wildlife refuge, off-limits to the public. Access to Cedar Lake via the canal. Access to Lake Calhoun via the lagoon. A winter hockey rink is built in the north arm and skate paths are cleared around the isles. Lake of the Isles is 102 acres with 2.86 miles of shoreline and a maximum depth of 54 feet.

LAKE CALHOUN: First named Lake of the Loons ("Mde Med'oza") by local Native Americans, the lake was renamed for **John Caldwell Calhoun**, the vice president from 1825 to 1832, who as secretary of war in James Monroe's cabinet established Fort Snelling. The northeast area includes a boat and canoe rental;

Hurray! Minnesota

rented canoe racks and sailboat buoys; boat access ramp for Calhoun, Isles and Cedar lakes; a fishing dock; and a snack counter. The first non-Native American dwelling in Minneapolis was the Pond brothers' cabin, built in June 1834 on the bluffs overlooking Calhoun at 35th Street. At that time there was also a Dakota settlement on the southwest shore. Lake Calhoun is 421.3 acres with 3.12 miles of shoreline and a maximum depth of 90 feet.

Lake Harriet: Named after **Harriet Lovejoy Leavenworth**, wife of Col. Leavenworth, this lake's present shape is not a result of dredging or filling. When the other three major lakes were being joined, it was discovered that Harriet was seven feet lower than Calhoun, and a planned Calhoun-Harriet connection was abandoned. Harriet empties intermittently, via an underwater culvert and an unnamed stream, into Minnehaha Creek.

The 353-acre area includes 2.68 miles of shoreline, the award-winning bandshell and refectory designed by Minneapolis architect **Milo Thompson**, rented canoe racks and sailboat buoys, a boat ramp, the dock for the "Queen of the Lakes" sternwheeler, and the Linden Hills station on the Harriet-Como Streetcar Line. Streetcars run a scenic one mile through the glen between Lake Harriet and Lake Calhoun. The two-mile, 15-minute round trip begins at Queen Avenue South and West 42nd Street on the west shore of Lake Harriet. Passengers can also board at East Lake Calhoun Parkway just south of West 36th Street. The Como-Harriet Streetcar Line operates daily through the summer until Labor Day and on weekends until November 1. Streetcars run until dusk, beginning at 12:30 p.m. on Sundays, 3:30 p.m. on Saturdays and 6:30 p.m. on weeknights. The fare is 75 cents per person; children under age 4 ride free. For charter information, call (612) 754-0303.

Just north of the lake is the **Thomas Sadler Roberts Bird Sanctuary** and the **Lyndale Park Rose and Rock Gardens**, the focus of which is the Japanese-style cedar footbridge built in 1985 over a dry stream bed. Coinciding with the 40th anniversary of the bombing of Hiroshima, the dedication of this peace bridge, as well as the Hiroshima peace stone on the southeast end of the bridge, occurred on August 6, 1985. (The peace stone was salvaged in 1982 from a spot near the site of the atomic bomb explosion and donated to Minneapolis and the Rock Garden. On August 9, 1986, the Nagasaki peace stone on the northwest corner of the bridge was dedicated — it was donated by a survivor of the Nagasaki bombing who lost seven family members on that day in 1945.)

Loring Lake: Man-made, the lake was part of this park's original design by **Frederick Law Olmstead**, who also designed New York's Central Park. The park contains 7.5 acres with .64 miles of shoreline. The lake has a maximum depth of 7 feet. The Ole Bull statue was designed by **Jakob Fjelde** in 1897, and the Berger Fountain by **Robert Woodward** in 1975.

Brownie Lake: The lake was named after **Brownie McNair**, the daughter of an early owner of the surrounding property. Lake access from Cedar Lake is via a narrow, navigable culvert. The lake is 18 acres with .18 miles of shoreline and a maximum depth of 53 feet.

Spring Lake: Spring-fed, this lake sits in a pocket of wilderness under Interstate 394. The marshy north and west sides harbor water birds. The lake is 2 acres with .22 miles of shoreline and a maximum depth of 22 feet.

Lake Nokomis: This lake offers fishing, swimming, picnic areas, a concession stand and a beautiful backdrop for walking, biking or in-line skating. Each lap around the lake is 2.7 miles, and you're just a quick bike ride away from Minnehaha Falls.

Powderhorn Lake/Park: This 65 1/2-acre park, bounded roughly by 32nd and 35th streets and 10th and 14th avenues south, was named for the small lake that lies within the park. In 1990, the colorful and multiethnic Powderhorn community celebrated the park's 100th birthday.

The lake was named by Fort Snelling military personnel who thought it was

Boom Island Park is one of the undiscovered treasures of downtown Minneapolis.

shaped like a powderhorn. The park opened in 1890 when the Minneapolis Park Board bought 25 acres surrounding the lake, and in 1923 the park reached its present size. The park flourished with the building boom that occurred in the area and became a popular spot for festivals and sporting events. A skating rink opened there in 1891, and one of Minneapolis' first playgrounds was built there in 1907. But Powderhorn has always been best known as a community park — the site of family picnics, neighborhood gatherings and fireworks.

MINNEHAHA CREEK/FALLS: The 22-mile creek flows from Lake Minnetonka through western Minneapolis suburbs and into the city, then dives over Minnehaha Falls and into the Mississippi. The 40-foot falls, located near the end of the creek, are mentioned in Longfellow's "Song of Hiawatha": "Where the falls of Minnehaha/Flash and gleam among the oak trees/Laugh and leap into the valley." Minnehaha Park was created in 1889 and the house of **John Stevens**, a Minneapolis pioneer, was towed to the site by 10,000 schoolchildren. The site of both weddings and suicides, the falls are visited by thousands of tourists and locals each year.

THEODORE WIRTH PARK: Originally known as Saratoga Springs and later as Glenwood Park, the core of the 957-acre park was acquired in 1889 and renamed in 1938 to honor Wirth's devotion and efforts in helping develop the premier municipal park system in this country.

Located 2 1/2 miles from downtown, the park contains massive plantings of evergreens; a golf course clubhouse modeled after a miniature Swiss chalet that Theodore Wirth and his wife brought back from their honeymoon trip to Switzerland in 1895; the 13-acre **Eloise Butler Wildflower Garden and Bird Sanctuary** (established in 1907, it is the oldest public wildflower garden in the state); a 5-acre, spring-fed tamarack bog that contains 200 mature tamaracks; the largest red maple tree in Minneapolis; several natural springs (an Englishman named William Fruen began the Glenwood-Inglewood Company here in the 1880s); a 1 1/2-acre 4H children's garden called the J.D. Rivers' Garden Project; and trails, signs guiding park visitors, picnic areas, a fishing dock, a bridge over Bassett's Creek, a pathway under Olson Highway, lighted and groomed cross-country ski trails, plantings and cedar fencing. For information on cross-country skiing and downhill ski lessons, call (612) 521-9731.

BOOM ISLAND PARK: Located near the Plymouth Avenue bridge on the Mississippi is an oasis for families that remains largely undiscovered by much of downtown. The park is well-designed, and from May through September the Padelford Packet Boat Company departs from the island. A ride downriver is still an incomparable experience. For more information, call (612) 348-9300.

Hurray! Minnesota   PHOTO BY NANCY CONROY

Downtown Minneapolis

DOWNTOWN MINNEAPOLIS consists of a number of areas, each with a flavor of its own. To the north along the Mississippi River is the area known as St. Anthony Mills or Mississippi Mile. Southwest of the river is the Warehouse District. Directly south, running perpendicular to the river and central to the city, is the Nicollet Mall. The government sector and the majority of the skyscraper office buildings are east of Nicollet Mall.

There are residential areas both north of downtown, in the Riverside and St. Anthony areas, and in the area near Loring park and Laurel Village on

Minneapolis Skyways

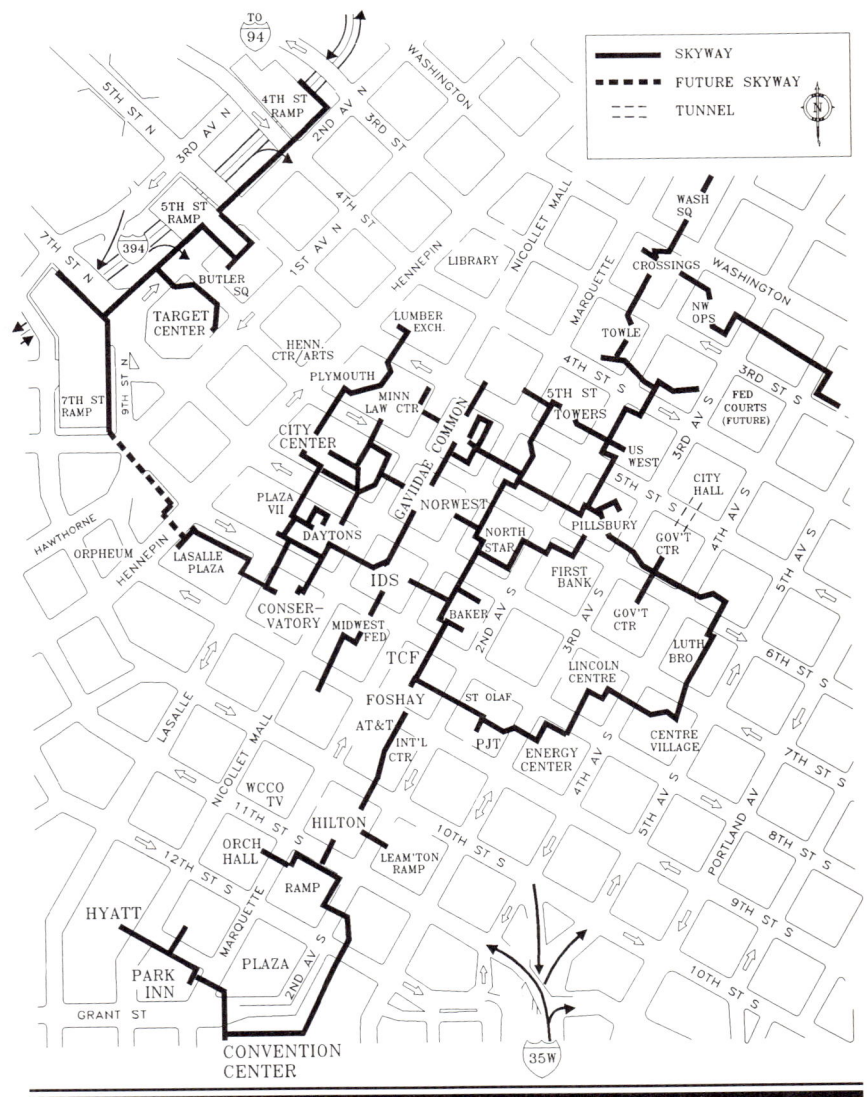

215 TWIN CITIES / MINNEAPOLIS

the southwest edge of the business district along Hennepin Avenue.

SKYWAYS

THE ARTERIES OF life for downtown Minneapolis are its skyways. These covered bridge-like tubes for pedestrians provide second floor access to downtown's stores, restaurants, hotels and parking. The skyway system is particularly convenient in the cold of winter and on rainy days, enabling workers, visitors and shoppers to stroll through most of downtown without a coat or rain gear.

The pathways through the skyways and the buildings cover some five miles and are traversed each work day by an

DOWNTOWN MINNEAPOLIS PARKING

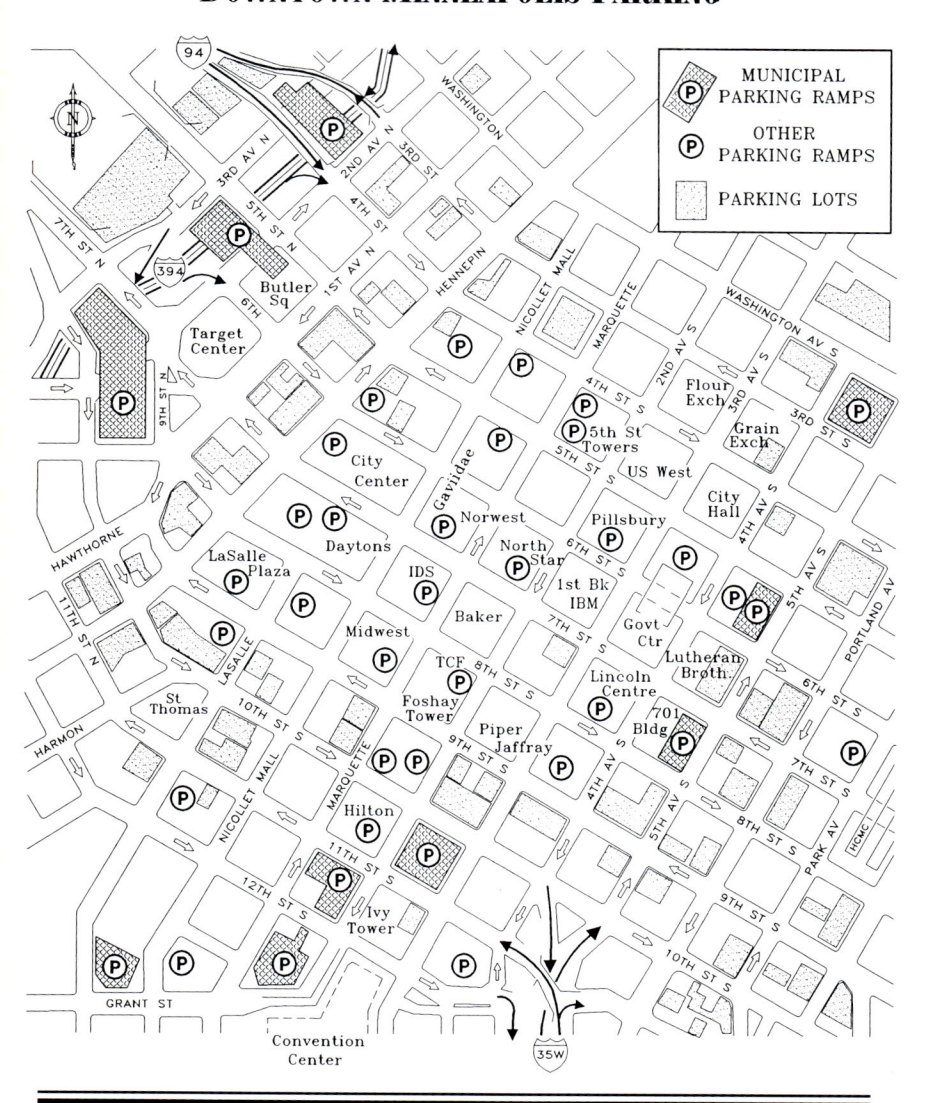

Hurray! Minnesota

The Farmer's market livens up Nicollet Mall every Thursday during the summer.

estimated 200,000 people. There are 60 skyway bridges that link nearly 50 blocks.

The first skyway was built in 1962 connecting two office buildings — the Cargill and Roanoke buildings. Colder climate cities in the northern United States and Canada have followed suit. The skyways are such a part of downtown Minneapolis life that one lively weekly downtown newspaper is named Skyway News.

The skyways in Minneapolis are open 6:30 a.m. to 10 p.m. Monday through Friday, 9:30 a.m. to 6 p.m. Saturdays and noon to 6 p.m. on Sundays.

PARKING

CITY OFFICIALS HAVE done their best to make downtown Minneapolis easily accessible by automobile. There are more than 50,000 spots to park your car and three different locations: in a lot or a ramp or at an on-street meter.

The city has recently put in thousands of parking spaces in three major ramps off Second Avenue North. These ramps, a real bargain, connect by skyway to Butler Square and Target Center, but do not yet reach the main skyway system. Other ramps throughout downtown connect directly to the skyways and many surface lots are close to buildings with skyway access. On the fringes of downtown, particularly north of Washington Avenue and west of Second Avenue North, are more outstanding parking bargains. After parking your car, any bus heading your direction downtown will take you for a quarter.

NICOLLET MALL

THE NICOLLET MALL was constructed in 1967 as a response to keep downtown alive in the face of suburban shopping mall competition and was substantially rebuilt in 1991. The mall is a softly curving trail of shaded sidewalks and pedestrian plazas extending 12 blocks south from Washington Avenue to 13th Street. Giving focus to the downtown area and interspersed with beautiful architectural highlights and sculptures, the mall is the heart of the shopping district, hub to the skyway system and part of an extended walkway that stretches almost two miles from the Mississippi River to the Walker Art Center. Only bus, taxi and emergency traffic are permitted on the mall. (See the Nicollet Mall map.)

Nicollet Avenue (the downtown portion is now Nicollet Mall) was named for **Joseph N. Nicollet**, a French scientist, cartographer and astronomer who created the first accurate map of the vast

STAFF PHOTO

Northwestern National Life Insurance Building.

area between the Missouri and Mississippi rivers in the late 1830s. The island in the Mississippi near downtown and the county in southern Minnesota were also named after Nicollet (originally pronounced Nick-o-LAY).

At the north end of the mall, majestically visible from blocks away, is the pillared **Northwestern National Life Insurance** Building designed by **Minoru Yamasaki**. It was built in 1964 in an extended form of Greek Revival style by using magnificently rich stained glass windows framed by stark white columns.

Just across Washington on the mall is the **Federal Reserve Bank Building**. Some controversy surrounds the federal government's plan to replace this building, which it has outgrown, with a new building along the river. Built in 1968, it is an exceptional architectural example of a suspension building. The floors are hung on cables suspended from two main cables connected to two corner piers. The cement plaza flows at a downward angle beneath the building's graceful bridge form — an irresistible challenge to skateboard enthusiasts — and is scattered with sculptures and a most unusual fountain.

Kitty-corner from the Federal Reserve Building, at 300 Nicollet Mall, is the **Minneapolis Public Library and Planetarium**. The Planetarium shows discovery tours of the earth and the heavens daily. **(612) 372-6646**. At the entrance to the Planetarium is the library's used-book shop. You'll find great bargains on books from A to Z.

Many of the buildings that line Nicollet Mall are architectural beauties. It is a tapestry of old and new that includes the nationally acclaimed 51-story, blue-glass **Investors Diversified Services (IDS)** office tower — the tallest building in Minneapolis and the tallest building between Chicago and the West Coast. Occupying the bottom three floors of the tower is the **Crystal Court**, an enclosed town square with shops and restaurants. Further along the mall is **The Conservatory**, a shopping complex where the new is built around the old, and the **Medical Arts** and **Young Quinlan** buildings, both on the National Register for Historic Places.

Just before you reach Peavey Plaza and Orchestra Hall, the bunker-like structure on the corner of 11th Street South with its forest of antennas is the studios of **WCCO-TV**, owned by the CBS Television network.

ORCHESTRA HALL AND PEAVEY PLAZA

A ceiling full of plaster cubes frozen like tumbling rocks is the secret behind the remarkable acoustics of Orchestra Hall,

Hurray! Minnesota   PHOTO BY GINGER ANDERSON

Nicollet Mall

Shopping
Hotels
Entertainment
Parking

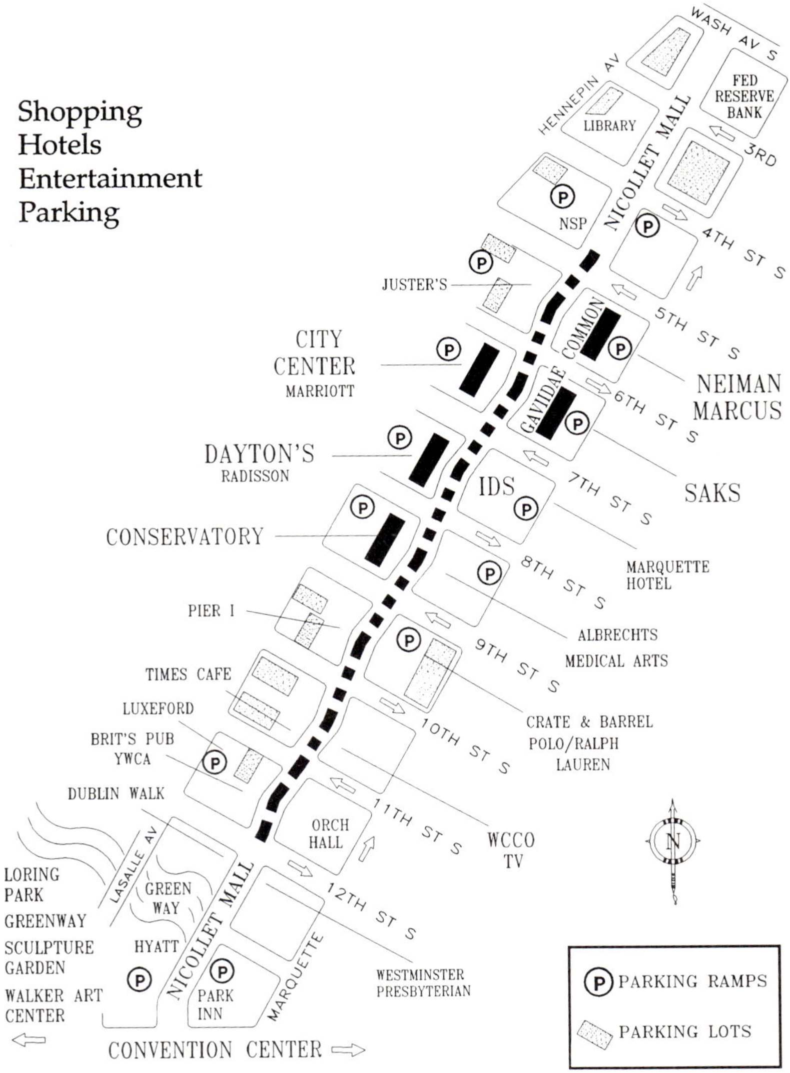
WASH AV S
HENNEPIN AV
FED RESERVE BANK
LIBRARY
3RD
NICOLLET MALL
NSP
4TH ST S
JUSTER'S
5TH ST S
COMMON
CITY CENTER
MARRIOTT
NEIMAN MARCUS
GAVIIDAE
6TH ST S
DAYTON'S
RADISSON
IDS
7TH ST S
SAKS
CONSERVATORY
8TH ST S
MARQUETTE HOTEL
PIER I
ALBRECHTS
MEDICAL ARTS
9TH ST S
TIMES CAFE
LUXEFORD
CRATE & BARREL
POLO/RALPH LAUREN
10TH ST S
BRIT'S PUB
YWCA
DUBLIN WALK
11TH ST S
ORCH HALL
WCCO TV
N
LASALLE AV
LORING PARK
GREEN WAY
12TH ST S
GREENWAY
SCULPTURE GARDEN
HYATT
NICOLLET MALL
MARQUETTE
WESTMINSTER PRESBYTERIAN
WALKER ART CENTER
PARK INN
PARKING RAMPS
PARKING LOTS
CONVENTION CENTER

which have garnered international praise. The acoustics are so good that you can feel them the moment before the first note and the moment after the last. Since hosting its inaugural concert in 1974, Orchestra Hall, located at 11th Street South and Nicollet Mall, has expanded its season to 52 weeks. (See Venues section.)

Peavey Plaza, located right on Nicollet Mall adjacent to Orchestra Hall, often shares in the activities of the hall, particularly for three weeks in July and early August during **Sommerfest**.

The Paul Granlund sculpture in front of Westminster Presbyterian Church.

For two hours before each evening concert, music by small groups fills the air and revelers dance in the plaza to Viennese waltzes and oom-pah-pah polkas. The upper levels of the plaza have garden tables and concessions serving tasty German delights such as apfel strudel, kaffee mit schlag, wurst, delicate wines and robust beers.

In winter the surface of the plaza pool is frozen, a warming house is erected and a parks representative plays Strauss or the cassette of your choice over the speakers. Bring your skates and glide across the ice under the lights and stars.

At the end of the mall just past 13th Avenue South are the **Park Inn International** and **Hyatt Regency** hotels. **Loring Greenway** is a right turn in the middle of the block just before the hotels. It's marked by a pyramid fountain across the street from the **Westminster Presbyterian Church** with the **Paul Granlund** sculpture out front. The Greenway is a fine city park. There are shaded alcoves, pyramid-like gardens and fountains, shuffleboard courts and a children's playground with slides that are slippery and wide enough for an adult. Go ahead — no one's looking!

Loring Greenway winds its way through apartment high rises and condominiums to **Loring Park**. This 36-acre park was the first major park established by the Minneapolis Park Board in 1883 and was named after the "father of the parks," **Charles M. Loring**.

A magnificent fountain made to look like a dandelion ready to burst its fluffy parachutes is at the entrance to the park from Loring Greenway. This fountain, modeled after a fountain in Australia, was donated in 1975 by **Benjamin Berger**, former owner of the Minneapolis Lakers, Schiek's Restaurant and 19 movie houses in Minnesota and North Dakota. To the north is **Jakob Fjelde's** statue of **Ole Bull**, a famous Norwegian violinist and composer. The first building in the park was the Loring Park Shelter, built in the Eastlake style in 1889. The California Mission-style pavilion was built in 1906.

The beautiful **Irene Hixon Whitney Bridge**, a pedestrian bridge on the west side of the park designed by **Siah Armajani**, not only conveys you across the busy Hennepin and Lyndale Avenues traffic to the **Walker Art Center** and the **Minneapolis Sculpture Garden**, but it also is a total art experience, from the play of light on the angular grid of the girders to the inscribed words of John Ashbery, read as you walk: ". . . A reason that picks you up and places you where you always wanted to be."

Hurray! Minnesota   PHOTO BY GINGER ANDERSON

SHOPPING

NICOLLET MALL IS the main shopping district in downtown Minneapolis. The business and activity that occur here daily bear witness to the fact that this is one of the major and finest shopping districts in the Twin Cities.

Along Nicollet Mall are four indoor shopping complexes: The Conservatory, City Center, the IDS Center and Gaviidae Common. All are connected by skyways that make shopping downtown comfortable no matter what nature is doing to Minneapolis. There are three major department stores. Neiman Marcus and Saks Fifth Avenue anchor the two separate wings of Gaviidae, and Dayton's is connected by skyway to the IDS Center, the Conservatory and City Center.

Thursdays during summer is farmer's market day on Nicollet Mall. The mall fills with farmers and local merchants selling homemade honey and breads and homegrown fruits, flowers and vegetables. Prices are great and the merchandise is fresh and sweet as only homegrown can be. Contributing to the festive atmosphere are local street musicians playing bagpipes, violins and an assortment of instruments.

Located for many years at Fifth Street and the mall, **Juster's**, a locally and privately owned men's and women's clothing store, has been a part of Minneapolis since 1912. It has recently moved across the street into the Neiman Marcus wing of Gaviidae. This innovative clothier has developed a reputation for fashionable clothing. In the early '20s, Juster's sponsored style clinics at which fraternity students were invited to give their opinions on features for current men's styles. These style changes put Juster's on the cutting edge of fashions for the times.

Between Fifth and Seventh streets is **Gaviidae Common**. Gaviidae has two wings spread over two blocks, anchored by **Neiman Marcus** and **Saks Fifth Avenue**. There are two skyways, on the second level and the fourth level, connecting the two five-story buildings. This is the only "double decker" skyway connection in Minneapolis. Gaviidae is from

Maybe These Glasses Aren't You. Maybe It Would Be Fun To Be Someone Else For A Change.

Glasses, contacts, sunglasses, eye exams, frame selection assistance, quick adjustment and repairs. Between Dayton's & Shinder's at 10 South 8th St. in Mpls. 332-7907

MOSS OPTICAL

the Latin word (Gavia immer) for Minnesota's state bird, the loon.

In the Neiman wing, don't miss the fountain that flows up instead of down — a fascinating feat of engineering. On the top floor of the Neiman wing is the **State Fair Food Court**, which features **McDonalds** and **Manchu Wok**, and the **FreshMarket Cafe**, a comfortable sit-down eatery. For fine dining, **Morton's of Chicago** is on the concourse level.

In the Saks wing, under the 230-foot-long, barrel-vaulted ceiling hand-painted to represent the Minnesota starry sky, are 18 apparel stores featuring high fashion quality clothes. The stores range from classic clothiers like **Olds Pendleton**, **Burberrys** and **The Custom Shop** to designer fashions such as **Laurel**, **Cache** and **Lillie Rubin**. There also are shoe stores, stores for leather goods and accessories and gift shops such as **Lenox China Company**, **The Museum Co.** and **Brentano's Books**. Brentano's exemplifies the stores in Gaviidae. It has the best in books — not the most — but a well-chosen selection such as the travel book with the most accurate information or baby books that educate as well as entertain.

The top level of the Saks wing has **Toulouse**, a deli-style restaurant where you can buy your food at the counter and eat it in the beautiful courtyard under the "starry" sky. In the corner, with large windows overlooking the mall, is **Azur**, a restaurant for fine dining.

City Center, the **Multifoods Tower** office building and the **Marriott Hotel** fill much of the block between Sixth and Seventh streets. Among the City Center shops are stores carrying casual ready-to-wear clothing such as **The Gap**, **The Limited** and **County Seat**. **Filene's Basement**, a discount designer-brand clothing store, is located in the basement. On the third floor of City Center is a large food court with 15 fast-food restaurants. At street level are **Mick's** restaurant and bar with its historic Art Deco interior, **Chi Chi's Mexican Restaurant** and an old Minneapolis favorite for Chinese food, the **Nankin**.

Between Seventh and Eight streets on Nicollet Mall is **Dayton's**, which has long dominated downtown shopping in Minneapolis. In fact, Dayton's has been a household word in the Twin Cities for generations, not just because it has been a homegrown department store, but also because the Dayton corporation and Dayton family have been generous participants in the Twin Cities business and arts communities for years. Generations of Twin Citians and Minnesotans have been brought up to anticipate the tradition of holiday visits to Dayton's downtown store to see the decorated window displays and to attend the elaborate holiday shows for children in the eighth-floor auditorium.

In 1896, **George Draper Dayton** purchased the land at Seventh and Nicollet that become the site of the first Dayton's. He built a six-story building, the bottom three floors of which were occupied by Goodfellow's Dry Goods. When Goodfellow's began to fail, Dayton purchased the stock and changed the name to Dayton's Dry Goods. The business has grown through the 20th century to become Dayton Hudson Corporation, a public company and one of the nation's retailing giants, by linking the Dayton's, Hudson's and Marshall Field's chains, by adding the Mervyn's chain of department stores, which extend across the South and up the West Coast, and developing the fast-growing Target quality discount stores.

Across the mall from Dayton's, connected by skyway, is the IDS tower with its Crystal Court. Under the windowed ceiling, shop for necessities at **Woolworth's**, feed your chocolate craving at **Godiva Chocolates** or shop for fine clothing from retailers such as **Benetton**, **Talbots** and **Naturalizer Shoes**. Throughout the year, particularly during holidays and special events, the court hosts entertainment and exhibits, performing the role of "town square" for Minneapolis.

For meals and snacks, the open court has **Au Bon Pain**, a French bakery and cafe with excellent breads, espresso, soups and sandwiches. Adjacent to the court in the IDS building is the **Marquette Hotel**, which operates the Jolliet restaurant. The **Jolliet** has a

Hurray! Minnesota

delightful balcony with a dozen tables overlooking the court. It's like a sidewalk cafe year-round. Two of the tables have plaques dedicated to Mary Tyler Moore, who played the lead role in an early 1970s series that took place in Minneapolis, and Barbara Flanagan, a longtime reporter and columnist for the Minneapolis Star (now the Star Tribune). Flanagan often used her column to chide leaders and residents for the betterment and development of Minneapolis, and particularly downtown.

At the top of the IDS tower is **Windows on Minnesota**, fine dining at its finest with the best view of the Twin Cities from its 50th-floor perch. The elevator ride to the top is a bit of a thrill and so are the floor-to-ceiling restroom windows. No acrophobiacs here!

Four-story glass atriums at either end and gracious staircases contribute to the atmosphere of elegance at **The Conservatory**. But atmosphere isn't all you'll find here. There are two award-winning restaurants, **Tejas** and **Goodfellow's**, and unique quality shops such as **Mark Shale**, the Chicago-based men's and women's clothier, **The Nature Company** and **The Sharper Image**. There is a cartoon art gallery on the street level, **Jean Stephen Galleries**, which is really fun to walk through. An original cartoon can be a priceless gift that at the same time is playful. Jean Stephen's main gallery is on the fourth floor of the Conservatory and features both originals and graphics of recently established contemporary artists on the rise.

Farther along Nicollet Mall on the corner of Ninth Street South, you'll find **Albrechts** in the Medical Arts Building selling fine women's clothing and, in the Young Quinlan building, the third-largest — after the stores in New York and California's Rodeo Drive — **Polo/Ralph Lauren**, where three levels of Ralph Lauren lifestyle fashions are featured. The Young Quinlan Building is the perfect building for the Lauren style of displaying merchandise. The antiques and understated refined clothing collections fit in this historic structure's high, arched ceilings, marble staircases and ornate elevators. In the same building is

Crate and Barrel, selling fine and unusual housewares.

Looking for a special Minnesota gift or souvenir? **Hello Minnesota**, with two locations downtown, has a large collection of Minnesota crafts, gourmet foods, clothing, books, tapes and more. One location is on Seventh Street South between the Nicollet Mall and Hennepin Avenue. The other is near the south end of the mall at 12th Street South. While at the mall store, be sure to check out **Dublin Walk**, which offers perhaps the finest selection of Irish gifts and memorabilia that you'll find anywhere.

Also along the mall among the many smaller stores, you'll find the **Men's Warehouse** in the colonial-fronted store in the courtyard across the mall from the Conservatory and **Hit or Miss** women's career fashions and **Pier 1 Imports** on the block between Ninth and 10th streets.

MINNEAPOLIS ARCHITECTURE

NEAR THE Nicollet Mall shopping district are the many skyscraper office buildings of the downtown area. From 1929 to 1973, the **Foshay Tower** was the tallest building on the Minneapolis skyline. Then the 57-story IDS center was built. But it wasn't until the 1980s that the real high-rise boom got started in Minneapolis with buildings like the 17-story rose-colored glass **Lutheran Brotherhood Building** and the 40-story **Pillsbury Center** on either side of the Hennepin County Building at South Third Avenue and Sixth Street. These were followed in close succession by **Multifoods Tower**, **701 Building**, the **Lincoln Centre**, the

Gifts from Around the World

Specializing in Irish Imports

𝕿𝖍𝖊 𝕯𝖚𝖇𝖑𝖎𝖓 𝖂𝖆𝖑𝖐

1200 Nicollet Mall
Mpls., MN 55403
(612) 338-5203

Basilica of Saint Mary

This magnificent feat of engineering and design is an expression of the Beaux Arts influence in church architecture and Minnesota's religious heritage. It was the first such church to be proclaimed a basilica in the United States.

Construction of the Roman Catholic Basilica at Hennepin and 16th Street was begun in 1907 with the laying of the Rockville granite foundation. The exterior walls reach 70 feet to the eave-line and are of white Vermont granite. The Basilica seats 1,600 people.

Though the church was dedicated in 1913, the interior decoration, windows and plaster work were not completed until 1926. That is also the year Pope Pius XI elevated the church to the rank of a minor basilica.

French architect Emmanuel Louis Masqueray designed both the Basilica and the Cathedral of St. Paul, but used a floor plan for the Basilica featuring a wide nave rather than the "Greek cross" plan of the Cathedral. Among some of the more noteworthy of the architectural features are: the dome, which rises 200 feet above floor level, painted blue and gold to represent the rays of glory of the heavens; and, above the main entrance, the 15-foot-diameter rose window facing into a huge choir loft.

On the same block with the Basilica, in a park-like setting, are the school, the resident house and convent. The school was built during the same period as the Basilica. It is currently rented by the Minneapolis Public School System operating as Chiron Junior High School, a field-based experimental school. The priests and the parish administration offices occupy the residence house, also constructed in the 1920s. The most recent addition, a convent, is currently being rented as office space.

The Basilica has been placed on the National Register of Historic Places and is undergoing extensive restoration and renovation. To restore and weather-seal the dome and repair and repaint the interior surfaces is expected to cost up to $16 million for all phases. For tour information, call (612) 333-1383.

Piper Jaffray Tower, **Fifth Street Towers**, **Norwest Center** and, most recently, **First Bank Place**.

The IDS is still the tallest building in Minneapolis at 775 feet, though two buildings were built in the 1980s that come within a few feet. The octagon-shaped IDS glass tower designed by **Philip Johnson** includes the beautiful several-story Crystal Court and the 51-floor tower. Beyond its architectural acclaim, it is well-known as the location for some of the opening scenes of the "Mary Tyler Moore Show," in which the star is shown riding the court's escalator and dining at the Jolliet.

Controversy over new glass and steel structures versus rapidly threatened historic buildings has heated up in the downtown area. Arguments against the dilution and sterilization of the personality of the city, losing the people-friendly atmosphere of diverse, rich exteriors and human-size doorways have brought downtown's older buildings into the limelight. But the beauty of the Minneapolis skyline is still there and improving thanks to the hard work and dedication of city council members, business interests and the **Heritage Preservation Committee**.

Walk the streets and look up. There is an eclectic array of flickering reflections, gargoyles and egg-and-dart cornices, and wonderful plays of light and angle throughout the downtown area. The **Norwest Center** tower is a Cinderella at night, with exterior lighting that has been lauded as a public work of art. Or experience the mental "Oh" when the sky's reflection is first discerned in the smoky glass of the IDS tower. In some areas old has been blended with new to the advantage of both, such as the LaSalle Plaza block.

LaSalle Plaza, the restored **State Theatre** and the old and new **YMCA** buildings occupy the block bounded by Hennepin and LaSalle avenues and Eighth and Ninth streets. It is a beautiful, well-planned blend of architectural styles meeting the needs of occupants and pedestrians in a free-flowing, two-level arcade and skyway. The simplicity of style of the new YMCA and LaSalle Plaza buildings, though at times dwarfing the original YMCA building, still sets off the intricate detailing of the older building's Collegiate Gothic style.

City Hall and the **Hennepin County Government Center** are another good example of the blending of old and new. City Hall, built in 1889, is connected to the 24-story Hennepin County Government Center by an underground tunnel. At the center's end of the connecting tunnel is a waterfall, part of the outdoor fountain on the Government Center Plaza, falling into a dramatic (and wet) courtyard. The center, which covers two city blocks, is built from the same stone as City Hall, only it has a smooth finish.

The City Hall building takes up the entire block between South Third and Fourth avenues and Fourth and Fifth streets. It was built of Ortonville red/pink granite between 1889 and 1905 and designed by the architectural firm of **Long and Kees**. The Richardsonian Romanesque style is castle-like with rough-faced massive stone walls, towers and gables. The building is five stories and is topped by a 400-foot four-face clock tower. It was said to be the largest working clock in the world when it was installed. There is a 14-bell carillon which, among other songs, can play the "Star Spangled Banner."

The impressive five-story interior courtyard is dominated by the statue entitled **Mississippi — Father of Waters**. (His big toe is the designated meeting site for many a rendezvous.) The massive flowing statue was sculpted by **Larkin G. Mead** of Florence, Italy, in 1904. At the entrance on Fifth Street is a statue of Hubert Humphrey, who began his political career as mayor of Minneapolis.

In 1889, the Minneapolis Tribune, writing on the construction of City Hall, stated that Minneapolis would not carry "down to future generations the taint of boodle and the crumbling evidences of bad architecture and worse construction." This prophecy has held true as time has testified to the excellent craftsmanship, construction and design of the building. The interior office space was designed to be changed as needs required with all floors supported by independent partitions. The County Adult Detention Center is on the top two floors.

When visiting City Hall, watch for ladies in hoop skirts or gentlemen with briefcases who glide through walls. Legend has it that City Hall is home to several ghosts who hide in mazes of stored furniture or glide across catwalks and creep up winding tower staircases, fueled by the emotions of politics and crime.

Around town are a number of other historic buildings in a variety of styles reflecting the era in which they were built.

The old **National Guard Armory** takes up the entire block at 500 South Sixth Street. The round-cornered exterior is simply decorated with monumental carved stone eagles with 14-foot wing spans at the entryways and field guns flanking the centrally located flagpole. The drill hall is covered by a hangar-shaped roof and has a concrete-slab floor with a wood-floor insert in the center intended for recreational activities such as dancing and basketball.

Built in the mid-1930s, it was the

Ivy Tower

Standing alone on the block at Second Avenue South between 11th and 12th streets is the beautiful Ivy Tower. It was to be one of four towers around a central dome for the Christian Scientist Church. Probably because of the Depression, only one tower was built in 1930. The ziggurat design (indented stepped pyramid) corresponds to the styles of the Empire State and Chrysler buildings in New York, which were built during the same period.

---

largest public works project built in Minnesota during the Depression era. This stark, massive, block-long hall is an excellent example of the Public Works Administration (PWA) Moderne style. As with all PWA projects, all materials were locally produced: granite from St. Cloud, limestone from Mankato, bricks and steel work from Minneapolis companies.

At one time the armory provided office space and drill grounds for as many as 27 units of the Minnesota National Guard and Naval Militia. Over the years it has been used for exhibits and spectator events such as wrestling, the Golden Gloves boxing tournament and Lakers' basketball.

The National Guard moved out in the early 1980s. Currently the building is not in use. It was purchased by Hennepin County in 1990 and, amidst much controversy, there is talk of demolishing it to clear a site for a new county jail.

Also built in PWA Moderne style is the **Minneapolis Post Office** at 201 South First Street. It was under construction from 1932 to 1935. This 540-foot long building has a granite foundation and limestone walls. The main hall contains a huge bronze chandelier, which is 350 feet long and weighs 16 tons. The chandelier also contains heating and air conditioning equipment.

On the 300 block of Fourth Avenue South are the **Grain Exchange** (1902) and the **Flour Exchange** (1892) buildings. Just 10 years made a remarkable difference in construction. The Flour Exchange is a masonry building where the walls, thicker and splayed at the base, bear the weight of the building. The Grain Exchange was a steel and beam construction. Both buildings are on the National Register of Historic Places.

The Flour Exchange has been converted into general offices but at the Grain Exchange, after interior and technical modernization over the years and a complete exterior restoration in 1981, grain is still actively traded in the octagonal pit under the gallery arches.

Minneapolis has an impressive number of buildings in the Art Deco style both old, such as the US West Building (formerly AT&T) across Third Avenue South from City Hall, and new, such as the nicely sculpted **Norwest Center** on Marquette between South Sixth and Seventh streets and the colorful, finely detailed **Lincoln Centre** on Third Avenue South between Seventh and Eighth streets.

The US West Building was designed

The Foshay Tower, still a Minneapolis landmark, nestles up against the IDS Tower.

like the New York City skyscrapers, with the upper stories indented in a series of steps to the top. The design was in response to a 1916 New York building code that regulated the size of the buildings at the top so that sunlight could reach the streets.

One of the best examples of Art Deco, the **Foshay Tower**, at the corner of Eighth Street South and Marquette Avenue, was built in 1929. It has 32 floors and is a perfect illustration of the excesses of the roaring '20s. John Philip Sousa was even commissioned to create a march for the three-day grand opening.

The Foshay Tower was Minneapolis' tallest structure until the IDS was built in 1973. The restoration, completed in 1992, restored the beautiful terrazzo floors and marbled walls of the art deco arcade to their original splendor. A carefully prepared citrus-based cleaner was used to restore the cream-colored limestone exterior walls. The Foshay is on the National Register of Historic Places.

On the 30th floor is the **Wilbur Foshay Tower Museum** with the history of the tower, its three-day grand opening and its builder, **Wilbur Foshay**. The building is patterned after the obelisk design of the Washington Monument. Foshay once said Washington was his idol and a man to be emulated.

Wilbur Foshay made most of his money in utilities. He came to Minneapolis from the East Coast with $200 in his pocket and, in less than 12 years, had turned it into $60 million. The stock market crash came two months after the completion of the tower. With the crash of the market came the crash of his fortune and a jail term for mail fraud. Even Foshay's $20,000 check to Sousa for his march bounced.

From the museum there is a short flight of stairs up to the observation deck. For many years, before numerous other skyscrapers were built, this was the highest vantage point in Minneapolis and all of the Upper Midwest. There is a $2 admission charge to the museum and observation deck. The concierge at the lobby information desk will take you up in the elevator.

THE UNIVERSITY OF MINNESOTA CAMPUS

The **University of Minnesota** actually has two campuses, thanks to the Mississippi River. The East Bank is the main campus and the original. Here you'll find administration, **Coffman Union**, the **James Ford Bell Natural History Museum**, **Northrop Auditorium** and numerous classroom and dormitory buildings. Since opening in 1929, the 4,850-seat Northrop has been the site of many graduations and countless performances by the great and near great, the former including **Igor Stravinsky** and **Sergei Rachmaninoff**. (See Venues section.)

Williams Arena, home of the basketball Gophers, and **Mariucci Arena**, where ice hockey is played, are on this campus. Both arenas are undergoing extensive renovations to be completed by the summer and fall of 1993.

Memorial Stadium, the "Brickhouse," where the Gophers did gridiron battle for 59 autumns between 1924 and 1971, fell to the wrecking ball in the summer of 1992. Football moved to the Metrodome beginning with the 1982 season. The university's **Aquatic Center**, with its 8-lane 50-meter competition pool and diving facilities, was built in 1990 on the football field within Memorial Stadium. It remains though the stadium walls fell around it.

Due to be completed in June of 1993 is the **Frederick R. Weisman Art Museum**. This is to be a teaching museum as well as a home for the university's art collection, which is currently being housed on the second floor of Northrop Auditorium. Frederick R. Weisman is a Los Angeles-based art collector who has donated $3 million and a portion of his collection for display in the new museum.

Other notable buildings are **Eddy Hall**, the fortress-like University of Minnesota **Armory**, the **Civil and Mineral Engineering Building**, extending six stories underground, and **Folwell Hall**, built in 1907.

Also on the East Bank is the **University Hospital and Clinic — Variety Club Children's Hospital**, a world-renowned institution famed for its work in organ transplants and cancer research.

Near the East Bank campus are **Stadium Village** and **Dinkytown**, university communities of shops, restaurants, coffeehouses and watering holes frequented by students and staff. Dinkytown, where **Bob Dylan** once lived above **Gray's Campus Drug**, has a number of restaurants where the bill won't shock you and the food is tasty and unique. There's a great coffee shop, **The Espresso Cafe**, for feeding your coffee and conversation habit.

On the West Bank, which is accessible via the Washington Avenue bridge and footbridge, are **Wilson Library**, **Carlson School of Management**, the **Humphrey Institute for Public Affairs** and the law school. Nearby is **Seven Corners**, more recently referred to as the **West Bank Theater District**. Here are shops, restaurants, and theaters such as **Mixed Blood Theatre**, the **Southern Theater**, **Theatre in the Round Players** and **Hey City Stage**, featuring its harmonic hit, "Forever Plaid." (See Theater section.)

THE WAREHOUSE DISTRICT

THE FIRST ATTRACTION that drew people to the Warehouse District was its buildings. Many buildings such as the Colwell Building, once a fur auction house, or the Butler Brothers Building, a sprawling warehouse, have been remodeled for contemporary use while preserving the historic significance and ambience of wood and old brick.

These buildings offer the small- to medium-sized business a comfortable and affordable alternative to high-rise glass and steel structures. Restaurants can achieve a comfortable, friendly atmosphere. And high ceilings and roomy interiors supply the light and space needed for galleries and nightclubs. This could be why, in roughly a 14-block area that includes the Warehouse District and its fringes, you'll find five theaters, six nightclubs, more than 15 restaurants and 20 art galleries. (See Warehouse District map, Eater's Digest and Nightlife sections.)

The district has a wide range of restaurants in both price and cuisine.

Choose fine dining at **D'Amico Cucina**, the original vegetarian cuisine found at **Brenda's Cafe** or the **Pickled Parrot**'s Caribbean fare, to name just a few.

For nightlife, it's hard to beat what the district has to offer. This is where they danced in the streets the night the Twins won the World Series. The area rocks, and revelers roam on Friday and Saturday nights or any evening there is an event at the Metrodome or Target Center. Or, if you would just like a little pub crawl, try starting with **Jose's** or **Rosen's Sports** bars. Don't miss a little of Gluek's own brew at **Gluek's Bar and Restaurant**. Gluek's is the place with the immense Venice mural on the outside wall painted by artist **Herman**

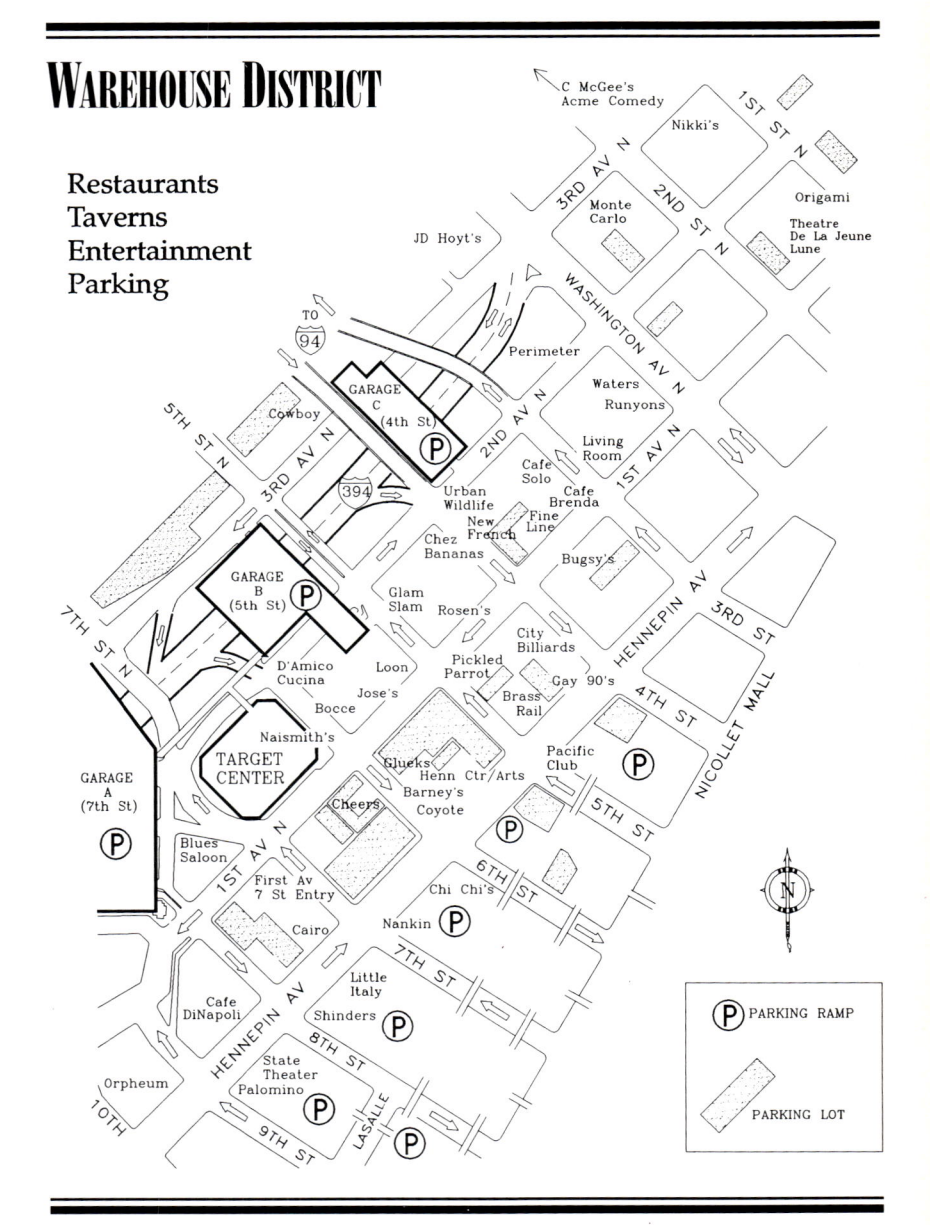

WAREHOUSE DISTRICT

Restaurants
Taverns
Entertainment
Parking

229 TWIN CITIES / MINNEAPOLIS

Krumpholz. Then round out the evening with late-night coffee and conversation at **Caffe Solo**. The cafe is open until 3 a.m. Friday and Saturday.

Besides a long list of bars, there are nightclubs such as **First Avenue** and **Glam Slam**, both associated with Minnesota's hometown boy, Prince. First Avenue was significant in the origin of the rock style called the "Minneapolis Sound." Or check out the **Fine Line** for contemporary national and local entertainers and an excellent meal or snack.

The official area of the Warehouse District, as defined in the National Register of Historic Places, is bounded on the north by First Street North, on the east by First Avenue North, on the south by Sixth Street North and on the west by 10th Avenue North. This area includes 157 buildings, brick and cobblestone streets and two steel bridges. As you stroll the streets, the cohesive style of the buildings arouses a definite sense of the period in which they were built.

The construction of the Warehouse District took place in the late 1800s and early 1900s and was the result of three major trends: a growth in wholesale selling, the ability of the railroads to transport large quantities of goods and the advancements in building construction and fireproofing.

Many of the district's buildings are considered to be excellent examples of the Chicago Commercial Style of architecture. The style features multi-story skeletal frame or post-and-beam construction, with large display windows on the ground floor. Typically the buildings are embellished in Richardsonian Romanesque or Gothic Revival styles.

BUTLER SQUARE
100 N. Sixth St.
The Butler Brothers Building was one of the first Warehouse District buildings to be renovated and put to new use. Built in 1906, the former warehouse reopened as a retail and office complex in the mid-'70s and now houses offices and commercial businesses along with four restaurants. The spacious interior has two open atriums exposing heavy wood timbers. Suspended in the west atrium is George Segal's sculpture "Acrobats."

THE LUMBER EXCHANGE
425 Hennepin Ave.
The great lumber barons of the Northwest territories were known to wheel and deal within these walls of granite and Lake Superior brownstone. In what has been termed Richardsonian Romanesque style, the Exchange was built between 1885 and 1890 and was a forerunner to the Chicago style of architecture that was to characterize the Warehouse District.

When the Minneapolis fire of 1891 left the Lumber Exchange relatively untouched, people realized buildings of this size could be fireproofed, making them a relatively sound investment. In the case of the Lumber Exchange, fireproofing was achieved by a terra-cotta sheath over the wood and iron beams. Today the 12-story Lumber Exchange houses mostly offices and the Pacific Club nightclub.

THE HISTORIC ORPHEUM THEATRE
910 Hennepin Ave.
(612) 339-7007
As in the past, the Orpheum still presents live Broadway, pop, jazz and rock events. The theater opened in 1921 starring the **Marx Brothers** and the best seat in the house was a whopping 47 cents. The Hennepin Theater, as it was called then, was the second largest vaudeville theater in the nation when it opened and a member of the prestigious Orpheum Circuit, one of the two major vaudeville circuits in the United States. Among the headliners the Orpheum featured were **Jack Benny**, **George Jessel**, **Fanny Brice** and, later in the 1940s, **Count Basie**, **Tommy Dorsey**, and **Benny Goodman**.

THE HISTORIC STATE THEATRE
805 Hennepin Ave.
(612) 339-7007
In 1991, after $8.8 million dollars in renovations, the State Theatre was reopened. The elegant Italian Renaissance interior with its painted wall murals, crystal chandeliers, and molded-plaster cherubs, festoons and figures, has been restored to its past glory along with the dazzling new marquees on Hennepin Avenue. In the years to come, it will once again play host to national performers, orchestras

and Broadway musicals. The theater originally opened in 1921 as a vaudeville house, then operated as a movie house and finally a hall for religious meetings until it was closed in 1985.

HENNEPIN CENTER FOR THE ARTS
528 Hennepin Ave.
(612) 332-4478
This stately sandstone "wedding cake" building at the corner of Hennepin and Sixth houses an impressive array of not-for-profit arts organizations and two popular restaurants. The building is in Richardsonian Romanesque style embellished with Syrian-arched balconies and was completed in 1890. It was designed by the architectural firm of Long and Kees. (The same firm also designed City Hall and the Lumber Exchange.)

Originally built as a Masonic Temple, this building, with its magnificent ballroom and fine meeting facilities, played a central role in the cultural and social scene of Minneapolis. With the advent of the automobile and the movement to the suburbs, the building slowly declined in use and importance, serving for a time as an office building and then a merchandise mart.

It was saved from the wrecking ball in the late 1970s by a coalition of civic leaders, businesses and foundations, who raised $5 million to acquire and restore the building and to adapt it for its present use — to house a variety of arts organizations. When Hennepin Center opened in 1979, 1,800 tap dancers performed on Hennepin Avenue, gaining a place in the Guinness Book of World Records for the most tappers doing a single routine.

Today, the Hennepin Center for the Arts seeks to encourage growth in the arts by providing significant spaces and reasonable rents for its tenants — several dance studios, theaters, musical groups and arts organizations. (See Theater, Music, Dance sections.)

WYMAN BUILDING GALLERIES
400 N. First Avenue
Though there are a large number of galleries in close proximity in the District, 10 of them are housed in the Wyman Building. Designed by Long and Kees in 1896, it once was the wholesale building for dry goods of Wyman Partridge and Co. Before taking the elevators to the galleries occupying almost every floor, examine the original floor mosaic at the Fourth Street entrance.

ARTSPACE PROJECT INC.
250 N. Third Ave.
The Artspace Project, Inc. is soon to be located in the old Appliance Parts Building, which has been placed on the National Register of Historic Places. When it opens in the fall of 1993, the six-story center will include studio space, living units, classroom and exhibition space for local artists.

TARGET CENTER
600 N. First Ave.
(612) 673-1637
Target Center, home of the Timberwolves professional basketball team, is customer-friendly to the 18,000 people it can accommodate. The arena boasts ample parking in adjacent lots, ample restroom facilities, elegant viewing suites and concert sound that's one of the best in the Twin Cities for the size of the hall. The main lobby is a visual sculpture of neon tubes. The exterior, though not in the style of the buildings that make up the rest of the Warehouse District, has been modified to blend by way of a Postmodern design.

In addition to Timberwolves' games, Target Center also hosts concerts by nationally prominent entertainers, circuses, ice shows, tennis matches and other major performances. Located below the arena is a complete health and exercise facility, which includes a track, pool, two basketball courts and racquet/handball courts.

THE COCA COLA SIGN
New to the area is the neon tube sculpture promoting Coca Cola located atop a building at Seventh Street and Hennepin Avenue South. The sign is 30 feet in diameter with 1,400 bulbs and 1,400 running feet of neon. It was built by a third-generation Kaufman from Kaufman Sign Company, the original builder of the neon Grain Belt bottle cap sign just across the Hennepin Avenue bridge from downtown.

Other historic buildings in the Warehouse District include the Trade Center

Building (500 N. First Ave.), Robitshek Building (21 N. Fourth St.), Textile Building (119 N. Fourth St.), Eide Saw Co. (300 Washington Ave.), Kingman Building (314 N. First Ave.), Hooker Building (311 N. First Ave.), the former Minneapolis Railroad Co. Building (200 N. Third Ave.) and the Minneapolis Van and Warehouse Co. Building at First Street and First Avenue North, which will to be the home of **Theatre de la Jeune Lune**.

MISSISSIPPI MILE

IN THE EARLY history of Minneapolis, the Mississippi River was the center of all activity. It transported goods and people and generated the power that produced flour and lumber. The river is still an important center of activity, but more for its natural beauty and recreational opportunities and less as the backbone of industry and transport. This area where the Mississippi flows through downtown Minneapolis, between Interstate 35W and the Plymouth Avenue Bridge, has been christened the Mississippi Mile. Here you can get a fine meal, dance in a nightclub or walk or bike in the peaceful parks of the riverbank.

Beginning at **Father Hennepin Bluff Park** at the south end of the Mississippi Mile on the east bank, take a moment to appreciate the 23 gracefully proportioned low limestone arches of the **Stone Arch Bridge**. Built by **James J. Hill** in 1893 to carry his Great Northern Railway into Minneapolis and westward, the bridge closed to railroad traffic in 1978. The good news is that it's scheduled to be opened soon to pedestrians, bicyclists and possibly rubber-wheeled trolley traffic.

The 23 arches, ranging in width from 40 to 100 feet, sweep across the river, curving to an end parallel with the west bank. Hill himself designed the bridge, and it cost a phenomenal sum in its day — $750,000 — earning for Hill the unflattering label "Jim Hill's folly." It is while on the bridge that one can best experience the size and power of the Mississippi, particularly because of its location just downstream from **St. Anthony Falls**.

When work to prepare the bridge for its new use is completed, it will be the southern connecting link between the east and west portions of the **St. Anthony Falls Heritage Trail**. The trail follows the river through the parks and among the buildings of the Mississippi Mile.

Father Hennepin Park is reputed to be the site from which the first white man to visit this area, **Father Louis Hennepin**, saw St. Anthony Falls in 1680. He named the falls after his patron saint, Anthony of Padua. Because of soft stone underpinnings, the falls has moved back almost four blocks from the spot where Hennepin first saw it.

Lumber mills first used St. Anthony Falls for power in the 1880s, followed by flour mills. By the turn of the century, Minneapolis was both the world's leading lumber market and the foremost flour milling city in the United States.

Across from Father Hennepin Park on Main Street is the **Pillsbury A Mill**. Built in 1881, this was once the largest mill in the country. The building has been placed on the National Register of Historic Places. The building is in commercial use, though on a limited basis.

MAIN STREET

MAIN STREET IS a picturesque neighborhood of cobblestone streets, historic buildings and outdoor cafes. Before World War II Main Street, on the east side of St. Anthony Falls, was a thriving center for the community. You could get everything and anything you wanted without ever going downtown. In fact, during the early history of Minneapolis, it served as downtown for the white men while the Indians lived on the west bank. After the war, the face of business changed from banks and retail establishments to warehouses and discount houses until the renovation that began in the mid-1970s.

The refurbishing and remodeling done to the warehouses along Main Street has resulted in a district devoted to recreational activities from jogging and biking to movies, restaurants, shopping and music.

Though many of the old buildings just off Main have been replaced with beautiful river-view condominiums and apartments, a few of the original estab-

Hurray! Minnesota

MISSISSIPPI MILE

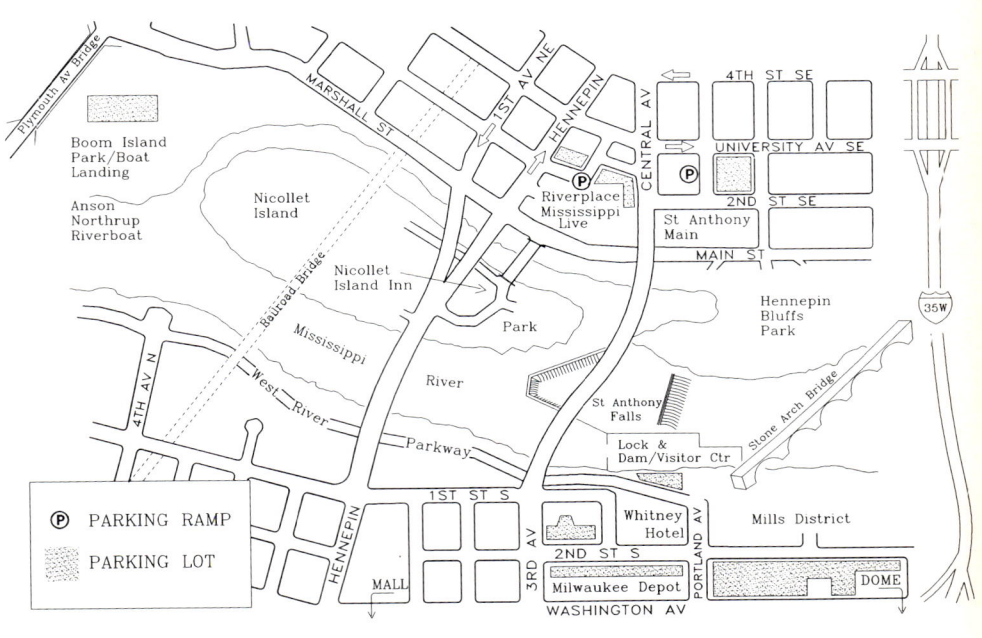

MISSISSIPPI MILE HOTLINE
(612) 348-9300
From historic tours to concerts to horse-drawn carriage parades, something is happening all the time on Mississippi Mile. Call weekdays for an update on activities.

lishments, such as **Nye's Polonaise Room**, still conduct a profitable business and retain some of the ethnic flavor of the neighborhood. This neighborhood has been home to many ethnic groups.

At the top of a horrendous flight of stairs just off Main Street is **Our Lady of Lourdes Church**. The church was built in 1857 and is Minneapolis' oldest continually operating house of worship. Nearby in Chute Square is the **Ard Godfrey House**, built in 1849. It is the oldest existing residence in Minneapolis. Godfrey ran the sawmill at St. Anthony Falls.

ST. ANTHONY MAIN
In the early 1970s, after a period of steady decline, what had been a string of run-down warehouses were renovated, revitalized and renamed St. Anthony Main. The 150,000 square feet of commercial/retailing space has had its financial ups and downs over the past decade. From its heyday in the late 1970s to what probably was its low point in 1987, St. Anthony Main appears to have found its competitive niche with the neighboring Riverplace, not only as an entertainment center but also as office space for service industries such as Minnesota Cable TV. The original restaurant establishments of **Pracna on Main** and **Anthony's Wharf** still serve up excellent fare, but now relatively new establishments such as **St. Anthony Main Theaters**, **The Comedy Gallery**, **Wild Bill's Comedy Safari**, **The Padded Cellar** and **Dirty Dick's Diner** have moved in.

Riverplace, just to the north of St. Anthony Main along Main Street, is a conglomerate of shops and restaurants.

Mississippi Live on a hot summer day.

The restaurants include: **J. Cousineau's**, home of the yard-long beer; **Kikugawa at Riverplace**, a Japanese restaurant; and Yvette, a French cafe with soft jazz and excellent food and wines. **Yvette** serves lunch and dinner, and it's the perfect place to stop after an event or to enjoy the outdoor cafe in the summer. Taking up a large portion of Riverplace is the three-level entertainment complex, Mississippi Live.

Mississippi Live is a subsidiary of Entertainment Centers of America, which has similar entertainment centers in New Orleans and Dallas. As you enter from the river side of the complex, to your left is a stainless steel Dairy-Queen-type server dispensing — other than soft-serve ice cream — slushy versions of margaritas, daiquiris, white Russians and six other favorites. Grab a slushy of the cocktail you fancy and sip away while you wander through the complex, sampling the smorgasbord of entertainment possibilities.

There are three levels of fun in 15 night spots. If you come before 7:30 p.m., the cover charge, which varies from $3 to $6, is waived. (See Nightlife Section.)

THE FATHER HENNEPIN SUSPENSION BRIDGE

From Riverplace, look across Main Street to the film-famous Hennepin Avenue Suspension Bridge, one of the newest landmarks in downtown Minneapolis. This is worth a pause and even a picture, particularly when it is lit. The bridge connects downtown and the Warehouse District with Nicollet Island and the east side of the river. County officials chose to spend more than twice what a conventional bridge would have cost just so that it would have that landmark quality. The bridge has six traffic lanes, two pedestrian lanes and one of the shortest suspension spans of any North American suspension bridge.

GRAIN BELT NEON SIGN

The Grain Belt Beer neon bottle cap sign, situated next to the Hennepin Bridge, is an old landmark. The sign is the only seven-tier neon sign left in the United States. It was first lit 52 years ago. After 14 years of darkness, it was re-lit in 1989 by the G. Heileman Brewing Co. of La Crosse, Wisconsin. A truckload of bird and squirrel nests was hauled away while 1,400 lights, 800 feet of exposed neon and 3,000 feet of wiring were replaced.

The sign is now owned and operated by **Minnesota Brewing Co.**, which bought the former Jacob Schmidt brewery from Heileman in 1991. Besides Grain Belt, Minnesota Brewing produces **Landmark**, **McMahon's Potato Ale** and the popular **Pig's Eye** brand beers.

THE GRAIN BELT BREWERY

1215 Marshall St. N.E.
Begun in 1891, the brewery is composed of the brewhouse, office building, warehouse and bottling plant. The imposing limestone facade of the main building is irregular both in height and style, having four distinct bays — the outer two are six stories high and the middle two are five stories high. Wolff and Lehle of Chicago, famous brewery architects, designed this brewery as well as Fitger's Brewery in Duluth. The brewery operated under the name of the **Minneapolis Brewing and Malting Co.** from 1890 to 1975.

Hurray! Minnesota

PHOTO BY GINGER ANDERSON

The brewery was purchased by the Minneapolis Community Development Agency in 1989. Concepts for development and management of the brewery buildings are still under review at this writing.

Nicollet Island

Just across the Merriam Street Bridge from Riverplace is Nicollet Island, which also can be reached from the Hennepin Street Bridge. Surrounded by the great river, with quiet streets and riverside parks, Nicollet Island is an oasis in time and place. The island has gone through a number of economically good and bad times. Today it is enjoying one of its best. During the 1870s, the island, particularly the south half, was a heavily industrialized area. What is now the **Nicollet Island Inn** was once home to a sash and door company. The park shelter was once the Boiler Works Building. The northern half of the island eventually gave rise to homes such as the Grove Street Flats and a few mansions. But by the end of World War II, many houses and businesses had fallen into disrepair.

In the 1960s, an urban renewal plan was proposed to remove all of the island's buildings and set aside the island as park land. That was when residents fought to have the island included on the National Register of Historic Places. Today the island is a balanced compromise with 22 residential plots, 50 percent park land, **De La Salle High School**, the Nicollet Island Inn and Nicollet Island Pavilion and Amphitheater, the site of summertime concerts and performances.

The Anson Northrup Paddleboat

Boom Island
(612) 227-1100

From the north end of Nicollet Island, following the Heritage River Trail, cross over the walking bridge to **Boom Island Park**. Or drive to Boom Island from the west side of the river across the Plymouth Avenue Bridge. Listen for echoes of banjo strings and laughter. For here, anchored on the east bank of the river, is the excursion boat **Anson Northrup**, a sidewheeler built specifically for the Minneapolis harbor. During warm-weather months, the Northrup conducts narrated trips as she plies the river three times a day. Fridays there is also a dinner cruise.

Upper St. Anthony Falls Lock and Dam

Portland Ave. and West River Parkway
(612) 332-3660

About a mile's walk or drive down the west bank of the river from the Plymouth Avenue Bridge are the St. Anthony Falls locks. The Visitors Center at the Upper St. Anthony Falls Lock and Dam has a large observation platform for watching the boats locking up and down the river. The center is open during the "nav season" (navigational season), which is from April to December. This lock is the first of 29 on the Mississippi between Minneapolis and the Gulf of Mexico. The observation deck also offers a good view of the Stone Arch Bridge.

Whitney Hotel

150 Portland
(612) 339-9300

Just up from the locks is the newly renovated Whitney Hotel, a four-star hotel. The open brick courtyard is a great place for light meals or for cocktails before or after an event. The service and facilities are equivalent to the best of the most exclusive small European hotels. The quiet elegance is felt the moment you step through the door, from the award-winning Whitney Grille to the 97 guest rooms and the five meeting salons.

The Old Milwaukee Road Depot and Freight House

201 S. Third Ave.

Completed in 1899, this is Minneapolis' oldest train station. Presently in poor repair and not in use, the building once echoed with the sounds of ladies in long traveling gowns and frock-coated men hurrying across the marble floors of the main station. Above are such architectural refinements as detailed plaster walls, carved wood ceilings and the 100-foot clock tower. The attached train shed is 6,254 feet long, 100 feet wide and 40 feet high. It is a stub-end type depot, meaning the tracks end at the station. There were five stub tracks coming into the station that have since been removed. The building recently was purchased by the Minneapolis Community Development Agency, which is committed to the development of the complex.

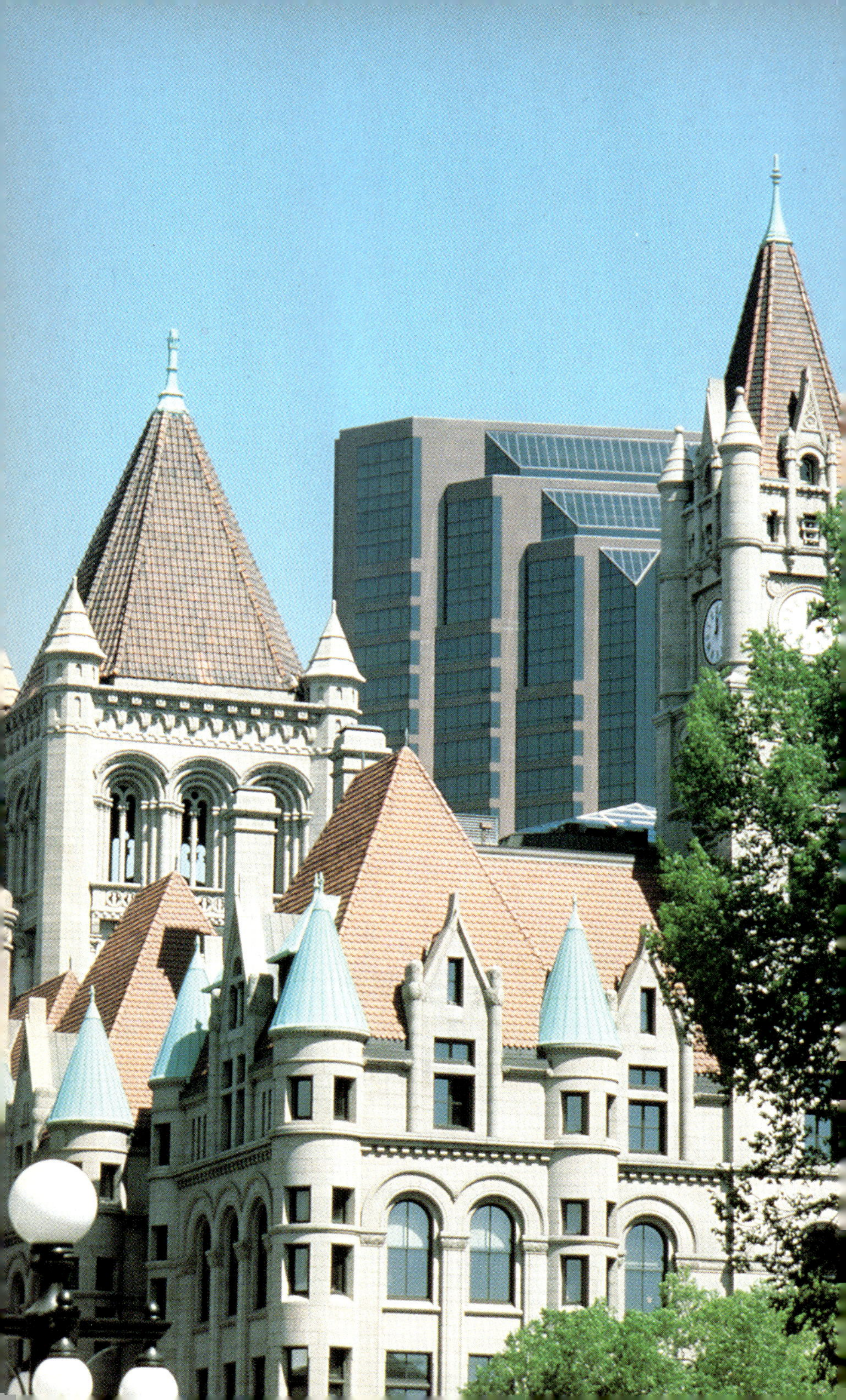

St. Paul

Kipling said, "Oh, East is East, and West is West, and never the twain shall meet." That may be true for the rest of the world, but Kipling never visited St. Paul. Yes, St. Paul is east of the Mississippi (that other little place, Minneapolis, is on the other side), but while you're crossing the river you might as well toss in your compass. The Mississippi flows from north to south, but as it enters St. Paul it curves toward the northeast. St. Paul grew up on the banks of the river, and as it twisted and turned, towns hiphopped across it and sprang up on both sides. So if you want to go to the West Side, for instance, go south (it's called the west side because to steamboat captains it was the *west bank* of the Mississippi, but it's actually south of downtown St. Paul).

Minneapolitans claim that they can't find their way around St. Paul because the streets don't make sense to them; their city is laid out in a nice grid, and street names run alphabetically. Because of St. Paul's hilly conformation, it was impossible for the city founders to plat the land in the same way. Nevertheless, it is an endearing testament to St. Paulites' resistance to change that many of the zigzagging downtown streets follow old paths leading from the river to the hills and that Snelling Avenue, West Seventh and I-94 were once Dakota trails.

St. Paul was an international center of trade before it was even a territorial capital. It outshone as well as outpeopled Minneapolis until 1880, when the population of Minneapolis surpassed St. Paul's. Over the decades Minneapolis continued to grow, St. Paul didn't, and St. Paul developed an inferiority complex. Now, St. Paul has finally stopped trying to compete with Minneapolis for the tallest skyscraper and the toniest retailers and is polishing up what it already has — culture, strong neighborhoods and natural and architectural beauty. Like a parent whose rowdy teenager has at last gone off to college, St. Paul has a kind of graceful world-weariness that comes from surviving a wild past of bootleggers, speakeasies and gangsters. "St. Paul," writes James Gray in "Pine, Stream and Prairie," "having tried everything already, is less easily dazzled [than is Minneapolis] by the promise of novelty. . . . It takes its pleasures less giddily than does Minneapolis. St. Paul has the greater poise of its greater age."

The city still has such an old-world flavor that it seems like only yesterday that **F. Scott Fitzgerald**, a St. Paul native, ran out onto **Summit Avenue** in 1920 with the good news that his first novel, "This Side of Paradise," was going to be published. The row house where he wrote it is still there (you can read about it on the plaque hanging above the door) at 599 Summit. Summit Avenue epitomizes the city's golden days, with massive houses ranging from the 32-room mansion built by railroad baron **James J. Hill**, the "Empire Builder," at number 240 to the governor's residence at 1006, home of **Minnesota Governor Arne Carlson**. Summit runs nearly five miles from the **Cathedral of St. Paul** west all the way to the Mississippi River, making it the longest span of intact Victorian mansions in the country.

It is said that Minneapolis is a small city and St. Paul a big town. Although this state capital is the second-largest city in Minnesota (after Minneapolis), it has a population of just 270,000. But in a space of only 52 square miles, St. Paul has managed to squeeze in all the amenities of a larger city. It has world-class cultural institutions such as **The Saint Paul Chamber Orchestra** and the **Science Museum of Minnesota and**

Landmark Center is one of St. Paul's oldest buildings.

Omni Theater. It hosts the oldest winter carnival in the United States, the **St. Paul Winter Carnival**, and the largest 12-day state fair in the country, the **Minnesota State Fair**. For its size it has an inordinately large number of colleges and universities, including **William Mitchell College of Law, Macalester College, The University of St. Thomas, The College of St. Catherine, Concordia College, Hamline University** and **Luther Northwestern Seminary**.

If St. Paul is conservative, it is because it was founded on two conservative businesses — railroading and banking. While those businesses no longer dominate the economy, St. Paul is known for local businesses such as **Ecolab, St. Paul Companies, 3M, Minnesota Mutual, H. B. Fuller** and **Minnesota Brewing Co.** (formerly **Schmidt Brewery**) that have grown into national and international concerns. St. Paul has been the breeding ground for such inventions as Scotch tape, the plastic drinking cup, the lithium-powered pacemaker and the shopping bag, which you will need if you stop at downtown's **Galtier Plaza** or **Saint Paul Center** shopping malls, or one of the smaller ethnic shops like **Old Mexico** or **Hmong Handiwork** on **Grand Avenue**.

Perhaps it isn't polite to discuss politics and religion, but without them St. Paul wouldn't even resemble what it is today. The **Minnesota State Capitol** dominates not only the skyline but also the political life of the city. And the **Cathedral of St. Paul**, another architectural treasure, attests to the fact that St. Paul is predominantly Catholic.

The Twin Cities are so identified with Scandinavians that people are often surprised to know that there are so many other ethnic groups in St. Paul. The land on which St. Paul stands was for centuries owned by the Ojibwa and Dakota Indians. In the 1600s it was settled by the French and French-Canadians, followed by the Irish, Germans, African Americans, Chinese, Italians, Swedes,

St. Paul's Summit Avenue, circa 1880, in a more leisurely era.

Norwegians, Slavs, Poles, Romanians, Hungarians, Greeks, Jews, Mexicans, Syrians, Lebanese and, more recently, Southeast Asians and Soviet Jews.

Like any major city, St. Paul has some famous natives: cartoonist **Charles Schultz**, artist **LeRoy Neiman**, actors **Loni Anderson** and **William Demarest** and Supreme Court Justice **Warren Burger**, to name a few. It even has some former residents who can't stay away. After living in Denmark and New York, **Garrison Keillor** has come back to St. Paul to broadcast "The American Radio Company" from the restored **World Theater** downtown.

In 1989, Newsweek magazine chose St. Paul as one of America's "hottest" cities. The article said that part of the reason the cities were hot was "because they don't see themselves that way." It's doubtful that anybody in St. Paul would argue with that. The word *hot* isn't even in their vocabulary.

Hurray! Minnesota

PHOTO COURTESY OF THE MINNESOTA HISTORICAL SOCIETY

History

In June of 1838, a Canadian voyageur named **Pierre "Pig's Eye" Parrant**, a "coarse, ill-looking, low-browed fellow with only one eye," settled into a log hut at Fountain Cave, near the present-day Interstate 35E bridge, and began selling whiskey illegally to Indians, **Fort Snelling** soldiers and French trappers. The cave had a stream that flowed out into the Mississippi River, so customers could paddle right up to Parrant's door and steamboats could conveniently unload his supplies. A year later, Parrant lost his claim to Fountain Cave and relocated to **Lowertown** at the foot of what is now Robert Street. One day, a young French Canadian in Parrant's tavern was dating a letter and needed a place name. "I looked up inquiringly at Parrant," he said, "and, seeing his old crooked eye scowling at me, it suddenly popped into my head to date it at Pig's Eye, feeling sure that the place would be recognized, as Parrant was well-known along the river. In a little while an answer was safely received, directed to me at Pig's Eye." The name stuck.

If it hadn't been for a Frenchman named **Father Lucien Galtier**, St. Paulites might still have Pig's Eye for a return address. Galtier was a missionary who came to minister to the French Catholics in the territory. In 1841 he built a chapel in Pig's Eye, dedicated it to Saint Paul and "expressed a wish, at that time, that the settlement would be known by the same name," and St. Paul was born.

If Father Galtier was St. Paul's spiritual guide, the Mississippi River was its lifeline. Even before it was a territorial capital, St. Paul's river advantage made it a world trade and commercial center. At one time, buffalo robes and pemmican arrived in St. Paul on Red River ox carts, were shipped via the Mississippi to eastern ports, and then on to British troops fighting in the Crimea.

Minnesota became a territory in 1849, with St. Paul as its capital. Eight years later, the town of St. Peter got greedy and plotted to have the capital moved, going so far as to build a new capital at its Third and Walnut streets. When the legislature passed a bill in 1857 to move the capital, the chairman of the committee, **Joseph Rolette**, tucked the bill into his pocket, locked it in a vault, and hid in a hotel room playing cards until the constitutional time limit for the bill to become law had expired.

In the same year, the legislature chartered the Minnesota and Pacific Railroad, and St. Paul changed forever. The railroads made St. Paul the transportation hub of the Upper Midwest, allowed the city to spread outward and brought in wave after wave of European immigrants. In 1888, a record eight million people passed through the old Union Depot. An enormous railroad empire was established by James J. Hill, one of the most important businessmen and philanthropists in St. Paul's history. Together, Hill and **Archbishop John Ireland**, who resettled hundreds of Irish families in Minnesota and spearheaded the building of the Cathedral of St. Paul, had perhaps a greater influence on the city and state than any other two people.

In the early 1900s St. Paul matured into a quiet, graceful city with tree-lined boulevards and beautifully landscaped parks. But in the 1920s, a crime wave swept St. Paul, and prostitution, gambling and bootlegging flourished. By the 1930s, St. Paul had become a haven for some of the nation's most wanted criminals. It began when Police Chief **John J. O'Connor** agreed to give shelter to gangsters such as **Ma Barker**, **Alvin Karpis**, **Homer Van Meter**, **Baby Face Nelson** and **John Dillinger** in return for their promising not to break the law within St. Paul. The O'Connor system, as it was known, worked for a while, until a federal agent searched out John Dillinger and knocked on his door at the Lincoln Court Apartments at 93-95 Lexington Parkway. The agent was greeted

239   Twin Cities / St. Paul

Lunchtime entertainment in the garden level of St. Paul's Town Square.

by submachine-gun fire and Dillinger escaped. The O'Connor truce with the gangsters ended when the Barker-Karpis gang violated the code and kidnapped St. Paul brewery owner **William Hamm Jr.**, and, later, banker **Edward Bremer**.

St. Paul weathered the Depression and two world wars as well as any city, but never returned to the boom times that characterized its settlement days. In the 1950s and '60s, like the rest of America, St. Paul faced aging neighborhoods, a population flight to the suburbs, a deserted downtown and a deteriorating infrastructure. It wasn't until the 1970s that the city began trying to bring people back into the inner city and saving its architectural treasures from demolition. With the election of **Mayor George Latimer** in 1976, a new age of urban renewal began. In the next decade and a half, **Town Square**, a hotel-shopping complex in the center of downtown, was built, the Old Federal Courts Building in **Rice Park** was reborn as **Landmark Center**, renovation of St. Paul's older urban neighborhoods began, the **Science Museum** opened its new building at Tenth and Wabasha, the beautiful old **World Theater** was restored, and the **Ordway Music Theatre** and **World Trade Center** were built, reestablishing St. Paul as a major commercial and cultural center.

St. Paul's present mayor, **Jim Scheibel**, has dreams of developing the riverfront, hoping to bring tourists and commerce to a vast underused resource. After all, it was on the river's terrace that the city's business district was born.

Neighborhoods

ST. PAUL IS and was made up of racial and ethnic neighborhoods and communities, many of which exist today in largely the same form, or in a reconfiguration caused by one of the waves of newer settlers that displaced or blended with previous residents. St. Paul has managed to make room for and welcome groups of people who found their way across the oceans and prairies to Minnesota.

Geography, religion and business were the primary influences on settlement in St. Paul, which was for a long time the end of the line for 19th-century pioneers who traveled by steamboat up the Mississippi. The Roman Catholic Church, with its parish system, also made a significant impact on the formation of the city. Virginia Brainard Kunz, author of "St. Paul: The First 150 Years," thinks St. Paul has a much stronger sense of neighborhood because

Hurray! Minnesota

of the Catholic religion than Minneapolis, which was primarily settled by Scandinavian Lutherans: "That's the reason those neighborhoods retained those ethnic colorations. Even though the people changed, the neighborhood remained intact." But the primary consideration for many people who settled here, from the French fur trappers in the 1600s to the Southeast Asians in the 1970s, was that St. Paul offered jobs. Current world upheavals have introduced new arrivals: Central Americans, Poles, Russian Jews and more Southeast Asians.

Before the Europeans arrived, the Dakota farmed and hunted in what is now the metro area, and they also lived and traded in the area they called **Mendota** near Fort Snelling and the confluence of the Minnesota and Mississippi rivers. Between 1680 and 1740, the Ojibwa moved into the area, forced east and south by white settlement. Many worked for the French in the fur trade. Treaties at Fort Snelling and Traverse des Sioux (near St. Peter) in 1851 forced Indians to leave the area for western Minnesota, not to return until labor shortages and changes in federal law following World War II.

The first Europeans in the area were French fur traders and Jesuits, including the two Frenchmen who officially settled St. Paul: Pierre "Pig's Eye" Parrant and Father Lucien Galtier, who both had a hand in naming the town. Three Irish-born soldiers discharged from Fort Snelling — **Edward Phelan**, **John Hays** and **William Evans** — staked claims in what is now the **West Seventh Street**, **downtown** and **Dayton's Bluff (East Side)** areas in 1838. The following year, Hays was killed and Phelan was charged with the city's first murder. (In 1851, the city's Irish population staged the first St. Patrick's Day celebration in Minnesota, and in 1878 **William Dawson** became the first of many Irish mayors of St. Paul.)

Revolution in Germany in 1848 brought refugees to the state. (By 1878, Germans held 54 of the area's 57 brewing licenses. By 1870, 37 percent of St. Paul's foreign-born residents were German.) During the early 1850s, Germans had settled throughout the new city, including a swampy area they named Froschburg (**Frogtown**), near the **Thomas-Dale/Midway** part of St. Paul. The Church of St. Agnes, built between 1900 and 1912, still holds Masses in Latin and as late as the 1960s, conducted confessions in German.

African Americans were living in Minnesota by the early 1800s, working the fur trade. Some of the officers at Fort Snelling later brought slaves: Dred Scott was one; James Thompson was another. He later became an Indian interpreter and the only black member of the St. Paul Old Settlers Society. Civil War labor shortages drew the first large number of blacks to St. Paul from the South. By 1900, African Americans had begun moving from the West Side into the **Rondo Avenue** neighborhood (near the **Selby-Dale** area), the heart of the black community until it was removed by Interstate 94 construction in the 1950s.

Poor rural Swedes settled in the 1850s in the Phalen Creek area of St. Paul still known as **Swede Hollow**. Later, they dominated the neighborhoods along Payne Avenue on the East Side. Many headed for Minneapolis, which was more Protestant and had less competition from Irish and Germans. Minnesota's first Norwegian periodical, Folkets Rost, was published in St. Paul in 1857. But Norwegians did not move heavily into urban areas until the 1890s and 1900s.

The first steamboat to arrive in the area in 1823, the Virginia, brought Italian nobleman and explorer **Giacomo Beltrami**. He was followed by Italian artisans and merchants in the 1850s, who settled below West Seventh Street in the Upper Levee area that became known as **Little Italy**. In the 1880s, unskilled Italians began replacing Irish and Scandinavians on railroads, settling in Swede Hollow and later on lower Payne Avenue.

Czechs first settled in the 1870s in St. Paul's **West Seventh Street** neighborhood, where they built Minnesota's first Czecho-Slovanic Benefit Society lodge. As late as the 1950s, Czech-language films were featured monthly at the Garden Theatre on West Seventh, drawing as many as 300 people.

Enough Poles had migrated to St.

St. Paul's Hmong citizens display their crafts.

Later arrivals were Russian and Polish Jews fleeing pogroms in their native lands; they formed the Sons of Jacob in 1872. Jews settled on the West Side river flats, east of the capitol and in the **Selby-Dale** area, later moving southwest to the **Highland Park** area. The community was heavily involved in social action and business; popular department stores in the early 20th century were Mannheimer's and, later, Dittenhofers' Golden Rule. Immigration of Russian Jews revived in the mid-1980s.

Mexican Americans, mostly U.S. citizens from Texas, began settling on the **West Side** in 1912, having arrived as migrant workers in the expanding sugar beet industry. By 1925, two-thirds of the community were working for meatpackers or railroads. Our Lady of Guadalupe Church was founded as a mission in 1931. In 1970, 6,500 St. Paul residents listed Spanish as their mother tongue.

Middle Easterners began settling on the West Side river flats in the 1880s. They moved quickly from railroad and meatpacking work into merchandising and organized St. George Syrian Orthodox Church in 1913 on the West Side and the Maronite Catholic Church of the Holy Family in 1915.

Driven from Laos by war and attracted to St. Paul by church sponsorship, 10,000 Hmong came to St. Paul between 1976 and 1980, settling in the **Summit-University**, West Side and Swede Hollow areas. Hmong, Vietnamese and Cambodian refugees have established businesses and moved rapidly into home ownership. A young woman elected to the St. Paul School Board in the 1991 elections became the first Hmong to hold public office in the Twin Cities.

Paul by the 1880s that the Polish National Alliance, a political and business group, held its annual convention in St. Paul in 1887. The Polish Catholic St. Stanilaus Church still stands on the west end, just off of West Seventh Street. South St. Paul's meatpacking industry drew Serbs, Croats, Bulgars, Hungarians and Romanians in the late 1880s. Many settled in St. Paul's **West Side** (south of downtown St. Paul) or clustered around St. Adalbert's Church in **Frogtown**.

Greeks immigrated to Minnesota cities about 1910. Of 26 Greek merchants in 1915, 12 owned restaurants. St. George Greek Orthodox Church was founded in a mansion at Summit and Lexington avenues in 1939. Greek-born Thomas Christie of St. Paul was elected to the legislature in 1946.

German Jews organized Mount Zion Hebrew congregation in 1856 in St. Paul.

St. Paul consists of more neighborhoods and communities than these, including the Groveland-Macalester area, more commonly called **Mac-Groveland**, which sprang up around Macalester College and surrounding educational institutions; the **Merriam Park** area, named for one of the city's early movers and shakers; the **Irvine Park** neighborhood, a cluster of grand homes centered around a small park named for another city father; and the **Crocus Hill** area, established along with Summit Avenue after the wealthiest St. Paulites moved up the hill and away from the river.

The mixture of cultures and steady influx of ideas in such a small, conservative place as St. Paul have not always proved harmonious over the years, but racial and ethnic differences have usually found acceptance and produced some interesting results, such as Morgan's Mexican-Lebanese Grocery on the West Side. Linda Schloff, director of the St. Paul-based Jewish History Society of the Upper Midwest, says, "Being part of an ethnic group in St. Paul has always been sort of kosher."

DOWNTOWN

IN DOWNTOWN Minneapolis, bigger and newer is better. But in downtown St. Paul, older and smaller are just perfect. In St. Paul you're more apt to find stalwart historical buildings, locally owned businesses, small ethnic restaurants, and reasonable (sometimes even free) parking. Minneapolis may have Saks and Neiman-Marcus, but St. Paul has the "cultural corridor," a pathway of theaters, museums, concert halls and restaurants stretching from the **Minnesota State Capitol** across Interstate 94 and down Cedar and Wabasha streets all the way to the Mississippi. The cultural corridor is actually a cornucopia shape that encompasses the **Minnesota History Center**, **Science Museum and Omnitheater**, the **Great American History Theatre**, **World Theater** and the **Penumbra Theatre**, among others. In 1993, the **Children's Museum** and the **Minnesota Museum of Art** will move to the corridor from their current locations at Bandana Square and St. Peter Street, respectively.

Some of St. Paul's major cultural and communications businesses, such as **Minnesota Public Radio** and the **Saint Paul Pioneer Press**, are downtown as well. Twin Cities Public Television stations **KTCA** and **KTCI** recently relocated to a brand-new high-tech facility called the Minnesota TeleCenter (for tour information, call 222-1717) in **Lowertown**, a warehouse district that has become a neighborhood for artists and a summer destination for **Farmer's Market** devotees.

Downtown St. Paul grew up on the banks of the Mississippi and is bounded by the river on the southeast, I-94 and the state capitol on the northwest and Ramsey Hill on the west, squeezed by nature, politics and commerce into an area of approximately five square miles. If the streets are confusing to you, you're not alone. In 1875 the city's peculiar layout was described as "perpetual misery inflicted on posterity." But it is the quirky narrow streets and compactness of the downtown that give St. Paul more of an Eastern than a Midwestern flavor.

If downtown St. Paul is known for one thing, it is probably its **skyway system**. At 4.7 miles, it's the largest publicly owned skyway system in the world. (In Minneapolis, the skyways are owned by the buildings they connect.) Started in 1967 to allow people to go from building to building without having to face subzero temperatures, skyways are now used year-round and have generated an entire second-story city.

While you'll find yourself using the skyways to get around downtown, you'll probably want to use the city streets as well so that you don't miss the architecture and public art. There are some excellent walking tours (for information, call the St. Paul Convention and Visitors Bureau at 297-6985 or visit one of the information centers at Town Square, the Norwest Bank Building, City Hall, Landmark Center, the Science Museum or the State Capitol). Surrounding **Rice Park** are the **Landmark Center**, a castle-like French Renaissance-style building that was once the Federal

St. Paul Parking

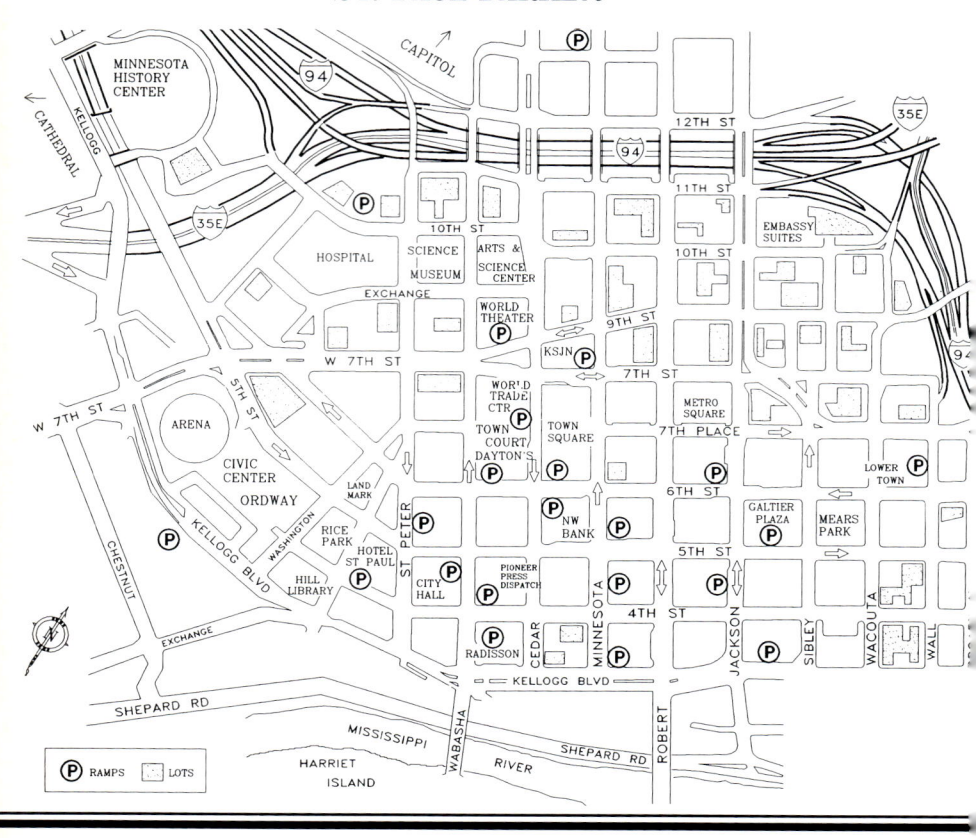

Courthouse; the **Ordway Music Theatre**, built in 1985 partly to house **The Saint Paul Chamber Orchestra** and modeled after some of the grand old concert houses of Europe (but with state-of-the-art acoustics); the **St. Paul Public Library and Hill Reference Library** building, commissioned by railroad king James J. Hill; and the **Saint Paul Hotel**, designed in 1910 by the same architects who did New York's Grand Central Station. Other buildings you won't want to miss are the Art Deco **City Hall-County Courthouse** building on Kellogg Boulevard with its Zigzag Moderne interior and rotating **God of Peace** statue by Carl Milles; the Minnesota Museum of Art's **Jemne Building**, one of the best examples of Art Deco architecture in the Twin Cities; and the neo-Classical **Union Depot**, built in 1917, a monument to the days when 12 major railroad lines came through the city.

Although **Saint Paul Center** has national anchor retailers such as Dayton's, much of downtown's shopping is small specialty stores. **Carriage Hill Plaza** has cobblestone walkways and picturesque indoor and street-level stores. **Galtier Plaza** in Lowertown is a multilevel complex built in 1987 that houses stores, restaurants, office space, condos, apartments and a four-screen movie theater. **Wabasha Street** between Fourth and Fifth streets contains some of St. Paul's oldest and most distinctive shops. And **West Seventh Street** leading southwest from downtown is lined with antique stores, ethnic restaurants and Irish pubs.

Hurray! Minnesota

St. Paul Skyways

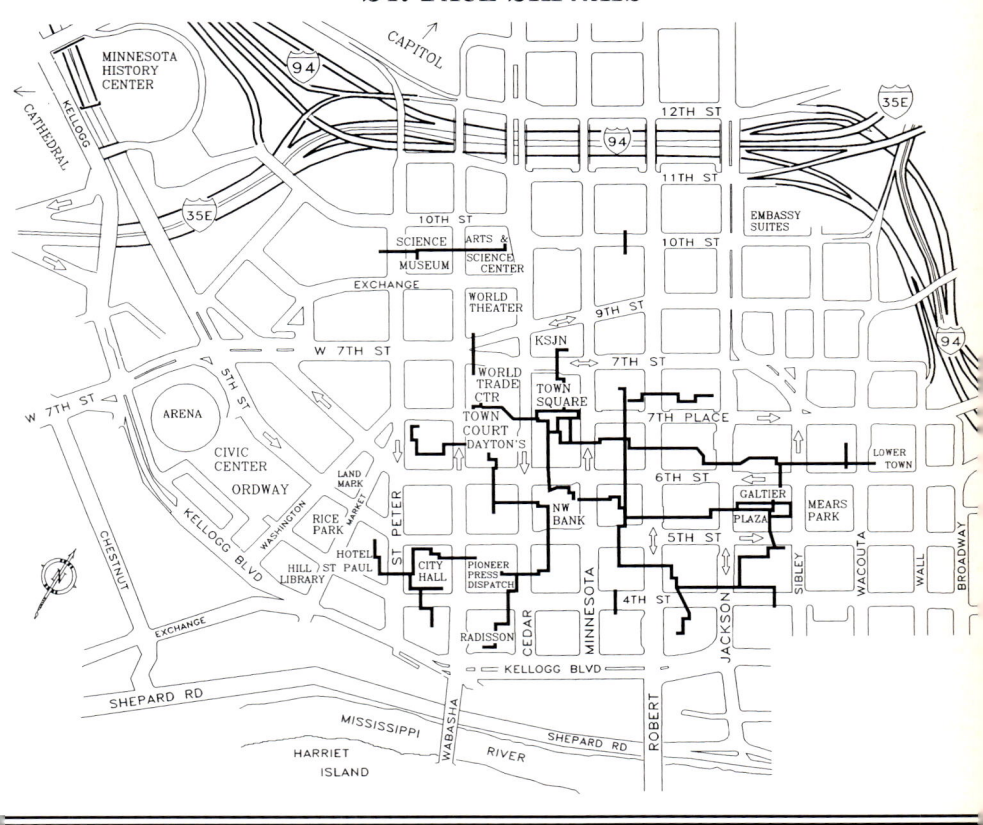

St. Paul's many ethnic groups are represented by restaurants such as **Cossetta's**, a generations-old family-run Italian market; **The Deco**, a Scandinavian smorgasbord in the Minnesota Museum of Art; **Sawatdee**, serving Thai food; and the Irish pubs and restaurants **Gallivan's**, **Patrick McGovern's Pub** and **Shannon Kelly's**, among others. **Le Carrousel** (not to be confused with **Cafesjian's Carousel**, a merry-go-round in Town Square Park), revolves atop the Radisson Hotel St. Paul, offering a sweeping view of downtown and beyond. And the new **Saint Paul Grill** in the Saint Paul Hotel, overlooking Rice Park, is one of the city's most popular restaurants.

Cass Gilbert, the architect of the state capitol, envisioned downtown St. Paul as a cultural capital with classical buildings and expansive malls linking government and culture, similar to places like Washington, D.C., and the Champs Elysees. Now city planners are looking to Gilbert and the past for a vision for the future. A major reconstruction of the capitol/I-94 area is under way, and the city has already begun to enhance its entry points, upgrading the bridges over the highways with Classical-style balustrades, globe lights and iron railings.

There are also plans to develop the riverfront, reclaiming an exquisite valley with high bluffs from decades of industrial wreckage. **Kellogg Mall Park**, a newly renovated promenade of plazas, walkways and fountains along the bluffs overlooking the Mississippi River, is a beautiful start.

245   Twin Cities / St. Paul

ATTRACTIONS

ASSUMPTION CATHOLIC CHURCH
51 W. Seventh Street (west of St. Peter)
St. Paul
(612) 224-7536

No existing building in St. Paul better exemplifies the city's strong German heritage than Assumption Catholic Church. Completed in 1871, it is the oldest Catholic church in St. Paul and the first in which German was spoken (services are no longer held in German). It was designed by **Edward Riedl**, architect to the king of Bavaria, and modeled after the German Romanesque Ludvigskirche in Munich. Masses are held daily at 7 a.m., 12 p.m. and 5:15 p.m. (5 p.m. on Saturdays); Sundays at 8 a.m., 9:30 a.m., 11 a.m. and 12:30 p.m. The church is open Monday through Saturday from 10 a.m. until the afternoon mass.

CAFESJIAN'S CAROUSEL
Town Square Park
Town Square
Seventh and Cedar
St. Paul
(612) 290-2774

Cafesjian's Carousel, formerly the State Fair Carousel, was a major attraction at the Minnesota State Fair for 75 years, until 1988, when the State Fair Board announced it would auction the merry-go-round. Minutes before some of the horses were scheduled to be sold individually to collectors in New York City, a nonprofit group of Twin Citians bought the 68-horse carousel for $1 million, saving it from dismemberment and keeping it in the Twin Cities. It was renamed Cafesjian's Carousel after **Gerard L. Cafesjian**, who donated the largest portion of the funds needed to save it. The carousel was built in 1914 by the Philadelphia Toboggan Company during a time when it employed its best carvers. Its four rows of brightly painted hand-carved basswood horses have been lovingly and painstakingly restored to their original splendor. Rides are $1 for adults and children over 1 year old. Hours: Thursday and Friday, noon to 7 p.m.; Saturday, 10 a.m. to 5 p.m.; Sunday, noon to 5 p.m. Call for holiday hours. Private rentals available.

CATHEDRAL OF ST. PAUL
239 Selby Avenue
St. Paul
(612) 228-1766

The magnificent Cathedral of St. Paul on the brow of St. Anthony Hill overlooking downtown was the inspiration of one of the most powerful figures in the city's history, **Archbishop John Ireland**. Ireland found a kindred spirit in the French architect **Emmanuel L. Masqueray**, the chief designer for the 1904 World's Fair in St. Louis, and brought him to Minnesota to design the cathedral as well as the Basilica of St. Mary in Minneapolis. (See Minneapolis section.) The cornerstone was laid in 1907, and it wasn't until 1954 that the inner dome was decorated. Modeled after St. Peter's in Rome, it is one of the largest church buildings in North America, able to seat 4,000 people. Among its many points of interest are the 175-foot-high copper dome; the baldachin (canopy) over the altar with its six black-and-gold Portora marble columns; the bronze grille at the rear of the sanctuary; and the six chapels called the Shrine of Nations, in which stand statues of the patron saints of the nations whose people settled St. Paul, carved out of marble imported from those countries. Open to the public 6 a.m. to 6 p.m. daily. Call for mass schedule.

CITY HALL-COUNTY COURTHOUSE
15 W. Kellogg Boulevard
St. Paul
(612) 298-4012

Harrison Fraker, architect and dean of the College of Architecture at the University of Minnesota, called the blue Belgian marble lobby of St. Paul City Hall "one of the best art deco spaces west of New York City." Thankfully, the 19-story building, designed in 1931 by Holabird and Root and Ellerbe Architects, has been preserved. Take note of the panels on the elevator doors, by **Albert Stewart** of New York, which depict the history of St. Paul. At the end of the Fourth Street lobby, which is called the War Memorial Concourse, is the famous "God of Peace" statue by the Swedish sculptor **Carl Milles**. The Indian, whose hand is extended in a gesture of friendli-

Hurray! Minnesota

The Cathedral of St. Paul is an integral part of St. Paul's skyline.

ness, was designed in plaster at the artist's studio in Stockholm and carved in Prapada Mexican onyx in a St. Paul workshop by **Giovanni Garatti** and 19 craftsmen. It was (and might still be) the largest carved onyx figure in the world. In the good old days, small souvenir replicas of the Indian by local sculptress **Evelyn Peabody** were distributed free to visitors. Open 8 a.m. to 4:30 p.m. weekdays.

FARMER'S MARKET
290 E. Fifth Street
St. Paul
(612) 227-6856

Downtown St. Paul has had a farmer's market for 140 years, and some of today's 160 growers have been coming to the market for generations. Like other immigrant groups before them, the Hmong people of Laos have recently brought a new element to the farmer's market and have helped introduce another ethnic cuisine to the area. In addition to the more familiar vegetables, they sell such produce as bittermelon, daikon, bok choy and Chinese long beans. The St. Paul Growers' Association allows only fresh, locally grown produce to be sold at the Farmer's Market. Also available are baked goods, cheese, poultry, buffalo meat, trout, eggs, honey, and plants and flowers, among other things. Hours: Saturdays, April 25 to November 14, 6 a.m. to 1 p.m.; Sundays, May 3 to October 25, 8 a.m. to 1 p.m. The Farmer's Market also operates eight satellite locations throughout the Twin Cities. Call for information.

HISTORIC FORT SNELLING
Fort Road at Highways 5 and 55
St. Paul
(612) 726-943

Hundreds of years before **Colonel Josiah Snelling** and his troops began construction of a fort on the bluffs overlooking the confluence of the Minnesota and Mississippi Rivers, this strategic spot had been well-known to Indians, fur traders and explorers. The fort was built in 1819 and for many years was the farthest northwest post of the army. **President Thomas Jefferson** predicted it would become a "center of civilization," and he was right. With its stone walls and massive towers it was not only an impressive military installation but also the center of civic and social life. In 1837, the famous American slave **Dred Scott** was married in one of its limestone lookouts. Fort Snelling was the site of Minnesota's first hospital, school and circulating library. Today, costumed guides re-create some of the activities and events that took place there in the 1820s. Admission: $3 (adults), $1 (children 6 through 15);

MINNESOTA MUSEUM OF ART
The Minnesota Museum of Art's permanent collection is housed in the Jemne Building, one of the finest examples of Art Deco architecture in St. Paul. The Deco restaurant, located in the same building, is known for its excellent cuisine and commanding view of the Mississippi.

children 5 and under are free. Hours: Monday through Saturday, 10 a.m. to 5 p.m.; Sunday, noon to 5 p.m. through October 31. For more information, call (612) 726-1111.

LANDMARK CENTER
75 W. Fifth Street
St. Paul
(612) 292-3225

What is now known as the Landmark Center was once a post office, customs house and federal courts building where gangsters of the Prohibition era were tried. When the building was scheduled for demolition in the 1960s, **Frank Marzitelli**, founder of the St. Paul/Ramsey Arts and Science Council, **Georgia DeCoster**, chairman of the St. Paul City Planning Commission's Historical Sites Committee, and **St. Paul Mayor Tom Byrne** organized the city's movers and shakers in business, politics, architecture and philanthropy to save the building. It was renovated in the early '70s at a cost of $13.5 million. Landmark Center was built in 1902 in a neo-Romanesque style using intricately carved pink granite from Stearns County, Minnesota. It's hard to believe that the ceilings had once been covered with acoustical tile and its spectacular marble lobbies, courtrooms and stained glass skylights painted government green. Landmark Center faces Rice Park and houses several arts organizations, including the Minnesota Museum of Art and The Saint Paul Chamber Orchestra. The Minnesota Museum of Art's temporary exhibitions are held there, and the Schubert Club Keyboard Instrument Museum has its permanent collection on the lower floor. (See Museums section.) Free tours Thursdays at 11 a.m., Sundays at 2 p.m. and by appointment. Open to the public every day. The Gladstone Cafe, on the first floor, is open Monday through Friday from 9:30 a.m. to 2:30 p.m.

MICKEY'S DINER
36 W. Seventh Street
St. Paul
(612) 222-5633

Mickey's Diner, built in 1938 to resemble a refitted railroad car, may not be famous for its food, but it has earned a spot on the National Register of Historic Places. That's one reason that when

Hurray! Minnesota

the city of St. Paul grows, it grows *around* Mickey's. Open 24 hours, it's one of the few places in St. Paul where you can satisfy that middle-of-the-night craving for eggs and hash browns. (See Restaurants section.)

MINNESOTA BREWING COMPANY
882 W. Seventh Street
St. Paul
(612) 228-9173
The old Schmidt Brewery has been a St. Paul landmark since 1855. When the brewery changed hands in October 1991, it was renamed Minnesota Brewing Company and a contest was held to name its signature beer. Although "Pig's Eye" was a public favorite, in the end a more dignified "Landmark" was chosen. In addition to Landmark Beer, the brewery produces Premium Grain Belt, Grain Belt, McMahon's Potato Ale and — in homage to that rascally one-eyed bootlegger Pig's Eye Parrant, after whom St. Paul was originally named — Pig's Eye Pilsner, which has become a popular seller. Minnesota Brewing Company is 100-percent Minnesota-owned and -operated, and 95 percent of its packaging and raw material comes from the state. Call for tour information.

MINNESOTA STATE CAPITOL
Cedar and Constitution streets
St. Paul
(612) 296-2881
When the Minnesota state government outgrew its second state capitol on Wabasha and 10th streets, the state held a nationwide competition in 1893 for a design for a new building. Of the many nationally known and established architects who submitted plans, a young St. Paul architect named **Cass Gilbert** was chosen. The capitol was Gilbert's first large commission. It was so successful that it served as a model for most of the state capitols built in the next 25 years and gained Gilbert national fame. He went on to design the Woolworth Building in New York and the Supreme Court Building in Washington, D.C., among other landmarks. The Italian Renaissance-style capitol was completed in 1904 at a cost of $4.5 million. The exterior is constructed of gray granite from St. Cloud, Minnesota, and Georgian marble. The two most striking features of the exterior are the central dome, which is a near-exact copy of St. Peter's in Rome, and the gold-leaf charioteer bearing Minnesota products. The interior uses more than 20 kinds of marble as well as several types of stone found in Minnesota. Wheat, corn, gophers, north stars, and ladyslipper flowers are used throughout as architectural motifs. Free 45-minute tours are given on the hour Monday through Friday, 9 a.m. to 4 p.m.; Saturdays, 10 a.m. to 3 p.m.; and Sundays, 1 p.m. to 3 p.m. Call in advance for groups of 10 or more. On the other side of Constitution Boulevard is a small park where you'll find two bronze figures by Minnesota sculptor **Paul Granlund**; they represent Little Falls native **Charles Lindbergh** as a young man and a small boy.

MINNESOTA STATE FAIRGROUNDS
Como and Snelling avenues
St. Paul
(612) 642-2200
At the end of every August through Labor Day, more than 1.5 million people come to the 350-acre fairgrounds in St. Paul for the "Great Minnesota Get-together," the largest 12-day state fair in North America. But after the Ferris wheels are broken down and trucked away, the fairgrounds are neither silent nor empty. They're home to a wide variety of events, such as horse, antique, classic car and country folk art shows; antique sales; and furniture, computer, electronics and recreational equipment liquidations.

ST. PAUL CIVIC CENTER
I. A. O'Shaughnessy Plaza
143 W. Fourth Street
St. Paul
(612) 224-7361
The 180,000-square-foot Civic Center is a multipurpose arena, auditorium and trade show space that has hosted hundreds of the nation's top conventions, concerts and special events, as well as many international conferences. Recent events and entertainers include a "Star Trek" convention, the Allman Brothers Band and a "Sesame Street" show. Every year the Civic Center hosts the fantastically popular Minnesota State High

The Como Ordway Memorial Japanese Garden is a haven of tranquility.

School League wrestling, basketball and hockey tournaments. Conveniently located near restaurants, hotels, shopping and sightseeing.

St. Paul Public Library
Fourth and Market streets
St. Paul
(612) 292-6341

Hill Reference Library
(612) 227-9531

The St. Paul Public Library and the Hill Reference Library, although two separate institutions, are housed in one building, designed by **Electus Litchfield** in the Italian Renaissance style and built in 1916. The library was donated to the city by railroad baron **James J. Hill**. It has an extensive collection for all ages and levels of interest. Free 45-minute guided tours: Monday through Thursday, 9 a.m. to 9 p.m.; Tuesday, Wednesday and Friday, 9 a.m. to 5:30 p.m. Call for library hours. The Hill Reference Library was established in 1921 through a million-dollar endowment fund by Hill and contains his own reference collection among its approximately 170,000 volumes on every imaginable subject. Call for library hours.

Summit Brewing Company
2264 University Ave.
St. Paul
(612) 645-5029

Summit is one of hundreds of small local breweries around the country producing classic high-quality beers. Summit beers have become St. Paul favorites and are available on tap in many local bars. Great Northern Porter, a full-bodied porter ale, won the top award at the 1987 Great American Beer Festival. Two-hour tours are given every Saturday starting at 1 p.m. Tours are free, but please make a reservation.

Parks

Cass Gilbert Memorial Park
750 N. Cedar
St. Paul
Park and observation lookout dedicated to Cass Gilbert. (See Minnesota State Capitol entry in Attractions section.)

Como Park, Lake, Zoo and Conservatory
1431 N. Lexington Parkway
St. Paul
(612) 489-1740 (conservatory)
(612) 488-5571 (zoo)
(612) 488-9213 (golf)
Como Park is one of St. Paul's most popular parks. It has a zoo, amusement park, picnic areas, swimming pool, ball fields, golf course, lake with walking and biking trails, cross-country skiing, floral conservatory and Japanese gardens designed by **Masami Matsuda** of Nagasaki, St. Paul's sister city. The 18-hole golf course was completely renovated in 1986. The Como Park pavilion on Como Lake was razed and is being rebuilt to resemble the original 1907 structure, with arched and snowflake-pattern windows, globe light fixtures and a tile roof. Conservatory hours: 10 a.m. to 6 p.m. daily. Free zoo open daily. April 1 to September 30: grounds open 8 a.m. to 8 p.m. and buildings open 10 a.m. to 6 p.m. October 1 to March 31: grounds open 8 a.m. to 5 p.m. and buildings open 10 a.m. to 4 p.m.

Highland Park
Montreal and Hamline avenues
St. Paul
(612) 292-7400
(612) 699-6082 (nine-hole course)
(612) 699-5825 (18-hole course)
Located in one of St. Paul's nicest neighborhoods, from some vantages Highland Park offers spectacular views of the Mississippi River Valley. Golf (18- and nine-hole courses), swimming pools and picnic areas. Cross-country skiing in winter.

Irvine Park
Walnut Street and Ryan Avenue
St. Paul
(612) 292-7400
One of the oldest and most charming parks in the city is named after **John R. Irvine**, who donated the land. Some of St. Paul's most distinguished families once lived in the elegant century-old houses lining the park.

Kellogg Mall Park
Kellogg Boulevard between Robert and Wabasha streets
St. Paul
This former eyesore has undergone a complete transformation. It is now an elegant promenade of plazas, walkways and fountains with arresting views of the Mississippi and the state capitol.

Mears Park
Sibley between Fifth and Sixth streets
St. Paul
(612) 292-7400
This downtown city park is near the farmer's market (see Attractions section) and Galtier Plaza (see Shopping section) and is being beautifully renovated.

Mounds Park
Mounds Boulevard and Burns Avenue
St. Paul
(612) 292-7400
The site of ancient Indian burial mounds. Of the 16 mounds once crowning the bluffs, only six remain. They date from the prehistoric era of the Hopewell mound builders, ancestors of the Dakota people. Excellent views of the Mississippi River and downtown St. Paul.

Phalen Park and Lake
Wheelock Parkway at Arcade Street
St. Paul
(612) 292-7400
(612) 778-0424 (skiing)
(612) 778-0413 (golf)
Picnic areas, fishing, swimming, boating, 18-hole golf course, walking and biking trails, tennis and downhill and cross-country skiing. The park also has an amphitheater, a St. Paul Winter Carnival Ice Palace Memorial and a Civilian Conservation Corps Memorial.

Rice Park
Market Street between Fourth and Fifth streets
St. Paul
(612) 292-7400
The circular-and-square downtown city park is said to be reminiscent of New York's Washington Square. There are plenty of benches and it's a perfect place to spend a lunch hour or take a break from sightseeing. It's surrounded by four of St. Paul's most beautiful buildings —

the public library, Ordway Music Theatre, Landmark Center and the St. Paul Hotel.

TOWN SQUARE PARK
Town Square
Seventh and Cedar streets
St. Paul
(612) 227-3307

One of the world's largest indoor public parks is in the heart of Town Square, a four-story shopping, office, dining and entertainment center. It's the new home of Cafesjian's Carousel, formerly the Minnesota State Fair Carousel. (See Attractions section.)

Special Celebrations

FESTIVAL OF NATIONS
St. Paul Civic Center
St. Paul
(612) 224-7361

This multi-ethnic festival celebrates the diversity of nationalities found in Minnesota. The food, crafts, costumes, music and dance of more than 80 ethnic groups are represented. Festival of Nations is usually held on the last weekend of April/first weekend of May. Admission: $7 (adults), $4 (children); children under 5 are free. For more information, call the International Institute of Minnesota at (612) 647-0191.

GRAND OLD DAY
Grand Avenue
St. Paul
(612) 224-3324

Summer officially begins in St. Paul on the first Sunday in June, when people come from all over the Twin Cities to stroll down Grand Avenue for the largest one-day streetfest in the Midwest. In 19 years, Grand Old Day has grown from a

Cold weather be darned at the Winter Carnival — everyone loves a parade.

small community festival into a party so large that the crowds often significantly outnumber the population of St. Paul (which, incidentally, is roughly a quarter of a million). The day starts early in the morning with an 8K run followed by a noon parade. There's something for everyone, from food, music and dance to carnival rides and games. Free.

St. Patrick's Day
St. Paul

There's at least one thing St. Paul has over Minneapolis, and that's more Irish. Although St. Patrick's Day celebrations are held in both cities, St. Paul is the place to be. There is a noonday parade through downtown St. Paul, an "Irish Celebration" at Landmark Center (292-3225) and lots of green beer at St. Paul's many Irish pubs. The best event, without a doubt, is the annual Worst Tenor Singing Contest, held at Mancini's Char House, itself a local institution (224-7345).

St. Paul Winter Carnival
St. Paul
(612) 297-6953

It all started when a New York reporter visited St. Paul in 1885 and wrote that the city was so cold it was worse than Siberia. A group of heated businessmen promptly hightailed it up to Montreal and stole the idea of a winter carnival to show the world just how much fun wind chills can be. The idea actually caught on, and the 12-day carnival has been held every year since 1886 (with time out for a few freakishly warm winters and a couple of world wars). Every year St. Paulites are chosen to represent King Boreas and the Queen of Snows (who reign over this icy kingdom) and Vulcanus Rex and his red-clad Krewe, who try to ruin the festivities and drive Boreas, and thus winter, out of the city. Winter Carnival events include an opening night parade, royal coronation, King Boreas Medallion Hunt and an ice-carving contest in Rice Park.

Every few years a palace is built from blocks of ice carved out of Minnesota lakes. At 150 feet high and 15 million pounds, the 1992 ice palace was the world's largest ice structure. It was designed by **Bill Rust** of Rust Architects in St. Paul and cost almost $1 million. The ice palace gained national and international attention because the 1992 Super Bowl, played at the Metrodome in Minneapolis, coincided with the Winter Carnival and drew journalists, photographers and celebrities to the Twin Cities. Among the 2.5 million people who visited the palace were **Jimmy** and **Rosalynn Carter**, **Paula Abdul**, **Dan Rather**, **Burt Reynolds** and **Donald Trump** and **Marla Maples**. In keeping with tradition, at 5:02 p.m. on February 3, 1992, three truckloads of rowdy Vulcans began demolishing the ice palace. "I think it's interfering with our reign," said Vulcanus Rex the 55th. "We've got to bring it down." The Winter Carnival is held the fourth Wednesday in January through the first Sunday in February.

• GRAND PORTAGE • BOUNDARY WATERS CANOE AREA WILDERNESS •

• GRAND MARAIS • TOFTE-LUTSEN • TWO HARBORS • THE NORTH SHORE • DULUTH • CLOQUET • HINCKLEY •

Downhill skiing
at Giants Ridge Ski Area.

PHOTO COURTESY OF MINNESOTA OFFICE OF TOURISM
ILLUSTRATION BY ERIC HANSON

• VIRGINIA • MOUNTAIN IRON • CHISHOLM • HIBBING • CALUMET •

THE ARROWHEAD

NORTHEASTERN MINNESOTA is called the Arrowhead because its cartographic shape actually resembles an arrowhead. It's the part of Minnesota that usually finds its way into the national travelogues. The Arrowhead encompasses the North Shore of Lake Superior, 160 miles of breathtaking natural beauty, arguably the most scenic stretch of accessible coastline in the country. There's also the north woods, whose showpieces are the 1.1-million-acre Boundary Waters Canoe Area Wilderness (BWCAW) and the adjoining Superior National Forest. The BWCAW, one of the great wilderness areas in the United States, combines with the adjacent Quetico Park in Canada to form the greatest canoeing and fishing area you may ever experience. Superior, with its wooded high hills, precious wildlife and island-studded glacial lakes, is rich in modern-day recreational opportunities and legends of the 18th- and 19th-century Voyageurs, pioneers and fur traders. Numerous other national and state parks add further to the Arrowhead's unequalled scenic splendor.

One of the most stunning attractions of the Arrowhead is Lake Superior, which forms the northeastern border of the state. Superior lives up to its name: It is quite possibly the most enchanting of the five Great Lakes. By one measure Lake

The Arrowhead

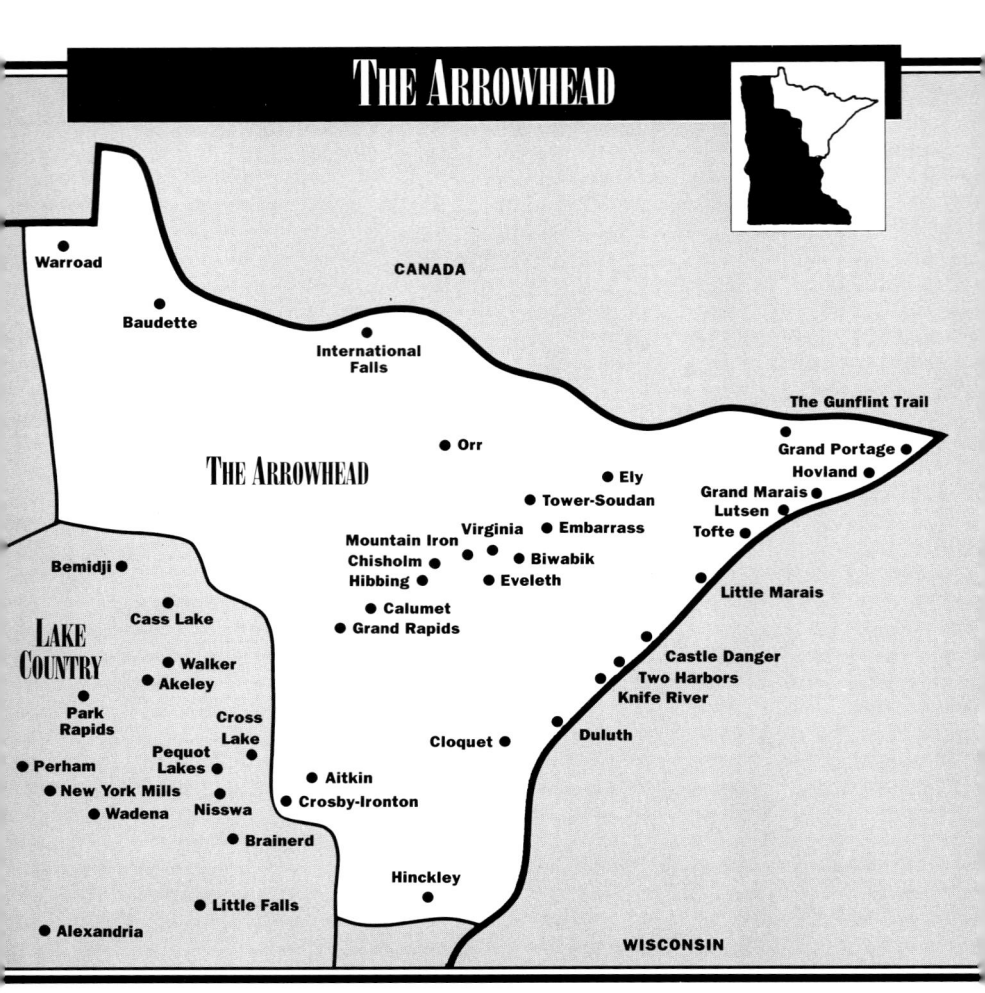

Superior is the world's largest freshwater lake. It has the largest surface — 31,700 square miles — but Lake Baikal in Russia has the most water — 5,518 cubic miles compared with Superior's 2,934 cubic miles. Lake Baikal, the world's oldest and deepest body of fresh water, is 25 million years old and 5,313 feet deep. Superior is 10,000 years old and 1,333 feet deep. Together, these giant lakes hold one-third of the fresh surface water on earth.

Lake Superior's main port city, and one of the major freshwater ports in the world, is Duluth, the eastern gateway to the Arrowhead and definitely one of Minnesota's fastest-changing cities. Tourism is becoming of ever-increasing importance in Duluth, and the city has spent literally millions of dollars in recent years to become visitor-friendly.

Downtown Duluth and the waterfront have undergone extensive renovation. The city has a new entertainment and convention center. The waterfront has been through extensive improvement. The Lakewalk, which runs for miles, is popular with walkers and joggers. And the Aerial Lift Bridge, one of only two in the world, continues as a major attraction. You can see the sights of Duluth and the surrounding area not only on foot or by car but via horse-drawn carriage, railroad car or the ever-popular harbor cruises.

As you move up the North Shore from Duluth, you experience the beauty of the lake and the forests and you can enjoy the fine resorts, the small towns, parks and attractions along the way that

Hurray! Minnesota

make a North Shore tour a truly memorable experience. Attractions along the way are numerous, including the famous Split Rock Lighthouse, the 1910 octagonal lighthouse that has just undergone extensive restoration; Lutsen Mountain, which in winter offers the best skiing in the Midwest and in summer offers breathtaking gondola rides; and Gooseberry Falls State Park, where the Gooseberry River tumbles over five waterfalls en route to Lake Superior.

Inland from Lake Superior lie some of the most prized timber stands in the country, along with what used to be one of the richest deposits of iron ore in the world. The Iron Range — actually comprised of the Vermilion, the Mesabi and the Cuyuna ranges — produced the iron ore from which was made much of the steel to produce 20th-century American buildings, bridges, vehicles and machinery. The Range now turns out taconite, a low-grade ore product.

There are many vestiges of the heyday of iron mining that can still be viewed in a trip around the Range. You can descend 2,341 feet below ground in an old mine at Tower-Soudan. You can tour Minntac, the world's largest taconite pellet plant, in Mountain Iron. You can explore the Minnesota Museum of Mining in Chisholm and visit Ironworld USA, which, in addition to depicting iron-mining heritage, presents a summer concert and festival venue.

In Hibbing, which incidentally is the hometown of folk musician **Bob Dylan** and Boston Celtics basketball star **Kevin McHale**, you can see the Hull Rust Mahoning Mine, the world's largest open-pit iron ore mine. Referred to as Minnesota's Grand Canyon, it's three miles long, two miles wide and 535 feet deep. Hibbing, by the way, is where the Greyhound Bus Line got its start back in 1914.

Just a few other attractions in Minnesota's Arrowhead include: Eagle Mountain, the highest point in Minnesota at 2,300 feet above sea level, located on the edge of the BWCAW; Grand Rapids, home of **Judy Garland**; Eveleth, "hockey capital of the nation," home of the U.S. Hockey Hall of Fame; Ely, "dog sledding capital of the Northwest," home of famous Arctic and Antarctic explorers **Will Steger** and **Paul Schurke** as well as wolf experts **Dan Groebner** and **Lori Schmidt**; International Falls, the "icebox of the nation" and hometown of football legend **Bronko Nagurski**; Baudette, the "walleye capital of the world"; Lake of the Woods, the most northerly lake in the United States; the Northwest Angle, a "chimney-shaped" piece of land atop the state that is the most northerly in the contiguous 48 states; and Angle Inlet, the most northerly town.

The Arrowhead offers almost every form of outdoor recreation, summer and winter. It offers incomparable scenery. It offers fascinating sights and history. And it offers all of this in whatever degree of comfort you choose — from a luxury resort to a tent in a wilderness campsite. Enjoy exploring!

HINCKLEY

SINCE THE AGE OF THE AUTOMObile, Hinckley has been known by those who travel between Duluth and the Twin Cities as the halfway point. Thanks to Tobie's and Cassidy's, it's a great place to stop and stretch your legs, grab a snack and fill up with gas.

For history enthusiasts, Hinckley is best remembered for the **Great Hinckley Fire** of 1894 in which more than 400 people died. To commemorate the catastrophe, the town created the **Hinckley Fire Museum** in an old railroad depot.

The exact cause of the fire is still conjecture, but the conditions were just right so that two smaller fires joined together into what was termed a fire storm. The entire town was destroyed. The individual stories of escape and harrowing rescues are worth the stop.

ATTRACTIONS
HINCKLEY FIRE MUSEUM
106 Old Highway 61
(612) 384-7338
Saturday, September 1, 1894, was the day one of the worst fires in the country blazed a trail of death and destruction through Hinckley and five neighboring towns. Despite the best efforts of Duluth railroad engineer James Root, whose daring nighttime train rescue saved 400 traumatized citizens, more than 400 others perished. Six towns, including Hinckley, were nothing but smoldering embers the next day.

The Hinckley Museum is located in the former St. Paul and Duluth Railroad Depot and is listed on the National Register of Historic Places. Visitors are given a chilling look at the events of the fire. There's a video show, walls of old photographs, old newspaper accounts and a souvenir shop. The museum is open May through October, 10 a.m. to 5 p.m.

ST. CROIX STATE PARK
Route 3, Box 450
Hinckley, MN 55037
(612) 384-6591
For a lush river valley, scenic bluffs, rolling hills and plenty of trails cut and groomed for summer and winter fun, stop at St. Croix State Park, located east of Hinckley on Highway 48. There are ample campgrounds and acres of hiking and cycling trails with a river view. Popular modes of transportation around here are mountain bike and horse.

SHOPPING
TOBIE'S MILL
Interstate 35 and Highway 48
(612) 384-7469
Featured are the sprawling world of Tobie's individual gift shops and an all-season, all-sport recreational equipment outfitter. Open every day.

EATING
TOBIE'S
Interstate 35 and Highway 48
(612) 384-6175
Since 1948, people traveling Interstate 35 have stopped at Tobie's between Duluth and the Twin Cities. The caramel rolls are the signature treat. Tobie's restaurant has plenty of seating, serving chicken-fried steak, burgers, hot soups and much more.

CASSIDY'S RESTAURANT
Interstate 35 and Highway 48
(612) 384-6129
Featuring a large salad bar with seven different breads. Fine dining. Open daily 6 a.m. to 9 p.m.

LODGING
AMERIC-INN MOTEL
Interstate 35 and Highway 48
Hinckley, MN 55037
(612) 384-7451
(800) 634-3444
Strategically situated, the Americ-Inn Motel has 29 modern motel units, with easy access to Tobie's as well as St. Croix State Park.

DAKOTA LODGE
Route 3, Box 178
Hinckley, MN 55037
(612) 384-6052
Ten comfortable rooms decorated in country-style plaid and oak themes. Each room has its own character and charm. Some rooms even have whirlpools and cozy fireplaces. The house sits just outside of Hinckley, a few miles from St. Croix State Park with great trails and hunting nearby. All-you-can-eat buttermilk pancakes and fresh fruit are served for breakfast. Shared baths.

▼ **FOR MORE INFORMATION...**
HINCKLEY AREA CHAMBER OF COMMERCE
Box 189
Hinckley, MN 55037
(612) 384-7837

CLOQUET
BETWEEN HINKLEY AND Duluth, in Cloquet, is the only gas station designed by **Frank Lloyd Wright**. A unique structure, it is a "must see" by any architecture enthusiast. Take note of the 32-foot copper canopy, unsupported by posts, covering the gas pumps; the angular glass-enclosed observation deck designed as a customers' waiting room (and ideally, a local meeting place); and the custom-made Phillips 66 sign in the center of the building, original but unreadable.

The Duluth Channel lighthouse.

Duluth

THERE'S A LOT GOING ON IN Duluth these days, more now than ever before. Duluth is less than three hours north of the Twin Cities. It has 11,000 acres of park land, 105 parks and playgrounds, two 27-hole public golf courses, 41 tennis courts, 44 miles of snowmobile trails, 24 miles of cross-country ski trails, and seven major hiking trails. Duluth is a friendly host. It is easy to navigate, with lots of free parking and a beautiful skyway system connecting the downtown shopping and office centers.

For a town of 95,000, Duluth is blessed with an incredible range of entertainment possibilities. Duluth has art, culture, universities, industry, history, charter fishing, old-world architecture, San Francisco-like city streets, lots of cobblestone (including 3.5 million new bricks), wrought-iron lampposts, tree-lined streets, a nationally recognized marathon, and, best of all, a front-row seat to Lake Superior. The lake front is increasingly more accessible to strollers, bicycles, in-line skates and general foot traffic.

To the native Duluthian, Duluth is divided into four regions: over-the-hill, downtown, East and West. Over-the-hill is the area in the vicinity of Miller Trunk Highway. This includes the **Miller Hill Mall** with Duluth's own retailers, **Glass Block** and **Maurices**, both of which are headquartered in Duluth. Along Miller Trunk are a number of smaller shopping plazas, large discount stores and major car dealerships.

West Duluth is an area of local shops and cafes with a strong blue-collar tradition. Major industries such as the **Lake Superior Paper Industries** plant, taconite and grain loading docks and storage facilities are located here.

East Duluth has the mansions of the old lumber and iron barons, such as the **Congdons**, **Whitesides** and **Dudleys**, along with the major hospitals and the universities. **Sinclair Lewis** once spent a year in one of these mansions, the former **John Williams** man-

PHOTO BY STEPHEN HERRERA

sion at 2601 East Second Street.

Finally, there is **downtown**. For the visitor, this area offers shops, brick-paved streets, skyways, the **Duluth Entertainment and Convention Center (DECC)** and attractions such as **The Depot** and **Canal Park**, where Duluth's colorful role as a historical transportation hub are portrayed. It also houses major employers such as **Minnesota Power** and the **Duluth News Tribune**. With an extensive skyway system, good restaurants and shopping, downtown is a fine place to work no matter what weather Lake Superior delivers.

Though Duluth's livelihood has historically been centered around the shipping, timber and iron ore industries, most recently tourism, retail and health care have helped to diversify and insulate against economic downturns.

Duluth has always been the launching point to the North Shore. People might stop, but not necessarily stay, on their way up the spectacular lakeshore drive. To change that, the city has spent $200 million over the past several years on the waterfront and another $60 million on street and storefront renovations all along Superior Street, making the town more tourist-friendly. Duluth's most prized assets, its history and lakeshore, are now easily accessible.

The Duluth Entertainment and Convention Center has been a major draw for trade shows, concerts and festivals on the waterfront. And after six years and $200 million in waterfront renovations, Duluth's waterfront is now one of the city's (and one of the state's) most popular attractions.

Today, the waterfront, with its lakewalk, museums, restaurants and shops is the place to be in Duluth. You won't find a better place to watch people and boats than at Canal Park, which sits in the shadow of the aerial lift bridge.

In 1991, 3 million people visited Duluth, spending $100 million in the process. And the waterfront wasn't even finished. It will be, for the most part, by the summer of '92, so there's never been a better year to see the city that Telly Savalas once called "one great lake and a whole lot more."

HISTORY

JUDGING BY THE pictographs on the ancient copper mines and earthen mounds just outside Duluth, there were people here as far back as 3,000 B.C. The Sioux, or Dakota as they called themselves, who are connected closely to the Algonquin Tribe of the St. Lawrence River Sioux, first came to the Duluth area around 1550. Later they were joined by the Chippewa, or Ojibwa. It wasn't until 1661 that this beautiful stretch of land, with its natural harbor at the foot of Lake Superior, was first visited by French fur trappers **Pierre Radisson** and **Medart Grosielliers**.

Later, in 1679, a French army commander, **Daniel Greysolon du Lhut**, was sent to claim the territory for New France. Then a small outpost of French fur trappers, known as Voyageurs, lived, trapped and traded with the Sioux and Chippewa. The land was eventually parceled out to steadily growing numbers of new European settlers in the 19th century.

In 1870 the Upper Midwest's first railroad lines came to Duluth, facilitating even greater trade and transportation. Duluth was officially incorporated the same year. One year later, despite strong controversy, ambitious industrialists saw the commercial potential of an access to the harbor from the Duluth side. They excavated a ship channel through a stretch of bog known as Minnesota Point, which opened a clear entrance to the Duluth side of the harbor. Today the Port of Duluth/Superior is the terminus of the 2,342-mile Great Lakes/St. Lawrence Seaway that connects America's heartland to the Atlantic and is the westernmost Atlantic seaport in the country.

THE BUSINESS OF DULUTH

DULUTH'S PRIMARY INDUSTRIES are tourism, shipping services, grain and ore storage, paper products, printing, health care and retail trade. Retail trade, including department stores, eating and drinking establishments, entertainment and lodging, produces $750 million in annual sales.

But, clearly, the most viable signs of

business activity, when you drive into Duluth, revolve around its Twin Ports shipping activity. Tens of million metric tons of grain and taconite are shipped and stored here in Duluth/Superior annually. The harbor, with its 50 miles of docking facilities, services more than 1,200 freighters each year. The majority of them are "Lakers," but anywhere from 100 to 120 are ocean-going freighters from all over the world.

Low-grade taconite iron ore, agricultural and forest products make up the bulk of the shipping cargo. Twenty million metric tons of domestic iron ore are shipped annually. While as much as 10 million tons of grain have passed through the port in a year, in the 1990 and 1991 seasons the amount has been less than half that. The trade in forest products, such as paper, pulp and wood, is growing, a reflection of the hard work and investment made by government and local businesses in this area.

During the 1980s, the city and private industry invested $1.2 billion in Duluth to update, expand and enhance both public and private facilities.

Miller Hill Mall, Duluth's major mall development located over the hill, spent $25 million on expansion and improvements. **U.S. West** spent $52 million on fiber optics and digital switching systems.

In other areas, the medical community alone has spent $119 million on general expansions; federal, state and city governments spent $200 million on Interstate 35 extensions; and local hotel management invested $11 million on hotel improvements, providing another 290 rooms.

Among the city's largest employers are **Minnesota Power** with its subsidiary, **Lake Superior Paper Industries**, a wood yard, pulp mill and paper processing firm; the schools and University of Minnesota-Duluth; **Advanstar**, a publisher of trade publications and an expositions and school supplies distributor; the medical facilities of **St. Mary's Medical Center**, the **Duluth Clinic** and **St. Luke's Hospital**; and the **Duluth, Mesabi and Iron Range Railway Co.**

EDUCATION

MORE THAN 60 percent of all Duluth high school graduates go on to further schooling. Duluth has 18 elementary schools, four middle schools and three high schools. Duluth also has several private, parochial and religious schools.

The University of Minnesota-Duluth (UMD) is one of four University of Minnesota campuses. It has almost 8,000 students, 70 major fields of study and 16 fields in the graduate program, as well as a curriculum for the first two years of medical school. The school was founded as the Duluth State Teachers College in 1902 and became a branch of the University of Minnesota in 1947.

The College of St. Scholastica is a four-year Benedictine liberal arts college founded in 1912. The main administration building is a beautiful stone edifice with a commanding view of Duluth and Lake Superior. Today, there are just under 2,000 students. It has 30 major programs of study and graduate programs in management, education, physical therapy, psychology of aging and nursing. The Benedictine Health Center is right on the campus.

In addition, Duluth has three two-year community colleges: **Duluth Business University**, **Duluth Community College** and **Duluth Technical College**.

THE WEATHER

DULUTH IS PROBABLY one of the most exciting Minnesota towns weather-wise. Lake Superior keeps things cooler until the air temperature drops below the lake temperature, which averages at 40 degrees Fahrenheit. Then the lake keeps things a little warmer until it freezes. In other words, it can be 80 degrees over the hill while a half mile away, down on Park Point next to the lake, it's 40 degrees. You never know what to expect, so dress in layers...T-shirt, sweater and down jacket.

If you have a northeast wind blowing across the lake (some natives call it a Nordeaster), this produces some dramatic, if not scary, conditions. This is true particularly in November, when the Lake Superior storms can whip up record waves of 31 feet and snowstorms in the two-foot range. Consequently, November has been the most fatal month in the shipping season for transport vessels of all sizes. More ships lie at the bottom of Lake Superior because of storms in November than from storms in any other month.

During January, the coldest month, the average low temperature is -3 degrees Fahrenheit and the average high is 16 degrees. In July, the hottest month, the average low is 54 degrees and average high is 76 degrees. The average annual precipitation is 29.68 inches, while the annual snowfall is 77.3 inches.

TRANSPORTATION

Duluth International Airport connects Duluth with the rest of the world by air. **Greyhound** and **Trailways** provide regional and national bus service. Locally, the **Duluth Transit Authority** (DTA), (218) 722-SAVE, operates nearly 90 buses, servicing 98 square miles with 22 routes. They also have a handicapped program, STRIDE, and in the summer months offer "Discover Duluth" sightseeing tours and the downtown Port Town Trolley.

PORT TOWN TROLLEY

This is a great way to get around and see all the downtown and Canal Park sights. The trolley travels in a circular path every half hour from the Depot to Bayfront, DECC, Canal Park, Fitger's, and back down Superior Street to the Depot. Tickets are 50 cents for adults, 25 cents for children or $1 for all day. Park in the huge convention lot, catch the trolley and see the sights. The trolley operates 11:20 a.m. to 6 p.m. daily, June 15 to Labor Day and weekends in September.

BAYFRONT HORSE-DRAWN CARRIAGE CO.
Bayfront Park
(218) 720-3567
Sure, there are faster ways to see the city and waterfront, but none as romantic as a horse-drawn carriage ride. Call for reservations.

TOP HAT CARRIAGE SERVICE
402 Canal Park Drive
(218) 399-2436
Top Hat has horse-drawn carriages or a horse-drawn trolley for larger groups. It picks up in the parking lot in Canal Park near the Marine Museum. Call for reservations.

NORTH SHORE SCENIC RAILROAD
506 W. Michigan St.
Amtrak Station at the Depot
(218) 722-1273
If you like North Shore scenery and old trains, this excursion is for you. **Trip #1** is a 5 1/2 hour trip from Duluth to Two Harbors with a layover on the waterfront in Two Harbors. **Trip #2** is a fairly quick one-hour journey to the Lester River, past the grand old mansions of Duluth. **Trip #3** takes around 2 1/2 hours, traveling from Duluth to Palmer's Siding, and explores the legacy of the old rail yards. At 6:30 p.m., Tuesday through Friday, is the "Pizza Train." Your ticket includes all-you-can-eat pizza. **Trip #4** takes you to Tom's Logging Camp and the sites of the Duluth, Mesabi and Iron Range's working yards.

HARBOR CRUISES
VISTA QUEEN AND VISTA KING
Harbor Drive, Duluth Entertainment and Convention Dock
Bayfront Park
(218) 722-6218. Call collect.
The entire family will enjoy the harbor boat excursion. Basically, the boats circumnavigate the harbor of Duluth/Superior, then go under the lift bridge out into the big lake, if the weather permits. Through an entertaining anecdotal narration, the knowledgeable tour staff present this harbor, this lake, its industry, history and scads of other pieces of trivia surrounding one of the largest inland ports in the world. There are daytime and evening cruises (often with music and cocktails) May 11 through October 13. Call for times and reservations.

LAKE SUPERIOR AND MISSISSIPPI RAILROAD
Grand Ave. and 71st St. W.
Western Waterfront Trail Parking Lot
(218) 624-7549 or 727-8025
This 90-minute, 12-mile round trip excursion along the banks of the scenic St. Louis River is the perfect way to relax. Snap some otherwise hard-to-get photos while indulging yourself on a beautifully restored vintage train. Operates from July 6 to September 1.

ATTRACTIONS
THE DULUTH WATERFRONT

The Duluth Waterfront is where it's happening. Along the lake, stretching several miles, is the **Lakewalk**. It begins at Bayfront Park, circles around the Convention Center, across the canal, under the aerial bridge and then north along the lake shore, past the Pickwick and Fitger's to Lief Erickson Park. There are plenty of park benches as well as a separate bicycle and carriage path.

Dominating the waterfront activities is the famous **Duluth Aerial Lift Bridge**. It is famous because the bridge lifts up, rather than separating in the middle, to let ships pass. The story goes that in 1871 the people of Duluth got together and dug the canal under the bridge, cutting through Minnesota Point. The waters of the big lake and Duluth harbor were joined just in the nick of time. A court order to stop digging, initiated by the town of Superior, was delivered just a few hours too late. It is rumored that "Grandma's Girls" (another bit of "historical gossip" states there was a bordello on the spot of what is today Grandma's restaurant) helped to dig that last few feet and participated in the celebration that followed.

At the eastern end of the Lakewalk, on Harbor Drive just east of Interstate 35, is **Bayfront Festival Park**. Here you'll find the Lake Superior sight-seeing boats and **Lake Superior Center**. From May to October a bright yellow tent goes up at Bayfront Park and it becomes the outdoor destination for clowns and other assorted performers, concerts, picnics and festivals. The Lake Superior Center features aquatic-theme exhibits from freshwater lakes around the world and other photographic and illustrative displays of Lake Superior and its sister, Lake Baikal in Russia.

Also, for the kids, there's Playfront, an outdoor collection of things to climb and play on, including a scaled-down version of the aerial lift bridge.

The huge complex between Bayfront and the canal is the **Duluth Entertainment and Convention Complex (DECC)**. Completed in 1990, it houses concert and convention facilities, the hockey arena (Duluthians are very supportive of the UMD Bulldogs), and the **Duluth Curling Club**, one of the finest curling rinks and past host to the **International Bonspiel**.

Just before you cross the **Minnesota Slip Drawbridge** is the **SS William A. Irvin**. The SS Irvin is a 110-foot retired U.S. Steel freighter that is moored in Bayfront Park. Inside you'll see massive cargo holds that held iron ore, the virtually spotless brass-railed engine room, the lavish executive/guest quarters and the crew bunk rooms. It is open daily 10 a.m. to 6 p.m., May to mid-October, for guided walking tours. (218) 722-5573 or (800) 628-8385.

Along the other side of the Minnesota Slip is **Grandma's Sports Garden** with indoor boccie and volleyball courts. Right next door, to be opened in the summer of '92, is **Grand Slam**, with indoor miniature golf, batting cages and electronic games.

Across the street, almost right under the bridge, is the famous **Grandma's** restaurant and **Mickey's Grill** complex. The food is great and the decor is unbelievable. A really fun place to grab a bite, a beverage or just gawk.

As you walk out the pier to the lighthouse, don't miss the **Canal Park Maritime Museum** with an authentic hands-on ship's control room and tales of Superior shipwrecks. Allow at least one hour to see the museum but don't be surprised if you spend more time. (See complete listing under Museums.)

Across the road from the Lakewalk is the **DeWitt-Seitz** building with shopping and restaurants. Farther along that

Welcome Aboard!

Guided tours aboard
William A. Irvin
flagship of the
Great Lakes Fleet
(218) 722-7876 or
1 (800) 628-8385

THE STEAMER
WILLIAM A. IRVIN

Downtown Duluth Waterfront District

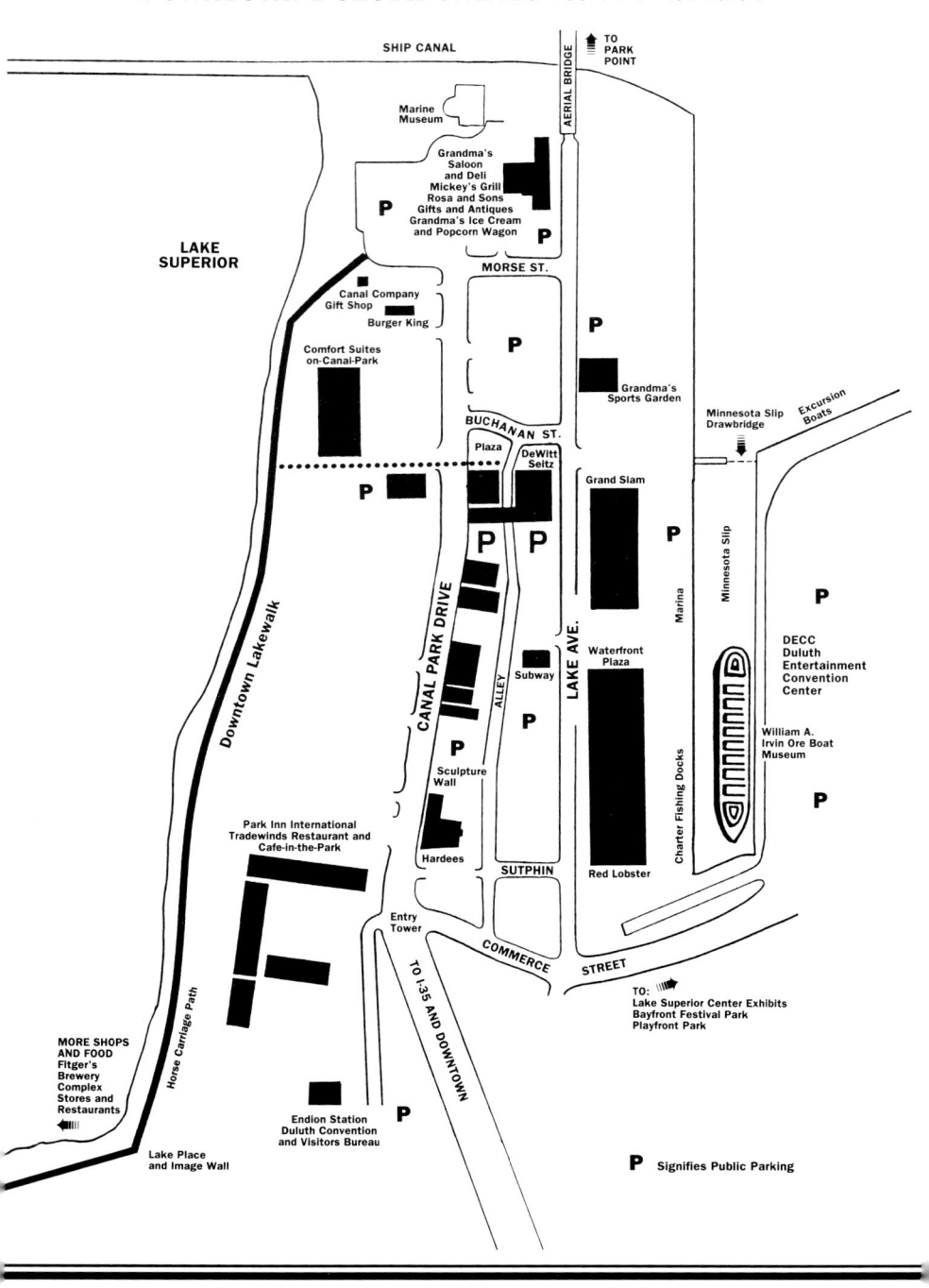

SHIP CANAL

TO PARK POINT

AERIAL BRIDGE

Marine Museum

Grandma's Saloon and Deli
Mickey's Grill
Rosa and Sons Gifts and Antiques
Grandma's Ice Cream and Popcorn Wagon

LAKE SUPERIOR

MORSE ST.

Canal Company Gift Shop

Burger King

Comfort Suites on-Canal-Park

Grandma's Sports Garden

Minnesota Slip Drawbridge

Excursion Boats

BUCHANAN ST.

Plaza

DeWitt Seitz

Grand Slam

Minnesota Slip

Downtown Lakewalk

CANAL PARK DRIVE

ALLEY

Subway

LAKE AVE.

Waterfront Plaza

Marina

DECC Duluth Entertainment Convention Center

Sculpture Wall

Charter Fishing Docks

William A. Irvin Ore Boat Museum

Hardees

SUTPHIN

Red Lobster

Park Inn International
Tradewinds Restaurant and
Cafe-in-the-Park

Entry Tower

COMMERCE STREET

TO:
Lake Superior Center Exhibits
Bayfront Festival Park
Playfront Park

Horse Carriage Path

TO I-35 AND DOWNTOWN

MORE SHOPS AND FOOD
Fitger's Brewery Complex Stores and Restaurants

Endion Station
Duluth Convention and Visitors Bureau

Lake Place and Image Wall

P Signifies Public Parking

Hurray! Minnesota

MAP COURTESY OF DULUTH CONVENTION AND VISITORS BUREAU

Canal Park Drive Shops
Kemp's Fish Market and Grill
Captain's Corner
Owens Yacht Sales
Bluestone
Winona Knits
Twin Ports Cyclery
The Duluth Pack Store
Blue Note Cafe
St. Croix Station
Courtney-Leigh
On The Limit
Gasoline Alley
Archer Classic Cars
Club Saratoga
Brass Bed Antiques

DeWitt-Seitz Shops
Art Dock
Big Crow Arts and Crafts
Blue Heron Trading Co.
Catherine Imports
Christal Center
Cruisin'
Duluth International Peace Center
Hepzibah's Sweet Shoppe
J-Skylark
Lake Avenue Cafe
Sandra Dee
Sweetcakes
Tales to Tell
Taste of Saigon
Window Works
Word Processing of Duluth

Lake Ave. Shops and Entertainment
Grand Slam
Grandma's Sports Garden
Lake Superior Magazine
Red Lobster
Subway
Waterfront Plaza Diner

same block are many more unique establishments offering entertainment and shopping such as **Brass Bed Antiques** and **Club Saratoga**.

Just before you cross the new extension to Interstate 35 is the **Duluth Convention and Visitors Bureau**. Personnel here will answer any questions about Duluth or provide information on current activities. On the other side of Interstate 35, you can leave the Lakewalk and enter downtown Duluth, which features delightful brick streets, wrought-iron street lights and benches. The stalwart citizens of Duluth suffered through the remodeling construction during the 1980s and, though the bricks can be slippery in winter, it requires no imagination to enjoy the ambience of downtown and to browse the shops.

The **Lakewalk** continues along the North Shore. On sunny days, the scenes of rocks, waves and water are breathtaking. But even if the weather is being influenced strongly by the lake, it can be an exhilarating and exciting experience to bundle up and face the elements, not unlike the freighter captains of old.

Some boats to look for on your walk are: the car ferry, called the **Incan Superior**, which plies a regular schedule between Duluth/Superior and Thunder Bay, transporting boxcars usually loaded with newsprint; the **Vista Queen**; sailboats racing on Wednesday evenings and Saturdays, and, of course, the huge freighters.

You can identify the freighters' owner/operators by the colors of the smokestack. The flag of the country of registration is flown at the stern of the ship. At the same time, the flag of the country of the port of destination (in this case the U.S. flag) is flown behind the smokestack. Listen for the four toots (long, short, long, short) from the laker and then the four toots of acknowledgment from the aerial lift bridge. This communication is no longer necessary, thanks to modern radio contact, but continues as an exciting Great Lakes tradition.

Check a few of the local book stores for some great books on the history of Great Lakes shipping or a book that shows the colors of the various shipping

The yellow tent of Bayfront Festival Park.

companies so that you can identify the ships coming into port. There is also a **Boatwatcher's Hotline (218) 722-6489** providing up-to-the-minute information on harbor activity.

The history of shipping on Lake Superior is one of boom, bust and bad weather. Shipping has followed the rise and fall of the timber, iron ore and grain industries. The last big bust was in the fall of 1979, when 470 grain millers went on strike. For three months dozens of ships were sitting in the harbor and even more were moored in the lake just outside the harbor. To the impartial observer, the lights of all those ships, lit up at night, made a spectacular background.

However, it was a real judgement call for the owners. Should they run the ships back empty and be sure to make it off Lake Superior before the locks froze in at **Sault St. Marie**? Or should they wait for a load, with the risk of spending an idle winter? Rumor was that the cost of an empty boat was in the $10,000-a-day range. This dealt a real blow to grain shipping out of Duluth/Superior. It is slowly recovering, but has yet to reach the yearly tonnage of that period, 8.5 million metric tons.

Lake Superior's history of shipwrecks, ghosts and lost sailors is engrossing, and there's no better place than Duluth to immerse your psyche in it.

There are plenty of stories to hear and it isn't hard to find someone who would be more than happy to talk about sunken freighters and debate the fine points of shipwrecks, such as the wreck of the **Edmund Fitzgerald**, lost in a storm on November 11, 1975.

At the west end of the Lakewalk is the **Pickwick**, **Fitger's Brewery Complex** and **Leif Ericson Park**. The Pickwick is a cozy restaurant with great food in the tradition of hearty German cooking and excellent charbroiled steaks, a fixture in the culture of Duluth. Fitger's Brewery Complex now contains a beautiful historic inn, a variety of unique and interesting shops and a couple of excellent restaurants.

The original brewery was established in 1859 but really became successful under a man named **Nicholas Decker**, who advertised that he would deliver beer to the home at $3 a barrel. In 1881, **August Fitger** bought into the brewery. Finally, in 1903, it was incorporated as the **Fitger Brewing Co.** The brewery remained in operation until 1972, switching to soft drinks and candy during prohibition.

FESTIVALS

DULUTH HOSTS A large number of festivals and special events throughout the year. Those definitely not to be missed and really fun for all ages are:

Grandma's Marathon, a 26.2-mile run along the North Shore held in June. The start is in Two Harbors and it finishes at Canal Park. Lots of activities for everyone under the tents at Canal Park. For more information: Scott Keenan, 600 E. Superior St., Duluth, MN 55802, (218) 727-0947.

The **John Beargrease Sled Dog Marathon** is held in January. This is the premier winter sled dog race in the lower 48 states. It is named after the Chippewa who delivered mail along the North Shore during its early history. The course begins in Duluth at 6:15 p.m. on a Tuesday. It takes mushers from around the globe approximately five days to reach Grand Portage via the North Shore, a distance of 500 miles. Celebrations and festivals are held along the trail. Beargrease Office, Box 500, Duluth, MN 55802, (218) 722-7631.

The **Bayfront Blues Festival** is in its fourth year and is held the first full weekend in August. Twenty-one regional and national bands perform on two stages over a three-day period at Bayfront Park. Free admission. Blues Fest Hotline (218) 726-0467.

MUSEUMS AND HISTORICAL EXHIBITS

CANAL PARK MARINE MUSEUM
Canal Park Drive
(218) 727-2497
Located in the shadow of the only aerial lift automobile bridge on this continent

(the only other aerial lift bridge in the world is located in Rouen, France), you'll find one of the most popular museums in Minnesota, the U.S. Army Corps of Engineers' Canal Park Marine Museum. Actually, it's an amazing portal into what life on the lake is all about for the people and ships that traverse it for a living. There are maps with shipwreck sites, ship cabin exhibits, an authentic control room, old diving gear, assorted items collected from shipwrecks, and even an exhibit of local and national paintings depicting the beauty and fury of the greatest of the Great Lakes.

THE DEPOT
506 W. Michigan St.
(218) 727-8025
Open daily all year.

This 1890s Norman Chateau Revival-inspired train depot is a popular spot for a variety of reasons, not the least being its large size (91,000 square feet), exhibit variety and convenient downtown location. The Depot is home to an assortment of Duluth arts organizations as well as three distinct museums that offer splendid collections of history about the area's logging, mining and railroad roots.

The **Lake Superior Museum of Transportation** is perhaps the best opportunity in the country to get hands-on experience with old locomotives. There is an acre of turn-of-the-century coal-fired locomotives. The Depot also houses the **A.M. Chisholm Museum** with exhibits portraying local natural history. Finally, **St. Louis County Historical Society** has displays exploring the early American Indian, the European explorer and the settler history of the area.

Several of Duluth's most prominent arts organizations make their home there too, including the **Duluth Ballet, Duluth Playhouse** and **Duluth Art Institute**. The Depot has a beautiful theater, which seats 280. Many of Duluth's arts organizations perform in its intimate, almost nostalgic, setting. In addition, the Depot still serves as a train station for the North Shore Scenic Railroad, which runs daily. (See Transportation.)

▼ **FOR MORE INFORMATION...**
A.M. CHISHOLM MUSEUM
(218) 722-8563
ST. LOUIS COUNTY HISTORICAL SOCIETY
(218) 722-8011
LAKE SUPERIOR MUSEUM OF TRANSPORTATION
(218) 727-0687

GLENSHEEN MANSION
3300 London Road
(218) 724-8864 for reservations.
(218) 724-8863 for general information.

Some mansion tours can really be quite sterile and uninformative. Not so at Glensheen. The tour begins with a slide show introduction to the grounds and the Jacobean-style mansion. Throughout the tour of Glensheen's 39 rooms you'll also get ample history and a glimpse into the lives of Glensheen's heart and soul, iron mogul Chester Congdon and his family.

Completed in 1908, this 22-acre country estate on the shore of Lake Superior at the northern edge of Duluth is a tribute to both wealth and ingenuity. The University of Minnesota operates Glensheen with the volunteer help of the Duluth Junior League. The guides do a fine job of explaining in detail the architecture, antiques, landscaping and Congdon family lore of the mansion as well as the carriage house. You might have to wait in line to get into Glensheen, but you can book ahead, which is advisable on weekends in the summer months. Allow plenty of time to explore the grounds after your tour.

LAKE SUPERIOR CENTER
Bayfront Park
Harbor Drive just east of Highway 35
(218) 720-3033

The Lake Superior Center is a combination freshwater think tank and laboratory along with an aquatic museum that chronicles the unique ecosystems in freshwater lakes. Using Lake Superior, the largest freshwater lake by area, and Lake Baikal in Russia, the largest by volume, the curators are building what they hope will become the world's preeminent

Hurray! Minnesota

The elegant Glensheen Mansion as seen from the lake.

center for the study of and the public's exposure to freshwater aquatic environments. As of 1991, it was still under construction, but preview exhibits are open to the public from June to September.

TWEED MUSEUM OF ART
University of Minnesota-Duluth
10 University Drive, Lot G
(218) 726-8222
This museum exhibits European and American historic and contemporary art. The Tweed has nine galleries on the University of Minnesota-Duluth campus. Five are dedicated to changing exhibitions while four hold a constantly expanding permanent collection.

DULUTH ART INSTITUTE
506 W. Michigan St.
(218) 727-8013
Located in the Depot, the Duluth Art Institute primarily displays contemporary art created by local, regional and national artists.

ENTERTAINMENT
DULUTH BALLET
The Depot
(218) 722-2314
This troupe stages both traditional and contemporary works. The 1992 season is the 26th for the only professional resident ballet company in Minnesota. The season, running from September through March, includes a fall series of three to four performances; the "Nutcracker" in December, again with three to four performances; and a spring series. Performances are held at the DECC, the Depot theater, and the Marshall Performing Arts Center at UMD.

CONCERT BY THE LAKE
Glensheen
(218) 724-8864
Local musicians gather on Wednesday evenings on the grounds of Glensheen Mansion from mid-June to mid-July.

DULUTH-SUPERIOR SYMPHONY ORCHESTRA
(218) 727-7429
This orchestra was constituted in 1932 and has performed every year since. The orchestra performs 10 subscription concerts each year — seven classical and three pops — at the DECC. The season runs from September through May with an annual holiday concert in mid-December featuring chorus and orchestra.

DULUTH PLAYHOUSE
The Depot
(218) 722-0349
This community theater has a year-round season of eight productions that includes a children's show. Performances are held at the theater in the Depot.

SPIRIT OF THE NORTH THEATER
600 E. Superior St.
(218) 727-5060 or 722-6337
This theater stages the Lake Superior Experience from Memorial Day through Labor Day, a multi-media show that chronicles life on the North Shore in a humorous, poignant style. Year-round there are concerts and live theater productions by such performing troupes as Renegade Theater and Colder by the Lake.

MATINEE MUSICALE
The Depot
(218) 727-8025
This group presents national talent in its Concert Artist Series. Season runs from September to May. Concerts take place at various places around the city.

FOND DU LUTH CASINO
129 E. Superior St.
(218) 727-0280
(800) 777-8638
Open daily. Blackjack, video slot machines and bingo.

PHOTO COURTESY OF DULUTH CONVENTION AND VISITORS BUREAU

Parks and Outdoor Recreation

Enger Memorial Tower
17th Ave. W. and Skyline Boulevard
This historical five-story octagonal watchtower, complete with a bonsai garden, is quite a structure and just happens to have the best view of the lake and harbor in Duluth. This is a place to watch a spectacular sunrise, have a picnic lunch and take a stroll through the gardens in the summer. Be sure to bring your camera and binoculars.

Hawk Ridge
East Skyline Parkway
Between Glenwood and Lester Park
Overlooking Lester Park, Hawk Ridge is the birdwatcher's destination of choice. It lies in the path of the migratory highway for thousands of birds during the spring and fall. The Minnesota Ornithologic Union schedules "Hawk Weekend" here in late September.

Lake Superior Zoo
(218) 624-1502
Grand Ave. and 72nd Ave. W.
Open year-round.
This zoo is expanding and continues to put more emphasis on true-to-life animal habitats. For the animals it means better living conditions. For zoogoers it means a more realistic picture of how polar bears and seals, for example, live in the wild. The zoo opened a new Australian exhibit in 1992.

Lester Park
Lester River Road and E. Superior St.
This scenic trail winds through what used to be Burlington Northern Railroad yards along the St. Louis River from South 63rd Avenue West and Waseca Street to Riverside Marina. This is another popular birdwatching environment that's dotted with fishing and swimming holes.

Park Point
At the end of Minnesota Ave.
Park Point has an easy four-mile hiking trail, a swimming beach, softball fields and even a bicycle and sailboat rental shop. It's rarely crowded, and if you follow the trail at the foot of Minnesota Avenue all the way out to the breakwater there are beautiful scenic vistas of the city of Superior across the bay and looking back across the lake to Duluth. There's also a classic turn-of-the-century lighthouse at the end of the trail.

Park Point also is a great place for birdwatching. In April and May you can see loons and hawks. In late May the shorebirds, such as sandpipers and killdeer, come out. During the summer you might spy a horned owl, and during the winter you can spot snowy owls.

Skyline Parkway
The Skyline Parkway is a well-marked scenic drive through Duluth offering vistas of the lake and the harbor and passing through most of the parks. It begins at the Visitors Center off of Interstate 35 at the very top of the hill and ends at Becks Road and 61st Avenue West.

Charter Fishing
There are more than 28 charter fishing companies operating out of Duluth harbor and surrounding ports, fishing for steelhead, salmon, trout and walleye. If nature and fish are what you're after — and unless you have your own boat, electronics, and knowledge of the open water — charter fishing is money well spent. Depending upon the time of year and day of the week, these angling sleuths can be booked solid. The charter season usually runs from April through October. It pays to make reservations early, especially when the salmon are running in the fall.

All **Charter Captains Association** members are licensed by the U.S. Coast Guard and the state of Minnesota. But there are also many independent charters and guides that can enhance your fishing experience on the big lake or in one of the 15 rivers funneling into Lake Superior.

Most charter operations offer comparably priced and outfitted fishing excursions. Depending upon the waters you're interested in, charter guides sport 14- to 40-foot boats that handle anywhere from one to six anglers. Most have years of experience and all the requisite deep sea necessities like U.S. Coast Guard safety equipment, marine radio, outriggers, cabin bathrooms, trolling gear, bait, tackle, radar, videograph-depth finders and a host of other electronic equalizers. Most of these charters are half-day and full-day expeditions,

Hurray! Minnesota

Public Golf Courses
Duluth's public courses each offer 27 holes of challenge. They are:
Enger Golf Course
1801 W. Skyline Parkway
(218) 722-5044
Lester Golf Course
1860 Lester River Road
(218) 525-1400

which are usually priced in the $200 and $400 range, respectively.

You're responsible for your own food, drink and clothing. Lake Superior creates its own weather patterns so expect anything at any time of the year. Most charters will refund your money if the weather is impossible. Also, bring an ice chest to pack your catch, which the crew will photograph, clean and dress.

You must have a Minnesota or Wisconsin fishing license and an appropriate fish stamp. Many captains sell these licenses. If not, they're for sale at bait and tackle shops and many other locations in and around Duluth.

As for details about the boats and the captain, if you really want to get the lowdown, write the North Shore Charter Captains Association at: Box 292, Duluth, MN 55801.

Spirit Mountain and Recreation Area
Boundary Ave., Exit 249 off Highway 35
(218) 628-2891
(800) 642-6377
Spirit Mountain has terrain for all types and levels of skiing. The downhill area boasts a 700-foot vertical drop and a high-speed quad chairlift, which is enclosed in case of inclement weather. There is a whole system of trails for the cross-country skier. There also is camping and hiking in the warmer months.

Boat Landings
Rice's Point
Under the Blatnik Bridge at the foot of Garfield Ave.
Munger Landing
At the base of Clyde Ave.
Boy Scout Landing
At the foot of Commonwealth Ave.

Park Point
At the base of Minnesota Ave.

Hiking Trails
Chester Park Trail
2.5 miles, challenging.
19th Ave. E. and Kent Road
Congdon Park Trail
1.5 miles, easy.
32nd Ave. E. and Superior St.
Kingsbury Creek Trail
1.3 miles, challenging.
7210 Fremont (above the zoo)
Lester Park Trail
.86 miles, easy.
E. Superior St. and Lester Park Road
Lincoln Park Trail
1.5 miles, easy.
25th Ave. W. and Third St.
Mission Creek Trail
3.25 miles, challenging.
Highway 23 and 131st Ave. W.
Park Point Trail
4 miles, easy.
Base of Minnesota Ave.
Western Waterfront Trail
5 miles, easy.
Grand Ave. and 72nd Ave. W.
Across from the zoo.

Shopping
Downtown
Bagley and Co.
315 W. Superior St.
(218) 727-2991
Bagley and Co. has been a part of downtown Duluth for more than a century. This historic gift shop features fine jewelry, china and gifts.
Explorations
127 W. Superior St.
Downtown Duluth
(218) 722-1651
If you come to Duluth with children, or happen to be shopping around for gifts for kids, this is your store. Explorations has a complete selection of toys, books, learning materials, tapes, records and other child-ready incidentals.
Holiday Center
207 W. Superior St.
There are a variety of shops in this two-level center, which is connected to the skyway system.

CANAL PARK
BRASS BED ANTIQUES
329 Canal Park Drive
(218) 722-1347
Just two blocks from Canal Park and the aerial lift bridge, Brass Bed Antiques deals in a wide assortment of antiques and collectibles. Free parking behind the building.

DEWITT-SEITZ MARKETPLACE
394 S. Lake Ave.
Canal Park
(218) 722-0047
Located in one of Duluth's beautifully restored historic warehouses and just one block from the aerial lift bridge, the DeWitt-Seitz Marketplace is a cornucopia of shops that cover the gamut from art, toys and chocolate to kitchen wares and greeting cards. There also are two wonderful cafes: the delightfully understated Lake Avenue Cafe and spicy Taste of Saigon.

DULUTH CAMERA EXCHANGE
321 S. Lake Ave.
Canal Park
(218) 722-0047
To capture your North Shore/Canal Park experience on film or video, here's the place to buy the camera and film, or have your film developed or videotape cartridge transferred in roughly the time it takes to have lunch.

EAST
FITGER'S BREWERY COMPLEX
600 E. Superior St.
(800) 777-8538
Fitger's is a restaurant, a hotel and also a great place to browse. The shops have one of the best views of the lake in the city, and there are plenty of windows to remind you just how close and magnificent Lake Superior really is. There are 14 shops that range from arts and crafts at Smiles Gift Shop to Christmas at Nana's.

MAINSTREET
4625 E. Superior St.
(218) 525-3755
Mainstreet is an artisans' marketplace. It has one of the region's largest selections of arts and crafts made by local artists as well as a host of Crabtree and Evelyn country home inspirations.

MILLER HILL MALL
Highway 53 at Trinity Road
(218) 727-8301

Glass Block, **Sears** and **Montgomery Ward** along with 110 smaller stores offer quite a selection. The remodeling done in 1987 nearly doubled the mall's size. There also is a three-screen cinema. Stroll the mall, grab a bite at the new food court and then view the latest movie, especially if Duluth's weather is not being cooperative.

EATING
AUGUSTINO'S PASTA, SEAFOOD AND STEAK HOUSE
Fitger's Brewery Complex
600 E. Superior St.
(218) 722-2787
Located below Fitger's Inn in the Fitger's Brewery Complex, Augustino's offers fine dining from a menu of both northern Italian and American cuisine and an excellent wine selection. There is a stellar view of Lake Superior and downtown Duluth from just outside on the lawn.

CHINESE LANTERN AND BRASS PHOENIX NIGHT CLUB
402 W. First St.
(218) 722-7486
Many regard the Chinese Lantern as being among the finest Chinese restaurants in Minnesota. Over the years it has developed a loyal following.

CONEY ISLAND DELUXE
112 W. First St.
(218) 722-2772
For half a century they've been serving some of the best Coney dogs, Greek gyros and assorted other Boardwalk and Greek fare right here in Duluth.

GRANDMA'S SALOON AND DELI
522 Lake Ave. S.
Canal Park
(218) 727-4192
Grandma's is an institution in Duluth and clearly a hot spot among both locals and tourists. It has location — right smack in the heart of Canal Park at the mouth of Duluth/Superior harbor, in the shadow of the aerial lift bridge — and serves up a bounty of fish, sandwich, steak and salad entrees. Despite the fact that Grandma's has two restaurants, a huge saloon, a deli, and even a dance club upstairs, there's often a wait. For the sports bar crowd

Hurray! Minnesota

there's **Grandma's Sports Garden** just across the street.

HOLIDAY CENTER
207 W. Superior St.
Porter's — Casual fine dining serving a complete menu. (218) 727-6746.
Porter's Pub — Sandwiches, burgers and snacks. (218) 722-1202.
The Grocery — Atrium-style cafe with European class and charm. Authentic French bread. (218) 727-3387.
Sneakers — Sports bar and grill. Serving gourmet burgers. Big screen TV. (218) 727-7494.

JOLLY FISHER RESTAURANT AND LOUNGE
W. Superior St. and Lake Ave.
(218) 722-4305
"If it swims, we have it." Fresh seafood featuring catch of the day and noon lunch specials.

KEMP'S FISH MARKET AND GRILL
11-15 Buchanan St.
(218) 727-4800
If it's fresh fish you want, this is the place.

LAKE AVENUE CAFE
DeWitt-Seitz Building
394 Lake Ave. S.
(218) 722-2355
The menu is inventive yet down to earth, the service exemplary and the food is all tantalizing. Lake Avenue Cafe serves homemade meals including sandwiches, pasta and chicken dishes as well as some real fine soups.

LOMBARDI'S CAFE
201 E. Superior St.
(218) 722-0190
Here's a place where you can get fresh pasta marinara, espresso and great service all for a rather palatable price. Lombardi's is one of Duluth's newest Italian restaurants.

NATCHIO'S GREEKTOWN
109 N. Second Ave. W.
(218) 722-6585
This has authentic cuisine and atmosphere, like a port town cafe in the Isles.

PICKWICK
508 E. Superior St.
(218) 727-8901
The Pickwick, just down the street from Fitger's, is a local favorite that many tourists have found. Consequently, there's often a wait during peak dinner and lunch hours. This place has been in the same family since 1914, so they've had plenty of time to perfect their mostly fish and steak fare. Relax, it's worth the wait.

SIR BENEDICT'S TAVERN ON THE LAKE
805 E. Superior St.
(218) 728-1192
A favorite spot for deli-style sandwiches served in an architecturally unique brick building built in 1939 as a Pure Oil gas station. Smoked chicken and ribs served on weekends. There are 120 different beers offered. Outdoor seating when weather permits.

TOP-OF-THE-HARBOR
Radisson Duluth
5th Ave. and Superior St.
(218) 727-8981
Located on the top of the Radisson, this revolving restaurant has excellent views of the Duluth harbor and surrounding hillside. Offering steaks, seafood and American cuisine, Top-of-the-Harbor is open for breakfast, lunch and dinner with daily specials.

LODGING

FITGER'S INN
600 E. Superior St.
Duluth, MN 55802
(218) 722-8826
This old brewery turned restaurant and inn is perched directly above Lake Superior, connected to Canal Park by the Lakewalk. Fitger's is old-world charm and elegance. The inn is a true experience in elegant lodging, with its character-steeped suites decorated in lace, linen and hardwoods and its restaurant, with the finest food and wine, sterling silver, and respectful protocol. It's also connected to a row of distinct arts and crafts shops. Fitger's has 48 rooms and six suites.

HOLIDAY INN DULUTH
207 W. Superior St.
Duluth, MN 55802
(218) 722-1202
The hotel has 350 rooms, two indoor pools, sauna and whirlpool. A sports bar, several restaurants and gift shops in the Holiday Center are adjacent to the hotel, which is connected to the Duluth Skyway.

RADISSON HOTEL
5th Ave. and Superior St.
Duluth, MN 55802
(218) 727-8981
(800) 333-3333
Blessed with a view of the harbor and situated in the heart of downtown Duluth, the Radisson is first-rate elegance. There are 268 rooms, an indoor pool, sauna, whirlpool and several fine restaurants, including the rooftop restaurant and lounge.

COMFORT SUITES
408 Canal Park
Duluth, MN 55802
(218) 727-1278 or (800) 228-5150
Situated right on the waterfront in the center of activity at Canal Park, there are 82 suites, all with microwaves and refrigerators. The facility has a pool and whirlpool.

PARK INN INTERNATIONAL
Duluth Lakeshore
250 Canal Park Drive
Duluth, MN 55802
(218) 727-8821
(800) 777-8560
This is a prime Canal Park location for strolling the waterfront and Canal Park but yet only a block away from the cobblestones of downtown Duluth. Park Inn, with 145 rooms, offers everything from stunning views of the harbor and downtown houses and businesses to accommodations that include luxury and family suites, sauna, indoor pool, hot tub, fine seafood and live music every night of the week.

THE MANSION
3600 London Road
Duluth, MN 55804
(218) 724-0739
Open from May to October.
Closed on Wednesdays.
Warren and Sue Monson are the proprietors of this beautifully restored 1930s bed and breakfast on Duluth's London Road. The Mansion is just down the road from Glensheen Mansion, and was built by Marjorie Congdon Dudley, a descendant of the Congdon family who built Glensheen. Perched on the shore of Lake Superior, the tailored lawns and towering trees frame a panoramic view of the lake.

There are 10 rooms in the main house and a three-bedroom apartment over the carriage house.

THE ELLERY HOUSE
28 S. 21st Ave. E.
Duluth, MN 55812
(218) 724-7639
Built in 1890 by Ellery C. Holiday, this is an elegant three-story Queen Anne Victorian. The Jeffries family, who moved in a few years after the home was built, was prominent in Duluth society in the early 1900s. Besides the wonderful ambience of the exquisitely-appointed rooms, this retreat also has lake views, antiques, fireplaces, full breakfast and room service. There are four guest rooms, all with private baths. The sleeping porch, a health fad during the tuberculosis scare, is now the sitting room for the three-room suite.

THE STANFORD INN
1415 E. Superior St.
Duluth, MN 55805
(218) 724-3044
This majestic 1886 Victorian estate is just blocks from Lake Superior in Duluth's historic district and pampers its guests with no less than a gourmet breakfast every morning. There are four rooms.

THE BARNUM HOUSE BED AND BREAKFAST
2211 E. Third St.
Duluth, MN 55812
(218) 724-5434
(800) 879-5437
Open all year.
Dave and Pam Wolff are the proprietors of this historic old turn-of-the-century B&B, once the home of one of Duluth's most respected benefactors, George Barnum, the man responsible for bringing the city its first passenger train. The Barnum House is nestled in a densely-wooded area of the historic east end. It has been refurbished to its original character and updated with modern conveniences. There are fireplaces, reading rooms, plenty of warm, cozy woodwork, and lots of wicker. There are five rooms with private baths.

MATTHEW S. BURROWS 1890 INN
1632 E. First St.
Duluth, MN 55812
(218) 724-4991

Hurray! Minnesota

Duluth's Aerial Lift Bridge is one of only two in the world.

▼ For More Information...

Duluth Convention and Visitors Bureau
100 Lake Place Drive
Duluth, MN 55802
(218) 722-4011
(800) 438-5884

Duluth Area Chamber of Commerce
118 E. Superior St.
Duluth, MN 55802
(218) 722-5501

Superior/Lester River Tourist Information Center
(218) 392-2773

Minnesota Office of Tourism Northeastern Regional Office
320 W. Second St.
Duluth, MN 55802
(218) 723-4692

General Information and Referral
(218) 727-2222
(800) 232-1300

Visitor Information For The Hearing/Speech-Impaired
(218) 722-4011 Voice/TDD
(800) 4-DULUTH Voice/TDD

Parks and Recreation Department
(218) 723-3337

U.S. Coast Guard
(218) 720-5412/720-5418

North Shore Bed and Breakfast Association
(800) 622-4014, ext. 4.

Back in 1890, Matthew S. Burrows, a famous clothier, built a splendid Victorian home in the hills overlooking Lake Superior as a cozy retreat. It was made into a B&B only a few years ago. This place has all the comforts plus big porches, stained glass windows, fireplaces, antiques, exquisite woodwork and ornate fixtures. Breakfast consists primarily of homemade breads, fruit, muffins, juice, coffee and tea. There are four rooms.

Camping

Jay Cooke State Park
500 E. Highway 210
Carlton, MN 55718
(218) 384-4610

Spirit Mountain
9500 Spirit Mountain Place
Boundary Ave., Exit 249 off Highway 35
(218) 628-2891
(800) 642-6377
Open May through October.

PHOTO BY STEPHEN HERRERA

Rock climbing on the North Shore provides thrilling vistas along with some of the highest vertical climbs in the state.

Notable climbs along the North Shore are Palisade Head, Shovel Point and Carlton Peak.

NORTH SHORE

THE SCENIC NORTH SHORE RUNS 160 miles along Lake Superior from Duluth to the Canadian border and is steeped in the history of commerce and trade. For the white man, this history dates back to the early 1700s; for the Indian, much further. The rivers and harbors of the North Shore were used to transport the furs of the wilderness, fish, timber, iron ore and grain. Today, though still a major route of transport, the North Shore has assumed the new role of providing access to nature at its finest and virtually unlimited recreation possibilities. Highway 61 along the North Shore provides access to more than 11 state parks and wayside rests.

The North Shore is best known for its magnificent scenic drive, including views of cliffs pounded by Lake Superior's crashing waves, gnarled trees, smooth shore rocks and tall pines. The North Shore can be experienced in the comfort of your car, with short walks along the rivers and picnics on the shore. Or it can be experienced at varying degrees of greater physical challenge by hiking or biking.

There is the **Superior Hiking Trail**, which is an interconnected trail through the parks from Two Harbors to the Canadian border. The trail runs parallel to the shore following the ridge line of the Sawtooth Mountains with views of the lake no less spectacular than from the highway. In the winter, it becomes a cross-country ski/snowshoe trail. You can make arrangements to ski or hike from lodge to lodge nearly all the way up the North Shore. There also are snowmobile, horseback riding and mountain biking trails along the shore and up a number of the rivers. Old Highway 61, between Duluth and Two Harbors, also has a beautiful biking lane.

Fishing along the many streams, the smaller lakes and Lake Superior is excellent. The **Cook County News-Herald** publishes several brochures with detailed information on the many different fishing opportunities. For more information contact the Cook County News-Herald, Box 757, Grand Marais, MN 55604, **(218) 387-1025**.

More information can be obtained about the facilities at the parks and along the North Shore from the Minnesota Office of Tourism **(612) 296-5029**. The **Lutsen-Tofte Tourism Association** publishes a nice little booklet twice a year called **"On the North Shore."** This can be obtained by writing the association at Box 2248, Tofte, MN 55615 or calling **(218) 663-7804**.

As you begin your drive up the North Shore from Duluth, you have a choice of directions. You can take the four-lane highway to Two Harbors or mosey up Old Highway 61. Both arrive at the same place. Your choice of paths depends on the amount of time you have to spend. The North Shore can be driven in a long day or deliciously savored over a week.

Old Highway 61 is a nice meander with lots of scenic views and stops. You can spend a whole afternoon just wandering with or without a picnic lunch, for there are a number of places to spread out your blanket or buy your lunch. Just past Two Harbors, the cliffs are a little steeper, the view may be considered a little more spectacular and it does begin to take on that wilderness aura. Short of time? Start meandering at Two Harbors.

EATING AND LODGING

SHORECREST SUPPER CLUB AND LOUNGE
5593 North Shore Drive
Duluth, MN 55804
(218) 525-2286
Serving steaks, seafood and light appetite specials. There also is a motel and cabins on the site.

DODGES LOG LODGES
5852 North Shore Drive
Duluth, MN 55804
(218) 525-4088
Located on scenic Highway 61 between

Two Harbors and Duluth, these six quaint log cabins sit right on the shore.

Shopping
Once Upon A Time
5103 North Shore Drive
Duluth
(218) 525-3029
This quaint little gingerbread house, resplendent in Victorian flavor, is packed wall-to-wall with knickknacks, collectibles and gifts for the home. There's a room full of the Minnesota experience and a plentiful array of Scandinavian arts, crafts and books. Open from April through December.

As you drive up the North Shore, the peaks and hills on your left are known as the Sawtooth Mountains. These worn-down volcanoes were formed billions of years ago at the same time as the basalt ridge and Superior Basin, which form the topography of the region. But Lake Superior was not really formed and filled with that clear cold water until relatively recently — only 10,000 years ago. This volcanic history makes rock collecting along the North Shore varied and rewarding. Keep your eyes open. You may find:
- **felsite** – red
- **rhyolite** – reddish and very fine grained
- **jaspar** – a very deep red
- **basalt** – gray or black
- **anorthosite** – transparent green
- **lintonite** – green
- **quartz** – white, pastel colors
- **thomsonite** – multi-colored (primarily pink, green and white). Gemstone quality thompsonite can be found in the Grand Marais-Lutsen area.
- **agate** – multicolored

Ever wonder why the rocks on the beach are relatively flat? It's the wave action. Waves bring them all up, but the round ones roll back in.

Knife River
Island View Resort
Box 25
Knife River, MN 55609
(218) 834-5886
Housekeeping cabins overlooking Lake Superior. Charter fishing and sightseeing tours available.

Two Harbors

Two Harbors is a friendly little North Shore community, founded in 1883, with a resident population under 4,000. For the tourist, this is a great place to pick up smoked salmon and cheese, Minnesota wild rice, freshly tapped maple syrup and clover honey.

However, it is still a port city, relying on commerce from the ore docks as much as tourism. In fact, outside of Duluth, Two Harbors is the most important ore shipping port in Minnesota. The twin ports of **Agate Bay** and **Burlington Bay**, which inspired the town's name, ship tons of ore every year from Iron Range mines.

Within the bay area you'll find the world's largest ore loading dock (more than 1,000 feet long), a moored 1895 tugboat named Edna G., a towering restored Mallet locomotive and a fascinating historical museum in the original turn-of-the-century depot.

Attractions
Lake County Historical Society Railroad Museum
The Depot at Agate Bay
Two Harbors
(218) 226-4372
To get a feel for the cultural and industrial heritage of this old logging, fishing and shipping town, take a detour to the Historical Museum at Agate Bay inside the old Duluth Mesabi and Iron Range Railroad Depot. There's plenty here for the train lover. Take a look at the giant Mallet locomotive, one of the world's most powerful at one time, and "Three Spot," the first steam engine to operate in Two Harbors, parked directly in front of the depot.

3M Dwan Museum
Waterfront Drive
Two Harbors
(218) 834-4898
Minnesota Mining and Manufacturing, more commonly known as 3M, was born in Two Harbors. The original office building was recently purchased by

3M and donated to the Historical Society for the museum. The Dwan Museum tells the history of sandpaper, the product that formed the cornerstone of 3M's present global enterprises.

THE WATERFRONT
At the east edge of Two Harbors in **Burlington Bay** is the **Paul H. Van Hoven Lake Front Park** and a campground. If it's been a warm summer, the water here in Burlington Bay is almost swimmable. At least for a short swim. You might find wading much more to your liking.

Viewed from Burlington Bay, the massive ore loading docks in Agate Bay are quite a sight. Next to the docks, in Agate Bay (check this bay, rock hunters!), is a good-sized public boat ramp operated by the Department of Natural Resources. There is no charge for launching your boat.

EDNA G. TUGBOAT
Retired, but still moored at the dock, is the Edna G. Named after the daughter of the president of the **DM&IR Railroad**, **J.L. Greatsinger**, this tugboat was built in 1896 by the **Cleveland Shipping Co.** specifically for the bay at Two Harbors. The bow is reinforced to deal with the icy waters of the bay. It is hoped the city council will soon be setting her up in dry dock for viewing. However, she currently affords a great photo opportunity. She has been in continuous service, except for a brief period from 1962 to 1966 when the port closed due to the slump in iron ore shipping. She was also commissioned for duty during World War I. The Edna G. was finally retired in 1982.

LIGHTHOUSE POINT AND HARBOR MUSEUM
(218) 834-4898
The lighthouse is still in active use. The harbor museum contains very interesting displays on the development of Two Harbors as an iron ore port. There also is a renovated pilot house from an ore boat that you can explore. There are fascinating exhibits on commercial fishing and another on shipwrecks, which could save you a lot of diving time. Quite a number of lakers have gone down in Superior over the years and their stories are engrossing. Open daily 9:30 a.m. to 6 p.m., Sunday through Thursday; closing at 8 p.m. Friday and Saturday, May through October. Open weekends, 10 a.m. to 5 p.m., November through April.

SHOPPING
BUDDY'S RICE
724 Seventh Ave.
Two Harbors
(218) 834-5823
Buddy has a broad assortment of Minnesota and Wisconsin wild rices, all grades of fresh-tapped maple syrup, and honey in all sizes from sampler up to gallon jugs. This little shop, right on the main street of Two Harbors, also has some incredible carved wood sculptures. This is a great slice of the North Shore.

EATING
BETTY'S PIES
215 Highway 61 E.
Two Harbors
(218) 834-3367
This is one of those places that just keeps getting better with time and tradition. Located just down the road from downtown Two Harbors, Betty's has been serving up some of the best homemade pies, wild rice soup and panfish plates on the North Shore for more than 30 years. Betty's is no secret to North Shore locals, so there may be a wait during peak lunch and dinner hours. Open May through October.

LODGING
SUPERIOR SHORES LODGE AND LAKE HOMES
Two Harbors, MN 55616
(800) 242-1988
This is a beautiful lodge secluded on a privately owned North Shore peninsula. There are rooms at the lodge or lake homes that feature fireplaces, a full kitchen and decks. There are outdoor and indoor pools, a spa and jacuzzi, tennis courts and a restaurant.

▼ FOR MORE INFORMATION...
TWO HARBORS AREA CHAMBER OF COMMERCE
Box 39
Two Harbors, MN 55616
(218) 834-2600

JUST NORTH OF Two Harbors is the first natural rock highway tunnel opened in the Midwest. Completed in November 1991, it was named the **Lafayette Tunnel** after the freighter that hit the rocks below during a November storm. The tunnel is part of a program to improve the safety, without destroying the dynamic beauty, of the 126-mile drive along the cliffs. It is 792 feet long, 55 feet wide and 28 feet high and is the most spacious mined tunnel in North America. Only the Alps has one higher and wider.

CASTLE DANGER

STAR HARBOR RESORT
1098 Highway 61
Castle Danger
(218) 834-3796

Star Harbor is reportedly the oldest resort on the North Shore. This delightful, relaxing compound of cabins, built in 1915, updated with handcrafted wood furnishings, spacious living rooms, plenty of windows, and the modern necessities, is truly luxury lodging with just enough rustic flavor to blend into the North Shore surroundings.

BOB'S CABINS ON LAKE SUPERIOR
WSR Box 101
Two Harbors, MN 55616
(218) 834-4583

With 1,000 feet of accessible shoreline and a spectacular view of Lake Superior, Bob's is a great place to hang your hat.

The Byrneses recently replaced the old cabins, built in 1919, with six new ones featuring lake view decks, fireplaces and full kitchens. Very rustic and very private. It is only minutes away from Gooseberry Falls and the Split Rock Lighthouse.

GOOSEBERRY FALLS STATE PARK
Highway 61
(218) 834-3855

Just 13 miles north of Two Harbors along scenic North Shore Highway 61 is Minnesota's famous Gooseberry Falls State Park. Gooseberry Park is 1,700 acres of wooded peaks and valleys, complete with an interpretive center, picnic tables, campsites, miles of marked hiking trails and, of course, the wild and scenic Gooseberry River that snakes through the park and over five waterfalls before reaching Lake Superior. The falls require, for the best vantage point, a short hike. But it's worth it, especially to see fall leaf colors.

SPLIT ROCK LIGHTHOUSE STATE PARK
2010 Highway 61 E.
(218) 226-4372

If you've ever seen a photograph of a North Shore lighthouse, chances are it was Split Rock, perched some 130 feet above the craggy Lake Superior shoreline 50 miles northeast of Duluth. Built in 1910, this 54-foot octagonal stone and steel tower, with its penetrating fog horn and revolving green signal, was a life-saving beacon to ship navigators. The official range of the light is 22 miles, but it has been spotted 60 miles away at Grand Marais. The lighthouse was decommissioned in 1969.

Many early freighters and fishing boats ran aground during storms and thick fog until lighthouses such as Split Rock were erected to warn them of perils ahead. Today Split Rock is on the National Register of Historic Places. Recently it went through an extensive restoration returning windows and color schemes to their original condition. To defray the cost of this restoration, there is a $3 admission charge for adults, $1 for children and senior citizens.

The museum is filled with Lake Superior maritime memorabilia and exhibits. There's a brief film on the history of this lighthouse and Lake Superior shipping, a tour, and the museum gift shop.

Since the lighthouse is located in a state park, you must have a parks permit to enter. Permits can be purchased at the gate and used at this park and other parks throughout the state: $4 for a day tag for your car or $18 for the year. State parks are open 8 a.m. to 10 p.m. year-round.

TETTEGOUCHE STATE PARK
474 Highway 61 E.
Silver Bay, MN 55614
(218) 226-3539

The park runs for one mile along Lake Superior. Within the park are four lakes and excellent salmon fishing along the Baptism River. There is a magnificent 80-foot waterfall on the Baptism River.

Hurray! Minnesota

Split Rock Lighthouse.

There are more than 14 miles of hiking and cross-country ski trails in the park plus an information center. Camping is available.

SILVER BAY GOLF COURSE
Silver Bay
(218) 226-3111
Nine-Hole

LITTLE MARAIS

STONE HEARTH INN
1118 Highway 61 E.
Little Marais, MN 55614
(218) 226-3020
Susan and Charlie Michels retained the 1920s atmosphere in this beautiful family homestead. The inn, nestled in a pungent grove of black spruce, has an old fashioned front porch with Adirondack chairs, perfect for contemplating the beautiful yard, which sits right on the water. There is a magnificent stone hearth fireplace and your hosts serve up a unique regional-cuisine — not your standard bacon and eggs — gourmet breakfast.

FENSTAD'S RESORT
1190 Highway 61 E., Dept. 6
Little Marais, MN 55614
(218) 226-4724
Housekeeping cabins along the lake. Open all year.

CARIBOU FALLS

THERE ARE HIKING trails and fishing at this small roadside park, which actually is part of the larger George H. Crosby Manitou State Park.

CROSS RIVER

THIS WAYSIDE REST is part of the Temperance River Park.

TEMPERANCE RIVER STATE PARK
(218) 663-7476
The spectacular Temperance River gorge is famous for its bare rock cliffs and potholes. There are good hiking trails for stretching your legs or really trucking. A picnic area and camping are available.

TOFTE

ROCK COLLECTORS, on **Good Harbor Bay** and **Agate Beach** in Tofte you might find one of those Lake Superior agates or thompsonites.

The scenic **Sawbill Trail** (Highway 2) heads out of Tofte and travels 50 miles up into the Superior National Forest to Sawbill Lake and campground. There are good views of the Temperance River.

BAYSIDE GIFT SHOP
Bluefin Bay
Tofte
(218) 663-7296
Loaded with local arts, crafts and jewelry, Bayside also has a fine selection of T-shirts and sweatshirts.

BLUEFIN RESTAURANT
Tofte
(218) 663-7296
Fresh fish, good service, plenty of wild rice and a room with a view. This is North Shore dining at its finest.

BLUE FIN BAY ON LAKE SUPERIOR
Highway 61
Tofte, MN 55615
(218) 663-7296
(800) BLUE FIN (258-3346)
The Blue Fin has been called the most romantic resort on Lake Superior. This cozy resort is in a spectacular location. Treat yourself to the ambience of a relaxing private whirlpool and warm crackling fire while waves lap at the shore and sea gulls soar above. Its two restaurants have been noted as "worth the drive" by Mpls./St. Paul magazine. The 87 units at Blue Fin have a centrally located indoor pool, sauna, whirlpool and spa. Boat tours and charter fishing can be arranged.

CHATEAU LEVEAUX
Box 115
Tofte, MN 55615
(218) 663-7223
(800) 445-5773
The Chateau has three motel rooms and 31 condominiums complete with kitchen and fireplace. All units have a view across the lawn of the lake. A pool, sauna, whirlpool and game room are centrally located.

RAY BERGLAND STATE WAYSIDE PARK
Trails, fishing and picnic facilities.

LUTSEN

LUTSEN IS OFTEN considered the playground of the North Shore. Located here is some of the best downhill skiing in the Midwest in winter and many of the larger resorts. In summer you can rent just about any piece of recreational equipment, plus there's the alpine slide and gondola rides on Lutsen Mountain.

Olympic star **Cindy Nelson**, who won a bronze medal for the downhill event in Alpine skiing in the 1976 Olympics, learned to ski here at Lutsen. She is the granddaughter of Charles Axel Nelson, who established Lutsen Resort in 1885.

ATTRACTIONS
LUTSEN MOUNTAINS GONDOLA RIDES AND ALPINE SLIDE
Box 128, County Road 36
Lutsen, MN 55612
(218) 663-7281
High above Superior National Forest in one of Lutsen's spectacular gondolas you can see for miles. When you reach the top there's a picnic experience awaiting you that beats a city park any day. If you're looking for something a little more hair-raising, try the alpine slide: a thrilling half-mile toboggan run that is safe for all ages. There also are mountain bikes and horses for rent here. Open mid-May through mid-October.

LUTSEN MOUNTAIN SKI AREA
Box 128, County Road 36
(218) 663-7281
Situated in the pine and birch woods of Superior National Forest, Lutsen has warm gondolas with a view, 1,500 acres of terrain, a vertical drop of nearly 1,000 feet, an awesome view of Lake Superior and clearly the best skiing in the Midwest. There are 27 runs spread over four mountains. There are four double chairs, a t-bar and the gondola to get you up the mountain. There are two restaurants with bars, one at Village Chalet and the other at Gondola Base Chalet. The mountain also has all the accompanying services, such as rentals, ski schools, ski shops and repair. Open late November to early April.

FAT TIRE TOURING
Lutsen
(218) 226-4724
Offering bicycle rentals and just what it takes to outfit and send you on a two-wheeled journey. There's also a shuttle service.

GOLF COURSES
LUTSEN ON LAKE SUPERIOR
(800) 346-1467
(218) 663-7212
This 18-hole championship golf course, designed by Don Herfort, has it all: the beauty of Lake Superior, the backdrop of the Sawtooth Mountain ridge and the roaring Poplar River. Lutsen is a wonderful experience, even if your golf score isn't.

LUTSEN GOLF COURSE
Lutsen
(218) 663-7863
Par 3, Nine-hole.

SHOPPING
CLEARVIEW GENERAL STORE
Lutsen
(218) 663-7478
If you need some last-minute provisions, this is your stop.

LUTSEN MOUNTAIN SHOP
Lutsen Mountain
(218) 663-7842
You'll find a great collection of outdoor gear. When you're done shopping, wander upstairs and examine the current display of local and regional art in the Sivertson Gallery.

KAH-NEE-TAH GALLERY
Highway 61 between Lutsen and Grand Marais
Grand Marais
(218) 387-2585
Kah-Nee-Tah exhibits a revolving collection of North Shore pottery, art, sculpture and stained glass.

LODGING
VILLAGE INN AND RESORT AT LUTSEN MOUNTAIN
County Road 36
Lutsen, MN 55612
(218) 663-7241
(800) 642-6036
The feel of an alpine village with the advantages of a resort. Choose from rooms at the inn or condos with loft, full kitchen, fireplace and deck. The Village is an all-season resort with tennis, hiking and swimming in the summer, downhill and cross-country skiing and snowshoeing in the winter.

LUTSEN RESORT
Box 9
Lutsen, MN 55612
(218) 663-7212
(800) 346-1467
One of the grandest of them all on the North Shore is Lutsen Resort. It is the oldest resort on record in the state. The resort was first established in 1885 by **Charles Axel Nelson**. There are all the

EATING
THE VILLAGE INN RESTAURANT AND SALOON
Box 87
Lutsen
(218) 663-7316
Located at the lodge on Lutsen Mountain.

LUTSEN RESORT DINING ROOM
Lutsen Resort
Lutsen
(218) 663-7212
The dining room has windows overlooking Lake Superior. Good home cooking is served at breakfast, lunch and dinner.

BETH'S FUDGE
Lutsen
(218) 663-7550
T-shirts, swim gear, assorted North Shore collectibles and, of course, mouth-watering fudge are featured at Beth's.

regular amenities of a resort, such as pool, sauna, tennis courts and championship golf, plus you can rent kayaks for exploring the North Shore coastline and bays, mountain bikes for Superior National Forest and a host of other recreational equipment. There are 100 units, either rooms or villas, a conference center and restaurant.

SOLBAKKEN RESORT
HCR-3, Box 170
Lutsen, MN 55612
(218) 663-7566
Perched on the North Shore hillside overlooking the vast expanse of Lake Superior, the luxurious Solbakken offers motel, cabin and lake-home accommodations. This resort also has a wonderful library to indulge in when you're not out playing.

LINDGREN'S BED AND BREAKFAST
Box 56
Lutsen, MN 55612
(218) 663-7450
Shirley Lindgren is the proprietor of this beautiful 1920s log home done in rustic knotty cedar. A hearty gourmet breakfast is served near the massive stone fireplace in the great room overlooking Lake Superior. The room is decorated with hunting trophies and a beautiful baby grand. There are four individually decorated sleeping rooms.

Caribou Trail (County Road 4) out of Lutsen is a designated scenic route that leads to Brule Lake, roughly 40 miles away. There is an access to the Boundary Waters Canoe Area Wilderness (BWCAW) from here.

Cascade River State Park is the place to be when the Chinook salmon run in the fall. There also are hiking trails, picnic grounds and camping. Call (218) 387-1543.

▼ **FOR MORE INFORMATION...**
LUTSEN/TOFTE TOURISM ASSOCIATION
Box 2248
Tofte, MN 55615
(218) 663-7804

GRAND MARAIS

LOCATED IN COOK COUNTY, Grand Marais is 110 miles northeast of Duluth on the North Shore of Lake Superior. According to the 1990 census, Grand Marais has a population of 1,171. Grand Marais is a final destination as well as a stopover point for hunting, fishing and canoeing expeditions in the surrounding **Superior National Forest** and **Boundary Waters Canoe Area Wilderness**. Also, the famous **Gunflint Trail** begins right here in the middle of town.

Grand Marais is a lively spot for people of all ages. Depending on the season, you can see camera-toting tourists snapping away at the seaplanes that fly into Grand Marais harbor, BWCAW-bound canoe enthusiasts indulging in one last taste of civilization at the donut shop or at **Sven and Ole's** restaurant, sled dog teams, skiers or friendly roughnecks from the logging camps.

Grand Marais, sandwiched between Superior and the north woods, has been an important outpost for years, beginning with the 17th century Voyageurs. These early visitors to the area used to purchase provisions here before heading off into the heart of the woods in search of beaver. Even though fur traders and postmaster **Richard B. Godfrey** set up a camp here in 1854, it wasn't until 1903 that settlers finally braved the long journey and difficult winter. During this century, Grand Marais, French for "big marsh," was mostly a logging town. In the 1960s, with the establishment of the BWCAW, it began attracting individuals who took advantage of homesteading opportunities around this beautiful area. The complexion of the town is mixed between logging, sports and recreation, and tourism.

Grand Marais, with its picturesque harbor and peninsula jutting out into the vast expanse of Lake Superior, is also the North Shore city of choice for artists searching for inspiration. Grand Marais has an active artists' colony, giving the town a distinctly creative aura. And, though the locals will disagree, unlike other towns of this size, there's also plenty of nightlife here.

Hurray! Minnesota

ATTRACTIONS

COOK COUNTY MUSEUM
First and Wisconsin streets
Grand Marais
This quaint little museum, housed in a building built in 1896, takes you back to the early days of Grand Marais when timber and trapping were the languages spoken and people had to test their mettle every winter to survive until spring thaw. It also examines how the local culture and landscape have changed over the years with the advent of mass transportation and tourism. Open May through October.

BIRCH TERRACE LOUNGE
Sixth Ave. W.
on Highway 61
Grand Marais
(218) 387-2215
For a bit of northwoods nightlife this place is great. There are lots of windows, good live music and atmosphere, from the bar to the cozy fireplace.

HARBOR LIGHT
Highway 61
Grand Marais
(218) 387-1142
Live music and lots of room on the dance floor make this a popular night spot for locals as well as for those who might have been out in the woods too long.

ARLEIGH JORGENSON DOG SLEDDING
Box 667, Star Route 1
Grand Marais
(218) 387-2498
When this crew isn't training for the Beargrease Sled Dog Marathon from Duluth to Grand Portage, they're taking guests out into Superior National Forest on dog sled expeditions. This is a year-round passion for Jorgenson, who has been running dogs for more than 20 years. In the summer, Jorgenson conducts seminars, demonstrations and rides with a team of 18-20 dogs using a specially designed cart.

EATING

ANGRY TROUT CAFE
Grand Marais Harbor
Grand Marais
(218) 387-1265
The Angry Trout provides an incredible meal of sandwiches, soups and some of the sweetest desserts around. The specialty of the house is fish and chips, which taste particularly good while you're sitting on the deck looking out over Grand Marais Harbor.

SVEN AND OLE'S AND THE PICKLED HERRING
9 W. Wisconsin St.
Grand Marais
(218) 387-1713
You've no doubt heard about Sven and Ole's. It's the place with the Scandinavian flavor. Actually, the flavor here is primarily found in the pizza and hot sandwiches, which are the big sellers. The interior is cozy, almost diner style. Sven and Ole's is worth a stop just to say you've been there. Don't forget to ask about the Uffda Zah and Lena's pastries. Upstairs is the Pickled Herring Club, which has a great selection of bottled and tap beer.

BLUE WATER CAFE
Corner of Wisconsin and First streets
Grand Marais
(218) 387-1597
This place is just a few steps up from the harbor, so it's a great place to have lunch and watch the seaplanes land and take off. It's the sort of place that serves a great cup of soup, sandwich, or meat and potatoes meal. Local residents gather here to "catch up."

OUTFITTERS

SINCE GRAND MARAIS is a launching point for canoe, hunting, fishing and dog sled journeys, it has many outfitters. All are basically competitive in pricing and offerings. What separates them most is the degree of knowledge of various parts of the BWCAW, Quetico and Superior National Forest. Most outfitters are experienced and can share the kind of information that makes the difference between a safe, fulfilling trip and a miserable ordeal. Don't be afraid to ask plenty of questions about any trip you may want to plan. (See the Gunflint Trail section for more outfitters.)

Bear Track Outfitting Co.
Highway 61
Grand Marais
(218) 387-1162

Located on the southern edge of Grand Marais, Bear Track Outfitting has it all: great canoes, plenty of camping gear, bait and tackle, and BWCAW advice on where to spot moose, catch northerns and walleye and find trailside raspberry thickets. Bear Track also has a group of rustic cabins for rent just inland from the shop.

Northwind Sailing
Box 973
Grand Marais Harbor
Grand Marais
(218) 387-1265

If you feel the waters of Lake Superior calling to you, this is the place to make your move. Northwind has charter sailboats ranging in size from 26 to 43 feet for day excursions or for overnight trips to the beautiful Isle Royale. Or you can book an excursion aboard the **Sawtooth Mountain Ferry**, a 26-foot motor launch. Northwind Sailing is run by the same folks who run the **Angry Trout Cafe**, so stop at the Angry Trout to inquire about charter sailing opportunities. Open May 20 through October 1.

Shopping

Lake Superior Trading Post
Located on the harbor
Grand Marais
(218) 387-2020

This fort-like trading post has the stuff you'll need for an extended stay in the BWCAW or just a walk along the shore of Grand Marais harbor. There's also a gift shop with locally inspired arts and crafts and other impulse shopping knickknacks.

The Edge Gallery
107 Wisconsin St.
Grand Marais
(218) 387-1752

Owner, jeweler and artist Stephan Hoglund uses beautiful indigenous stones, such as thompsonite and Lake Superior agate, to create some of the most unique gold and silver jewelry on the North Shore. He sells artwork by local artists and has an evolving collection of select works from Russian artist Aleksei Ivanov, who has actually lived and worked in Grand Marais.

Lodging

Cascade Lodge and Restaurant
Box 490
Grand Marais, MN 55604
(218) 387-1112
(800) 322-9543

The Cascade has a variety of ways for guests to get back to nature. The pristine surroundings adjoin **Cascade River State Park**. Guests have a choice of private cabins or the main lodge with its mammoth moosehead. There's snowshoeing, ice fishing, cross-country skiing and snowmobiling and, of course, hiking, fishing, canoeing and mountain bike riding. Cascade Lodge has been featured in Country Inns and America's Wonderful Little Inns and Hotels.

Harbor Inn Restaurant and Motel
Box 669
Grand Marais, MN 55604
(218) 387-1191
(800) 245-5806

Great rooms overlooking the harbor. The restaurant serves breakfast, lunch and dinner with lunch and dinner specials every day. Open May through October.

East Bay Hotel
Box 246
Grand Marais, MN 55604
(218) 387-2800

This delightful historic hotel in downtown Grand Marais has a very comfortable front porch. Clearly the best view of the lake can be found in the East Bay dining room. A great setting for great food.

Bally Creek Camp
State Road 158
Grand Marais, MN 55604
(218) 387-1162

Bally Creek is a rustic cabin experience for the traveler who wants to shed all the trappings of modern civilization and really get back to the basics. There's no running water, no phone and no electricity, only wood-fueled stoves for warmth. Bally Creek is a perfect place to stay before and after BWCAW trips. The camp is six miles inland from Highway 61 on the south edge of Grand Marais.

GRAND MARAIS RECREATION AREA
Box 62
Grand Marais, MN 55604
(218) 387-1712
These grounds feature 300 campsites, RV hookups, trailer parking, and a nearby marina complete with a fuel station. Beautiful indoor pool with sauna, whirlpool and wading pool operated year-round. Open May through October.

▼ FOR MORE INFORMATION...

TIP OF THE ARROWHEAD ASSOCIATION
Box 1048
Grand Marais, MN 55604
(218) 387-2020

HOVLAND

Arrowhead Trail (Route 16), out of Hovland, is a designated scenic drive, though it is 36 miles of gravel. It leads into the BWCAW and terminates at the Canadian border.

NANIBOUJOU LODGE AND RESTAURANT
HC 1, Box 505
Grand Marais, MN 55604
(218) 387-2688
About 15 miles east of Grand Marais on Highway 61 lies one of the most sought-after resorts on the North Shore. It was originally built in 1929 as a private resort. It is on the National Register of Historic Places. The rooms range in character from basic to luxurious. Many of the larger suites upstairs are rooms with a view of Lake Superior and a fireplace. The main dining area is also quite grand with a 10- by 20-foot stone fireplace. The Naniboujou sits on some gorgeous North Shore terrain with plenty of beach to stroll. The restaurant is excellent, serving local dishes with lots of fresh fruit and vegetables, walleye, wild rice and heavenly sauces.

KODANCE RIVER STATE ROADSIDE PARK
Trails to stretch your legs and pools in the river for fishing.

JUDGE C. MAGNEY STATE PARK
(218) 387-2929
The 4,500 acres of forests and the Brule River provide camping, picnicking, hiking and fishing. Here the Brule River divides into two branches. One branch visibly flows over a falls and on into Lake Superior. The other branch flows into the **Devil's Kettle**, a pothole into which the water "disappears." Many a Ping-Pong ball has been tossed into the Kettle, never to be seen again.

GRAND PORTAGE

THE NORTH SHORE view doesn't get any better than this. Close to the Canadian border, Grand Portage exhibits the best of the Lake Superior shoreline and the great north woods. It also is a launching point to Isle Royale, the BWCAW and the southern forests of Ontario.

Grand Portage started as a fishing village in 1730 and evolved by 1778 into a trading post for the **Northwest Co.** Grand Portage was reportedly the first permanent white settlement in the state. The settlers were merchants living off the fur trade and bounty of the Voyageurs. The Voyageurs traveled throughout the north woods by canoe, collecting the rich furs and mapping the territory.

Every year the Voyageurs would hold a summer festival called the Rendezvous and trade with the Cree, Ojibwa and various traveling salesmen. It was designed both as a celebration and a swap meet for supplies and furs. In honor of that festival, modern-day Grand Portage holds its own Rendezvous Days and Powwow every year celebrating the Voyageur heritage with dancing, reveling, ax-throwing contests, birch-bark canoe races and Indian leg wrestling. (See Minnesota Festivals and Events.)

Our Lady of the Rosary Catholic Church, built in 1865, is the original tamarack log church under the plaster. The parish, founded as a mission in 1839, is the oldest Roman Catholic parish in Minnesota.

ACTIVITIES
TRAIL CENTER
Grand Portage
(800) 232-1384
For more information on the more than 100 miles of hiking trails through the Grand Portage Indian reservation.

GRAND PORTAGE STATE PARK
This is Minnesota's freshman state park, having been inaugurated in 1991. The highlight of this new Arrowhead destination is 94-foot Big Falls on the Pigeon River, which divides Minnesota from Ontario. It is the state's highest falls. For more information about facilities as they open, call the DNR Information Center in St. Paul at **(800) 652-9747**.

GRAND PORTAGE CASINO
Box 306
Grand Portage, MN 55605
(800) 232-1384
There are direct pay gaming machines, blackjack and bingo.

LODGING
GRAND PORTAGE LODGE AND RESTAURANT
Box 306
Highway 61
Grand Portage, MN 55605
(218) 475-2401
(800) 232-1384
Adjacent to Grand Portage Casino, this resort certainly doesn't lack beautiful surroundings, character or ambience. It has history, lake views and superior facilities that include dining, tennis, sauna, a banquet room, and easy access to everything from cross-country ski trails in the winter to cycling trails in the summer. There are more than 100 guest rooms, so Grand Portage Lodge is big enough to handle large meetings and gatherings. Grand Portage also provides Isle Royale boat service and charter fishing out of the marina.

GRAND PORTAGE NATIONAL MONUMENT/WITCH TREE
Highway 61
Grand Portage
This famous 400-year-old tree thrives stoically on the rocky cliffs of the North Shore, inspiring artists from around the globe. However, you won't find in all of this art the depth of feeling evoked by a personal visit. The Witch Tree is sacred to the local Cree and Ojibwa and is soon to be turned over to the Lake Superior Band of Chippewa Indians to become a permanent part of their lands.

The national monument, built from a reconstructed fur-trading post, pays tribute to the days of the 18th century when this land was nothing more than marsh, trees and lakes. You can tour inside the fort with authentically dressed guides. Be sure to visit the Great Hall and the canoe warehouse.

Boasting the best natural harbor on the North Shore, Grand Portage Bay, Grand Portage National Monument marks the "great carrying place," the 8 1/2-mile trail that took the Voyageurs and their canoes to the Pigeon River and the beginning of the 1,000-mile water trade route now called the Boundary Waters Canoe Area Wilderness (BWCAW).

Hurray! Minnesota

Annual Grand Portage Powwow.

ISLE ROYALE

ISLE ROYALE IS the largest island in Lake Superior. Though closer to Minnesota, the island is really a part of the state of Michigan and is under its jurisdiction.

The island is 45 miles long and seven miles wide. The island was of interest to both the Indian and white man because of its copper deposits, though it was never profitably mined. You may have heard of it in reference to the balance of nature studies conducted on the wolf and moose populations. These studies were possible because of the island's isolation.

The island is now a national park and maintained by the federal government. There are camping sites and hiking trails to take around the island. It can be reached by boat or float plane from Grand Portage. It is a 22-mile trip and takes three hours by boat. Reservations for transport are needed and can be made at a number of places, such as Grand Portage National Monument, Sivertson's Isle Royale Excursions **(218) 728-1237** or Northwind Sailing **(218) 387-1265**. Camping permits can be obtained from any federal ranger station or call **(218) 387-2788**. Open mid-May to October.

▼ **FOR MORE INFORMATION...**

TIP OF THE ARROWHEAD ASSOCIATION
Box 1048
Grand Marais, MN 55604
(218) 387-2524
(800) 622-4014

GRAND PORTAGE AREA INFORMATION
Box 307
Grand Portage, MN 55605
(800) 232-1384

The Gunflint Trail and BWCAW

THE GUNFLINT TRAIL IS A THUMB of land surrounded by the Boundary Waters Canoe Area Wilderness (BWCAW). If you love nature, water, camping, fishing and canoeing, it doesn't get any better than this. Anywhere. The BWCAW is 1.1 million acres of pristine lakes, rivers, streams and wilderness. Most lakes are dotted with islands. Black bear, moose, loons, deer and eagles are just a sample of the wildlife you might encounter. It's still possible to paddle for days without seeing or hearing another human being. And if that's not enough, at night the Northern Lights often put on a brilliant display of night light and shimmering colors.

The thousands of BWCAW lakes are connected by streams and portage trails. These woods and lakes have been traveled for hundreds of years in much the same way, first by Indians and then by fur traders and trappers. To traverse the densely wooded land of marsh and woods, campers portage their canoe and gear from lake to lake via portage trails. The landscape is mapped out in fine detail. There are designated campsites throughout the BWCAW that provide a clearing for tents and a fire pit for overnight stopovers.

A quota system during the summer keeps the BWCAW sparsely populated, so make your permit reservation with the Forest Service as early as possible. Permits are free but there is a $5 reservation charge. Keep in mind that if the route or lake you had hoped for is booked, there are 1,500 miles of canoe routes. The BWCAW borders with the Quetico, a continuation of the wilderness area only under Canadian jurisdiction. If in your chosen route you will be crossing the border, you must either pass through a customs checkpoint or obtain a Remote Area Border Crossing Permit from the Canadian Immigration Service. The Gunflint Trail provides numerous places to "put-in" (meaning begin your wilderness excursion), whether it is by canoe, skis, snowshoes, dog sled or on foot. There are no motorized vehicles permitted in the wilderness area. The basic formula for success in the BWCAW is to plan ahead for the elements, pack light, and bring a compass, small flashlight and a spare map. Also, don't forget your camera (with a Ziploc bag for film) and binoculars. Outfitters supply maps, route suggestions, canoe-towing, fly-in possibilities and permits. There are plenty of books on BWCAW routes and canoeing fundamentals.

Justine Kerfoot, a pioneer of the Gunflint Trail, is well-known for her books "Woman of the Boundary Waters" and "Gunflint: Reflections on the Trail," a collection of anecdotes about the region. Both are great take-along reading for the trail. Born in 1907, Kerfoot has been on the Gunflint her entire life. Her parents, and then she, ran the Gunflint Lodge. In addition to being an author, she has been a county commissioner, Republican party delegate, conservationist, canoe guide and is a great-grandmother.

Attractions
Gunflint Hills Golf Course
Four miles up the Gunflint Trail
(218) 387-9988
If you don't mind an occasional wildlife hazard or losing a few golf balls, this is a beautiful golf course in its wilderness splendor.

Hiking Trails
There are more than 33 trails of various length off the Gunflint Trail. The two major routes are: the Kekekabic Trail, which travels through the BWCAW to Ely; and the Border Route Trail, travel-

Hurray! Minnesota

ing from Grand Portage to the head of the Kekekabic trail.

There are numerous short stretch-your-legs trails along the Gunflint, such as the 10-minute hike to Honeymoon Rock on a bluff overlooking Hungry Jack Lake. Another short hike is to the marker for the Laurentian Divide at the overlook on Birch Lake. The waters flowing down the east side of this watershed flow into the Atlantic through the Great Lakes. Waters on the west side of the Divide flow into Hudson Bay.

EAGLE MOUNTAIN
Gunflint Trail
Located right on the fringe of the BWCAW, Eagle Mountain is the highest point in the state. The hike to the top is fairly easy, with wonderful flora and fauna along the way. Don't expect a typical view from the top. These woods are so dense and the surrounding terrain so similar that Eagle Mountain's allure lies mostly in the satisfaction of knowing that you've made it to the 2,300-foot peak after starting in Grand Marais at roughly 600 feet above sea level.

ARCHAEOLOGICAL DIG
On the shore of East Bearskin Lake in the BWCAW, about 23 miles north of Grand Marais, is an archaeological dig sponsored by the Superior National Forest and the University of Minnesota-Duluth. The dig has been open to visitors and is on the site of a Paleo-Indian camp dating back roughly 10,000 years.

EATING

POPLAR LAKE LODGE RESTAURANT
500 Gunflint Trail
Grand Marais, MN 55604
(218) 388-2214
Open seven days a week from 7 a.m. to 9 p.m. Good food at reasonable prices. Featuring burgers and thick malts as well as dinners of walleye and juicy steaks.

NOR'WESTER LODGE
Poplar Lake, Gunflint Trail
Grand Marais, MN 55604
(218) 388-2252
(800) 992-4FUN

Catching northern in the BWCAW.

The beautiful, historic log dining room sets the atmosphere for this wonderful lodge on the Gunflint. There are secluded lakefront cabins, a sand beach and playground for the kids, hiking trails, campground and canoe outfitting. Open all year.

ROCKWOOD LODGE AND OUTFITTERS
625 Gunflint Trail
Grand Marais, MN 55604
(218) 388-2242
(800) 942-2922
The **Gaslight Dining Room** has a beautiful view of Poplar Lake. It is the only fine dining on the Gunflint. The dress is casual. The restaurant features homemade breads, pastries, soups and desserts. The lodge also has 11 housekeeping cabins.

THE LOON LAKE LODGE
710 Gunflint Trail
Grand Marais, MN 55604
(218) 388-2232
(800) 552-6351
Serving breakfast and dinner family style. Reservations required.

PHOTO BY TIM A. BOGENSCHUTZ

THE GUNFLINT PINES
755 Gunflint Trail
Grand Marais, MN 55604
(218) 388-4454
(800) 533-5814
The Pines serves snacks, pizza and hot dogs at the lodge all day. There are six housekeeping cabins, 18 campsites, small store, marina and mountain bike rental.

SEA ISLAND LODGE RESTAURANT
On Sea Gull Lake
925 Gunflint Trail
Grand Marais, MN 55604
(218) 388-2261
(800) 346-8906
Delicious home-style dinners in a warm, welcoming north-woods dining room. The menu features homemade breads and soups. Entrees include fish, chicken, ribs and steaks. There are four housekeeping cabins.

LODGING
BEARSKIN LODGE
275 Gunflint Trail
Grand Marais, MN 55604
(218) 388-2292
(800) 338-4170
The lodge is located on East Bearskin Lake just a holler away from the BWCAW. This old lodge has been spruced up and modernized into a year-round resort. There are 12 housekeeping accommodations, private boat docks, the Hot Tub Hus and all the BWCAW recreational opportunities. The dining room in the main lodge serves family-style meals.

GOLDEN EAGLE LODGE
325 Gunflint Trail
Grand Marais, MN 55604
(218) 388-2203
(800) 346-2203
This is a resort for the family on Flour Lake. There are 10 housekeeping cabins on the secluded lake shore. Two of the cabins are barrier-free for people with disabilities. There is a full-time naturalist on staff in the summer along with all the other wilderness activities.

CLEARWATER LODGE AND CANOE OUTFITTERS
355-R Gunflint Trail
Grand Marais, MN 55604
(218) 388-2254
(800) 527-0554
This log lodge is on the National Register of Historic Places. Three-quarters of Clearwater Lake is in the BWCAW and this is the only lodge on the lake. Clearwater offers complete and professional outfitting so you can start your BWCAW experience right from here after a good night's sleep and a hearty breakfast. There are six cabins on the lake and five B&B rooms. Open May to October.

HUNGRY JACK CANOE OUTFITTERS AND CABINS
434 Gunflint Trail
Grand Marais, MN 55604
(218) 388-2275
(800) 648-2922
If you want to make your start deep in the heart of the BWCAW, Hungry Jack is a great place to rent your canoe and pick up bait, tackle and maps. They have a bunkhouse, a Saganaga Lake tow service that can save you paddling time and offer plenty of good tips on fishing holes. The Gateway restaurant serves breakfast, lunch and dinner. Reservations required. Open May to October.

YOUNG'S ISLAND BED AND BREAKFAST
590 Gunflint Trail
Grand Marais, MN 55604
(218) 388-4487
(800) 322-8327
Wake up in a 60-year-old split log home on a private 18-acre island to baked eggs and homemade muffins or an outstanding French toast with praline ice cream in the recipe. There's only one room for rent here but the Youngs also have accommodations in a secluded cabin next to the BWCAW. In addition, the Youngs operate a yurt-to-yurt ski-touring program and participate in the Gunflint Trail's winter lodge-to-lodge ski program. For the record, a yurt is a canvas-covered structure on a wood platform with a fireplace and skylight. On a cold winter's day, it's like a cozy cocoon.

GUNFLINT LODGE
750 Gunflint Trail
Grand Marais, MN 55604
(218) 388-2294
(800) 328-3325
Bruce and Sue are the third generation of Kerfoots to operate the Gunflint Lodge, a family resort with wilderness

Hurray! Minnesota

activities to please everyone. Thanks to the resident fishing pro, his staff of eight professional fishing guides and a fleet of boats, the lodge has one of the best programs for fishermen. There are 24 cabins, either housekeeping or American plan. The dining room serves breakfast, lunch and dinner to the public. Reservations are needed for dinner. Menus feature specials and your choice of chicken, fish or steak.

BORDERLAND LODGE
855 Gunflint Trail
Grand Marais, MN 55604
(218) 388-2233
(800) 451-1667
The Borderland Lodge, an all-season resort located on the north end of Gunflint Lake, maintains one of the largest private ski-trail systems in the state with more than 60 miles of groomed and mapped trails. Gunflint Lake has some of the best fishing around and the lodge has the people to help you find the big ones, including maps, bait and tackle recommendations. There are villas, cabins, and the new Cedar Hus cabins for a total of 13 units, all with full kitchens, private baths and lake views.

TUSCARORA LODGE AND CANOE OUTFITTERS
870 Gunflint Trail
Grand Marais, MN 55604
(218) 388-2221
(800) 544-3843
Owners Jim and Ann Leeds have everything here for the traveler: five cozy units, day trips to the BWCAW and Quetico, canoes, touring gear, bait, tackle and licenses. The Tuscarora also has a nice gift shop filled with local crafts and assorted knickknacks.

WAY OF THE WILDERNESS
Canoe Outfitter, Trading Post and Campground
947 Gunflint Trail
Grand Marais, MN 55604
(218) 388-2212
(800) 346-6225
Located at the end of the trail, Way of the Wilderness has easy access to many of the circle canoe routes, including one of the most scenic, the rugged Hunter Island route. Bunkhouse, showers and 33 campsites. Open May through September.

Cross-country skiing off the Gunflint Trail.

▼ **FOR MORE INFORMATION...**

TIP OF THE ARROWHEAD ASSOCIATION
Box 1048
Grand Marais, MN 55604
(218) 387-2524
(800) 622-4014

GUNFLINT TRAIL ASSOCIATION
Box 205
Grand Marais, MN 55604
(800) 338-6932
The association publishes a number of guides to different activities along the Gunflint and in the BWCAW. Some of those are: Cross-Country Ski Guide, Visitor's Guide, Camping on the Trail, Hiking on the Trail and Fishing on the Trail.

U.S. FOREST SERVICE
Gunflint Ranger Station
Grand Marais, MN 55604
(218) 387-1750

BWCAW PERMITS AND RESERVATIONS
Superior National Forest
Box 338
Duluth, MN 55801
(218) 720-5440

QUETICO PARK PERMITS
District Manager
Ministry of Natural Resources
Atikokan, Ontario P0T 1C0
Canada
(807) 597-2735

ELY

NESTLED ON THE SOUTHERN perimeter of the sprawling **Boundary Waters Canoe Area Wilderness (BWCAW)**, Ely has evolved into a world-class center for wilderness outfitters as well as for wolf and black bear research. The international media has focused its attention on a number of famous Ely personalities and their respective outdoor passions. Some of Ely's more notable inhabitants include explorers **Will Steger** and **Paul Schurke** as well as international wolf experts **Dan Groebner** and **Lori Schmidt**. Nature writer and environmentalist **Sigurd Olson** made Ely his home.

Charles Kuralt, veteran CBS correspondent who is best known for his reports from on the road throughout the United States, says Ely is his favorite summer place. Kuralt wrote in a May 1992 issue of TV Guide: "It's possible to walk into Ely dressed in a business suit and within one hour be fully charged, outfitted, equipped and paddling a canoe on wilderness waterways." He added, "The people who live here say that you could paddle a canoe for 100 years and visit a different lake every day." (His other favorites: Rockport, Maine; San Francisco; Glacier National Park, and Sitka, Alaska.)

Ely is one of the principal entry points to the BWCAW. Another is the **Gunflint Trail**. (See the **North Shore** section.) Out of Ely, you can enjoy the wilderness to any extent you desire. There are outfitters to provide the necessary equipment for roughing it, there are isolated campgrounds, rustic hotels and relaxing resorts. Ely can supply as much or as little of nature as you would like.

Thanks to Will Steger and Paul Schurke, 20th-century polar explorers, Ely has developed a close association with Arctic expeditions. Some of the excitement can be experienced firsthand in the local museum. Here is displayed a sled used by Steger and Schurke in 1986 on the first documented expedition to the North Pole made on foot without re-supplying. There also are pictures of the Steger-led expedition to the South Pole.

Ely also is home to the Steger mukluk and Wintergreen outerwear. **Susan Hendrickson Schurke** designs and manufactures, under the name of Wintergreen, a line of outerwear specializing in an anorak, a fur-lined jacket modeled after those worn by the Eskimos. This line is sold at Wintergreen Designs in Ely or by mail order. **Patti Steger**, whose shop, Steger Mukluks, is just down the street, does the same for a line of mukluks, which are fur-lined boots, again modeled after those of the Eskimo.

Ely is also called the "Dog Sledding Capital of the Northwest." The **Ely All American Sled Dog Races** are held every mid-January. It is the biggest sprint race in the lower 48 states. In conjunction with the race is a big weekend festival. A relatively new event introduced at this festival has been ski-jouring. In this sport, a pair of dogs are attached to a specially designed harness and then pull a cross-country skier. A new twist to skiing, or maybe just the lazy man's way of walking the dog.

For the individual who would like a unique, more personal experience, there are overnight dog sled expeditions, either camping or lodge-to-lodge trips, which can be arranged out of Ely. For more information, contact the Ely Chamber of Commerce at **(218) 365-6123** or Wintergreen Lodge at **(218) 365-6022**.

There also is the **Wilderness Trek Ski Race**, held every February. It is a beautiful 50-kilometer race along the edge of the BWCAW. Again, the Ely Chamber of Commerce has more information.

The **Wolf Center**, in coordination with **Vermilion Community College Environmental Studies Center**, **(800) 657-3609**, offers a wonderful wilderness experience. Every Monday, Wednesday and Friday, June through August, the center offers the "Howling Program." It begins with a short presentation on wolf communications and hierarchy practices. Your group is then taken to a spot where wolves have been recently radio-tracked. After a few lessons in the proper method of howling, attempts are made to get the wolves to respond to a human howl. When successful, which it often is, the experience is unbelievably rewarding.

The Environmental Studies Center also offers Saturday field trips with a naturalist/instructor. Besides the wolf, these trips concentrate on other animals, such as the black bear, eagle, osprey and loon. In addition, there are winter wolf weekends, in which wolves are sighted and followed by plane, dog sled or cross-country skis, plus elderhostel dog sled expeditions with a naturalist/instructor.

HISTORY

THE FIRST RECORDED inhabitants of Ely were the **Laurel Indians** as early as 500 B.C. The **Ojibwa Indians** were joined by the **Voyageurs**, who set up trading posts in the 1700s. Iron ore was discovered on what became the **Vermilion Range** in 1883. By 1888, the town of Ely had been incorporated and the railroad from Duluth and Tower was in operation.

Ely is set on the southern shore of **Lake Shagawa**. It is named after **Arthur Ely**, an Ohio businessman who was involved in the development of the mines and railroad in the region. There have been 11 mines between the **Chandler Mine**, opened in 1888, and the closing of the **Pioneer Mine** in 1967. Today the mining of taconite still contributes to the economy of the region.

Soudan Underground Mine is the oldest and deepest iron ore mine in Minnesota. It is now a state park open for visitors during the summer months from 9:30 a.m. to 4 p.m. daily.

Another major economic contributor to the region came from logging and lumber. Logging went largely unchecked, destroying large tracts of white pine and virgin forests, until 1909 when 36,000 acres was established as the **Superior National Forest**. Today these same forests still contribute to the economic welfare of the community, but now it's through controlled logging.

ACTIVITIES

VERMILION INTERPRETIVE CENTER AND HISTORY MUSEUM
1900 E. Camp St.
Ely, MN 55731
(218) 365-3226
Located in Vermilion Community College, this fascinating collection of exhibits chronicles the region's logging, mining, trapping and explorer past and present. Open daily 10 a.m. to 4 p.m. May to October; Wednesday through Saturday 1 to 4 p.m. October to May.

VOYAGEUR VISITOR CENTER
East of Ely on Highway 169
(218) 365-6126
This headquarters for the U.S. Forest Service has information, maps and displays about Superior National Forest and BWCAW permit information. Open daily 6 a.m. to 6 p.m. during the summer.

ELY STEAM BATH
127 S. First Ave. E.
(218) 365-6728
Bath houses in Europe have been a popular and therapeutic meeting place for centuries — a place to cleanse the body and soul and to mix with friends, associates and neighbors in a decidedly relaxed atmosphere. Well, the same is true for the Ely Steam Bath. In existence for just a little more than a half century, it's every bit as vital and functional in Ely as the steam baths of Europe. There are separate public rooms for men and women and even private suites for couples. Open all year.

ELY GOLF COURSE
Highway 21
(218) 365-5932
If you don't mind the contour of the land (read that to be a bit rocky and bumpy), this is a beautiful nine-hole course.

WINTERGREEN LODGE
1101 Ring Rock Road
Ely, MN 55731
(218) 365-6022
Paul Schurke operates a winter adventure travel program touring the BWCAW by dog sled or cross-country skis. You can camp, travel hut-to-hut or lodge-to-lodge, depending on your desire for the amenities of civilization. Schurke also leads expeditions to the northeast regions of Siberia, following reindeer herds or, in the summer, river rafting.

Shopping

Bobby Johns
145 E. Chapman St.
Ely
(218) 365-6081
Closed Sundays.
For those lucky enough to live here and those who merely visit, this is the place to bring the kids to shop. It's sort of a mecca for small dudes.

Pengal's Main Street Outfitters
137 Sheridan St.
Ely
(218) 365-3134
In operation since 1914 providing practical outdoor clothing. Also a fine selection of silk-screen shirts and gifts.

Piragis' Northwoods Co.
105 N. Central Ave.
Ely
(218) 365-6745
A canoe-camping shop featuring quality gear and functional clothing. Seasonal.

Mealey's
124 N. Central Ave.
Ely
(218) 365-3639
A 19th-century general store, complete with original hardware, hardwood, fixtures and even the storefront. Offers a variety of gift items, such as hand-carved wood collectibles, hand-woven rugs and assorted glassware.

Wintergreen
1708 Savoy Road
Ely
(218) 365-6022
Paul Schurke, the North Pole explorer and dog sled enthusiast, has teamed up with his wife to operate this outdoor garment design and manufacturing company. The Schurkes' garment district here in Ely produces some of the best outdoor gear money can buy, thanks to his North Pole and Bering Strait experiences.

Outfitters

Ely is the outfitter capital of the lower 48, so there are scads of them to choose from. Here are a few suggestions:

Canadian Border Outfitters
Box 117
Ely, MN 55731
(218) 365-5847
(800) 247-7530

Hill's Wilderness Trips
Box 715 E.
Ely, MN 55731
(218) 365-6515
(800) 950-2709

Voyageur North Outfitters
1829 E. Sheridan St.
Ely, MN 55731
(218) 365-3251
(800) 848-5530

Wilderness Adventures
943 E. Sheridan St.
Ely, MN 55731
(218) 365-3416
(800) 843-2922

Portage Air
1583A Highway 1
Ely, MN 55731
(218) 365-6013
Portage Air can drop into those hard-to-reach spots or simply take you away on an aerial sightseeing foray into the north woods or up into Canada to catch a glimpse of polar bears, wolves and a host of other wilderness inhabitants that you wouldn't otherwise see.

Eating and Lodging

Aki Nibi Resort
Rural Route 1, Box 3137
Ely, MN 55731
(218) 365-4370
If a resort can be quaint, John Kennedy's Aki Nibi Resort is it. It's basically a low-key stopover on Farm Lake that puts its emphasis on quality more than quantity. There are only seven cottage units, so call ahead.

Breakers On Snowbank
Box 128
Ely, MN 55731
(218) 365-6032
(800) 777-7162
Built on the banks of lovely Snowbank Lake, Breakers has full service and convenience with all the trimmings. There are even heated ice fishing huts, hiking and skiing trails that lead practically to your doorstep and motor/canoe rentals just down the shore.

Camp Van Vac
2714 Van Vac Lane
Ely, MN 55731
(218) 365-3782 (summer)
(612) 927-0892 (winter)

There are 24 beautiful log and stone cabins on Fall Lake, as fun to look at as to stay in. Beautiful sandy beach, guide service, trails and towing to the BWCAW.

CHOCOLATE MOOSE
Corner of Sheridan St. and Central Ave.
(218) 365-6343
Look for the log cabin. Featuring homemade ice cream, breakfasts and lunches.

CRANBERRY'S RESTAURANT, STEAK ROOM AND SALOON
47 E. Sheridan St.
(218) 365-4301
American and Mexican cuisine, including burgers, steak and seafood. Large salad bar.

DON BELAND'S NORTH COUNTRY LODGE, WILDERNESS CANOE TRIPS AND CAMPGROUND
Box 808
Ely, MN 55731
(218) 365-5811
(800) 777-4431
Situated on Moose Lake, Beland's is the largest resort in town, with 18 cabins, three rooms and eight campsites. They also will happily set you up on one of their canoe trips into the BWCAW. Restaurant and bar. Open year-round. Call early for reservations.

BURNTSIDE LODGE
2755 Burntside Lodge Road
Ely, MN 55731
(218) 365-3894
Established in 1914 and listed on the National Register of Historic Places. Housekeeping cabins, boating, dining room and lounge, game room and sandy beach.

BRITTON'S CAFE
5 E. Chapman St.
(218) 365-3195
Serving breakfast, lunch and dinner year-round.

LUDLOW'S ISLAND LODGE
Box 92 MRA
Cook, MN 55723
(218) 666-5407
(800) 777-8480
There are 19 luxury cabins with fireplaces and decks tucked away on an island in Lake Vermilion. All water-related sports are available along with tennis and indoor racquetball. Family Circle magazine rated Ludlow's as one of the best in the United States.

NORTH COUNTRY RETREAT CENTER
Vermilion River
Buyck, MN 55731
(218) 666-3104
(800) 458-2403
Since most of the state's lodges and resorts are situated on lakes, North Country is a cozy change of pace. Situated on the Vermilion River, this place has wonderfully secluded cabins complete with wood stoves. There are only four cabins, so call ahead for reservations.

NORTHWIND LODGE
Box 690
Ely, MN 55731
(218) 365-5489
Fine dining on beautiful Jasper Lake on the Fernberg Trail. Open for breakfast. Dinner reservations required.

WILDERNESS BAY LODGE
Box 127
Ely, MN 55731
(218) 365-4311
The lodge is hidden away on beautiful Snowbank Lake and accessible only by seaplane or canoe, with highly attentive service, epic wilderness scenery and secluded housekeeping cabins.

TIMBER BAY LODGE AND HOUSEBOATS
Box 248E
Babbitt, MN 55706
(218) 827-3682
Rent a fully-equipped houseboat and navigate 20-mile-long Birch Lake. Excellent fishing and swimming. Sleeps two to 10. The lodge also has 11 housekeeping cabins. In winter: 10040 Colorado Road, Bloomington, MN 55438, (612) 831-0043.

▼ FOR MORE INFORMATION...

ELY CHAMBER OF COMMERCE
1600 E. Sheridan
Ely, MN 55731
(218) 365-6123

BWCAW PERMITS AND RESERVATIONS
Superior National Forest
Box 338
Duluth, MN 55801
(218) 720-5440

QUETICO PARK PERMITS
District Manager
Ministry of Natural Resources
Atikokan, Ontario P0T 1C0
Canada
(807) 507-2735

Voyageurs canoe trip offered by the Voyageurs National Park Service.

Northern Arrowhead

THE NORTHERN PORTION OF Minnesota's Arrowhead region is the longest inland lake waterway on this continent. The eight largest lakes that form this border waterway are: **Rainy**, **Kabetogama**, **Namakan**, **Sand Point**, **Lac La Croix**, **Saganaga**, **Basswood** and **Gunflint**. Much of this area is protected wilderness, parks and national forests. The towns located along the lakes' borders swell with summer and now, more and more, winter visitors who come seeking adventure in the spirit of the Voyageurs.

Hurray! Minnesota

use or size. You can explore it by canoe or luxurious cruiser. Voyageurs includes the larger lakes of Rainy, Kabetogama, Namakan and Sand Point. The park service offers interpretive hikes, Voyageur canoe trips and the Sight-Sea-er and Pride of Rainy Lake tour boats guided by naturalists. These begin at **Rainy Lake Visitors Center** (Highway 11, about 11 miles east of International Falls) or **Kabetogama Lake Visitors Center** (off Highway 53 on County Road 123). There are both day and evening programs. **(218) 286-5470**.

▼ For More Information...
VOYAGEURS NATIONAL PARK
Box 50
International Falls, MN 56649
(218) 283-9821

ORR

ORR, A TOWN of 283 people, is on the edge of beautiful Pelican Lake and in close proximity to Voyageurs National Park. It has a history founded in the timber and logging industries. Today, thanks to the beauty of nature and fishing and hunting in the area, it prospers from the tourist trade. Pelican Lake, the largest lake in the immediate area, has a number of modern resorts. Many are open year-round.

For those interested in original and unusual gifts, the Chippewa of the Boise Fort Indian Reservation make beautiful beaded hand-crafted items. These can be found in local gift shops.

ATTRACTIONS
VERMILION FALLS
Turn right off Highway 53 on to County Road 180 and continue to bear right at the next two junctions to reach Vermilion Falls. There is a short hiking trail to this beautiful falls. The Falls' history dates back to the gold-rush days.

VOYAGEURS NATIONAL PARK

JUST WEST OF the Boundary Waters Canoe Area Wilderness (BWCAW) is the 218,000 acres of the Voyageurs National Park. Voyageurs is the largest water-based park in the national park system, having 83,000 acres of wilderness waterways. The park requires no permits and has no restrictions on motorboat

Vermilion Gorge has a "gorge"-ous 1 1/2-mile hiking trail that begins just past the Voyageurs National Park office on Highway 24 in Crane Lake. The trail ends at the Vermilion River Gorge with a view of awesome granite cliffs and huge rock outcrops. Crane Lake was once a fur trading post.

The Fire and Ice Geological Interpretive Walk describes how the glacial period and the 1970 fire worked together to determine the types of forests in the area. Turn off County Road 23/24 on to Echo Trail (116) approximately 37 miles north of Orr. The walk is at a wayside 18 miles down Echo Trail.

KETTLE FALLS HOTEL
Ash River Trail
Orr, MN 55771
(800) 322-0886

Located on the Kabetogama Peninsula, this hotel can only be reached by boat. Built in 1913, the hotel was purchased in 1918 by the Williams family for four barrels of whiskey and $1,000. After the national park was established, the Williams family operated the concession under the park service until 1992, when Darrell and Joan Knutson became the new proprietors.

In 1985, because the foundation of the hotel deteriorated to such a point that the floors literally rolled in waves from wall to wall, the park service rebuilt the hotel to original specifications, with as much as possible of the original lumber. However, the heaving floors were left in one area of the hotel, the Tilton Hilton Bar. Most of the original furnishings are intact along with additional antiques and reproductions in keeping with the period. There are 12 rooms with 10 new villas, dining room and guide service. It is interesting to note that the hotel looks south into Canada.

▼ FOR MORE INFORMATION...
ORR TOURIST INFORMATION CENTER
Highway 53
Orr, MN 55771
(218) 757-3932

PELICAN LAKE-ORR RESORT ASSOCIATION
Box A
Orr, MN 55771
(218) 757-3932 or 757-3479

INTERNATIONAL FALLS

EVERYONE KNOWS International Falls, with a mean annual temperature of 36.4 degrees Fahrenheit, as the "Icebox of the Nation." Unfortunately, to some people that moniker tends to paint a not-so-favorable picture of this beautiful northern Minnesota town. It is true that there is a giant thermometer in the middle of town for reality checks, and it's also true that International Falls has a national testing facility to evaluate product performance, such as cars and batteries, under the coldest of weather conditions. But there's more to International Falls than inspiration for **Rocky** and **Bullwinkle's Frostbite Falls** and frigid weather reports.

International Falls sits on the edge of **Voyageurs National Park** (which it shares with Ontario to the north), the great **Boreal Forest**, **Superior National Forest** (home of the state's largest black spruce) and the **BWCAW**. International Falls takes its name from the rushing falls that once danced down the Rainy River. Those falls have since put their force into generating hydroelectricity that helps power the community and its paper industry.

International Falls used to be merely a stopover for the French fur trappers, the Voyageurs, but today it's very much a final destination for those who appreciate the spectacular recreational possibilities that this northern paradise provides.

In 1903 Congress gave permission for the construction of the International Bridge to connect the Falls with Fort Francis in Canada. Then, in 1906, the Falls became the county seat for Koochiching County. International Falls is now a city of 10,000.

At one time International Falls might have been better know for its famous son, **Bronko Nagurski**, than its extreme temperatures. Nagurski has been referred to as one of the top 101 athletes of the century. He began his football career playing for the University of Minnesota. He played fullback on offense and tackle on defense. In 1929, he became the only player ever named All-

Hurray! Minnesota

American at two positions in the same year. The high point of his career was when he led the Chicago Bears to the first pro championship in 1933. After retiring in the mid-'50s, Nagurski returned to live in International Falls until his death in 1990.

ATTRACTIONS

GRAND MOUND
Highway 11
Due west of International Falls on Highway 11 is a uniquely Upper Midwest experience known as the Grand Mound, an ancient Indian burial ground of the **Laurel Indians**. It's a place of extreme reverence. There is an information center nearby to explain the historical and archeological significance of these mounds and a patchwork of nature trails you can hike.

KOOCHICHING COUNTY HISTORICAL MUSEUM
Smokey Bear Park
International Falls
(218) 283-4316
Exciting exhibits covering Indian artifacts, the gold rush, logging and homesteading. Open Memorial Day through Labor Day. Admission $1 for adults, 50 cents for grades K-12.

Smokey Bear Park is a good spot for a picnic and to get your picture taken with the gigantic 82-ton statue of Smokey the Bear.

Boise Cascade, one of the largest employers in town, offers tours of its paper-making mill. Tours are conducted June 1 through August 31, Monday through Friday, at 9 and 11 a.m. and 12:30 and 2:30 p.m. **(218) 285-5312**.

Ice Box Days each January features the Freeze Yer Gizzard Blizzard 10k foot race, the 12k and 24k cross-country ski Voyageur Loppet, along with softball, volleyball, broomball and many more tournaments. Holding these summer events in January adds real challenge to the sports and rids the soul of cabin fever. **(800) 325-5766**.

SNOWMOBILE TRAILS
The Lake of the Woods County snowmobile trails link with other northwestern trail systems and the famous Can-Am Trail.

SHOPPING

RONNINGS BORDER BARGAINS
Downtown International Falls
Hudson Bay blankets, souvenir T-shirts, sweatshirts and caps. In fact, some say you will find the largest selection here.

INTERNATIONAL MALL
Highway 11-71
It is nice to have enclosed shopping in this town of cold weather. The mall includes a Super Valu Store, small shops and restaurants.

PORT RAINER
Quaint shops, art gallery and old-time general store make this the perfect place to browse. Arrangements can be made to have the "Pride of Rainy Lake" tour boat stop here so you can make a real day of it. (218) 286-5470.

EATING

SPOT SUPPER CLUB AND FIRESIDE LOUNGE
Highway 53 S.
International Falls
(218) 283-4475
Family owned and operated since 1934. Serving American favorites.

BARNEY'S
1319 Third St.
International Falls
(218) 283-3333
Serving good home cooking for breakfast, lunch and dinner.

LODGING

ARROWHEAD LODGE
10473 Waltz Road, Box RG
Ray, MN 56669
(218) 875-2141
The beautiful rustic lodge dining room and lounge reflect the north woods atmosphere. There are 12 rooms and 10 housekeeping cottages. The lodge can provide an excellent fishing guide service.

HOLIDAY INN
Highways 11 and 71
International Falls, MN 56649
(218) 283-4451
If you're traveling with or without an entourage and looking for a name you can count on, go with this beautifully remodeled Holiday Inn on the Rainy River. It has 126 rooms, a lounge, pool, sauna and meeting rooms.

ISLAND VIEW LODGE
HCR-8, Box 411
International Falls, MN 56649
(218) 286-3511
(800) 777-7856

The Island View, just outside of International Falls, has what you need to get the most out of your stay on Rainy Lake. They have paddle boats, canoes, snowmobiles and knowledgeable guides on hand for Voyageurs National Park. They can tell you where the fish are biting and the moose are grazing.

NELSON'S RESORT
Department R92
Crane Lake, MN 55725
(218) 993-2295

This 1930s-style resort offers 28 cozy lakeshore log cabins, guides and some of the best home-cooked meals you'll encounter in northern Minnesota. Nelson's is on the border of Voyageurs and the BWCAW. It is at the end of the road, in the wilderness, but still a first-class full-service facility. Private hiking trail, excellent swimming beach, dining room and cocktail lounge. Open May to October.

RAINY LAKE HOUSEBOATS
Route 8, Box 408
International Falls, MN 56649
(218) 286-5391

A wonderful way to relax, sightsee and explore Voyageurs National Park in comfort and style. Open mid-May to October.

THUNDERBIRD LODGE AND MOTOR INN
Route 8, Box 407
International Falls, MN 56649
(218) 286-3151

Located right on Rainy Lake, the Thunderbird has 15 rooms and 10 housekeeping cabins. Tennis courts and guided fishing are available. The restaurant and lounge have a spectacular view of Rainy Lake. Open all year.

VOYAGEURS PARK LODGE
10436 Waltz Road
Ray, MN 56669
(800) 331-5694

Located on scenic Kabetogama Lake, Voyageurs Park Lodge is a thoroughly modern resort while maintaining the spell of the wilderness. There are wonderful dining facilities, lodge suites and 11 cabins.

A wilderness vacation...with all the comforts of home!

Deep in Minnesota's Northwoods there is a peacefulness that is difficult to match anywhere in North America. A quiet serenity punctuated only by the lapping of water by the shore, the songs of birds and the whisper of breezes through the tall pines.

This is the setting for Nelson's Resort, with its 27 individually designed and decorated cabins, first-rate dining and loads of activities for the whole family!

The Voyageur's National Park, Boundary Waters Canoe Area and Canada's Quetico Park are *literally* at your doorstep, with over 40 miles of continuous water teeming with walleyes, northerns, lake trout and bass! We'll furnish you with everything you'll need — even a guide to show you where they are!

And if it's just relaxing you're after, there are hiking trails, a sauna, swimming beach, canoes, shuffleboard, horseshoes, sailing and water-skiing!

But a word of caution: as soon as you have determined the best time for your Wilderness Vacation, let us know so we can reserve the American or Modified Plan cabin that's best for you.
Ask about our new video.

Nelson's Resort
Crane Lake, Minnesota 55725
Write or call us collect
(218) 993-2295

Hurray! Minnesota

OLSON'S BORDERLAND LODGE AND OUTFITTERS
Crane Lake, MN 55725
(218) 993-2233
Olson's has all the gear you'll need for a wonderful trip into the BWCAW or one of the many lakes or rivers in and around Voyageurs National Park. Olson's also has cabins to ease you into and then back out of the wilderness.

▼ **FOR MORE INFORMATION...**
INTERNATIONAL FALLS VISITORS AND CONVENTION BUREAU
Box 169
International Falls, MN 56649
(218) 283-9400 or (800) 325-5766

LAKE OF THE WOODS AREA

Baudette is the county seat for Lake of the Woods County and has approximately 1,200 residents. Located on the Rainy River at the southwest corner of Lake of the Woods, it proudly refers to itself as the "Walleye Capital of the World."

Baudette's economy was founded on lumber milling and logging and, secondarily, commercial fishing. **Wilhelm Zippel** was the first resident and a commercial fisherman. A by-product of commercial fishing was the establishment of the **Folvay Pharmaceutical** manufacturing facility, formerly Reid-Rowell. The company was founded in the early 1930s by Theodore Rowell for the sale of liver oil from Lake of the Woods' burbot fish. The oil, potent in Vitamins A and D, was refined and sold as a tonic.

In addition, during the 1950s, a local potato quarantine was established and the area became a large producer of disease-free certified seed potatoes. Today, these businesses still play an important part in the economy of the area along with tourism.

Warroad, at the western edge of Lake of the Woods, is home to Marvin Windows, the largest employer in northern Minnesota. However, not all of the town's 2,200 residents work at Marvin. The **Christian brothers, Roger** and **Billy**, have built a business manufacturing hockey sticks and have captured eight to 10 percent of the world market. This business, employing 60 people, is appropriate for "Hockey-Town U.S.A." and also fitting for the Christian brothers, who were instrumental in the 1960 Winter Olympic games when the U.S. hockey team won its first gold medal. Roger scored four of nine goals against Czechoslovakia and Billy scored the tying and winning goals against the Soviet team in the semifinals.

The Warroad River and Warroad, at one time the largest Chippewa village on Lake of the Woods, received their names from what the Sioux called the Red and Roseau rivers, which meet here at the mouth of the Warroad River. The Sioux, in the fight for control of the rice fields, used these rivers as their "road to war" in the attacks on the Chippewa.

Lake of the Woods, the most northerly lake in the country, is partly in the United States and partly in Canada. It is a glacial remnant lake that began forming some 72,000 years ago. It is famous for its fishing, particularly walleye

---

A "REEL" DEAL!

Looking for a vacation spot that the family, grandma & grandpa or the fishing buddies can enjoy?

We have "reel" deal for you!

• World-class fishing
• First-class hospitality
• Camping, golfing, swimming, boating, nature trails, historical sites, shopping

For a free brochure write or call:
Lake of the Woods Area
Tourism Bureau
Box 518 HMN
Baudette, MN 56623

minnesota's **LAKE OF THE WOODS** *area*

1-800-382-FISH

ATTRACTIONS

ZIPPEL BAY STATE PARK
Williams, MN 56686
(218) 783-6252
Named for Wilhelm Zippel, the first official white resident of Lake of the Woods county. A beautiful white sand beach and ocean-like waves are attractions at this park. There are campsites, hiking, horseback riding and snowmobile trails.

LAKE OF THE WOODS HISTORICAL MUSEUM
Baudette
(218) 634-1200
Exhibits are about the Laurel, Blackduck and Chippewa tribes, commercial fishing, logging history, the 1910 fire and early agriculture. Open May 1 to October 1, Tuesday through Saturday, 10 a.m. to 4 p.m.

OAK HARBOR GOLF COURSE AND TNS CLUB, INC.
Baudette
(218) 634-9939
Beautiful course along the Rainy River.

FORT ST. CHARLES
This fort is located at the tip of the Northwest Angle on Magnussen Island. It is a restored fort on the site of the 1732 fortress and trading post established by Pierre La Verendrye. Since 1951 the Knights of Columbus organization has been maintaining and improving the fort area. The fort, which is only accessible by water, has a self-guided tour.

WILDERNESS TRAIL DRIVE
Lake of the Woods County has designated and marked drives through the Beltrami Island State Forest. A great opportunity to view many forms of wildlife. Maps are available.

CHRISTIAN BROTHERS HOCKEY EQUIPMENT
Box C, 1001 N. State Ave.
Warroad, MN 56763
(218) 386-1111
Located on Highway 89 across from Marvin Windows. Open for 20-minute tours Monday through Friday, 10:30 a.m. and 3 p.m.

---

because of the ideal habitat provided by the many bays, inlets and 14,000 islands in its 2,000 square miles. In fact, the record walleye of 13 pounds, 8 ounces was caught through the ice here in April 1987. There is also great fishing for muskie, northern and small mouth bass.

The Northwest Angle, the little "chimney" of land on top of the state, is accessible by road, boat or plane and is about 60 miles out of Warroad or 40 miles across the lake from Baudette. This is the most northerly U.S. land of the 48 contiguous states. Likewise, Angle Inlet, the main town on the Angle, is the most northerly town at 49.22 degrees N. longitude. The Northwest Angle is surrounded on three sides by Canada. In

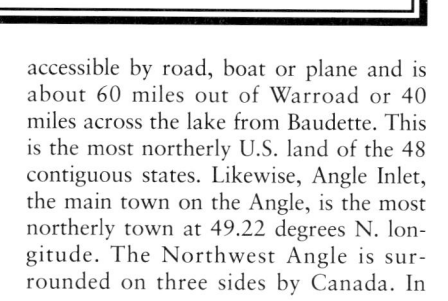

Hurray! Minnesota

fact, it would have been part of Canada if it were not for an error in the 1775 map used for setting the U.S. borders with Canada in the Treaty of Paris.

Rainy River, which, surprisingly, flows east to west from Rainy Lake to Lake of the Woods, was a main artery in the Voyageurs trade route. Today the river forms part of the border between Canada and the United States. This beautiful scenic river is an excellent source of fishing and recreational opportunities.

EATING

COUNTRY HOUSE
One mile west of Baudette on Highway 11
Baudette
(218) 634-2383
Open for lunch and dinner. Serving steaks, seafood, ribs and chicken. Cocktails available.

THE RANCH HOUSE
203 W. Main St.
Baudette
(218) 634-2420
Fine and casual dining. Serving breakfast, lunch and dinner. Open year-round.

LODGING

ANGLE INN LODGE
Box 3
Oak Island, MN 56741
(218) 442-5013
(218) 843-3465
Peace and tranquility are found at this homey lodge located on Oak Island in the heart of Lake of the Woods. Home-cooked meals. Boats, motors and guides. Also open for ice fishing.

BALLARD'S RESORT
Box 176
Baudette, MN 56623
(218) 634-1849
Besides full-service fishing and dock services, this beautiful resort, at the mouth of the Rainy River, has a heated outdoor pool, hot tub and sauna, 15 housekeeping cabins of different sizes and a full-service restaurant with a select-and-grill-your-own charbroil pit. In winter there is guided ice fishing via a ride to a heated fishing house.

DANNY GIBBONS
(218) 634-1564
Sleeper ice houses.

SPORTSMAN'S LODGE
Route 1, Box 167
Baudette, MN 56623
(218) 634-1342
(800) 862-8602
Rooms in a handsome lodge, housekeeping cottages and indoor pool with hot tub are some of the features that make "roughing it" a luxury. There are two dining rooms, two lounges, charter fishing and boat/motor rentals. Open all year.

SPRINGSTEEL RESORT
HC-02, Box 124
Warroad, MN 56763
(218) 386-1000
Lakefront housekeeping cabins, camping, seasonal docking and lodge with dining facilities. Open year-round.

WIGWAM LODGE/TRAILS END RESORT
Route 1, Box 200
Baudette, MN 56623
(218) 634-2168
(800) 488-9260
Choose a beautiful lodge room or housekeeping cabin. Depending on the season, you can catch your fish on a guided charter, rented boat/motor or a heated fishing house. There's a full-service restaurant, lounge, snowmobile trails and campground. Open all year.

YOUNG'S BAY RESORT
Box 127B
Angle Inlet, MN 56711 (summer)
Route 3, Box 70B
Warroad, MN 56763 (winter)
(218) 386-2497
The perfect place for great fishing or duck hunting. Housekeeping cabins and campsites. Boat ramp with protected harbor. Store, gas and boat/motor rentals. Open May through October.

▼ FOR MORE INFORMATION...

LAKE OF THE WOODS AREA TOURISM BUREAU
Box 518
Baudette, MN 56623
(800) 382-FISH (in Minnesota)
(800) 351-FISH (out-of-state)

WARROAD AREA CHAMBER OF COMMERCE, INC.
Box 7
Warroad, MN 56763
(800) 328-4455 (out-of-state)
(218) 386-3543

IRON RANGE

THE TOWNS OF THE IRON RANGE (often referred to as just "The Range") offer many forms of recreation. There are historic centers to explore and relive the past of the iron ore and timber industries; restored mine pits, whose clear, cold water has been stocked with rainbow and brook trout or put to use as aquafarms; the beautiful recreational lakes that northern Minnesota is famous for; and acres and acres of forests and park lands for cross-country skiing, snowmobiling, hiking and even hills for downhill skiing.

Northern Minnesota actually has three iron ranges: the **Vermilion Range**, under Tower and Ely; the **Mesabi Range**, which runs from Grand Rapids to Babbitt; and the **Cuyuna Range**, at Crosby-Ironton.

Beginning with Tower on the Vermilion Range, Highway 169 acts as a main artery between the Range towns all the way down to Aitkin, on the edge of the Cuyuna Range.

The most northerly of the three ranges is Vermilion. It is composed of very hard rock ore deposits. These deposits were tilted by geological upheavals. To remove the ore, vertical shafts were dug deep into the bowels of the earth. Today one of those mines, the Soudan Underground Mine State Park, is open to the public for tours.

The term Mesabi, meaning sleeping giant, originally came from the Indians and refers to the silhouette of the range. The ore on this range lies in horizontal masses, like a sleeping giant, at a depth of 200 feet. The ore, soft and almost dusty in texture, merely had to be scooped out of the earth and hauled away. First, however, new furnaces that didn't clog from the dust had to be developed to handle the soft ore.

Leonidas Merritt opened the first mine on the Mesabi Range in 1890, called **Mountain Iron**. After a costly legal battle, the Merritts eventually lost control to the wealthier **J.D. Rockefeller**. The mine at Mountain Iron is still operated by U.S. Steel.

The Cuyuna Range, the most southerly range, was named for the prospector **Cuyler Adams** and his dog **Una**. Adams discovered the range in 1895. The Kennedy Mine, the first mine worked on this range, opened in 1911. Like the Vermilion Range, the ore is very hard, lies in vertical lenses and is mined by shafts.

The year 1937 saw the greatest annual production from all three ranges at 48,700,000 gross tons. As the rich ore ran out and new technology was developed, the mines began to produce taconite, a lower grade iron ore. Current production rates of taconite have been around 45 million tons annually for the past five years. The iron mining industry has consistently contributed an estimated $1 billion to the state's annual economy.

▼ **FOR MORE INFORMATION...**
IRON TRAIL CONVENTION AND VISITORS BUREAU
Box 559
Eveleth, MN 55734
(218) 744-2441
(800) 777-8497

TOWER-SOUDAN

TOWER IS WHERE mining began on the Iron Range back in 1865. The Soudan Mine was Minnesota's first, deepest and richest iron ore mine, and was dubbed "the cradle of the iron mining industry." Since 1962, when the mine ceased operations, having essentially run out of high grade iron ore, the Tower-Soudan area has been supported more by the offshoots of tourism from nearby Lake Vermilion, with its 365 islands, lakeside resorts and campgrounds; by the mine and its fantastic underground tour; and by hiking available on trails into some of the area's largest abandoned open pit mines.

ATTRACTIONS
SOUDAN UNDERGROUND MINE STATE PARK
Box 335 (on Highway 169)
Soudan, MN 55782
(218) 753-2245
If you can handle descending to a depth of 2,341 feet below the earth's surface, you're in for quite a tour. Moving about in an old railcar, visitors are transported to the once-famous Montana ore body. You'll see parts of the mine and the formerly ore-rich caverns that were last worked nearly 30 years ago. You will have the opportunity to explore and climb a spiral staircase into the cavity where the ore was actually found. Don't forget a coat. Even in the middle of August it gets a bit drafty nearly half a mile below ground. (Hard hats are provided.) Open daily, Memorial weekend to Labor Day, 9:30 a.m. to 4 p.m.

FORTUNE BAY CASINO
1430 Bois Forte Road
Tower
(218) 753-6400
(800) 992-PLAY
Bingo, slot machines, blackjack and keno. Restaurant.

▼ FOR MORE INFORMATION...
TOWER-SOUDAN CHAMBER OF COMMERCE
Box 776B
Tower, MN 55790
(218) 753-2301

EMBARRASS

THANKS TO THE townspeople through the Sisu Heritage organization, seven log buildings (almost a whole town) have been restored and placed on the National Register of Historic Places. The organization also offers tours, which include restored homesteads, craft shops, a house-barn and an old Finnish sauna.

▼ FOR MORE INFORMATION...
TOWN OF EMBARRASS
7503 Lavender Road
Embarrass, MN 55732
(218) 984-2672

SISU HERITAGE
Box 127
Embarrass, MN 55732
(218) 984-2672

BIWABIK

GIANTS RIDGE
Box 190, Biwabik, MN 55708
(218) 865-4143
(800) 475-7669
A family recreational ski area with four lifts, 19 runs and more than 55 kilometers of groomed cross-country ski trails, Giants Ridge has been host to a number of national and world-class events.

EVELETH

THIS IRON MINING town is considered the birthplace of hockey in North America and has spawned the likes of hockey greats **Sam LoPresti** and **Frank Brimsek**. It stands to reason that the town with the nickname "Hockey Capital of the Nation" should be the site of the U.S. Hockey Hall of Fame. Taconite might be the work of this community, but ever since that first game in 1903, Eveleth's recreation has been hockey.

ATTRACTIONS
U.S. HOCKEY HALL OF FAME
Downtown Eveleth
(218) 744-5167
See the greats enshrined forever in wall-to-wall exhibits of photos, original sticks, uniforms, trading cards and other player memorabilia. A quadrant of this museum is devoted to the U.S. Olympic Hockey Team, complete with running videotape of the great games, including the 1980 U.S.-USSR gold medal game.

LEONIDAS OVERLOOK
This man-made summit provides a splendid observation stand for photographing or just plain gazing at the Eveleth Taconite Operations, Minntac Mine and the lush green forest.

SHOPPING
WINDFALL STUDIO
Grant at Jones St.
Eveleth
(218) 744-3004
If you're looking for a great sample of

Mountain Iron

THE LARGEST IRON ore pellet plant in the world is the Minntac Plant in Mountain Iron. Taconite capacity is 14 million tons annually. The first production from this mine began in 1892. Tours, lasting 1 1/2 hours, are offered by Minntac. They begin at 10 a.m. and 1 p.m. on Fridays at the Senior Center in Mountain Iron, Memorial Day through Labor Day. Reservations are not necessary. Minntac **(218) 749-7469**.

Minnesota artists, this is the place. There also are plenty of national artists represented.

THE UNUSUAL PLACE
113 Grant Ave.
Eveleth
(218) 744-4714
This is a star attraction in Eveleth. The Unusual Place is just that, a tidy collection of antiques, collectibles, classic furniture and a wide assortment of enchanting gifts from yesteryear. Open Monday through Saturday.

THE GARDEN COTTAGE
Highway 53 and 16E
Eveleth
(218) 744-5199
This place is almost a destination in and of itself. Situated just down from the Swanson greenhouse, the Garden Cottage sits on the edge of a duck pond surrounded by sweet-smelling shrubs, flowers and trees.

This is a great place to do a little browsing for antiques and collectibles, and then step outside and take in the beauty of the north woods.

EATING
THE LANTERN FAMILY RESTAURANT
3147 Miller Trunk Road
(Junction of Highways 53 and 57)
Eveleth
(218) 744-9931
For more than a half century the Lantern has been serving up home-cooked family-style ribs, steak and potatoes and pan fish. It's still a popular eating spot among the locals. The price is right, the servings are ample,

and the service is friendly. Open all year.

LODGING
HOLIDAY INN
Highway 53
Eveleth, MN 55734
(218) 744-2703
(800) 465-4329
A vacation unto itself. Families often take the weekend, especially when it's really cold, to rent a poolside room and enjoy the pool, whirlpool and sauna. Restaurant and lounge. 145 rooms.

▼ FOR MORE INFORMATION...
EVELETH CONVENTION AND VISITORS BUREAU
Box 559
Eveleth, MN 55734
(218) 744-4714

Virginia

LIKE OTHER IRON RANGE towns, Virginia made its mark in the early 20th century as a mining and logging town. Virginia's mines, the largest in the world, are famous for taconite, the abundant low grade iron ore. Taconite is processed into hailstone-sized balls that can be seen piled high along the North Shore ore loading docks outside of Silver Bay, Two Harbors and Duluth. The largest taconite mine in the world, Minntac, is still operating in Mountain Iron next to Virginia.

ATTRACTIONS
ROUCHLEAU MINE/MINE VIEW IN THE SKY
On the south end of town you can park and stare out at the cavernous Rouchleau Mine from the Mine View in the Sky observation deck. The observation deck is open daily, Memorial Day to September.

OLCOTT PARK
N. Ninth St. and Ninth Ave.
Olcott contains the **Virginia Municipal Golf Course**, tennis courts, a playground, plenty of picnic tables and a greenhouse. It remains a favorite spot among Virginians.

Hurray! Minnesota

LAURENTIAN DIVIDE FITNESS TRAIL
The trail on Highway 53 is named for the fact that Virginia straddles the Laurentian Divide, the point at which all water on one side flows into Lake Superior and on the other side flows north into Hudson Bay.

VIRGINIA HISTORICAL SOCIETY HERITAGE CENTER
N. Fourth St. and Sixth Ave.
Virginia
(218) 741-1136
Historical artifacts and exhibits of north St. Louis County. Open Monday through Friday, 8 a.m. to 4 p.m. Free admission.

FINNTOWN NEIGHBORHOOD
This is the only section of Virginia that escaped a 1900 fire that leveled the rest of the city. It remains a historical remnant of Virginia's past. There is a self-guided tour available for the area, which includes information on the Lincoln Building, Kaleva Hall, a 1907 Finnish Temperance Hall, and the two-room log house which is now the Virginia Heritage Museum housing the Peace Flag exhibit.

SHOPPING

MESABI RECREATION
1116 S. Eighth St.
Virginia
(218) 749-6719
A full line of quality sportswear and equipment.

THUNDERBIRD MALL
Virginia
(218) 741-9228
Herberger's, J.C. Penney, K-Mart and more than 30 stores occupy the 236,344 square feet of this newly remodeled indoor mall.

IRMA'S FINLAND HOUSE
Across from Northgate Plaza
Virginia
(218) 741-0204
Irma's has a wonderful collection of gifts for the home, such as glassware, sauna accessories, hand-woven blankets and classic cookware.

EATING

ITALIAN BAKERY
205 S. First St.
Virginia
(218) 741-3464
This frankly-named bakery is an institution that's been serving up delectable pastries, breads, muffins and fruitcake since 1910. Today it still adheres to the original family recipes for its time-honored classics, such as its fruitcakes and baked potica. The Italian Bakery also has a thriving mail-order business in case you want to ship a parcel of potica (or a fruitcake) home. Open Monday through Saturday.

RAINY LAKE SALOON AND DELI
207 Chestnut St.
Virginia
(218) 741-6247
At Rainy Lake they serve up real helpings and the service is decidedly homespun. It's a meat and potatoes place for sure, but one that also knows what to do with fish, chicken and fresh crisp salads.

AMANDA'S SUPPER CLUB
103 Chestnut St.
Virginia
(218) 741-6449
Lots of oak woodwork gives this family dining restaurant a real homey atmosphere. Amanda's serves lunch and dinner, featuring a full menu that includes sandwiches, steaks, pastas, seafood and salad bar. Entertainment on Sundays in the full-service lounge.

LODGING

COATES PLAZA HOTEL
502 Chestnut St.
Virginia, MN 55792
(218) 749-1000
(800) 777-4699
Located in downtown Virginia, only a few blocks from the shops and close to Ironworld and Giants Ridge, the Coates has 80 rooms with all of the amenities, such as pool, sauna, dining room and lounge.

Coates also offers a host of recreational packages, such as cross-country skiing, hiking and fishing, for year-round outdoor adventures.

▼ FOR MORE INFORMATION...

VIRGINIA AREA CHAMBER OF COMMERCE
233 Chestnut St.
Virginia, MN 55792
(218) 741-2717

CHISHOLM

CHISHOLM HAS DEVELOPED into a popular Iron Range destination, thanks to Ironworld USA. With mining economics constantly riding a down-bound train, city leaders realized long ago that their future lies in tourism more than mining. This theme park, built around the area's rich mining history, is a hit among both young people and adults.

The town rolls out the red carpet for tourists and makes the most of who and what the town is: a historic mining community comprised of a cornucopia of nationalities.

ATTRACTIONS
BRIDGE OF PEACE
As a major tribute to its multiethnic heritage, Ironworld has erected a giant bridge festooned with flags of nations from around the world to promote the idea of both cultural common ground and diversity. The bridge spans downtown Chisholm.

IRONWORLD USA
Highway 169
Chisholm
(218) 254-3321
(800) 372-6437
Ironworld is no small undertaking. This is a colorful living museum with shopping and rides. The observation decks stare out on a sprawling landscape of reality rather than pure fantasy.

There is a wonderfully crafted Festival Park designed to resemble a river and stream environment with arching bridges, waterfalls and babbling brook. There also are cafes with wafting scents of home-cooked food inspired by cultures from around the world. There are local arts and craft exhibits, assorted gift shops and interpretive exhibits that depict life on the Iron Range. After you've combed the shops and exhibits you can take a trolley or a touring train to the open pit Glen Mine.

During the summer, Ironworld presents a concert venue of a wide range of national musical talent plus several festivals, such as the Polka Fest. The amphitheater is a great place to catch one of these concerts and to enjoy a picnic in the sun.

MINNESOTA MUSEUM OF MINING
Highway 169
(Across from Ironworld USA)
Chisholm
(218) 254-7158
For a broad historical perspective on Minnesota's mining past, pay a visit to the Minnesota Museum of Mining. The museum has everything from interpretive displays of mining villages to a scale model of a taconite mining operation. For heavy equipment lovers, there is a collection of water cannons, dinosaur-sized dredge buckets and other mechanical hulks like backhoes, ore carts and giant ore scoops once employed in the service of the mining trade.

There is even something for train lovers here: a restored wide-belly, turn-of-the-century steam-powered locomotive. But the focal point and emotional heart of this museum is the 36-foot brass-sculpted Iron Man Memorial, which pays homage to the generations of miners who made their livelihood in this difficult and dangerous vocation. Open May through September.

SHOPPING
DREAM COTTAGE ANTIQUES
300 First St. N.W.
Chisholm
(218) 254-2153
Usually it's a safe bet that an antique store is only as good as the culture and history of the surroundings. Thanks to this region's highly varied immigrant roots, the Dream Cottage is packed with some of the most collectible antiques in northern Minnesota. There's furniture, jewelry, lamps, pictures, old magazines and a wide array of mining-related antique hardware. Open Tuesday through Thursday and Saturday and Sunday during the summer; Thursdays and Saturdays in the winter.

EATING
VALENTINI'S
31 W. Lake St.
Chisholm
(218) 254-2607
In this case, family owned and operated really means homemade Italian foods, which include seafood, steaks, chops

The trolley at the Hill Annex Mine.

CALUMET

HILL MINE ANNEX STATE PARK
Box 376 (on Highway 169, 15 miles northeast of Grand Rapids)
Calumet, MN 55716
(218) 247-7215
Listed on the National Register of Historic Places, this is the only remaining ore mine in Minnesota with the majority of its original buildings. The Hill mine was ranked as sixth-largest U.S. producer in the first half of the century. More than 63 million tons of ore were extracted from the mine between 1914 and 1978. Visitors can ride the trolley and tour the open pit mine. Open daily 10 a.m. to 4 p.m. Memorial Day through Labor Day.

and fresh Minnesota Aquafarms salmon daily. After 58 years Valentini's really knows how to cook.

▼ FOR MORE INFORMATION...
CHISHOLM CHAMBER OF COMMERCE
327 W. Lake St.
Chisholm, MN 55719
(218) 254-3600
(800) 422-0806

HIBBING

HIBBING WAS incorporated in 1893, not long after a forward-looking German immigrant, **Frank Hibbing**, established the fact that there was iron ore on the sight. Today it's the site of the world's largest open pit iron ore mine, more than three miles long, two miles wide and 535 feet deep. The Hull Rust Mahoning Mine produced more than a quarter of this nation's iron ore by the middle of the 1940s. Iron ore from Hull Rust was shipped through the Great Lakes to the steel mills of Pittsburgh.

Due to this rich deposit of iron ore, the original town of 188 buildings was forced in 1919 to relocate a few miles to the south. Engineers discovered that the small village was built on acres of high grade iron ore. The only remnants of the original Hibbing are a patchwork of dirt-covered sidewalks and a few outlines of old foundations.

The new town, thanks to the investment of nearly $21 million by the **Oliver Mining Co.**, was given impressive new buildings, such as the City Hall and the Androy Hotel. At one time Hibbing had the national reputation as "the richest little village in the world."

Hibbing is the birthplace of a number of famous persons and companies, such as **Robert Zimmerman**, better known to most of the world as folk musician **Bob Dylan**. Thanks to such songs as "Blowin' in the Wind" and "Like a

Rolling Stone," musicians from all over the world have named Dylan's lyrical genius as their source of inspiration. This also is the hometown of University of Minnesota and Boston Celtics basketball star **Kevin McHale**.

In the realm of business, the **Greyhound Bus Line Co.** began in Hibbing back in 1914 as a transportation system to cart miners around to the various mines on the Iron Range. Plus **Jeno Paulucci**, a feisty entrepreneur who built a financial empire in Duluth on Chinese food and later, pizzas, was born in Hibbing in 1919.

Paulucci grew up in poverty during the Depression. To help feed the family, he made a position for himself as a produce "barker" when he was only 16. He managed to make a little profit off a case of "slightly" brown bananas by offering them as Argentine bananas at a "slightly" inflated price. He moved on to bean sprouts and eventually his first company, **Chun King**, which he sold in 1966.

ATTRACTIONS

HULL RUST MAHONING MINE OVERLOOK
Northeast Hibbing

You won't believe your eyes when you gaze out from this eagle's nest on the Hull Rust mining operation at work below. The mine has been referred to as the Grand Canyon of the north. More than 1.4 billion tons of dirt have been moved from here. Take your binoculars for a closer look. This mine is so vast and so deep you'll need them to see the dinosaur-sized front-end loaders, cranes and dump trucks and to watch the mine crews blasting and hauling away the giant slabs of raw yellow, brown and black bedrock.

HULL RUST MAHONING MINE TOURS
Open May 15 through September 30. Call the Chamber of Commerce for tour reservations. **(218) 262-3895**.

HIBBING HISTORICAL SOCIETY/FIRST SETTLER'S MUSEUM
21st St. and E. Fourth Ave.
Hibbing
(218) 262-3486

This museum chronicles the rich mining history of this region and the world of the immigrants who made their living digging and blasting the heavy ore from the gaping pits of the Hull Rust Mine. Housed in the historic city hall, the First Settler's Museum is a fine collection of artifacts, photographs and mining, logging, American Indian and early explorer memorabilia. It's named after the First Settler's Association, whose members helped settle the early mining community of Hibbing in 1893.

PAULUCCI SPACE THEATRE
Arrowhead Hibbing Community College
Highway 169 and E. 23rd St.
Hibbing
(218) 262-6720

The Paulucci Foundation worked with several other civic and private organizations to get this wonderful space theater off the ground. The result is an amazing planetarium whose throbbing fish-eye projection lens, supporting cast of slide projectors, and surround sound offers viewers a front row seat to a different space and time. Needless to say, this is a place for kids of all ages.

GREYHOUND BUS ORIGIN CENTER
Fifth Ave. and 23rd St.
Hibbing
(218) 263-5814

Thanks to **Andrew "Bus Andy" Anderson** and **Carl Wickman**, who provided transport to the miners, Hibbing is the home of the Greyhound Bus Lines. The Center houses displays, audio-visuals and memorabilia of that era and the company. Included is a 1913 Hupmobile automobile.

EATING

4 SEASONS FAMILY RESTAURANT AND BAR
Junction Highways 53 and 169
Hibbing
(218) 741-4200

The specialties are barbecue ribs and the Friday night fresh fish fry. There are good home-cooked specials on Sunday.

LODGINGS

ADAMS HOUSE BED AND BREAKFAST
201 E. 23rd St.
Hibbing, MN 55746
(218) 263-9742

This historic English Tudor mansion was built in 1927 by one of the first doctors in town. There are lots of antiques and

Hurray! Minnesota

five unique guest rooms, all with old English style and comfort.

DAYS INN
1520 Highway 37 E.
Hibbing, MN 55746
(218) 263-8306
Clean, economical and convenient. 61 units.

REGENCY INN AND CONFERENCE CENTER
1402 E. Howard St.
Hibbing, MN 55746
(218) 262-3481
(800) 662-5708 (in Minnesota)
(800) 346-3552 (out-of-state)
Excellent restaurant, lounge, pool and sauna. Seven minutes to Ironworld. 125 rooms.

▼ FOR MORE INFORMATION...
HIBBING CHAMBER OF COMMERCE
Box 727
Hibbing, MN 55746
(218) 262-3895

GRAND RAPIDS

GRAND RAPIDS, named for the three-and-one-half mile stretch of rapids that blocked further traffic up the Mississippi, was once a pine-covered wilderness. The surrounding woods supplied many of the builders along the Mississippi River Valley with timber, cut and transported via steamship to the mills in Minneapolis and Winona.

In 1901 the power of those rapids was harnessed by the **Itasca Paper Co.**, helping to form the new industrial base needed to replace the depleted forest products. Financial magnate **C. K. Blandin** purchased the plant and began the expansion to what it is today. Blandin employs approximately 1,200 people in the paper mill and another 200 in the wood products subsidiary. **The Blandin Foundation**, founded in 1940, has added to the quality of life for those in the region with projects such as the **Myles Reif Performing Arts Center**.

Today, depending upon whom you ask, Grand Rapids, with a population of more than 7,000, is either a farming community, a lumber town, an iron ore distribution center, which some say is the real mother lode, or the birthplace of

The springboard chopping contest at Tall Timber Days in Grand Rapids.

Frances Ethel Gumm, otherwise known as **Judy Garland**. Her childhood home, a modest white frame structure, still stands at 727 Second Avenue N.E. and is a private residence.

To commemorate its rich history, Grand Rapids celebrates every summer with the Judy Garland Festival in June and Tall Timber Days in August, both of which draw people from across the nation. More than anything, visitors to Grand Rapids can't help but notice that this is a clean, friendly, wonderfully scenic town. It's surrounded by pristine lakes and has the Mississippi running through the middle of town. Some of the town's most captivating 19th-century structures are still standing.

ATTRACTIONS
FOREST HISTORY CENTER
Highways 169 and 2
Grand Rapids
(218) 327-4482
This well-kept museum brings to life the

Above, the childhood home of Judy Garland at Second Avenue Northeast.

Left, Central School has been remodeled into a cultural arts center.

timber industry that made Grand Rapids what it is today. There's a 1900 logging camp replica, interpretive building with running films and exhibits, a Minnesota Forest Service cabin complete with costumed guide, a collection of primitive and modern logging equipment and plenty of old logging archive photographs. After all that, visitors can walk the Woodland Trail next to the Mississippi and apply their newfound tree knowledge. Open year-round. Limited hours in winter.

BLANDIN PAPER CO.
115 S.W. First St.
Grand Rapids
(218) 326-8531
See how raw wood pulp is bleached, coated and rolled into the massive paper rolls that provide the pages for many of the world's magazines. Open for tours during the summer.

CENTRAL SCHOOL
10 N.W. Fifth St.
Grand Rapids
(218) 327-1843

JUDY GARLAND MUSEUM
ITASCA COUNTY HISTORY MUSEUM
If you love architecture and history, this is your escape in Grand Rapids. When built in 1895, Central was the only schoolhouse within miles. Today, after a million-dollar restoration, this beautiful example of Romanesque Revivalist architecture houses two museums, shops and a restaurant. In many respects, Central School is to Grand Rapids what the Depot is to Duluth, a historical landmark renovated into a cultural arts center.

On the first floor is a collection of shops, from crafts to antiques, and the **First Grade Restaurant**. Upstairs is the enchanting Judy Garland Museum, filled with memorabilia from Garland's now-famous storybook childhood starring on the silver screen, including, of course, her role in "The Wizard of Oz." There are volumes of movie stills from Garland's film and stage career, starting with her first childhood performances in vaudeville acts with her sisters in Grand

Rapids. You can learn about Garland's meteoric rise to fame and the pressures of Hollywood, which ultimately hooked her on the drugs that caused her death. This museum captures the thrill and tragedy of Garland's life in vivid detail. There is even a yellow brick road leading to the entrance of the building.

The **Itasca County Museum** captures the essence of this region's rich history: the early pioneers, the iron ore and the white pine bounty of the surrounding forests.

POKEGAMA DAM PARK
Highway 2 W.
Located on the banks of the Mississippi, Pokegama is a favorite spot to just plain relax, read a good book and listen to the soothing flow of the tumbling river below or the gentle swells of Pokegama Lake above.

RIVERSIDE PARK
Highway 2 E.
When you have a river like the Mississippi running through your town, you make the most of it. For Grand Rapids, Riverside serves as a tranquil spot with plenty of benches, tables and trails along the bank. Great for picnics and recreation.

WABANA TRAIL AND WILDFLOWER SANCTUARY
County Road 59
Grand Rapids
(218) 326-6619
Wabana has rich bouquets of wildflowers of all colors, shapes and sizes sprawled across acres of rolling countryside. The intricate trail system also accommodates hiking, walking or cycling in the summer and snowmobiling and cross-country skiing in the winter.

QUADNA MOUNTAIN
100 Quadna Road
Hill City
(218) 697-8444
(800) 422-6649
For downhill skiing there is a 365-foot vertical drop with four lifts. There is also an extensive system of cross-country and snowmobile trails.

SHOWBOAT
16th Ave. W. and Third St.
Grand Rapids, MN 55744
(218) 327-1823
(800) 722-7814
Captain Andy and a cast of more than 60 will entertain you as the minstrels, vaudeville stars and orchestras entertained on this mighty river in the late 1800s. Running three weekends in July through August. Call for reservations.

EATING

BLACK CHERRY LOUNGE
5200 S. Highway 169
Grand Rapids
(218) 326-0621
Good home cooking. Daily luncheon and dinner specials.

FOREST LAKE RESTAURANT AND LOUNGE
Highway 2 W.
Grand Rapids
(218) 326-3423
The cozy log setting overlooking Forest Lake makes this a great place for breakfast, lunch or dinner. American cuisine.

FRONTIER CAKE AND STEAK
600 N.E. Third St.
Grand Rapids
(218) 326-4112
This 24-hour restaurant serves breakfast, lunch and dinner. Among the best in local food and atmosphere.

SHAY'S FAMILY RESTAURANT
20 N.W. Third St.
Grand Rapids
(218) 326-2272
Home-cooked meals. Breakfast is served anytime. Open 5 a.m. to 9 p.m.

LODGINGS

BEST WESTERN RAINBOW INN
1300 Highway 169 E.
Grand Rapids, MN 55744
(218) 326-9655
It's within walking distance to most everything in Grand Rapids. The Rainbow Inn is large enough to handle large groups, too. There are 81 guest rooms. The lounge often features live music.

SAWMILL INN
2301 S. Pokegama Ave. and Highway 169
Grand Rapids, MN 55744
(218) 326-8501
(800) 235-6455
Brimming with hand-carved, honey-stained wood planks and beams and a big cozy fireplace, the Sawmill Inn lives up to its name in period motif. It features lots of carved wood, old saws and

great old black-and-white photographs from the turn of the century. The Sawmill is thoroughly modern with all the amenities. There are banquet facilities, sauna, swimming, even putting greens. If you have a reunion or business retreat in mind, there is plenty of convention space as well as a lounge and nightclub with live music. Moreover, the staff is knowledgeable about the surrounding area's fishing, hunting, hiking and cycling possibilities. The inn has 124 rooms.

SPIDER SHORE RESORT
Marcell, MN 56657
(800) 88-BOATS
Situated on beautiful Spider Lake, Spider Shore is a comfortable collection of 10 guest cabins just outside of Grand Rapids and affords visitors easy access to cross-country skiing, cycling, hiking and snowmobile trails as well as a lake filled with fish.

BUCKHORN ON CARIBOU LAKE
Box R
Marcell, MN 56657
(218) 832-3723

A hideaway of five unique cottages with decks on beautiful Caribou Lake. Forty acres of nature trails and tall pines.

QUADNA FOUR SEASONS RESORT
100 Quadna Road
Hill City, MN 55748
(218) 697-8444
(800) 422-6649
This beautiful resort has it all. Tennis, golf, boating and swimming in summer. Downhill and cross-country skiing and snowmobiling in winter. Between the motel and lodge, there are 200 rooms.

▼ **FOR MORE INFORMATION...**
1000 GRAND LAKES VISITOR AND CONVENTION BUREAU
1 Third St. N.W.
Grand Rapids, MN 55744
(218) 326-1281
(800) 472-6366
GRAND RAPIDS VISITOR AND CONVENTION BUREAU
(800) 472-6366
CHIPPEWA NATIONAL FOREST
(218) 832-3161
ITASCA COUNTY PARK AND RECREATION DIVISION
(218) 327-2855

AITKIN

SITUATED ON THE Mississippi River, Aitkin is 125 miles north of Minneapolis/St. Paul. The river, being a main route for travel, first brought the Sioux and Chippewa, and then early explorers such a **Greysolon du Lhut**, **Zebulon Pike**, **Father Louis Hennepin** and **Joseph N. Nicollet**. But it was **William A. Aitkin** who established the first permanent settlement here in 1831.

When the railroad was built, Aitkin became a transportation hub and an important player in logging and lumber-related industries. Today the Mississippi and the many lakes in the area provide the visitor with numerous recreational opportunities.

ATTRACTIONS
AITKIN RIVERBOAT DAYS
Held in July, Riverboat Days is a celebration of Aitkin's role as a major landing point for the Mississippi riverboats.

A TIME TO REMEMBER

Quadna Four Seasons Resort
100 Quadna Road • Hill City

- Challenging golf & tennis
- Indoor & outdoor pools & sauna
- 30 km mountain bike trail
- Lakeside lodge, Northwoods motel
- Restaurant
- Fishing, canoeing, pontoons

Call for reservations now at our Lakeside Lodge, Northwoods motel or comfortable townhomes.

A complete conference facility
(218) 697-8444 • (800) 422-6649

Hurray! Minnesota

There are black-powder shoots, parades, dances and more. **(218) 927-2316**.

SHOPPING
BUTLER'S V STORE
Downtown Aitkin
(218) 927-2185
When you step into Butler's, you step into another era. Located in the historic Aitkin opera house building, Butler's, a department store, features displays of Victorian antiques and artifacts among the men's, women's and children's clothing. Butler's also has three departments devoted to a wide selection of fabrics.

EATING
40 CLUB INN AND RESTAURANT
Highway 210 W.
Aitkin
(218) 927-7090 (restaurant)
(218) 927-2903 (motel)
Serving a full menu from steaks and lobster to hamburgers. Luncheon buffet 11 a.m. to 2 p.m., daily except Saturday. Daily dinner specials and dinner buffet on Thursday. The motel has 27 rooms, hot tub and sauna.

LODGING
EDGEWATER BEACH RESORT
Route 3, Box 108 (on Cedar Lake)
Aitkin, MN 56431
(218) 927-2895
You have to love a place that hosts a potluck dinner every Wednesday night. The Edgewater is a homespun resort with the conveniences of bait, gas and groceries on the premises. There is a conference room that accommodates up to 40 people. The staff will direct you to the best places for cross-country skiing or snowmobiling.

MORNINGSIDE RESORT
Route 3, Box 163 (on Cedar Lake)
Aitkin, MN 56431
(218) 927-2708
(800) 346-6166
There are 10 cozy lakeside cabins that come with canoes and paddle boats. There's plenty of open space in front of the lake for volleyball, croquet and picnics. Morningside also has two 120-foot fishing piers just outside your cabin door. Open May to October 1.

▼ FOR MORE INFORMATION...
AITKIN CHAMBER OF COMMERCE
Box 127
Aitkin, MN 56431
(218) 927-2316

CROSBY-IRONTON
CROFT MINE HISTORICAL PARK
Box 97
Crosby-Ironton, MN 56455
(218) 546-5466
On display at the park are mining machinery and artifacts, interpretives, dioramas, the office of Cuyler Adams, the prospector who discovered the Cuyuna Range, and historic mining buildings. Open daily 10 a.m. to 6 p.m., Memorial Day through Labor Day.

CUYUNA RANGE HISTORICAL MUSEUM
Downtown Crosby
This museum is located in the old railroad depot, which is of the same era as the exhibits and artifacts on display. There are mining and logging displays of tools and artifacts and an 1880s general store and dining kitchen. Open Monday thru Friday 10 a.m. to 4 p.m.

LODGING
WALDEN WOODS BED AND BREAKFAST
Route 1, Box 193
Deerwood, MN 56444
(612) 692-4379
Four beautiful rooms in this hand-built log home sitting on the edge of a private lake surrounded by 40 wooded acres. Thoreau would have enjoyed contemplating here. Full breakfast and evening refreshments.

HALLETT HOUSE
Box 247
Crosby, MN 56441
(218) 546-5433
Built in 1920, there are five rooms with private baths in this Colonial-style home. Equipped with chair-lift. Near lakes and ski trails.

▼ FOR MORE INFORMATION...
IRON TRAIL CONVENTION AND VISITORS BUREAU
Box 559
Eveleth, MN 55734
(218) 744-2441
(800) 777-8497

THE ARROWHEAD

• CASS LAKE • BEMIDJI • AKELEY • PARK RAPIDS • ALEXANDRIA •

• ST. CLOUD • MILLE LACS • LITTLE FALLS • BRAINERD • NISSWA • PEQUOT LAKES • CROSS LAKE • WALKER •

GOLFING AT MADDEN'S RESORT ON
GULL LAKE NEAR BRAINERD.

PHOTO COURTESY OF MINNESOTA OFFICE OF TOURISM
ILLUSTRATION BY ERIC HANSON

• COLD SPRING • BEMIDJI • WALKER • FERGUS FALLS • ASHBY •

LAKE COUNTRY

THERE ARE THREE major concentrations of lakes in the region "Hurray! Minnesota" defines as "Lake Country." One is the center of the state, anchored by the city of Brainerd, with lakes to the north of Brainerd up to the Whitefish Chain and with Mille Lacs, one of the state's largest and most prominent, to the west of Brainerd. Another concentration occurs in the west central part of the state, with three cities as important anchors — Alexandria, Detroit Lakes and Fergus Falls. The third is north-centrally located in the Itasca Headwaters of the Mississippi River area, anchored by Walker, Bemidji and Park Rapids and including such major lakes as Leech and Winnibigoshish.

These areas are cottage and resort country and are an integral part of Minnesota culture. When Minnesotans say they're going "up to the lake," most often they're headed to one of these areas, whether to a cottage, resort or campground. You can ask any one of these people and they'll tell you that their lake is the very best in Minnesota.

This migration northward on Friday afternoons and back south to the Twin Cities on Sunday evening causes a unique phenomenon called the "Minnesota Tilt." When you hear this expression you know that it refers to the population shift from

LAKE COUNTRY

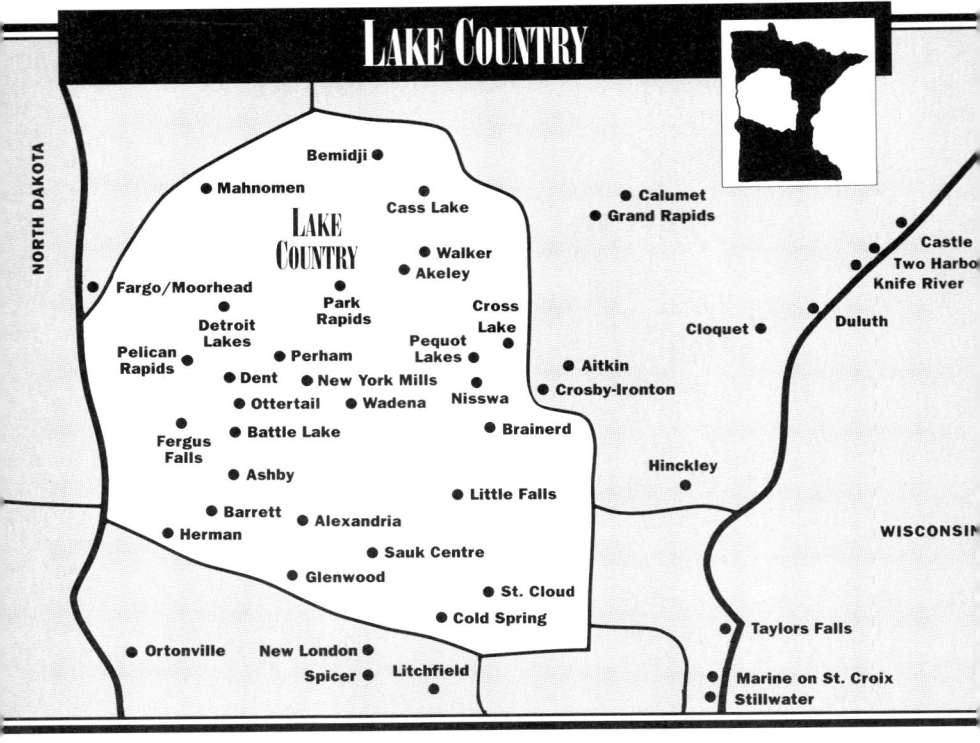

metro to lakes and back to metro. The heaviest "tilt" begins with the opening of fishing in May and begins to taper off around Labor Day and the start of school in the fall.

And why not? There are thousands of pristine lakes surrounded by forests of red and white pine or by rolling acres of maple, oak, and birch, adding up to a unique recreational experience that is distinctly Minnesotan.

With the spotlight on the lakes and water-related activities, Lake Country has some of the poshest resorts in Minnesota and features some of the finest golf courses and tennis facilities. Certainly there are resorts for every pocketbook, but the Brainerd area particularly features several resorts that have facilities, amenities and service to compare with hospitality anywhere.

Although nature gets much of the attention in Lake Country, it's worth pointing out that there are plenty of other attractions in Lake Country. For example, Alexandria, just 130 miles northwest of the Twin Cities on Interstate 94, has a rather compelling legend that causes the area to claim the distinction of being the "Birthplace of America." Runic etchings on what is now known as the **Kensington Runestone** indicate that America's real discoverers were Vikings and that they visited Kensington, just north of Alexandria, 130 years before Christopher Columbus set foot on this continent.

The **Runestone Museum** in downtown Alexandria houses the Kensington Runestone that in 1889 Olaf Ohman found wrapped in the roots of an aspen tree on his farm.

St. Cloud, on the southern edge of Lake Country, is the fastest-growing metropolitan area in the state. It's the world's largest producer of granite as well as a leader in optics and the paper/printing industries.

The first American to win the Nobel Prize for literature grew up in Sauk Centre between St. Cloud and Alexandria. Sinclair Lewis based "Main Street" on the experiences he had growing up in Sauk Centre. Today his boyhood home is restored and open to the public along with the **Sinclair Lewis Interpretive Center and Museum**.

Hurray! Minnesota

The famous **Charles Lindbergh**, the first man to complete a solo crossing of the Atlantic by plane, spent boyhood summers in Little Falls. Here, too, you can tour the **Lindbergh House and Interpretive Center** and see replicas of the planes he flew and other Lindbergh memorabilia.

Farther north the tales grow dramatically taller and certainly more lighthearted. Indeed, no description of Lake Country is complete without mention of the fabled giant lumberjack, **Paul Bunyan**, and his big blue ox, **Babe**. It is said that Bunyan is responsible for Minnesota's 10,000 lakes and thousands of miles of rivers. Statues of this famous pair can be found in both Bemidji and Brainerd as well as his cradle in Akeley and his tombstone in Kelliher.

Lake Country is a fascinating part of Minnesota. Get out your fishing rod and your lawn chair, find your lake and your quaint town, get some exercise, enjoy a festival, visit one of the sites and, most of all, relax.

THE ST. CLOUD AREA

IT'S HARD TO ENVISION ST. CLOUD without conjuring images of granite quarries, paper companies and **Lake Wobegon**, the mythical community somewhere near here made internationally famous by public radio show host **Garrison Keillor**.

St. Cloud each year produces the world's largest supply of granite from a single source. Nearly half of all prescription glass optics are manufactured here. And one of the oldest Benedictine abbeys in the United States is still operating in nearby **Collegeville**. But there's also a great deal more to St. Cloud.

Both in terms of business and overall mentality, St. Cloud likes to say that it is a big little town. You don't have to look far to see just how big this city has become to realize that it has become a regional destination, with many of the advantages of a major metropolis.

On the flip side, the St. Cloud metro area is still small enough to be friendly and open to visitors. And small enough that when someone like **Louie Wippich** builds what's been called the largest rock garden in the Upper Midwest, it's news. You can see this unusual rock garden and its 45-foot granite Tower of Babel in nearby **Sauk Rapids**.

HISTORY

ST. CLOUD BEGAN as a lumber town in 1856. Sawmill builder **John Lyman Wilson** paid $250 to secure the 325 acres that would become St. Cloud. St. Cloud is named after the city **Napoleon** built for **Empress Josephine**. Early St. Cloud was the culmination of three distinct communities: German Catholic immigrants, settlers from the southeastern seaboard and New England Protestants. Despite their religious differences and strongly divided views on slavery, they banded together for mutual survival and methodically grew into a major force in Mississippi River traffic and distribution.

In the same year, Minnesota's first liberal arts college, St. John's, and the Benedictine abbey were founded just west of St. Cloud in Collegeville.

The commerce created by the river's advantage in distribution and shipping caused the population to explode in the 1860s. Then, in 1868, a mountain of the most beautiful granite the region had ever seen was discovered. But it wasn't until the railroad arrived in 1890 that St. Cloud really took off as a major supplier of granite, timber and agricultural products.

The granite quarries provided wealth and prosperity to St. Cloud, much as the Iron Range communities achieved through iron ore during roughly the same period. St. Cloud's granite quarries continue to produce millions of tons of granite every year. On the **Mall Germaine**, in downtown St. Cloud, there's a sculpture titled **"Granite Trio"** in honor of this heritage. The **Minnesota State Capitol**, **Cathedral of St. Paul**

The Mississippi River as it flows through St. Cloud.

and **Statue of Liberty** all have granite from St. Cloud quarries.

Even St. Cloud's once famous minor league baseball team, the **Rox**, took its name in honor of the city's great granite history. During the team's existence from 1946 to 1971, two Hall of Famers played their first pro games here, pitcher **Gaylord Perry** in 1958 and outfielder **Lou Brock** in 1961. Perry won over 300 games during his major league career, which began with the San Francisco Giants. Brock achieved the all-time record for stolen bases during his career with the St. Louis Cardinals.

THE BUSINESS OF ST. CLOUD

ST. CLOUD HAS been adept at creating new jobs in a variety of industries, including health care, manufacturing and creative services. According to the Minnesota Department of Jobs and Training, since the 1982-83 recession, St. Cloud has developed new jobs faster than any other city in Minnesota, the Dakotas, Montana, Nebraska, Wyoming, Iowa or Wisconsin.

Corporations like direct marketing giant **Fingerhut** have expanded or taken up new residency in St. Cloud because of the city's favorable tax climate, affordable real estate, skilled and educated labor force, low crime rate and high quality of life. St. Cloud also was recently awarded a $3.1 million grant by the state of Minnesota to establish a **Central Minnesota Manufacturing Technology Center**.

Despite this growth, which materialized substantially during the 1980s, St. Cloud's heart and soul still revolves around its big three industries: granite, optics and paper/printing, all of which have long histories in this area.

Ever since the vast deposits of granite were discovered, this multi-colored stone has played a vital role in the city's economy. St. Cloud's **Cold Spring Granite** quarries produce more granite than any other place in the world.

St. Cloud's printing and paper industry, which began with **Watab Paper** (now **Champion International**, located just outside of St. Cloud in nearby Sartell) in 1905, continues to hum as one of the largest in the nation. St. Cloud paper companies produce more lightweight coated paper (the paper used in consumer magazines and catalogs) than any other city in the nation. Champion alone supplies the paper for 20 of 25 of the nation's largest magazines. With no fewer than 19 full-service web and sheet-fed printers operating around the clock, St. Cloud has one of the highest concentrations of printing power between the Twin Cities and the West Coast, according to city promoters.

Most people have heard about St. Cloud's granite and printing prominence, but many are surprised to learn about the city's optics industry. St. Cloud's 16 optics manufacturers turn out 47 percent of America's prescription lenses every year.

Agriculture continues to play a large role in the St. Cloud business mix. St. Cloud is the county seat for a healthy farming community. Stearns County, which stretches west from St. Cloud, remains the state's largest dairy and swine producing area.

Herberger's Department Store was founded in St. Cloud in the early 1900s by G.R. Herberger. St. Cloud continues to be the headquarters for the 37 stores, which are located throughout northern Minnesota, Montana and Wyoming.

DEMOGRAPHICS

ST. CLOUD IS the fastest growing city in Minnesota. The city of St. Cloud itself has a population of 46,158. Add the suburbs and that number swells to 81,755. The neighboring cities of **Sartell**, **Sauk Rapids**, **St. Joseph** and **Waite Park**, as part of a three-county metropolitan area, bring the total population to 175,000. It is this last number that state forecasters predict will increase by 25 percent within the next decade.

EDUCATION

ST. CLOUD'S HIGH school graduation rate is 96 percent. That's five percent higher than the state average, which is already ranked as one of the best in the country, and 20 percent higher than the national average. The city's SAT college entrance exam scores rank in the top 20th percentile nationally.

St. Cloud is home to **St. Cloud State University**, the fastest growing campus in the state university system, and the state's third largest university overall (17,000 students). Collegeville and St. Joseph to the west are home to **St. John's University**, the oldest educational institution for men in Minnesota, and **The College of St. Benedict**, a liberal arts college for women. St. John's University is home to the world-renowned **Hill Monastic Manuscript Library**, the largest medieval manuscript collection in the world.

The city also has **St. Cloud Technical Institute**, with 35 technical programs, plus a business college and two cosmetology schools.

HEALTH SERVICES AND INDUSTRY

BETWEEN THE **St. Cloud Hospital** and **St. Cloud VA Hospital**, the city is both a major health care provider and also employer. The hallmark of St. Cloud's medical profile is its **Mid-Minnesota Health Clinic**, which was established in 1990 to provide uninsured and underinsured residents within a 30-mile radius with quality health care.

ATTRACTIONS

STEPHEN B. HUMPHREY THEATER
St. John's University
Collegeville
(612) 363-2734
This theater hosts an international film festival, drama, comedy, lectures, musical concerts and dance performances throughout the academic year.

ST. CLOUD SYMPHONY ORCHESTRA
St. Cloud
(612) 259-4015
This gifted orchestra, in its 18th season, performs four concerts each year, featuring renowned local and visiting soloists. The season runs from October through April with a special Christmas concert and a young performers of Minnesota competition. Conductor Lawrence Eckerling is from Chicago.

COUNTY STEARNS THEATRICAL CO.
22 S. Fifth Ave.
St. Cloud
(612) 253-8242
Comedy, drama and musicals are all part of the package here at St. Cloud's preeminent theater company. The season runs from September through May.

NEW TRADITION THEATER CO.
913 W. St. Germaine St.
St. Cloud
(612) 253-9722
This theater's offerings include a wide variety of modern and traditional dra-

matic interpretations. It's located in downtown St. Cloud in the renovated historic Paramount Theatre. The season runs from September to April with a different show every month.

BENEDICTA ARTS CENTER
College of St. Benedict
St. Joseph
(612) 363-5777
Located on campus at the College of St. Benedict, this arts center has a collection of national, regional and local art on display throughout the year.

NATURE'S STUDIO
419 W. St. Germaine
St. Cloud
(612) 259-6484
This gallery and custom frame shop has a wide selection of original and poster art as well as limited-edition wildlife, aviation and marine-inspired paintings and drawings.

LOUIS C. WIPPICH ROCK GARDEN
The Garden of Infinity
Third Ave. and Sixth St.
Sauk Rapids
In nearby Sauk Rapids is one of the largest rock gardens in the Upper Midwest, if not the country. This is a theosophical reincarnation garden, which was built over 30 years by an eccentric (now deceased) ex-railroad worker named Louie Wippich. There's a 45-foot modern-day Tower of Babel and various other structures surrounding a massive rock garden that is supposed to provide the place for Louie to return to as a bird in his next life. This is such a fascinating architectural memorial that visitors come from across the country. The Walker Art Center of Minneapolis has featured Louie in its American Eccentrics exhibit titled "Naives and Visionaries."

MUNSINGER GARDENS
Riverside Drive S. and Michigan Ave.
St. Cloud
Just across the Mississippi River from St. Cloud State University is a magical rock and flower garden filled with 35,000 trees, flowers and assorted greenery. Flower Park also has walkways, picnic tables and lots of trees for a relaxing lunch overlooking the scenic Mississippi.

PIRATE'S COVE PADDLEBOAT DINING CRUISES
7355 N.E. River Road
(off Highway 10 on the Mississippi)
Sauk Rapids
(612) 252-8400
The Anne Bonny, a paddleboat replica, travels the Mississippi. It's a spectacular photo opportunity as well as a relaxing way to get close to the water and beautiful bluffs. The Anne Bonny is available for charter trips for dinner, Sunday brunch or evening cocktail cruises. Public cruises are given Friday through Sunday. There are three restaurants at the Cove serving lunches and dinners. For fine dining, the main dining room upstairs, with huge windows overlooking the river, serves American and continental cuisine with evening specials. For those who like to boat in, the Gazebo Bar has deck seating along the river and serves sandwiches and snacks. The Garden Court downstairs has live entertainment every night.

OLIVER H. KELLEY FARM
15788 Kelley Farm Road
(off Highway 10)
Elk River
(612) 441-6896
South of St. Cloud 35 miles is an opportunity to step back in time and see how farms used to be worked. This 1867 farm, built by Oliver Kelley, the founder of the Patrons of Husbandry during the farmer's protest movement, is an interpretive center and museum today. The staff dresses in period Victorian clothing, churns butter by hand, and even plows the nearby fields with oxen and draft horses.

CHATEAU DEVENOIS WINERY
150 N.W. 125th St.
Rice
(612) 393-WINE
Just 15 miles north of St. Cloud lies a wonderful winery that has blossomed from the rich soil of the Langola Valley. Chateau Devenois, or House of Deven, named after the Kaminski family's daughter Deven, has a winery, vineyard, tasting rooms, banquet facilities large enough to serve 250 people and dining and picnic areas. Call for tour availability. Tasting room open Friday through Sunday, noon to 6 p.m.

Hurray! Minnesota

CHAMPION INTERNATIONAL PAPER MILL
Sartell
(612) 251-6511
Along the banks of the Mississippi you can see Champion, one of the nation's largest manufacturers of lightweight coated stock paper, the kind used in publications such as TV Guide or the Sears catalog. Here the mammoth rolls of pressed, bleached and treated wood pulp and chemicals come together to form the raw sheet paper for many of the world's magazines and catalogs. This is a walking tour so don't forget your walking shoes. Call for tour reservations.

MOLITOR'S TROUT HEAVEN
425 N.E. 35th St.
Sauk Rapids
(612) 253-1672
If you want to fish but don't have the gear, time or patience to test your skill and luck in the traditional way, try Molitor's Trout Heaven in Sauk Rapids. Molitor's has gear, cleaning and dressing services, and a scenic fishing pond stocked with rainbow trout. Molitor's also features some of the tastiest cherry and apple wood-smoked trout in the area for sale at the main shop.

ROCKVILLE GRANITE QUARRY
Highway 23
Rockville
At this open pit granite quarry you can observe the granite being quarried for transport to processing plants.

GOLDEN SHOE TOURS
St. Cloud
(612) 253-4132
Find the car a bit stifling? See the historic and beautiful sights of downtown St. Cloud by romantic horse-drawn carriage. Trolley and motorcoach tours also available. Call for reservations.

HISTORICAL SITES

ST. CLOUD HAS an impressive collection of architecture preserved from its past. There's the Cold Spring Brewers' Houses, First National Bank and Stearns County Courthouse, just to name a few of the more than 19 places on the National Register. Phone for a list of the St. Cloud homes and buildings listed on the National Register of Historic Places.
(612) 253-8424.

Illuminated 15th-century manuscript page.

HILL MONASTIC MANUSCRIPT LIBRARY
Bush Center
St. John's University
Collegeville
(612) 363-3514
The world's largest, most precious collection of manuscripts from the medieval, Renaissance and early modern periods are housed at St. John's University, the state's oldest liberal arts college. The museum has no fewer than 72,000 manuscripts, 122,000 papyri and volumes of assorted archives from all over Europe and Ethiopia.

Some of the pieces in this collection exist here only on microfilm, while others are preserved under glass. You'll be astonished at the vivid mosaic patterns of artwork and sketchings that adorn these pages. These are the authentic words and images that shaped western civilization for centuries. Included are writings of culture, religion, music and civics that date back to the Crusades. This is a working research center for academics and clerics from around the world.

Ask to see the slide show for a beginning understanding of the magnitude of this collection.

Powerboat racing on the Mississippi River.

RECREATION

THE METRO AREA has 566 parks, six full-service health clubs, two municipal ice arenas, and the U.S. Olympic ice training arena. City boosters point out that St. Cloud has more tennis courts per capita than almost any other city in the nation. St. Cloud has eight golf courses within a 25-mile radius of the city. There also are miles of winter sports trails and paths as well as a host of fishing opportunities in the surrounding rivers and lakes.

MUSEUMS

STEARNS COUNTY HERITAGE CENTER AND HISTORICAL SOCIETY
235 S. 33rd Ave.
St. Cloud
(612) 253-8424

With a collection of nearly 10,000 museum items, 200,000 old photographs and 10,000 local biographies, the Stearns County Historical Society Museum is one of the largest historical museums outside of the Twin Cities and one of the few accredited by the American Association of Museums. The multi-floor visual and educational experience in the museum and adjacent heritage center includes elaborate scale exhibits of a two-story granite quarry replica, dairy farming implements, fur trading with the Ojibwa and Dakota peoples, timber and sawmill operations, and the 26 seasons of St. Cloud's beloved minor league baseball

Shopping

DOWNTOWN HAS **Herberger's** and a beautiful four-block open walking mall with a number of specialty stores. West of town on Division Highway 23 is the **Crossroads Shopping Center**, an enclosed mall with 102 stores including a **Sears**, **J.C. Penney**, **Dayton's** and **Target**.

Arts Co-op
619 Mall Germaine
St. Cloud
(612) 252-3242
There is a gift shop and a permanent collection of artwork for sale that includes weavings, Victorian collectibles, stained glass, pottery, wood carvings and other handmade crafts from local artists.

A Little Bit Country
3333 W. Division St.
St. Cloud
(612) 259-7923
This cozy store claims to have the largest selection of hand-crafted country collectibles in central Minnesota. There's a bounty of arts and crafts for the home, some from local artists. It's all on display in a quaint country village setting with a boardwalk and old-fashioned park square.

Jennings Decoy Co.
601 Franklin Ave. N.E.
St. Cloud
(612) 253-2253
Jennings sells carving supplies for those who like to carve birds and fish and also reproductions for those who like to just do the finishing work. They also have a beautiful display with more than 500 finished decoys for sale.

---

team, The Rox. Open Tuesday through Saturday 10 a.m. to 4 p.m.; Sunday noon to 4 p.m.

Benton County Historical Society
218 First St. N.
Sauk Rapids
(612) 253-9614
Here you'll find the complete history of the fur trading, timber and farming communities just east of St. Cloud in Benton County.

Eating

Anton's
2001 Division St.
Waite Park
(612) 253-3611
This is a beautiful spot on the Sauk River. It was built in the 1920s as a speakeasy called Bricky's. After Prohibition it became a bar and continued to prosper. By the front door is a still that is rumored to have distilled "Minnesota 13," popular Prohibition spirits from the area. Anton's serves seafood and steaks with a special every night. Try their baked turtle or prime rib specials. Lunch, dinner and full-service bar. Just west of St. Cloud off County Road 75.

Bravo Burritos Mexicatessen and Bar
26 Fifth Ave. S.
St. Cloud
(612) 252-8700
This Mexican deli, where the menu is

painted on the wall above the ordering counter, is low-key, ala carte-style dining for sure. But don't be fooled by the casual motif and non-traditional style; the food is some of the best Mexican food around. The menu is complete, the servings are huge and the prices are designed for college students. Serving lunch and dinner.

CHARLIE'S
102 Sixth Ave. S.
St. Cloud
(612) 252-4538
Charlie's, located in downtown St. Cloud, is one of those dining experiences where you can still have great service, a tasty meal of pasta, chicken dishes, or catch of the day, all for a decent price. Open daily 10:30 a.m. to 1 a.m.

D.B. SEARLE'S
18 S. Fifth Ave.
St. Cloud
(612) 253-0655
D.B. Searle's offers some of the tastiest lunches and dinners you'll have in St. Cloud in one of the most unique settings. The restaurant is built in a fully-restored 1886 four-story warehouse in St. Cloud's historic downtown. There's great steak and seafood, as well as burgers and sandwiches. The place is well known for its French onion soup and stuffed popovers.

CHINESE PHOENIX RESTAURANT AND LOUNGE
Crossroads Cinema Complex
St. Cloud
(612) 255-1103
The Phoenix offers a lunch and dinner buffet or full dinner menu cooked without MSG. Enjoy a cocktail or tropical cocktail in an atmosphere authentically Chinese.

HEMSINGS DELICATESSEN
30 S. Fifth Ave. (Highway 10)
St. Cloud
(612) 251-5524
Hemsings Deli is a local favorite that's been named best deli in St. Cloud. The deli's selections include hot and cold sub sandwiches, homemade soup and salads, cheeses, ice cream and a whole gamut of other deli food. This is the home of the famous breakfast bagel. Open Monday through Saturday 8 a.m. to 2 a.m.

LODGING

RADISSON SUITE HOTEL
404 W. St. Germaine St.
St. Cloud. MN 56301
(612) 654-2940
(800) 333-3333
This is St. Cloud's newest hotel. Located in the heart of downtown, the Radisson has all the amenities for a luxurious stay, including whirlpool, entertainment suites, swimming pool and suite-style rooms that come equipped with a refrigerator, microwave and wet bar.

SUNWOOD INN AND CONVENTION CENTER
1 Sunwood Plaza
St. Cloud, MN 56301
(612) 253-0606
(800) 321-4151
Beautiful location on the Mississippi in downtown St. Cloud, with a fine dining restaurant and lounge. There are 230 rooms, indoor pool, whirlpool and sauna.

HOLIDAY INN
75 S. 37th Ave.
St. Cloud, MN 56301
(612) 253-9000
(800) HOLIDAY
This is the place for a summer vacation during a Minnesota winter with four indoor pools (two regular, whirlpool and wading pool), sauna, fitness room, game room, and play area with basketball, volleyball, badminton and Ping-Pong. Family rates available.

PILLOW, PILLAR AND PINE
419 Main St.
Cold Spring, MN 56320
(612) 685-3828
On the historic Red River Trail, this Greek Revival three-story mansion was built in 1908. It has three guest rooms, shared and private baths and a double whirlpool. Lovely woodwork, stained glass and antiques.

▼ **FOR MORE INFORMATION...**
ST. CLOUD CONVENTION AND VISITORS BUREAU
30 Sixth Ave. S.
St. Cloud, MN 56301
(612) 251-2940
(800) 937-6606

LAKE MILLE LACS

MILLE LACS IS THE SECond largest lake in Minnesota with borders completely within the state. Being only 90 minutes from the Twin Cities, it's a popular fishing and recreational area. For its size, it is not a deep lake and as a result can be very dangerous when the winds rile it up. The waves come big and close together.

Around the lake there are more than 80 resorts and the towns of **Isle**, **Wahcon**, **Cove**, **Onamia**, **Vineland**, **Garrison**, **Cutler**, **Wealthwood** and **Malmo**. The west shore is the location of the **Mille Lacs Chippewa Indian Reservation**.

Launch fishing on a lake the size of Mille Lacs lends the sport an oceangoing sensation — without the salt.

Fishing by Indians and recreational fishermen yields 500,000 pounds of walleye annually. Fishing is not limited just to summer months; each winter as many as 3,000 to 5,000 fish houses appear on the lake. The Crystal Carnival in February captures the fun and camaraderie of these Lake Mille Lacs towns, with costumed characters Eelpout Eddie and Edith bringing fun and good cheer to all.

Fishing Hotspots, a waterproof map of Mille Lacs Lake, can be obtained from **Box 1167, Rhinelander, WI, 54501, (715) 369-5555 or (800) 338-5957**.

ATTRACTIONS
FATHER HENNEPIN STATE PARK
Box 397 (Highway 27)
Isle, Mn 56342
(612) 676-8763
Located on the southeast shore of Mille Lacs next to Isle, this 316-acre park offers a beautiful sandy beach, fishing, hiking and boat access to Mille Lacs.

WEALTHWOOD ROD AND GUN CLUB
North end of Mille Lacs
(218) 678-2281
Near Wealthwood State Forest, the club is open to the public. There are 28 target ranges for trap and skeet.

MILLE LACS KATHIO STATE PARK
HC-67 Box 85 (Highway 169, eight miles north of Onamia)
Onamia, MN 56359
(612) 532-3523
The park has an excellent interpretive center that traces the human habitation around the lake as far back as 5,000 years.

FORT MILLE LACS VILLAGE
(612) 532-3651
The village has an art gallery, Indian room and shop and museum. For the younger set, the animal forest and paddle boats are entertaining. There is a great family restaurant, Granny's Kitchen, which is famous for its all-you-can-eat Sunday turkey dinner. Open May through September.

MILLE LACS INDIAN MUSEUM
Highway 169
Onamia
(612) 532-3632
Beautiful life-sized dioramas illustrate the life of the Ojibwa in each season. Artifacts from area tribes depict the history and culture. There also is a museum shop with handcrafted items for sale. Open May through October, Monday through Saturday, 10 a.m. to 5 p.m. and Sunday noon through 5 p.m.

TERRY'S BOAT HARBOR MARINA
Star Route 169
Garrison
(612) 692-4430
(800) 325-4380
Guide service for trophy walleye, northern and muskie fishing. Launch fishing trips, charters boats and boat launching facilities.

GRAND CASINO
Highway 169, West Shore
Mille Lacs Indian Reservation
(612) 532-7777
(800) 626-LUCK
Just east of Hinckley near Lake Mille Lacs, the casino has blackjack, video slots, bingo and the Gold Rush Grill. Operated by the Mille Lacs band of Ojibwa.

SHOPPING
STONE HOUSE
(218) 678-2683
Beautiful gifts and antiques can be found in this quaint old house. It's just a fun place to stop and browse. Located four miles north of Garrison on old Highway 169 or No. 37.

TUTT'S BAIT AND TACKLE
Highway 18 W.
Garrison
(612) 692-4341
Tutt's carries a large selection of bait, a complete line of lures for all types of fish and hunting supplies. Open daily 6 a.m. to 9 p.m. year-round.

EATING
BLUE GOOSE INN
Highway 169
Garrison
(612) 692-4330
This gourmet restaurant has a full-service cocktail lounge and live entertainment on Friday and Saturday. It's a great place to stop for a hot toddy, since it's right on the snowmobile trails.

HEADQUARTERS LODGE
Highway 169
Garrison
(612) 692-4346
American and continental cuisine served in a casual rustic atmosphere that has an outstanding view of Mille Lacs. Open year-round.

GATEWAY CAFE
Highway 169
(One mile south of Onamia)
Onamia
(612) 532-3787
This family restaurant serves homemade soups and pies. Open seven days a week, 24 hours a day in summer.

FLAGSHIP INN, INC.
HC-69, Box 204A
Isle
(612) 676-3693
The dining room has lots of windows to really get a view of the lake in comfort, no matter what the weather. Open for breakfast, lunch and dinner. Full-service cocktail lounge.

LODGING
IZATYS GOLF AND YACHT CLUB
Route 1, Mille Lacs Lake
Onamia, MN 56359
(612) 532-3101
(800) 533-1728
Stay in one of 70 shoreline town homes and villas and play the 18-hole championship golf course. There's a driving range to practice your swing and a pro shop for support. In between games, try the indoor and outdoor pools, sauna, spa and lighted tennis courts. There is a sheltered harbor with 120 boat slips and a full-service marina. There are trails and facilities for all the winter activities such as cross-country skiing, skating and ice fishing. Izatys' gorgeous clubhouse features gourmet dining. There are meeting facilities for groups of various sizes. This is one of Minnesota's premier resorts.

RUTTGER'S BAY LAKE LODGE
Box 400
Deerwood, MN 56444
(218) 678-2885
(800) 247-0402 (MN)
(800) 328-0312 (USA)
This is a wonderful family resort with a history dating back to 1898. Legend has it that this was the first resort in Minnesota, originally begun to house the loggers in the area. There are 30 motel rooms, 35 cabins and 100 condos. Recreation includes indoor and outdoor pools, 27 holes of golf, tennis and hiking. The beautiful log dining room has a lake view. Open mid-April through October.

Hurray! Minnesota

ORR'S CAMPGROUND AND SUPPER CLUB
Star Route
Isle, MN 56342
(612) 684-2380
The full-service restaurant serves steaks and seafood. There are more than 100 camping and RV sites and a couple of cabins. There is a sandy beach and protected harbor with launch service. Boats and bait are available on the premises.

▼ **FOR MORE INFORMATION...**
MILLE LACS AREA TOURISM ASSOCIATION
Box 692
Isle, MN 56342
(612) 532-3634
(800) 346-9375

LITTLE FALLS

AFTER PRESIDENT Thomas Jefferson bought Minnesota from France in the Louisiana Purchase, he sent explorer **Zebulon Pike** to find the headwaters of the Mississippi River and to map the area for future settlement. In 1805 Pike landed on the west side of the Mississippi at the mouth of the Swan River, just south of where Little Falls sits today. He built Fort Pike, which is considered the first U.S. presence in Minnesota. Since 1925, the fort has been submerged under the waters of the Blanchard Dam and reservoir. In 1983 and again in 1987, the waters of the reservoir needed to be lowered for dam repair and archeologists were given the opportunity to excavate the site. They found the outline of the old fort and a number of artifacts.

Little Falls, a small community nestled on the banks of the Mississippi River, was the childhood summer home of **Charles Lindbergh Jr.**, the first person to fly nonstop across the Atlantic. He accomplished this feat on May 20, 1927. A portion of the original Lindbergh farm has been turned into a park and Lindbergh's childhood home is now a popular museum and interpretive center.

This river town also has plenty of other well-preserved history, including the Charles A. Weyerhaeuser Museum, the stately Our Lady of Lourdes Polish church and a collection of 19th-century Victorian/Romanesque homes and buildings. Just a few miles north of Little Falls you'll find **Camp Ripley**, the nation's largest National Guard camp, which also has the Camp Ripley Military Museum.

Little Falls is well-known for its annual arts and crafts fair in September. Now in its 20th year, this weekend event is billed as the largest of its kind in the Midwest. Little Falls also is home to **Crestliner**, one of the country's major boat manufacturers.

ATTRACTIONS
HISTORICAL SITES
A WALKING TOUR in Little Falls reveals excellent examples of turn-of-the-century architecture, such as the 1899 Railroad Depot designed by **Cass Gilbert**, the Morrison County Courthouse and the Dewey-Radke Mansion. The Little Falls Chamber of Commerce has a map and information on the sites. **(612) 632-5155** or **(800) 325-5916**.

DEWEY-RADKE MANSION
Highway 27 W.
Little Falls
(218) 632-5155
A completely restored and refurnished home of the late 1800s. Open weekends, Memorial Day through Labor Day.

LINDBERGH HOUSE/CHARLES A. LINDBERGH STATE PARK
Route 3, Lindbergh Drive
(two miles south of Little Falls)
Little Falls
(612) 632-3154
Charles Lindbergh's father was a congressman so the family lived most of the year in Washington, D.C., during young Lindbergh's formative years. But he loved his home on the farm in Little Falls and spent his childhood summers here with his mother.

This farm home is now a captivating historical landmark that's been turned into a museum, park and interpretive center. Three generations of Lindberghs are represented through photos, archives, clothing and other memorabilia, which include replicas of Lindbergh's planes, the Spirit of St. Louis and the Jenny. This is a fitting tribute to the man who made the world's first trans-Atlantic airplane flight in 1927 and achieved distinction as a wingwalker, parachutist, inventor and environmentalist.

Just across from the Lindbergh home is Lindbergh State Park, where you can camp, picnic, hike or ski along a scenic and wooded Mississippi River trail. There are restrooms, hot showers, a shelter cabin and groomed trails. Open May through Labor Day, daily 10 a.m. to 5 p.m.; September 7 through April 26, Saturday 10 a.m. to 4 p.m. and Sunday noon to 4 p.m.

Charles A. Weyerhaeuser Memorial Museum
S. Lindbergh Drive
Little Falls
(612) 632-4007

Minnesota paper giant Charles Weyerhaeuser contributed this museum to Morrison County. On display are the history and heritage of Little Falls and the surrounding county's early 19th-century industry, lifestyles and noteworthy personalities. Open May through October, Tuesday through Saturday, 10 a.m. to 5 p.m., Sunday 1 to 5 p.m.

Minnesota Military Museum
Camp Ripley, Highway 371 S.
Little Falls
(612) 632-6631

Operated by the Minnesota Military Historical Society and located between Little Falls and Brainerd, the Minnesota Military Museum is located on the grounds of Camp Ripley, the 53,000-acre National Guard training facility, the largest year-round facility of its kind in the nation.

The museum has displays on each war from the time of the frontier forts to Desert Storm. Special exhibits of the 1992 season: E. B. Miller — By Way of Bataan and Women in the Military — 50 Years. There are weapons exhibits from frontier days to the present, including weapons used in Desert Storm. The library and research area are open to individuals by appointment. An outdoor display features tanks, trucks and other military equipment, such as an L19 plane and the 1949 French Boxcar. Open June through August, Wednesday through Sunday, 10 a.m. to 5 p.m. Closed national holidays. Free admission. For more information: Director Col. (Ret.) Richard L. Hayes **(612) 422-9731**.

Pine Grove Municipal Park and Zoo
Highway 27 W.
Little Falls

Next to a towering stand of virgin white pine, from which this park gets its name, is a delightful zoo featuring elk, buffalo, bear, wolves and other animals native to this part of Minnesota.

Little Falls Annual Arts and Crafts Show
Little Falls

Begun in 1972 and held the weekend after Labor Day, the Arts and Crafts Show has more than 800 exhibitors. Sponsored by the Chamber of Commerce, it includes music, entertainment and lots of food. Parking is at the Middle School in downtown Little Falls, with shuttle bus service to the exhibits.

Eating
Charlie's Pizza
1006 N.E. Fifth St.
(612) 632-6727

If you're in the mood for pizza, this is the place to go in Little Falls. It's a cozy place where you still get a pizza the size of your table at a small price.

The Kitchen
1201 N.E. First Ave.
Little Falls
(612) 632-2384

Standard American fare with daily specials. Extensive soup and salad bar.

Lodging
Anderson Pine Edge Inn and Motel
U.S. 10 and Highway 371
Little Falls, MN 56345
(612) 632-6681

A historic country inn on the banks of the Mississippi. There are 54 rooms, heated outdoor pool, meeting rooms and coffee shop. The Coach House Dining Room, with the charm and atmosphere of a true country inn, serves traditional fare with daily specials.

▼ **For More Information...**
Little Falls Area Chamber of Commerce
202 S.E. First Ave.
Little Falls, MN 56345
(612) 632-5155
(800) 325-5916

Hurray! Minnesota

BRAINERD LAKES AREA

WITHIN 25 MILES OF BRAINERD there are 464 lakes as well as the Mississippi, the Crow Wing, the Nokasippi and Pine rivers. This area is sometimes called Paul Bunyan's Playground. Legend has it that Paul and his big blue ox, Babe, were wrestling one afternoon after there had been a long rainy spell. The two of them were full of "vip and vinegar." The wilder they got, the harder they tromped and stomped until wherever they landed — a foot here, a horn there — the spot filled with water. Today, these are the lakes of the Brainerd area.

Brainerd is the southern point of the Gull Lake and Whitefish chains of lakes and the largest town in the immediate area, with a population of 12,350. Brainerd was founded in 1871 by the **Northern Pacific Railroad** when the decision was made to put the Mississippi railroad crossing at this point. The town was officially organized in March of 1873. **Brainerd** is the maiden name of the wife of the first president of the Northern Pacific Railroad Co., **J. Gregory Smith**.

The Crow Wing trading post was the first established settlement in the area, surrounded by a village of Chippewa, with the earliest record of trading occurring around 1826. Crow Wing, now the name of the county of which Brainerd is the county seat, originally came from the Indian name for the river meaning "wing of the raven." However, the white men, who came from the east, were not familiar with the raven (also a black bird, though much larger), so they named it "crow." By 1837, Crow Wing was the center for Indian trade for the entire upper country and the location of the general supply store.

The **Chiefs Hole-in-the-Day** (Older and Younger), who came from this area, were two of the foremost leaders of the Chippewa tribe. During the mid-1800s, they worked hard to protect the land rights of the Indians, negotiating treaties and rights to reservation lands. Hole-in-the-Day the Younger journeyed six times to Washington, once meeting with President Lincoln, to negotiate treaty rights. At the age of 40, Hole-in-the-Day the Younger was assassinated, and his murderers were never brought to justice.

There is a very complete, sometimes entertaining, history of the area written by **Carl Zapffe**. It has been published in installments by the Country Echo newspaper of Pequot Lakes (218) 568-8521.

As you drive through Brainerd, look for the **Brainerd Water Tower** at the corner of Highways 371 and 210 in the center of town. It is on the National Register of Historic Places. The hippo-shaped water fountain at its base also has been around for a long time.

Just outside of Brainerd, 12 miles west on Sylvan Lake, is **Camp Confidence**. One hundred forty acres have been set aside for those with disabilities. The camp operates year-round. It was founded in 1967 by **Dick Endres**, its executive director.

Just north of Brainerd and the Baxter strip, Highway 371 becomes a beautiful

The Brainerd Water Tower, finished in 1922, was the first all-concrete elevated tank in the United States.

drive around lakes and through forests as it meanders past the Gull Lake chain, then the Whitefish chain through Pine River to Leech Lake, finally ending at Cross Lake.

The **Gull Lake chain** is one of the more developed lake chains in Minnesota, in part because a number of major Minnesota resorts are located here, including **Madden's**, **Grand View**, **Kavanaugh's**, **Cragun's** and **the Quarterdeck**. There also are a number of popular restaurants that can be reached by car or boat, such as those at the resorts, as well as **Lost Lake Lodge**, **Bar Harbor**, the **Channel Inn** (with Taco Tuesday) and the **Butcher Block**.

Nisswa, at the north end of Gull Lake, is an excellent little town for shopping. There are a number of Minnesota shops, such as **Anthony's**, featuring the latest in men's and women's clothing. Quaint Bavarian-style architecture creates a festive atmosphere in Nisswa. Don't miss the turtle races that date back to 1965, held every Wednesday afternoon at 2 p.m. in front of **Earl's Furniture**. Bring your own turtle or rent one from the stable of racing turtles.

Up Highway 371, under the **Paul Bunyan Fishing Bobber** water tower (Paul left a little of himself everywhere) you'll find **Pequot Lakes**. It is the home of the **Country Echo**. This newspaper has traveled the world with local residents, as demonstrated in a regular feature photo of locals reading the Echo in far-away places. Pick up a copy. You'll get news of local happenings and activities for the whole lakes area in this weekly.

Near the Echo, just off Highway 371, is the **Oasis**, which features great food and excellent caramel rolls, but you have to get there early because the rolls go fast. Turn left off 371 at the stop light for the **Jack Pine Center**. This small mall has a number of unique shops and a great spot for lunch called **Beverly's**.

To get to **Breezy Point** and **Pelican Lake**, head east on County Road 11 out of Pequot Lakes. As you travel on 11 around Pelican, head north on County Road 3 to reach **Cross Lake** and the east end of the Whitefish chain. Also in the Whitefish area is the **Ossawinnamakee chain**.

The **Whitefish chain** consists of 14 navigable lakes that empty into the **Pine River**, which is a state canoe route. There are launching sites along the river on the way to Brainerd.

Breezy Point Resort is located on Pelican Lake. The famous resort, which lends its name to the town, has been in existence since 1921 and has an early history of catering to famous guests, such as movie stars **John Wayne**, **Clark Gable** and **Carol Lombard**, sports figures **Jack Dempsey** and **Walter Hagen**, and Minnesota writers **Margaret C. Banning** and **Sinclair Lewis**. Breezy was owned by **Billy Fawcett** of Fawcett Publications during the 1920s and '30s. Fawcett Publications owned a movie magazine, and oftentimes those being interviewed would spend a few days at the resort.

The main lodge burned in 1959 and again in 1976 but has been rebuilt and expanded over the years to include a large number of rooms, cabins, and condominiums. The main dining room has just received a facelift.

ATTRACTIONS
CROW WING COUNTY HISTORICAL SOCIETY MUSEUM
320 Laurel St.
Brainerd
(218) 829-3268
Housed in the old Crow Wing County jail, the museum's exhibits include the restoration of a 1917 home. Besides the resident exhibits, this museum also participates in the Historical Society's traveling exhibition program. Open June through August, Monday through Saturday, 9 a.m. to 5 p.m.; September through May, 1 to 5 p.m.

THIS OLD FARM
7344 Highway 18 E.
Brainerd
(218) 764-2915
Exhibits dating around the 1920s and '30s of a log cabin schoolhouse, old steam-driven farm equipment and tools, barns and a little store. Open weekends only, Memorial to Labor Day. There is a threshing show the second weekend in

Hurray! Minnesota

August. See steam-operated threshing machines in operation, logs being cut at the sawmill and shingle- and rope-making. The equipment and farm are operated by the Rademacher family. The farm has been in the family for more than 25 years.

ACTIVITIES
PAUL BUNYAN FUN CENTER
Highways 210 and 371
Brainerd/Baxter
(218) 829-6342
Stop by and have a chat with the animated Paul Bunyan. Rides, attractions and souvenirs. One admission fee is good for all rides all day. Open daily, Memorial weekend through Labor Day weekend. The helicopter ride, just outside the entrance, takes you for a wonderful ride down the river valley.

BRAINERD INTERNATIONAL RACEWAY
Highway 371
Brainerd
(218) 829-9836
The raceway sponsors a number of races throughout the season, such as the SCCA Nationals road race on the raceway's high-speed three-mile road course with 10 turns; the Champion Auto Stores Winston Drag Racing Series, on the 5,200-foot main strip, with cars reaching 200 miles per hour; and the Champion Auto Funny Car Nationals. For race information write: 17113 Minnetonka Boulevard, Suite 214, Minnetonka, MN 55345, (612) 475-1500. The schedule begins in May and runs through August. There are 500 acres with camping for tents, trailers and motor homes. Free admission for children under 12.

DEERLAND ZOO
North of Brainerd on Highway 371
Brainerd
(218) 829-0440
Exhibits of many animals native to Minnesota and some that are not. Hand feed the tame deer. Gifts and souvenirs. Open daily, 9 a.m. to 8 p.m., Memorial Day to Labor Day; 10 a.m. to 5 p.m., September and October.

LUMBERTOWN U.S.A.
Box 387
Brainerd
(218) 829-8872
Visit a refurbished historical 1870 logging village on the grounds of Madden's Resort on Gull Lake. Take a riverboat ride or a jaunt around the park on an authentic replica of the first Northern Pacific locomotive. There is a wax museum, ice cream parlor and gift shops. Open daily at 9:30 a.m. May through September.

VACATIONLAND PARK
Five miles north of Brainerd on
Highway 371
(218) 829-4963
Cam-Am go-karts, kiddy karts, toddler karts, video arcade barn, 18-hole mini golf, bumper boats and batting cages. Open daily, 10 a.m. to dusk during the summer, weekends fall and spring.

THE VIKING WATER SLIDE
Junction of Highways 371 and 77
Nisswa
(218) 963-3545
Daily, 11 a.m.-8 p.m.

BUMP•N•PUTT FAMILY FUN PARK
Four miles north of Nisswa on
Highway 371
(218) 963-2805
Miniature golf, bumper boats, water wars, Hoops! USA, pedal powered go-carts and kids play area. Open daily 10 a.m.

The **PAUL BUNYAN** Center
Home of World's Largest Animated Man

Unlimited rides for one low price

Open daily at 10 a.m.
Memorial Day — Labor Day

Located at junction of Hwys 210 & 371
**Brainerd, Minnesota
Call 218.829.6342**

LAKE COUNTRY

AREA DRIVES AND POINTS OF INTEREST

DRIVE #1
For a back road trip, head north out of Brainerd on County Road 25. You'll see red-winged blackbirds perched on cattails, weathered barns and frequent glimpses of small lakes and resorts through the trees. As you travel northward, you will pass the **Chaparral**, a very "local" bar, and the small town of Merrifield. Just past **Merrifield**, at the "Y" store, which is now called **D and D's** — though it's really still referred to as the "Y" store — you can choose either County Road 3 or 4. They both take you up to the Whitefish chain. County Road 4 passes through Breezy Point and the west side of Pelican Lake, while 3 goes along the east side straight to Cross Lake.

(Above) Bridge over the Gull River.
(Below) A great blue heron.

DRIVE #2
On Highway 13, between Highway 371 and County 4, is the old **Lake Hubert Depot**. Across the street, right on Lake Hubert, is the Lake Hubert store. Go in for a soda and a step into the past.

DRIVE #3
The drive around Gull Lake on County Road 77 is beautiful and scenic during all seasons. Catch Highway 77 off of Highway 371 at the Madden's turnoff. As you're heading north, two or three miles past Madden's but before you reach the **Pillsbury State Forest**, there is a swamp with a heronry of great blue herons on the left side of the road. There are more than 50 nests. The herons can best be seen at sunrise or sunset when they are leaving or returning to the nest after feeding. These birds are approximately four feet tall, so they're hard to miss.

Be sure to stop at the **Swedish Timber House** and **Sherwood Forest** on your trip around the lake. There is shopping at both, and the buildings are unique and delightful to examine. Sherwood Forest also serves an elegant afternoon tea with delicious cakes and sandwiches.

DRIVE #4
Just north of Crosslake on County Road 6 there is a huge occupied eagle's nest in a pine next to the road. The nest is one-half mile past **Moonlight Bay** on the west side of the road. Immediately after you pass the **Ox Lake Tavern** on the right, look up to the tallest pine on your left (one block away from the tavern). At the top of the pine is a huge eagle's nest that looks out over Ox Lake to the east and Rush Lake to the west. Bring your binoculars because the nest is way up there. Eagles have been spotted in the nest both in 1991 and 1992. If you reach a stone wall with a wagon wheel, you have gone too far. Stop, turn around and look up.

RED BARN RIDING STABLES
Breezy Point
Pequot Lakes
(218) 562-4377
CROSSLAKE SUPERSLIDES
Crosslake (downtown)
(218) 692-3111

SKIING/SNOWMOBILING

THERE ARE 136 kilometers of cross-country ski trails in the Brainerd area on eight separate systems with both ski-touring and ski-skating trails.

There are more than 1,000 miles of groomed snowmobile trails over the lakes and through the woods with access to many resorts, restaurants and bars. These are maintained by 11 local snowmobile clubs.

Maps for both trail systems can be obtained from the **Brainerd Lakes Area Chamber of Commerce**, Washington and Sixth Street, Brainerd, MN 56401, **(218) 829-2838, (800) 432-3775, ext. 89**.

There also is a Brainerd Snow Report at (800) 432-3775, ext. 80.

SKI GULL
Pillsbury State Park (Gull Lake)
Highway 77
Brainerd
(218) 963-4353
Fourteen runs, triple chairlift, snowmaking and lodge.

GOLF COURSES

THERE ARE 16 golf courses in the Brainerd Lakes area. Madden's, Breezy Point and Grand View resorts have 36 holes each.

A complete list can be obtained from the Brainerd Lakes Area Chamber of Commerce, Washington and Sixth Street, Brainerd, MN 56401, **(218) 829-2838, (800) 432-3775, ext. 89**.

PARKS

PILLSBURY STATE FOREST
Highway 77
Lake Shore
(218) 828-2565
On the shores of Gull Lake, the Pillsbury State Forest has beautiful trails for hiking in the summer or cross-country skiing in the winter.

PAUL BUNYAN ARBORETUM
Brainerd
(218) 829-8770
The Arboretum's 583 acres of wooded area was established in 1977 to preserve, educate and provide areas for research and recreation. There are more than 12 miles of trails for hiking and cross-country skiing. It is open daily throughout the year.

THE DEEP PORTAGE CONSERVATION RESERVE
Highway 84
Hackensack
(218) 682-2325
There are more than 6,000 acres of hills, ridges, lakes, rivers, bogs and ponds in this reserve, which was set aside in 1973. It is a rare and beautiful glacial moraine formed by the meeting of two glaciers.

SHOPPING

THERE ARE THREE major shopping districts in Brainerd: downtown, a small mall on the east end of town with a J.C. Penney Store, and the Westgate Mall, which is a larger mall and contains Herberger's and K Mart.

THE FINISHING TOUCH GIFTS
Westgate Mall
Brainerd
(218) 828-2067
A beautiful gift shop, carrying Dept. 56 collectibles.

MOREY'S FISH HOUSE
Highway 371 N.
Brainerd
(218) 829-8248
Large selection of fresh and frozen fish. Morey's serves an excellent clam chowder.

SOMEONE'S HOUSE GIFTS
4995 Highway 371 N.
Brainerd
(218) 829-7984
A unique assortment of gifts presented in a delightfully decorated house.

MARV KOEP'S NISSWA BAIT AND TACKLE
Highway 371
Nisswa
(218) 963-2547
Even if you don't fish you will still enjoy a visit to Marv Koep's. There are more than 80 mounted fish on display plus a collection of wood carvings of world

record fish. The current record fish are frozen in the freezer at the front door. There also are gifts for the visitor and the fisherperson. It is the home of the **Nisswa Guides League**. If you want a guide, you're sure to get the best one here or the best advice on what's biting and where. Marv's has the latest in tackle and the freshest in bait.

DOWNTOWN NISSWA
There's great shopping with a wide range of stores for browsing. For clothes, look into the **Town and Lake**, **Winona Knits**, **Zaisers**, **Lundrigen's** and the famous **Anthony's**. For unique gift items and souvenirs, **Totem Pole** has been around for a long time; sometimes you'd think they have some of their original merchandise. There is also the **Merchant of Nisswa**, **Rainbow's End Jewelry**, **Windsong**, **Carriage Gallery**, **Carson's Fine Jewelry**, **Martin's**, **Yellow Brick Road** and the **Stony Brook Antique Mall**.

SWEDISH TIMBER HOUSE
7678 Interlachen Road
Nisswa
(218) 963-7897
You'll find the finest of Scandinavian handicrafts and gifts in this beautiful log house tucked away in the forest. If you're lucky enough to be there in the spring, ask Ingrid Anderson about some of the wild flowers that grow around the Timber House. Beginning in early May, the woods are carpeted in bloodroot, hepatica, rue anemone, Dutchman's-breeches, wild ginger and many different kinds of ferns. They are followed by the jack-in-the-pulpit, meadow rue, bellwort, blue cohosh, and the most magnificent display of white trillium, which is a protected flower. At the end of May and into the beginning of June, you'll see the false solomon seal, violets of every hue, columbine, the Virginia waterleaf, and maybe, if you're lucky, the yellow lady's slipper, the official state flower.

WORLD OF CHRISTMAS
Highway 371
Four miles north of Nisswa
Pequot Lakes
(218) 568-5509
An excellent Christmas store, carrying a unique assortment of Christmas paraphernalia, designer and collectors' series ornaments.

PINE CONE GALLERY
130 W. Front St.
Pequot Lakes
(218) 568-8239
Open daily, 9:30 a.m. to 5:30 p.m. (call for winter hours).

DUBOIS WOODCARVING SHOPPE AND GALLERY
County Road 6
Crosslake
(218) 692-4258
Open daily, 10 a.m. to 5 p.m. in summer; by appointment in the winter.

JUDY'S HOUSE OF GIFTS
Crosslake
(218) 692-3123
Open 9:30 a.m. to 5 p.m., Monday through Saturday; 10 a.m. to 3 p.m., Sunday, Memorial Day to Labor Day. The shop is closed Monday and Tuesday in the winter.

BEACHCOMBERS CLOTHING
Crosslake
(218) 692-3700

EATING
BRAINERD
BUSTER'S RESTAURANT AND SPORTS LOUNGE
1360 Highway 210
Brainerd
(218) 829-4162
Buster's is the place to go in Brainerd. Sandwiches, steaks and Mexican food. Daily happy hour. Food served until midnight. Sixteen large TVs and a large screen for all sporting events. Music and dancing nightly.

HASSIE'S FAMILY RESTAURANT
2131 Highway 210
Brainerd
(218) 829-3487

HASSIE'S II
Highway 371
Baxter
(218) 839-3750
Serving one of the best burgers in the Brainerd area and definitely the best ribs.

PAULINE'S AND THE LAST TURN SALOON
Highways 210 and 371
(behind Paul Bunyan)
Brainerd
(218) 829-2318

Hurray! Minnesota

Casual dining featuring prime rib, walleye and piping hot popovers. Specials daily.

BUSTER'S SPORTLAND CAFE
9 Smiley Road
(Highway 371 and County Road 77)
Nisswa
(218) 963-4602
Local family restaurant. If local tradesmen don't answer their office phone, you can often find them here.

IVEN'S ON THE BAY
5195 North Highway 371
Brainerd
(218) 829-9872
Located at the south end of North Long Lake. Renowned for savory seafood, with a fresh fish featured daily. Fantastic Sunday brunch with Belgian waffles, omelettes and fresh fruit.

GULL LAKE CHAIN
BAR HARBOR SUPPER CLUB
6512 Interlachen Road (County Road 77)
Lakeshore/Nisswa
(218) 963-2568
A favorite stop by boat, snowmobile, car or plane. The charcoal steak, giant lobster and walleye are some of the best on the lake. Entertainment and dancing and a barefoot patio bar.

SHERWOOD FOREST LODGE
7669 Interlachen Road
Lakeshore/Nisswa
(218) 963-2516
Breakfast and lunch is served in an enchanting outdoor atmosphere on the screened veranda, featuring croissant sandwiches and a variety of salads and specialty dessert items. They also serve an excellent afternoon tea, ice cream drinks or cocktails in the lounge. The lodge is on the National Register of Historic Places and has two rooms for bed-and-breakfast guests.

CHANNEL INN AND GRANNY'S PUB
6401 Lost Lake Road (County Road 77)
(218) 963-4790
Casual dining featuring Cajun, chops and walleye upstairs with a piano bar and dancing. Downstairs is action-packed with live entertainment year-round. Boat docks are on the channel (access to Gull Lake chain) in front of the patio bar, featuring tacos and burger baskets. Stop by for volleyball or to watch a great sunset.

LOST LAKE LODGE
6415 Lost Lake Road
Nisswa
(218) 963-2681
Consider calling ahead because the food is home cooked and so good the restaurant is often full. The breads are fresh baked from flour ground at the mill on the premises. The lodge maintains a remarkable wine list and is on the Gull Lake chain so you can reach it by boat.

DOWNTOWN NISSWA
There are several small restaurants right downtown, such as the **Nisswa Inn**, **Country Cookin'**, **Tower Pizza**, coffee shops, and, for ice cream, **Nisswa Country Store**. The **Bierstube** and **Ye Old Pickle Factory** serve a good drink.

PEQUOT LAKES
BEVERLY'S RESTAURANT
Jack Pine Center
Pequot Lakes
(218) 568-4901
Great lunches in a garden atmosphere. Sunday brunch buffet. Sunday liquor.

BUTCHER BLOCK STEAKHOUSE AND SALOON
Pequot Lakes
(218) 568-9950
Inside there's an open barbecue at which you cook your own steaks, fish or chicken. Choose your meat. They provide baked potato, thick-sliced bread, which you can drench in garlic butter and toast on the grill, and salad bar. Mmmmm-Mmmmm.

A-PINE FAMILY RESTAURANT
Highway 371 and County Road 16
Pequot Lakes
(218) 568-8353
Serving famous recipe chicken with buckets-to-go. Homemade malts, beer-battered onion rings and old-fashioned strawberry shortcake.

You also can get information here on the **Clamshell Queen** cruises, a two-hour dinner cruise around the islands of the Whitefish chain.

BREEZY POINT AREA
THE COMMANDER BAR
Breezy Point
(218) 562-9494
The regulars of Breezy stop in often. Good place for burgers and the American standards.

CHARLIE'S
Breezy Point
(218) 562-7180
This is the lodge of an old ski hill. Open May through September.

CROSSLAKE AREA
PINE PEAKS FAMILY RESTAURANT
Crosslake
(218) 692-4100
Serving breakfast, lunch and dinner. Different specials daily.

THE EXCHANGE NIGHTCLUB
Crosslake
(218) 692-4866

MOONLIGHT BAY
Crosslake
(218) 692-3575
They have a nice view of Cross Lake. Serving ribs, chicken and burgers.

OX LAKE TAVERN
Crosslake
Has a comfortable screen porch that overlooks Ox Lake. Just down the road from the eagle's nest.

ECHO RIDGE SUPPER CLUB
Crosslake
(218) 692-4800
Seasonal.

NORWAY RIDGE
County Road 39 (south of Ideal Corners)
(218) 543-6136
Featuring home-smoked ribs, whale-sized walleye and sourdough appetizers. A rustic lodge overlooking beautiful Kimble Lake. Reservations recommended.

YE OLD WHARF
County Road 16
Crosslake
(218) 692-3454
An eating and drinking establishment that can be reached by car, snowmobile or boat on the Whitefish chain. Has two great decks right on the channel between Cross Lake and Rush Lake. Food to go. Pontoon rental and gas available.

WILD ACRES HUNTING LODGE AND GAME FARM
HCR 1 (County Road 16)
Pequot Lake, MN 56472
(218) 568-5024
Hunting reminiscent of the early '40s is available August through April. Mary Ebnet and her family run an authentic lodge for hunting pheasant, quail, chukker partridge, wild turkey and wild mallard. The farm is in a rolling wooded area with ponds and small fields. The lodge is very rustic and sleeps six. Bed and breakfast available in the summer. Wild game dinners available by reservation, catering and to go. In summer the area is available for working hunting dogs and trap shooting.

LODGING
IN THE Brainerd Lakes area, there are a number of resorts, both large and small. There also is a **Holiday Inn**, **Super 8 Motel**, **America Inn** and **Daystop**. Some of the resorts are:

GRAND VIEW LODGE AND RESORT
North shore Gull Lake/County Road 77
134 Nokomis Ave. S.
Nisswa, MN 56468
(218) 963-2234
(800) 432-3788
Completed in 1923, the main lodge at Grand View looks much as it did then. The lodge has been placed on the National Register of Historic Places. The lodge has 10 rooms and also houses registration and the restaurant serving longtime favorites. There also are 75 cabins in the woods and on the beach, each with its own private setting and deck. The cabins vary in size and number of bedrooms.

Grand View has one of the nicest beaches on Gull Lake with all the water sports, an indoor pool, tennis courts and pro shop with tennis pro and tournaments hosted during the season. There is a nine-hole golf course and the brand new 36-hole Pines championship course. Open May to mid-October.

LOST LAKE LODGE
6417 Lost Lake Road
Nisswa, MN 56468
(218) 963-2681
(800) 450-2681
Intimate resort with uncommonly good food. Ten delightful cottages overlook either the channel on the Gull Lake chain or the resort's own Lost Lake. There are 80 acres of woods with hiking trails and a family-created hands-on interpretive center. Lost Lake is a privately stocked fishing lake with a safe sandy beach for swimming. Lost Lake's grist

mill is still in operation, grinding grains for the fresh goods they bake daily.

GULL FOUR SEASONS RESORT
Gull Lake
1336 Colombo Road S.
Brainerd, MN 56401
(218) 963-7969
Family resort with 27 housekeeping units. There also are one- to four-bedroom condos. Activities for all four seasons, including golf.

MADDEN'S ON GULL LAKE
8001 Pine Beach Peninsula
Brainerd, MN 56401
(218) 829-2811
(800) 247-1040 (in Minnesota)
(800) 233-2934 (out-of-state)
1992 is Madden's 50th anniversary season. This is a huge, beautiful north woods resort located on the south end of Gull Lake. It is definitely one of those places that has something for everyone, and all of the highest quality. Golf (45 holes on premises), tennis and croquet club, lawn bowling, six swimming pools (three indoor with spa facilities), boating, restaurants, convention facilities and a recreation director who can provide planning or instruction so you can make the most of your stay. There are 286 rooms ranging from cabins to suites with fireplaces and whirlpools. Open mid-April through mid-October. Lumbertown USA, a historic amusement center, is located on the grounds.

KAVANAUGH'S
Sylvan Lake
2300 Kavanaugh Drive S.W.
Brainerd, MN 56401
(218) 829-5226
(800) 562-7061
This resort features 43 townhouse units on Sylvan lake and an excellent gourmet restaurant with large windows framing a beautiful view of the lake.

CRAGUN'S LODGE, RESORT AND SPA
2001 Pine Beach Road
Brainerd, MN 56401
(210) 829-3591
(800) CRAGUNS
Cragun's is a beautiful resort with a half-mile sandy beach on Gull Lake. Cottages or rooms with a lakeview and fireplace. Indoor and outdoor pools, marina, tennis and spa with whirlpool, sauna and massage. Open all year.

GRAND VIEW LODGE
GOLF AND TENNIS CLUB

Vacations for the entire family

Enjoy. . .
Golf • Tennis • Swimming
Fine Dining • Entertainment
Children's Programs
and golf the Pines

CALL FOR INFORMATION
1 (800) 432-3788 MN
On Gull Lake in Brainerd, MN

D iscover cozy lakeside cottages and taste-tempting meals on over 80 acres of secluded woods. Explore 7 lakes from our docks on Gull Lake Narrows or relax on the sandy beach of our private 14 acre lake. Children's counselors plan special activities for ages 3 and up. Vacations include breakfast and supper, unique nature programs and much more.

Come Discover Lost Lake Lodge

6415H LOST LAKE ROAD
BRAINERD - LAKE SHORE, MN 56468

1-800-450-2681
MINNESOTA TOLL-FREE

1-218-963-2681
OUTSIDE MINNESOTA

Lost Lake Lodge
ON THE GULL LAKE NARROWS

QUARTERDECK RESORT AND RESTAURANT
Gull Lake
1588 Quarterdeck Road W.
Nisswa, MN 56468
(218) 963-2482
(800) 950-5596
This is a great family resort on Gull Lake with docking facilities. Many of the 30 cabins and villas are on the beach. Excellent restaurant and lounge with entertainment.

SHERWOOD FOREST LODGE
7669 Interlachen Road
Lake Shore, Nisswa MN 56468
(218) 963-2516
The lodge is on the National Register of Historic Places and features the largest cut-stone fireplace in the Northwest. There are two rooms available for bed and breakfast and a one-bedroom cabin. Open seasonally.

SANDY BEACH RESORT
Gull Lake
7894 Sandy Point Road
Lake Shore, Nisswa, MN 56468
(218) 963-4458.
An ideal family resort with 27 one- to four-bedroom units. Furnished housekeeping cottages on a safe sandy beach. Playground, picnic tables, boats and small store.

DAYSTOP
Highway 371
Nisswa, MN 56468
(218) 963-3500
(800) 325-2525
Indoor pool, sauna and guest laundry. Forty-six rooms.

STONEHOUSE BED AND BREAKFAST
HCR 2, Box 9
Pequot Lakes
(218) 568-4255
A delightful handmade stone cottage for rent.

BREEZY POINT RESORT
Big Pelican Lake
Breezy Point, MN 56472
(218) 562-7811
(800) 432-3777 (in Minnesota)
(800) 328-2284 (out-of-state)
Your choice of 300 condos or rooms at the lodge. Beautiful 36-hole golf course, tennis, complete boat marina and 57-foot cruise boat. You have your choice of pools, saunas, whirlpools and beach. There are three restaurants, two

Come Visit Us During Our 50th Anniversary Celebratory Season!

Enjoy...

- 45 holes on premises golf
- Supervised children's program
- Luxurious accommodations
- Tennis, croquet, lawn bowling
- Dining room, lounge, pub, coffee shop, pizza & sub shoppe

For your COMPLETE vacation, call
1-800-642-5363
Brainerd Lakes Area

Madden's on Gull Lake — 1942-1992

Hurray! Minnesota

of which overlook the lake. Live entertainment.

CHASTAIN'S PINEWOOD CABANAS, INC.
Big Pelican Lake
Box 269
Breezy Point, MN 56472
(218) 562-4777
(800) 343-4152
Located in Breezy Point. Heated outdoor pool and picnic grounds. Open year-round. Sixty rooms.

BOYD LODGE
Whitefish Lake
HC-83, Box 667
Crosslake, MN 56442
(218) 543-4125
(800) 450-BOYD, ext. 4
The 34 housekeeping cabins have redwood decks and fireplaces. Sandy beach, tennis, heated pool and wading pool. All types of water and winter sports available. Planned activities. Open May through October and January through March.

CHAIN O'LAKES HOUSEBOATS
Crosslake-Whitefish Chain
Box 15E
Crosslake, MN 56442
(218) 692-4677
(800) 247-1932
Houseboat rental with housekeeping. Boats sleeping two to eight are available to cruise the Whitefish chain.

**DRIFTWOOD FAMILY RESORT
AND GOLF COURSE**
Whitefish Chain of Lakes
Route 1, Box 404, Dept. M92
Pine River, MN 56474
(218) 568-4221
The Driftwood is run by a family for families. Meals or housekeeping plans are available. There are 24 cabins, four constructed of logs, and complete watersports program, tennis, pony rides, sailing school and a nine-hole golf course. Open May through September. Visit the **Minnesota Resort Museum**.

**MCGUIRE'S PINEY RIDGE LODGE AND
IRISH HILL GOLF**
Upper Whitefish Lake
Route 1, Box 315 R
Pine River, MN 56474
(218) 587-2196
Beautiful family resort with more than 50 activities available. Choice of 27 cabins or eight villas.

CAMPING

THERE ARE A large number of resorts with campgrounds plus smaller campgrounds on the Pine River, Daggett Brook, Gull and Love Lake and Lake Emily. For a complete list: **Brainerd Lakes Area Chamber of Commerce**, Washington and Sixth Street, Brainerd, MN 56401, **(218) 829-2838** or **(800) 432-3775, ext. 89**.

DON AND MAYVA'S CROW WING LAKE CAMPGROUND
8831 Crow Wing Camp Road
Brainerd, MN 56401
(218) 829-6468
Just south of Brainerd off Highway 371. Ninety trailer sites and 10 tent sites.

HIGHVIEW CAMPGROUND AND RV PARK
HC 83, Box 1084
Breezy Point, MN 56472
(218) 543-4526
(612) 424-9525 (winter)
There are 100 trailer sites and 30 tent sites on Lake Ossawinnamakee.

▼ FOR MORE INFORMATION...

BRAINERD LAKES AREA CHAMBER OF COMMERCE
Washington and Sixth Street
Brainerd, MN 56401
(218) 829-2838
(800) 432-3775, ext. 89.

NISSWA CHAMBER OF COMMERCE
Box 185
Nisswa, MN 56468
(218) 963-2620
(800) 950-9610
(Next to the Caboose in Nisswa)

PEQUOT LAKES CHAMBER OF COMMERCE
Box 208
Pequot Lakes, MN 56472
(800) 950-0291
(218) 568-8911

CROSSLAKE CHAMBER OF COMMERCE
Box 315
Crosslake, MN 5644
(218) 692-40272
Memorial Day through Labor Day.

MINNESOTA OFFICE OF TOURISM
North Central/West Regional Office
Box 443
1901 S. Sixth St.
Brainerd, MN 56401
(218) 828-2334
(800) 345-2537

Only in Itasca State Park can you walk across the Mississippi River.

ITASCA HEADWATERS

SURROUNDING LAKE ITASCA, THE headwaters of the Mississippi River, are small towns, vast tracts of woods and wetlands and other tranquil lakes. Area residents proudly refer to the region as Paul Bunyan's playland. Legend has it Paul was born at **Akeley** and buried at **Kelliher**. He and Babe, his blue ox, grew to such enormous proportions because there was plenty of room for them to grow in these north woods.

The legend of Paul Bunyan, world's greatest lumberjack, holds that the Mississippi River was formed one winter when the huge tank wagon Babe was hauling sprung a leak. The rushing waters created Lakes Bemidji and Itasca and the overflow trickled down to New Orleans, forming the Mississippi.

Within 60 miles of the headwaters of the Mississippi there are no fewer than nine state forests, one national forest, two wildlife management areas, a state park and the three largest Indian reservations in Minnesota.

White Earth Indian Reservation is 1,200 square miles with approximately 8,000 residents. Every year on June 14 there is a celebration of the arrival, in 1868, of the first band of Indians on the reservation. The three principal bands

Hurray! Minnesota

PHOTO COURTESY OF GRAND RAPIDS
CONVENTION AND VISITORS BUREAU

INTERNATIONAL EELPOUT FESTIVAL
(800) 833-1118, ext. 92
Visitors from around the globe attend this unique festival, held each February. For one weekend thousands of people bring hundreds of ice fishing houses, and practically whole towns are set up on Leech Lake. There is lots of partying and many different activities from the Eelpout Peelout (5-mile run) to softball and golf tournaments on the frozen lake, plus thousands of dollars in prizes for those who bag the eelpouts. The eelpout is a bottom feeding fish, considered by many to be the ugliest fish in Minnesota waters.

Prizewinning catch at the International Leech Lake Eelpout Festival.

were the Mississippi Band, from Crow Wing and Gull Lake; the Pembina Band, from the upper Red River Valley; and the Otter Tail Pillagers, from Otter Tail Lake.

The Red Lake Indian Reservation lands were set aside in 1863. Unlike the other reservations, the land was retained by the Chippewa and never sold to the white man. Red Lake is the largest lake in Minnesota. Indian lands encompass more than three-quarters of the lakeshore. Indians have established a cooperative fish processing plant at Redby.

Similarly, the Leech Lake reservation encompasses a good portion of the Leech Lake shoreline and extends north around Lake Winnibigoshish.

WALKER

THE TOWN OF Walker on the shores of Leech Lake is steeped in history. The first known inhabitants were the Dakota branch of the Sioux Indians followed by the Ojibwa. Zebulon Pike raised the U.S. flag at Ottertail Point in 1806. In 1896, the town of Walker was incorporated and the inglorious Battle of Sugar Point occurred, one of the final battles between white men and Indians.

Today Walker, a town of just under 1,000 people, has a thriving year-round tourist economy taking advantage of the excellent recreational lakes and forests in the area.

ATTRACTIONS
MUSEUMS
In downtown Walker, the history of Walker, its wildlife and inhabitants are clearly presented in the Museum of Natural History, the Cass County Historical Museum, and the Old Pioneer School House located next door. All are open Memorial Day to Labor Day.

LEECH LAKE FISH HATCHERY AND INTERPRETIVE CENTER
Walker
(218) 755-4027
(800) 833-1118
The center is capable of incubating 27 million walleye each year. An education center is open to the public.

HEARTLAND STATE TRAIL
Thirty miles of old railroad bed has been made into a beautiful trail winding along rivers, lakes and through forests for biking, hiking and snowmobiling.

LODGING
CHASE ON THE LAKE
Box 206
Walker, MN 56484
(218) 547-1531
On the National Register of Historic Places, this is a delightful B&B inn with a sandy beech on Leech Lake. The dining room has recently been remodeled, so come by boat or car for cocktails and dinner overlooking the lake. There's entertainment nightly in the summer.

HUDDLE'S RESORT
HCR 84, Box 67
Walker, MN 56484
(218) 836-2420
(800) 358-5516
This full-service resort has 19 housekeeping units, some with fireplaces, a beautiful sandy beach and a swimming pool. Boats, motors and fishing guide services are available. The lodge has a dining room open to the public.

BAYVIEW RESORT AND CAMPGROUND
Box 58
Walker, MN 56484
(218) 547-1595
There are 31 housekeeping units along with a full-service campground with both tent and RV sites. There is a harbor for boats, sandy beach and a snack shop.

TIANNA FARMS B&B
Box 629
Walker, MN 56484
(218) 547-1306
All five large rooms have private baths and beautiful views of the lake and grounds. This is a wonderful 1920s farmhouse loaded with local history and surrounded by gardens. There are screened porches, swimming, tennis and hot tub. Open all year.

PEACECLIFF
HCR 73, Box 998D
Walker, MN 56484
(218) 547-2832
Spectacular view of Leech Lake from this Tudor house sitting high on the bluff. Five charming guest rooms are furnished with antiques and old books. A full breakfast is served.

THE PARK STREET INN
Route 1, Box 254
Nevis, MN 56467
(612) 599-4762
(218) 652-4500
One block from the Heartland Trail, this B&B has four guest rooms with private baths and is filled with country antiques and homemade quilts. Full breakfast.

▼ FOR MORE INFORMATION...
LEECH LAKE AREA CHAMBER OF COMMERCE
Box 1089-H2
Walker, MN 56484
(800) 833-1118, ext. 6

HACKENSACK AREA CHAMBER OF COMMERCE
Box 373
Hackensack, MN 56452
(218) 675-6135
(800) 279-6932

Bemidji
First City On The Mississippi

BEMIDJI

BEMIDJI IS PROUD to be the first town on the Mississippi. It was named for the Ojibwa chief, who was named after Lake Bemidji. Loosely translated, Bemidji means lake which is divided by the river current. The Mississippi flows in from the center of the east side and flows out the center of the west.

In Bemidji you can experience the area as did the Indians and settlers. Float a canoe down the winding Mississippi or Turtle rivers as the two rivers flow through and around Bemidji. There are accesses set up on both rivers. If you find you like river canoeing, there are a dozen more rivers in the area. The Department of Natural Resources has detailed maps of all the rivers that include some of the more historic landmarks. **(612) 296-6157** or **(800) 652-5484**.

Paul Bunyan, being indigenous to the area, has been honored by Bemidji. Statues of Paul and Babe stand 18 feet tall at Lakeside park. These world-famous statues, erected in 1937, are among the Midwest's most photographed attractions. Next door is the Paul Bunyan House with some of Paul's more impressive mementos and many tales to be learned, such as how he and Babe formed the lakes and the Mississippi.

Also located on the shores of Lake Bemidji, Bemidji State University offers nearly 70 major fields of study. In summer Bemidji State hosts a variety of youth camps, Concordia Language Villages and Elderhostel programs.

Hurray! Minnesota

ATTRACTIONS
PAUL BUNYAN'S ANIMAL LAND
Highway 2 East
Bemidji
(218) 759-1533
Animal Land has a petting zoo, trout pond and unique toy museum. There also is a playground and picnic area.
RED LAKE FISHERIES
Highway 1
Redby
(218) 679-3813
If you're passing this way in June through September, the fisheries have an observation room for the processing plant, which is open to the public.
PIONEER PARK WORKING MUSEUM
Solway
(218) 467-3230
This authentic working farm museum has guided tours with working corn shellers, 1871 flour miller, 1873 grain seeder, 1880 reaper and other late-1800s farm equipment. There is a ghost town, Conestoga wagon and lots of working farm animals. Reservations are not necessary but requested.
HISTORICAL AND WILDLIFE MUSEUM
300 Bemidji Ave.
Bemidji
(218)751-3540
Indian and pioneer artifacts and exhibits from the early days of Bemidji.
BUENA VISTA SKI AREA
County Road 15
(12 miles north of Bemidji)
Bemidji
(218) 243-2231
The vertical drop is 230 feet. You can reach the top of the mountain by two triple chair lifts, two double chair lifts or a beginner tow rope. The roomy three-story chalet has three fireplaces, cafeteria and rentals. There also are 25 kilometers of groomed and tracked cross-country ski trails. Buena Vista is host to the Finlandia international cross-country ski marathon and Logging Days Festival held in February. Open late November to March.
PALACE BINGO
Highway 2
Bemidji
(800) 228-6676
Slots, high-stakes bingo and blackjack.

BLACKDUCK WOOD CARVERS FESTIVAL
Box 60
Blackduck
This festival is held the last Saturday in July at Wayside Park, Blackduck. The festival includes exhibits, demonstrations and purchasing opportunities. There are more than 50 exhibitors, local and from around the country and Canada.

SHOPPING
PAUL BUNYAN MALL
Highway 2
Bemidji
More than 40 stores, open all week.
BEMIDJI WOOLEN MILLS
Third and Irvine Ave.
Bemidji
(218) 751-5166
No middleman here. Goods are direct from the factory, including yarn, fabrics, blankets, sportswear, deerskin gloves and sweaters.
CHOCOLATES PLUS
102 First St. (Union Square)
Bemidji
(218) 759-1175
Their specialty is truffles, fresh from the kettle.
THE OLD SCHOOLHOUSE
2335 Monroe Ave. S.W.
Bemidji
(218) 751-4723
Works of more than 500 artists and craftsmen fill the rooms of this old schoolhouse. You can buy crafts, original artwork and supplies. Head south on 197 to Carr Lake and Old Schoolhouse Road, then west one mile.

EATING
THE BACK YARD
Highways 2 and 71
Bemidji
(218) 751-7853
Fine dining featuring baron of beef buffet at noon and specials every night. Great salad bar and Sunday brunch. Full cocktail service.
GRIFFY'S EATING ESTABLISHMENT
319 Minnesota Ave.
Bemidji
(218) 751-3609
They serve deli-style breakfast and lunch. Griffy's is best known for their

delicious soups, which are made from scratch.

HOOK'S HORSESHOE LODGE
Route 2
Cass Lake
(218) 335-8875
Good homemade breakfast and dinner. Full-service cocktails. The resort has housekeeping cabins, beach, playground and an excellent harbor.

STATS SPORTS BAR AND DINER
102 First St. N.
Bemidji
(218) 751-0441
Stats has windows right on Lake Bemidji so you can view the lake or a sports event on one of 17 TVs. The diner serves steaks, seafood, pasta and burgers.

LODGING

RUTTGER'S BIRCHMONT LODGE
530 Birchmont Beach Road N.E.
Bemidji, MN 56601
(218) 751-1630
(800) 726-3866
Located on the shore of Lake Bemidji, the lodge offers lakeside cottages or lakefront lodge rooms, many with fireplaces. There's a beautiful dining room and bar. Swimming is available on the 1,700-foot beach or the indoor/outdoor pools. Children's programs, tennis courts and fishing are offered.

▼ **FOR MORE INFORMATION...**

BEMIDJI CONVENTION AND VISITORS BUREAU
Box 66
Bemidji, MN 56601
(218) 751-3541
(800) 458-2223, ext. 50

CASS LAKE AREA CIVIC AND COMMERCE
Box 548
Cass Lake, MN 56633
(800) 356-8215

BLACKDUCK CIVIC AND COMMERCE
Box 373
Blackduck, MN 56630
(218) 835-7788
(800) 323-2975

KOHL'S RESORT
15707 Big Turtle Drive N.E.
Bemidji, MN 56601
(218) 243-2131
Two-, three- and four-bedroom cottages, condos and inside poolside suites in a beautiful park-like setting, some with decks, fireplaces, screened porches and whirlpools. Kohl's has a beautiful sandy beach and marina. Open year-round.

A PLACE IN THE WOODS
11380 Turtle River Lake Road N.E.
Bemidji, MN 56601
(218) 586-2345
(800) 676-4547
There are 10 housekeeping units at this intimate family resort, which has a sand beach, fireplaces and whirlpool. Open four seasons.

RAINBOW RESORT ON TURTLE RIVER LAKE
Route 6, Box 266
Bemidji, MN 56601
(218) 586-2673
A small tranquil resort in the Buena Vista Forest that has nine clean, comfortable cabins, some with screened porches. There is a small beach with safe swim area and lots of dock space. Fishing plus a variety of wildlife is abundant. Open mid-May to mid-October.

WOLF LAKE FAMILY RESORT AND CAMPGROUND
12150 Walleye Lane S.E.
Bemidji, MN 56601
(218) 751-5749
(800) 322-0281, ext.10
When not fishing, you can relax in the pool, sauna or whirlpool. Of 16 housekeeping units, some are larger to accommodate groups or families. Wolf Lake features a sandy beach with all types of waterfront entertainment, playground and rec room for the kids. There also is a shaded 60-site campground. Open year-round.

FRONTIER RESORT
Route 1, Box 317
Pinewood, MN 56664
(218) 243-2700
The ideal resort for a family vacation in the north woods. Six lakeside cabins, all with decks. Cabin 2 is the perfect place to spend your honeymoon. Frontier has a sandy beach, volleyball court, boat dock and playground.

Hurray! Minnesota

MAHNOMEN

MAHNOMEN IS ONE of the state's major wild rice-producing areas. In fact, mahnomen is the Dakota word for wild rice. Outdoor recreation opportunities in both summer and winter are some of the best in the state, including hunting, fishing, hiking, cross-country skiing and snowmobiling.

THE SHOOTING STAR CASINO
Highway 59
Mahnomen
(800) 453-STAR
Keno, blackjack, nearly 750 slot machines, cabaret lounge, full-service hotel and RV park.

▼ FOR MORE INFORMATION...
MAHNOMEN COUNTY
CHAMBER OF COMMERCE
Box 36
Mahnomen, MN 56557
(218) 935-5758

PARK RAPIDS

WHAT STARTED AS a farming and logging community in the late 1800s has quickly evolved into a premier resort destination. With a rich array of natural wonders, an inventory of more than 400 lakes and nearly as many resorts, cabins and lodges, Park Rapids is a wonderful place to kick back and enjoy the good life. While you're here, don't miss Lake Itasca State Park, home of the headwaters of the greatest river in the nation, the mighty Mississippi.

ATTRACTIONS
ITASCA STATE PARK
Highway 71
(28 miles north of Park Rapids)
(218) 266-3654
(800) 652-9747
It is here at Itasca Lake that you can actually walk from stone to stone across the Mississippi as it begins its 2,552-mile journey to the Gulf of Mexico. The 32,000 acres of the park were dedicated in 1891. It is the oldest Minnesota state park.

You can take a tour of Lake Itasca aboard the **Chester Charles**, which follows the historic Schoolcraft route across Lake Itasca right up to the headwaters of the Mississippi. (**Henry Schoolcraft** is credited with discovering the source of the Mississippi.) You'll learn all about this beautiful land and its wildlife.

Or, you can simply traverse the park on foot, bicycle or by car. There are plenty of trails, a scenic drive and miles of scenic cycling trails. This park has ancient 1,000-year-old burial mounds and remnants of 8,000-year-old Indian artifacts. Itasca Park has an area called Preacher's Grove that still has 250-year-old red pine trees standing majestically next to the water's edge. Camping and lodging is available on a limited basis. Call ahead for reservations. Open Memorial Day through September.

SILVER STAR CITY
Highway 34 E.
Park Rapids
(218) 732-4443
Silver Star City is a re-created 1890s lumber town with live music, staged shootouts and arrests and a working steam-powered sawmill. There's a stagecoach that rides into town and actors mill about in period costumes. Silver Star City also has a handmade-crafts gift shop. Open Memorial Day through Labor Day 9 a.m. to 6 p.m.

HUBBARD COUNTY COURTHOUSE
Junction of Third and Court St.
Park Rapids
(218) 732-5237
The old county courthouse houses both the **Hubbard County Historical Museum** and the **North County Museum of Arts**. The museum displays highlight the Civil War and late 19th-century history of Park Rapids. Among the many fine art exhibits on display at North County is a permanent collection of 16th- to 19th-century European oils and watercolors. North County also features traveling exhibits of local and national art. Open seasonally.

HEARTLAND TRAIL
For 50 miles from Park Rapids through **Dorset**, **Nevis** and **Akeley** to **Walker** and then on up to **Cass Lake**, this trail follows the old abandoned railway through the forests and along the lakes. Between Park Rapids and Walker, 27 miles have been surfaced for biking.

Along the way, check out Paul Bunyan's cradle in Akeley and have a bite to eat in Dorset, which boasts an unusually large number of good restaurants for its size.

Shopping

Smoky Hills Arts Community
Highway 34
Osage
(218) 573-3300
Tucked in the woods nine miles west of Park Rapids on Highway 34 is this little community of 15 cottages and two restaurants connected by a boardwalk. Craftsmen and artisans sell their wares and demonstrate their trade in these shops and galleries. Open Memorial Day through Labor Day. Admission charge.

Summerhill Farm and Sun Porch Restaurant
Highway 71 North
(Seven miles north of Park Rapids)
Park Rapids
(218) 732-3865
Summerhill Farm is a quaint place to stroll and browse. The grounds are beautiful with hanging dried-flower racks, fragrant flower gardens, cobblestone footpaths and white picket fences. There are five different gift shops. It's a good place to shop for locally made gifts, including Minnesota jams and jellies. To round it out, stop in at the Sun Porch Restaurant and enjoy a cup of wild rice soup and a sandwich. Open May through September.

The Schoolcraft Gallery Collection
Highway 71
Lake George
(218) 266-3977
The focal point of this original and unique collection of art and gifts is the 1905 log schoolhouse. Hamilton's stoneware and Pat Shannon's pottery are featured along with Ojibwa crafts and quilts. Don't miss the Teddy Bear House, with shelf upon shelf of cuddly teddy bears, or the Books 'n' Print Shop.

Eating

Compadres del Norte
Downtown
Park Rapids
(218) 732-7624
Admittedly, authentic Mexican food seems unlikely in this neck of the woods, but here at Compadres del Norte you can have a smothered burrito with homemade green or red chili. The real surprise is the seafood enchilada and Mexican pizza.

Dorset Cafe
Downtown
Park Rapids
(218) 732-9565
A full-service American restaurant serving broasted chicken and ribs. Cocktails. Open for dinner Monday through Friday. Lunch and dinner on Saturday and Sunday.

The Great Northern Cafe
Highway 34 E.
Park Rapids
(218) 732-9565
Family restaurant serving breakfast, lunch and dinner. Open all week.

Long Van
703 E. First St.
Park Rapids
(218) 732-5491
The spice and flavor of Long Van's Cantonese-style spiced chicken in black bean sauce or lo mein is a real Epicurean pleasure. Open for lunch and dinner.

Shipwreck Restaurant
Northern Pine Road (off Highway 71)
Park Rapids
(218) 732-9708
Shipwreck Restaurant is part of the North Beach Resort near the shore of Potato Lake. The Shipwreck is famous for its all-you-can-eat crab legs dinner. They also serve delectable steak and fresh fish entrees.

Rapid River Logging Camp
County Road 18
(Four miles east of Highway 71)
Park Rapids
(218) 732-3444
Family style all-you-can-eat breakfasts, lunches and dinners are served in this rustic replica of a lumber camp dining hall. Open Memorial Day to Labor Day.

Lodging

Dorset Schoolhouse Bed and Breakfast
Box 201
Park Rapids, MN 56470
(218) 732-1377

Not far from Itasca State Park, this B&B, located in a 1920s schoolhouse, has just as much charm as it does history. There are six rooms, each packed with country-style antiques and floral linens. Also, each room has a door that leads to a patio deck, lots of windows, high ceilings and beautiful honey-stained maple floors.

FREMONT'S POINT
Route 1, Box 119P
Nevis, MN 56467
(218) 652-3299
(800) 221-0713
A pair of bald eagles nesting on the adjacent island love this wilderness setting and so will you. Fremont's, on the National Register of Historic Places, is on Big Mantrap Lake. It is near the Paul Bunyan State Forest and the Heartland Trail. There are five cabins with fireplaces, swimming beach, boat dock and boat rental.

EVERGREEN LODGE
HC06, Box 267
Park Rapids, MN 56470
(218) 732-4766
On beautiful Big Sand Lake you have all the comforts of a large resort and the intimacy of a small one. There are 19 housekeeping cabins and a beautiful 1,000-foot sandy beach. Tennis, golf, rentals and supervised playtime for children.

GRAMMA'S BED AND BREAKFAST
Route 2, Box 1
Park Rapids, MN 56470
(218) 732-0987
This is a lovely log cottage on the Fish Hook River. Biking and hiking trails are nearby. It is located within walking distance of local businesses and there is free use of the dock, canoe and rowboats. Open Memorial Day to Labor Day.

SUNNY POINT RESORT
Route 2, Box 371
Nevis, MN 56467
(218) 732-5310
(800) 279-3464
Sunny Point has a beautiful timbered lodge with game room and 11 cabins. It is located on 2nd Crow Wing Lake of the Crow Wing Chain of 11 lakes. These lakes are great for canoeing and fishing. There is a safe sandy beach and free use of the boats, canoes and paddleboat.

THE TIMBERLANE LODGE
Box 168-S
Park Rapids, Mn 56470
(218) 732-8489
These 18 housekeeping units are tucked away on the shores of Long Lake. Amenities include: swimming pool, whirlpool and sauna, beach with paddle bikes and boats, and tennis courts. Open year-round.

VACATIONAIRE
HC 05, Box 181
Park Rapids, MN 56470
(218) 732-5270
This comfortable resort motel and supper club on Island Lake caters to both families and business groups. There are lake activities, indoor pool, sauna and game room. Open year-round.

NORTH BEACH VILLAS
HC-6, Box 126
Park Rapids, MN 56470
(218) 732-9708
(800) 450-9708
You'll love staying in one of the 32 two-bedroom villas situated on a beautiful sandy beach on Potato Lake. There is an indoor pool and game room plus tennis, volleyball and excellent fishing. Open all year.

▼ FOR MORE INFORMATION...

PARK RAPIDS CHAMBER OF COMMERCE
Box 249G
Park Rapids, MN 56470
(218) 732-4111
(800) 247-0054

ITASCA WEST RECREATIONAL AREA ASSOCIATION
Box 71E
Waubun, MN 56589
(218) 983-3230

LAKE GEORGE AREA ASSOCIATION
Box 1635B
Lake George, MN 56458
(218) 266-3977

AKELEY CIVIC AND COMMERCE
Box 222
Akeley, MN 65433
(800) 356-3915

NEVIS CIVIC AND COMMERCE
Box FISH
Nevis, MN 56467
(218) 652-FISH

WEST CENTRAL MINNESOTA

The Detroit Lakes area has the trails and facilities for exciting snowmobiling.

DETROIT LAKES

DETROIT LAKES HAS been inviting to the visitor ever since 1877 with the arrival of **John K. West**. He initiated many programs to enhance the enjoyment of the area. One of these was a scenic steamship line that plied the lakes.

Detroit Lakes became the Becker County seat in 1877 and was incorporated in 1881.

Today, next to farming, tourism is the major industry in the area. The Fourth of July celebration that takes place here is proof of that. To stake out your spot on Detroit Lakes beach you may have to get up by 6 a.m. on Independence Day. Word is that this celebration is one of the largest in terms of revelers (and in enthusiasm) in the state, if not in the nation.

This also is serious walleye country. The Detroit Lakes area is sometimes known as the "412 Lakes Area." With this many lakes within a 25-mile region there's more than ample opportunity for fishing and other water sports.

There are plenty of bait and tackle shops, cabins, lodges and resorts to accommodate visitors. The public beach in town has more than a mile of open beach. And Detroit Lakes has plenty to offer browsers, such as antique shops and craft stores filled with Minnesota memorabilia. Nearby Itasca State Park has mile after mile of scenic wooded trails and overlooks. Like other Lake Country destinations, Detroit Lakes is an all-season experience, with activities for almost everyone.

As a note of interest, the main street of Detroit Lakes sits on the highest point of land between Winnipeg and New Orleans. The waters west of main street flow to the Red River and then north to Hudson Bay. The waters east of main

IN WEST CENTRAL MINNESOTA there are thousands of lakes in the area encircled by Detroit Lakes to the north, Fergus Falls to the west, Wadena to the east and Alexandria to the south. The larger of these lakes are Lake Lida and Lake Lizzie to the north and Otter Tail Lake to the south. This area differs from the Brainerd lakes area and the lakes of the Itasca headwaters in that the woods are more hardwood than pine, the soil is a little blacker and the people are of pioneer stock and close-knit communities.

▼ **FOR MORE INFORMATION...**
CENTRAL LAKES TOURISM ASSOCIATION
Box 273
Paynesville, MN 56362
(612) 597-2473

Hurray! Minnesota

PHOTO COURTESY OF DETROIT LAKES CHAMBER OF COMMERCE

street flow to the Mississippi and south to the Gulf of Mexico.

ATTRACTIONS
ISLAND GIRL YACHT AND DINNER CRUISE
Highway 10 E.
Detroit Lakes
(218) 847-1618
The Island Girl travels Detroit Lake in style. There are beer and pizza cruises as well as full dinner excursions with stuffed chicken breast or a prime cut of beef. The 68-foot yacht also is available for weddings and special parties. It departs from the Holiday Inn on Detroit Lake.

TAMARAC NATIONAL WILDLIFE REFUGE
County Roads 26 and 29
Rochert
(218) 847-2641
Tamarac is for anyone who wants to see and experience nature. With a little patience you can spot timber wolves, white-tailed deer, beaver, fox and a host of migratory birds, including several nesting bald eagles. Spring brings delicate shadings of wildflowers everywhere whose colors become bolder as the season matures until, finally, in the fall, colors are the boldest. Look for the tamarack in the swampy areas. They turn a brilliant gold in the fall and shed their needles just like deciduous trees.

Tamarac's 43,000 acres are flanked by the White Earth Indian Reservation, the White Earth State Forest and Smoky Hills State Forest. Open Memorial Day to Labor Day.

BECKER COUNTY HISTORICAL MUSEUM
Summit and W. Front
Detroit Lakes
(218) 847-2938
For a nice diversion from the resort world, visit the Becker County Museum. There's a century's worth of history and heritage on display here in a fascinating array of exhibits, archives and photographs of fur trappers and logging pioneers that settled this part of Minnesota.

TRADING POST
Highway 34 and County Road 29
Detroit Lakes
(218) 847-2808
Spend a few hours tubing down the Otter Tail River on a hot summer day. Tube rentals are available at the Trading Post, which also has a petting zoo and displays of Indian artifacts.

DETROIT COUNTRY CLUB
Highway 59
Detroit Lakes
There are two 18-hole courses. The Pine to Palm Course is a little more challenging and is home to the Pine to Palm Golf Classic. Pine To Palm, (218) 847-5790. Lakeview Executive Course, (218) 847-8942.

TRI-STATE DIVING
Route 2, Box 396
Detroit Lakes
(218) 847-4868
This part of the state has many deep, clear, spring-fed lakes, some with traces of the logging, trapping and timber trade. You can often find old tools and antiquated hardware from the late 1800s on the lake bottoms. The shop has Saturday group dives at 10 a.m. every weekend from June through August. The shop rents and sells all the accessories you'll need for a lake dive or a Lake Superior excursion and offers all levels of scuba training.

MIKE'S MARINA
Washington Ave. (Detroit Lakes beach)
Detroit Lakes
(218) 847-7291
Founded in the 1880s, Mike's is water activity headquarters. Full marina with docking, storage and boat lifts. Or you can rent canoes, windsurfers, paddle boats, kayaks, fishing boats and bumper boats.

WE FEST
Soo Pass Ranch
Detroit Lakes
(218) 847-1681
In August, the Detroit Lakes population swells from 7,000 to more than 90,000 for this three-day event. People come from near and far to see one of the greatest country music extravaganzas in the country. In the 19-acre concert bowl such country greats as Merle Haggard, Johnny Cash, Dolly Parton, the Nitty Gritty Dirt Band and many more have taken turns performing during the festival's 39 hours of country music. There are six campgrounds plus food, drink and other vendors galore.

SKIING AND SNOWMOBILING
For a free map of cross-country and snowmobile trails in the Detroit Lakes area phone **(800) 542-3992**.

DETROIT MOUNTAIN
One mile south of Detroit Lakes
Off Highway 34
(218) 847-1661
Detroit Mountain has runs for every level of skier. There is one chair lift, two T-bars and four rope tows. There are 15 kilometers of marked and groomed cross-country ski trails.

SHOPPING
THE RED WILLOW
1160 S. Washington Ave.
Detroit Lakes
(218) 847-6297
The Red Willow features fixtures, furniture and wall and window treatments. Like a cozy B&B, each room in this store is decorated and stocked with something distinct. There's the northwoods cabin motif, a children's room, back to the country, and several other complete theme rooms. There's even a collection of Christmas gifts.

WORLD OF CHRISTMAS
Highway 10 W.
Detroit Lakes
(218) 847-1334
World of Christmas specializes in Christmas ornaments, collectibles and festive home trimmings. There really is no time like the present to start thinking about Christmas. This place, especially its candy shop, will definitely put you into that holiday spirit no matter what the time of year. Open May through Christmas season.

WASHINGTON SQUARE MALL
808 Washington Ave.
Detroit Lakes
(218) 847-1679
Restaurants, entertainment and more than 30 stores.

LODGING
MAPLELAG RESORT
Little Sugarbush Lake
Route 1, Box 53A
Callaway, MN 56521
(218) 375-4466
(800) 654-7711
Cross-country ski enthusiasts find their paradise, all 53 groomed kilometers of it, at Maplelag Resort. USA Today newspaper called Maplelag, named for the majestic maple trees that surround this compound, one of the top 10 cross-country ski resorts in the country.

The food is spectacular, the atmosphere is laid back, the 16 cabins, with their wood stoves and great views, are rustic but cozy, and there's plenty to do when not skiing. At the old lodge you'll find hearty food, lots of homemade baked goods and plenty of hot coffee to chase away the cold.

The interior of the main lodge is decorated with old skiing memorabilia. There's also a fish decoy museum (claimed to be the world's largest), saunas, steam room, and an enticing outdoor hot tub big enough to accommodate the whole crew and then some. In the summer Maplelag turns into a language camp for people between the ages of seven and 18. Open Labor Day through Memorial Day.

FAIR HILLS RESORT
Box 6 MR
Detroit Lakes, MN 56501
(218) 847-7638
(800) 323-2849
On Pelican Lake southwest of Detroit Lakes off Highway 59, Fair Hills is one of the area's more luxurious resorts. Fair Hills is a year-round resort with golf, tennis, horse stables and a private fishing lake. Fair Hills can accommodate groups of up to 350 people in its spacious conference facilities. It has 105 units.

ICE CRACKING LODGE
Route 1, Box 272
Ponsford, MN 56575
(218) 573-3631
There are nine lakeshore cabins on the edge of the Tamarac National Wildlife Refuge. Four have been winterized and have new fireplaces and decks. There is a cozy lodge with dining. This is the place for both summer and winter sports. Activities include a sandy beach, fishing, hiking, cross-country skiing and snowmobiling. There is plenty of wildlife in the neighborhood if you just want to observe.

HOLIDAY INN–INN ON THE LAKE
Highway 10 E.
Detroit Lakes, MN 56501
(218) 847-2121
(800) HOLIDAY

Eating

Main Street Restaurant
900 Washington Ave.
Detroit Lakes
(218) 847-2884
Great family restaurant with a tremendous selection of homemade pies. Daily specials. Serving breakfast, lunch and dinner.

Sedona's On The Lake
12375 W. Lake Drive
Detroit Lakes
(218) 847-8828
When the spirit and mystique of Sedona, Arizona, comes to Detroit Lakes, this is what you get: a lot of atmosphere and menu pages of great Southwestern cuisine steeped in cayenne, green and red chilies and jalapeno. There also are menu items as American as barbecued ribs and fresh walleye. Sedona's has dancing, live music and in summer a bar and volleyball area next to the lake. Open for lunch and dinner in the summer, dinner only in the winter.

The Fireside
East Shore Drive
Detroit Lakes
(218) 847-8192
If you're looking for fine dining in Detroit Lakes, try the place that sits right on the banks of Detroit Lake. The Fireside serves lobster, fresh fish, tender steaks and all the local accompaniments, including wild rice and fresh vegetables. Open daily April to November.

Lakeside 1891
200 W. Lake Drive
Detroit Lakes
(218) 847-7887
The Lakeside 1891 is named for its century-old history as an institution in Detroit Lakes. Though there have been additions, the original structure, built on the shore of Detroit Lake, is intact. Today the old Lakeside stands out for its fine dining more than its historic relevance. You'll find exquisitely prepared fresh fish, marinated prime rib and a delicious assortment of appetizers and homemade soups.

Holiday Inns in other towns should be so lucky. Built on the sandy shores of Lake Detroit, this facility has no less than 500 feet of beach. Like other Holiday Inns, there is a Holidome Fun Center for the kids. 103 units.

Oak Ridge Golf and RV Resort
Route 1, Box 6
Detroit Lakes, MN 56501
(218) 439-6192
(800) 879-1717
Stay in a two-bedroom poolside suite, modern cottage or a site in the 200-site campground. There is a nine-hole golf course, fitness center, indoor pool, hot tub and sauna. The hiking and biking trails are great for both summer and winter activities. The restaurant serves lunch and dinner. Open April to November.

▼ For More Information...

Detroit Lakes Regional Chamber of Commerce
Box 348
Detroit Lakes, MN 566501
(800) 542-3992

PELICAN RAPIDS

BILLED AS THE world's largest pelican, the Pelican Statue of Pelican Rapids stands at the base of Mill Pond Dam on the Pelican River. The pelican is 15.5 feet tall and was erected in 1957 by volunteers who, by hand, wheeled 120 bags of cement down the steep bank just for the base.

MAPLEWOOD STATE PARK
Route 3, Box 422 (off Highway 108)
Pelican Rapids, MN 56572
(218) 863-8383
Maplewood park is located at the south end of Lake Lida. The eight major lakes in the 9,250 acres of hardwood forest park can be explored via a beautiful five-mile drive through the park or via the 25 miles of hiking trails. In the fall the colors of the maple leaves are absolutely magnificent. The park has cabins, modern campgrounds, hiking and snowmobile trails and great lakes for fishing.

LODGING

OAK LODGE RESORT
Route 3, Box 344P
Pelican Rapids, MN 56572
(218) 863-5800
This is a great family resort located on Lake Lida. There are 20 lakefront cabins and all the necessary equipment for fishing. For family fun there are paddleboats, shuffleboard and volleyball courts and a swimming area with raft.

PRAIRIE VIEW ESTATE
BED AND BREAKFAST
Route 2, Box 443
Pelican Rapids, MN 56572
(218) 863-4321
There are three large guest rooms in this Scandinavian farmstead home with a warm friendly atmosphere. You can choose either a full or continental breakfast.

MAPLE BEACH RESORT
Route 3, Box 358
Pelican Rapids, MN 56572
(218) 863-5248
This fun-filled family fishing resort on Lake Lida has a sandy beach and playground. The 11 modern cabins come with boats. There is also a store with a coffee shop and grill serving burgers and fries. Open mid-May to October.

▼ **FOR MORE INFORMATION...**
PELICAN RAPIDS AREA CHAMBER OF COMMERCE
Box 206
Pelican Rapids, MN 56572
(218) 863-5701
(800) 545-3711

DENT

DISTRICT 166 RESTAURANT
Silent Lakes Road
Dent
(218) 758-2310
Serving Scandinavian dinner specialties seven nights a week and Sunday lunch. Located four miles east of Lake Lida.

PERHAM

TURTLE RACES
Downtown Perham
If you haven't the time to train your own turtle, you can rent one for the race. Races are held every Wednesday at 10:30 a.m.

PERHAM LAKESIDE COUNTRY CLUB
County Road 8
Perham
(218) 346-6070
Perham offers a beautiful 18-hole course, driving range, rentals and snack shop with full bar.

▼ **FOR MORE INFORMATION...**
PERHAM AREA CHAMBER OF COMMERCE
155 E. Main St.
Perham, MN 56573
(218) 346-7710
(800) 634-6112

NEW YORK MILLS

FINN CREEK MUSEUM
Minnesota 106
(2.5 miles south of Highway 10)
New York Mills
(218) 385-2233
On display is a log house and sauna built in 1890 by Finnish settlers. There also is a reconstructed granary and summer kitchen.

The hardwood trees produce brilliant fall colors at Maplewood State Park.

WADENA

WADENA IS A town of 4,000. The name was taken from an Ojibwa word meaning sloping or rounded hills. The original site, the old Wadena Trading Post, was a ferry crossing on the Crow Wing River and a stop for the fur traders' oxcarts on the Red River Trail. It was moved 15 miles west to its present location when the Northern Pacific came through.

WADENA AREA CHAMBER OF COMMERCE
222 Second St. S.E.
Wadena, MN 56482
(218) 631-1345

OTTERTAIL

SHOPPING
OTTERTAIL OAKS POTTERY
Highway 78
Ottertail
(218) 367-2022
Offering a variety of items made on the premises, such as routed wood signs, stoneware pottery and unusual gift items.

EATING
THE OTTER SUPPER CLUB
Highway 78
Ottertail
(218) 367-2525
They're rumored to have the finest Sunday smorgasbord in the county. There's also an all-you-can-eat daily smorgasbord from 11 a.m. to 2 p.m. Serving lunch and dinner. Live entertainment and cocktails.

JERRY'S VILLAGE INN
Highway 108 (1 mile east of Highway 7)
Ottertail
(218) 367-2810
Jerry's features savory steaks, juicy ribs, chicken and seafood. They have a tremendous Sunday brunch and evening dinner specials. Serving breakfast, lunch, dinner and cocktails.

LODGING
SHADY GROVE RESORT
Route 1, Box 436C
Ottertail, MN 56571
(218) 346-6040
Lots of family fun at this beautiful resort with 19 cabins that include new luxury condo units. The pool, fishing and boating facilities and a lodge with rec room will make your stay complete.

LIMMER'S RESORT
Route 1, Box 537M
Ottertail, MN 56571
(218) 376-2790 (summer)
(612) 646-4707 (winter)
On the shore of Rush Lake, this is a friendly little fishing resort of nine cabins. There also is a lodge with refreshments. Limmer's can provide all you need for a great fishing trip, including license.

▼ FOR MORE INFORMATION...
OTTER TAIL COUNTY TOURISM ASSOCIATION
Box 1000
Ottertail, MN 56571
(218)346-6133

BATTLE LAKE

ATTRACTIONS
BALMORAL GOLF COURSE
Highway 78
Battle Lake
(218) 864-5414
(218) 367-2055
This challenging 18-hole regulation course is open daily to the public.

TURTLE RACES
The races are held in downtown Battle Lake every Wednesday during the summer at 1 p.m.

SHOPPING
ART OF THE LAKES GALLERY
Highway 78
Battle Lake
The old township hall is now a gallery for the display of work by local artists. You'll find beautiful paintings, pottery and other art forms on display and for sale. Open Memorial Day through Labor Day.

EATING
STUB'S DINING HALL AND SALOON
Battle Lake
(218) 864-9929
Home of the affordable feast. Piano bar every Wednesday through Thursday during the summer months.

Lodging

Three Seasons Lodge
Route 2, Box 268
Battle Lake, MN 56515
(218) 495-2954
There are 14 modern cabins on this beautiful sandy beach of Otter Tail Lake. The lodge is well equipped to provide the best in fishing with boat and motor rentals, docks and bait.

Holly's Resort
Route 2, Box 224
Battle Lake, MN 56515
(218) 495-3456
(800) 237-5331
Holly's has a dozen wonderful vacation homes with deck, patio or screened porch set on park-like grounds on Otter Tail Lake. The resort has tennis courts, clear sand-bottom lake and exceptional playground.

Woodlawn Resort
Route 2, Box 365M
Battle Lake, MN 56515
(218) 864-5389 (summer)
(402) 435-5858 (winter)
Woodlawn gets its name from the dense forest that surrounds this facility of nine beautifully paneled cabins on Blanche Lake. There are several lakes within walking distance, tennis courts, a variety of recreational boats and plenty of lakeside chairs for reading and relaxing on the sandy lakeshore. Open June to September.

Fergus Falls

VISITORS TO FERGUS FALLS can still see the wonderful Victorian architecture that graced Fergus Falls more than 100 years ago.

James Fergus financed the expedition that staked out the townsite of Fergus Falls back in 1856. The village was finally incorporated in 1872 and is now the county seat for Otter Tail County.

Fergus Falls is graced by five scenic lakes within the city limits and more than 1,000 in the county. A recent multimillion-dollar redevelopment of the downtown has created Riverwalk, five shady blocks of stores carrying both specialty and necessity items. This is a delightful park-like setting to while away an afternoon or take care of a few errands.

Attractions

Fergus Falls Center for the Arts
124 W. Lincoln
Fergus Falls
(218) 736-5453
The center sponsors a variety of theater productions during the season. Open May to October.

Otter Tail County Historical Museum
1110 W. Lincoln
Fergus Falls
(218) 736-6038
The exhibits, expertly designed and complete, are of a Midwestern farm, main street and Indian dwelling along with local history and geography formations. The museum also rents cassettes for a self-guided historical tour of the area by car.

Phelps Mill Park
This is a pretty little park on the Otter Tail River with an 1889 mill open for viewing.

Pebble Lake Golf Club
Highway 59
Fergus Falls
(218) 736-7404
Located two miles south of Fergus Falls, this beautiful 18-hole golf course is open to the public. There is a pro shop, restaurant and lounge.

Shopping

The Quilter's Cottage
715 Pebble Lake Road
Fergus Falls
(218) 739-9652
If you've always wanted to make a quilt but never knew just exactly how, here's your answer. The Quilter's Cottage can teach you the finer points of this almost forgotten American art. They have all the equipment and materials to get you started on a quilt of your own.

Ashby

INSPIRATION PEAK STATE PARK
Urbank
This park has the second highest spot in Minnesota at 1,750 feet. Eagle Mountain near the Boundary Waters Canoe Area Wilderness is the highest point in Minnesota at 2,301 feet. There is a breathtaking view of the lakes and forest of three counties. On a plaque at the site is a quote by Sinclair Lewis describing the beauty of the spot as: "...some 50 lakes scattered among fields and pastures, like sequins fallen on an old Paisley shawl."

The view from Inspiration Peak, the second-highest spot in Minnesota.

SEVEN SISTERS PRAIRIE
This is an ecologically unusual Western prairie on the north shore of Lake Christina. The hill crowned with seven knolls supports a large variety of Western prairie plants not commonly found in Minnesota.

EGRET ISLAND
This 34-acre island is located on Pelican Lake just south of Ashby. In its woodlands and marshes is the greatest concentration of colonial birds in Minnesota. You'll find nesting sites of the great blue heron, black-crowned night herons, egrets and double-crested cormorants.

Eating

THE PEAK SUPPER CLUB
Highway 38
Clitherall
(218) 267-5491
Family dining is at its best in this restaurant located at the base of Inspiration Peak. Featuring nightly specials, steaks, ribs, turtle, chicken, seafood and a Sunday smorgasbord. Open weekends for breakfast, lunch and dinner. Serving only dinner Tuesday through Friday.

VICTOR LUNDEEN CO.
126 W. Lincoln
Fergus Falls
(218) 736-5433
Victor Lundeen Co. is the oldest store in town and one of the oldest printers in the area. The book, stationery and card shop is next door to the printing plant.

COUNTRY FANCIES
426 W. Lincoln Ave.
Fergus Falls
(218) 739-4828

Just as the name implies, Country Fancies is filled with all of the things that help make your home a little bit country. You'll find furniture, wall hangings, window treatments, handmade crafts and lots of lace.

THE PHELPS MILL STORE
Highway 210
Underwood
(218) 826-6158
It's not every day that you find an operating general store that's made the National Register of Historic Places,

Hurray! Minnesota

BARRETT

ATTRACTIONS
PRAIRIE WIND PLAYERS DINNER THEATER
Roosevelt Hall
Barrett
(612) 528-2386
Historic Roosevelt Hall adds atmosphere to this fun dinner theater. It is an entertaining and inexpensive evening at only $13 for dinner and the show.

HERMAN

LODGING
LAWNDALE FARM
Route 2, Box 50, Herman, MN 56248
(612) 677-2687
Gordon Ekberg has received numerous well-deserved honors from wildlife groups around the country for restoring the habitat of many species of birds that now winter here, including 37 species of wild ducks, 14 species of wild geese, plus trumpeter and tundra swans. On his farm he has dedicated 103 acres to native switchgrass and constructed a system of ponds. After years of hard work he has created a habitat for the perpetuation of many wildfowl species. More than 5,000 people annually visit this farm for guided tours through the grasses and wetlands. Ekberg operates a separate guest cottage as a B&B. There is a wonderful deck on the cottage overlooking the wildlife ponds. You also can spend your days exploring the trails, observing nature at its best. A great breakfast, usually with Belgian waffles, is served.

especially one that still runs as it did a century ago. Phelps is just that sort of store. It's the place where you used to get a pound of sugar, a rope of licorice and a bar of soap. Today Phelps is still selling sundry items, including Minnesota gifts, stick candy, rugs, ice cream and gift baskets. Open Memorial Day through Labor Day.

WESTRIDGE MALL
Highway 210 W.
Fergus Falls
(218) 739-4439
More than 50 businesses are located in this climate-controlled shopping mall.

EATING
BAO CUISINE
108 E. Lincoln
Fergus Falls
(218) 739-2106
Bao Cuisine, named after its chef, serves authentic Chinese food, with all the hot and sour trimmings, in a relaxing small-town atmosphere. Bao is located in the historic district of downtown Fergus Falls.

VIKING CAFE
2103 W. Lincoln Ave.
Fergus Falls
(218) 736-6660
The Viking Cafe is where regulars gather for breakfast to catch up on the local news. It's also the place visitors have come for years for hearty, homecooked meat-and-potatoes-type lunches and dinners. Don't miss the hand-cut bacon ham and homemade rolls for breakfast.

MABEL MURPHY'S
Interstate 94 and Highway 210 W.
Fergus Falls
(218) 739-4406
Mabel's Irish stew is just about as legendary as Mabel around Fergus Falls. She's quite a character, with more than a few stories to tell, but more important, she's quite a cook. This is a place for fresh walleye, duck and other fresh game and fish.

Lodging
Nims Bakketopp Hus
Route 2, Box 187A
Fergus Falls, MN 56537
(218) 739-2915

Just north of Fergus Falls among the woods and rolling hills sits a popular Norwegian-style B&B atop one of the more scenic hilltops. Bakketopp Hus, which literally means house on the hill, is beautifully decorated in Norwegian motif. There are three rooms, each with its own distinct personality, and lots of Norwegian country charm. The experience comes complete with spa, recreation room and full breakfast.

Fergus Falls Holiday Inn
Interstate 94 and Highway 210
Fergus Falls, MN 56537
(218) 739-2211
(800) HOLIDAY

This Holiday Inn has 99 rooms and a Holidome indoor fun area. There also is a restaurant and lounge with entertainment.

▼ For More Information...
Fergus Falls Area Chamber of Commerce
202 S. Court St.
Fergus Falls, MN 56537
(218) 736-6951

Alexandria

ALEXANDRIA'S PERMANENT population of around 8,000 nearly triples in the summer. What makes it grow is lakes — nearly 200 of them in and around Alex, (as the residents call their city). Alexandria is 135 miles northwest of the Twin Cities on Interstate 94.

When the weather warms and school is out, cottage owners arrive for a summer of fun. Arriving at the same time are vacationers who stay at the more than five dozen resorts or at campgrounds, motels and B&Bs in this friendly community. One estimate says that during the summer 40 percent of the people in residence are making their home on a lake.

Water-related activities, including fishing, boating, swimming and water skiing, are the main attractions, of course. In addition to pan fish, there are plentiful catches of bass, walleye and northern pike. Some avid fisherpeople call Alexandria the prime bass-fishing area in the state. But there's also plenty of golf and other outdoor activities.

Winter sports include ice fishing, snowmobiling and cross-country and downhill skiing. Both downhill and cross-country are available at **Andes Tower Hills**, 15 miles west of Alexandria, (612) 965-2455. Groomed cross-country trails also are available at the **Radisson Arrowwood Resort** on Lake Darling and at **Lake Carlos State Park** at the north end of Lake Carlos.

Whereas tourism is big business, agriculture continues as a strong part of the backbone of the regional economy, with dairy farming being the main enterprise. Larger employers include a **3M Co.** sandpaper plant, a **Fingerhut Manufacturing Co.** mailing facility, **Douglas Machine** and **Continental Bridge**. Serving the retail needs of a large surrounding area is another important part of the economic picture. Residents are rightly proud of **Alexandria Technical College**, which has been recognized by the National Center for Research on Vocational Education as one of the top 10 vocational schools in the United States.

Alexandria is named for **Alexander Kinkead**, who with his brother, William, first settled in the community in 1858. The city is the seat of Douglas County, named for Illinois Senator **Stephen Douglas**, who pushed to passage the bill making Minnesota a state. Chippewa and Sioux Indians inhabited the area for many years before settlers arrived. But the possibility that there were other visitors, Vikings from Norway in 1362, gives rise to interesting lore and a "must see" tourist attraction, even though a certain controversy as to the authenticity of the Viking experience continues to this day.

The controversy revolves around the **Kensington Runestone**. Its story is this: In 1898 a Swedish farmer, **Olaf Ohman**, and his 10-year-old son were clearing trees on their farm near Kensington, a small community just north of Alexandria. They found a large flat stone embedded in the roots of an aspen tree. The stone contained inscriptions carved on its face and on one edge. The stone is a native rock called graywacke and measures 31 inches long, 16 inches wide, and 6 inches thick. It weighs 202 pounds. The inscription was in runic, an alphabet used by ancient Scandinavian and Germanic people. The generally accepted translation is:

8 Goths and 22 Norwegians on exploration journey from Vinland over the West We had camp by 2 skerries on days journey north from this stone. We were and fished one day. After we came home found 10 men red with blood and dead Ave Maria Save from evil. *On the edge of the stone:* Have 10 of our party by the sea to look after our ships 14 days journey from this island Year 1362.

A skerry is a rocky island. In corroboration of the story, boat mooring stones and 14th-century Scandinavian implements have been found in the vicinity of the route the party is believed to have taken to the Alexandria area — from Hudson Bay, down the Nelson River to Lake Winnipeg, then down the Red River of the North and finally to Cormorant Lake in what is Becker County, to the north of where the stone was found.

Scholars have taken both sides in the debate over the authenticity of the stone. Olaf Ohman and his son both went to their graves staunchly maintaining the story of the stone's discovery. If true, Christopher Columbus truly was a "come lately" and the Vikings are discoverers of America.

If true, Alexandria is entitled to its claim: **Birthplace of America**.

GOLF COURSES
ALEXANDRIA GOLF CLUB
County Road 42
(612) 763-3604

A championship 18-hole course first established in 1915 on the northern edge of Alexandria. Alexandria Golf Course has become well-known for hosting the Resorters Golf Tournament, held every year since its founding in 1921. The Resorters attracts many of the best amateurs from Minnesota and many other states. AGC also is well-known for its seventh hole, the "Minnesota hole." A water-filled moat guards the green on three sides. You drive from elevated tees overlooking Lake Darling. The view is spectacular, if not a little unnerving to the weekend golfer.

SHOPPING

THERE ARE A wide variety of shopping opportunities available in and around Alex, including a mall, several major discounters, several antique shops and a number of interesting shops downtown.

FROM THE HEART
522 Broadway
Alexandria
(612) 762-1754

From the Heart features fine gifts, cards and collectibles, many not found at other stores in the area. China, woodcarvings, linens, glassware and candles are among the selections at this location, which was once an opera house.

MY FAVORITE THINGS
515 Broadway
Alexandria
(612) 762-8750

This shop is truly unique, featuring Victorian and country gifts and collector pieces. You'll find handmade collector porcelain dolls, rag dolls, collectible teddy bears and santas, baskets, books, wicker and lace. Central Minnesota's largest dollhouse is part of My Favorite Things. Craft supplies and classes are featured in the lower level, called My Favorite Dungeon.

LITTLE RIVER STORE AND GALLERY
529 Broadway
Alexandria
(612) 762-5333

Featuring quality art and craft works of more than 100 artisans. The thousands of handcrafted items include country decor, baskets, rugs, artwork by local artists, woodworking, floral arrangement, rosemaling, pottery and much more.

THE FARMHOUSE COUNTRY STORE
609 N. Nokomis
Alexandria
(612) 762-2243

Not far from downtown is a home that had been part of a working farm until Alexandria grew up around it. The Farmhouse features nine rooms with handcrafted Amish furniture, dolls, quilts, brass and pewter accessories, baskets, dishes, toys and many more items. Holiday seasons feature special displays and themes.

EATING
THE WHARF
2710 N. Nokomis (Highway 42)
Alexandria
(612) 846-7055

The Wharf bills itself as "Alex's Number One Hot Spot," a claim that probably doesn't come under much challenge. The Wharf is located on Lake Le Homme Dieu. They feature good food for lunch and dinner — appetizers, salads, burgers, sandwiches, and steak and fish dinners. In warm weather service also is available on a large deck. But the Wharf is best know for fun, and owners Craig and Cathy Dunmire have fun events organized year-round. In the summer there are volleyball tournaments, pig roasts, boat radar runs and tubing contests. Winter activities include snowmobile radar runs and golf and softball on the ice. There's dancing every night during the summer and five nights a week during the winter (Monday and Tuesday excepted). On Sunday evenings you can sing along with the karaoke machine.

FIRESIDE STEAK HOUSE
Highway 27
Alexandria
(612) 763-6677

A short distance east of Alex is a unique dining experience for a couple of reasons. One is that you can dine either in the restaurant or in an attached, refurbished green-and-yellow Spokane, Portland and Seattle railroad car. The other is owner Sonny Osterberg, who is in his 24th year of preparing steaks, walleye and other delicious entrees over the charcoal grill. You can visit with Sonny as he prepares your dinner exactly to your liking. Fireside is open daily at 5 p.m., except Mondays. Reservations are accepted beginning at 4 p.m.

TRAVELER'S INN RESTAURANT
511 Broadway
Alexandria
(612) 763-4000

Traveler's has been dishing out good food for the entire family since 1928, making it Alexandria's oldest eating establishment. Located in the heart of downtown, Travelers offers a complete menu for breakfast, lunch and dinner, including homemade fresh-baked pastries.

DEPOT EXPRESS RESTAURANT AND LOUNGE
104 Broadway
Alexandria
(612) 763-7712

Just a short distance from the Runestone Museum and Big Ole, this restaurant is housed in the former Great Northern passenger depot. The depot is built of red fire brick with stone trimming and first opened its doors June 27, 1907. Passenger service to Alexandria was stopped in 1967 and by 1976 the depot was closed for all railroad service. The depot was purchased in 1985 by **Bill Seykora** and **Ken Neumann**, who gutted the inside of the building and had it remodeled into a restaurant and lounge. A solarium was placed over the loading dock, and the original ceiling and floor in what became the lounge area were sandblasted. In the restaurant area, tin ceiling panels were installed and all walls were wainscoted four feet high like the original Great Northern Depot. Decor inside includes many antiques, old railroad memorabilia and wildlife artwork. Depot Express Restaurant and Lounge opened for business May 6, 1985, and that same year the building was designated as a National Historic Site. Trains still pass by on the adjacent tracks. Otherwise, your view of nearby Lake Agnes is unobstructed.

The menu is 10 pages long and is wide-ranging to include a variety of appetizers, soup and salad specialties, basic sandwiches, popovers and potato dishes, Mexican-American fare, stir-fry, low-calorie offerings, pastas, seafood, chicken dishes, steaks, chops and ribs. There are plenty of dessert items to choose from and a menu for the kids.

LODGING
ARROWWOOD, A RADISSON RESORT
2100 Arrowwood Lane
Alexandria, MN 56308
(612) 762-1124
(800) 333-3333

Alexandria is home to one of Minnesota's finest resorts. Arrowwood is located on Lake Darling, just a few minutes out of

ATTRACTIONS
RUNESTONE MUSEUM
206 Broadway
Alexandria
(612) 763-3160

The museum is at the far end of downtown Alexandria's main street, Broadway. You can't miss it because the statue of **Big Ole** stands in the middle of the street outside the museum. The museum houses the Kensington Runestone, which is encased in glass. A small theater features a videotape telling the story of the visit of the Vikings and the discovery of the stone.

The museum also features an exhibit of wildlife of the area and an antique gun collection, and you can tour the adjoining Fort Alexandria, where you'll find assorted vintage cars, a 1917 fire engine, an 1885 schoolhouse and exhibits depicting 19th-century life in the region.

BIG OLE
Standing in the middle of Broadway outside the Runestone Museum is Big Ole, the world's largest Viking. Ole is made of fiberglass, stands 28 feet tall and weighs more than 12,000 pounds. On his shield in large letters is the inscription, "Alexandria, Birthplace of America."

Big Ole was produced in time to accompany the Runestone to the 1965 World's Fair in New York, both becoming part of the Minnesota exhibit. Big Ole traveled to and from New York via flatbed truck. Upon returning from the fair, he was put on display in Alexandria. It's said that visitors are photographed more with Ole than with stringers of big fish from Alexandria area lakes.

Big Ole in Alexandria.

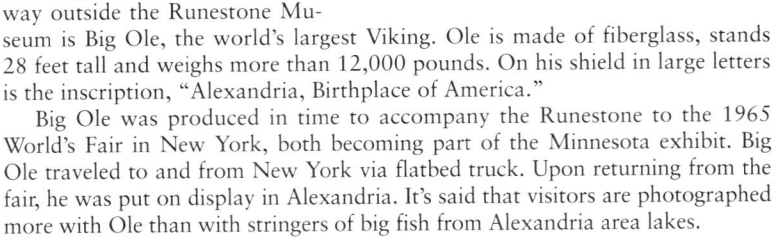

KNUTE NELSON HOUSE
1219 S. Nokomis
Alexandria
(612) 762-0382

Built in 1872 and listed on the National Register of Historic Places, this was once the home of former Minnesota Governor and U.S. Senator Knute Nelson. It houses a museum operated by the Douglas County Historical Society.

THEATRE L'HOMME DIEU
(612) 846-3150

This professional summer stock theater is located north of Alexandria on County Road 42, then a short distance east on County Road 20. It is close to Lake Le Homme Dieu. An affiliate of St. Cloud State University, each summer Theatre L'Homme Dieu stages eight plays that run the gamut from comedies to musicals to murder mysteries. Open June through August, performances are Wednesday through Sunday evenings at 8 p.m.

Alex. It is situated on 450 acres on the site of the former Lake Darling Dude Ranch. Arrowwood has 170 guest rooms, 15,000 square feet of conference space and nearly every activity available in the Minnesota fine resort experience. If you're wondering about quality of facility and service, consider that Arrowwood is the recipient of the AAA Four Diamond rating. Arrowwood has been managed by Radisson since the mid-1970s.

Arrowwood features tennis, archery, an 18-hole golf course, fishing, boating, horseback riding, and children's activities through Camp Arrowwood, for kids four through 12. Swimming pools, indoor and out, sauna and whirlpool are available. In the winter Arrowwood offers cross-country skiing, skating, snowmobiling and sleigh rides. The Lake Cafe offers a full and varied menu and is a favorite dining spot of guests and local residents as well as vacationers from throughout the area.

THE ROBARDS HOUSE
518 Sixth Ave. W.
Alexandria, MN 56308
(612) 763-4073
This country inn is located on Lake Winona within walking distance of downtown Alexandria. More than 100 years old, the house originally was owned by **Oscar Robards**, an early Alexandria businessman. Four exquisitely appointed rooms are named after families important in the history of the community — Cowing, Pederson, LeRoy and Kinkead. A penthouse suite on the third floor has a sunken living room, small library, dining area and private patio.

CARRINGTON HOUSE
Route 5, Box 88
Alexandria, MN 56308
(612) 846-7400
This bed and breakfast is a restored 1911 mansion on the shores of Lake Carlos just north of Alexandria off Highway 42. There are four guest rooms in the main house and a honeymoon cottage with a double whirlpool tub. The living room features an eight-foot fireplace, and the lakeside porch has a wood-burning stove to provide warmth on chilly evenings. Theatre L'Homme Dieu is nearby, as is the Interlachen Inn restaurant, which features steaks and walleye pike.

▼ FOR MORE INFORMATION...
RESORT CONVENTION AND VISITORS BUREAU
206 Broadway
Alexandria, MN 56308
(612) 763-3161
(800) 235-9441

SAUK CENTRE

THERE ARE TWO exits off Interstate 94 into **Sauk Centre** — Main Street and Sinclair Lewis Avenue. As you head into town on Main Street, oversized street signs proclaim that this is not just any Main Street, it is "The Original Main Street."

If you weren't aware before, it becomes abundantly clear that celebrating the memory of native son **Sinclair Lewis** is an important part of the fabric, and even the economy, of Sauk Centre.

Lewis, America's first and Minnesota's only winner of the Nobel Prize for Literature, was born in Sauk Centre February 7, 1885. He died in Italy on January 10, 1951, and his ashes were flown to Sauk Centre for burial in the Lewis family plot in Greenwood Cemetery.

Harry Sinclair (Red) Lewis enraged the people of his home town in 1920 with "Main Street," the book that candidly portrayed life in small-town America. This fictional small town was named Gopher Prairie, which clearly was heavily based on his growing-up experiences in Sauk Centre.

The anger subsided quickly, though, as his work won him the Nobel and he went on to become celebrated internationally for his literary accomplishments. Lewis wrote 23 novels, five of which were considered his major works — "Main Street," "Babbitt," "Arrowsmith," "Elmer Gantry" and "Dodsworth."

Lewis also became celebrated for a literary prize that he did not win, or at least did not accept. After being rejected for a Pulitzer for "Main Street" in March 1921, Lewis became embittered. When named a Pulitzer Prize-winner for

Hurray! Minnesota

Attractions
THE SINCLAIR LEWIS BOYHOOD HOME
612 Sinclair Ave.
Sauk Centre
(612) 352-5201
When Lewis was four, he moved to this home with his parents, Dr. and Mrs. E. J. Lewis, and older brothers Fred and Claude. The home is on the National and State Registries of Historic Places. The home has been restored and furnished to the period of the famous author's boyhood.

SINCLAIR LEWIS INTERPRETIVE CENTER AND MUSEUM
Interstate 94 and Highway 71
Sauk Centre
(612) 352-5201
The Center has exhibits on Sinclair Lewis and the history of the area in which he grew up. Included are photos, memoranda, plot notes and summaries of his major books. The center is open daily during the summer and on weekdays from 8 a.m. to 3 p.m. the rest of the year.

The boyhood home of Sinclair Lewis at 612 Sinclair Lewis Avenue has been refurbished and is open to the public.

his 1925 novel "Arrowsmith," he declined the award. "Main Street," he knew, was a much better piece of work than "Arrowsmith."

Located on the Sauk River and Sauk Lake, Sauk Centre was first settled in 1857 and was incorporated as a village in February 1876. A good place to begin exploring this community is the Sinclair Lewis Interpretive Center and Museum, just off Interstate 94.

Lodging and Eating
THE PALMER HOUSE HOTEL
Main St. and Sinclair Lewis Ave.
(612) 352-3431
The Palmer House derived much of its fame from the fact that Sinclair Lewis worked there during his spare time while a high school student. Word is that he was fired for daydreaming and reading on the job.

The three-story brick building was built in 1901 by **R. L. Palmer**, and it was a year later that Lewis got his part-time job there. The Palmer House was the Minniemashie House in "Main Street" and the American House in "Work of Art." The hotel has changed little over the years since the days when salesmen paid $3 per night for a room. The hotel has 37 rooms, 27 in use. Given inflation, room rates haven't changed much. A room with private bath costs $27.69 per night. A room with shared bath goes for $25.44 per night.

All restored rooms are furnished with antiques, including original basswood writing desks designed by R. L. Palmer for the convenience of his salesmen guests. Ask to see some of the rooms. Also, the walls of the lobby and restaurant feature many historic photographs.

The Palmer House — now on the National Register of Historic Places — has been owned since 1974 by **Al Tingley** and **Dick Schwartz**, who have done much restoration, including raising the building four inches to install new footings and installation of an automatic sprinkler system.

Do not just tour the Palmer House. Enjoy a meal there. Al Tingley does much of the cooking, and the food is like grandma used to make. And the prices are less than you spend on tips at metro-area fine dining spots. The Saturday lunch special is spareribs and sauerkraut, served in generous portions with mashed potatoes, corn and homemade whole wheat bread. The price: $4. The Sunday chicken dinner is $3.90, just $3.50 for senior citizens. The special each Thursday is spaghetti.

Also, be sure to talk with Tingley, who's almost always around during the day. He's a great source of history about Sinclair Lewis as well as the Palmer House. He's a former Methodist minister who subsequently worked for the Citizens League of Minneapolis and the Minnesota Medical Association before teaming up with Schwartz to purchase the Palmer House. With only short notice, Tingley will whip up a multi-course gourmet meal for groups of up to 20 people. He has authored a cookbook and a book called "Corner on Main Street," which relates 10 years of experience at the Palmer House. Both books are available for purchase at the hotel.

WALKING TOUR

The Interpretive Center will provide you with a map and short historic descriptions of several stops on a walking tour. In addition to the Lewis Boyhood Home and the Palmer House, you can see an old mill; the small cottage in which the Lewis family lived until Sinclair was age four; the Corner Drug, built in 1903, above which Dr. E. J. Lewis had his office; churches; a stockade built as a defense against the Sioux Indians in the uprising of 1862; and other buildings and historic sites.

▼ **FOR MORE INFORMATION...**
SAUK CENTRE CHAMBER OF COMMERCE
Box 222
Sauk Centre, MN 56378
(612) 352-5201

GLENWOOD

GLENWOOD, the Pope County seat, is situated on the shores of Lake Minnewaska. The lake was named after the beautiful daughter of a Dakota Indian chief. She drowned in the lake when she fled with her warrior, Pezhekee. Glenwood is the center of activity for the county during the summer months, playing host to Waterama, an activity-filled water festival, and the Pope County Fair.

ATTRACTIONS
STATE AREA DNR FISHERIES HEADQUARTERS
North Lakeshore Drive
Glenwood
(612) 634-4573
Stocking fish are grown here for a four-county area. There are trout ponds where you can see the fish in various stages of their growth. The walleye hatching period is from mid-April to mid-May.

POPE COUNTY HISTORICAL MUSEUM
809 S. Lakeshore Drive
Glenwood
(612) 634-3293
This museum houses the history of the county, a display of farm machinery and Indian artifacts.

GLACIAL LAKES STATE PARK
Route 2, Box 126
Starbuck, MN 56381
(612) 239-2860
The 1,880 acres in this park are divided between prairie, hardwood forests, lakes and marshes. The wide band of glacial hills is a terrain like no other in the state. The park, located on Highway 41, has a modern campground, lake swimming and numerous recreational trails.

HISTORIC MILL DISTRICT
Terrace
(612) 278-3289
Listed on the National Register of Historic Places, the Terrace Mill is one of

Hurray! Minnesota

the last 12 remaining mills of the nearly 1,000 that operated in Minnesota at one time. In addition to the mill, there are a number of other turn-of-the-century structures, such as the Keystone Arch Bridge and dam, fieldstone miller's home and log cabin. This area also is host to several art and cultural festivals during the summer months.

EATING
MINNEWASKA HOUSE
Highways 28 and 29
Glenwood
(612) 634-4566
(800) 828-0882
The open-hearth grill charbroils to perfection the meat that has been hand-cut on the premises. Specialties include 13 cuts of steak, pork and lamb chops, and ribs. There is live music on Friday and Saturday.

LODGING
PETER'S SUNSET BEACH AND GOLF CLUB
2500 S. Lakeshore Drive
Glenwood, MN 56334
(612) 634-4501
Listed on the National Register of Historic Places, Peter's has been treating visitors to that vacation on the lake for more than 75 years. There is a choice of cottages, town homes or hotel rooms. For recreation there are tennis and racquetball courts, golf, a beautiful sandy beach and fishing services. The dining room and Pezhekee Club Cocktail Lounge are open to the public.

BAYSIDE RESORT AND RV PARK
Box 37
Glenwood, MN 56334
(612) 634-3233
(800) 342-5189
These 16 cabins on the shore of Minnewaska are a great place for a family vacation. The resort offers safe swimming, a playground, fishing and boating services.

▼ **FOR MORE INFORMATION...**
GLENWOOD/STARBUCK AREA CHAMBER OF COMMERCE
137 E. Minnesota
Glenwood, MN 56334
(612) 634-3636
(800) 782-9937

COLD SPRING

COLD SPRING GOT its name from the fact that the vicinity abounds in natural mineral springs. Cold Spring Brewery, one of the few remaining Minnesota breweries, established headquarters here in 1874.

ATTRACTIONS
MACDOUGALL HOMESTEAD
County Highway 23
(1.1 miles off County Highway 26)
Cold Spring
This is the site of a great blue heron colony. You can see more than 1,000 nesting sites. The herons nest from April through August. The best time to see them is in the early morning or evening just before sundown when they're not feeding. The house and barn are on the National Register of Historic Places. Bring your binoculars.

EATING AND LODGING
THE BLUE HERON SUPPER CLUB
305 Fifth Ave. S.
Cold Spring, MN 56320
(612) 685-3831
The Blue Heron offers traditional American cuisine featuring prime rib and combination steak dinners in an atmosphere of fine dining. Live entertainment is offered occasionally in the cocktail lounge.

PILLOW, PILLAR AND PINE
419 Main St.
Cold Spring, MN 56320
(612) 685-3828
(800) 332-6774
There are three guest rooms in this beautiful Greek Revival mansion built in 1908. You'll enjoy the warm colors of the stained and leaded glass, oak and maple floors and fireplaces. There also is a comfortable wrap-around porch. A continental breakfast is served either in your room or in the dining room.

▼ **FOR MORE INFORMATION...**
COLD SPRING AREA CHAMBER OF COMMERCE
Box 328
Cold Spring, MN 56320
(612) 685-4186

• FRONTENAC • LAKE CITY • WABASHA • WINONA • LA CRESCENT •

TAYLORS FALLS • MARINE ON ST. CROIX • STILLWATER • BAYPORT • AFTON • HASTINGS • RED WING • AUSTIN •

SUGAR LOAF, ONE OF THE MOST SPECTACULAR LANDMARKS IN BLUFF COUNTRY, STANDS GUARD OVER WINONA.

PHOTO COURTESY OF WINONA CHAMBER OF COMMERCE
ILLUSTRATION BY ERIC HANSON

• ALBERT LEA • OWATONNA • FARIBAULT • NORTHFIELD • BAYPORT •

BLUFF COUNTRY

THE EARLY AMERICAN explorer **Zebulon Pike** said in 1805 upon seeing the Mississippi River Valley in Minnesota's Bluff Country, "It was altogether a prospect so variegated and romantic that a man may scarcely expect to enjoy such a one but twice or thrice in the course of his life." Fortunately, we can enjoy "such a one" as often as we choose.

The Bluff Country of Minnesota gets its name from the river-flanked limestone bluffs that form the Minnesota-Wisconsin border from St. Croix State Park to the east of Hinckley on down through the southeastern corner of the state. These rust-colored bluffs are the handiwork of centuries of creeping prehistoric glacial action, followed by the steady gouging of post-ice-age erosion from the St. Croix and Mississippi rivers.

Reaching skyward along the banks of the St. Croix River, these bluffs frame a perfectly serene picture that extends past Taylors Falls and Stillwater on the north end down to Hastings, where the St. Croix and the Mississippi meet and meander south past Red Wing and Winona.

In certain spots along the river — near Taylors Falls, for example — these cliffs rise nearly 300 feet from the river bottom. During the summer these flat-faced cliffs lure rock climbers

Bluff Country

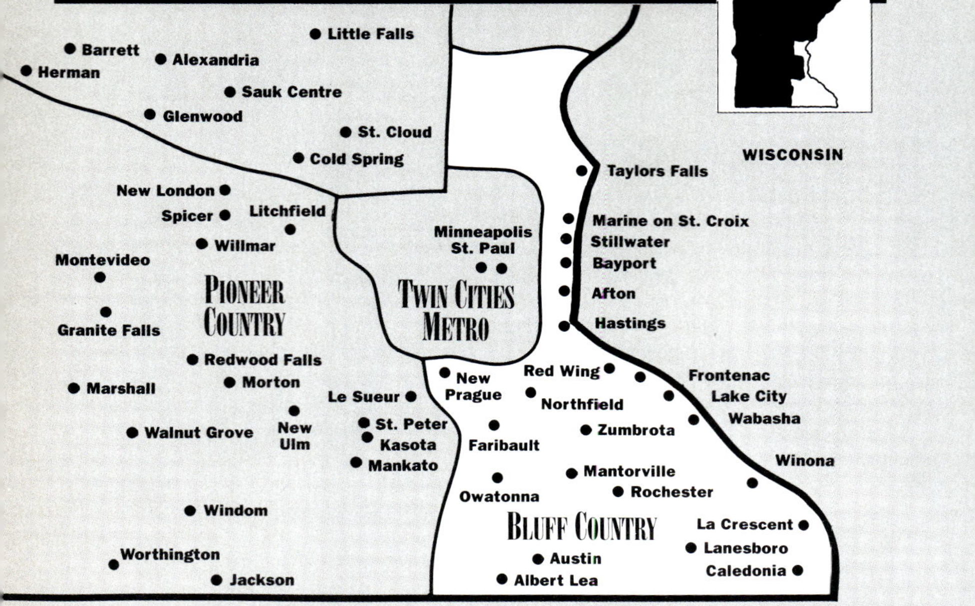

Little Falls
Barrett
Alexandria
Herman
Sauk Centre
Glenwood
St. Cloud
Cold Spring
WISCONSIN
Taylors Falls
New London
Spicer
Litchfield
Willmar
Marine on St. Croix
Stillwater
Bayport
Afton
Hastings
Minneapolis
St. Paul
Montevideo
Granite Falls
PIONEER COUNTRY
TWIN CITIES METRO
Redwood Falls
Morton
Marshall
Le Sueur
New Prague
Red Wing
Frontenac
Lake City
Wabasha
Northfield
Walnut Grove
New Ulm
St. Peter
Kasota
Mankato
Faribault
Zumbrota
Winona
Mantorville
Owatonna
Rochester
Windom
BLUFF COUNTRY
La Crescent
Lanesboro
Caledonia
Austin
Albert Lea
Worthington
Jackson

The Dragon Boat Races during Lumberjack Days in Stillwater.

from all over the region, and the tumbling flow of the St. Croix draws both recreational and competitive kayak and canoe enthusiasts. The outlying hills are prime birdwatching, sightseeing, cycling and jogging terrain in the summer months and a scenic environ for cross-country skiing and snowshoeing in the winter. Birdwatchers, in particular, come from miles around to see the bald eagles, red-tailed hawks and herons that make their seasonal homes in the trees along the river banks outside of Taylors Falls and especially the tiny community of Reads Landing near Wabasha.

These river towns are some of Minnesota's oldest. Stillwater and Winona sprang up along the St. Croix and Mississippi, respectively, in the mid-1800s as farming, logging, fur trading and flour milling towns. Various support industries, such as saloons, inns, blacksmith shops, knitting mills, potteries and mercantile operations, captured the imagination of enterprising East Coast entrepreneurs and homesteaders and European immigrants.

Many of these Bluff Country towns are much the same as they were decades ago. Some of the cottage industries that took root early on, such as manufacturing, pottery making, milling and dairy farming, are still part of the fabric of this region. Several of these towns with links to the past have evolved into minor tourist meccas, in large part because they have found a way to maintain their heritage, identity and 19th-century charm.

PHOTOS BY DEB CHIAL

RIVER TOWNS

TAYLORS FALLS

TAYLORS FALLS, like so many other river towns in Minnesota, was a logging town. Its namesake, **Jesse Taylor**, was a logger who laid claim to these woods in 1838, although timber baron and state senator **William Folsom** founded the city 20 years later.

Taylors Falls was an affluent community, thanks to the logging boom of the late 19th century. The Federal, Victorian and Greek Revival architecture of its grand old homes and commercial buildings speaks volumes about the amount of money that lumber brought to this town. But it wasn't just money that made Taylors Falls: The mentality and style of its many transplanted New Englanders shaped the town's look and feel and are still visible in some of its old neighborhoods.

Due to its beautiful St. Croix River Valley location, its lavish old homes, such as the W.H.C. Folsom House, and its close proximity to the Twin Cities, Taylors Falls has become a popular tourist destination. Visitors can enjoy neighborhood walking tours of the Angel Hill Historic District, which contains several 19th-century buildings listed on the National Register of Historic Places, as well as hiking, skiing, canoeing, kayaking and rock climbing. The Dalles of the St. Croix, located just outside of Taylors Falls, are a fascinating geological treasure bed of fossils entombed in layers of limestone and shale.

ATTRACTIONS

WILDWOOD CAMPGROUND
Box 68
Taylors Falls, MN 55084
(612) 465-7161 (seasonal)
(612) 257-2075 (year-round)
Located three miles west of Taylors Falls on U.S. Highway 8.
Open late April/early May through late September/early October.
Wildwood is a privately owned campground offering a heated pool and wading pool, large wooded sites, free hot showers, flush toilets, tables, a store, firewood, ice, a lighted 18-hole mini golf course and horseshoes, volleyball, a

A riverboat cruise down the St. Croix.

Wild Mountain
Box 225
Taylors Falls, MN 55084
(612) 465-6315; 462-7550 (Twin Cities toll free) or (800) 447-4958 (outside the Twin Cities)
Open Memorial Day through Labor Day.
Featuring wet, dry, slow and fast rides at this water park extraordinaire. Aside from water slides, Wild Mountain features horseshoes, volleyball, picnic areas, boat rides, canoe rentals and chairlift rides.

One of the wet and wild rides at Wild Mountain in Taylors Falls.

nature trail and playground. No boat rental or fishing is available.

Taylors Falls Scenic Boat Tours, Canoe Rentals and Dinner Cruises
Taylors Falls
(612) 462-6315
462-7550 (Twin Cities toll free)
(800) 447-4958 (outside the Twin Cities)
Located in Interstate State Park, Highways 8 and 95.
Open Memorial Day through Labor Day (with the exception of fall leaf cruises, which can run into October).

IF YOU EVER wanted to canoe the wild and scenic St. Croix, past the bluffs and dense woods of birch and maple, this is your ticket. Trips start from Taylors Falls and wind downstream to Osceola or farther south to William O'Brien Park. Along the way, you'll find plenty of river banks with soft sand and picnic space. Transport service is available to shuttle canoeists back to their starting point in Taylors Falls. Or climb aboard a double-decker paddleboat for a three- or seven-mile trip down the St. Croix. You get a front row seat for your ride past the towering bluffs and a chance to spot the wildlife of this region.

Interstate State Park
Box 254
Taylors Falls, MN 55084
(612) 465- 5711
Located one mile south of Taylors Falls on Highways 8 and 95.
Open May through mid-October for full camp facilities; all year-round for rustic camping.

Nearly 300 acres of scenic wooded park land contain massive natural holes in the rocks' surface caused by lava flows centuries ago. There is a hiking trail, a naturalist on duty and an interpretive center full of the tales and wares of the logging industry. Canoe, fishing and excursion boat rentals available.

Dalles of the St. Croix
These fossil-bearing layers of limestone and shale contain the keys to the river's past. From afar, they appear to be nothing more than some odd limestone formations, but a closer look into these gorges reveals fossil imprints. Though the dam blocks the view of much of the formation known as St. Croix Falls, the surrounding 200-foot-high cliffs, which tower over the rushing, 100-foot-deep water far below, are a spectacular sight.

Shopping
THE VILLAGE OFFERS a variety of small shops and stores where you can find antiques, crafts, collectibles, homemade candies, souvenirs and up-to-the-minute fashions.

Eating
Chisago House Restaurant
311 Bench St.
(612) 465-5245
This restaurant features home-cooked meals, with weekend buffets served family style. Homemade desserts are a special-

MARINE ON ST. CROIX

PLATTED IN 1839, Marine on St. Croix was the site of the first sawmill on the river. The entire downtown of Marine on St. Croix is listed on the National Register of Historic Places.

THE STONE HOUSE MUSEUM
Oak and Fifth streets
(612) 433-2061
Open July 4 through Labor Day or by appointment.
Built in 1872 from local sandstone, the museum contains artifacts from early New England and Swedish settlers. The Marine Restoration Society, **(612) 433-2049**, was organized to restore and preserve the 1888 Marine Village Hall and promote historical preservation of other area sites, such as the first sawmill, the old red bridge and the general store.

ASA PARKER HOUSE
17500 St. Croix Trail N.
Marine on St. Croix, MN 55047
(612) 433-5248
This restored 1856 lumberman's home in the historic village overlooks the river valley. There are five antique-filled bedrooms with English wallcoverings and decor and a whirlpool suite, a double parlor, wicker-filled porch, private tennis court, gazebo and a marina with canoes. A sumptuous breakfast is provided. Bike and ski trails at the back door enable visitors to enjoy William O'Brien State Park.

The General Store is part of historic Marine on St. Croix.

ty. Open for breakfast, lunch and dinner.
PALMDALE TAP AND GRILL
18345 N. St. Croix Trail
(612) 583-3113
Enjoy fine food and liquors, family dining for lunch and dinner, a game room and live music. Luncheon specials are served Monday through Friday.

LODGING
THE PINES MOTEL
Rivers Street
Taylors Falls, MN 55084
(612) 465-3422
Located two blocks from the center of town, the Pines offers a serene atmosphere, cheerful accommodations, free continental breakfast on Saturday and Sunday, and easy access to shops and restaurants in town as well as the area's many scenic wonders.

THE OLD JAIL CO. BED AND BREAKFAST
100 Government Road
Box 203
Taylors Falls, MN 55084
(612) 465-3112
Choose between the private guest room in a restored jail or one of two large suites in the historic Shottmuller Building next door. All rooms contain bath, sitting room, small kitchen and private entrance. Located a half block from town and the St. Croix River.

▼ FOR MORE INFORMATION...
TAYLORS FALLS CHAMBER OF COMMERCE
Taylors Falls, MN 55084
(612) 465-6661
Washington County has much to offer the history buff. After you leave Taylors Falls, consider making a stop at **Scandia**. Even a casual visitor to Scandia will

The Minnesota Zephyr on its scenic run.

MINNESOTA ZEPHYR
601 N. Main St.
(612) 430-3000
Call for reservations. Boarding times: Friday and Saturday, 6:30 p.m.; Sunday, 11:30 a.m.
The Zephyr is a railroad dining experience you won't soon forget. This romantic three-and-a-quarter hour excursion aboard a 1940s-vintage train consisting of five dining cars and a Vista Dome club car takes you on a scenic ride through Stillwater, along the St. Croix River and up through the lush green St. Croix River Valley.

---

see that it doesn't take its Swedish heritage lightly. **Gammelgarden** is the location of the first Swedish settlement in Minnesota. The 11-acre site houses six structures built between 1850 and 1880, including one of the oldest log churches and log parsonages in the state and a log immigrant house from 1855. Open May through October, Gammelgarden is located at County Road 3 and Highway 52. (612) 433-5053. **Historic Corner** is a four-acre site at the junction of County Road 3 and Old Marine Trail that contains three major attractions recognizing the Swedish influence in Minnesota: Johannes Erickson Log House Museum, Hay Lake School, and Hay Lake Settlers Monument. Open May through November. (612) 433-5972.

STILLWATER

A TRIP TO Stillwater is a trip to Minnesota's yesteryear. Located on the sparkling blue St. Croix River, Stillwater lays claims to being Minnesota's oldest town, and it was the birthplace of the Minnesota Territory in 1849. From the 19th-century Greek Revival and Victorian mansions perched on the south hill to the brownstone warehouses and storefronts that line Main Street, Stillwater is steeped in history and beautiful natural surroundings.

Settled in 1843, Stillwater was a community long before Minnesota became a state in 1858, and it was the site of the convention that drew up the state's territorial charter. Stillwater is the home of the state penitentiary — the first state prison in the country and publisher of the nation's oldest continuously published prison newspaper — one of the oldest lift bridges in the Upper Midwest, an enviable quality of life and a stable indigenous population that hovers just below 15,000. For commuters, Stillwater is close enough to the Twin Cities to be practical, yet far enough away to feel like country living.

Stillwater is a popular tourist destination. In the summer months, especially on weekends, Highway 36 from the Twin Cities and Highway 95, leading in from the south, are clogged with incoming traffic trying to squeeze into the city's tiny downtown quarter. Visitors come to sample the restaurants, to browse, to boat on the river, to shop for antiques and to cross the bridge to Wisconsin. Be warned, this is an old town that was

Hurray! Minnesota   PHOTOS BY DEB CHIAL

> **WIEDERKEHR BALLOONS**
> 130 N. St. Croix Trail
> Lakeland, MN 55043
> (612) 436-8172
> The oldest hot-air balloon company in the country, Wiederkehr's is open all year, weather permitting. Soar the St. Croix, winter and summer. Call for information and restrictions.

built on bluffs, so the streets are steep and narrow and often crowded. One thing is sure, however: Stillwater may not be the easiest town to funnel into on the weekends, but it is certainly one of Minnesota's easiest towns to fall in love with.

ATTRACTIONS
RIVERTOWN TROLLEY
305 Water St.
(612) 430-0352
This quaint trolley, modeled after an 1889 city trolley, takes riders on a 40-minute narrated tour of the beautiful and historic community of Stillwater, a town of Gothic churches, Victorian-inspired homes and a central downtown area that still bears much of its original false-front architecture.

ANDIAMO SHOWBOAT
225 E. Nelson
(612) 430-1234
Open Tuesday through Sunday, mid-May through mid-October.
If you love atmosphere with your food, you should try this riverboat dining experience. The lunch and dinner cruises treat you to a fine meal amidst the beauty of the limestone bluffs along the scenic St. Croix River.

STILLWATER WALKING TOUR
Rivertown Restoration Walking Tour Brochures with information and lore pertinent to your self-guided walking tours of historic Stillwater are available at the Chamber of Commerce on Main Street.

WILLIAM O'BRIEN STATE PARK
16821 N. O'Brien Trail
Marine on St. Croix, MN 55047
(612) 433-0500
Open most of the year; call to verify.

Hot-air ballooning provides a superior perspective of the St. Croix River Valley.

Located 15 miles north of Stillwater on Highway 95, the park offers full facilities for camping, fishing, hiking, picnicking, canoe rentals and swimming. Rustic camping is available in spring and winter.

JOSEPH WOLF BREWERY CAVES
402 S. Main St.
(612) 439-3588
Open daily Memorial Day through Labor Day. Available for group reservations all year.
The hand-hewn caves with the natural springs were used by fur trappers before they became the site of a brewery in the mid-1800s. Prohibition was the beginning of the end for the business, and the caves were abandoned for a time. But they were reopened for sightseers in the early 1950s and, under the ownership of Vittorio's Restaurant since the late 1960s, are still open to visitors.

WARDEN'S HOME MUSEUM
602 N. Main St.
(612) 439-5956
Open May through October.
This 1853 home for 11 wardens who managed the first territorial prison in

this part of the country contains a large collection of pioneer artifacts.

WASHINGTON COUNTY HISTORIC COURTHOUSE
101 W. Pine St.
(612) 430-6233
Completed in 1870, this is the oldest surviving courthouse in the state. Visitors to the historic site can see exhibitions and inspect the old jail.

GOLDEN ACRES RV PARK AND PICNIC AREA
15150 N. Square Lake Trail
Stillwater, MN 55082
(612) 439-1147 or 430-1374
Open May 15 through September 15. Apart from Square Lake, the park has 54 campsites, a boat ramp, fishing boat rentals, a large swimming beach, refreshments, firewood, ice, a playground, picnic tables and shuffleboard. Waterskiing is allowed on the lake.

SHOPPING

THERE ARE PLENTY of galleries, shops and antique shops in Stillwater. Browse to your heart's content.

KELLEY FRAME AND FINE ART GALLERY
312 S. Main St.
(612) 439-6246
Kelley Fine Art has a knowledgeable exhibition staff and leans towards locally produced art.

MULBERRY POINT ANTIQUES
270 N. Main St.
(612) 430-3630

MORE ANTIQUES
312 N. Main St.
(612) 439-1110

THE MILL ANTIQUES
410 N. Main St.
(612) 430-1816
One of three buildings lodged in the historic 1869 Isaac Staples Sawmill Complex, the Mill Antiques offers one of the largest displays of antiques in the St. Croix Valley. The Sawmill Complex itself houses more than 18,000 square feet of space in which 80 dealers offer their selection of vintage clothing, linens, textiles, kitchenware and other antiques.

SOUTH MAIN MERCANTILE
125 S. Main St.
(612) 439-1223

Hurray! Minnesota

EATING

GASTHAUS BAVARIAN HUNTER
8390 Lofton Ave.
(612) 439-7128
Located two miles west of Stillwater and two-and-a-half miles north of Highway 36. Everything in this chalet restaurant is authentic, from the traditional Bavarian food to the music and furnishings. Even the owner, Carl Schoene Jr., is German. Open for lunch and dinner. Prepare for a taste treat from the old country, because there's no American food on the menu.

KATIE'S SECRET GARDENS
122 N. Main St., upstairs
(612) 430-4372
Katie's is a newcomer to downtown Stillwater. Katie's is what happens when "light" cuisine, which in this case means salads, sandwiches, and chicken and fish entrees basking in fresh, homegrown herbs, meets Victorian decorum. In addition to its herb-conscious menu, which also includes gourmet coffees and homemade pastries, Katie's employs antique lace effects, classic furniture and a splendid view of the St. Croix River to create a blend of the best from the past with the taste of today.

BRINE'S
219 S. Main St.
(612) 439-7556
A casual atmosphere enhances the consumption of deli sandwiches, great burgers with homemade buns, and malts made with real ice cream. Open for breakfast, lunch and dinner, seven days a week.

ESTEBAN'S
324 S. Main St.
(612) 430-1543
Mexican food is presented in a fresh way. The lunch buffet includes tacos, salads, soups, fruit, rice, beans, burritos, enchiladas, ribs and desserts, and features a daily special.

TRUMPS
317 S. Main St.
(612) 439-0024
Trumps boasts good, old-fashioned American food that's tasty, especially chicken and pasta dishes, and features a Sunday country-style breakfast that's served family style. Open for lunch and dinner.

FREIGHTHOUSE RESTAURANT
305 S. Water St.
(612) 439-5718
Enjoy casual riverside dining — on the deck when the weather permits — and cuisine consisting of salads, steaks, burgers and seafood. Open for lunch and dinner, with a Sunday breakfast buffet.

VITTORIO'S
402 S. Main St.
(612) 439-3588
Vittorio's specializes in strictly Italian food that leans toward northern Italian delicacies (except for the pizza). Built into the caves, Vittorio's utilizes the ambience of the old Joseph Wolf brewery in its Grotto dining room. Open for lunch and dinner.

DOCK CAFE
425 E. Nelson St.
(612) 430-3770
The Dock Cafe serves American cuisine of fresh seafood, chicken, steaks, fresh salads, sandwiches and appetizers, featuring daily specials. The veranda is open in the summer, and windows overlook the river all year round. Open for lunch and dinner, with breakfast served on Sundays.

LODGING

THE RIVERTOWN INN
306 W. Olive
Stillwater, MN 55082
(612) 430-2955 or (800) 562-3632
In a beautifully restored 1882 three-story lumberman's mansion, guest rooms are decorated with Victorian antiques, and some are equipped with whirlpools and fireplaces. A full breakfast is served. The inn overlooks Stillwater and the river valley and is close to historic Main Street.

WILLIAM SAUNTRY MANSION
626 N. Fourth St.
Stillwater, MN 55082
(612) 430-2653
This Queen Anne/Eastlake-style lumber baron's mansion, built in 1890, has documented wallpapers, historically correct room settings and is entirely furnished with antiques. The mansion has five fireplaces, stained glass windows, parquet floors and original light fixtures. Guest rooms are air-conditioned with private baths. Full breakfast is served.

THE ANN BEAN HOUSE
319 W. Pine
Stillwater, MN 55082
(612) 430-0355
Lumber baron Jacob Bean bought this house in 1880 and later gave it to his daughter, Ann, and her husband. Because the mansion stayed in the family until 1957, it retained much of its period furnishings and fine Victorian design and is being restored to its turn-of-the-century splendor. Guest rooms include private baths. A three-course breakfast is served to guests either in the dining room near the fireplace or in bed. A social hour at 6:30 p.m. gives visitors a chance to share appetizers, seasonal homemade beverages and conversation.

THE LOWELL INN
102 N. Second St.
Stillwater, MN 55082
(612) 439-1100
The Lowell Inn is the first full-service country inn in the Upper Midwest. Opened in 1927, the inn is built in colonial Williamsburg style and known as the "Mount Vernon of the West." Management of the inn has been the Palmer family business since 1930: the second and third generations of the family are represented by Art and Maureen Palmer and their children, Mary Simon and Steve Palmer. The inn has 21 rooms, all decorated with period linens, lace and hardwood antiques. There are stained- and leaded-glass windows and a comfortable veranda, and guest rooms are furnished with sitting and dining areas and complimentary wine.

The Lowell Inn is also known for its fine dining. The Garden Room and George Washington Room serve a full menu, and the Matterhorn Room takes reservations for its preset meal of fondues and wines.

▼ **FOR MORE INFORMATION...**
STILLWATER CHAMBER OF COMMERCE
423 S. Main St.
Stillwater, MN 55082
(612) 439-7700

The Bayport Marina.

BAYPORT

BAYPORT BEGAN as a river town with an economy based on lumber and farming. The first settler, **Francis Bruce**, built a block house at Central Avenue and Main Street in 1842, and the first permanent settlement was established in 1852. Three villages — Bangor, Baytown and Middletown — merged in 1873 under the name South Stillwater, which was changed to Bayport in 1922. If the spectacular scenery or a day spent in pursuit of history works up an appetite, here's a suggestion:

CLYDE'S ON THE ST. CROIX
101 5th St.
Bayport
(612) 439-6554
Clyde's is synonymous with casual dining right on the river. It offers a dining room with a view, free docking for boats, a summer menu for the closed-in porch and the open deck, prime rib on weekends, a fish fry on Friday nights, steak, seafood, pasta, chicken, stir fry, salads and sandwiches. Open for lunch and dinner.

AFTON

THE TINY New England-inspired village of Afton, settled in 1861, sits on the banks of the St. Croix River due east of the Twin Cities. If you blink you'll miss it, so keep your eyes open when you're traveling south on Highway 95 from Stillwater. State records indicate that 150 years ago, the New Englanders that tilled and farmed the land in and around what is now Afton harvested their crops with the first steam-powered thresher and built Minnesota's first bona fide flour milling operation.

What you'll find is a quaint river town nestled in the trough of the St. Croix River Valley at the foot of several towering bluffs, right in the midst of acres of rolling corn fields. Afton has been flooded several times over the years. (To see just how high the flood level of the St. Croix can get, look at the flood marker above the door at Selma's Ice Cream Parlor.)

ATTRACTIONS

AFTON ALPS SKI AREA
Intersection of County Roads 20 and 21 (from Interstate 94 East, take Washington County Road 15 South and follow the signs).
(612) 436-5245
Open early November through early April. The largest ski area in the metro area, Afton Alps has 36 trails with 18 chair lifts, night skiing, 100-percent snowmaking, four chalets and three rental shops. There's a ski run to suit every level of expertise.

AFTON HISTORICAL MUSEUM
3165 S. St. Croix Trail
Downtown Afton, in the old Afton Village Hall.
(612) 436-8895
Open Memorial Sunday through mid-October.
Built in 1868 as the American Church, the museum features farming displays, since the state's first farm was established in Afton by **Joseph Haskell** in 1839. The museum also houses a large photo collection of Afton personalities, events and architecture, and includes special displays and area artifacts.

Hurray! Minnesota

EATING

THE AFTON HOUSE INN AND CATFISH SALOON
3291 S. St. Croix Trail Ave.
(612) 436-8883
The restaurant features fine dining with tableside cooking in a dignified, old-fashioned atmosphere. The Catfish Saloon is a bit more casual, serves hearty burgers and snacks, and is a great place to gather with friends after boating or skiing.

SELMA'S ICE CREAM PARLOR
Downtown Afton
Selma's specializes in homemade waffle cones and delicious ice cream and is a veritable beehive of activity during the summer months.

LERK'S BAR
Downtown Afton
Home of the Lerk Burger. Closed in winter. No phone. Discovering Afton and Lerk's is pure serendipity.

Lerk's Bar in Afton Village.

SHOPPING

AFTON HAS MANY small shops in which to browse on a quiet afternoon, including: The Little Red House, known for its beeswax candles, jewelry and gifts (612) 436-7102; The Berry Patch Loft, which sells fine yarns and needle art (612) 436-7447; Village Wood and Brass, two unique shops rolled into one (612) 436-8067; Country Interiors, which handles unique decorative accessories and gifts (612) 436-7910; and the Afton Toy Shop, a place visited by nearly everyone who passes through town (612) 436-1150.

LODGING

THE AFTON HOUSE INN
3291 S. St. Croix Trail Ave.
Afton, MN 55001
(612) 436-8883
This inn was renovated in 1867 and is located in the village. The 12 rooms are individually decorated with country antiques and have private baths. Four rooms with balconies and whirlpools overlook the St. Croix. It's close to the launch point for public cruises on the St. Croix, Afton Alps ski area, specialty shops, the marina and bike trails.

AFTON COUNTRY BED AND BREAKFAST
210 S. Indian Trail
Afton, MN 55001
(612) 436-5090
A contemporary home with country decor, this B&B offers two guest rooms with queen-size beds and private baths. One room has a whirlpool and fireplace. Full breakfast is served. The entire home is handicapped-accessible and is near the St. Croix River, bike and snowmobile trails, shops and stores.

▼ FOR MORE INFORMATION...

THE CITY OF AFTON
Box 386
Afton, MN 55001
(612) 436-5090

HASTINGS

THE DOWNTOWN district of Hastings, perched on the river's edge, looks much the same as it did a century ago. Storefronts, old lamp posts and the friendly demeanor of the locals cast a comforting light over this town. Hastings sits on the banks of the junction where the St. Croix and Vermillion rivers hook up with the Mississippi and substantially increase its volume from Hastings southward. This area was a favorite hunting, fishing and trading site for the Dakota Indians, who lived here for centuries before East Coast settlers and European immigrants arrived in this fertile plain in the mid-1800s.

Like many of Minnesota's river towns, Hastings became a trading post and distribution center for industries such as steamboat transportation, logging and farming.

Named after Minnesota's first governor, **Henry Hastings Sibley**, this town is perhaps best known today for the wealth of Greek Revival, Gothic, Italian and Victorian architecture to be found in the historic section of Hastings. Many of these old mansions and civic buildings, such as the LeDuc-Simmons Mansion and the old courthouse, are open to the public as part of a 30-stop walking tour. Hastings is only a half-hour southeast of the Twin Cities on Highway 61 out of St. Paul.

ATTRACTIONS

WALKING TOUR OF HISTORIC HASTINGS
Brochures for a self-guided walking tour of the historic district of town are available from the Chamber of Commerce and several local businesses on Second Street. The LeDuc-Simmons Mansion, the Olson House, the Pringle-Judge House, the Thorne Lowell House, the Dakota County Courthouse and the Thorwood and Rosewood Inn are just a few of the architectural treats on the tour. Some of the buildings are not open to the public and can be viewed only from the outside; the guidebook provides current information and historical data.

ALEXIS BAILLY VINEYARD
18200 Kirby Ave.
(612) 437-1413
Open June through October, Friday through Sunday, noon to 5 p.m.
Explore the vineyards and wine cellars. See how wine is made and sample the results. During the first two weekends in June, the family-run vineyard celebrates the opening of the season by releasing a new vintage, and during the first weekend in November, the vineyard commemorates the end of the season with a harvest wine tasting.

CARPENTER ST. CROIX VALLEY NATURE CENTER
12805 St. Croix Trail
(612) 437-4359
Located one mile north of Highway 10 between Hastings and Prescott on the Minnesota side of the river.
Open daily during business hours, this is a place to hike, picnic, birdwatch, snowshoe in the winter, observe bird-banding, learn about the latest bird research and even catch a glimpse of raptor rehabilitation.

WELCH VILLAGE SKI AREA
(800) 421-0699
15 miles south of Hastings, Highway 61 to Welch Village Road (County Road 7), in Welch
Open early November through mid-March.
This ski area has 33 runs with nine lifts, night skiing, 100-percent snow-making, two chalets with cafeterias and a complete rental facility.

LOCK AND DAM NO. 2
1350 Dam Road
Hastings, MN 55033
(612) 437-3150
Located a mile north of the city, the 1931 dam includes an observation platform from which to view the barges as they pass through on their way upriver to St. Paul. For a tour of the works, phone the lock master.

EATING

MISSISSIPPI BELLE
101 Second St.
(612) 437-5694
Enjoy dining in a riverboat atmosphere. Known for its traditional, hearty fare of steaks, ribs, chicken and seafood, the restaurant has been in business for 30 years and features baked seafood au gratin and homemade desserts. Open for lunch and dinner.

EMILY'S BAKERY AND DELI
1212 Vermillion St.
Bakery: (612) 437-3338
Deli: (612) 437-2491
If you're hankering for a fresh cup of soup, sandwich and homemade breads and pastries, Emily's has that and more. The service is friendly and the atmosphere a far cry from noisy, big-city delis.

This is simply a casual place with great made-to-order food.

STEAMBOAT INN
307 N. Lake St.
Prescott, WI 54021
Four miles from Hastings on Highway 10 and the St. Croix River.
(715) 262-5858 or (800) 262-8232
Family-style dining overlooking the St. Croix. Savor hearty, homemade meals in a riverboat atmosphere, featuring daily specials and a Friday chicken and fish fry. Open for lunch and dinner from May through October; for dinner only during the winter; Sunday brunch and buffet all year round. Though located in Wisconsin, the Steamboat Inn is one of few border restaurants included in "Hurray! Minnesota," a tribute to its popularity among Minnesotans.

JURY'S INN FOOD AND SPIRITS
314 Vermillion St.
(612) 437-4145
The menu ranges from lighter fare to steaks and seafood with a salad bar in a warm English setting.

LEVEE CAFE
119 E. Second St.
(612) 437-7577
Famous for nightly specials that include homemade pasta, biscuits, rolls and real mashed potatoes.

LODGING
THORWOOD
315 Pine St.
Hastings, MN 55033
(612) 437-3297
A French Second Empire home built in 1880, Thorwood first opened as a B&B in 1979 and was the first B&B to operate in Hastings. Some rooms have a double whirlpool and/or fireplace. The rooms are air-conditioned with private baths. A welcome snack and large breakfast to suit guests' schedules are served in the suite or dining room.

ROSEWOOD INN
620 Ramsey
Hastings, MN 55033
(612) 437-3297 or (800) 657-4630
This Queen Anne home, built in 1880, has nine fireplaces and several porches. A welcome snack and large breakfast to suit guests' schedules are served in the

rooms or a dining alcove. Private baths, queen-size beds, air-conditioned. Most rooms have a double whirlpool and fireplace. There are several unique suites and dinner packages available.

▼ **FOR MORE INFORMATION...**
HASTINGS AREA CHAMBER OF COMMERCE
1304 Vermillion St.
Hastings, MN 55033
(612) 437-6775

RED WING

THE LAND THAT Red Wing occupies today was once known to the Dakota Indians in this region as Koo-poo-hoo-sha, which meant, roughly, "wing of the scarlet swan." Then came Barn Bluff, a name the traveling Voyageurs gave this particular stretch of land along the Mississippi. The city founders declared that the town be named in honor of **Chief Red Wing**, a Dakota leader who helped Swiss missionaries find food and shelter.

Less than 50 miles from the Twin Cities, nestled in the rolling hills of the Hiawatha Valley and the shadows of its bluffs, Red Wing is a city that has both intriguing history and captivating scenery. **Barn Bluff** was one of three historical navigation points along the river; **Coffee Mill** in Wabasha and **Sugar Loaf** in Winona were the other landmarks that helped guide boats on their journey downriver. Known throughout the country for Red Wing Shoes and Red Wing Stoneware, the town and surrounding countryside are favorite local destinations for hikers, cyclists, canoeists, shoppers and weekend visitors.

ATTRACTIONS
AMERICAN MUSEUM OF WILDLIFE ART
3303 N. Service Drive on Highway 61
Red Wing
(612) 388-0755
Founded in 1987, the museum dedicates itself to the preservation and exhibition of wildlife art by the foremost artists of the genre. The museum, under the direction of **Byron G. Webster**, includes a reference library of books, magazines, limited edition prints, photographs and audiovisual tapes of wildlife.

THE T.B. SHELDON PERFORMING ARTS THEATRE
Third St. at East Ave.
Red Wing
(612) 388-2806
Described as a jewel box when it opened in 1904, the nation's first municipal theater has been restored to its original beauty and again hosts a variety of entertainment: theater productions, musical concerts, family programs and films.

MISSISSIPPI NATIONAL GOLF LINKS
409 Golf Links Drive
Red Wing
(612) 388-1874
Open April through October.
The 27-hole public golf course, set amidst the bluffs along the river, combines 19th-century charm with 20th-century convenience. The colonial-style clubhouse features a bar/grill and a banquet room, and the course offers a full-line pro shop, cart rentals, a driving range and group and private lessons by PGA professionals.

SHOPPING

ST. JAMES HOTEL SHOPPING COURT
406 Main St.
Red Wing
(612) 388-2846
(800) 252-1875
Twelve specialty shops surround the lobby in this historic hotel, offering a variety of quality merchandise and unique items for shoppers who like ambience while they browse.

THE UFFDA SHOP
Corner of Main and Bush (across from the St. James Hotel)
(612) 388-8436 or (800) 488-3332
Call for seasonal hours.
This is a shop overflowing with imports from Scandinavia, including ornaments, nutcrackers, nativity scenes, crystal, porcelain, pewter and jewelry.

RED WING STONEWARE CO.
4909 Moundview Drive off Highway 61
(612) 388-4610
Open daily.
Red Wing pottery, with its distinctive early-American designs, helped make the town a favorite tourist stop. The works closed in 1964, but were reopened in 1984 by **John Falconer**, who is continuing a 130-year-old tradition and adding his own contemporary designs to the existing line of pottery. Visitors can watch the pottery being made in the showroom as well as purchase it.

POTTERY PLACE
2000 W. Main St.
(612) 388-1428
Open May through December 23.
Former home of the original Red Wing Pottery, this building, listed on the National Register of Historic Places, now houses Minnesota's first factory outlet center. Specialty shops, antique dealers and restaurants round out the variety contained in this shopping complex.

RED WING POTTERY SALESROOM
1995 W. Main St.
(612) 388-3562 or (800) 228-0174
Open daily.
The white salesroom offers pottery dinnerware, glassware, china and crystal from around the world, as well as seasonal dinnerware, fine collectibles, garden pottery and old-fashioned crockery, homemade fudge and candy, and an annex filled with discontinued items.

RIVERFRONT GALLERY
320 Main St.
(612) 388-3103
Open daily.
This gallery offers a wide selection of limited-edition prints that will delight collectors of portraits, Americana, wildlife and Western art.

TEAHOUSE ANTIQUES
927 W. Third St.
(612) 388-3669
Open daily.
Off the beaten path but just right for the antique collector, this shop is housed in a historic, octagonally shaped home built in 1857. You'll find a full range of antiques, including china, glassware, silver, Red Wing pottery, furniture, linens and vintage clothing.

EATING

ST. JAMES HOTEL
406 Main St.
(612) 388-2846 or (800) 252-1875
The historic hotel offers a choice of fine dining and entertainment in the Port of Red Wing restaurant, bar and lounge, or an elegant breakfast, lunch or dinner in

A ferry heading across the river toward Red Wing, circa 1895.

the Veranda Cafe overlooking the Mississippi. Outdoor dining is available, weather permitting. Jimmy's, an English pub located upstairs and overlooking the city, and the Library are two quiet nooks where visitors can relax.

LIBERTY RESTAURANT
303 W. Third St.
(612) 388-8877
Open for breakfast, lunch and dinner. Renowned for its pizza creations and its antique setting in a century-old building, the Liberty also offers American, Mexican and Italian dishes, Sunday brunch, and a chicken, fish and shrimp buffet on Fridays. For those staying in nearby motels or visiting the Marina, Liberty's provides complimentary shuttle service.

LODGINGS

PRATT-TABER INN
706 W. Fourth St.
Red Wing, MN 55066
(612) 388-5945
Built in 1876 by **A.W. Pratt**, one of Red Wing's first bankers, the inn is within walking distance of downtown and the river. The inn's furnishings reflect the Italianate, Renaissance Revival and Country Victorian styles in its six guest rooms and throughout the house. A full breakfast is served. Guests arriving by boat, train or bus can choose to be met and toured along the scenic skyline bluff drive on the way to the inn.

CANDLE LIGHT INN
818 W. Third St.
Red Wing, MN 55066
(612) 388-8034
True to its historic roots, this 1877 Victorian home still displays the original stained glass, light fixtures and polished wooden mantelpieces throughout. The inn is comprised of seven bedrooms, two living rooms, a library, kitchen, six bathrooms, two screened porches and five fireplaces. It's also close to downtown and the river.

SWANSON-JOHNSON INN
Rural Route 2
Red Wing, MN 55066
(612) 388-FARM or (800) 657-4740
Located in Vasa, one of Minnesota's oldest Swedish communities, the inn boasts a copy of the deed signed by Abraham Lincoln. The Swanson-Johnson Inn offers a taste of genuine country life complete with hearty meals, farm animals, open spaces and authentic Americana decor. It's located near cross-country skiing and hiking trails and Welch Ski Village.

ST. JAMES HOTEL
406 Main St.
Red Wing, MN 55066
(612) 388-2846 or (800) 252-1875
The centerpiece of Red Wing, this Victorian hotel was restored to its 1875 elegance in 1977 and is listed on the National Register of Historic Places. Each of the 60 rooms is decorated with authentic period furnishings, named after a Mississippi riverboat and offers a splendid view of the river and the bluffs. The hotel provides a choice of packages that include various amenities, dinner, theater and breakfast.

▼ FOR MORE INFORMATION...

RED WING AREA CHAMBER OF COMMERCE
Box 133B
Red Wing, MN 55066
(612) 388-4719

LAKE CITY

ROUGHLY HALFWAY between Red Wing and Wabasha on Highway 61 is Lake Pepin, a bona fide lake-size bulge in the river. Lake City is built on the banks of this spectacular wide spot. Make no mistake, this is still the Mississippi River, only wider, much wider — plenty of room for those houseboats or your 43-foot ketch. Lake Pepin is 28 miles long and three miles wide, with the largest marina on the Mississippi. It was here in 1922 that water-skiing was invented by a teenager named **Ralph Samuelson**, who used two pine planks strapped to his feet.

Lake City originally made its living as a port market for grain until the railroads virtually wiped out river traffic, and the barges of soft white pine from northern Wisconsin and Minnesota became scarce. Modern Lake City has evolved into a tourist and recreation town centered around water sports such as canoeing, kayaking, waterskiing and sailing. Lake City is also a great place for bird watchers to see bald eagles, pelicans, gulls, herons and other assorted waterfowl.

ATTRACTIONS
WILD WINGS GALLERY
A mile south of Lake City on Highway 61
(612) 345-3663
Wild Wings Gallery is the work and labor of love of **Bill Webster**, the duck stamp print collector who created the whole Wild Wings concept in the early 1970s while working out of his home in Frontenac. What began as purely a small gallery idea to sell a few wildlife prints in Edina has since taken on much greater proportion and now includes 10 galleries, seven franchises and roughly 700 wholesale outlets. Wild Wings publishes the work of many famous artists, among them **Robert Abbett**, **David Maass**, **Rosemary Millette** and **Nancy Glazier**.

SHOPPING
LITTLE BRICK JAIL HOUSE
110 E. Marion St.
(612) 345-5343
Call for seasonal hours.
This turn-of-the-century jail house has long since been replaced by a more modern version, but the old one-story, two-room jail lives on as an antique and collectibles shop. If you like Victoriana, this is the place. You'll find plenty of lace, porcelain, and boxes of Victorian items. This place is also something of an old country general store, with homemade jams, scented soaps and candles and a host of other country pleasantries for your home.

EATING
WATERMAN'S RESTAURANT
1702 N. Lakeshore Drive
(612) 345-5353
Call for seasonal hours.
Waterman's definitely has a room with a view, being located practically on the water. Food here has that homemade character, with plenty to eat, a relaxed atmosphere, and some of the best fresh fish, steak and boneless poultry dishes on the river. In addition to the wonderful dining experience, Waterman's also has a lounge, boat rental, slips, bait and tackle shop and plenty of knowledgeable people on staff who can give you inside tips on getting more out of Lake Pepin, Lake City and the surrounding area.

HARBOR VIEW CAFE
Pepin, WI
(715) 442-3893
Call for seasonal hours.
People go out of their way and stand in line for a chance to dine at the Harbor View. The small cafe on the Wisconsin side of Lake Pepin serves lunches and dinners that combine nouvelle cuisine with healthy and homemade. The result is so creative that most diners think it well worth the trip.

LODGING
RED GABLES INN
403 N. High St.
Lake City, MN 55041
(612) 345-2605
This Greek Revival/Italianate home was built in 1865 by a Wisconsin wheat-farming family in the rolling hills along the bluffs overlooking Lake Pepin. The atmosphere of Victorian elegance extends to the five individually decorated guest rooms, a generous breakfast buffet,

Lake Pepin is an idyllic setting for this popular summertime sport.

gourmet picnics, period decor and other extras to make each guest feel pampered.

THE VICTORIAN BED AND BREAKFAST
620 S. High St.
Lake City, MN 55041
(612) 345-2167

If you're looking for Victorian charm and an unimpeded view of Lake Pepin, this is the place. As its name implies, this B&B has all the trappings of a turn-of-the-century home, including lace, homemade quilts and brass beds. The Victorian was built in 1896 and has three rooms from which to choose.

THE PEPIN HOUSE
120 S. Prairie St.
Lake City, MN 55041
(612) 345-4454

This restored Picturesque Victorian home, built by a local brewer in 1905, has stained glass windows, a carved staircase, two parlors — one with a fireplace — and three guest rooms. The largest has a private bath, balcony and canopy bed.

EVERGREEN KNOLL ACRES
Rural Route 1, Box 145
Lake City, MN 55041
(612) 345-2257

In the family since 1919, the Evergreen B&B is definitely a cozy, quaint home away from home. All three rooms exhibit a lot of attention to detail, both in their woodwork as well as the fixtures. Each room has a big, comfortable bed, old-fashioned picture frames, prints and photographs, window treatments, and assorted antique furniture and collectibles. There's a relaxing reading area next to a fireplace in the main room and a working dairy farm out back that just might need an extra pair of hands.

LAKE CITY COUNTRY INN
1401 N. Lakeshore Drive
Lake City, MN 55041
(612) 345-5351

Located just a few steps from Lake Pepin, the Country Inn is an easy choice if you want ready access to the marina as well as the highway for a day trip. The Country Inn is a varied assortment of 26 rooms that range from strictly utilitarian to luxurious.

▼ **FOR MORE INFORMATION...**

LAKE CITY CHAMBER OF COMMERCE
212 S. Washington St.
Lake City, MN 55041
(612) 345-4123

Frontenac

A TURN FROM Highway 61 onto County Road 2 leads you into Frontenac, a quiet village that looks as though it stepped from the pages of history. Its unpaved streets and stately frame homes, many of Greek Revival style built during the 1850s and 1860s, place Old Frontenac in another era of history. Back in the 1870s, this was a charming resort town on the Mississippi; guests arrived by riverboat.

The town is encompassed by **Frontenac State Park** (612) 345-3401, which affords panoramic views of Lake Pepin from its many scenic overlooks. The wonderful landscape of rolling hills, swaying trees and hiking trails is sprinkled with picnic areas and lots of places to just sit and take in the scenery.

MT. FRONTENAC/MT. FRONTENAC GOLF COURSE
Highway 61
Frontenac
(612) 388-5826

The 18-hole links on Mt. Frontenac are as beautiful as they are challenging, with a hillside lie on practically every hole. With these views of Lake Pepin and the scenic, wooded surroundings here in the river valley, what else could a golfer want except a mulligan for every shot that ends up in the woods.

If the links happen to be covered in four feet of the white stuff, the only thing left to do is ski to your heart's content. With a 400-foot vertical drop, simply gorgeous views of Hiawatha Valley and Lake Pepin, and a collection of runs that meet most every degree of difficulty, Mt. Frontenac is a fine choice for winter recreation.

▼ **FOR MORE INFORMATION...**
LAKE CITY CHAMBER OF COMMERCE
212 S. Washington St.
Lake City, MN 55041
(612) 345-4123

Wabasha

WABASHA IS ONE of the oldest towns on the entire upper Mississippi River. It has been occupied continuously since 1826. Government records and the second treaty of Prairie du Chien in 1830 could conclusively establish Wabasha as the oldest town in Minnesota. The early white settlers found a wise and gracious soul in Dakota **Chief Wa-pa-shaw** when they first came to the Hiawatha Valley. It is in his honor that they named their town. The early days in Wabasha were centered around fur trading, riverboat commerce, logging and, of course, flour milling from the vast acreages of wheat and soybeans in the surrounding river valley.

Today Wabasha is primarily a tourist stopover on scenic Highway 61 between Red Wing and Winona. Located on the shores of the Upper Mississippi U.S. Fish and Wildlife Refuge, it is also a wintering spot for bald eagles. This county seat has a general store, scads of apple orchards, a ski hill, museum, seaplane and boat slips, and mile after mile of cycling, cross-country skiing and snowmobile trails.

The town of **Reads Landing**, just north of Wabasha, displays its own pieces of pioneer and river-town history and provides another ideal location for eagle watching. The Mississippi River Valley is an important ecosystem and migratory stopover for hundreds of species of birds, including bald eagles, golden eagles and red-tailed hawks. You

Hurray! Minnesota

can see these great raptors along the river from Winona up through Lake City. In March, before the trees have leaves, you can easily spot some of these beautiful birds just off Highway 61 and along both sides of the river banks.

Bald eagles also nest in the trees just off the river's edge in and around the town of **Camp Lacupolis**. Although bald eagles are still on the endangered species list, their numbers are growing in Minnesota. Fortunately, there are plenty of riverside rest stops from which to view these birds. Don't forget your binoculars and camera. A telephoto lens helps. **Kellogg**, just south of Wabasha, is the home of a toy and woodcarving factory that makes a stop entertaining for people of all ages. The artistry and creativity of woodcarving reach new heights in this out-of-the-way town. **Rollingstone**, located approximately 20 miles south of Kellogg on Highway 248, is one of the country's oldest Luxembourger settlements. A walking tour of the old town, which was established in 1855, includes 28 preserved structures that played a part in the early life and heritage of this agrarian community.

ATTRACTIONS
WABASHA COUNTY MUSEUM
Reads Landing on Highway 61
(612) 565-4251
Open weekends, mid-May through October 1.
The Reads Landing four-room schoolhouse was built in 1870 at a time when the village was a thriving center of early steamboat and logging operations. Displays include reminders of the industries as well as the daily lives of the people of Wabasha County from pioneer days in the mid-1800s until about World War II. Visitors can examine Indian artifacts, steamboat models, navigation lights, logging equipment, farm tools, old photographs, maps, clothing and an early Edison phonograph with a morning-glory horn, and then visit replicas of a general store, a school room, a pioneer kitchen and a doctor's office.

Wabasha plays host to nesting bald eagles.

COFFEE MILL SKI AREA
Intersection of Highways 60 and 61
Wabasha
(612) 565-2777
Open November through March.
Coffee Mill, named for another historic navigation site along the river, offers the best of coulee skiing, while its "bowl" arrangement inside the bluffs provides shelter from the winter winds and convenient lift accessibility. Skiers on any of the extra-long 10 runs have breathtaking views of the river valley.

ARROWHEAD BLUFFS EXHIBITS/MUSEUM
Highway 60
Rural Route 2
(612) 565-3829
Open May through December.
The museum seeks to take visitors on a trip into the past and present of our great American heritage through displays of early Indian and pioneer artifacts, a wildlife exhibition of North American animals, wildlife art and an exclusive collection of Winchesters — one of every model sold from 1866 through 1982 — as well as other unique firearms from the past.

GREAT RIVER HOUSEBOATS
1009 E. Main St.
Wabasha, MN 55981
(612) 565-3376
For a unique type of vacation or weekend trip, captain a houseboat for a cruise in the Upper Mississippi Wildlife Refuge. Visit historic river towns, fish, swim, or just laze on the deck and enjoy river life. Arrange the trip and the type of boat to suit your vacation schedule and accommodate a variety of interests. And then you and your traveling com-

One of the Anderson House cats du jour.

Eating and Lodging
The Anderson House
333 W. Main St.
(612) 565-4524
(800) 862-9702 (in Minnesota)
(800) 325-2270 (outside Minnesota)
A country inn listed on the National Register of Historic Places, the Anderson House opened in 1856 and has been run by the Anderson family since 1896. Its 32 rooms are decorated with furnishings and antiques dating back to the inn's early days, and the daily menus feature recipes used by Grandma Anderson. Renowned for its food, the inn has published two cookbooks filled with its most popular recipes. Another of the inn's famous services is its cat rentals — any guests who wish feline companionship during their stay may choose a house cat and voilà, you have an instant pet. The Anderson House furnishes food and a litter box for your furry companion.

panions are as free as Huck Finn to set out for an adventure.

Perennial Design
Reads Landing
A mile off Highway 61
(612) 565-2112
Open April through September.
Located on top of a bluff, landscape artist Beth Tidwell's Perennial Designs offers visitors large displays of flowers and landscape design ideas to view and purchase.

Shopping
Country Bouquet Outlet
317 W. Main St.
(612) 565-3808
This shop features quality carved Santas and birds, collector dolls, furniture, miniature villages, gifts and crafts.

Dick's Frame and Uptown Gallery
164 Pembroke
(612) 565-4793
This gallery offers a fine collection of limited-edition prints by local Minnesota artists as well as wildlife prints, wood works and carvings, handcrafted collectibles, paintings and sculptures. Custom framing and gift wrapping.

L.A.R.K. Toys
Lark Lane
Kellogg (on Highway 61)
(507) 767-3387

Call for seasonal hours.
Imagination and quality craftsmanship create a fantastic world of handcarved rocking horses, toys, animals and full-size carousel animals that spell L.A.R.K. (Lost Arts Revival by Kreofsky), designer and manufacturer of wooden toys sold across the country.

Owner **Donn Kreofsky** started the business in 1983 and in 1990 added a year-round Christmas Shop to the carving studio and woodshop. Visitors of all ages can watch toys and carousel animals in the making.

Old City Hall
257 W. Main St.
Wabasha
(612) 565-2585
Wabasha's old city hall, built in 1894, has been lovingly renovated and now houses a handful of craft, antique and specialty shops. Annie B's, an ice cream and candy shop located in the former jail, ships caramels made in the shop around the world. In the marketplace, the site of the former fire hall, several area businesses sell their wares.

▼ **For More Information...**
Wabasha Chamber of Commerce
Box 105
Wabasha, MN 55981
(612) 565-4158

Hurray! Minnesota

PHOTO COURTESY OF THE ANDERSON HOUSE

Downtown Winona displays a quiet charm reminiscent of its early days.

WINONA

MANY CITIES IN Minnesota claim to be the gateway to the West, but none has more legitimate claim to that distinction than Winona, which captures the essence of Bluff Country in both its geography and culture. Tucked away in the southeastern corner of the state, Winona was a portal that bridged the gap between the parochial East and the rugged West during the 19th century.

In 1851, steamboat **Captain Orrin Smith** landed three men on the sandbar upon which Winona was founded. The town was named after **We-no-nah**, the eldest daughter of an Indian chief. She jumped to her death from Maiden Rock overlooking Lake Pepin because she had not been allowed to marry the brave of her choice. We-no-nah remains a symbol of the city, and her statue is found in Levee Park.

Winona's early citizenry, a cross section of Polish and German immigrants mixed in with westward-ho Easterners, certainly was an enterprising lot. Some of this state's first millionaires, such as lumber baron **William Laird**, grocery tycoon **John Latsch** and Winona founding fathers **Verrazano Simpson**, **Henry Huff** and **Henry Lamberton** made their fortunes in this bustling little river town.

Moreover, some of the state and nation's most distinguished politicians came from Winona as well: **U.S. Senator Daniel Norton**, famous for his role in the impeachment proceedings of **President Andrew Johnson**; **Minnesota Supreme Court Chief Justice William Mitchell**, for whom the St. Paul law school is named; and **William Windom**, who served in both houses of Congress, lent his likeness to the $2 bill and also served as secretary of the treasury in the Garfield administration.

Incorporated in 1857, Winona attracted people from far and wide looking for a piece of the action in the booming lumber, railroad and flour-milling industries. By 1880, three-quarters of this town's population were immigrants or the children of immigrants. You can still observe this influence in the vast array of residential, commercial and church architecture. Some of Minnesota's most splendid examples of residential Victorian, Tuscan, Spanish Mission and Georgian architectural design are still standing in the neighborhoods of Winona. Likewise, Winona's commercial district downtown bears an equally impressive assortment of Art Deco, Egyptian Revival, Romanesque Revival and Richardsonian Romanesque architecture — a testament to the wealth, culture and spirit that flourished in Winona in its earlier days.

Much of this wealth came from lumber and flour milling. In 1892 Winona was the eighth-largest lumber producer in the nation. And when flour milling peaked in the mid-1870s, Winona had 13 flour mills and was generally regarded as the fourth-largest grain market in the country. The largest of these flour milling operations, built in 1875, later became the Bay State Milling Co., which still operates in Winona.

The demise of Winona as a regional economic powerhouse, brought on by ever-vanishing supplies of white pine trees in northern Minnesota and Wisconsin, was not unlike that of the Iron Range when the profitable iron ore market disappeared after the ground could yield no more. Adding to the town's economic misery was the milling industry's gradual exodus from Winona. By the turn of the century, Winona was a shadow of its earlier self.

To gain some perspective on Winona, consider this: With a population of 3,000, Winona was the third-largest city in the state in 1857. But as the timber and flour milling jobs went elsewhere, the population growth was stunted dramatically. Since 1900, Winona's population has increased by only 6,000. Today the population is approximately 25,400. In some ways this town really hasn't changed much over the years, and that's what makes it such a find. And like many other historic enclaves around Minnesota, Winona is fortunate enough to have some preservation-minded residents who have made it their passion to save what remains of the town's historic grandeur.

Winona is a fine example of 19th-century Americana and is naturally blessed with a landscape for all seasons. It is the hometown of U of M Athletic Director and former All-American football player **Paul Giel**. Winona is also the home of: the two largest manufacturers of stained glass in the country — Hauser Art Glass and Conway Universal Studios; the Hal Leonard Publishing Corporation, founded in 1947, publishers of printed music and music education materials; the 260-mile-long Upper Mississippi National Wildlife Refuge; the C.A. Rohrer Rose Garden; the campuses of Saint Mary's College of Minnesota, Winona State University, the College of St. Teresa and Winona Technical College; and some of the most majestic bluffs in Bluff Country. Steamboat Days, an annual celebration held near the 4th of July, brings together Winona's entire summer social scene and involves visitors and residents alike. Visitors should also note that because the Mississippi runs from east to west in Winona, the process of giving and receiving directions in this town requires a minor readjustment of one's compass points.

ATTRACTIONS
CONWAY UNIVERSAL STUDIOS
503 Center St.
(507) 452-9209
By appointment only.
One of the country's largest stained glass manufacturing companies operates in Winona. Conway Universal offers tours upon request for stained glass aficionados. It's an opportunity to see how these massive sheets of glass are stained, cut, trimmed and etched for churches and homes around the world.

SUGAR LOAF
Off Highway 61 on the southeast edge of Winona
Winona has some of the largest river bluffs in the state, and this is one of the most photographed. This 500-foot-high slab of limestone was called Wa-pa-sha's Cap because of its original shape and color. The bluff was named in honor of the chief of a tribe of Dakota Sioux who wintered at the mountain's base, and it held an important place in the lore of the

tribe. After Winona was founded, Sugar Loaf became a debarkation point for settlers and a navigational landmark for steamboat captains. When the shape of the mountain began to change at the hands of quarrymen in the 1870s, the name Sugar Loaf was adopted because of the appearance of the mountaintop as a result of the mining. Quarrying was halted in 1888, and in 1950 the Daughters of the American Revolution purchased the site and deeded it to the city of Winona. Since 1983, the bluff has been floodlit at night. When the lights are on, the outline of a cross is visible in the side of the bluff that faces the city. Sugar Loaf's summit is accessible to the public.

JULIUS C. WILKIE STEAMBOAT MUSEUM
Main St. at Levee Park
(507) 454-6880
Open Memorial Day through Labor Day.
A century ago, before the advent of the railroad and automobile, travel between river towns usually meant travel on the river. Steamboats were almost as common on the Mississippi and St. Croix as the bus is today on city streets. With the arrival of the railroads in the late 1800s, the slower and less-direct steamboats became virtually obsolete.

If you ever wondered what these old steamboats were all about, how they navigated, how fast they traveled, how many people they could carry, how people ate meals en route to their destination, or merely what they looked like on the inside, this is the place to find out. The Julius C. Wilkie, a replica of a retired Mississippi River steamboat, is now a museum that exhibits the history and utility of these once-prominent river transport boats. Tours are available by day and in the evening by appointment.

GARVIN HEIGHTS PARK
Garvin Heights Road (across Highway 61 at the south end of Huff St.)
On a clear day, you can see for 20 miles in any direction. For the best view in the house, take Huff Street south out of town across the highway and follow Garvin Heights Road up the winding bluffside road to Garvin Heights. There are plenty of photo opportunities, picnic tables and hiking trails here atop this 575-foot-high bluff that towers above downtown Winona, the river valley and the distant rolling hills of Wisconsin.

WINONA COUNTY HISTORICAL SOCIETY MUSEUMS
WINONA ARMORY MUSEUM
160 Johnson St.
(507) 454-2723
Open almost every day of the year.
This is a great place to lose yourself for a few hours. It's a combination interpretive center, museum, general store and bookstore. The Armory Museum, located in the same building, gives visitors a good slice of what early life here on the river was all about, from logging and flour milling to high society and its European base.

THE BUNNELL HOUSE
At Highways 61 and 14
Homer
(507) 454-2723
Open Memorial Day through Labor Day.
Perched majestically above the Mississippi, this Gothic Revival-style three-story home is listed on the National Register of Historic Places. Located just five minutes south of Winona, the house

Free Bird Poster!
Winona, MN, abounds in native & migratory birds! Call for a free color poster with tour maps and birding tips.
Also, ask us about these events:
- Tundra Swan Watch, Nov. 7-8, 1992
- Spring Eagle Watch, March 6-7, 1993

Winona Convention & Visitors Bureau
Box 870, Winona, MN 55987-087H
Call toll-free: 1-800-657-4972

was built by **Willard Bunnell**, former Great Lakes steamboat captain, in the early 1850s. Bunnell and his family were the first permanent white settlers in the county and were also true friends to Chief Wapasha, whose band of Dakota lived in this valley. The Bunnell House is filled with artifacts from the days when settlers had to make their living off the land and did so in part through customs they picked up from the Dakota.

Arches Museum
Highway 14 (11 miles west of Winona)
(507) 454-2723
Named for the stone railway arches nearby, the museum features early agricultural equipment, tools and household items. Displays include an authentic one-room schoolhouse, log cabin and barn.

Pickwick Mill
On Big Trout Creek off County Road 7
Pickwick
(507) 452-9658 or 452-7341
Open May through October.
The Pickwick Mill was one of Minnesota's first viable flour mills. It's a six-story limestone structure built in 1854 that ground grain used to feed Union soldiers in the Civil War, and the mill remained in use until 1978. Today the Pickwick Mill, just about 10 miles south of Winona, is an incredible photo opportunity and a visible link to Minnesota's grain-dominated past.

Polish Cultural Institute
102 Liberty St.
(507) 454-3431
Open May through November.
The institute was founded in 1976 to preserve the diligence, culture and pride of the early Polish immigrants who helped build Winona into one of the wealthiest river towns in the Midwest. Housed in a wonderful old warehouse, the museum celebrates Winona's active Polish community, which accounted for more than a third of the city's population for many years. The institute also has one of the Bluff Country's most active genealogical research centers. Displays include historic and religious icons, texts, photographs and fourth-generation family heirlooms passed down from some of Winona's prominent Polish families.

Winona Walking Tour
A self-guided walking tour of historic downtown Winona will acquaint you with the city's diverse architectural styles and history: Watkins Incorporated on Liberty Street is a 1913 two-story, block-long building that incorporates Viennese classical elements with local ornamental imagery in the manner of the Prairie School and still carries on business as usual, furnishing the complete Watkins product line from spices and gifts to personal care products; the Watkins Home on East Wabasha Street, donated by the family in 1956 to be used as a senior citizens' residence, is often referred to as "the house vanilla built." It was constructed in the late 1920s by **Paul Watkins**, second president of Watkins Incorporated and nephew of founder **J.R. Watkins**, and is an English Tudor-style building that houses a large Aeolian organ with nearly 6,000 pipes and a Steinway concert piano; the Winona Arts Center on Fifth and Franklin streets is the oldest wooden structure in town; Merchants National Bank on East Third Street is a Prairie School building designed by Purcell, Elmslie and Feich and completed in 1912; Winona National and Savings Bank on Main Street is an Egyptian Revival-style building with a Prairie School interior and stained glass and bronze work made by the Tiffany Studios of New York; and the remarkable St. Stanislaus Catholic Church on East Fourth Street was designed in 1894 by architect **Charles Maybury**, who took a Greek cross plan, grafted on Romanesque and Baroque elements, and topped it with a silver dome and the statue of St. Stanislaus.

Shopping
The Oaks Gallery and Country Store
425 Cottonwood Drive
(507) 453-3603
A visit to this establishment is a visit to the days when the country store sold everything from arts and crafts to crackers and chocolate. The gallery section is a good place to find works by local and national artists, including a strong collection of wildlife art.

Hurray! Minnesota

EATING

ZACH'S ON THE TRACKS
Corner of Front and Center streets
(507) 454-6939
The Winona and St. Peter Railroad was the first in these parts and played a role in both putting the steamboats out of business and helping to bring prosperity to this river valley. Some of that history is still parked out back of this restaurant. This is a favorite of Winona families and college students. It's basically American homestyle here, with plenty of meat and potatoes and a smattering of poultry and fish entrees. Zach's is decidedly casual and comfortably homespun Winona.

HOT FISH SHOP
Highway 14/61
(507) 452-5002
Closed Mondays.
Located just below Sugar Loaf, the Hot Fish Shop has been run by the Coshenet family for the three generations since it opened. Famous for its batter-fried walleye, the restaurant serves a full menu at breakfast, lunch and dinner with daily specials. The Hot Fish Shop also has a fish market stocked with imported and seasonal seafood.

WINONA KNITS SWEATERS
720 E. Highway 61 at Sugar Loaf
(507) 454-1724 or (800) 888-2007
In New England there's L.L. Bean. Here in the Midwest, the company people have been turning to for reliable clothing quality for generations is Winona Knits. Moreover, like L.L. Bean, Winona Knits is a conscientious corporate citizen that supports local festivals, sporting events and charities.

Winona Knits has been in the **Woodworth** family in downtown Winona since 1943 and continues to produce some of the finest knit sweaters in the Midwest as well as a host of other knitted products, such as scarves and blankets. Today Winona Knits has 25 retail outlet stores throughout Minnesota and the Midwest. And Winona Knits plans to expand beyond the Midwest as well. Not bad for a concept that started next door to the old Winona Knits Mill purely as a place to sell and get rid of blemished sweaters.

HEART'S DESIRE
Second and Center streets
(507) 452-5621
Two floors of unique gifts and decorations are located inside this restored 19th-century bank building.

IN SEASON
79 Plaza E.
(507) 452-6398
Decorations can be found here for every holiday you can imagine, but Christmas collectibles are a hot item. The store will ship anywhere in the country.

LODGING

CARRIAGE HOUSE BED AND BREAKFAST
420 Main St.
Winona, MN 55987
(507) 452-8256
This 1870 three-story carriage house, located just across the street from Winona State University, introduces guests to old-fashioned country charm and decor. Each of the four rooms has its own distinct character, including one room that still uses the original hayloft sliding door. Proprietors Deb and Don Salyards are a wealth of information about the city and surrounding areas.

BEST WESTERN RIVERPORT INN AND SUITES
900 Bruski Drive
Winona, MN 55987
(507) 452-0606 or (800) 782-9422
Located just below Sugar Loaf and across from the Hot Fish Shop, the

La Crescent bursts into full flower during apple blossom season.

three-story, 106-room hotel is brand new and features in-room whirlpools, a two-story grill and pub and four fantasy suites complete with old cars and a drive-in motif.

▼ **FOR MORE INFORMATION...**
WINONA AREA CHAMBER OF COMMERCE AND CONVENTION AND VISITORS BUREAU
67 Main St.
Winona, MN 55987
(507) 452-2272 or (800) 657-4972

LA CRESCENT

HOUSTON COUNTY IS full of well-kept secrets. One of them is the town of La Crescent, located south of Winona just across the river from La Crosse, Wisconsin. Known as the "apple capital of Minnesota," La Crescent affords visitors a chance to see spectacular scenery on the eight-mile **Apple Blossom Trail**, which is particularly beautiful when the blossoms are at their peak in early to mid-May. Some say this drive is second in beauty only to the North Shore Drive. Bicycle enthusiasts from all across the Midwest find the steep Apple Blossom Trail extremely challenging.

Each September, the annual Applefest celebrates the harvest with a weekend of activities and culminates with the King Apple Grand Parade. La Crescent is also known for its excellent hunting and fishing locales, its apple, flower, and produce stands and its bike trails. The 35-mile **Root River Trail**, built on an old railroad bed and running from Fountain to Rushford, will soon be extended to La Crescent.

▼ **FOR MORE INFORMATION...**
LA CRESCENT CHAMBER OF COMMERCE
Box 132
La Crescent, MN 55947
(507) 895-2800

CALEDONIA

ANOTHER SECRET IS tucked away in the southeast corner of Minnesota, just in from the Iowa-Wisconsin border. Caledonia, settled by Scottish immigrants who came to the area to farm the fertile fields of the river valley, is a pleasant little hideaway surrounded by river bluffs just minutes away from one of the widest spots in the Mississippi River.

Many of the local farms are still in the hands of second- and third-generation Scots, who also put their time and money into flour milling enterprises. The vestiges of the industry are still found today in **Scheck's Mill**, the only water-driven mill still operating in Minnesota.

Caledonia is known to hunters as the wild turkey capital of the world. It's also one of the stopovers on the way to the **Richard J. Dorer Memorial Hardwood Forest**, one of the state's few remaining hardwood forests.

▼ **FOR MORE INFORMATION...**
CALEDONIA AREA CHAMBER OF COMMERCE
Box 24B
Caledonia, MN 55921
(507) 724-2511

ROCHESTER

ROCHESTER IS THE HOME OF the Mayo Clinic, regarded by many as the finest medical institution in the world, especially in the area of clinical research. In 1991, U.S. News and World Report ranked the Mayo Clinic as one of the 10 "best of the best" hospitals in the nation. The same survey rated it as among the best in 12 specialty areas: cancer, cardiology, endocrinology, gastroenterology, gynecology, neurology, orthopedics, otolaryngology, psychiatry, rehabilitation, rheumatology and urology.

The Mayo Clinic is the legacy of **Dr. William Worall Mayo**, who arrived at the 10-year-old Rochester settlement in 1863 to act as examining surgeon for men being inducted into the Union Army. After the war, Mayo went into private practice in Rochester. His sons, **Drs. Charles** and **William Mayo Jr.**, joined the practice and the Mayo Clinic evolved from the family partnership. In the 1920s, Dr. Charles Mayo's sons, **Dr. Charles W.** and **Dr. Joseph G. Mayo**, helped form the Mayo Clinic into an internationally recognized institution known for leadership in the research and treatment of medical illness. Today, 130 years after its founding, the Mayo Clinic still shapes Rochester's personality. Few cities in the world have such a flourishing concentration of medical talent, all in a town of roughly 80,000. Nearly four times that many people visit Rochester every year for treatment at Mayo.

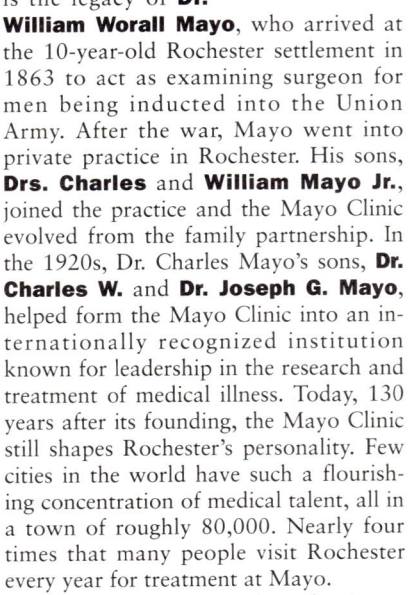

Although the Mayo Clinic dominates downtown Rochester, with its vast medical treatment and support facilities, the suburbs are largely IBM country. Big Blue has one of its largest American divisions here in Rochester, which, combined with Mayo Medical Center, St. Mary's Hospital and Rochester Methodist Hospital, makes for a well-educated, well-paid populace.

Consequently, although Rochester is built near a gorgeous landscape of rolling hills, fertile farmlands and the Zumbro River Valley, most people tend to think of Rochester more for Mayo and IBM than the Bluff Country beauty that surrounds it. But Rochester and the surrounding area offer a variety of sights and activities for the visitor: There's Mayowood, the sprawling Mayo mansion just outside of Rochester; the Quarry Hill Nature Center (named for the numerous limestone quarries that have operated around the Zumbro River Valley for decades); Whitewater State Park; Silver Lake Park, home to a huge number of Canadian geese all year long; the Rochester Art Center, which provides residents and visitors with classes and art exhibitions by regional and national artists; Rochester Civic Theater; Mayo Civic Center; Mystery Cave, located 32 miles south of Rochester; Rochester Civic Music, the parent organization of the Rochester Symphony Orchestra and Chorale, the Rochester Symphony Chamber Orchestra, the RSO Ensembles and the Summer Music in the Park series. St. Mary's Hospital, Federal Medical Center and the Mayo Clinic provide tours of the facilities.

ATTRACTIONS

MAYOWOOD
Box 6411
Rochester
(507) 282-9447
Reservations required. Tours leave from the Olmsted County Historical Center. The former home of Dr. Charles H. Mayo and his son, Dr. Charles W. Mayo

The new Seibens Clinic adds color and dimension to downtown Rochester.

(Dr. Chuck and Dr. Charlie, respectively), this grand mansion overlooking the Zumbro River Valley was once the center of a 3,000-acre estate. In 1970, Mayowood was named to the National Register of Historic Places. The Mayo family donated the 1911 residence to the Olmsted County Historical Society 15 years ago, and guides sprinkle their tour talks with anecdotes about the Mayos, including the story of the house itself. Dr. Chuck's family went one day to their favorite picnic place, sat under a giant oak, and watched Dr. Chuck as he took a ball of string from his pocket and showed them the outline of their future house. That oak still stands in the center of the courtyard. In its time, Mayowood has served as a cultural and social center for the region: The guestbook includes the

Hurray! Minnesota

PHOTOS BY JACK B. HUHNERKOCH

Mayowood, the former home of two Mayos and their families.

names **Helen Keller**, **Franklin D. Roosevelt**, **Adlai Stevenson**, the **King of Nepal** and **King Faisal** of Saudi Arabia.

PLUMMER HOUSE OF THE ARTS
1091 Plummer Lane
(507) 281-6184
(507) 281-6160
Open June through August.
Call for hours and information.
In 1917 **Dr. Henry S. Plummer** built "Quarry Hill," later known as Plummer House. The 49-room house was part of a 65-acre estate, which currently consists of 11 acres of landscaped grounds. Plummer was asked by Dr. Mayo to join the Mayo Clinic staff in 1901, and he spent the next 35 years there. Plummer is credited with several inventions and improvements at the clinic; his wife, **Daisy Plummer**, a patron of the arts, donated the house and grounds to the Art Center in 1969.

QUARRY HILL NATURE CENTER
701 N.W. Silver Creek Road
(507) 281-6114
Open daily.
The center's 212 acres contain five miles of hiking trails through meadow, flood plain and upland forest habitats; a two-acre fishing pond; a historic limestone quarry embedded with fossils; sandstone caves; and recreational facilities for the whole family.

SHOPPING

ROCHESTER OFFERS ITS many visitors more than 25 mall and shopping areas that include all the major anchor stores as well as small specialty and gift shops and boutiques. Many of these shops are geared to accommodate the needs of patients and/or visitors shopping for patients. Many shopping venues are conveniently located near the medical facilities and lodgings, and during the winter, visitors and temporary residents can enjoy shopping and walking in covered malls.

EATING

BROADSTREET CAFE AND BAR
300 N.W. First Ave.
(507) 281-2451
Located in a renovated historic warehouse, the Broadstreet Cafe is a charming American bistro with a downstairs restaurant, the Redwood Room, serving Mediterranean food. Open for lunch, dinner and Sunday brunch, the Broadstreet changes its menu weekly. Dinner specialties include grilled swordfish, broiled breast of duck or seafood pasta, while the

Redwood Room offers a tasty pizza topped with lamb sausage, chevre and red onion, shrimp, marinara and Monterey jack cheese. Live music Wednesday through Saturday.

MICHAEL'S RESTAURANT
15 S. Broadway
(507) 288-2020
One of downtown's premier restaurants since 1951, Michael's is well-known for its old country charm and excellent food and service. The restaurant, which seats 400, contains five individual rooms for casual or elegant dining and is open for lunch and dinner. Specialties range from Midwestern favorites to native Greek cuisine. The lounge features live piano music, and the Greek Haraka dining rooms are available evenings for private parties or meetings.

HENRY WELLINGTON
216 S. First Ave.
(507) 289-1949
A turn-of-the-century building filled with antiques and memorabilia offers several intimate rooms in which to dine. Specialties on the extensive lunch and dinner menus include New England clam chowder and homemade soups and salad dressings. Upstairs in Newt's Bar and Grill, enjoy sandwiches and lighter fare.

SANDY POINT SUPPER CLUB
Rural Route 4
(507) 367-4983
The "out of town place" has been a local favorite for more than 40 years, offering a lovely river location, friendly service and one of the largest menus in the state. Lunch and dinner specialties include seafood, prime rib, barbecued ribs, Cornish game hens, chicken Kiev and teriyaki selections.

THE 7TH RIB
Highway 63
(507) 378-7427 (RIBS) or (800) 658-2553
Closed Mondays.
A seventh heaven for diners and dancers, the 7th Rib is located 15 miles south of Rochester and is the oldest family-owned restaurant in southeastern Minnesota. The rustic but contemporary setting is the backdrop for lunch and dinner cuisine featuring steaks, ribs, chops, fish and broiled seafood. The 7th Rib is also home to "the Challenger," a 72-ounce New York strip steak: Any guest who can finish it in 45 minutes eats free. The Sunday brunch buffet is an old standard, and so is the '50s and '60s music played in the new Cabaret Lounge on weekends.

LODGING

ROCHESTER HAS MORE than its share of hotels, motels, inns, guest homes and other accommodations. Following are a few of the biggest and best-known.

KAHLER LODGING
20 S.W. Second Ave.
Rochester, MN 55904
(507) 282-2581 or (800) 533-1655
In 1912, a man named **John Kahler** built the Zumbro Hotel to provide lodging for Mayo Clinic patients and their families. Today, Kahler Lodging is in the same business, but it has grown to include the Kahler Hotel (700 rooms), Clinic View Inn (142), Holiday Inn Downtown (172 rooms owned and operated under the Holiday Inn franchise) and the Kahler Plaza Hotel (194 rooms). A pedestrian subway connects the Clinic View Inn with the Mayo medical complex, Rochester Methodist Hospital and Kahler Hotel. The Kahler Hotel offers a nursing service, and the AAA's four-diamond-rated Kahler Plaza Hotel offers luxury accommodations to medical guests and corporate travelers as well as excellent downtown service to leisure and business travelers.

RADISSON HOTEL CENTERPLACE
150 S. Broadway
Rochester, MN 55904
(507) 281-8000
Located in downtown Rochester, the AAA's four-diamond-rated Radisson is minutes away from the airport and IBM and is accessible by skyway from the Mayo Clinic, shopping areas and theaters. Two fine restaurants, **The Meadows** and **McCormick's Restaurant and Bar**, provide visitors a choice of unique or casual dining: The Meadows features homemade pastas, poultry and seafood; McCormick's offers soups, sandwiches and daily specials.

SOLDIERS FIELD BEST WESTERN SUITES
410 S.W. Sixth St.
Rochester, MN 55904
(507) 288-2677 or (800) 366-2067

Located in a residential area just four blocks from downtown and less than two blocks from the Mayo Clinic subway, this motel and entertainment complex has 128 units and 90 kitchen suites on eight floors. Summertime rooftop dining, singing waiters and light entrees make dining here an upbeat experience. The complex also offers guests a bar, pool, Jacuzzi, sauna, playroom, meeting and recreation rooms, gift shop, beauty shop, bakery and mini-grocery.

▼ **FOR MORE INFORMATION...**
ROCHESTER CONVENTION AND VISITORS BUREAU
150 S. Broadway
Rochester, MN 55904
(507) 288-4331 or (800) 634-8277

MANTORVILLE

THE ENTIRE 12-BLOCK downtown Mantorville is listed on the National Register of Historic Places, which puts it on a par, technically, with Historic Williamsburg, Gettysburg and Freedom Square in Philadelphia. Mantorville was, and still is, a town centered around the limestone quarries just outside of town. And like other Bluff Country towns, Mantorville's geography was shaped by a river. Founded in 1853 by the **Mantor brothers** along the north branch of the middle fork of the Zumbro River, Mantorville was built of a local limestone known as Mantorville stone.

A boardwalk runs through the town, linking the old buildings and leading the way for the visitor's journey into the past. The structures are a testament to a lifestyle that has long since disappeared, but the spirit has been carefully preserved. Mantorville is less than 15 miles west of Rochester on Highway 14 and close to **the Douglas Trail**, located between Pine Island and Rochester, a 13-mile trail with two separate treadways for biking and horseback riding.

ATTRACTIONS
WALKING TOUR OF MANTORVILLE
Follow the boardwalk to nearly 40 historic structures, including: the Dodge County Historical Museum, located in the 1869 St. John's Episcopal Church, richly stocked with Dodge County memorabilia; the Dodge County Courthouse, built in 1871, Minnesota's oldest working courthouse; The Opera House, built in 1918, which houses the Mantorville Theater Co. (Its melodramas on summer weekends invite the audience to hiss, clap and boo along with the performance); and Restoration House, built five years before the Civil War, restored to resemble its early appearance. A log cabin built in the 1850s, original home of the cooper who made barrels for the local brewery, is located near the house. The tour takes visitors to many fascinating buildings, some of which house modern-day shops and stores. There are plenty of antique shops and working businesses housed in 19th-century limestone buildings This is a town made for strolling.

SHOPPING
MANTORVILLE MERCANTILE CO.
Highway 57
(507) 635-5132
The oldest continuously operated pre-Civil War retail store in Dodge County, this store features handmade oak furniture, antiques and collectibles in an old-fashioned atmosphere.

EATING
THE HUBBELL HOUSE
Main St.
(507) 635-2331
Established in 1854 as a stagecoach stop and hotel, the Hubbell House serves outstanding meals in an old-time atmosphere complete with Civil War mementos and 19th-century furnishings.

LODGING
GRAND OLD MANSION
501 Clay St.
(507) 635-3231
Call for seasonal hours.
This old mansion is as much a museum as a B&B. It is open for tours and also has three guest rooms available, as well as a rustic log cabin out back for extra guests. Owner Irene Stussy Felker has restored the home to its original design and gives tours of the house and Mantorville.

The covered bridge in Zumbrota once rang with the clatter of coaches and horses' hooves.

The Victorian home contains the original woodwork, prism-cut glass and hand-carved staircase, and a wide selection of antiques. A full breakfast is included for overnight visitors.

▼ For More Information...
MANTORVILLE CHAMBER OF COMMERCE
Box 358
Mantorville, MN 55955
(507) 635-3231 or 635-2481

ZUMBROTA

LOCATED 20 MILES north of Rochester in the Zumbro Valley, Zumbrota is the home of the only remaining covered bridge in Minnesota. Listed on the National Register of Historic Places, the bridge was built in 1869 by New England pioneers, is 120 feet long and is completely preserved. In its original location over the Zumbro River, the white pine bridge channeled the stagecoach traffic between Dubuque, Iowa, and St. Paul through the village of Zumbrota. The bridge now stands in **Covered Bridge Park**, approximately a thousand feet from its original location, and is the centerpiece of a group of historic structures. The park also furnishes complete camping and picnic facilities for tourists.

Sherwood Forest, located three miles north of Zumbrota on Highway 52, also provides excellent camping and picnic facilities and summertime activities. The **Covered Bridge Restaurant, Lounge and Motel**, located a mile from Covered Bridge Park, accommodates visitors who are hungry, thirsty and uninterested in camping, and the **Zumbrota Clay Pits** attract fossil hunters from all over the area. The **Zumbro River Valley** is also a hotbed of antique sales and shopping. The towns of Zumbrota, **Pine Island**, **Oronoco**, **Elgin**, **Zumbro Falls** and **Mazeppa** are bound to please antique lovers of all stripes.

▼ For More Information...
CITY OF ZUMBROTA
Box 158
Zumbrota, MN 55992
(507) 732-7362

LANESBORO

LANESBORO LIES ALONG the Root River in a deep valley edged on three sides by sheer, wooded limestone and sandstone bluffs. This part of southeastern Minnesota is known as "the driftless area" — so called because the glaciers didn't flatten it. The runoff from the melting glaciers carved valleys and gorges and created springs and rivers that, over the eons, fashioned a roller-coaster landscape of highland and flatland. Whether you come from the Twin Cities, Wisconsin, or Iowa, you drive *down* into Lanesboro. The Root River makes a hairpin turn around Lanesboro before it resumes its eastward course across Fillmore County toward the Mississippi.

In 1867, a group of scouts discovered Lanesboro. They were sent by East Coast investors to find a western resort site, and the Lanesboro Townsite Co. was born. When the company dammed up the Root River to create a lake for their resort, they discovered a power supply that led them to scrap the idea of a resort in favor of flour milling. The Southern Minnesota Railroad soon laid tracks near the town and the mills were in business.

The wheatlands gave out, and the mills burned down (most by 1900 and another in 1931). The power-processing plant built at the turn of the century still allows Lanesboro to sell electricity. Lanesboro has also been home to a canning factory and a turkey-processing plant, but agriculture has always been the mainstay of the area. Today, thanks in large part to the Root River Trail, Lanesboro has become a hub of tourist activity. People from all over the region come for the trail and then discover the charm of the town and the hidden valley in which it rests, as well as the surrounding towns and countryside.

Lanesboro is located in the heart of a locale rich with history and scenic wonders: **Forestville State Park**, located in **Preston**; **Lake Louise State Park**, located in **Le Roy**; **Beaver Creek Valley State Park**, located in **Caledonia**; and Minnesota's two largest and only operating caves (**Mystery Cave**, operated by Forestville State Park, (507) 352-5111, near Preston; and **Niagara Cave**, two miles south of **Harmony** and then two miles west on Niagara Road, (507) 886-6606). Both offer tours to the public Memorial Day through Labor Day, and both have off-season hours. The Amish settlement of Harmony welcomes visitors on guided tours and offers some of its handmade crafts for sale. Tours are available through **Michel's Amish Tours**, (507) 886-5392, or **Amish Country Tours**, (507) 886-2302.

Stewartville, a town that began as a trading post in 1853, has had a block of the town restored to its 1899 appearance by the Minnesota Historical Society. It reopened the **Meighan Store** and Meighan family residence for the public. The store was the economic and social hub of the community. Closed in 1910, it was designated a historical site in 1968 and is now open from July 1 through Labor Day as part of **Historic Forestville**.

ATTRACTIONS
THE ROOT RIVER TRAIL
Built on the old railroad bed, the Root River Trail now runs for 35 miles from Rushford to Fountain and is being expanded. The trail is perfect for hiking, birdwatching, cross-country skiing, horseback riding and strolling. Since it opened in 1989, the trail has put Lanesboro and the Root River Valley back on the map. For a complete look at the trail and the towns it touches, write the **Root River Trail Towns, Box 411, Lanesboro, MN 55949**. If you want to expand your investigation of the trail, two places in town can supply your needs: **Michael's Adventure Outfitters**, (507) 467-2622, rents horses and takes horseback tours along the trail and into Cribben Valley. Michael's also will customize horseback trips. **Brewster's Outfitters**, (507) 467-3400, rents canoes, bikes, skis and other essentials tailored to enhance vistors' enjoyment of the trail and state parks.

WALKING TOUR OF LANESBORO
The historic downtown, an area roughly a block and a half long, is listed on the National Register of Historic Places. The exteriors of these buildings have changed little since the town was founded, but modern businesses have sprung up behind the 19th-century facades. The Merchant of Lanesboro building, which sold dry goods since the town's early days, houses an antique shop. The 1895 Galligan Block, a two-story brick commercial building, is a plumbing and heating store. The Com-

monweal Theatre Co. has revitalized the old Elite Theatre, now called the St. Mane, which was once a furniture store and movie house. A Chinese laundry, a millinery shop and two apartments were located in what is now the Lanesboro Historic Museum. Some of the town's fine restaurants and bed-and-breakfast inns occupy old buildings as well. The local Chamber of Commerce, located in the St. Mane Theatre on North Parkway Avenue, can furnish information on the numerous sites along the walking tour, and visitors will quickly discover the best places to shop for antiques and collectibles.

SCENIC VALLEY WINERY
101 Coffee St.
(507) 467-2958
Open daily May 1 through January 1.
Located in what used to be the old creamery, Scenic Valley Winery offers tours to groups of 15 or more and invites guests to ask questions, look around and sample its selection of strawberry, raspberry, apple, elderberry and wild plum wines.

RIVER VALLEY CHEESE
208 N. Parkway Ave.
(507) 467-7000
Open daily.
Located in a remodeled storefront with a large viewing window into the cheesemaking room, River Valley Cheese is a relative newcomer to town, though its cheesemaking methods are very old-fashioned. This is a cooperative venture between a Midwest cheesemaker and about 80 local Amish farmers who supply the milk. Visitors can watch as the milk is slowly turned into cheese and sample and purchase the results: colby, Monterery jack, colby-jack, Muenster, cheddar, pepper jack or baby Swiss.

FOREST RESOURCE CENTER
Rural Route 2, Box 156A
Lanesboro, MN 55949
(507) 467-2437
A private, nonprofit corporation promoting the wise use of natural resources, the center is located six miles outside of Lanesboro and is surrounded by 900 acres of state forest land. Visitors can see ways in which land management practices that are both ecologically and commercially viable can be put in action in the nearby hardwood forest. A good example of that sort of common sense is apparent in the center's shiitake mushroom cultivation project, which is not only turning a profit but proving beneficial to the ecostructure of the area.

DNR FISH HATCHERY
One mile west of Lanesboro on Highway 16
(507) 467-3771
Open all year during business hours.
The hatchery welcomes visitors. It raises rainbow, lake and brown trout for fishing lakes throughout the state, and even people who don't fish will be fascinated by the thousands of trout of different ages swimming in the spring-fed ponds. A favorite with guests and fishing enthusiasts is the tank holding the huge granddaddy trout — just like the ones that always get away in fishing tall tales.

ST. MANE THEATRE
206 N. Parkway Ave.
(507) 467-2525
High-quality professional seasonal theater by the Commonweal Theatre Co. typically includes romantic action plays and musicals such as "Tom Jones" or a Wild West version of "The Taming of the Shrew," as well as a traveling puppet show for children and occasional short works that address current social issues. Matinee performances for large groups can be booked in advance and include lunch. The 140-seat St. Mane Theatre is an intimate and comfortable venue for lively theater and family entertainment.

STORYTELLING BY DUKE ADDICKS
August through October at the Sons of Norway Lodge at 8:30 p.m., Duke Addicks presents "Who Haunts Here?" The program is composed of Addicks' specialty: true ghost stories and tales from the Root River region, with a few Twin Cities stories thrown in for good measure. Every Sunday afternoon at 1:30 from July through September, Addicks conducts a walking tour of Lanesboro, which begins at the Lanesboro Historical Museum. The tours include the local history and legends that are part of the town lore.

Eating and Lodging

Mrs. B's Historic Lanesboro Inn and Restaurant
103 Parkway
Lanesboro, MN 55949
(507) 467-2154
Remodeled and restored from an 1872 commercial building situated on the Root River, Mrs. B's has 10 guest rooms, each with an individual character. Each has a private bath, but some have a fireplace, some a balcony, and some look out on the river. The parlor and dining room are comfortable and beautifully furnished. Breakfast is served daily with dinner served five evenings a week by reservation. Owners Nancy and Jack Bratrud offer a five-course dinner that features locally grown produce, meats, dairy products, mushrooms and fish, and their liquor selections include local wines and beers.

Carrolton Country Inn
Rural Route 2, Box 139
Lanesboro, MN 55949
(507) 467-2257
The inn is an 1880s farmhouse that belonged to the same family for more than a hundred years. Current owners Charles and Gloria Ruen renovated the home and its four guest rooms and provide accommodations for bed and breakfast, whole house rental and family reunions. The inn is located near the bike trail, the river, the town and the original three-story log home built in 1856.

Scanlon House Bed and Breakfast
709 S. Parkway Ave.
Lanesboro, MN 55949
(507) 467-2158
Built in 1889 by the son of Lanesboro's founder and one of the many buildings in town listed on the National Register of Historic Places, the house is Queen Anne Victorian in style and is beautifully restored. Five guest rooms are available, all with air conditioning and the graceful decor of the period.

Cady Hayes House
500 Calhoun Ave.
Lanesboro, MN 55949
(507) 467-2621
The house of nine gables (and one turret) has beveled glass windows, restored authentic stenciling on coved ceilings, a game room, music rooms, a parlor and a spacious front porch. The Cady Hayes home is Queen Anne Victorian in style and more than 100 years old. The owners have three guest rooms: the Garden Suite, the Amish Room and the Norwegian Room, each decorated and embellished appropriately by local craftspeople, including the rosemaling in the Norwegian room. A full breakfast is served daily. Other features available are trail lunches and arrangements for bikes, skis, canoes, inner tubes or horseback tours.

Sunnyside Cottage at Forestville
Rural Route 2, Box 119
Preston, MN 55965
(507) 765-3357
Located just a few miles west of Lanesboro on Highway 16, this modern country three-bedroom house is available for one party of guests. A continental breakfast is furnished, and guests can enjoy being situated on a working farm complete with dairy and beef cattle, chickens, geese, ducks and wild waterfowl. Sunnyside Cottage is adjacent to Forestville State Park, Mystery Cave, the Root River Trail and some great fishing holes.

The Victorian House
709 S. Parkway
(507) 467-3457
Authentic French cooking in a Victorian setting. The house was built for **Senator Samuel Nelson** of Lanesboro in 1870; the interior retains the original white oak and stained glass and is furnished with antiques from around the world. Dinners are served Wednesday through Sunday, by reservation only. Guests are seated in small, intimate dining rooms, choose from among several authentic entrees, and then sit back and enjoy each course as it arrives, prepared and served by the owners, chef Jean Claude Venant and Sonja Venant.

▼ For More Information...

Chamber of Commerce
206 N. Parkway Ave.
Lanesboro, MN 55949
(507) 467-2525 or (800) 657-7025

Historic Bluff Country
Box 609
45 Center St., Harmony, MN 55939
(507) 886-2230

Prairie Towns

Austin

THE HOMETOWN OF Pulitzer Prize-winning poet **Richard Eberhart**, and football coach and broadcaster **John Madden** and host town to the Miss Minnesota Pageant, Austin is also the birthplace of the Ladies Floral Club, founded in 1869, the oldest women's club in the state and the second oldest in the country. Austin spawned the Weyerhaeuser Co. and the Austin Plow and Harrow Co., organized in 1878, which invented the everlasting harrow, made of steel instead of wood. Austin is famous throughout the country, however, as the home of the multinational George A. Hormel and Co., founded in 1887. The city and company grew up together; by the turn of the century, the population had increased from 400 in 1864 to nearly 7,000.

The $2 billion-plus-in-sales Hormel is famous for products such as Jennie-O turkeys, canned ham, Dinty Moore beef stew, Canadian bacon, Hormel chili and the ever-popular, often-ridiculed Spam. More recently, Hormel has introduced products such as Chicken-by-George, microwavable bacon, microwavable meals called Dinty Moore American Classics and Top Shelf, a line of dinner entrees that require no refrigeration.

Austin was named after frontiersman **Austin Nichols**, the first settler in the area, who drove a claim stake into the ground in June 1854. He sold his claim to **Chauncey Leverich**, who erected the first sawmill and the first frame structure. Located on the Cedar River, which powered the sawmills and flour mills that sprang up in the town, Austin is surrounded by acres of corn and soybean fields and contains more than 20 parks within its city limits.

SHOPPING

DOWNTOWN AUSTIN OFFERS Main Street to visitors as one of its most pleasant shopping venues. Brick-lined sidewalks, tree-shaded benches and the sound of a fountain accompany the relaxed shopper to a variety of specialty shops. Farther up the street in the area called North Main, you'll find a discount store, video store and several restaurants. Oak Park Mall and Sterling Shopping Center should be able to supply any shopping needs unfulfilled by a foray through downtown Austin.

EATING

THE OLD MILL
Two miles north of Interstate 90; exit at Sixth St. N.E.
(507) 437-2076
Closed Sundays.
Open for lunch and dinner, this restaurant is situated on historic Ramsey Dam over the Red Cedar River and offers a perfect combination of American food and quaint atmosphere. Ramsey Mill was built in 1872 and was a working mill until a few years before it was remodeled and opened as a restaurant in 1950. The original feel of the three-story mill complements the menu of seafood, steak, fish and tempting desserts.

LANSING CORNERS SUPPER CLUB
Four miles north of Interstate 90 and Oak Park Mall on Highway 218 N.
(507) 433-8985
Famous for its barbecued ribs, this restaurant also serves steaks, chicken and seafood, and it sells homemade baked beans and dressings. Families and tour groups are welcomed. The supper club is closed Mondays, open for lunch and dinner on Sunday and for dinner all other nights.

TORGE'S PUB AND GRILL
Holiday Inn and Austin Conference Center
Interstate 90 at N.W. Fourth St.
(507) 433-1000
For informal dining and live entertainment, Torge's is a good place to try. It boasts an open-air grill, horseshoe bar, game room and dance floor, and this restaurant claims to serve the best half-pound burger in the country. Enjoy lunch or dinner daily.

ATTRACTIONS
HORMEL HOME
208 N.W. Fourth Ave.
(507) 433-4243
Built in 1871 by Austin mayor **John Cook** and purchased in 1901 by **George A. Hormel**, the home is listed on the National Register of Historic Places. Though it was originally Italianate in style, Hormel remodeled it into the Classical Revival style. In 1927, the Hormels donated their home to the Austin YWCA, which is still housed there. It is open to the public and available for open houses, receptions, weddings and tours.

JAY C. HORMEL NATURE CENTER
1304 N.E. 21st St.
(507) 437-7519
Located a quarter-mile northeast of Austin, the 300-acre nature sanctuary includes six miles of groomed trails for guided or self-guided tours and an interpretive center, exhibit area and a naturalist that encourage visitors to learn about the preservation of marshes, wetlands, woodlands and prairies. The center sponsors activities such as cider pressing, maple syruping, bird watching, meteor and star gazing, cross-country skiing and snowshoeing, campouts and cookouts.

MOWER COUNTY HISTORICAL CENTER
S.E. 12th St. between Fourth and Sixth avenues
(507) 437-6082
The center contains 20 exhibits, each one a miniature museum, including: the original Hormel building; the Rural Life Museum housed in the original Mower County Fair building; the Rahilly Museum of restored horse-drawn vehicles, featuring a one-horse open sleigh; the Fireman's Museum; a working blacksmith shop; a log cabin from 1862; a windmill; and the Railroad Museum, which contains a depot, passenger coach, baggage coach, steam locomotive, refrigerator car and caboose.

AUSTIN AREA FINE ARTS CENTER
1419 S.W. First Ave. in Sterling State Bank
(507) 433-8451
Open May through September.
Austin's art gallery features local artists who display their work in all mediums. The gallery is open for special exhibitions throughout the year, including wildlife, nature and Christmas themes.

LODGING
AUSTIN OFFERS VISITORS a wide selection of motels and accommodations throughout the area, including the Best Western Countryside Inn, the Holiday Inn Holidome, the Airport Inn, the Sterling Motel and a Super 8 Motel.

▼ FOR MORE INFORMATION...
AUSTIN CONVENTION AND VISITORS BUREAU
300 N. Main St.
Box 864
Austin, MN 55912-0864
(507) 437-4563 or (800) 444-5713

Albert Lea

THE LARGEST TOWN in Freeborn County is Albert Lea, named after **Lieutenant Albert Miller Lea**, a member of an expedition of United States Dragoons that passed through the area in 1835. Lea was a cartographer who sketched the outline of the lake that later bore his name. The settlement that grew up along the northwest edge of the lake also took his name.

Albert Lea is located in the heart of a productive agricultural area that was settled by Scandinavian and German farmers attracted to the rich soil. During

ATTRACTIONS

FREEBORN COUNTY HISTORICAL MUSEUM/PIONEER VILLAGE
1031 N. Bridge
(507) 373-8003
Call for hours.

The museum exhibitions range from a mammoth tusk and bones that are between 10,000 and 12,000 years old to a 1950s Packard. In between those extremes, visitors will find old-time kitchen items, doll collections, farm tools and machinery, a covered wagon, a toy shop and more.

The village is made up of a fine collection of 19th-century buildings that were moved to the site and arranged to present town life in the last century. The structures include a Lutheran church built in 1872, a one-room schoolhouse that was in use until 1958, a general store, post office, hardware store, blacksmith shop, jail, bank and barber shop. A tiny two-room log cabin built in 1853, which is thought to be the first residence in the county, was the home of five different families during a 50-year period.

The 19th-century Pioneer Village at Albert Lea.

WALKING TOUR OF ALBERT LEA
The tour originates among the residences surrounding **Fountain Lake Park**, a residential community in the heart of the city, and includes about 27 buildings. Four of these are listed on the National Register of Historic Places, including the Liquor Rail Depot, the former City Hall and the Jones Residence. Two structures that merit a close look are the Romanesque Freeborn County Courthouse and the French Classical Albert Lea Art Center.

MYRE-BIG ISLAND STATE PARK
Route 3; take Interstate 35 exit 11
(507) 373-5084

Visit the waterfowl blind during spring migration, or come in the fall to spot white pelicans. The Esker Trail and the Big Island Trail are favorites with campers and visitors to the park, as is the display of Native American artifacts. The first weekend in October, visit the park for the Big Island Rendezvous and Festival, one of the state's largest reenactments of an 1840s fur trader encampment, including 200 teepees and lodges, black-powder shooting, Native American dances and ethnic foods.

the late 1850s the first businesses were opened, followed by a school and a flour mill. The city was platted in 1859.

A progressive city of lakes, residences, commerce, parks and industry, Albert Lea is the smallest city west of the Mississippi served by two interstate highways: Interstates 35 and 90. Agricultural products in Freeborn County include dairy, potatoes, poultry, corn, hogs and soybeans, which have helped place it in the top three percentile of all agriculture-producing counties in the nation. It is also the home of two leading meat-processing firms.

Shopping

ALBERT LEA OFFERS shoppers the wares and specialty items found on Broadway Avenue downtown and on South Broadway, including antiques, books, collectibles and art for the discerning buyer, and good selections of prairie- and country-style gifts. Northbridge Mall Shopping Center is located on Bridge Avenue, which is off Interstate 90 on the County Road 22 exit.

Eating

DINING EXPERIENCES IN Albert Lea can be as varied as your mood. Choose between family, elegant, casual or ethnic foods and atmospheres, as well as bakeries, delis and the usual assortment of fast foods for people in a hurry. Some of the places to choose from are: Hong Kong Restaurant at 212 E. Clark (507) 373-1033; Golden Corral Steak House at 1604 E. Main St. (507) 373-7283; Philadelphia Bar and Grill at 804 E. Main St. (507) 373-2450; Trumble's Family Restaurant at 1811 E. Main St. (507) 373-2638; Best Western Albert Lea Inn Country Peddler at 2301 E. Main St. (507) 373-8291; and the Edgewater Restaurant on Route 2 just off W. Richway (507) 377-1683.

Lodging

FOUNTAIN VIEW INN
310 N. Washington Ave.
Albert Lea, MN 56007
(507) 377-9425
Formerly owned by opera singer **Beatrice Bessesen**, the house is located in the heart of town on Fountain Lake. All three guest rooms have a lake view, private bath and air conditioning. Continental breakfast in the morning can be followed up with the very short walk or drive to the state park, the golf course, the lake, downtown Albert Lea or the Freeborn County Museum.

THE VICTORIAN ROSE INN
609 W. Fountain St.
Albert Lea, MN 56007
(507) 373-7602 or (800) 252-6558
Built in 1898 in Queen Anne Victorian style, the Victorian Rose lives up to the majesty of its architecture. Stained glass windows, handcrafted woodwork and other authentic fixtures have been proudly maintained. Four rooms are available for guests, and a full breakfast is served in the morning.

▼ For More Information...

ALBERT LEA CONVENTION AND VISITORS BUREAU
202 N. Broadway
Box 686
Albert Lea, MN 56007
(507) 373-3938 or (800) 345-8414

Owatonna

LEGEND HAS IT that Owatonna is named for a frail Indian princess who sought the curative powers of the local mineral springs. When the bubbling waters restored her health, the tribe decided to settle here and name the area for the chief's fortunate daughter. The first white settlers arrived in 1854, and the town was incorporated in 1858.

Today, the 38-acre **Mineral Springs Park** is one of the city's 19 parks and three golf courses. Owatonna is a thriving community of nearly 20,000, the cultural and economic center of Steele County, one of the wealthiest cities in the state and home to more than 40 industrial business firms, such as SPx Corporation, Federated Insurance, Viracon, Inc. and the Wenger Corporation. Jostens, Inc., founded in 1897 by the **Gainey** family as manufacturers of high school rings and now an internationally known company, still operates three plants in Owatonna. The city offers visitors and residents a variety of recreational and cultural venues; it is a city that respects its historic past, manages the success of the present and keeps an eye turned toward the future.

ATTRACTIONS
UNION DEPOT AND OLD ENGINE 201
Eisenhower Drive
(507) 451-3798
In 1866, the railroad tracks that would link Chicago to the Twin Cities were joined together in Owatonna, cutting travel time between the Twin Cities and Chicago to 28 hours. Owatonna was now a crossroads of some importance and a link between East and West. It was also host to the 1883 and 1884 Minnesota State Fair, another event that brought many travelers to town. In 1887, the Chicago, Milwaukee and St. Paul Railway Co. and the Chicago and Northwestern combined to build a new depot in Owatonna, which served the city until its closing in 1976. It was moved, with Engine 201, to its present site and restored to its original condition.

Engine 201 was one of a batch of 125 steam locomotives produced in 1880 by Rogers Locomotive and Machine Works in New Jersey. In 1893, **Casey Jones** drove Engine 201 for the Illinois Central Railroad, shuttling more than 100,000 visitors to the World's Columbian Exposition in Chicago. Engine 201 was retired in 1926, put on exhibition in the Chicago Museum of Science and Industry and elsewhere, and in 1975 was moved, with its tracks, to its new home in Owatonna.

NORWEST BANK
101 N. Cedar Ave.
(507) 451-5670
Designed by renowned architect **Louis Sullivan** in 1908 as the National Farmers' Bank of Owatonna, the Norwest Bank embodies what is known as Prairie School architecture and is listed on the National Register of Historic Places. Sullivan called his bank a "color tone poem" and almost everyone else calls it one of his finest Midwestern banks. Inside and out, down to the tiniest detail, the materials, shapes and colors found in the bank echo the prairie theme and Sullivan's revolutionary dictum that "form follows function."

THE VILLAGE OF YESTERYEAR
1448 Austin Road
Fairgrounds at the southeast corner of Owatonna
(507) 451-1420
A growing collection of mid-1800s Steele County buildings relocated to this site form the Village of Yesteryear. A stroll through this village will allow visitors to see cabins, an early Catholic church, a railroad depot, a schoolhouse, a blacksmith shop, a general store and the historic Dunnell House, a mansion built in 1868-69 by scholar and educator **Mark Hill Dunnell**.

The Steele County Courthouse in Owatonna.

STEELE COUNTY COURTHOUSE
111 E. Main
(507) 451-8040
Built in 1891 in the Romanesque style and still in use, the courthouse blends the past with the present and is located across the street from **Central Park**, the location of a fountain that was cast in 1873.

RICE LAKE STATE PARK
Located seven miles east of Owatonna on Steele County Highway 19
(507) 451-7406
This park is a haven for waterfowl, flocks of birds, deer and a variety of wildflowers. Camping, swimming, boating, cross-country skiing and self-guided hiking are only a few of the activities visitors can enjoy.

KAPLAN'S WOODS PARKWAY
Runs along the river and Mosher Ave.
(507) 455-0800
This 225-acre wooded wonderland provides an ideal setting for hiking, biking, jogging, picnicking, cross-country skiing, and observing nature. Enjoy swimming, fishing, canoeing and sailing on Lake Kohlmier.

WEST HILLS COMPLEX
540 W. Hill Circle
(507) 451-4540
This 75-acre complex contains the **Owatonna Arts Center**, the **Sculpture Garden**, the **Little Theater of Owatonna** and a Romanesque masterpiece built in 1887 that now serves as **City Hall** and is on the National Register of Historic Places. Many of the cultural performances and programs of the city take place at the complex and attract visitors and local residents alike.

SHOPPING AND EATING

IN A CITY as large and prosperous as Owatonna, a variety of stores, shops, motels, hotels, restaurants and activities are at your fingertips.

LODGING

NORTHROP-OFTEDAHL HOUSE
358 E. Main St.
Owatonna, MN 55060
(507) 451-4040
A bed and breakfast in an 1898 Victorian home offers guests a choice of five rooms and provides them with a turn-of-the-century ambience complete with stained glass windows, oak woodwork, brass chandeliers and a grand piano in the west parlor. Owned by the Northrop family since 1943, the house was turned into a B&B in 1987. The guest rooms are named for some of the distinguished members of the family, including **Cyrus Atwood Northrop**, second president of the University of Minnesota and the man for whom Northrop Auditorium was named.

▼ FOR MORE INFORMATION...

OWATONNA CONVENTION AND VISITORS BUREAU
320 Hoffman Drive
Box 331
Owatonna, MN 55060
(507) 451-7970 or (800) 423-6466

FARIBAULT

IN 1853, Faribault was an outpost for **Alexander Faribault**, who made a living trading his furs with the local Dakota Sioux. The location, near the confluence of the Straight and Cannon rivers, was conducive to trade; before long, teepees dotted the landscape, and the town soon attracted scores of British and New England settlers.

Faribault grew rapidly due to the area's abundant natural resources — the rivers, forest and surrounding farmland — and its proximity to St. Paul. Early businesses included flour milling, wool production, lumber milling, breweries and drygoods stores to provide the new community and farmers with supplies and food staples. In 1865, the first railroad line into Faribault was constructed, and the introduction of railroads increased the number and variety of businesses and industries serving the community. By 1904, three rail companies with main roads, branch lines and a large network of connections linked Faribault with larger cities in the Midwest and with both coasts.

Unlike many towns, Faribault grew under the direction of its resident namesake. Alexander Faribault financed the construction of the first church in the town in 1855, gave land and money for other churches, schools, parks, and institutions, and served on the town's first school board in 1856. He was one of the first to exploit local water power by establishing flour mills on the Straight and Cannon rivers in the late 1850s and early 1860s. His views and ambitions were complemented by those of **Bishop Henry B. Whipple**, who was encouraged by Faribault and early Episcopal missionaries to establish the Minnesota Diocesan See in Faribault. Both men's friendships with Indian groups and commitment to education and religion profoundly affected the flavor of early Faribault and the community's evolution.

Faribault's colorful history is reflected in the types of buildings constructed and the variety of architectural styles and building materials used. It was here in Faribault that the country's first Gothic Episcopal cathedral was built. Faribault's original home is still standing and open to visitors. The town also is the headquarters of the world famous Faribault Woolen Mill Co., home of the classic Faribo blanket.

ATTRACTIONS

WALKING TOUR OF HISTORIC FARIBAULT
With block after block of Neoclassical, Victorian, Greek Revival, Gothic Revival, Italianate, Colonial Revival, Prairie and Moderne buildings, churches, schools and homes to see — many of which are listed on the National Register of Historic Places — Faribault is a popular city for both walking and driving tours. An excellent guidebook/history, produced through the Minnesota Historical Society, is available from the Chamber of Commerce.

Some of the historic places on the tour include: The site of Alexander Faribault's Trading Post and Log House, built in 1835, part of a cluster of log buildings seasonally occupied by Faribault and used as a stopping place and trading post for traders and travelers; the Alexander Faribault House, a Greek Revival structure that was the first frame house in town, built in 1853 with lumber hauled by oxen from St. Paul for a total cost of $4,000; the site of Breck School, a coeducational primary school opened in 1858 and the beginning of the school system later known as Shattuck, St. Mary's and St. James' Schools; the Faribault Historic Commercial District on Central Avenue between North Second and Third Street, a group of late 19th-century commercial buildings that formed the "Main Street" of the period; Faribault City Hall, built in 1894; the first English Lutheran church, built in 1931; the Rice County Jail, built in 1910; the Cathedral of Our Merciful Saviour, completed in 1869, with a stained glass window depicting the diocesan seal chosen by Bishop Whipple, First Bishop of Minnesota, picturing a broken tomahawk, a peace pipe beneath the cross, the Bishop's mitre and a Latin inscription saying "Peace through the blood of the cross"; the site of the Old St. Mary's School for Girls (in 1866 this residence became part of the school, until a new St. Mary's site was chosen in 1883); the State School for the Blind (in 1874, Alexander Faribault's donation to the state of Minnesota of his second home and 97 acres prompted the completion of a complex devoted expressly to the eduction of and services for the blind); the State School for the Feeble Minded/Faribault Regional Center, built in 1879; the State School for the Deaf/Minnesota State Academy for the Deaf, built in 1864; and the Shattuck Historic District, the central focus of Faribault's Episcopal schools, which includes 21 structures, four of which were placed on the National Register of Historic Places before the entire district won nomination and one of which was designed by **Cass Gilbert**, architect of the State Capitol building in St. Paul.

FARIBAULT WOOLEN MILL CO.
1500 N.W. Second Ave. (factory and offices)
1819 N.W. Second Ave. (factory outlet store)
(507) 334-1644
This family-owned company began operations in 1865 with a one-horse treadmill, survived three fires before 1892 and expanded from selling yarn to producing fine woven cloth. Today, the company is one of only a few "fully vertical" woolen

Hurray! Minnesota

Eating

The Lavender Inn
2424 Lyndale Ave.
(507) 334-3500
Known as a "little oasis" 50 miles south of the Twin Cities, the inn began as a drive-in restaurant during the late 1950s. Now consisting of three dining rooms, the Lavender Inn serves lunch and dinner, featuring broasted chicken, seafood, prime rib and other Midwestern favorites. Aside from the dining rooms, the Lavender Inn has an art gallery with work by popular wildlife, landscape and impressionist artists, as well as porcelain collectors' items, crystal and jewelry.

---

mills in existence in this country, which means that all the processes necessary to change raw wool into woven blankets occur under one roof. In the Faribault Woolens Factory Store, visitors will find throws, blankets, clothing and other high-quality products for sale.

Rice County Museum of History
1814 N.W. Second St.
(507) 332-2121
Open Memorial Day through Labor Day. Dedicated to the preservation, promotion and advancement of the area's heritage, the museum contains artifacts, video presentations and displays pertaining to the people of various backgrounds who helped build Rice County and Faribault.

River Bend Nature Center
East of Faribault Regional Center on Rustad Road
(507) 332-7151
Open all year.
The center encompasses more than 600 acres of carefully preserved habitat, including wetlands, river valleys, grassland prairie and hardwood forest. Naturalists are available for tours or visitors can take self-guided walks. Trails are groomed in winter for skiing and snowmobiling.

Sakatah-Singing Hills Trail
Starting near the Comfort Inn just off Highway 60 and Interstate 35 and extending 50 miles toward Mankato, this trail of crushed limestone is groomed for snowmobiling in the winter. The trail parallels some area lakes and is surrounded by forest land. This area is rich with lakes and parks, including **Nerstrand Woods State Park** (11 miles northeast of Faribault) and **Sakatah Lake State Park** (14 miles west of Faribault on Highway 60), as well as several parks within the Faribault city limits and at least eight in Rice County.

Shopping

Downtown Faribault is filled with carefully restored shops that cater to all kinds of interests. The Faribault West Mall houses more than 60 shops and the newly renovated Town Square is an ideal venue for bargains, collectibles and unique gifts, including locally produced **Treasure Cave Blue Cheese**.

Lodging

Hutchinson House
305 N.W. Second St.
Faribault, MN 55021
(507) 332-7519
Listed on the National Register of Historic Place, the 1892 Queen Anne mansion was built by **John Hutchinson**, a furniture maker, mill owner and mortician who was also a state legislator and served in the volunteer infantry during the Sioux uprising. The five guest rooms have private baths and are decorated with antiques, elaborate woodwork and Oriental rugs. A three-course breakfast and complimentary desserts

are served. In the early evening, beverages and hors d'oeuvres are served.

CHERUB HILL
105 N.W. First Ave.
Faribault, MN 55021
(507) 332-2024

This Victorian home was designed in 1896 for **Dr. Jonathan Noyes** by **Olaf Hanson**, the first deaf architect in the country. Noyes was one of the first headmasters at the Minnesota Academy for the Deaf and was instrumental in founding the school for the blind and mentally disabled children in Faribault. Owners Keith and Kristi LeMieux have restored the home and ensured that Cherub Hill's three guest rooms each bear the look and flavor of another era. A full breakfast is served on weekends; a continental breakfast during the week. Cherub Hill is also available for occasions such as weddings or teas.

▼ **FOR MORE INFORMATION...**
FARIBAULT CHAMBER OF COMMERCE
Box 434
Faribault, MN 55021
(507) 334-4381 or (800) 658-2354

NORTHFIELD

NORTHFIELD SPRANG UP on the banks of the Cannon River in 1855 as an agricultural and flour-milling community and has been known for many years as "the City of Cows, Colleges and Contentment." The site of the first mill is the location of Malt-O-Meal headquarters. By 1880, dairy farming had virtually replaced wheat as the major industry of the area, and the town had grown to 2,300 people. During the 19th century, Northfield also became the home of two nationally known liberal arts colleges: Carleton College, founded by Congregationalists in 1866 and named after early benefactor **William Carleton**; and St. Olaf College, a seat of Norwegian culture founded in 1874 by Norwegian Lutheran immigrants, among them the **Reverend Bernt Julius Muus**.

Some of Carleton's more famous graduates include: **Thorstein Veblen**, one of the most celebrated economists and social critics of the 19th century, who coined the phrase "conspicuous consumption" and wrote "Theory of the Leisure Class" and "The Theory of Business Enterprise"; **Supreme Court Justice Pierce Butler**; **U.S. Secretary of Defense Melvin Laird**; and NBC news anchor **Garrick Utley**. **Senator Paul Wellstone** taught at Carleton before he waged his successful campaign to oust incumbent Rudy Boschwitz. St. Olaf's famous alumni include: **Governor Karl Rolvaag**, son of author **Ole Rolvaag**, who taught at St. Olaf and wrote "Giants in the Earth"; **Governor Al Quie**; and Oscar- and Emmy-winning writer **Barry Morrow**, who wrote the screenplay for the movie "Rain Man." St. Olaf has also been the country's foremost exponent of choral

Hurray! Minnesota   414   PHOTO COURTESY OF NORTHFIELD CHAMBER OF COMMERCE

A reenactment of the infamous 1876 bank robbery during the annual Defeat of Jesse James Days in Northfield.

music: Its world-famous a cappella choir carries on the tradition of founder **F. Melius Christiansen**.

Northfield rates a mention for several other reasons: It is the birthplace of **Governor Edward Thye**, a Republican who took office in 1943, as well as former ABC news anchor **Sylvia Chase**; St. Olaf's public radio station became the first listener-supported radio station in the country in 1924; the first baseball game played in Minnesota (in the late 1860s) took place on the high school square; it is the site of the first YMCA in "outstate" Minnesota, built in 1866. **Mark Twain** paid the town a visit for the grand opening and signed himself in the guest book as a "Professional Tramp."

Northfield earned a permanent place in U.S. history, however, not because of its noteworthy accomplishments and residents, but because of an accident of fate and the events of one infamous afternoon. On September 7, 1876, this peaceful farming community was terrorized by the notorious James gang. While eight of the outlaws fired their pistols and rode through town threatening to kill anyone who didn't clear the streets (and killing a Swedish immigrant who couldn't understand English), three others entered the

415 BLUFF COUNTRY

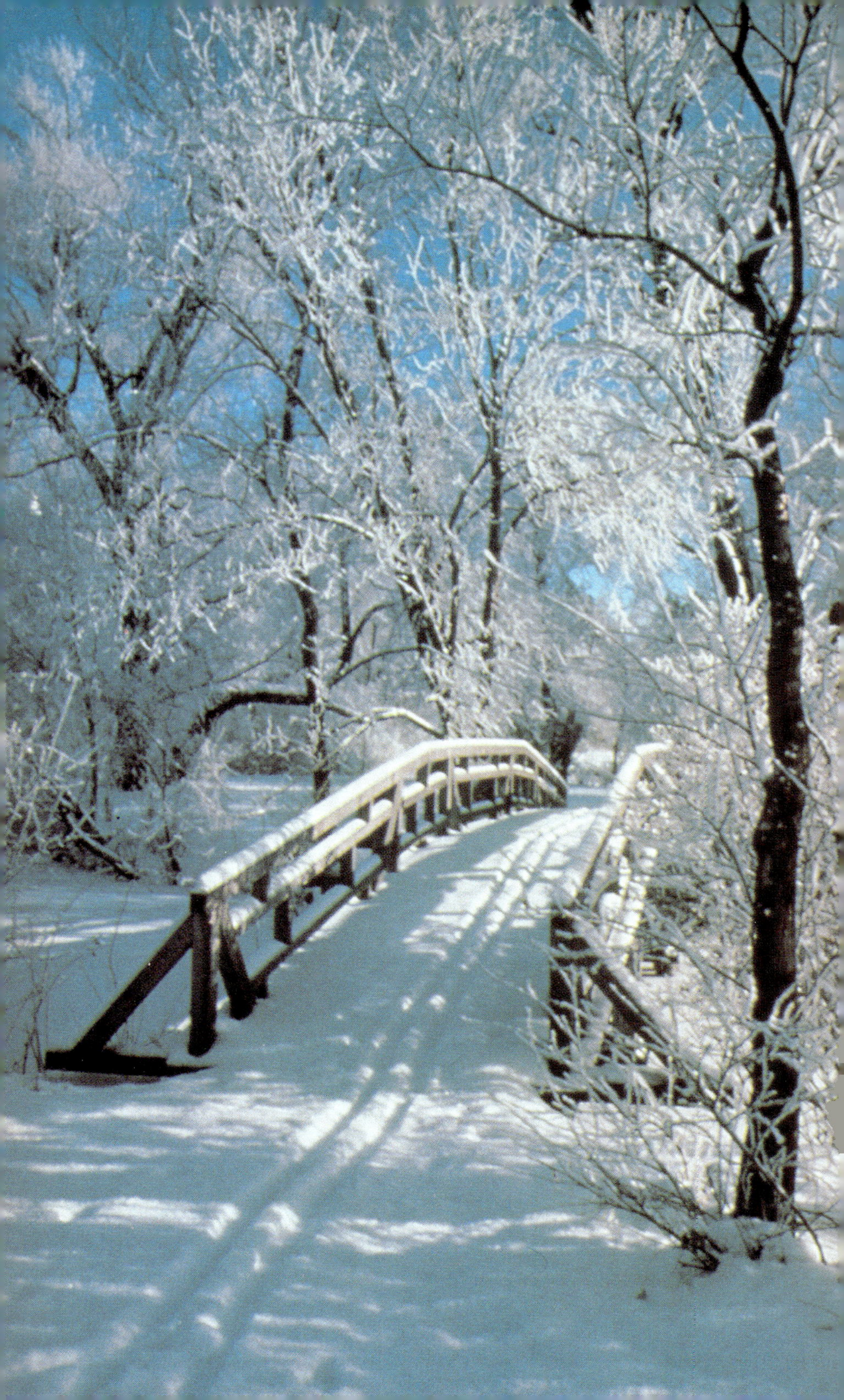

First National Bank. Acting cashier **Joseph Lee Heywood** refused to open the safe and was shot to death. The citizenry, meanwhile, opened fire on the bank robbers, killing two and putting the rest to flight. **Jesse James**, **Cole Younger** and the others rode out of Northfield along what is now called the Outlaw Trail. Part of the gang was ambushed at Madelia, where one more was killed. **Frank** and **Jesse James**, who had taken off on their own, escaped, but Cole Younger and his two brothers were sent to Stillwater State Prison. Jesse James was later murdered in St. Joseph, Missouri, in 1882, and Frank James was cleared of all crimes and died an old man.

The town of Northfield uses the memory of that foiled bank robbery as a symbol of community pride and commemorates the event annually (the weekend following Labor Day) with the Defeat of Jesse James Days, complete with a reenactment of the bank robbery in tribute to Joseph Heywood, a man "faithful unto death."

The neighboring town of **Dundas**, just three miles away, was founded in 1867 by **John Sidney Archibald**, his brother, and his cousin. They developed milling processes that are still in use by the food industry today, and they made Dundas an important flour-milling town. The old Archibald Mill on the Cannon River is listed on the National Register of Historic Places.

ATTRACTIONS
A WALKING TOUR OF NORTHFIELD
The history of the town is reflected in its architecture, and many of the buildings have been renovated for contemporary use. The tour includes The Scriver Building, on Bridge Square (in the center of town), which housed the First National Bank at the time of the attempted robbery. Built in 1868 by **Hiram Scriver**, first mayor of Northfield, it was the town's first large commercial structure; its limestone exterior is fashioned in the Romanesque Revival style. Today, it houses the restored bank and

SHOPPING
Bridge Square is the city's focal point. An antique popcorn wagon that still works is located near the fountain, and many visitors take a break here from their touring and browsing through stores that feature antiques, dry goods, Scandinavian wares, arts, crafts, dolls and miniatures, yarns and fibers, pottery, woodwork, jewelry, gourmet candies, ice cream and gifts for all occasions.

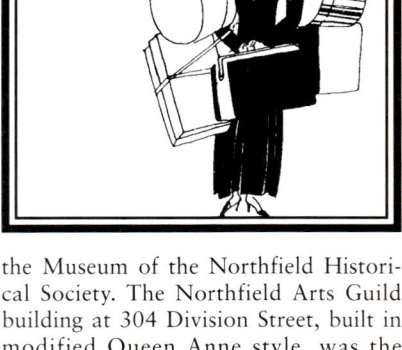

the Museum of the Northfield Historical Society. The Northfield Arts Guild building at 304 Division Street, built in modified Queen Anne style, was the first YMCA in rural Minnesota, served as the city hall for years, and now houses a gallery, gift shop, and facilities for educational programs that include drawing, painting, sculpture, dance, music and photography. The Heiberg dental office at 109 E. Fourth St. is the oldest building in town. City founder **John C. North** built it in 1857 as the Lyceum, and pioneers used it for meetings, debates, lectures and a library. The old Ware Auditorium, built in 1899 and designed in the Federal Revival style by Minneapolis architect Harry Carter, was the community's major civic facility. With the advent of movies, the Lyceum became the Grand, and now is a restaurant of the same name. All Saints Church, at 419 Washington St., was constructed in 1866 and consecrated by Bishop Henry Whipple. The Ole Rolvaag House is located at 311 Manitou. The Archer House is bounded by

Winter in Northfield.

the Cannon River and Division Street; built in 1877 as a hotel, the inn was in use for more than 100 years before it fell into disrepair. Now restored, the Archer House serves as a hotel and a centerpiece for stores and eating establishments.

EATING

QUALITY BAKERY
410 Division St.
(507) 645-8392
Located next door to the Northfield Historical Society building, Quality Bakery has been in operation for more than a century. The Klinkhammer family has owned and run the bakery since 1949. They bake everything from scratch and are reputed to have the largest variety of baked goods in the state. The Klinkhammers fill orders from around the world, make exam week gift boxes of baked goods, and created a program called Rice County Cakes — for parents of Carleton and St. Olaf students who want to call in cake orders for special occasions.

THE OLE STORE
1011 St. Olaf Ave.
(507) 645-5558
A combination restaurant and convenience store is located in what used to be a locker plant and run by Robert and Susan Stangler. Home of the famous "Ole Roll," the restaurant serves breakfast and lunch, complete with homemade rolls, breads and pies, and features daily specials and Sunday brunch.

RUEB-N-STEIN
503 Division St.
(507) 645-6691
Home of a very good Rueben sandwich — what else? This establishment also serves grilled foods and short orders to go with a salad bar and imported beers. Open for lunch and dinner.

JESSE JAMES COUNTRY INN
1700 S. Highway 3
(507) 645-6062
Located a mile from Northfield, the restaurant is open for lunch and dinner and features one of the best Sunday buffets in the state, complete with homemade desserts and popovers with lemon butter. Come for the fish fry on Friday nights, too.

L AND M BAR AND GRILL
224 N. Railway St.
(507) 645-8987
Closed Sundays.
One of the oldest bars in the state, the L and M is more than 110 years old. Soak in the ambience while you savor the taste of fine beverages accompanied by burgers, sandwiches and grilled chicken. The outdoor beer garden is open when the weather permits.

NORTHFIELD ABOUNDS WITH eateries other than the ones mentioned. Fast food and pizza places supply the hurried visitor, as can Grundy's Corner Bar and Grill, featuring the best burger in town, or Uncle Dave's Downtown Dogs, featuring nothing but hot dogs, chili dogs, draft root beer and ice cream. Castle Garden Supper Club and the Mandarin Garden Restaurant specialize in family and casual dining. Visitors will also discover deli, Mexican and Italian food in town.

LODGING

MARTIN OAKS
107 First St.
Dundas, MN 55019
(507) 645-4644
Martin Oaks, listed on the National Register of Historic Places, blends its 1869 Victorian Italianate elegance with a bucolic setting. Three second-floor guest rooms are filled with antiques, brass beds, down comforters, porcelain fixtures and honey-stained oak floors and mouldings. The second "B" in this B&B is nothing short of gourmet — all five courses of it. Marie and Frank Gery are the owners.

THE ARCHER HOUSE
212 Division St.
Northfield, MN 55057
(507) 645-5661
After more than a century of accommodating weary travelers, the 1877 four-story Archer House is one of Minnesota's finest examples of Victorian charm. Current owners Dallas and Sandra Haas renovated the French Second Empire building and endowed each of the 38 rooms with country charm and individuality. The feel is homespun, rus-

Hurray! Minnesota

tic and quaint, but guests are assured of up-to-date conveniences to accompany the antique charm. The Archer House has space for conferences and receptions and is the center of a complex containing a variety of shops and restaurants.

THE LOG HOUSE
6575 145th St.
Northfield, MN 55057
(507) 645-5325
Overlooking a valley six miles south of Northfield, this 1856 house features a downstairs bedroom with an upstairs parlor. Hosts Anne and Mike Mikkelsen have decorated the house with antiques and handmade quilts. The house is surrounded by herb gardens in the summer and ski trails in the winter. Breakfast is included, and dinner can be arranged. French cooking is the specialty of the house.

MOSES HOUSE
1100 S. Division St.
Northfield, MN 55057
(507) 663-1563
Northfield's first B&B, this Cape Cod-style home was built in 1931 and contains four guest rooms and several other rooms in which to relax and feel at home. It's located just a short distance from historic downtown. Breakfasts are tailored to individual wishes. The entire house is available for rental arrangements.

QUILL AND QUILT
615 W. Hoffman St.
Cannon Falls, MN 55009
(507) 263-5507
This Colonial Revival house, built in 1897, has four guest rooms and spacious common areas rich with oak woodwork, early-American stenciling, antiques and handmade quilts. The rooms have private baths, and one suite features a double whirlpool. Enjoy both the full breakfast and the complimentary social hour. Cannon Falls, several miles east of Northfield on Highway 19, is conveniently close to biking, hiking and skiing venues.

▼ **FOR MORE INFORMATION...**
NORTHFIELD CONVENTION AND VISITORS BUREAU
Box 198
Northfield, MN 55057
(507) 645-5604 or (800) 658-2548

NEW PRAGUE

IN 1856, a group of pioneers from Bavaria and Bohemia looking for a new life settled in what they called "Praha," in a section of the state south of Shakopee known as the big woods. **Anton Philipp** was the first settler in New Prague and was soon joined by several other immigrants who had been on their way to St. Cloud but got on the wrong steamboat and the wrong river. They had headed west on the Minnesota rather than the Mississippi River and arrived in Shakopee before discovering their error, so they decided to join Philipp in Praha.

New Prague came into its own after 1877 — the year the grasshopper plague ended, the settlement was incorporated into a village and the first train arrived. The railroad changed life for the villagers, and New Prague became a center of trade for neighboring communities.

In spite of its beginnings as a settlement founded by men who turned left when they meant to turn right, New Prague managed to retain its ethnic flavor rather than lose it to the great American melting pot. One thing that sets New Prague apart are the recently commissioned murals on commercial buildings depicting the history of the town and its links to the old country. Two of the town's biggest landmarks are St. Wenceslaus Church and Schumacher's New Prague Hotel. The church was built in 1906, a combination of Romanesque and Bohemian architecture capped with twin, copper-covered domes, and was one of the largest churches in the state at the time it was constructed. The hotel was designed in 1898 by Library of Congress and Minnesota State Capitol architect **Cass Gilbert**, and it boasts an elegant Bavarian decor to complement the red brick Greek Revival exterior. New Prague is also the birthplace of Robin Hood Flour, the product of the mill built in 1896 by **Francis Atherton Bean Sr.**, with a little help from his friends in the community. That old mill, still visible today, formed the nucleus of what is today International Multifoods, headquartered in Minneapolis.

New Prague, more than many towns, is embodied by its citizens: The blend of rich and lively cultures and industrious characteristics native to them forms a background against which the town thrives. The community celebrates its mixed heritage each year on the fourth Saturday in September with Dozinky — A Czechoslovakian Harvest Festival. The streets are filled with costumed dancers and musicians, ethnic music, Czech and German and harvest foods, traditional arts and crafts, historical demonstrations and agricultural displays.

ATTRACTIONS

A VISIT TO New Prague is far from complete unless a walking tour of town is included. The tour includes Schumacher's New Prague Hotel; the First National Bank Building, listed on the National Register of Historic Places; the Bruzek Homestead Site, home of one of the first settlers; the Bean Mansion; the Anton Philipp Home; the railroad depot; St. Wenceslaus Church; and the historic flour mill. The tour is spiced with murals: the New Prague Philharmonic Orchestra Mural, the New Prague Fireman Mural, the New Prague Schoolhouse Mural, the Bohemian Brass Band Mural, the Czech Festive Costume Mural, the New Prague Power Plant Mural and the New Prague Threshing Mural.

SHOPPING

THE WALKING TOUR of town will take visitors past the Country Store, which offers handmade Amish quilts and wall-hangings; New Prague Antiques; and the Elegant Era, which features hand-embroidered linens, Victorian keepsakes, floral arrangements, gourmet cooking and dining accessories and coffees roasted in New Prague. **Lau's Bohemian Bakery** specializes in ethnic pastries filled with poppy seeds, apricots and prunes: Eat them there or take them home.

EATING AND LODGING

SCHUMACHER'S NEW PRAGUE HOTEL
212 W. Main St.
New Prague, MN 56071
(612) 758-2133
(612) 445-7285 (metro area)
Each of the 11 rooms is individually decorated with its own central European and seasonal theme. Owners John and Kathleen Schumacher combine the elegance of the building with the comfort of the rooms and serve an impressive bill of fare in the three distinctive dining rooms. Open for breakfast, lunch and dinner seven days a week, the restaurant dishes up more than 50 Czech and German delicacies, as well as furnishing imported Czech and German beers. Everything in the kitchen is homemade, from the sausage to the cucumber pickles to the kolackys. It might be best to take the walking tour of New Prague *after* a meal at Schumacher's.

▼ FOR MORE INFORMATION...
NEW PRAGUE CHAMBER OF COMMERCE
217 W. Main St.
Box 191
New Prague, MN 56071
(612) 758-4360

SCHUMACHER'S
New Prague Hotel

Quite possibly,
the most romantic place
in Minnesota ...

*Superb Central
European Cuisine,
Lodging and Gifts*

reservations recommended

212 WEST MAIN STREET,
NEW PRAGUE, MN 56071
(612) 758-2133

This stone memorial, dedicated in 1987 during the Year of Reconciliation, is located near the 1862 Sioux execution site in Mankato.

western Minnesota's leading metropolis. It has a population of 40,000 and ranks as the major trade, medical and educational center of southern Minnesota, complete with Mankato State University, several colleges, hospitals and a flourishing cultural life including several theaters and the Mankato Symphony Orchestra. Industry and agriculture merge in Mankato; its location still enables the

The R.D. Hubbard House, built in 1870, was one of the grandest residences in Mankato.

town to be a natural trade center for southwestern Minnesota, parts of Iowa and South Dakota. Mankato is home to some of Minnesota's largest companies, such as Carlson Craft (one of the largest printing operations in the country), Hubbard Milling (the world's largest processor of private label pet food) and Johnson Fishing, a leading international producer of fishing rods and reels). The Happy Chef chain of family restaurants had its beginnings in Mankato.

There are many fine historical buildings in town, including the Carnegie Library and the Queen Anne-style Judge Lorin P. Cray Mansion. **Mount Kato**, for people who love to ski, features eight chairlifts, 18 slopes and a chalet and rental shop. For hikers and bikers, the 39-mile **Sakatah Singing Hills Trail** winds through rich farmland along an abandoned railway line, and the **Flood Wall Trail** runs along the Minnesota River.

Some of Mankato's best-known events are: the Minnesota Vikings Training Camp, held on Blakeslee Field at Mankato State University in the late summer; the Mahkato Mdewakaton Powwow, complete with dancing, traditional foods and authentic crafts, held in the fall; the 1800s Historic Festival, featuring fur traders, historic artifacts, music and family activities, held in mid-November; and the Celebration of Lights, a monthlong event held all over town during the Christmas season.

ATTRACTIONS
LINCOLN PARK AREA
Lincoln, Pleasant, Clark streets
Minnesota Valley Regional Library
100 E. Main St.
Mankato

Welcome to Deep Valley, the town beloved by readers as the setting for the **"Betsy-Tacy"** children's books written by Mankato author **Maud Hart Lovelace** about her hometown. Many of the scenes from the stories are listed on the self-guided walking tour, including Lovelace's birthplace on Clark Street.

The library has a Lovelace wing where visitors can find information and see a keepsake scrapbook from the author, as well as a mural depicting scenes from the stories and Lovelace's life. Many of the scenes from the stories are listed on the self-guided walking tour of the area.

BLUE EARTH COUNTY COURTHOUSE
204 S. Fifth St.
Mankato

Built in 1889, the courthouse makes elaborate use of local Mankato stone in French and Haitian Renaissance architecture. The building has recently been completely renovated.

WINTER WARRIOR
Riverfront Drive

Located at the Minnesota Valley Regional Library, the sculpture is made of local stone and is a tribute to the Year of Reconciliation, which marked the 125th year after the U.S.-Dakota Conflict in

1862. Beside the sculpture stands a special marker noting the site where 38 Dakota Sioux Indians were hanged for the part they played in the uprising.

MINNEOPA STATE PARK/SEPPMAN'S MILL
Six miles west of Mankato on Highway 60 is a 917-acre state park named after the Dakota word for "two falls." It is situated along Minneopa Creek, where two scenic waterfalls drop 50 feet into a gorge surrounded by steep bluffs. Included in the park is an old stone windmill built by **Louis Seppman** in 1864. The mill is 32 feet high and has a millstone that Seppman brought from St. Louis at a cost of $6,000. Seppman's mill ground flour until 1880 and was used as a feed mill for local farmers until 1890. The park was donated by the Blue Earth Historical Society to the state park system in 1931. It is only a short drive down into the Minneopa Valley, where you can park and walk the hundred or so feet to the falls.

HERITAGE CENTER MUSEUM
415 Cherry St.
Mankato
(507) 345-5566
The museum highlights the history of Blue Earth County and Mankato settlement, development and culture. Attractions include artifacts, a Native American collection, farming and industrial displays and a Maud Hart Lovelace exhibit. The museum has a research library available for use by the public and sponsors special programs that include tours of historic homes. A gift shop offers handmade items from the area as well as period gifts and books on local history.

R.D. HUBBARD HOUSE
606 S. Broad St.
Mankato
(507) 345-5566 or 345-4154
This is the residence of **Rensselaer D. Hubbard**, founder of Hubbard Milling Co. Built around 1870, the French Empire-style home designed with local red brick is listed on the National Register of Historic Places, and so is the carriage house. The interior features green silk-brocade wall fabric, Tiffany light fixtures and marble fireplaces, as well as a gift shop offering period gifts and books of area history.

SHOPPING

MANKATO OFFERS SEVERAL shopping venues: the Mankato Mall, River Hills Mall, Madison East Center, Old Town Shopping, downtown North Mankato, the Belle Mar Mall, University Square and Village East.

EATING

CALEDONIA LOUNGE
Madison East Center
Mankato
(507) 625-9622
Open daily, the Caledonia Lounge offers nightly entertainment — country western and '50s and '60s rock and roll — and specializes in terrific pizza and sandwiches.

EXCHANGE
1655 Mankato Mall
Mankato
(507) 625-1655
Open daily, the Exchange serves pasta, appetizers, salads and an all-you-can-eat Sunday champagne brunch.

CHARLEY'S RESTAURANT AND LOUNGE
920 Madison Ave.
Mankato
(507) 388-6845
You haven't savored a steak like this until you bite into Charley's 24-ounce prime rib. And for only $9.99. Complete menu. Open daily for breakfast, lunch and dinner. Closing time on Saturday is 11 p.m.

MEXICAN VILLAGE
1630 Madison Ave.
Mankato
(507) 387-4455
Enjoy authentic Mexican and American food in a comfortable atmosphere. Open daily for your convenience.

HILLTOP TAVERN
1021 Madison Ave.
Mankato
(507) 625-9787
This is where the locals go, and they call it "hamburger heaven." Compare the Hilltop's burgers with your favorites from elsewhere. Mankatoans say you'll be impressed. While you're there, have homemade soup of the day and the Hilltop's outstanding potato salad. Open daily 11 a.m. to 9 p.m. but closed on Sundays.

433   PIONEER COUNTRY

METTLER'S BAR AND RESTAURANT
117 S. Front St.
Mankato
(507) 625-9660
Open daily for dinner, Mettler's provides live entertainment nightly.

SADAKA'S FAMILY BUFFET
1325 Madison Ave.
Mankato
(507) 388-2491
Get in line and select from a bountiful spread of quality foods at reasonable prices. Open 11 a.m. to 9 p.m. daily.

HOLIDAY INN–SAULPAUGH DINING ROOM/ BLAZER LOUNGE
101 Main St.
Mankato
(507) 345-1234
Open daily, the dining room and lounge offer a variety of fine dining with three different menus that appeal to everyone's taste.

LODGING

MANKATO CAN accommodate quantities of visitors in the Holiday Inn Downtown, Cliff Kyes Motel, Redwood Motel, Sunset Motel, Kato Motel, Days Inn, Super 8 Motel, Best Western Garden Inn and Budgetel Inn.

CEDAR KNOLL BED AND BREAKFAST
Route 2, Box 147
Good Thunder, MN 56037
(507) 524-3813
Located about 10 miles south of Mankato, the Cedar Knoll B&B offers three guest rooms decorated in a blend of local and Eastern antiques. Situated on a working farm with animals, woods, ravines, orchards and mowed walking trails, this B&B invites guests to use the huge screened porch and outdoor fireplace. A full breakfast is served each morning, and visitors will find the flourishing artists' colony and public wall murals of **Good Thunder** an added attraction to their stay here.

▼ FOR MORE INFORMATION...

MANKATO AREA CONVENTION AND VISITORS BUREAU
Box 999
Mankato, MN 56001
(507) 345-4519
(800) 657-4733

NEW ULM

NEW ULM IS located on high land that was once an island in the Glacial River Warren, at the confluence of the Cottonwood and Minnesota rivers. The town was built on three different terraces formed by these rivers. In 1854, members of the German Land Society of Chicago arrived in New Ulm to lay out the town, named for Ulm in Wurttemberg, Germany. Like the cities in their beloved homeland, New Ulm was carefully planned to include parks, market squares and public areas. Within a year, the town had developed around craftsmen, bankers, brewers and farmers. By 1880, there were more than 653 Germans living in New Ulm who maintained their native language and customs.

New Ulm was the site of an important battle during the Sioux uprising of 1862. Settlers from surrounding areas sought protection in New Ulm as word spread that **Chief Little Crow** was leading a large party of Dakota warriors into battle against them. The Sioux had been unsuccessful in their attack on Fort Ridgely, located upriver, and mounted an attack on New Ulm on August 23, 1862. **Charles Flandrau**, a St. Peter judge, led the residents of New Ulm in a successful defense against the prolonged attack by 800 warriors, but much of the town was burned, 26 people were killed and scores wounded. **Dr. William W. Mayo** of Le Sueur was one of the doctors who came to the aid of the wounded. Shortly after the attack, Judge Flandrau evacuated the entire town of some 1200 people to Mankato.

Today, the town's German culture flourishes through the colorful celebrations of ethnic music, food and dance at festivals celebrated each year: Heritagefest, Oktoberfest, Marktstrasse, Fasching (New Ulm's version of Mardi Gras) and the Minnesota Festival of Music. Some of the businesses located in New Ulm are throwbacks to the town's beginnings, such as the August Schell Brewing Co., a successful specialty beer brewer founded in 1860 and family-owned ever since. Other companies situated in town are Kraft Inc. and several large trucking

Hurray! Minnesota

firms. The little utopia envisioned by the founding fathers still reflects some of the best elements of both the old world and the new, and New Ulm gladly shares its gemutlichkeit with visitors.

ATTRACTIONS
AUGUST SCHELL BREWERY/AUGUST SCHELL HOUSE
Schell Park
New Ulm
(507) 354-5528
New Ulm's oldest industry, the brewery has been under the ownership and direction of August Schell's descendants since it opened in 1860. The rising popularity of premium-quality "specialty" beers made in small breweries has been a boon to Schell's, which is known for its premium Weiss and Pilsner beers. The Schell Brewery, which produces 25,000 barrels of beer annually, is housed in the original brick buildings next to the Schell mansion, gardens and deer park. Visitors can tour the brewery, the gardens and the Schell Museum of Brewing, which was built in 1987. Open Memorial Day through Labor Day.

WANDA GAG HOUSE
226 N. Washington St.
New Ulm
(507) 359-2632
Wanda Gag, author, artist and illustrator of "Millions of Cats," the book commonly considered a children's classic and the work for which she is perhaps best-known, grew up in New Ulm. She was the daughter of local artist Anton Gag, whose murals can be found in the New Ulm Cathedral. Wanda Gag's Queen Anne-style childhood home is located three blocks west of New Ulm's downtown district and is listed on the National Register of Historic Places.

JOHN LIND HOME
Center and State streets
New Ulm
(507) 354-8802
The house was built in 1887 for John Lind, Minnesota's 14th governor. A Queen Anne-style home listed on the National Register of Historic Places, the governor's residence was often the center of community and social activities in its time.

New Ulm's famous musical landmark charms visitors.

GLOCKENSPIEL
North Fourth and Minnesota streets
This free-standing carillon clock tower is 45 feet high, and the total weight of the bells is 2 1/2 tons. The bells chime the time of day in Westminster style, play programmed pieces at noon, 3 and 5 p.m., and can be played on a portable keyboard housed in the base of the tower. On the west side of the tower, beneath the bells and clock face, three animated polka band figures perform 10 months out of the year, replaced by a nativity scene displayed from Thanksgiving until early January. Directly beneath the figures, a door slides up and a stage projects from the tower to reveal 3-foot-high animated figurines that depict the history and development of New Ulm.

HERMANN MONUMENT
Center and Monument streets
New Ulm
(507) 354-4910
The monument was erected in 1897 in memory of an ancient Teutonic hero,

Hermann (or Arminius, as the Romans called him) of Cherusci. He is honored as the liberator of Germany and the father of Germanic independence. The 102-foot-tall statue towers over the city from its place in **Hermann Heights Park** and provides one of the best vantage points from which to view New Ulm and the Minnesota River Valley. Open Memorial Day through Labor Day and on Oktoberfest weekends.

ALEXANDER HARKIN STORE
Brown County Historical Society
(507) 354-2016
Located eight miles northwest of New Ulm on Nicollet County Highway 21, the Alexander Harkin Store was the center of the thriving town of West Newton in 1870. At the general store/post office, trade and talk flourished and goods, news and ideas changed hands. All the settlers gathered at the Harkin store. By 1901, river commerce had dwindled and the town with it. The store was closed and, in 1938, reopened as a museum by the Harkins' granddaughter. Today, restored to its 1870 appearance by the Minnesota Historical Society, the store contains much of its original stock and has the smell and feel of the old store. Visitors can inhale the fragrance of cinnamon, cloves, camphor and lemon extract, have a look around, play a game of checkers, grind their own coffee or just sit a spell on the front porch. Open Memorial Day through Labor Day and weekends in May and September.

FORT RIDGELY STATE PARK
Seven miles south of Fairfax on Highway 4
Rural Route 1, Box 32
Fairfax, MN 55332
(507) 426-7888 or 697-6321
This historic fort was constructed in 1853 on a high plateau near the Minnesota River to protect settlers in southwestern Minnesota from Indian attacks. In the opinion of many soldiers banished to this western outpost, the fort was impossible to defend because of the deep, wooded ravines surrounding it on three sides. In 1862, the soldiers had a chance to test their theory when the Dakota Sioux living on the nearby reservation attacked the fort. The yearly June payment for their ceded lands hadn't reached the Sioux as late as August, and years of pent-up tensions exploded with this August 20 declaration of war. The Sioux were unsuccessful in taking the fort and engaged in skirmishes up and down the upper Minnesota River Valley until their surrender a month later.

Very little remains of Fort Ridgely today. After the war, the Sioux were forced to relocate to the Dakotas or Nebraska, the fort was closed and the settlers tore down the buildings to use for their own homes and barns. A restored stone commissary and a handful of stone foundations on the windy plateau are all that remain to mark the site of the fort. The Minnesota Historical Society operates exhibits and a gift shop on the grounds and enlightens visitors about the last Indian war in the state. Open May 1 through Labor Day.

FLANDRAU STATE PARK
Located just south of New Ulm is an 800-acre state park situated in the heavily-wooded Cottonwood River Valley. In this park there are 90 campsites, seven miles of trails, boat rentals and a park naturalist to answer questions.

SHOPPING
THE SAUSAGE SHOP
N. Third and Broadway
New Ulm
(507) 354-3300
Experience the taste that blends perfectly with New Ulm's German tradition.

THE CREATIVE TOUCH
18 1/4 N. Minnesota
New Ulm
(507) 354-7000
This shop features a large display of handcrafted gifts for all seasons, including furniture, bunnies, bears, baskets, wreaths, pottery and more.

HERITAGE ANTIQUES
121 N. Broadway
New Ulm
(507) 359-5150
Heritage Antiques is a mall with more than 30 dealers and a wide variety of antiques and collectibles. It's just like stepping back in time, and visitors to Heritage Antiques will be reminded of

A rendezvous reminiscent of a bygone era at Fort Ridgeley State Park during Historical Festival weekend.

the mall's motto: We have everything Grandma had, except Grandpa.

Domeiers
1020 S. Minnesota
New Ulm
(507) 354-4231
A rich assortment of German treasures fill the shelves of Domeiers, New Ulm's German store. It's like taking a trip to the old country when you step into this store.

Der Ulmer Spatz, Inc.
16 S. Broadway
New Ulm
(507) 354-1313
This intriguing, castle-like house contains original paintings, pottery, wood works, Indian art, needlework, jewelry, South American baskets, locally crafted items and unique imports from around the world.

Spielladen
Marktplatz Mall
101 N. German St.
New Ulm
(507) 354-7755
This specialty toy store features toys and games from Germany, plus a wonderful selection of children's books, plush animals, dolls and educational games.

Country Loft and Doll House
204 N. Minnesota St.
New Ulm
(507) 354-8493
This store offers a large selection of country crafts from more than 500 craftspeople around the country.

Fudge and Stuff
210 N. Minnesota St.
New Ulm
(507) 359-5272
Gnomemade Fudge is one of the chief attractions of this shop, and it's reputed to be the creamiest in the world. Visitors will also find pasta, gourmet coffee, tea, herb vinegars and unique gift items.

Lambrecht's and the Christmas Haus
119 N. Minnesota St.
New Ulm
(507) 354-4313
New Ulm's largest gift shop, Lambrecht's, is filled with German crystal, collectible gnomes, hummels, music boxes, lace, leather goods, souvenirs and more. The Christmas Haus features 11 rooms stocked year-round with nutcrackers, steins, smokers, santas, angels, dolls, nativity scenes and a wonderland of trees and ornaments.

Eating

Glockenspiel Haus Restaurant and Lounge
400 N. Minnesota
New Ulm
(507) 354-5593
This restaurant offers German-American

cuisine for dinner, breakfast with authentic German pastry, a Sunday brunch and quality handmade candy.

CAT 'N' FIDDLE SUPPER CLUB
Seven miles southeast of New Ulm on Highway 68
(507) 354-6911
The weekend smorgasbord features a variety of meats, salads, soups and desserts.

HERMANN'S HEIDELBERG AND STEIN–HOLIDAY INN
2101 S. Broadway
New Ulm
(507) 359-2941
The monthly lunch and dinner specials cater to diners' appetites for German and American cuisine. Try the Sunday brunch or come for the live entertainment Monday through Saturday nights.

VEIGEL'S KAISERHOFF
221 N. Minnesota
New Ulm
(507) 359-2071
This well-known restaurant is the home of "those famous barbecue ribs" as well as great steaks, chicken, seafood, salads, soups and sandwiches. Open daily for lunch and dinner. Check the daily specials.

LODGING

NEW ULM OFFERS visitors their choice of accommodations: Budget Holiday Motel and Colonial Inn on North Broadway; or Holiday Inn, Super 8 Motel and New Ulm Motel on South Broadway.

▼ FOR MORE INFORMATION...

NEW ULM AREA CHAMBER OF COMMERCE
220 N. Minnesota
Box 384 W
New Ulm, MN 56073
(507) 354-4217 or (507) 354-1504

MORTON

THE LOWER SIOUX AGENCY INTERPRETIVE CENTER
Nine miles east of Redwood Falls on County Highway 2
Rural Route 1, Box 125
Morton, MN 56270
(507) 697-6181
One of two administrative agencies built by the federal government to oversee the Indian reservation, the Lower Sioux Agency now presents the history of the Dakota people through displays and a video presentation. The remains of the site of the old Indian agency, destroyed in 1862, mark the scene of the first organized Indian attack in the U.S.-Dakota Conflict. Just up the road is St. Cornelia's Episcopal Church/Bishop Whipple Mission, listed on the National Register of Historic Places. Completed in 1890, the church was built from unhewn prairie stone selected by **Chief Wabasha** and is the mother parish of Dakota Episcopal congregations throughout the Midwest.

Symbols of Dakota heritage are painted on the hand-thrown pottery made on the grounds at Tipi Maka Duta and sold at the **Lower Sioux Trading Post**, along with other native crafts such as pipestone carvings, paintings and beadwork made by community residents. A yearly powwow (Wacipi) is held on the site.

JACKPOT JUNCTION
Lower Sioux Agency
(800) Letter-X
The Lower Sioux Tribal Council sponsors Jackpot Junction: 67,000 square feet of bingo, slot machines, "21" tables and keno. Visitors who come to play in the middle of a cornfield in the center of the river valley will also find a 24-hour restaurant, **Impressions**, famous for its breakfast, lunch and dinner buffets as well as a complete menu selection. A mural depicting Dakota culture graces a wall in the restaurant. An entertainment center at the site can accommodate more than 200 people for dinner and shows.

Hurray! Minnesota

Several monuments in Redwood County bear witness to the U.S.–Dakota Conflict. James Lynde, a white trader, was the first to die at the Lower Sioux Agency on August 19, 1862.

Lodging

Country Oaks Inn Bed and Breakfast
Route 4, Box 40
Redwood Falls, MN 56283
(507) 644-3111
Located just one-and-a-half miles from Jackpot Junction, the Country Oaks has four guest rooms, one whirlpool suite and a lounge area with a fireplace for visitors. A continental breakfast is served and free shuttle service to Jackpot Junction is provided.

Stanhope Bed and Breakfast
Rural Route 4, Box 14
Redwood Falls, MN 56283
(507) 644-2882
The Stanhope offers guests a quiet, comfortable country place overlooking the scenic Minnesota River Valley, located three miles east of Redwood Falls on Highways 19 and 71 and less than two miles from Jackpot Junction. Horse pasturage is available to visitors.

Redwood Falls

REDWOOD FALLS IS located at the junction of the Redwood and Minnesota rivers. The Dakota Sioux had inhabited the area since the early 18th century; they had found the sheltered valleys and surrounding prairie a good place to hunt, fish and grow crops. European settlers, primarily of English and German heritage, also liked the area and began arriving in the 1850s. After the signing of the Traverse des Sioux treaty in 1851, the settlers arrived in waves, and the government set up the Lower Sioux Agency.

The settlers built a sawmill in 1855 at the falls of the Redwood River. By 1862 a church, school and several trading

PHOTO BY CONNIE WANNER

Stone Bridge in Ramsey Park, the largest municipal park in the state.

posts had sprung up in the area. In the meantime, the Sioux were being pressured to adopt "white man's ways" and were becoming increasingly resentful at the influx of settlers and the loss of their traditional way of life, their land, game and crops. The mismanagement by federal government agents compounded the problem and helped spark the tragic U.S.-Dakota Conflict of 1862.

The war destroyed the European settlement and wreaked havoc on the Dakota people, driving them from the state for more than a generation. After the war, the settlers returned to the area and formed a community. Redwood Falls was founded in 1864 by Colonel **Sam McPhail**, who platted and helped develop the town. The village prospered, grew into an agricultural trade center and was incorporated as a city in 1891.

Today, Redwood Falls is a town of almost 5,000. Agriculture still forms the primary economic base, along with manufacturing and tourism. The town is the regional headquarters for the Evangelical Lutheran Church of America (ELCA), Peacepipe Girl Scout Council and Minnesota Technology, Inc.-Redwood Falls. The current major employers are Jackpot Junction, Zytec Corporation and Central Bi-Products, plus more than 200 manufacturing, retail, service and government offices that offer diverse career opportunities to residents of the community and surrounding area.

Redwood Falls is also the birthplace of Sears, which got its start when a jewelry company mistakenly shipped some gold watches to a local jeweler, a North Redwood rail station agent named **Richard Warren Sears**. He bought the unwanted watches and sold them to other station agents. This small event in 1886 launched the nation's largest retailer: Sears, Roebuck, and Co. From Chicago headquarters, the company went into the mail-order business and in 1925 opened the first Sears retail store. Today, the diversified company employs more than 480,000 people and includes the Sears Merchandise Group, All-State Insurance, Coldwell Banker Real Estate and Dean Witter Financial Services.

Hurray! Minnesota

PHOTO BY MICHAEL R. SCHREIER/
TRAVEL SOUTHWEST MINNESOTA

MINNESOTA INVENTORS CONGRESS, INC.
Box 71
Redwood Falls, MN 56283-0071
(507) 637-2344
(800) INVENT-1 (in Minnesota)
Redwood Falls is the site of the annual convention of the Minnesota Inventors Congress (MIC). Since 1958, the MIC has evolved into an effective support system for national and international inventors and a hotbed of ideas bright enough to have pleased Thomas Edison. It is both an annual convention and a resource center that inventors and businesses draw on year-round. More than 10,000 visitors — manufacturers, marketers, investors, licensees seeking new products, and folks fascinated with innovative ideas — travel to Redwood Falls during the second full weekend in June to view the hundreds of inventions on display at the convention.

The Nada-Chair Back-Up, invented by Victor Toso, goes everywhere — sporting events, hunting, camping or the office.

Company headquarters saluted North Redwood on the 100th anniversary of its incorporation in 1984. A Sears catalog store still operates in Redwood Falls.

ATTRACTIONS

BUILDINGS LISTED ON the National Register of Historic Places include the Redwood Falls Public Library, the swayback bridge, the building on the corner of Mill and Second streets and the house on the corner of Fourth and Minnesota streets. The Redwood county courthouse, located on the square at the corner of Jefferson and Third streets, celebrated a century of serving the residents of the county in 1991. The Birch Coulee Battlefield, located seven miles northeast of Redwood Falls on Highway 71 and Renville County Road 2, is the site where Dakota warriors trapped a force of U.S. cavalry for 72 hours. A marker commemorates the spot. Other markers and monuments noting events from the area's historic past can be found on short drives throughout the Minnesota River Valley.

REDWOOD FALLS COUNTY MUSEUM
West of Redwood Falls on Highway 19
(507) 637-3329
Originally a county poor farm, the 30-room building displays artifacts from middle-class life in the late-19th and early-20th centuries, including farm tools, doctors' equipment, a one-room school, military memorabilia and photos. Special sections include a rare bird collection from the 1930s, the Minnesota Hall of Fame and Women Inventors Who Changed the World. Open May 1 through September 30 and by appointment.

ALEXANDER RAMSEY PARK
Just off Highways 19 and 71
Named for the first governor of the state (1860–1863), this is the largest municipal park in Minnesota. Its 217 beautiful acres encompass Ramsey Falls, a stone swayback bridge, part of the Redwood River, wooden playgrounds, stone and wood picnic shelters, paved walkways, the Ramsey Falls observation area, the Ramsey Park Zoo, the Vita Course (a 10-station, half-mile exercise run), nature trails, a campground with space for

28 units, cross-country ski trails and a golf course.

TWO MOON COUNTRY/FARMERS' MURALS
Travelers driving west through Redwood Falls on Highway 19 will be struck by the 40-by-60-foot mural that employs the changing seasons in Ramsey Park as a backdrop to the central theme of past and present relationships between the Dakota and European residents of this land. A prominent part of the mural is the "Two Moon Country Color Wheel," which Indian nations used to teach their children the universal truths about the unfolding of the seasons and the passage of life.

On the east side of Mill Street in downtown Redwood Falls, travelers can see a brilliant mural in yellows and greens depicting the mainstay of rural life: agriculture. Several other murals by local artists can be found in the area. Look for outdoors murals by **Gary Butzer**, a wildlife artist from Morton, on the VFW on Highways 19 and 71; on the Firestone Building on Highways 19 and 71; and at the Redwood County Fairgrounds.

SHOPPING

THE BOOKMARK
Armory Square Mall
Redwood Falls
(507) 637-3732
Quality at an affordable price and a friendly atmosphere are the trademarks of a shop that features cards, books, bibles, cassettes, plaques and jewelry.

UNIQUE BOUTIQUE
120 E. Second
Redwood Falls
(507) 637-3131
This shop features dollhouses, miniatures and collectibles.

ATTIC ANTIQUES AND COLLECTIBLES
238 S. Mill
Redwood Falls
(507) 637-3056
The name of the store says it all. Stop in and browse.

CHANLEY CHEESE AND GIFTS
Morton
(507) 697-6294
Located just a few miles southeast of Redwood Falls, this store offers Minnesota souvenirs, T-shirts, sweatshirts, jewelry, clocks, cheese, candy, collectibles and unique gifts.

EATING

VALLEY SUPPER CLUB
North Redwood, 10 minutes from Jackpot Junction
(507) 637-5541
Fine dining. Open for lunch and dinner Monday through Friday and breakfast and lunch on Sundays.

FA CHOY HOUSE
226 S. Mill St.
Redwood Falls
(507) 637-8144
Fine Chinese cuisine is served at lunch and dinner Monday through Saturday. On Tuesdays, enjoy a buffet selection.

THE FOOD GALLERY
807 E. Bridge St.
Redwood Falls
(507) 637-3460
A full line of home-style cooking as well as great sandwiches await the hungry diner at the Food Gallery.

LODGING

THE VICTORIAN LADY BED AND BREAKFAST
Rural Route 2, Box 109-1A
Wabasso, MN 56293
(507) 747-2170
Located a few miles south of Redwood Falls and six-and-a-half miles north of Wabasso, this B&B is a century-old Victorian country home with beautiful oak woodwork, stained glass windows, an open, ornate wooden staircase and parquet hardwood floors. Full breakfast.

REDWOOD INN
Bridge Street (Highways 19 and 71)
Redwood Falls, MN 56283
(507) 637-3521
A two-story accommodation with 60 rooms, the inn houses Sneakers Sports Lounge and Pizza Ranch as well.

▼ FOR MORE INFORMATION...

REDWOOD FALLS AREA CHAMBER OF COMMERCE
Minnesota's Dakota Country Tourism Bureau
140 E. Bridge St.
Redwood Falls, MN 56283
(507) 637-2828
(800) 657-7070

WALNUT GROVE

MORE THAN A century ago, a young girl named Laura Ingalls lived on the Minnesota prairie. One of the places her pioneer family called home was a dugout on the banks of Plum Creek. When **Laura Ingalls Wilder** wrote about her childhood, she immortalized Walnut Grove through a series of children's books (particularly "On the Banks of Plum Creek," first published in 1937) that formed the basis for the TV show "Little House on the Prairie." The **Laura Ingalls Wilder Museum** (507) 859-2358, is open daily during the summer; it houses items from the late 1800s that give visitors a sense of what life was like in those days. The museum also contains Ingalls family memorabilia such as Laura's hand-stitched quilt, her calling card and a bench from the church the Ingalls family attended. The museum is located a block off Highway 14 in Walnut Grove.

Each summer, the residents of Walnut Grove re-create Laura Ingalls Wilder's life in a pageant called **"Fragments of a Dream,"** written by James Merchant and presented on the banks of the creek. The story is told through the eyes of Caroline (Ma) Ingalls and details the lives and struggles of pioneers and their dreams for a better future for their children. The building of the church in 1874 and the beginnings of the town of Walnut Grove are major events in the pageant. Charles Ingalls, Laura's father, gave his last three dollars so that the church could purchase a new bell. That bell still rings on Sunday mornings from the belfry of the present English Lutheran Church in Walnut Grove.

After surveys in 1866, the Winona and St. Peter Railroad, a subsidiary of Chicago Northwestern Railroad, began service to the area in 1873, bringing hundreds of families, businessmen, educators and farmers to settle here. It was on this tide of westerly pioneers that the Ingalls family came from Wisconsin via Kansas to Walnut Grove in 1873, when Laura was six years old, and they stayed for three years. Their first home was the dugout along Plum Creek, two miles north of present-day Walnut Grove on what is now the Gordon farm in North Hero township. In 1961, the Redwood Historical Society placed a granite marker at the farm on County Road 5 at the site of the Ingalls' dugout, which has been nominated to the National Register of Historic Places.

Another local site, now known as lower **Plum Creek County Park** southwest of town, has been nominated to the National Register of Historic Places. Archeological finds have shown that this area — an oasis of black walnut trees set in a small hollow encircled by steep bluffs amid vast grasslands — has been continuously inhabited since 200 A.D. until the coming of the white man. The native peoples who lived here would have found natural shelter from the fierce northwest winds and prairie fires and easy access to the game in the valley below.

Walnut Grove is now a town of 750 in the heart of a thriving agricultural area rich in soybeans, corn, and dairy, hog and sheep farming. Since 1975, Continental Grain has operated a multimillion dollar grain terminal in Walnut Grove. The 210-acre Plum Creek County Park provides recreation year-round with a picnic area, softball diamonds, playgrounds, scenic nature trails, campground, swimming beach and trails for cross-country skiing and snowmobiling. Hundreds of black walnut trees flourish on the grounds. Visitors who come for the pageant or to see the Ingalls site can enjoy the park and can find ample lodging in the nearby towns.

▼ FOR MORE INFORMATION...

LAURA INGALLS WILDER FREE MUSEUM AND TOURIST CENTER
Box 58
Walnut Grove, MN 56180
(507) 859-2358 or 859-2155

JUST EAST OF **Sanborn**, which is about 15 miles due east of Walnut Grove on the Cottonwood River, is the **McCone Sod House** (507) 723-5138. When pioneers first came to the Minnesota prairies, they built their houses of sod, since lumber was scarce on the grassy plains. The McCone family built two authentic sod houses on their farm in the southwestern part of the state. The houses are open for tours and also for overnight rentals. One is very basic, with a dirt floor. The other, a more upscale "soddie," has plastered walls, wood flooring and Victorian-style furniture.

WINDOM

THE VILLAGE OF Windom, located on the Des Moines River, was platted in 1871 and incorporated as a village in 1875. The Des Moines River (French for "River of Monks") and the river valley became part of the Minnesota frontier during the 1850s when such towns as Windom and Jackson were established. The first settlers of Windom came from Scandinavian and French stock. Windom was named in honor of prominent statesman **William Windom**, who had served the nation for 33 years, beginning in 1858, as U.S. Representative, Senator and Secretary of the Treasury. After the Sioux City and St. Paul Railroad was built through Windom in 1871, eight trains daily passed through the town, which meant settlers no longer had to market their crops at Mankato or New Ulm. The trains also brought passengers, until service stopped in October 1959.

Windom was named county seat of Cottonwood County in 1872. By 1890, the population was 835; by 1910, it was 1749. Today, Windom is a community of 4,500. Highways 71, 60 and 62 connect the city to the Twin Cities and Sioux Falls, South Dakota, and the town is also served by a 3,600-foot airport, Greyhound Bus Line and the Chicago Northwestern Railroad. Windom is the home of southwestern Minnesota's largest indoor arena, some of the best hunting and fishing in the area because of its many marshes, lakes and parks, and major industries such as Toro Corporation, the Caldwell Packing Co. and Northwest Cedar Products. The annual Riverfest celebration draws more than 1,500 people to enjoy fireworks, a parade, street dancing and entertainment in June. At Christmas each year, the community participates in "Charles Dickens' Christmas in Windom," an event that includes the production of Dickens' "A Christmas Carol," with its scenes set in various businesses in town.

ATTRACTIONS
COTTONWOOD COUNTY HISTORICAL SOCIETY
812 Fourth Ave.
Windom
(507) 831-1134
Established in 1901, the Cottonwood County Historical Society has occupied the old Co-op Oil Association building since 1973. The society features tool and rural exhibits showing the lifestyle of pioneers as they opened the prairie. Exhibits include a 19th-century one-room schoolhouse, a general store/post office, a parlor arrangement, old clocks, household utensils, guns and the Earlewine big-game trophy collection.

COTTONWOOD COUNTY COURTHOUSE
Courthouse Square
Windom
Windom is known as the town with the "courthouse on the square." Built in 1904 by **J.B. Nelson** of North Mankato for $59,949, the courthouse is listed on the National Register of Historic Places. The building features Corinthian-style marble columns, a 12-foot gold statue of the Greek goddess of justice, four interior murals in the rotunda that represent government, justice, freedom of the press and freedom of religion, and corner emblems on the dome called history, government, art and science. Open weekdays.

JEFFERS PETROGLYPHS
Located nears Jeffers on County Road 2, 15 miles north of Windom
(507) 877-3647
(612) 726-1171
Open daily during the summer.
Long before pioneers homesteaded the Little Cottonwood River Valley, Indians lived on the prairie and left their carvings on the ancient red quartzite bedrock. The nearly 2,000 carvings at the 80-acre Jeffers site comprise the largest petroglyph group in Minnesota. Other carvings are known to have existed throughout the state, but most of them have been destroyed.

Hurray! Minnesota

Some of the petroglyphs at the Jeffers site date back to 3,000 B.C.

Archeologists and anthropologists have unraveled only some of the mystery that surrounds this primitive art and the peoples who created it. The petroglyphs at Jeffers appear to date from two major archeological periods: the Late Archaic-Early Woodland period (3,000 B.C. to A.D. 500) and the Late Woodland period (A.D. 900 to 1750). A walking tour will take visitors to 18 petroglyphs that span the noted time periods and depict animal and human forms.

Pork Chop Ridge Farms
Located seven miles north of Windom on the west side of Highway 71, this farm provides an agri-tour that takes a firsthand look at southern Minnesota farming, machinery, crops, buildings and livestock. The farrow-to-farrow hog operation is owned by a father and son, who also raise corn and soybeans on 900 acres.

Area Parks
The Windom area contains several parks for recreation and entertainment: Mayflower Park, Tegels Park, Dynamite Park, Talcot County Park, Pat's Grove County Park, Witt Park, Mountain County Park, Kilen Woods State Park, Abby Park and Island Park.

Eating
Pine Inn
Junction Highways 60-71 and 62
Windom
(507) 831-2726
Enjoy the salad and taco bar, daily specials, frozen yogurt, broasted chicken or a delicious picnic to savor in one of Windom's parks.

The Seventy-One Club
Two miles north of Windom on Highway 71
(507) 831-5936
Treat yourself to a dinner of some of the largest, most delicious steaks around. Sundowner specials are served Monday through Thursday from 4 to 6 p.m., and check the nightly menu specials, which often include all-you-can-eat fare. The Sunday buffet runs from 11 a.m. to 2 p.m.

COZY CAFE
923 Third Ave.
Windom
(507) 831-4711
Open for breakfast, lunch or afternoon coffee Monday through Saturday. This restaurant features home cooking away from home.

CORNER CAFE
Corner of Third Ave. and 10th St.
Windom
(507) 831-3100
Come in for home-cooked daily specials, homemade pies and pastries and the Sunday family-style roast pork, beef, ham loaf or fried chicken dinners.

LODGING
JOHNSON MOTEL
Junction Highways 60-71 N.
Windom, MN 56101
(507) 831-3111
Large, clean rooms, some with queen-size beds, free cable TV and HBO are only some of the amenities this motel offers. Suites available.

WINDOM MOTEL
Highways 60-71
South Windom
(507) 831-1120
Conveniently located between Hardee's and Godfather's, the Windom Motel offers guests clean, comfortable accommodations near restaurants and parks.

▼ FOR MORE INFORMATION...
WINDOM AREA CHAMBER OF COMMERCE
920 Highway 60 and 71
Box 8
Windom, MN 56101
(507) 831-2752

JACKSON

HERE ALONG THE fertile, tree-lined valley of the Des Moines River is the site of the first white settlement in this area. In 1856, a dozen or so people settled around a shanty store near a ford in the river and named it Springfield. **William Wood** opened a log store on the west bank of the river, while most of the other cabins were scattered on the east side. The settlers' first winter here was severe, since the hurriedly built cabins were drafty and hard to heat. Food was scarce and fresh game was hard to find. The closest village was 50 miles away and being caught in a prairie blizzard meant almost certain death, particularly if one couldn't make the protection of a wooded river bottom.

But after surviving that first winter, a different kind of problem arose for the hamlet, which had changed its name to Jackson. Settlements had been budding across the prairie, farther and farther into what had been, for thousands of years, the Indians' hunting grounds. The Dakota had ceded southern Minnesota in the treaties of 1851 made at Mendota and Traverse des Sioux. But during the spring of 1857, a small band of Dakota became uneasy about the influx of whites to this region. Led by an Indian named **Inkpaduta** (Scarlet Point), the band attacked a small settlement eight miles south of Jackson at Spirit Lake, Iowa. Inkpaduta's appearance was frightening to the settlers. He was 60 years old, 6 feet tall, and his face was badly scarred from small pox.

It was a bloody encounter at Spirit Lake. Thirty-two pioneers and their children were killed by Inkpaduta's warriors. From there, the chief and his band escaped north toward Springfield (Jackson), where they attacked the scattered cabins along the river. At one site, the two Wood brothers and all their livestock were killed as their small store was looted. Several others were also killed at Springfield. Inkpaduta fled to South Dakota with 12 braves, their women and children, and three captives. Their escape was successful, but it was still cold that March and several of their horses starved before they reached South Dakota. Inkpaduta's notorious reputation grew and since he was never captured, fear spread among the settlers of southwestern Minnesota. (Inkpaduta was later reported to have aided in the battle against General Custer at the Little Big Horn. Today, a replica of Inkpaduta's camp can be found in Jackson.)

Five years later in 1862, the U.S.-Dakota Conflict reached this region. A cavalry unit was dispatched to the county. Soldiers found nine pioneer bodies,

Fort Belmont
Two miles south of Interstate 90 and Highway 71
(507) 847-5840

Fort Belmont was one of the first forts in the Upper Midwest and was used for protection from the roaming bands of Sioux. It was built by settlers in 1864, following the Springfield and Belmont uprisings led by Chiefs Inkpaduta and White Lodge. This authentic replica includes a sod house complete with period furnishing, the only water wheel-operated flour mill in the Midwest, a log chapel and a historical museum. From atop the high lookout tower, visitors can get a splendid view of the Des Moines River Valley. Open daily June through August.

This log house is located near Fort Belmont, one of the oldest forts in the Upper Midwest.

---

buried them, and reported that the rest of the county was entirely deserted. For one year, Jackson County was devoid of settlers until the fall of 1863, when small groups started to trickle back.

Besides the whites' fear of Indians and their struggles with fierce weather and claim jumpers, they also had to contend with prairie fires and insects. In 1872, Jackson residents fought a raging prairie fire to the outskirts of town, barely saving it. A year later, grasshoppers destroyed the crops and continued to plague the settlers for the next several years.

Today, Jackson is a city with a population of 3,797, nestled between two ridges of hills on the river, just north of the Iowa-Minnesota state line. It is the county seat of Jackson County. Its proximity to both the Twin Cities and Sioux Falls, South Dakota, and its connections with major highways in four directions place it in an advantageous position for marketing, distribution, tourism and trade. Jackson is widely known for its corn, soybean and hog production and is the home of some nationally known manufacturing and processing companies, such as Ag-Chem Equipment Co., Astoria Industries, Technical Services for Electronics, Yellow Freight Systems and Pioneer Hi-Bred International, Inc.

ATTRACTIONS
JACKSON COUNTY COURTHOUSE
Fifth and Sherman streets
Jackson
(507) 847-2763

Constructed in 1908, the courthouse is a neoclassic structure embellished inside with painted murals executed by regional artists and craftsmen. The building is listed on the National Register of Historic Places. Visitors can also see collections of rock fossils and Indian relics when they enter the courthouse. Open during business hours.

JACKSON COUNTY HISTORICAL MUSEUM
307 N. Highway 86
Lakefield (10 minutes west of Jackson on Interstate 90)
(507) 662-5505

Thirty displays depicting historic settings and manuscript, book and photo libraries are part of the collection at the museum. Special events are held frequently as well. Open Memorial Day through Labor Day. The mural on the exterior wall of the museum tells of the county's past. Native animals and

PHOTO BY MICHAEL R. SCHREIER/
TRAVEL SOUTHWEST MINNESOTA

Eating

Charlie the Greek
Highway 71 and Sherman St.
Jackson
(507) 847-4726
Food and cocktails Monday through Saturday from 11 a.m. to 10 p.m. Carry-out service available.

Dick's Place
207 Sherman St.
Jackson
(507) 847-3830
This newly remodeled "home of the wild ones" serves fast food, mixed drinks and off-sale beer. Open daily.

Bob and Jan's Family Restaurant
412 Second St.
Jackson
(507) 847-3102
Located in the historic downtown district, this restaurant offers a full menu of homestyle cooking with daily noon specials. The specialty of the house is pizza, and the chicken and burgers aren't bad, either. They deliver.

plants, early transportation and architecture, and the vastness of land and water are depicted.

History of Jackson County Fair Village
Jackson County Fairgrounds on the east edge of Jackson
(507) 847-4218 or 847-3891
Several restored historic buildings have been relocated to the fairgrounds, including a log cabin built in 1866, the old District 5 schoolhouse, the Alpha depot and the Depot Hill store and hotel (all built in the 1880s). The "village" also includes furnished doctor, dentist and attorney offices, a caboose, church, farmhouse, print shop and working blacksmith shop. Visit a piece of the past from August through Labor Day.

Jackson Speedway
Jackson Fairgrounds
Box 43
Jackson, MN 56143
(507) 847-3869
(712) 362-4355

The racing season runs Memorial Day through Labor Day. Races are held every Saturday night, with warmups starting at 7:30 p.m. Enjoy the fastest half-mile around driven by some of the best drivers in all classes.

Hoxie Rathbun Dugout
Kilen Woods State Park (nine miles northeast of Lakefield) County Highway 24, five miles east of Minnesota Highway 86
(507) 847-2240
The "Ole Holthe Cabin" is a well-preserved pioneer home and the nearby dugout is the site of the first recorded death in Jackson County in 1856. Mr. Hoxie Rathbun, a mail carrier, was the victim of a winter storm.

Shopping

Santee Crossing
Interstate 90 and U.S. Highway 71
(507) 847-3841
This place offers everything: shopping, food and accommodations. The Red Barn features handcrafts, art, antiques and gifts. The Earth Inn Motel is located in the same complex, as well as Santee Crossing, which offers a complete breakfast, lunch and dinner menu and a cocktail lounge that specializes in a stress-beating Whoopee Hour Monday through Friday.

The Country Clipboard
Downtown Jackson
(507) 847-5890
The shop has an endless array of unique gifts and home decor, as well as an old-fashioned candy counter. Open Monday through Saturday.

Red Wagon Antiques and Farm Toys
308 W. Ashley
Jackson
(507) 847-4679
This shop features general antiques and farm toys, both to buy and sell. Open Tuesday through Friday or by appointment or chance.

Hurray! Minnesota

Lodging

Prairie Winds Motel
N. Highway 71
Jackson, MN 56143
(507) 847-2020
This Budget Host motel offers convenient and comfortable accommodations for the traveler.

Country Manor Inn
Highway 71 and Interstate 90, Exit 73
Jackson, MN 56143
(507) 847-3110
Located halfway between Chicago and the Black Hills, the Country Manor Inn is a Best Western with a 24-hour coffee shop, lounge, indoor pool, restaurant, tennis and golf, and banquet and meeting facilities.

▼ For More Information...

Jackson Area Chamber of Commerce
603 Third St.
Jackson, MN 56143
(507) 847-3867

Jackson County Parks Department
Box 64
Jackson, MN 56143
(507) 847-2240

Worthington

WEST OF JACKSON, the freeway runs along the division of the Des Moines River basin draining south into Iowa and the Missouri River basin draining west into the Missouri river. One of the most obvious physical features of this prairie country is a prominent ridge crossing the region north to south, just west of the Des Moines River. Glaciers deposited this ridge during the most recent ice age. In some places, its crest rises to 1,500 feet above sea level. In the vicinity of Worthington, a series of terminal moraines, or north-south valleys and ridges, mark the western extension of the Keewatin Glacier. (Terminal moraines are the rolling hills and debris formed along the edges of a glacier.) This natural phenomenon occurred during the last ice age that ended some 11,000 years ago. It was the Coteau des Prairies, or "Highland of the Prairies," that resisted any further westward glacial extension.

Worthington, county seat of Nobles, has a population of 10,234 and is known as the turkey capital of the world. It was for many years the home of **Paul Gruchow**, who has written for regional and national publications and is the author of "The Necessity of Empty Places," among other books. Nobles County was named after **William H. Nobles**, a member of the 1856 territorial legislature who advocated the construction of a road running from southern Minnesota through a pass he discovered in the Sierra Nevada mountains a few years earlier. This road would be built for the purpose of helping California immigration. Eventually, trains connected St. Paul to California through that same pass.

Worthington was settled in 1871 by the National Colony Co., a temperance group that first called their settlement Okabena, a Dakota word meaning "nesting place of herons." Liquor sales were prohibited in Okabena, but if one tried hard enough, the illegal "firewater" could still be found behind some store counters. The nearby lake is still called Okabena, but the town was renamed Worthington in honor of a founder of the National Colony Co.

In 1873, the grasshoppers made the first of several destructive raids to southwestern Minnesota. Farmers showed an average yield that year of just nine bushels per acre in wheat, oats and corn. Money was in such short supply that the local newspaper offered to take anything in trade for subscriptions, except grasshoppers. Appeals went out to the entire nation seeking relief-aid for the thousands of destitute families. When farming failed, many of the pioneers turned to trapping as a means of existence. In the winter of 1874-75, 28,000 muskrat skins were shipped from Worthington.

During the early 1900s, Worthington had a local polo team that maintained a national rating. It is also the home of the Okabena apple, developed in orchards on the southern shore of Lake Okabena, and Worthington Community College.

Today, Worthington is the major trading center in southwestern Minnesota, with turkey production a major

Eating

WORTHINGTON OFFERS residents and visitors a variety of fast food and fine dining experiences, both in and outside the malls, including: Delmonico's Steak House at 206 10th St.; Brandywine (Holiday Inn) on Highway 59 North; Gobbler by the Mall at 1861 Oxford St.; Hunan Village at 1719 East Ave.; Michael's Restaurant at 1305 Spring; Windmill Cafe at 609 Kragness; and the Panda House at 913 Fourth Avenue.

income producer. It has two major meat-processing plants (Campbell Soup Co. and Monfort) in addition to grain elevators, feed mills and related industries, among them Cargill, Inc. Many of the farms in the Worthington area are Century Farms, so-called because they have continued in the same family ownership through more than 100 years. Crop farming consists primarily of corn and soybeans, as well as wheat, oats and alfalfa. Specialty crops range from orchards to fields of sunflowers. Livestock farming and production are big industries, including dairying, beef, pork, poultry and sheep operations. Jackson, along with Nobles, is one of the top farm-income counties in Minnesota.

Attractions

Nobles County Pioneer Village

West of the Nobles County Fairgrounds
(507) 376-4431
Open daily May through September.
In 1957 the Nobles County Historical Society acquired a rural schoolhouse. That was the beginning of the preservation of several buildings and many artifacts in the "village" that are a tribute to the pioneers of old. Some of the things visitors will see here are a sod house, a blacksmith shop, a prairie house, an old fire hall, a World War I cannon, a church, a replica of Main Street circa 1900, and a plaque marking the settlement of Worthington.

Peace Avenue of Flags

Highway 59 entrance to the city.
Worthington was designated as a World Brotherhood city in 1958, with its sister city being Crailsheim, Germany. Peace Avenue seasonally flies the flags of all peaceful countries belonging to the United Nations.

King Turkey Day

In September on the second weekend following Labor Day. Turkey and the poultry industry played a significant role in Worthington's return to economic prosperity after the Depression. The festival was patterned after one held in Cuero, Texas, called the Turkey Trot, which featured (and still features) a parade of turkeys marching down the street. Worthington started King Turkey Day both to promote the poultry industry and to offer tangible thanks to farm people for their patronage. With the exception of the war years, King Turkey Day has been held annually since 1939.

A political sideshow as well as a community festival, King Turkey Day, over the years, has been the forum for speakers such as Lyndon Johnson, Nelson Rockefeller, Estes Kefauver, Richard Nixon, Adlai Stevenson, Averill Harriman, Jesse Jackson and Rudy Boschwitz. Eight Turkey Day buttons have been designed by Worthington wildlife artist **Jerry Raedeke**, who did the 50th-anniversary commemorative button in 1990. The festival includes the Great Gobbler Gallop, featuring Worthington's entry, Paycheck, running against Cuero's Ruby Begonia since 1973.

Shopping

CITY CENTER, Northland Mall and the Beltline provide locals and visitors with all the shopping opportunities they could wish. City Center has been rated by U.S. government demographers as a complete shopping center, one that satisfies the basic needs of contemporary Americans for day-to-day goods and services. Northland Mall, on Worthington's

The old depot is one of the structures preserved at Worthington's Pioneer Village.

Hurray! Minnesota

PHOTO BY MICHAEL R. SCHREIER/
TRAVEL SOUTHWEST MINNESOTA

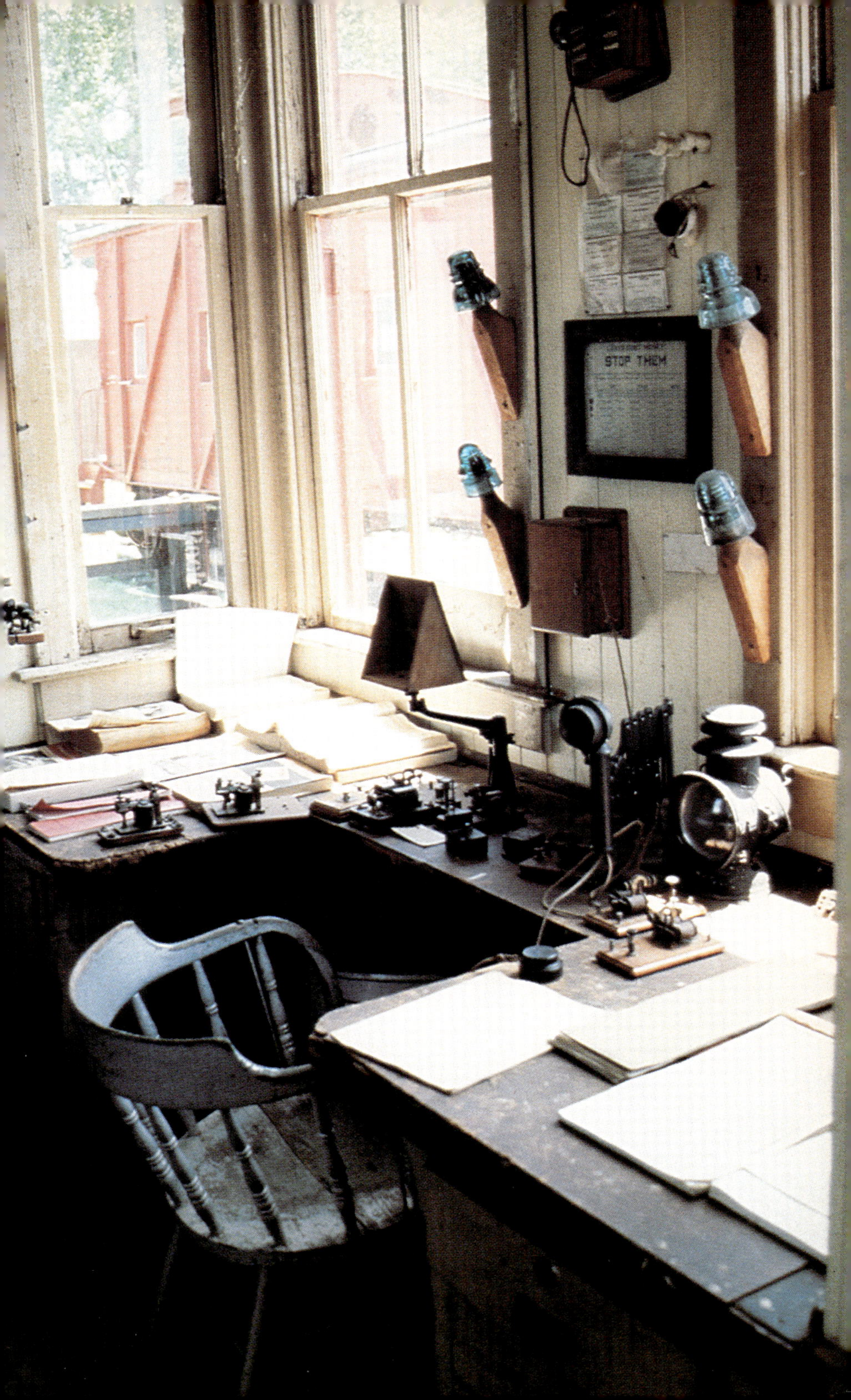
STOP THEM

Oxford Street, is a 32-acre center with two major department stores and a supermarket as well as specialty shops and movie theaters. The Beltline is a succession of retail and professional offices, shops and stores in a semicircle around the city's north, east and south edges.

Lodging
Best Western Motel
1923 Dover St.
Worthington, MN 56187
(507) 376-4146
(800) 528-1234
Waterbeds, air-conditioned rooms, color TV, free HBO and a meeting room are only part of the amenities. A lounge with entertainment and dancing is close at hand.

Budget Host
207 Oxford St.
Worthington, MN 56187
(507) 376-6155
(800) 333-3102
Economical lodging in beautiful, newly redecorated rooms with color cable TV and free HBO is what visitors find here. Family rooms are available.

Holiday Inn
2015 Humiston Ave.
Worthington, MN 56187
(507) 372-2991
(800) HOLIDAY
A hotel/convention center with indoor pool, whirlpool, restaurant, cocktail lounge, banquet and meeting rooms are all part of the facilities.

Oxford Motel
1801 Oxford St.
Worthington, MN 56187
(507) 376-6126
This motel offers economical lodging in comfortable rooms with color TV with free cable and HBO. Truck parking is available, and the motel is located close to a shopping center, restaurants and lounge entertainment.

▼ For More Information...
Worthington Convention and Visitors Bureau
1018 Fourth Ave.
Box 608
Worthington, MN 56187
(507) 372-2919

Pipestone

Less than a mile north of the city of Pipestone lies a quarry, described in Native American legends as a square-cut jewel lying upon folds of shimmering green velvet. This is a literal description of the red quartzite almost hidden by the vast prairie grasses. Designated a national monument by the United States in 1937, the quarry is as rich in Native American history as it is in the red stone for which it is named.

Pipestone National Monument is located on the west slope of a high plateau that French explorers called Coteau des Prairies — the dividing ridge between the Mississippi and Missouri rivers. To the east of the square-mile area lies a red quartzite ledge; to the south, an outcropping of flat red rock. Pipestone Creek and Lake Hiawatha border the northern edge, and to the west lies a thin line of upturned earth and rock.

Visitors to Pipestone National Monument can see Spotted Pipe Quarry, an active quarry named for the light-colored spots that speckle the pipestone; Nicollet Marker, where the names chiseled by members of Nicollet's 1838 expedition are still visible; Leaping Rock, a place where young braves, to prove their valor, leaped across a chasm and placed an arrow in the crack atop Leaping Rock; Quartzite Ledge, a point at which the layer of pipestone is more than 100 feet below the surface; and the Three Maidens, large granite boulders probably carried by the glacier to this spot as one huge boulder 50 to 60 feet in diameter. Legend has it that the spirits of the maidens who disappeared under the boulders for shelter remained to guard the quarry.

The pipestone originated, according to Lakota oral tradition, when the Great Spirit sent floods to cleanse the earth, and red pipestone — the blood of their ancestors — was all that remained. After the flood, the Great Spirit gave the Lakota a pipe carved from red stone, which was to be used only for religious and ceremonial purposes.

Another account was recorded by author/artist **George Catlin** during his vis-

Hurray! Minnesota

Blue Mound State Park: A home where the buffalo roam.

LUVERNE

RELIVE A PART of the American heritage that included a time when huge herds of bison roamed the prairie. Seven miles north of Luverne, on the Rock River in the southwest corner of the state, **Blue Mound State Park** is home to a herd of about 50 buffalo that graze in a large, fenced-off grasslands area. Naturalist-guided tours on a specially designed pickup truck take visitors out to the buffalo herd, and the park also has four miles of trails. The park took its name from the massive bluff of red quartzite that is flecked with blue from weathering. Early explorers such as Nicollet could see this bluff for miles on the level horizon and used it to guide their travels. Indians drove herds of buffalo over the bluff to obtain food and hides. It was also in these hills that **Jesse** and **Frank James** hid after their raid on Northfield in 1876 failed and the rest of their gang had been captured in a marsh northwest of Madelia. (507) 283-4892.

Luverne is also the home of writer/ naturalist **Frederick Manfred**, author of numerous books about the region.

it to the quarry in 1836:

At an ancient time the Great Spirit, in the form of a large bird, stood upon the wall of rock and called all the tribes around him, and breaking out a piece of the red stone formed it into a pipe and smoked it. He then told his red children that this stone was their flesh, that they were made from it, that they must all smoke to him through it, that they must use it for nothing but pipes; and as it belonged alike to all the tribes, the ground was sacred and no weapons must be used or brought upon it.

Catlin's writings about Native American activities at the quarry, as well as his paintings, inspired author **Henry Wadsworth Longfellow** to include the sacred quarry in his poem "The Song of Hiawatha," written in 1855.

According to geologists, pipestone was formed when a stream system deposited layer upon layer of sand and other sediment. The sand was eventually compressed into sandstone, and the red clay under it into clay stone. Some sediment was removed by one of the four glaciers that traveled through the area and scraped the land down to the sandstone. Under the weight of the glaciers and with extremely high temperatures, the sandstone became quartzite and the red clay sediment turned into pipestone.

Outcroppings of pipestone are also found in Montana, Arizona, Kansas, South Dakota, Wisconsin and Ohio.

Winnewissa Falls glistens in the spring sunlight at Pipestone National Monument.

Pieces of pipestone from Minnesota's quarry have been found in burial mounds in many different sections of North America, leading historians to believe that various tribes journeyed thousands of miles to quarry here. Catlin records that as Indian nations believed the ground was sacred, strict peace was observed in the vicinity.

Native Americans smoked "kinnikinnick," a mixture of dried leaves, bark and tobacco, ceremoniously: when rallying for warfare, when trading goods or hostages, during ritual dances, when signing treaties and during medicine ceremonies. The pipes became widely known as peace pipes because whites only encountered them at treaty ceremonies.

There were as many variations in pipe design as there were makers. By the time Catlin arrived at the quarry, the simple tubes of earlier times had developed into elbow and disk forms, as well as elaborate animal and human effigies. The Pawnee and Sioux were master effigy carvers. A popular pipe form was the T-shaped calumet, which was the type most often seen at treaty ceremonies.

Not long after the first white men visited the quarries — **Philander Prescott** in 1831, Catlin, and **Joseph Nicollet**, a French scientist sent by the U.S. government to map the area in 1838 — the decades-long struggle of the U.S. government to gain control of this territory began. In 1851, the federal government offered $15,000 to resident Native Americans for the title to all of their Minnesota lands, which included most of southern Minnesota. The Sisseton and Wahpeton bands ceded their lands, including the pipestone quarry, in the Traverse des Sioux treaty.

Charles Bennett, a druggist from Le Mars, Iowa, traveled to the pipestone quarry in 1873 with a party of four others and decided it would be an ideal place to establish a town. He built a five-foot-tall building with lumber hauled from Luverne and moved to Pipestone permanently in 1875. A grasshopper plague in 1876 drove some of the new residents away, but Bennett and a few others stayed on and platted the town of Pipestone. By 1878, Pipestone was a small but thriving trade center, and Bennett was instrumental in bringing both the railroad and a firm of English realtors to the area. In 1883, architect **Wallace Dow** began using the local quartzite for exterior building block material, and more than 30 commercial structures were built with quartzite within a year. Stone block products were sold to cities as far away as Chicago, and the quarry flourished as an important early industry.

Today, Pipestone's biggest draw may be its annual presentation of the **Song of Hiawatha Pageant**, based on Longfellow's poem, held July 17 through 19, 24 through 26, and July 31 through August 2. Members of the community began performing the pageant in 1949; they chose the land near the quarry entrance as a stage. Today, the stage has quadrupled in

Hurray! Minnesota

PHOTO BY CONNIE WANNER

size to a 5,000-seat amphitheater complete with stereophonic equipment. The 200-member cast consists of local men, women and children who donate their summer months to rehearse and perform the pageant.

Pipestone's "other" summer happening is the **Water Tower Park Festival**, which celebrates one of only a few cement water towers in the world. Built in 1921, the water tower was recently restored. Pipestone also hosts the **Civil War Days Festival**. The county's Civil War Roundtable Society, members of whom appeared in the opening of "Dances With Wolves," sponsors the event, which marks the 105th anniversary of an encampment of war veterans in Pipestone. The festival will feature dozens of Civil War re-enactors, battle scenarios, food booths, historic site tours and a luncheon for descendants of people who played a part in the Civil War.

The Calumet Hotel was first built one block north of its present site and was destroyed by fire in 1886. The present Calumet opened in 1888 as part of a new bank. In 1900 an addition was built on to the rear and by 1913 a fourth floor and 30 rooms were added. The hotel was restored to its former grandeur in 1979, and it now has 38 guest rooms and a lounge in what used to be the bank. The Calumet also features a dining room, pub, meeting room, board room, ice cream shop and gift shop. At Christmastime, the Calumet Hotel hosts the **Festival of Trees**.

The Calumet anchors Pipestone's historic district, which encompasses about a dozen blocks of downtown. The historic buildings are all in use and their rich architecture bears the hallmark of red quartzite exteriors. Visitors can see: the Moore Block, built in 1896, a building adorned by gargoyle heads carved in sandstone by sculptor and contractor **Leo H. Moore**, who also designed Soldier's Memorial, located on the courthouse grounds and dedicated in 1901 to veterans of the Civil and Spanish-American wars; Syndicate Block, an Italianate-

A Dutch windmill near Edgerton catches the breeze in Pipestone County.

style building that is the oldest in the district, built in 1884, featuring a ceremonial pipe crossed with bow and arrow; the Courthouse, built in 1900 in Richardson Romanesque-style and designed by **George Pass**; and Old City Hall, now the home of the Pipestone County Museum, which served as the city hall from 1896 to 1960. The museum is divided into interpretive galleries with displays that include George Catlin paintings, a Native American exhibit, a military room and pioneer lifestyles in several period settings.

Visitors to Pipestone for the pageant and festivals or to tour the town and quarry will find many places to browse for antiques and mementos and can find food and lodging at several places in the area. The Calumet (507) 825-5871 or (800) 535-7610, in addition to its ambience, offers an entertainment season of dinner concerts and special events. One of the packages offered by the inn is the Calumet and **Royal River**

Casino Junket, which takes guests to the casino 18 miles away in Flandreau, South Dakota, to play blackjack, slot machines and bingo. Call for information.

▼ For More Information...
Pipestone Area Chamber of Commerce Convention and Visitors Bureau
117 S.E. Eighth Ave., Box 8
Pipestone, MN 56164
(507) 825-3316

Marshall

Marshall became the county seat of Lyon County in 1873 and is the oldest existing town in the county. Like many other towns in southwestern Minnesota, Marshall grew up near what had been a gathering place and residence of Native Americans. The big bend of the Redwood River had been a spot often used by the Indians to make their camps while hunting or waging war. Trails extended from the spot in four directions: north to Lac qui Parle; south to the Cottonwood River country and Lake Shetek; southwest up the Redwood River to the Lynd woods and the Pipestone quarries; and northeast down the Redwood River to the present site of Redwood Falls and the Minnesota River.

The first white land claimants were **C.H. Whitney** and **C.H. Upton** in 1869. But Marshall, unlike many prairie towns, was the creation of railroad enterprise. The building of this section in 1872 of the Winona and St. Peter Railroad secured the expectation that a city would grow up in the bend of the Redwood River.

Marshall is an agricultural community, producing beef, pork and poultry for world markets, as well as corn, soybeans and grain crops. National leaders in food and agricultural product processing, such as Heartland Foods, Schwan's Sales Enterprises, Minnesota Corn Processors, Pepper's Pride Pet Foods and Ralco Products began in Marshall. Southwest State University, one of the seven institutions that comprise the Minnesota State University System, is located here. The town also is home to the Marshall Men's Chorus, the Marshall Municipal Band and the Southwest Minnesota Orchestra. And two well-known Minnesota artists hail from the windswept prairie country surrounding Marshall: Cottonwood is the home of humorist/writer **Howard Mohr**, author of "How to Talk Minnesotan"; and Minneota is the home of writer/musician/teacher Bill Holm, author of "Boxelder Bug Variations" and "Coming Home Crazy: An Alphabet of China Essays."

One of the country's newest industries has a home base in Marshall: **Minnesota Windpower, Inc.**, a wind farm inaugurated by Dan Juhl and his partner, Lars Olsen, to harness the hot, dry, constant winds that sweep the area and that used to drive early settlers to despair. Juhl's farm is the first one in Minnesota; his five generators can create enough electricity to power 200 homes per year and produce a clean, renewable source of energy that may spark a new industry in the state. Minnesota Windpower, Inc. is negotiating to build 250 generators on Buffalo Ridge in southwestern Minnesota and will produce 50 megawatts of electricity (almost one-third the output of NSP's Black Dog 4 coal-burning plant). Studies have shown that the winds on Buffalo Ridge alone could provide 20 percent of the state's electrical power.

Attractions
Lyon County Historical Museum
607 W. Main
Lyon County Courthouse, Marshall
The museum displays include an original 1892 courtroom that is intact, Indian artifacts, county history, pioneer kitchen and parlor, rural school exhibit and a research library. Open Monday through Friday during business hours. Closed in January.

Natural Science Museum
Southwest State University campus
(507) 537-6178 or 537-7110
The museum records the history of southwestern Minnesota and features exhibits on flora and fauna of the area.

William Whipple Art Gallery
Southwest State University campus
(507) 537-7110
The gallery displays art in a wide variety of media and styles by international, national and regional artists.

Hurray! Minnesota

Eating

Aunt Nellie's
1104 E. Main St.
Marshall
(507) 537-1439
An American cafe with country/antique atmosphere, Aunt Nellie's specializes in country food made from scratch, especially charbroiled steaks and burgers, ribs, chops, chicken and fish followed by homemade desserts. Open for breakfast, lunch and dinner. Mexican food is served on Thursdays. A buffet is served on Sundays.

Camden Country Inn
Junction Highway 19 and 23
Marshall
(507) 532-3221
This restaurant features fine dining with hometown hospitality. Featuring a Sunday champagne brunch ending at 1:30 p.m. Open for breakfast, lunch and dinner Monday through Saturday.

Hunan Lion
236 W. Main
Marshall
(507) 532-9733
This restaurant serves Chinese, Hunan Szechuan and Cantonese food. Open daily for lunch and dinner.

Foxfire
1407 E. College Drive
Marshall
(507) 532-7330
Featuring lunches and dinners, dancing and live music. Happy hours Monday through Friday.

Southwest State Historical Center
Southwest State University campus
(507) 537-7373
This regional research center houses the Prairieland Genealogical Society. Collections found at the center include regional census records from 1865, newspapers from 1875, family, church, town and oral histories and photograph collections.

Shopping

DOWNTOWN MARSHALL features specialty shops in a beautiful park-like setting. The Marshall Square Mall offers shoppers a complete line of specialty shops, personal service providers and diverse stores. On Marshall's arterial streets, you'll find stores with even more variety.

Lodging

Best Western–Marshall Inn
East College Drive
Marshall, MN 56258
(507) 532-3221
(800) 422-0897
The inn offers guests a choice of 100 rooms and three suites, with dining and lounge facilities.

El Rancho Motel
South Highway 23
Marshall, MN 56258
(507) 532-3203
The motel provides 13 rooms, three with kitchenettes, and free HBO.

Traveler's Lodge Motel
1425 E. College Drive
Marshall, MN 56258
(507) 532-5721
A choice of 90 rooms awaits visitors. The motel is adjacent to dining and lounge facilities, the university and Marshall Square Mall. Complimentary coffee and doughnuts. A conference room is available.

Comfort Inn
1511 E. College Drive
Marshall, MN 56258
(507) 532-3070
(800) 228-5150
This inn offers a free continental breakfast, waterbeds, cable TV, queen-size beds, a whirlpool suite, outside plug-ins and truck parking.

▼ For More Information...

Marshall Convention and Visitors Bureau
501 W. Main St.
Marshall, MN 56258
(507) 537-1865

Granite Falls

GRANITE FALLS HAS a population of 3,000. It is the county seat for **Yellow Medicine County** and has been nicknamed "Scenic City in the Valley."

Granite Falls lays claim to the oldest rock in the world. Granite outcroppings have been dated to between 2.65 and 3.65 billion years old. This does, of course, give solid footing to the town's name. The falls were created by the Minnesota River cutting a beautiful pathway through the area that was to be downtown and tumbling over a 38-foot falls. Today that falls has been turned into a dam with a beautiful park.

Near Granite Falls also was found, in 1989, the oldest archeological site in the state, dating to more than 8,000 years ago. The archeologists believe it was the site of a huge bison barbecue. They have estimated that some of the bison weighed more than 2,000 pounds.

ATTRACTIONS
MINNESOTA RIVER
The state has designated the Minnesota River as a scenic and recreational river. There are marked portages, rustic campgrounds and picnic areas along the 9.5 miles that wind through Granite Falls. The unique scenery includes light rapids and awesome granite outcroppings.

WESTERN FEST AND RODEO
Lee-Mar Ranch
Highway 212
Granite Falls
(612) 564-4039
Held at the end of June, the Fest has a smorgasbord of events that include a professional rodeo with calf roping, steer wrestling and the family favorites, the rodeo clowns. There also are street dances, beer gardens, flea markets, craft shows and a kids' fishing contest.

UPPER SIOUX AGENCY STATE PARK
Route 2, Box 92
Highway 67
Granite Falls, MN 56241
(612) 564-4777
In the mid-1800s, the government initiated a plan to teach the Indians to farm and incorporate them into the mainstream culture. The Upper Sioux Agency was part of that plan. The plan ended in disaster when the government, financially strapped and embroiled in the Civil War, failed to make good its promise of support. As the Indians starved, their resentment grew and the troubles between the federal government and the Sioux multiplied until the war known as the U.S.-Dakota Conflict broke out.

Today, the site houses an interpretive center presenting the history of the agency and a touch-and-see room as part of the natural history exhibit. The 1,100-acre park has canoeing, camping and miles of recreational trails.

Possible sites of Dakota burial mounds are often found on the edge of fields such as this one near the Upper Sioux Agency State Park.

BLUE DEVIL PRESERVE
Highway 67
Granite Falls
In this nature conservancy along the Minnesota River, you can find among the ancient granite outcroppings a five-lined skink. (No, it's not a misspelling of skunk.) The skink is a rare protected amphibian that lives in the cracks and crevices of the rock. The short hike takes you through woodland and prairies abounding with many rare plant species.

ANDREW VOLSTEAD HOUSE
163 S. Ninth Ave.
Granite Falls
(612) 564-3011
The Honorable **Andrew J. Volstead** was elected to the House of Representatives in 1912 and served until his retirement in 1923. In 1919 he permitted his name to be attached to a bill that provided the means of enforcement for the Wartime Prohibition Act. It passed both houses over President Wilson's veto. The Wartime

Prohibition Act prohibited the manufacture, use of materials and distribution of any alcoholic product containing more than .5 percent alcohol in volume.

Though he was a crusading prohibitionist, his lasting legacy was the work he did for the farmer: He wrote and championed the Capper-Volstead act, which permitted farmers to form cooperatives for the sale of their produce.

Volstead attended St. Olaf College and Decorah Institute for Law. He moved to Granite Falls in 1886. He served as city attorney, mayor of Granite Falls, and prosecuting attorney for Yellow Medicine County for 14 years. He had a reputation for impartial enforcement of the law. The restored home of Andrew Volstead is now a museum shown by appointment and also houses the Southwest Minnesota Initiative fund.

YELLOW MEDICINE COUNTY MUSEUM
Highways 23 and 67
Granite Falls
(612) 564-4479
The museum has a representative display of county pioneer and Indian artifacts. But what makes this museum really worth the visit is the display of ancient, exposed rock. Geologists have identified it as among the oldest in the world, placing it somewhere around 3.6 billion years of age.

FIREFLY CREEK CASINO
Highway 67 E.
Granite Falls
(612) 564-2121
(800) 232-1439
This casino is operated by the Upper Sioux Community. It has blackjack, video slot machines and pull tabs. The Firefly Creek Restaurant and Cafe has short-order menu items, full service dining and buffets Monday through Wednesday.

EATING

NINETY-FIFTH CLUB
Highway 212
Granite Falls
(612) 564-4003
This supper club serves excellent steaks, prime rib and walleye. They have full-service cocktails and the capacity to host large parties of up to 400.

FIREFLY CREEK CASINO
Upper Sioux Community

FEEL THE SPIRIT ◆ LIVE THE EXCITEMENT

OPEN DAILY
MON-THURS 10 AM-2 AM
FRI-SUN 24 HOURS

LIVE BLACKJACK
Hundreds of VIDEO SLOTS
PULL TABS ◆ RESTAURANT
SMOKE and GIFT SHOP

Next door to campgrounds, golf course and state park.
5 miles SE of GF on Hwy 67E

1 (800) 232-1439
(612) 564-2121
E. Hwy. 67, Granite Falls, MN 56241

Hurray! Minnesota

Chippewa City Pioneer Village on the edge of Montevideo.

THE FALLS RESTAURANT
Downtown Granite Falls
(612) 564-3880
Across the street from the walking bridge that crosses the Minnesota River to Rice Park is a cafe that serves homemade meals. The Falls serves breakfast and lunch specials and all homemade desserts, such as bread puddings, cobblers and pies.

WEDGEWOOD DINING AND LOUNGE
Highway 67
Granite Falls
(612) 564-4141
This restaurant has beautiful views from the lounge and dining room overlooking the eighth and ninth greens of the Granite Falls Golf Course. Wedgewood serves everything from burgers to prime rib, with the largest selection of seafood in the area. Open for lunch and dinner seven days a week.

DETOY'S FAMILY RESTAURANT
844 Highway 212 W.
Granite Falls
(612) 564-2280
This family restaurant, right next door to the new Super 8, serves a broasted chicken that has been marinated for sixteen hours and is unbelievably good. The beer-battered walleye is light and flavorful. (Only cholesterol-free oil is used to fry foods.) A particular favorite is a really tasty lasagna. Breakfast is served any time.

▼ **FOR MORE INFORMATION...**
GRANITE FALLS AREA CHAMBER OF COMMERCE
Box 220 A
Granite Falls, MN 56241
(612) 564-4039

MONTEVIDEO

MONTEVIDEO, the capital of Uruguay, was the inspiration to **Cornelius Nelson** when he platted this town and gave it its name. It is a very appropriate name, since the view of the twin valleys of the Minnesota and Chippewa rivers is truly a "mountain of vision."

The town has expanded the relationship with Uruguay over the past 50 years, trading delegates and tokens of goodwill. These tokens include the statue of **Jose Artigas**, which dominates the town square. To complement the atmosphere set by the statue, the town has added seating, lighting and festive music. Also in adhering to the Spanish theme, Montevideo hosts Fiesta Days in June.

ATTRACTIONS
CHIPPEWA CITY PIONEER VILLAGE
Highways 7 and 59
Montevideo
(612) 296-7636
The village is located on the edge of Montevideo. It began with a schoolhouse in 1965 and today there are 23 buildings

The bell tower of the reconstructed mission church at Lac qui Parle Mission. Exhibits within the church recall the missionaries' work with the Dakota.

connected by wooden sidewalks. All have been authentically restored right down to the furnishings and decorations, which include such things as twisted prairie grass logs once used for fuel by the pioneers.

OLOF SWENSSON FARM
Chippewa County 6
Montevideo
(612) 269-7636
The farm is operated by the historical society and includes 67 acres, a barn, a 22-room house, grist mill and farm equipment. It is an excellent example of the hard work and self-sufficiency displayed by the early settlers. Open Sunday afternoons in the summer.

LAC QUI PARLE MISSION
County Highway 13
Montevideo
(612) 269-7636
A replica chapel stands on the site of the original chapel, which was the second church established in the state. The mission operated from 1835 to 1854. There is a marked walking path to tour the area where the Protestant missionary families lived. The chapel houses artifacts and memorabilia of the missionaries and the school.

LAC QUI PARLE STATE PARK
Route 5, Box 74A
Montevideo, MN 56265
(612) 752-4736
The translation of the name of this park is "the lake that speaks." The park is five miles northwest of Watson off Highway 59 at the southeast end of Lac qui Parle Lake. The lake is home to thousands of birds, particularly waterfowl. There are facilities for camping and swimming and trails for hiking and horseback riding.

Marsh Lake, an impoundment on the

Madison

LUTEFISK CAPITAL U.S.A
Lou T. Fisk, the 24-foot cod, resides in one of Madison's six parks. Madison, Lutefisk Capital U.S.A., is located just west of the Lac qui Parle State Park and is the county seat for Lac qui Parle County.

Minnesota River near Appleton, is part of the Lac qui Parle Wildlife Sanctuary. On an island and peninsula in Marsh Lake are two of Minnesota's three breeding colonies of American white pelicans. The pelicans, which breed in ground nests, have produced upwards of 5,000 offspring annually at the Marsh Lake sites.

In the middle of June when the young are a couple weeks old, approximately six to 10 people head out to the island very early in the morning to band the new pelicans. The colony has been so healthy the past few years that they usually run out of bands before they do baby pelicans.

When the humans land on the island, the adult pelicans leave their young, making the job of banding the pelicans relatively easy. However, banding these little birds does get to be a bit unpleasant, particularly as the day warms up, since the little pelicans tend to toss up their fishy breakfast when they become frightened.

There are usually two birds in a nest with a maximum of four. The baby pelicans cannot really be described as cute. In fact, they are more the kind of child that only a mother could love. About a month after they're born, they begin swimming and looking for food on their own.

You'll see non-breeding pelicans anywhere in the state but most often in the agriculture region. They prefer shallower lakes where it is easier for them to find food. Pelicans primarily winter in the Gulf of Mexico area.

▼ **FOR MORE INFORMATION...**
MONTEVIDEO CHAMBER OF COMMERCE
Artigas Plaza
Montevideo, MN 56265
(612) 269-5527

American white pelicans on the wing.

ORTONVILLE

ATTRACTIONS
BIG STONE LAKE STATE PARK
Route 1, Box 153
Ortonville, MN 56278
(612) 839-3663
The park, located off Highway 7 just north of Ortonville, has more than 1,000 acres. There are only 10 rustic campsites that are right on the lake. The sites are often open during the week, but you should book ahead for the weekends. Walleye fishing on Big Stone Lake, which is 26 miles long, is reputed to be among the best in the state.

BIG STONE NATIONAL WILDLIFE REFUGE
25 N.W. Second St.
Ortonville, MN 56278
(612) 839-3700
Located on the Minnesota River, on Highway 7 south of Ortonville, is a wildlife refuge in a sea of agriculture. This is a prairie refuge, as opposed to a forest refuge, which is what the majority of the refuges around the state are. When completed, there will be 14,000 acres: 4,000 acres of marsh and water, 800-1,000 acres of flood plain forest, 100 acres of granite outcrop and the rest in domestic prairies and seeded native grasslands.

When you follow the hiking trails or the self-guided car route, you can see tall grass prairie birds, prairie wildlife, woodland wildlife and waterfowl.

LITTLE CROW LAKE REGION
Kandiyohi County and the cities of Willmar, Spicer and New London are sometimes referred to as the Little Crow Lake Region. In this area is the Little Crow River and 361 lakes that were carved out by the glaciers. Of these pristine lakes, 10 have resorts or camping accommodations. The Department of Natural Resources also maintains public access to many of the others.

GLACIAL RIDGE TRAIL
Kandiyohi County
This is a driving tour following hard-surface and graded roads through Kandiyohi County. The route is scenic, and historically significant sites are marked.

GLACIAL LAKES TRAIL
Kandiyohi County
This is a gravel-base trail along the old railroad roadbeds. It travels from Willmar through Spicer and New London to Hawick. It is great for biking, horseback riding or hiking and is groomed for snowmobiling in the winter.

WILLMAR

BUILT ON THE banks of two lakes, Willmar was founded by **Leon Willmar**, a Belgian who obtained the bond title for the section when the railroad was built. Willmar was established as the county seat for Kandiyohi County in 1871 and incorporated as a city in 1901.

Agriculture forms the base of the city's economic life. Industries such as Jennie-O Foods, Supersweet Feeds and ASI-AGRI Products employ a large number of the 18,000 people living in Willmar.

Along with agriculture, tourism is beginning to play a larger role in the city's economy. Willmar, in the heart of the Little Crow Lakes region, acts as the recreational hub for the many lakes in the area.

ATTRACTIONS

KANDIYOHI COUNTY MUSEUM
610 Highway 71 N.E.
Willmar
(612) 235-1881
The museum has an extensive collection of county artifacts. Most impressive is Locomotive 2523, which is right out front. Also on the museum grounds is the restored **Sperry House**. The house looks just as it did when it was built in 1893.

BARN THEATRE
321 W. Fourth St.
Willmar
(612) 235-9500
In 1965 the community of Willmar, under the guidance of a local doctor and many of the local businesses, worked together to convert a donated barn into a theater. Today the community theater group has new digs in downtown Willmar, but it is still a community-supported operation. There are six productions during the year and a children's theater workshop.

SHOPPING

THE HOUSE OF JACOBS
421 W. Litchfield Ave.
Willmar
(612) 235-2191

The Great Northern steam locomotive #2523 stands impressively out front of the Kandiyohi County Museum.

In reflection of the heritage of the area, this shop has authentic Scandinavian gift items. But the real reason to stop is that they make the "world's best lefse."

EATING

T. J. WEBER'S
1108 N. Highway 71
Willmar
(612) 235-3402
There are five beautiful dining rooms, three with fireplaces. Weber's specializes in steaks and seafood, or you can choose your own live lobster. For those with a light appetite, there are juicy burgers, sandwiches and finger foods available.

MCMILLAN'S
2620 S. Highway 71
Willmar
(612) 235-7213
McMillan's is open 24 hours a day. Homemade pastries, soups and fresh pies daily are a treat for the whole family.

Sonshine Christian music festival at the Civic Center in Willmar.

SONSHINE
Box 1444
Willmar
(612) 235-7593

More than 10,000 people attend this outdoor Christian music festival held in early July. Music groups from all over the nation perform beginning at 3 p.m. on a Friday and continuing through Saturday evening. The festival is held on the grounds of the Civic Center and camping is available.

SIMON'S
500 S.E. 19th St.
Willmar
(612) 235-9190

Simon's is a place for fun along with a family restaurant, which often features a buffet at lunch and dinner. There is a lounge with DJ, bowling lanes, and an upstairs ballroom that seats up to 1,200 people for special events.

LODGING

HOLIDAY INN–WILLMAR CONFERENCE CENTER
E. Highway 12
Willmar, MN 56201
(612) 235-6060

There is an indoor pool, sauna and whirlpool for use by guests in the 159 rooms. There also is a game room and **Torge's** lounge, which features live entertainment playing the top 40 every night except Sunday. The **Hardanger**, a traditional fine dining restaurant, is open for breakfast, lunch and dinner.

WILLMAR AMERICINN MOTEL
2404 E. Highway 12
Willmar, MN 56201
(612) 231-1962
(800) 634-3444

AmericInn has 30 rooms, an indoor pool, whirlpool and sauna. They also serve a free continental breakfast.

▼ FOR MORE INFORMATION...
WILLMAR AREA CHAMBER OF COMMERCE OR WILLMAR CONVENTION AND VISITORS BUREAU
518 W. Litchfield
Willmar, MN 56201
(612) 235-0300
(800) 845-TRIP

Hurray! Minnesota

SPICER

SHOPPING

MINNESOTA COUNTRY
12011 Highway 71 N.E.
Spicer
(612) 796-2199
You'll find a nice collection of country crafts and hand-crafted original items here. To complement the rustic look of your home or lake cabin, Minnesota Country sells well-made country pine furniture. Open daily all year.

EATING

LITTLE MELVIN'S ON THE LAKE
Spicer
(612) 796-2195
Melvin's is located on the south shore of Green Lake; you can come by boat or by car. On a sunny day, you'll run into a number of friends at Melvin's outdoor grill and bar.

LODGING

SPICER CASTLE BED AND BREAKFAST
11600 Indian Beach Road
Spicer, MN 56288
(612) 796-5243

John Spicer built this elegant Tudor home in 1893, and his grandson, the current owner, lived in it during the summers when he was a boy. The house has been faithfully preserved, because Spicer's grandson says his mother wouldn't let him change a thing. The house is on the National Register of Historic Places and a landmark to locals on Green Lake. There are four guest rooms plus two guest cottages. The home sits peacefully surrounded by trees, and it overlooks the lake. Guests have private baths and are served a full breakfast and afternoon tea.

INDIAN BEACH RESORT
Box VG92
Spicer, MN 56288
(612) 796-5616
Look for the teepee at this resort on Green Lake, which is designed to entertain the whole family. The 23 one- to four-bedroom housekeeping cottages are situated around a sheltered harbor. Bring your own boat, since there's a lot of dock space, or rent the watercraft of your choice. There's a sandy beach with a water playground and water recreational equipment. The resort center has a game room, lounge and convenience center. There is even a Frisbee golf course. During the summer, a barbecue is held once a week for the guests and includes a scavenger hunt for the kids. On fall weekends, special events are planned, such as an Oktoberfest weekend or fishing weekend.

▼ FOR MORE INFORMATION...

SPICER COMMERCIAL CLUB
(612) 796-0066

New London

Attractions

Sibley State Park
800 Sibley Park Road N.E.
New London, MN 56273
(612) 354-2055
This park of 2,400 acres is covered with virgin hardwoods and has a mile-long sandy shore on Lake Andrew. There are 138 campsites along with a complete trail system for everyone from hikers and horses to skiers and snowmobilers. Nature programs are conducted almost every weekend at the Interpretive Center all year long.

You can see why Mount Tom, located within the park, was a lookout point for the Dakota Indians. From the top, at 190 feet, you can see for miles.

Antique Car Run
New London
The run travels 120 miles from New London to New Brighton. It is patterned after the London-to-Brighton tour in England, which was first run in 1896 and is still being held. The Minnesota run is held at the end of August and features pre-1908 or one- and two-cylinder vehicles. The start is at 7 a.m. in New London, and the race usually takes all day since many of the vehicles travel not much over 18 miles per hour. Other activities surrounding the event include a vintage-clothes contest, steak fry, ski show and street parade.

Little Crow Water Ski Shows
Near Park
New London
The Little Crow Ski Club, a group of professional skiers from the region, puts on shows every Friday at 7:30 p.m. in June and July and 7 p.m. in August. Other shows and tournaments are held on weekends throughout the summer months.

Litchfield

LITCHFIELD IS ON Lake Ripley, one of the 100 lakes in tiny Meeker County. If you ever wanted to live in a Mayberry-type town, Litchfield is it. On a hot summer day, as the locusts buzz away, you can really hear corn growing in the surrounding fields and bass jumping in Lake Ripley. Or so the natives say.

But don't let that fool you: The town is a hive of small industries, such as **Fieldgate Cheese**; **Litchfield Woolens**, manufacturer of Jack Pine blankets and other woolen products; **Forest Time Products**, which produces those darling wood reindeer made from sticks and logs that you've seen around Minnesota; and **B. Lease and Sons, Inc.**, manufacturer of decorator wood products.

Attractions

Grand Army of the Republic Hall
Central Park
Litchfield
(612) 693-8911
This fortress was built in 1885 to commemorate the Civil War Union soldiers. If the light is right, look up at the round window at the very top of the hall. Etched in the glass window is a likeness of Abraham Lincoln. The Meeker County Museum is loaded with county history and is adjacent to the Civil War museum. There also is an exhibit of books and pictures of the late Dr. William Nolan, author of "Surgeon Under the Knife" and other books, who lived in Litchfield.

International Peanut Butter and Milk Festival
Litchfield
In an ingenious exchange of goodwill between industries and towns, Litchfield invites a delegation from the peanut industry and the Peanut Queen of Dothan, Alabama, to Litchfield in February for a banquet and weekend of winter fun. This weekend has been dubbed the Peanut Butter and Milk Festival. In exchange, Litchfield sends a delegation from the milk industry and the Dairy Princess to Alabama for its festival in the summer.

Birdwing Spa
21389 575th Ave.
Litchfield
(612) 693-6064
Birdwing is the only full-service European spa in the state of Minnesota. People from all over the world have repeatedly come to this intimate facility

Hurray! Minnesota

A wildlife refuge in a sea of agriculture: the river terrace prairie at Big Stone Wildlife Refuge.

known for its individual attention and pampering and for the beautiful natural surroundings of scenic countryside with two-and-one-half miles of private lakeshore.

SHOPPING
MAGOON'S OLD FASHIONED TOY CO.
25067 628th Ave.
Litchfield
(612) 693-7337
The Magoons really are Santa's helpers. They have their own workshop here in Litchfield making little desks, rocking horses and toys for little girls and boys.

EATING
PARKVIEW LUNCH
311 N. Sibley
Litchfield
(612) 693-8168

In Parkview you will experience real hamburgers where real meat has been molded into patties by hand and not by machine. They also have milkshakes served in metal containers, just like at the old corner drugstore.

MAIN STREET CAFE
226 N. Sibley
Litchfield
(612) 693-9067
Pictures of Litchfield in the early days adorn the walls. The cafe serves such specialties as Norwegian meatballs. Open for breakfast, lunch and dinner. Featuring good home cooking.

▼ FOR MORE INFORMATION...
LITCHFIELD CHAMBER OF COMMERCE
219 N. Sibley Ave.
Litchfield, MN 55355
(612) 693-8184

• ST. VINCENT • HUMBOLDT • HALLOCK • KENNEDY • DONALDSON •

• FARGO/MOORHEAD • CROOKSTON • EAST GRAND FORKS • THIEF RIVER FALLS • ARGYLE • LAKE BRONSON •

THE RECORD CATFISH OF THE RED RIVER ATTRACT FISHERMEN FROM AROUND NORTH AMERICA.

PHOTO COURTESY OF MINNESOTA OFFICE OF TOURISM
ILLUSTRATION BY ERIC HANSON

• NIELSVILLE • HENDRUM • DILWORTH • GEORGETOWN • FELTON •

The Red River Valley

The Red River of the North is the only river in the continental United States to flow north. The river is formed by the confluence of the **Otter Tail** and **Bois de Sioux** rivers at **Breckenridge, Minnesota**, and **Wahpeton, North Dakota**. At this point they become the Red River traveling north through Fargo/Moorhead, Grand Forks and Winnipeg before reaching its final destination in Hudson Bay.

The entire Red River Valley was once covered by the glacial **Lake Agassiz**. As the glacial waters receded, deposits of silt were spread across the land, leaving an immense, flat, fertile valley of rich farmland. In fact, the flat of the Red River Valley is said to be flatter than the flat of the northern plains, which, as you know, have the reputation for being flat.

The Red River was the main artery for transport as early as 1362 when a party of Vikings under the leadership of **Baron Paul Knutson** traveled up the Red River (which actually is the direction south), reaching as far as Douglas County. Evidence

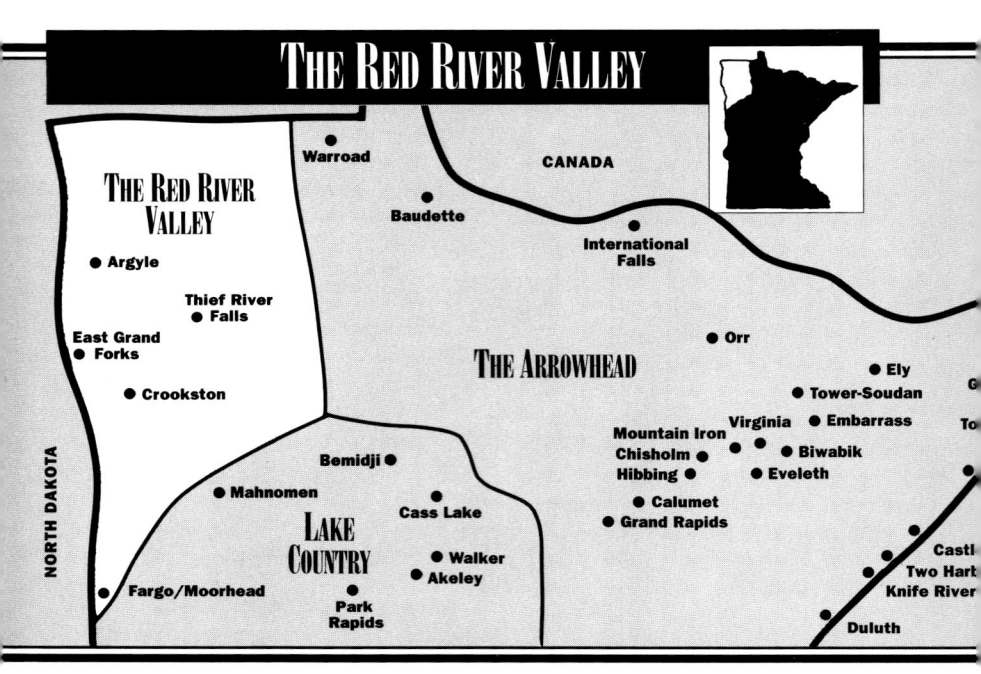

The Red River Valley

The Red River Valley
- Argyle
- Thief River Falls
- East Grand Forks
- Crookston
- Mahnomen
- Fargo/Moorhead

Warroad
Baudette
CANADA
International Falls

The Arrowhead
- Orr
- Ely
- Tower-Soudan
- Mountain Iron
- Virginia
- Embarrass
- Chisholm
- Biwabik
- Hibbing
- Eveleth
- Calumet
- Grand Rapids

Lake Country
- Bemidji
- Cass Lake
- Walker
- Akeley
- Park Rapids

Castl
Two Hart
Knife River
Duluth

NORTH DAKOTA

Hurray! Minnesota   **472**   PHOTO COURTESY OF THE MINNESOTA HISTORICAL SOCIETY

of their feat was found near Kensington, Minnesota: the Kensington Runestone.

The Red River Valley did not follow the usual order of settlement of the rest of the state, which was first the transient fur trader followed by the farmer. Instead, the farmers/settlers arrived first, drawn by the rich soil.

The first settlement in the Red River Valley was at Winnipeg by Scottish **Lord Selkirk** in 1811. This settlement was abandoned in 1820 because of the hardships and the isolation. The settlement had three routes for supplies and trade. The exchange of goods took many months, if not years, to complete. One of the routes was via the Hudson Bay, another via Lake Superior and a third via the Red River to Minneapolis. The Red River route was by far the easiest and safest of the three. It became a lifeline for the people of the valley. After leaving Winnipeg, it was natural that these people enter the United States and settle closer to sources of supply.

In time the Red River became part of the famous oxcart trails forming the major fur trade route from the Twin Cities to Winnipeg. Trains with hundreds of oxcarts driven by métis creaked over these trails. The métis (may-teé) were descendants of Frenchmen who had married Indian women and settled along the Red River Valley.

It was around the campfires on the oxcart trails that the melancholy tune "The Red River Valley" was created. The song is the tale of a lonely heartbroken métis woman whose blue-eyed lover returned East. Chorus:
*So consider a while ere you leave me,
Do not hasten to bid me adieu,
But remember the Red River Valley,
And the maiden that loved you so true.*

The sad tune was so popular that it traveled throughout the lonely West. People adapted the words to fit their region, such as the ranchers on the Red River between Texas and Oklahoma changing the last line of the chorus to "the cowboy who loves you so true."

The Valley began its first real settlement boom with the bonanza farms in the 1870s and the golden age of wheat. The owners of the railroads financed these farms to grow and harvest thousands of acres of wheat, thereby increasing traffic on the new railroads and settlement in the area.

As time passed, the wheat prices dropped, and the soil grew poor. A change of crop was needed. The farmers turned from wheat to beets. By 1924 the western Minnesota beet growers had incorporated and built the second state sugar beet refinery at Grand Forks.

By the mid-1980s there were four plants located in Minnesota, refining nine million hundredweight of sugar. Sugar beets were ranked fourth among crops in farm cash receipts and generated close to $300 million in economic benefits to Minnesota.

Driving the oxcarts over the Red River Valley trade route between Winnipeg and the Twin Cities was a lonely business.

Fargo/Moorhead

IN MANY WAYS, FARGO, NORTH Dakota, and Moorhead, Minnesota, are separated only by the Red River of the North. Many of their civic and social programs are joint efforts, particularly in the areas of public entertainment and tourism. Citizens enjoy the advantages of friendliness, safety and community spirit found in a small town while having the services, culture and sophistication afforded by a big city. Moorhead has a population of 32,300, while the metropolitan area, which includes Fargo, the suburbs and Cass and Clay counties, is 153,346.

Because of the isolating geography of this region, the towns of Clay County were built on the railroad lines. Moorhead, the county seat, was established on the completion of the Northern Pacific line from Duluth to the Red River in 1871. The town had also been a key transfer point on the oxcart trail. It was named for **William G. Moorhead** of Pennsylvania, who was a director of the Northern Pacific. Moorhead incorporated as a city in 1881. Fargo, its sister-city, was named after **William George Fargo**, founder of **Wells, Fargo Express Co.**

As the business hub of the Red River Valley, Fargo-Moorhead is the center for agribusiness processing, marketing and research. Companies such as **American Crystal Sugar** and **Anheuser Busch** operate plants here for processing raw food products into consumer products before worldwide distribution.

Moorhead has been a scholastic center for the region since the establishment of **Concordia Lutheran College** in 1891. The college is the site of the world-renowned Hvidsten Hall of Music. This conservatory of music is chiefly staffed by the professors of Concordia music department. A long list of fine artists and composers have gone on from here to world fame, such as opera singers **Phyllis Bryn-Julson** and **Karan Armstrong**.

In addition, there is **Moorhead State University**, part of the University of Minnesota system, and **Moorhead Technical College**. Moorhead State University sponsors the **Barlage Center for Science**, which conducts programs in science, technology and environmental education. The center also is responsible for the **Planetarium** and the **Buffalo River Site**, an environmental education program.

The largest major medical community between Minneapolis and the West Coast is located in Fargo-Moorhead with five hospitals and more than 500 physicians.

As an important transportation hub and the gateway between the Twin Ports, the Twin Cities and the northern Great Plains, Fargo-Moorhead is serviced by: three airlines, **Northwest Airlines** being the major airline; three bus companies, **Greyhound**, **Trailways** and **Jack Rabbit**; and is on the main rail line with both passenger (Amtrack) and freight service (Burlington Northern).

ATTRACTIONS

FARGO/MOORHEAD CIVIC OPERA
429 E. Main St.
West Fargo
(701) 282-3703
This full-time professional opera company presents three operas per season.

FARGO/MOORHEAD SYMPHONY ORCHESTRA
810 S. Fourth Ave.
Moorhead
(218) 233-8379
For more than half a century, residents of northwestern Minnesota and eastern North Dakota have enjoyed this symphony's music. The current music director is Joel Revzen. The season runs from October to April.

FARGO/MOORHEAD COMMUNITY THEATRE
333 S. Fourth St.
Fargo
(701) 235-1901
The theater stages several major productions each year and has been ranked among the top community theaters in the country.

Hurray! Minnesota

The Red River Dance and Performing Company stages a wonderful Christmas Holiday Show each season, showcasing a variety of talented dancers and musicians.

RED RIVER DANCE AND PERFORMING COMPANY
824 Main St.
Fargo
(701) 280-0004
The company performs several productions a year, featuring classical, jazz and tap dance.

LAKE AGASSIZ ARTS COUNCIL
806 Northern Pacific Ave.
Fargo
(701) 237-6133
The council serves and supports 30 Fargo/Moorhead arts organizations and maintains a master calendar of arts events.

PLAINS ART MUSEUM
521 Main Ave.
Moorhead
(218) 236-7383
The museum houses exhibits and works by contemporary regional artists, featuring American Indian art. The museum shop has a collection of unique items relevant to the museum's exhibits. There also are tours and children's activities.

MOORHEAD UNIVERSITY BARLAGE CENTER FOR SCIENCE
Highway 10
Glyndon
(218) 236-2904

In addition to conducting educational programs in science, technology and the environment, the center sponsors the Planetarium and the Buffalo River Site. The Planetarium, located on the university campus, concentrates on the heavens while the Buffalo River Site, next to Buffalo River State Park, concentrates on Mother Earth. The center also hosts a number of special public events and a series of Lawn Chair Lectures. Both the Planetarium and Buffalo River have programs for youth and adult groups and the general public throughout the year.

BUFFALO RIVER STATE PARK
Route 2, Box 118 (off Highway 10)
Glyndon, MN 56545
(218) 498-2124
Grasslands, wildflowers and hardwood forests abound on the more than 1,200 acres of this park in the Buffalo River Valley. To explore the park, there are

COMSTOCK HISTORIC HOUSE
506 Eighth St.
Moorhead
(218) 233-0848
This house was built in 1882 by Solomon G. Comstock, head of one of the Red River Valley's leading families. The original furnishings and many of the artifacts are still intact. There are exhibits on the history of the Red River Valley and the life history of Solomon G. Comstock and his daughter, Ada, the first dean of women at the University of Minnesota. In addition to regular visiting hours, the Comstock House Society hosts a Strawberry Festival on the lawn in July and Holiday Candlelight tours, featuring Victorian holiday decorations, in December. Both events are open to the public. Open May 25 through Labor Day, Saturday and Sunday, 1 to 5 p.m.

The Comstock Historic House in Moorhead was the home of Solomon Comstock, prominent early citizen of Moorhead whose daughter, Ada, served as president of Radcliffe College.

winding trails along the river, trails to the glacial beach ridge for views of the surrounding territory or trails stretching across open grasslands where you can see for miles and prairie wildlife is abundant with more than 200 species of plants. The Minnesota Department of Natural Resources, in conjunction with the Buffalo River Science Center, conducts a series of free naturalist programs at the park. There are 44 campsites, picnic grounds, a swimming beach and a nature trail.

BAGG BONANZA FARM
Box 702
Mooreton, ND
(701) 274-8989
On the National Register of Historic Places, this farm is the only remaining bonanza farm in the United States. It is located 45 miles south of Fargo and one mile west of Interstate 29. Open Memorial Day through Labor Day.

CHILDREN'S MUSEUM AT YUNKER FARM
1201 N. 28th Ave.
Fargo
(701) 232-0848
There are more than 50 hands-on exhibits for children housed in a century-old farmhouse. Children can play with such things as a bubble-making machine, a puppet theater, weaving looms, prehistoric bones or in the medical and dental corners or in build-a-house.

GOLF COURSES
PONDEROSA
Highway 10
Moorhead
(218) 498-2201
This nine-hole course along the Buffalo River is owned by Moorhead State University and is adjacent to the state park. There is a clubhouse, driving range and practice greens.

EDGEWOOD MUNICIPAL GOLF COURSE
N. 36th Ave. and Elm St.
Fargo
(701) 232-2824
This is an 18-hole championship course on rolling wooded hills. The course also has a driving range and offers a full-service pro shop.

MAPLE RIVER
Mapleton Exit off Interstate 94
Fargo
(701) 282-5415
This is a nine-hole championship course.

Since its voyage to Norway, the Hjemkomst, a replica of the early Viking ships, has been on display at the Heritage-Hjemkomst Interpretive Center.

HERITAGE–HJEMKOMST INTERPRETIVE CENTER
202 N. First Ave.
Moorhead
(218) 233-5604

The center, located on 11 acres of beautiful park land along the Red River, houses five different organizations. There is the Clay County Museum, Heritage Hall-Traveling Exhibits, the Heritage Shop, the Hjemkomst Center and the offices of the Red River Valley Heritage Society.

The **Heritage Hall-Traveling Exhibits** has 7,000 square feet for presenting history and science exhibits from such prestigious museums as the Smithsonian. The exhibits change every four months. The **Hjemkomst Center** features the full-scale authentic Viking sailing ship built by Robert Asp of Moorhead, which sailed the 6,000 miles from Duluth to Bergen, Norway, in 1982. The exhibits of the **Clay County Museum** explore the history of the towns of Clay County. The **Heritage Shop** carries educational and gift items representative of the center's exhibits.

SHOPPING
MOORHEAD CENTER MALL
Fifth St. and Cedar Ave.
Moorhead
(218) 233-6117

This convenient downtown mall is located just a few blocks from the river and has recently been beautifully remodeled and updated. There are 48 stores; 12 of them feature clothing. The Herberger department store is the largest in the Herberger chain.

WEST ACRES SHOPPING MALL
Interstate 94 and S. 13th Ave.
Fargo
(701) 282-2222

There are more than 100 retail and entertainment establishments under one roof including Dayton's, deLendrecie's, Sears and J.C. Penney. Also located in West Acres is the **Roger Maris Museum**, dedicated to the famous New York Yankee outfielder who broke Babe Ruth's home run record in 1961.

ARCHIE'S WEST UNLIMITED
Highway 10
Dilworth
(218) 236-0775

This gallery and museum features Western paintings and bronzes along with an extensive collection of American wildlife paintings and Victorian paintings dating back to 1874. The Gift Gallery has a large selection of gift and collectors' items featuring an Old Fashioned Christmas Store in the fall.

Looking north over the Heritage-Hjemkomst Interpretive Center toward Fargo, North Dakota.

PERSNICKETY GIFTS
1111 S. 38th St.
Fargo
(701) 282-7375
Occupying a corner of Fuddrucker's Restaurant, Persnickety carries a little bit of country, some special collectibles and a variety of gift items.

NORDIC NEEDLE
1314 Gateway Drive
Fargo
(701) 235-5231
Nordic Needle specializes in fine needlework, particularly hardanger and counted cross-stitch. Hardanger is a Norwegian counted openwork embroidery. Nordic Needle has published 70 books on the craft. They carry all the supplies, such as fabric, threads and patterns, for hardanger and a number of other fine embroideries. On display in the store are more than 1,000 finished models. Classes are available.

EATING

PARADISO
801 S. 38th St.
Fargo
(701) 282-5747
A little of old Mexico can be found here in one of Fargo's largest restaurants, which, of course, features Mexican and

American cuisine. The house specialties are chimichangas and fajitas. There is a full service lounge and outdoor patio.

SPEAK EASY
1001 S. 30th Ave.
Moorhead
(218) 233-1326
Speak Easy serves American and Italian cuisine, including calzone, in a setting right out of a 1930s gangster movie. Don't miss tasting the beer-battered onion rings or trying one of the 300 different cocktails served in the dining room and two lounges.

TRADER AND TRAPPER
617 Center Ave.
Moorhead
(218) 236-0202
The heavy wooden beams and multilevel seating create an intimate atmosphere in this restaurant serving steaks, seafood and chicken. The specialty of the house is prime rib.

TREE TOP RESTAURANT AND LOUNGE
403 Center Ave.
Moorhead
(218) 233-1393
Large windows frame an expansive view of the Red River and Fargo in this attractive restaurant. Tree Top features such specialties as salmon in phyllo and pork-chop fettucini, a double chop marinated in bourbon sauce served with fettucini prepared at your table. Lunch and dinner are served Monday through Saturday.

VALLEY KITCHEN OF MOORHEAD
3101 S. Eighth St.
Moorhead
(218) 236-5407
The Valley serves good home-style cooking for breakfast, lunch and dinner of such American favorites as burgers, chicken and hot sandwiches.

WINDBREAK
Interstate 19 and S. 32nd Ave.
Fargo
(701) 282-5585
This is a great restaurant for the interstate traveler. Open 24 hours a day, the menu features family favorites with a Mexican flair. Windbreak has a full service lounge with entertainment Tuesday through Saturday. The sign at the door to the lounge instructs the patron that "Fun is required by all."

LODGING

DAYS INN CONFERENCE CENTER
600 S. 30th Ave.
Moorhead, MN 56560
(218) 233-6171
(800) 325-2525
The Days Inn has 175 rooms with a complete indoor recreational facility that includes a health club, pool, sauna and whirlpool. There also is a restaurant and game room.

FARGO HOLIDAY INN
3803 S. 13th Ave.
Fargo, ND 58106
(701) 282-2700
(800) 465-4329
This is the largest hotel in the area with 308 rooms. There are conference facilities,

The University of Minnesota–Crookston has a comprehensive agricultural program and sponsors the Northwest Agricultural Experiment Station.

a health club, pool, sauna and whirlpool. The Gallery Terrace and Cafe are located on the premises along with a lounge that has live entertainment and gambling.

RADISSON HOTEL FARGO
201 N. Fifth St.
Fargo, ND 58102
(710) 232-7363
(800) 333-3333
This Radisson has 151 rooms, Passages Cafe and a lounge with live entertainment and gambling. The Radisson also has complete conference facilities, health club, pool, whirlpool and sauna.

REGENCY INN AND CONFERENCE CENTER
1010 S. 28th Ave.
Moorhead, MN 56560
(218) 233-7531
(800) 662-5708
Along with 192 guest rooms, the Regency has meeting and banquet facilities, a restaurant, game room, pool, whirlpool and waterbeds.

SUPER 8 MOTEL
Highway 75 and Interstate 94 S.
Moorhead, MN 56560
(218) 233-8880
(800) 437-4682
This Super 8 has 61 rooms.

▼ **FOR MORE INFORMATION...**
FARGO/MOORHEAD CONVENTION AND VISITORS BUREAU
Box 2164
Fargo, ND 58107
(701) 237-6134
(800) 235-7654

CROOKSTON

CROOKSTON WAS NAMED for the pioneer railroad man **Colonel William Crooks**, who was the chief engineer in locating the first railroad in Minnesota. Crookston is the county seat of Polk County and was first settled in 1872. It was incorporated in 1879. Downtown Crookston has dozens of turn-of-the-century commercial buildings on the National Register of Historic Places.

The Red Lake River flows through the city on its 165 mile westward journey from Red Lake to join the Red River of the North in East Grand Forks. There is a designated canoe route along the Red Lake River. The route passes through Crookston along with a variety of different topographical areas. Maps on the

Hurray! Minnesota

route can be obtained from the Crookston Area Chamber of Commerce.

One of the University of Minnesota's four campuses is here in Crookston, which includes the very important Northwest Agricultural Experiment Station of the University.

As in Moorhead, much of the town's industry is directed toward processing crops of the Red River Valley, such as sugar beets, sunflowers, potatoes and barley.

ATTRACTIONS
POLK COUNTY MUSEUM
Highway 2
Crookston
(218) 281-1038
The exhibits feature an 1872 log home built by a Norwegian settler and an 1890 schoolhouse.

RED RIVER VALLEY WINTER SHOW BUILDING
Highways 2 and 75 N.
Crookston
(218) 281-2900
A number of organizations around the region keep the nearly two acres of exhibition space in constant use with trade shows, competitions, exhibitions and events. You'll see everything from rodeos to the International Sugar Beet Institute trade show. The hall has a unique clay-sand combination floor that can be dug up for livestock shows, popular in this agriculture region, or packed down as hard as cement for exhibitions and trade shows.

EATING
BALONEY BILL'S
423 N. Main St.
Crookston
(218) 281-9922
Bill's specializes in all kinds of sausages,

Harvesting the fertile fields of the Red River Valley.

such as brats, Polish, hot Italian sausage and chorizo. This is a family restaurant where folks are folks.

IRISHMAN'S SHANTY
1501 S. Main St.
Crookston
(218) 281-9912
The Shanty has been serving local gentry for more than 46 years. Well-known for their ribs and the half-pound shanty burger, they also serve delicious steaks and seafood. There are homemade specials for lunch. Also open for breakfast.

RBJ'S RESTAURANT
622 University
Crookston
(218) 281-3636
This family restaurant serves breakfast, lunch and dinner. They have a great buffet and salad bar, and don't miss a piece of their fresh pie or a muffin or cookie.

ROOTER'S SPORTS BAR AND GRILL
223 N. Main St.
Crookston
(218) 281-1916
Rooter's serves great burgers, a variety of sandwiches, chicken and salads. The big screen TV and a number of other TVs provide good viewing for current sporting events.

PHOTO BY TWYLA ALTEPETER

LODGING

ELM STREET INN B&B
422 Elm St.
Crookston, MN 56716
(218) 281-2343
(218) 281-1721

There are four guest rooms with shared baths in this 1910 house built during the Arts and Crafts Movement. The style was named Mission, reflecting its straight look and simple lines. The three-story home has beautiful oak woodwork, pocket doors, stained and leaded glass and sponge-painted walls. You'll be served a truly memorable made-from-scratch breakfast by candlelight in the dining room.

NORTHLAND INN
Highways 2 and 75
Crookston, MN 56716
(218) 281-5210

The University Station restaurant is located in the inn. There are 60 rooms, banquet and meeting facilities, pool, whirlpool and winter plug-ins.

▼ FOR MORE INFORMATION...

CROOKSTON AREA CHAMBER OF COMMERCE
114 S. Main St., Suite A
Crookston, MN 56716
(218) 281-4320

THIEF RIVER FALLS

THE AREA AROUND and north of Thief River Falls is replete with parks, wildlife sanctuaries, refuges and management areas. They provide wildlife with such diverse habitats as Red River prairielands, Aspen parklands, swamps and marshlands. And, to be expected, the region abounds in wildlife. If you want to see waterfowl, a moose or even an elk, there are excellent opportunities in areas such as **Wetland, Pines and Prairie Sanctuary, Wapiti Trail, Roseau Bog Owl Management Unit, Pembina Wildlife Management Area, Thief Lake Wildlife Management Area, Beltrami Island State Forest** and the 100 square miles of **Agassiz National Wildlife Refuge**.

ATTRACTIONS

PENNINGTON COUNTY PIONEER VILLAGE
Oakland Park Road (off Highway 32)
Thief River Falls
(218) 681-5767

You won't find as many vintage buildings in larger well-funded museums as you will here. There are 14 historic buildings that have been carted to the site and, in some cases, reconstructed, including the Soo Line Depot from downtown Thief River Falls. There also is a museum committed to representing and preserving what remains of the lifestyles of the Pennington County settlers.

ARTCO INDUSTRIES
600 Brooks Ave.
Thief River Falls
(218) 681-8558

The manufacturer of Arctic Cat snowmobile operates tours Monday through Friday at 1 p.m. during the production season, which is approximately March through November. The tour, lasting one hour, takes you down the production line to see firsthand how the sleds are built.

AGASSIZ NATIONAL WILDLIFE REFUGE
County Road 7 (off Highway 32)
Middle River, MN 56737
(218) 449-4115

Agassiz Pool and 15 other broad, shallow ponds are central to the thousands of acres that form this unique refuge.

Hurray! Minnesota

Agassiz is home to 274 species of birds, including white pelicans, five species of heron, rare peregrine falcons and scores of songbirds. If you're observant, you may see as many as 49 species of mammals, including an occasional elk. Agassiz is the only refuge in the lower 48 states to have a resident wolf pack.

Visit the refuge headquarters to find the locations of the latest wildlife sightings and pick up maps and brochures outlining self-guided walking and driving tours. Dawn and dusk are the best wildlife-observation periods. Don't forget your binoculars.

SHOPPING
END OF THE TRAIL INDIAN CRAFT SHOP
Highway 1 E.
Goodrich
(218) 378-4322
This Chippewa craft shop features Indian quill work, willow baskets, ceramics, beadwork and necklaces that are handmade on the reservation. Closed Tuesday.

EATING
HANDY FARMS COUNTRY COOKING
Highway 59 S.
Thief River Falls
(218) 681-7686
A family restaurant that serves breakfast, lunch and dinner.

LON'S RESTAURANT AND PUB
Oakland Park Road
Thief River Falls
(218) 681-3138
Generous helpings are served in the dining room in an atmosphere reminiscent of a Tudor pub. Specialties include baron of beef, roast loin of pork, seafood, steaks and chicken. They also have full-service cocktails and a lounge.

LANTERN RESTAURANT AND PUB
Oakland Park Road
Thief River Falls
(218) 681-8211
Open for lunch and dinner Monday through Saturday. Featuring steaks, ribs, chicken and seafood.

REX CAFE
218 N. LaBree Ave.
Thief River Falls
(218) 681-1122

A salad bar and good home cooking makes this a good place to eat Monday through Saturday. A banquet room is available.

LODGING
BEST WESTERN INN OF THIEF RIVER FALLS
1060 Highway 32S
Thief River Falls, MN 56701
(218) 681-7721
The inn has 78 rooms, a heated indoor pool, sauna and whirlpool. Winter plug-ins are another great perk. The Sundance Dining Room is open seven days a week and has a Sunday brunch.

▼ FOR MORE INFORMATION...
THIEF RIVER FALLS CHAMBER OF COMMERCE
2017 S.E. Highway 59
Thief River Falls, MN 56701
(218) 681-3720
(800) 827-1629

ARGYLE
OLD MILL STATE PARK
Route 1, Box 42
Argyle, MN 56713
(218) 437-8174
Explore the old flour mill and log cabin in this 287-acre park. For recreation, there is a good swimming beach, woodland trails, volleyball and horseshoes. There are 26 campsites with shower facilities.

LAKE BRONSON
Lake Bronson State Park
Box 9
Lake Bronson, MN 56734
(218) 754-2200
Bald eagle nests and moose are some of the larger wildlife species you'll see in the 3,000 acres of this park. You can hike across prairie or through trees on 14 miles of trails including five miles of bike trails. There are 194 camping sites in three different campgrounds and a lake for swimming, boating and other water sports. On weekends, the park sponsors nature hikes and movies on the seasonal wildlife activity in the park such as currently blooming wild flowers or habits and instincts of nesting birds.

East Grand Forks

A TOWN OF almost 9,000, East Grand Forks is just across the river from Grand Forks, North Dakota, a town of almost 50,000. The towns were formed and named for the junction of the Red Lake River and the Red River of the North, which converge at this point. These rivers provide some of the finest catfish fishing in North America.

Eating

BEAVER'S FAMILY RESTAURANT
1304 N.E. Central Ave.
East Grand Forks
(218) 773-8533
You'll find good home cooking for breakfast, lunch or dinner at Beaver's. They have a large salad bar and a Sunday buffet.

RIVERBEND SUPPER CLUB
Highway 2 E.
East Grand Forks
(218) 773-2493
Steak and seafood are served in an atmosphere of fine dining overlooking the river. Open for lunch and dinner with a brunch on Sunday. Banquet facilities for groups up to 150.

WHITEY'S CAFE
109 DeMers Ave.
East Grand Forks
(218) 773-1831
Whitey's is a traditional community landmark of East Grand Forks. Thanks to the 40 nightclubs and restaurants that lined DeMers Avenue back in the early 1920s, East Grand Forks was once known as "little Chicago." This is where Whitey built the first stainless steel horseshoe bar in the United States

Whitey's "Wonder Bar" in East Grand Forks.
PHOTO COURTESY OF WHITEY'S CAFE

Grand Forks riverfront.

Hurray! Minnesota

486

PHOTOS COURTESY OF GRAND FORKS
CONVENTION AND VISITORS BUREAU

ATTRACTIONS
CATFISH DAYS
Central to the event is the Cat's Incredible Fishing Tournament. Fishermen from all over North America attend this event intent on catching the heaviest catfish and a cash purse of $2,500. Down by the river is the sight of all the action with concessions, a garage band contest, bike racing and dancing and live entertainment in the evening. Catfish Days are held the third weekend in July.

DAKOTA QUEEN
Downtown
Grand Forks
(701) 775-5656
Experience the river through a family sightseeing cruise, riverboat dinner, Sunday brunch cruise or a moonlight party.

The Dakota Queen.

back in 1930, calling it Whitey's Wonder Bar. The bar, now the only establishment to survive the era, is a magnificent example of Art Deco. In 1973 the bar was expanded to appeal to all age groups. There now are three distinct atmospheres ranging from popcorn and pool tables to fashionable cocktails.

LODGING
ACROSS THE RIVER in Grand Forks, North Dakota, there are six large conference hotels, each with more than 100 rooms and the usual facilities. East Grand Forks has a number of smaller motels.

EAST GATE MOTEL
Highway 2 E.
East Grand Forks, MN
(218) 773-9822
Complimentary coffee 24 hours a day and free local phone calls make this 60-room motel a great value.

▼ FOR MORE INFORMATION...
EAST GRAND FORKS AREA CHAMBER OF COMMERCE
218 N.W. Fourth St.
East Grand Forks, MN 56721
(218) 773-7481
(800) 866-4566

THE RED RIVER VALLEY

INDEX

"Antie Clare's" Doll Hospital and Museum   91
3M Dwan Museum   278
50th and France   141
Aamodt's Apple Farm   81
Aerial Lift Bridge   263
Afton   380
Afton Alps Ski Area   380
Afton Historical Museum   380
Agassiz National Wildlife Refuge   482
AIM Powwow   55
Aitkin   316
Aitkin Riverboat Days   316
Akeley   351
Albert Lea   408
Albert Lea Walking Tour   408
Alexander Harkin Store   436
Alexander Ramsey House   90
Alexander Ramsey Park   441
Alexandria   362
Alexis Bailly Vineyard   382
American Museum of Wildlife Art   383
American Swedish Institute   90
Andiamo Showboat   377
Andrew Volstead House   459
Annual Tri-State Band Festival   56
Annual Winter Art Show   46
Anoka   57
Anson Northrup Paddleboat   235
Antique Car Run   468
Antique Show   48
Antique Spectacular   56
Apple Cider Days   56
Apple Days   55
Apple Festival   55
Aquatennial   51
Arches Museum   394
Ard Godfrey House   90
Argyle   483
Arrowhead Bluffs Exhibits/Museum   389
Artco Industries   482
Arthur Upson Room, Kerlan Collection   87
Arts in the Park   50
Artspace Project Inc.   231
Ashby   360
Assumption Catholic Church   246
August Schell Brewery   435
August Schell House   435

Austin   406
Austin Area Fine Arts Center   407
Austin Farmfest   53
Bach Society Chorus   101
Bagg Bonanza Farm   476
Baker Park Reserve   86
Ballet Arts of Minnesota   120
Ballet of the Dolls   120
Balloon Fest   43
Bandana Square   141
Barn Theatre   465
Barrett   361
Basilica of Saint Mary   224
Battle Creek   51
Battle Lake   358
Baudette   305
Bavarian Sommerfest   52
Bayfront Blues Festival   55, 267
Bayfront Horse-Drawn Carriage Co.   262
Bayport   380
Bean Hole Days   51
Becker County Historical Museum   353
Bel Canto Voices   101
Belgian-American Days   53
Bemidji   346
Benedicta Arts Center   324
Benton County Historical Society Museum   327
Big Bucks Casino   74
Big Ole   365
Big Island Rendezvous   56
Big Stone Lake State Park   464
Big Stone National Wildlife Refuge   464
Birdwing Spa   468
Biwabik   307
Blackduck Wood Carvers Festival   52, 347
Blandin Paper Co.   314
Bloomington   79, 146
Blue Devil Preserve   459
Blue Earth County Courthouse   432
Blue Mound State Park   453
Blue Winds Theatre   110
Blueberry Arts Festival   52
Boise Cascade   301
Boom Island Park   214
Bower Hawthorne Theater   123
Brainerd   333, 338
Brainerd International Raceway   335

Hurray! Minnesota

Breezy Point   339
Bridge of Peace   310
Brookdale Center   140
Brooklyn Park   56
Brownie Lake   213
Bryant Lake Regional Park   86
Buena Vista Ski Area   347
Buffalo River State Park   475
Bunnell House   393
Burnsville Center   140
Butler Square   230
C.A.S.T. Theatre   110
Cafesjian's Carousel   246
Caledonia   396
Calumet   311
Campus Live Theater   110
Canal Park   263
Canal Park Marine Museum   267
Caribou Falls   281
Caribou Trail   284
Carpenter St. Croix Valley Nature Center   382
Carver Park Reserve   86
Cascade River State Park   284
Cass Gilbert Memorial Park   251
Castle Danger   280
Catfish Days   487
Cathedral of St. Paul   246
Catholic Digest   136
Cedar Lake   212
Central School   314
Champion International Paper Mill   325
Chanhassen   56
Chanhassen Dinner Theatres   110
Charles Dickens' Christmas   57
Charles A. Lindbergh State Park   331
Charles A. Weyerhaeuser Memorial Museum   332
Chateau Devenois Winery   324
Child's Play Theatre Company   111
Children's Museum   91
Children's Museum at Yunker Farm   476
Children's Theatre Company   110
Chippewa City Pioneer Village   461
Chisholm   310
Christian Brothers Hockey Equipment   304
Christmas in a 1900 Logging Camp   57
Cinco De Mayo   48
CityBusiness   137
City Center   222
City Hall   225
City Hall-County Courthouse   246
City Pages   137
Civic Orchestra of Minneapolis   108

Civil War Weekend   49
Cleary Lake Regional Park   86
Cloquet   258
Coca Cola Neon Sign   231
Coffee Mill Ski Area   389
Cold Spring   369
Collaborative Theatre   112
College of St. Scholastica   261
College of St. Thomas Celtic Library   88
Collegeville   48
Como Park, Lake, Zoo and Conservatory   251
Comstock Historic House   476
Concentus Musicus Renaissance Ensemble   101
Concert by the Lake   269
Conway Universal Studios   392
Cook County Museum   285
Coon Rapids Dam Regional Park   86
Corporate Report Minnesota   136
Cottonwood County Courthouse   444
Cottonwood County Historical Society   444
County Stearns Theatrical Co.   323
E. St. Julien Cox House   428
Cricket Theatre   111
Croft Mine State Park   317
Crookston   480
Crosby-Ironton   317
Cross River   281
Crosslake   340
Crow-Hassan Park Reserve   86
Crow Wing County Historical Society Museum   334
Crystal Carnival   46
Cuyuna Range Historical Museum   317
Dakota Queen   487
Dale Warland Singers   101
Dalles of the St. Croix   374
Deep Portage Conservation Reserve   337
Deerland Zoo   335
Defeat of Jesse James Days   55
Dent   356
Depot   268
Detroit Lakes   352
Detroit Mountain   354
Dewey-Radke Mansion   331
DNR Fish Hatchery, Lanesboro   404
Dog Days Celebration   53
Downtowner   137
Dozinky: A Czechoslovakian Harvest Festival   56
Dudley Riggs' Brave New Workshop   112
Duluth   259

Duluth Art Institute 269
Duluth Ballet 269
Duluth Playhouse 269
Duluth Superior Symphony Orchestra 269
Dutch Festival 51
Eagle Creek Rendezvous 48
Eagle Mountain 291
East Grand Forks 484
Eden Prairie Center 141
Edgerton 51
Edina 141
Edna G. Tugboat 279
Egret Island 360
Elk River 56, 324
Elm Creek Park Reserve 86
Eloise Butler Wildflower Garden and Bird Sanctuary 214
Ely 294
Embarrass 307
Enger Memorial Tower 270
Ensemble Capriccio 102
Ethnic Dance Theatre 120
Eveleth 307
Excelsior 55
Excelsior Arts Festivals 50
Eye of the Storm 112
Fall Festival 56
Faribault 411
Faribault Walking Tour 412
Faribault Woolen Mill Co. 412
Farmer's Market 247
Fasching & Bock Beer Festival 46
Father Hennepin State Park 329
Father Hennepin Suspension Bridge 234
Fergus Falls 359
Fergus Falls Center for the Arts 359
Festival of Nations 48, 252
Festival of Trees 57
Finn Creek Museum 356
Finn Fest 56
Finntown Neighborhood 309
Fire and Ice Geological Interpretive Walk 300
Firefly Casino 74, 460
First Settler's Museum 312
Fish Lake Regional Park 86
Fisherman's Picnic 53
Fitger's Brewery 272
Flandrau State Park 436
Folkways of Christmas 57
Fond-du-Luth Casino 74, 269
Forest History Center 313
Forest Resource Center, Lanesboro 404
Fort Belmont 447

Fort Belmont Days 51
Fort Mille Lacs Village 329
Fort Ridgeley State Park 436
Fort St. Charles 304
Fortune Bay Casino 74
Foshay Tower 227
Frank Theatre 112
Frazee
Frederic Chopin Society 102
Freeborn County Historical Museum/Pioneer Village 408
French Regional Park 86
Frontenac 388
Frontenac State Park 388
Garvin Heights Park 393
Gaviidae Common 221
Georgia Stephens Contemporary Dance Theater 120
Ghent 53
Ghost Squadron Air Display 53
Giants Ridge 307
Gibbs Farm Museum 91
Gilbert and Sullivan Very Light Opera Company 112
Glacial Lakes State Park 368
Glacial Lakes Trail 464
Glensheen Mansion 268
Glenwood 368
Glockenspiel 435
Golden Shoe Tours 325
Goldstein Gallery and Collections 91
Gooseberry Falls State Park 280
Governor's Residence 82
Grain Belt Brewery 234
Grain Belt Neon Sign 234
Grand Army of the Republic Hall 468
Grand Avenue 142
Grand Casino 76, 330
Grand Garage Theatre 112
Grand Marais 284
Grand Mound 301
Grand Old Day 252
Grand Portage 287
Grand Portage Casino 76, 288
Grand Portage National Monument 288
Grand Portage State Park 287
Grand Rapids 313
Grand Vinterslass 46
Grandma's Marathon 267
Grandma's Oktoberfest 56
Granite Falls 458
Great American History Theatre 113
Great Pumpkin Festival 56

Hurray! Minnesota

Great River Houseboats 389
Greater Twin Cities Youth Symphonies 102
Greek Festival 55
Greyhound Bus Origin Center 312
Gull Lake Chain 339
Gull Lake Chain Drives 336
Gull Lake Fun Regatta 52
Guthrie Theater 114, 123
Halloween Festival 57
Hastings 381
Hastings Walking Tour 382
Hawk Migration Weekend 55
Hawk Ridge 270
Heartland State Trail 345
Heartland Trail 349
Hennepin Center for the Arts 123, 231
Hennepin Parks 85
Hennepin History Museum 92
Heritage Center Museum, Mankato 433
Heritage Hjemkomst Interpretive Center 477
Herman 361
Hermann Monument 435
Hey City Stage 114
Hibbing 311
High School Rodeo 55
Highland Park 251
Hill Mine Annex State Park 311
Hill Monastic Manuscript Library 325
Hill Reference Library 250
Hinckley 257
Hinckley Fire Museum 258
Historic Fort Snelling 247
Historic Mill District 368
Historic Mississippi River Cruises 81
Historic Murphy's Landing 92
Historic Orpheum Theatre 123, 125
Historic State Theatre 125-127
Historical and Wildlife Museum Bemidji 347
History of Jackson County Fair Village 448
Hopkins 48
Hormel Home 407
Hotel Sofitel 203
Hovland 287
Hoxie Rathbun Dugout 448
Hubbard County Courthouse 349
Hubert H. Humphrey Metrodome 128
Hull Rust Mahoning Mine Overlook 312
Humphrey Forum 93
Hyatt Regency Minneapolis 203
Hyland Lake 85
Ice Box Days 46, 301
Illusion Theater 114
In the Heart of the Beast Puppet and

Mask Theatre 114
InitialStage Theatre Collective 115
Inspiration Peak State Park 360
International Eelpout Festival 46, 345
International Falls 300
International Festival 48
International Market Square 140
International Peanut Butter and Milk Festival 468
International Polkafest 50
Interstate State Park 374
Iron Country Hoedown 53
Ironworld USA 310
Irvine Park 251
Island Girl Yacht 352
Isle 46
Isle Royale 289
Itasca County History Museum 314
Itasca State Park 349
Ivy Tower 226
Jackpot Junction 76
Jackson 446
Jackson Speedway 448
Jackson County Courthouse 447
Jackson County Historical Museum 447
James Ford Bell Museum of Natural History 92
James J. Hill House 93
James J. Hill Reference Library 88
Jawaahir Dance Company 120
Jay C. Hormel Nature Center 407
Jazz Party 55
Jeffers Petroglyphs 444
Jerome Hill Theater 129
John Beargrease Sled Dog Marathon 267
John Lind Home 435
Joseph Wolf Brewery Caves 377
Judy Garland Museum 314
Julius C. Wilkie Steamboat Museum 393
Jungle Theater 115
Kandiyohi County Museum 465
Kaplan's Woods Parkway 411
Kasota 430
Kellogg Mall Park 251
Kerlan Collection, Walter Library 87
King Turkey Days and the Great Gobler Gallop 55, 450
Knife River 278
Knott's Camp Snoopy 148
Knute Nelson House 365
Koochiching County Historical Museum 301
Korn & Klover Karnival 51
La Crescent 396

491

Lac qui Parle Mission   462
Lac qui Parle State Park   462
Lake Benton   50
Lake Bronson   483
Lake Calhoun   212
Lake City   386
Lake County Historical Society Railroad
   Museum   278
Lake George   351
Lake Harriet   213
Lake Minnetonka   85
Lake Nokomis   213
Lake of the Isles   212
Lake of the Woods   303
Lake of the Woods Casino   76
Lake of the Woods Historical Museum   304
Lake of the Woods Steam & Gas Engine
   Show   53
Lake Pepin   386
Lake Rebecca Park Reserve   86
Lake Superior and Mississippi Railroad   262
Lake Superior Center   268
Lake Superior Zoo   270
Lakewalk   263-267
Landmark Center   248
Lanesboro   402
Lanesboro Walking Tour   403
Laura Ingalls Wilder Free Museum   443
Laurentian Divide Fitness Trail   309
Lawndale Farm   361
Le Sueur   426
Le Sueur Museum   427
Leech Lake Fish Hatchery and Interpretive
   Center   345
Leonidas Overlook   307
Lester Park   270
Lighthouse Point and Harbor Museum   279
Limelight   115
Lincoln Park Area   432
Lindbergh House   331
Lindstrom   46
Litchfield   468
Little Crow Lake Region   464
Little Crow Water Ski Shows   468
Little Falls   331
Little Falls Annual Arts and Crafts Show   332
Little Marais   281
Little Six Bingo and Casino   76
Lock and Dam No. 2   382
Loft   87
Longville   53
Loring Greenway   220
Loring Lake   213

Loring Park   220
Loring Playhouse Theatre Company   115
Louis C. Wippich Rock Garden   324
Lower Sioux Agency Interpretive Center   438
Loyce Houlton's Minnesota Dance Theatre
   and School   120
Lumber Exchange   230
Lumbertown U.S.A.   335
Lutsen   282
Lutsen Mountain Ski Area   282
Luverne   453
Lyon County Historical Museum   456
Lyric Theatre   115
MacDougall Homestead   369
Madison   57
Mahnomen   349
Mainstreet Days Fine Arts Fair   48
Mall of America   146
Mankato   430
Mantorville   401
Mantorville Walking Tour   401
Maple Syrup Festival   48
Maplewood Mall   142
Maplewood State Park   356
Mardi Gras North   46
Marine on St. Croix   375
Marquette   203
Marshall   456
Matinee Musical   269
Mayo Clinic   397, 398
Mayowood   397
MCAD Gallery   93
Mears Park   251
Media in the Twin Cities   136-139
Met Center   130
Mickey's Diner   248
Mid-Winter Festival   46
Mille Lacs Indian Museum   329
Mille Lacs Kathio State Park   329
Minneapolis Chamber Symphony   102
Minneapolis Convention Center   129
Minneapolis Hilton and Towers   203
Minneapolis Institute of Arts   93
Minneapolis Marriott City Center   203
Minneapolis Sculpture Garden   82
Minneapolis Trombone Choir   109
Minnehaha Falls   214
Minneopa State Park   433
Minnesota Air Guard Museum   94
Minnesota Brewing Company   249
Minnesota Centennial Showboat   116
Minnesota Center for Book Arts   87
Minnesota Chorale   103

Hurray! Minnesota

Minnesota Composers Forum   103
Minnesota Dance Alliance   121
Minnesota Ethnic Days   50
Minnesota Festival of Music   48
Minnesota Freedom Band   109
Minnesota Genealogical Society Library   89
Minnesota Harvest Apple Orchard   83
Minnesota History Center   88, 95
Minnesota Inventors Congress   49, 441
Minnesota Landscape Arboretum   83, 88
Minnesota Military Museum   332
Minnesota Monthly   136
Minnesota Museum of Art   95
Minnesota Museum of Mining   310
Minnesota Music Festival   50
Minnesota Opera Company   103
Minnesota Orchestra   104
Minnesota Prairie Day Celebration   53
Minnesota Public Radio   138
Minnesota Renaissance Festival   53
Minnesota River   458
Minnesota Sinfonia   104
Minnesota Square Dance Convention   50
Minnesota State Band   109
Minnesota State Capital   249
Minnesota State Fair   53
Minnesota State Fairgrounds   249
Minnesota TubaChristmas   109
Minnesota Valley National Wildlife Refuge   85
Minnesota Women's Press   137
Minnesota Youth Symphonies   105
Minnesota Zephyr   83, 376
Minnesota Zoo   83
Minnetonka   17, 85
Minnetonka Orchestral Association   109
Mississippi Live   234
Mississippi National Golf Links   384
Mixed Blood Theatre   116
Molitor's Trout Heaven   325
Montevideo   461
Montrose   52
Moorhead University Barlage Center for Science   475
Morton   438
Mounds Park   251
Mounds View   50
Mountain Iron   308
Mower County Historical Center   407
Mpls/St. Paul   136
Mt. Frontenac   388
Munsinger Gardens   324
Murphy-Hanrehan Park Reserve   86

Museum of Questionable Medical Devices   95
Music in the Park Series   105
Myre-Big Island State Park   408
Mystery Cafe   116
Mystery Cave   403
Mystic Lake Casino   76
Nancy Hauser Dance Company   122
National Sports Center   131
Natural Science Museum   456
Nature's Studio   324
Nerstrand Woods State Park   413
Nevis   351
New Classic Theatre   116
New Dance Performance Laboratory   122
New London   468
New Music-Theater Ensemble   116
New Prague   419
New Tradition Theater Co.   323
New Ulm   434
New York Mills   356
Niagara Cave   403
Nicollet County Historical Museum   429
Nicollet Island   235
Nicollet Island Inn   203
Nisswa   52, 338, 339
Nobles County Pioneer Village   450
Noerenberg Memorial County Park   86
Norsefest   57
North Shore Scenic Railroad   262
Northern Lights Gaming Casino   76
Northern Sign Theatre   116
Northfield   414
Northfield Walking Tour   417
Northland Inn and Executive Conference Center   203
Northrop Auditorium   131
Northtown Mall   142
Northwest Angle   304
Norwest Bank Building   410
O'Shaugnessy Auditorium   133
Oktoberfest   57
Olcott Park   308
Old Log Theatre   117
Old Mill State Park   483
Old Milwaukee Road Depot and Freight House   235
Ole & Lena Days   46
Oliver H. Kelley Farm   324
Olof Swensson Farm   462
Omni Northstar Hotel   203
Omnitheater   97
One Voice Mixed Chorus   109
Opera 101 Theater Company   105

493

Orchestra Hall   131, 218
Ordway Music Theatre   132
Original Baseball Hall of Fame of Minneapolis   95
Orpheum Theatre   230
Orr   299
Ortonville   464
Ottertail   358
Otter Tail County Historical Museum   359
Owatonna   409
Palace Bingo   76, 347
Palisade
Park Inn International   203
Park Point   270
Park Rapids   349
Park Square Theatre Company   117
Paul Bunyan Arboretum   337
Paul Bunyan Fun Center   335
Paul Bunyan's Animal Land   347
Paulucci Space Theatre   312
Pavek Museum of Broadcasting   96
Peace Avenue of Flags   450
Peavey Plaza   219
Pebble Lake Golf Club   359
Pelican Rapids   356
Pennington County Pioneer Village   482
Penumbra Theatre   117
People's Art Festival   57
Pepo Alfajiri Dance and Drum Theatre   122
Pequot Lakes   339
Perennial Design   390
Perham   356
Phalen Park and Lake   251
Phelps Mill Park   359
Phelps Mill Summer Festival   51
Pickwick Mill   394
Pig Patch Days   56
Pillsbury State Forest   337
Pine Grove Municipal Park and Zoo   332
Pioneer Festival   50
Pioneer Park Working Museum   347
Pipestone   452
Pipestone National Monument   452
Pirate's Cove Paddleboat   324
Plains Art Museum   475
Planes of Fame Air Museum   96
Playwrights' Center   88
Plum Creek County Park   441
Plummer House of Arts   399
Plymouth Music Series of Minnesota   105
Plymouth Playhouse   117
Pokegama Dam Park   315
Polish Cultural Institute   394

Polk County Museum   481
Pope County Historical Museum   368
Pork Chop Ridge Farms   445
Port Town Trolley   262
Powderhorn Lake and Park   213
Prairie Sugar, Sorghum & Molasses   56
Prairie Wind Players Dinner Theater   361
Prehistoric Activities Day   49
Preston   48, 403
Quadna Mountain   315
Quarry Hill Nature Center   399
R.D. Hubbard Museum   433
Radisson Hotel South and Plaza Tower   203
Radisson Hotel St. Paul   203
Radisson Plaza Hotel Minneapolis   203
Rainbo Children's Theatre Company   117
Rainy River   305
Red Eye Collaboration   117
Red Lake Fisheries   347
Red River Valley Winter Show Building   481
Red Wing   383
Redwood Falls   439
Redwood Falls County Museum   441
Refreshment Committee   117
Rice County Museum of History   413
Rice Lake State Park   411
Rice Park   251
Ridgedale Shopping Center   140
River Bend Nature Center   413
River City Days   53
River Park   427
River Valley Cheese   404
Riverplace   143, 233
Riverside Park   315
Rivertown Fall Colors Festival   56
Rivertown Trolley   377
Rochester   397
Rockville Granite Quarry   325
Root River Trail   403
Rosedale Shopping Center   140
Roseville Big Band   109
Rouchleau Mine   308
Runestone Museum   365
Saddle Horse Days   50
Sakatah Lake State Park   413
Sakatah-Singing Hills Trail   413
Sauk Centre   366
Scandia   53, 375
Scenic Valley Winery   404
Schubert Club   105
Schubert Club Keyboard Instrument Museum   96
Science Museum of Minnesota and

Hurray! Minnesota   **494**

Omnitheater 97
Scottish Country Fair & Highland Games 48
Seppman's Mill 433
Sequoia Theatre 118
Seven Sisters Prairie 360
Shakopee 48
Sheepdog Trials 53
Sherburn 56
Shiver River Days 46
Shooting Star Casino 76, 349
Showboat 315
Sibley State Park 468
Silver Star City 349
Sinclair Lewis Boyhood Home 367
Sinclair Lewis Interpretive Center and Museum 367
Skyline Parkway 270
Skyway News 137
Smokey Bear Park 301
Snelling Lake 85
Sommerfest 51, 219
Song of Hiawatha Pageant 50
Sonshine 466
Soudan Underground Mine State Park 306
Southdale Center 140
Southern Theater 118
Southwest State Historical Center 457
Spelmansstamma 53
Spicer 467
Spirit Mountain Recreation Area 271
Spirit of the North Theater 269
Split Rock Lighthouse State Park 280
Spring Lake 213
SS William A. Irvin 263
St. Anthony Main 143, 233
St. Cloud 321
St. Cloud Symphony Orchestra 323
St. Croix State Park 258
St. Mane Theatre 404
St. Patrick's Day 253
St. Paul Chamber Orchestra 106
St. Paul Civic Center 249
St. Paul Civic Symphony 109
St. Paul Hotel 203
St. Paul Pioneer Press 137
St. Paul Public Library 250
St. Paul Winter Carnival 46, 253
St. Peter 428
Star Tribune 136
State Area DNR Fisheries Headquarters 368
State Theatre 230
Stearns County Heritage Center 326
Steele County Courthouse 411

Stephen B. Humphrey Theater 323
SteppingStone Theatre for Youth Development 118
Stevie Ray's Comedy Theatre and Cabaret 118
Stewartville 403
Stiftungsfest 52
Stillwater 376
Stillwater Walking Tour 377
Stone House Museum 375
Stories from the Heartland 47
Storytelling by Duke Addicks 404
Sugar Loaf 392
Summit Brewing Company 250
Superior Hiking Trail 277
Swayed Pines Folk Fest 48
Swissfest 53
T.B. Sheldon Performing Arts Theatre 384
Tall Timber Days 50
Tamarac National Wildlife Refuge 353
Target Center 133, 231
Taste of Minnesota 50
Taylors Falls 373
Temperance River State Park 281
Terry's Boat Harbor Marina 330
Tettegouche State Park 280
Theatre 65 118
Theatre de la Jeune Lune 119
Theatre Exchange 118
Theatre in the Round Players 119
Theatre L'Homme Dieu 365
Theodore Wirth Park 214
Thief River Falls 482
This Old Farm 334
Thursday Musical 107
Tofte 282
Tower-Soudan 306
Town Square Park 252
Trading Post 353
Treasure Island Casino 76
Troupe America 119
Trout Days 48
Turkey Days 52
Tweed Museum of Art 269
Twin Cities Collectors' Car Show 55
Twin Cities Gay Men's Chorus 107
Twin Cities Jazz Society 107
Twin Cities Reader 137
Twin City Model Railroad Club Inc. 84
Two Harbors 278
Two Moon Country/Farmers' Murals 442
U.S. Hockey Hall of Fame 307
Ugly Truck Contest 52

495

Unicorn Theatre 119
Union Depot and Old Engine 201 410
University Art Museum 97
University of Minnesota - Duluth 261
University of Minnesota School of Music 107
University Theatre 119
Upper St. Anthony Falls Lock and Dam 235
Upper Sioux Agency State Park 458
Uptown 142
Uptown Art Fair 52
Utne Reader 136
Vacationland Park 335
Valleyfair! 84
Vermilion Falls 300
Vermilion Gorge 300
Vermilion Interpretive Center and History Museum 290
Victoria Crossing 142
Village of Yesteryear 410
Virginia 308
Virginia Historical Society Heritage Center 309
Vista Queen and Vista King 262
Voyageur Visitor Center 295
Voyageurs National Park 299
W.W. Mayo House 427
Wabana Trail and Wildflower Sanctuary 315
Wabasha 388
Wabasha County Museum 389
Wadena 356
Walker 345
Walker Art Center 97
Walnut Grove 443
Wanda Gag House 435
Warden's Home Museum 377
Warroad 305

Washington County Historic Courthouse 378
Wayzata 143
WCCO Radio 138
We Fest 53, 353
Wealthwood Rod and Gun Club 329
Welch Village Ski Area 382
West Hills Complex 411
Western Fest and Rodeo 458
White Bear Lake 85
Whitey's Cafe 484
Whitney Hotel 203, 235
Wiederkehr Balloons 377
Wild Wings Gallery 386
Wild Mountain 374
Wilderness Trail Drive 304
William O'Brien State Park 377
William Whipple Art Gallery 456
Willmar 465
Windom 444
Winona 391
Winona Armory Museum 393
Winona Walking Tour 394
Winter Warrior 432
Witch Tree 288
Wolverines 107
Wood Carvers Festival 52
World Theater 134
Worthington 449
Wyman Building Galleries 231
Yellow Medicine County Museum 460
Zeitgeist 108
Zenon Dance Company and School, Inc. 122
Zippel Bay State Park 304
Zorongo Flamenco Dance Theatre 122
Zumbrota 402

Hurray! Minnesota